JAWAHARLAL NEHRU

A Biography

VOLUME ONE
1889-1947

Sarvepalli Gopal

JAWAHARLAL NEHRU

A Biography

VOLUME ONE
1889-1947

HARVARD UNIVERSITY PRESS
CAMBRIDGE, MASSACHUSETTS
1976

Preface

Jawaharlal Nehru played a decisive role in the history of the twentieth century—as a leader of the Indian people, as a representative of the new mood of Asia, and as a spokesman of the international conscience. So, striking as was his personality, any study of him is bound to be more than merely the personal biography of a great man. This first volume, which covers the period when he strove for India's freedom, has become, because of his influential position, almost a history of the last thirty years of the Indian nationalist movement. While the focus is on the man, and matters in which his interest was peripheral have been skirted over, yet the range is necessarily broad. In the next two volumes, which will cover his seventeen years as Prime Minister, the approach will be the same.

Throughout this volume I have referred to him as Jawaharlal and not as Jawaharlal Nehru. This has the advantage of making it easy to distinguish him from his father, Motilal Nehru, who figures prominently in the first half of the book. But there is also a wider justification. This volume deals primarily with the Indian scene; and to the people of India, who took him to their hearts, he was, and is, Jawaharlal.

This has not been an easy book to write. Jawaharlal was the hero of my youth. Then, for nearly ten years, I served him in the Ministry of External Affairs; and over a fairly long period, from April 1959 to December 1962, I saw him almost every day. He was the Prime Minister, and I among the most junior of his officials. But my memory is crowded with instances of his personal generosity and affection. So to me his image still glows.

It is hard for me, therefore, to be objective about Jawaharlal Nehru. Yet I have tried; and I have been helped in this by the knowledge that this is what he himself would have wanted. His constant criticism of biographical writing in India was that it tended to be eulogistic and failed to assess the historical and impersonal forces at work.

This work has only been made possible by Shrimathi Indira Gandhi, who has given me unlimited access to her father's papers and placed no restriction on my freedom of opinion and judgement. These papers are now open up to

September 1946 and lodged in the Nehru Memorial Museum and Library at New Delhi. When no references are given, the quotations are from these papers. References to some papers which were at Anand Bhawan, Jawaharlal Nehru's residence at Allahabad, are given as Anand Bhawan papers. References to documents of the period after 1947 are given as from the Nehru papers. Many of Jawaharlal Nehru's letters, articles and statements are being published in the *Selected Works of Jawaharlal Nehru,* being brought out by the Jawaharlal Nehru Memorial Fund. Six volumes, covering the years up to the summer of 1936, have so far appeared, and references to these have been cited.

The official records consulted, unless otherwise stated, are those of the Government of India in the National Archives of India at New Delhi.

I am grateful to the Jawaharlal Nehru Memorial Fund which invited me to take up this work and granted me various facilities. Many people have talked to me about him, and this has been acknowledged in the footnotes. Sir Olaf Caroe has allowed me to consult his papers. Access was given to me by Dame Isobel Cripps to such of the Cripps papers as are at Nuffield College, Oxford; by Lady Beatrix Evison to the papers of her father, A.V. Alexander (later Earl Alexander of Hillsborough), at Churchill College, Cambridge; by Mr Robin Hallett to the papers of his father, Sir Maurice Hallett, in the India Office Library; and by the Librarian of the British Library of Political and Economic Science in the London School of Economics to the diaries of Beatrice Webb in the Passfield papers. Dorothy Woodman permitted me to go through the Kingsley Martin papers and the Laski papers which were then in her possession. Shankar has been good enough to let me reprint one of his cartoons.

Mr Christopher Hill most kindly read the manuscript and made many valuable suggestions. Mr Martin Gilbert has helped me with the proofs. I have exploited to the full the goodwill and scholarship of my colleagues at the Centre for Historical Studies in the Jawaharlal Nehru University. I am grateful to all of them.

Contents

Abbreviations

AICC	All-India Congress Committee
C.I.D.	Criminal Intelligence Department
Dep.	Deposit
D.I.B.	Director, Intelligence Bureau
D.S.V.A.	Draft second volume of autobiography
Gov.-Gen.	Governor-General
H.M.S.O.	Her. Majesty's Stationery Office
I.C.S.	Indian Civil Service
I.N.A.	Indian National Army
I.O.L.	India Office Library
Mss. Eur.	Manuscripts European
N.A.I.	National Archives of India
N.M.M.L.	Nehru Memorial Museum and Library
NWFP	North-West Frontier Province
Pol.	Political
S.W.	Selected Works
U.P.	United Provinces
U.P.P.C.C.	United Provinces Provincial Congress Committee

Illustrations

Illustrations in the text

Maps

Picture credits

The author and publishers would like to thank the following for permission to reproduce copyright material in the illustrations:

Associated Press Ltd: Plate 4
Jawaharlal Nehru Memorial Fund: Plates 1, 5, 6, 7, 9, 15, 17, 21, 22, 23, 24, 25, 26, 27, 28, 29, 31, 33, 34, 35; Illustrations in the text on pp. 190 and 347
Keystone Press Agency, 32
Press Association Ltd: Plates 10, 11, 12, 14, 18, 19, 20
Press Information Bureau, Government of India: Plates 2, 37
Radio Times Hulton Picture Library: Plates 3, 8, 13, 16, 30, 36
K. Shankar Pillai (Shankar): illustration in the text on p. 285

Picture research by Robyn Wallis.

Prologue

The years after the suppression of the revolt in 1858 marked the heyday of the *raj* in India. The British regarded themselves as a superior race ruling by right of conquest, and they saw no reason why they should not remain in India indefinitely. There was little hesitancy about accepting this position. Even Gladstone, who spoke normally in terms of holding India in trust and training Indians in self-government, could write in one of his unbuttoned moods, 'when we go, if we are ever to go . . . ' [1] Efficient administration was all that seemed to be required in order to maintain India within the empire in the interests of the British. They led the world in trade and manufacture, and India fitted smoothly into this pattern of world domination. Railways were laid down, with great profit to British investors and manufacturers but with little advantage to economic growth in India. There was a decline in the production of foodgrains and an incentive to grow cotton and jute, which were required by the factories in Britain, and indigo and opium, which sold at high prices abroad. India's export surplus was utilized to balance Britain's deficits with Europe and the United States; but British capital was mostly invested in 'white settler' countries. The banks in India were largely foreign and made no effort to attract Indian capital and direct it to the promotion of Indian industry. The refusal to permit industrialization on any major scale not only arrested progress but distorted the existing economy by increasing the pressure on land, with all the attendant evils of rural indebtedness, absentee landlordism and a large increase in landless labour and seasonal unemployment. The annual *per capita* income in 1875 has been officially estimated at about £2; and nearly 29 millions are thought to have died of starvation in the years from 1854 to 1901.

It was taken for granted that efficiency in administration meant that it would be, at any level that mattered, untouched by Indian hands. Education in the English language had been introduced in schools, and in 1857, the year that the revolt broke out, universities were established in the three leading

[1] Gladstone to Northbrook, 15 October 1872, Northbrook papers, India Office Library, Mss. Eur.C. 144, vol. 20, part I, p. 74.

towns of Calcutta, Bombay and Madras. But the products of these institutions were recruited to no higher posts than those of clerks. Entry by competitive examination into the higher official ranks was in theory open to Indians, but was made in practice almost impossible. All the senior appointments in the civil service were closed to Indians; and in the army, of course, there were no Indian officers at all. Indians were not permitted even to enlist in the volunteer corps.

Yet this unbroken monopoly of power had to be maintained in a vast country distant from the ultimate seat of authority, and by a civil service and troops which were numerically insignifi‿nt in comparison to those over whom they ruled. The revolt left with most British a legacy of hatred for Indians as well as an acceptance of the expediency of buttressing their rule with Indian support, if this could be obtained without compromise of their control. The obvious answer seemed to lie in an arrangement with the feudal classes. There were the 662 Indian Princes, with their principalities scattered over the country. Some, like Hyderabad, were as large as an Indian province, others were no more than small estates. But all these Princes had in common a total dependence on the British, who allowed them, in return for loyalty, to exercise despotic power over their subjects. In British India itself were the rural gentry, the *zamindars* of Bengal, the *talukdars* of the United Provinces and the landlords in other parts of the country. The revenue payable by them to the Government had been settled either in perpetuity or for long terms. It was on these men, whose economic interests were tied to those of the colonial system, that the British relied. It was from their ranks that nominees were chosen for the powerless legislative councils. Other empty, loud-sounding forms were also created to bind the conservative elements of Indian society to the empire without devolving any power or even influence. The Queen was declared Empress of India, an Imperial Assembly was held at Delhi, all the leading Indian Princes were given the title of Counsellors to the Empress, and uneducated young men of high birth were recruited to the lower levels of the public service.

There was, however, another class in India, the small, growing, élite of Indians educated in the English language. By 1885 they were not more than about 50,000. Some of them went into official service; but the majority, the lawyers, the doctors and the journalists, familiar with English political literature, were eager for wider avenues of public work. They were not revolutionaries, asserted their loyalty, and sought only greater opportunities of official employment, administrative reform, facilities for trade and a measure of elections to the legislative councils. For a time, in the years after 1880 when Gladstone was Prime Minister, an attempt was made to rely on this educated sector rather than on the upper classes. But even in the short term the attempt did not succeed. Local self-government never took root, while the effort to win middle-class support for the central government was broken by the weakness of the authorities and the fierce hostility of the British community in India.

The only result was a further quickening of political awareness and the formation of various associations, culminating with the establishment of the Indian National Congress in 1885.

The British Government were not happy about this, but could find no rational grounds for complaint. The Congress was not so much a party in opposition as an over-eager suppliant. Its supporters hoped that the British, who had, for their own reasons, helped to unify India, would now proceed to introduce modern technology and economic organization as well as representative government. That their rulers should reject such proposals, dismiss the Congress as a tiny group which represented nobody and encourage divisive trends in Indian politics were all shocks to their innocence.

1

Unformative Years

The broad details of the early life of Jawaharlal Nehru are by now well known. He himself, in his *Autobiography*, looked back with an untinted eye and provided a fairly detached, and even critical, account which has since been frequently paraphrased, and sometimes embroidered, by later writers. He was born at 11.30 p.m. on 14 November 1889 at Allahabad, to which place his father, Motilal Nehru, had moved three years earlier from Kanpur. Jawaharlal — the name was one which its owner never greatly fancied — was doted on by his parents; and this is not surprising, as Motilal had lost both a wife and son, had married again, and had lost another son before Jawaharlal, who remained an only child for eleven years.

Nothing, therefore, was going to be denied to Jawaharlal. A pampered child surrounded by luxury, with a private swimming pool and tennis court, Jawaharlal ran the risk of being smothered by devotion and affluence. Though Motilal's explosive temper frequently mitigated his spoiling of his son, there were no checks on the adulation Jawaharlal received from his mother, Swaruprani Nehru. As so often happened in Indian families of those days, the lack of companionship between husband and wife led to the mother building her life and her affections round her son.

The mother's influence ensured an Indian environment. The atmosphere of Hindu custom and folklore was not lacking in the Nehru home, and Jawaharlal picked up a great deal of legend from the women and indulged in temple-going and Ganga-bathing. When, in 1900, the father bought what was later known as Swaraj Bhawan, the boy was no doubt often told that this was on the site where, according to story, the *rishi* Bharadwaja had had his university, and that across the road where once the Ganga had flowed Rama was reported to have halted on his way to exile. But the Nehru family was never fully integrated into the high-caste Hindu society of Allahabad, for not only was Motilal a relative newcomer but he had been excommunicated in 1899 for his refusal to make atonement for having travelled overseas. This insulated the Nehrus from the revivalism then rampant in Hindu orthodox circles in Allahabad, and even cut them off from the more orthodox sections among the Kashmiri Pandits. Even as late as 1919, there was always a problem about the women of the Nehru household dining together with other Kashmiri women at weddings and other ceremonies.[1]

However, the Kashmiri Pandit community derived certain incidental advantages which distinguished it from the other Hindus. Among the Hindus of Kashmir, there were no castes below the Brahmins;[2] and so while the Pandits were very conscious of their status, inter-caste antagonisms did not enter deeply into their lives. There was also, among the Kashmiri Pandits, often little feeling of separateness from the Muslims. A small enclave community totalling never more than five to seven per cent in a State where the majority was Muslim, many of its members learnt Persian and sought official service. This eclectic, cosmopolitan tendency continued even among those who migrated southwards to the plains. Motilal himself was, like his ancestors, more fluent in Arabic and Persian and in Urdu than in any other Indian language. The chief retainer of his household was a Muslim, and it was from Mubarak Ali that Jawaharlal heard innumerable stories of heroism and tragedy of the years of the revolt.

The fortunes of the Nehrus had for generations been tied to Muslim patrons. There is no evidence for saying that in the early eighteenth century, Farruksiyar, the Mogul emperor, had invited Raj Kaul to join his court at Delhi. All that we do know is that Raj Kaul came to Delhi, and gradually the Kauls assumed the double-barrelled name of Kaul-Nehrus, because, it is said, their house was situated on the banks of a canal (*nahar* in Urdu).[3] Then, after the revolt of 1858, and the final collapse of the Mogul, the Kaul-Nehrus moved to Agra. They had left the canal, but it was the Kaul part of the name that gradually dropped out. The use of surnames in India was the result of British influence, and it is possible that as the Kaul-Nehrus were drawn into the British administrative network, they began to use that surname which was less indicative of their caste origins. If this be so, it hides an irony. The use of the surname Nehru did not become common till much later,[4] and even after it did, both father and son were commonly addressed as Pandit Motilal and Pandit Jawaharlal. Hard as he tried, Jawaharlal could never shake off this prefix which he found distasteful, and was referred to respectfully by his countrymen as 'Panditji'.[5]

The Nehrus were one of the many Indian families who took advantage of the conditions and opportunities created by the *raj*. At Delhi their landed estate had gradually dwindled, and Motilal's father, Ganga Dhar Nehru, was a minor police official. A portrait of him that exists depicts him in Mogul costume. He

[1] Urmila Haksar, *The Future That Was* (Delhi, 1972), p.24.

[2] See T. N. Madan, *Family and Kinship*, a study of the Pandits of rural Kashmir (London, 1965), p. 18.

[3] This was Motilal's theory, to which Jawaharlal gave currency in his *Autobiography*; but on the other hand, it has to be remembered that there were Nehrus even in Kashmir.

[4] As late as 1888 the list of delegates to the Congress session at Allahabad mentions not Motilal Nehru but 'Pandit Motilal, Hindu, Brahmin, Vakil High Court, North West Provinces.'

[5] 'Ji' denotes respect.

died in 1861, three months before the birth of Motilal, but the two older brothers, who themselves had taken service directly under the British or in a neighbouring Indian state, saw to it that Motilal received a proper education in the English language. He was a bright pupil, though he never graduated, and set up legal practice, first in Kanpur and then in Allahabad. The vast web of litigation created in the North-West Provinces by the *talukdari* system, debt, alienation, succession and transfers, and the enforcements of the revenue law made the province a paradise for an ambitious lawyer.[1] Specializing in these branches of the civil law, with many clients among the *zamindars* and *talukdars* and links doubtless with the Kashmiri Pandits who had infiltrated into the landed estates,[2] soon Motilal became one of the leaders of the Allahabad Bar.

Though Motilal had been born poor, had acquired many responsibilities at an early age as head of a large Hindu joint family, and was professionally equipped rather than generally educated, he had no complexes. A cheerful extrovert, full of the confidence and inner balance that come from self-made success, he set about living the life of an English gentleman. A photograph taken in 1894 shows him attired in English style, his wife, who was from an orthodox family of Lahore, in traditional Kashmiri dress, and his five-year-old son in a sailor suit. It is the kind of photograph a bourgeois English family would have had taken on a visit to Brighton.

Even the fact that his country was under alien rule did not subdue Motilal. He was too busy making money, and enjoying what money could buy. As soon as he could, he moved away from the traditional residential area of the Hindu middle class, and, till he bought a house of his own, lived in the Civil Lines where his neighbours were mostly British. He entertained generously, and his natural courtesy enabled him to overcome the restrictions of Anglo-Indian society and to make a number of English friends. His house was fitted with the latest gadgets imported from Europe. Like most members of the educated Indian élite, he took an interest in politics and dutifully attended as many sessions of the Indian National Congress as he could. But these were the years when the Congress was a loyalist organization, interested not in subverting British rule, not even in extracting concessions from it, but in pleading for greater opportunities for service.

So it was but natural that Motilal should want for his son the best that British education could offer. He first engaged two English governesses, and then sent his son for a few months to a local convent and finally decided on private instruction at home. The great Sanskrit scholar, Pandit Ganganatha Jha, tried, with no noticeable success, to teach Jawaharlal Sanskrit.[3] But the main emphasis was on a British tutor. A young and ardent Irish-French theosophist, F. T. Brooks, who had been recommended by Mrs Annie Besant, was in charge of Jawaharlal's education from 1901 to 1904. Brooks would seem to

---

[1] See the chapter 'The Frustration of Legal Remedy' in E. Whitcombe, *Agrarian Conditions in Northern India*, vol. 1 (Los Angeles, 1972), pp. 205ff.
[2] P. J. Musgrave, 'Landlords and Lords of the Land', *Modern Asian Studies*, July 1972, p. 269.
[3] See Jawaharlal's message on the death of Amaranatha Jha, 19 September 1955.

have been more interested in spreading theosophy in Allahabad, where he founded three lodges,[1] than in coaching his pupil; but he had a considerable influence on his impressionable charge. He introduced him to English poetry and literature and developed in him an interest in science by improvising a tiny laboratory in his rooms. He also, by allowing Jawaharlal to be present at his regular discourses on theosophy, planted in the boy's mind the idea that there might be more in religion than myth and miracle. The concept of ethics is what Jawaharlal perhaps rather vaguely comprehended when, at Brooks's instance, he read the not-too-easy *Upanishads* and the *Bhagavad Gita*. Certainly he was sufficiently engaged to seek and secure, at the age of thirteen, his father's permission to become a theosophist; and Mrs Besant herself initiated him at a solemn ceremony in Banaras. Motilal was right in not taking this seriously, and soon, once Brooks's influence was removed, Jawaharlal forgot all about the episode. But it was, in fact, more than a charade, and indicative of the delicacy of the young mind and spirit. Theosophy would also seem to have had a more permanent, though not major, influence, probably at a subconscious level, than Jawaharlal ever acknowledged. He always, for instance, unlike his father, favoured an austerity of diet.

Dissatisfied with private tuition, and in particular with Brooks, in May 1905 Motilal took his family to Britain and secured admission for his son at Harrow. Jawaharlal was now a boy of fifteen. Not very tall, and slightly built, he was handsome with a fair skin, clear features and well-brushed black hair which was, however, never very thick. For some time he sported a moustache, not so much because he fancied it as to please his father, who did not like his son's shaven face. In other words, you look like a fool.'[2] He was good at his school work and impressed his teachers. 'He looks very well and happy' wrote the headmaster to his father,[3] 'and is doing remarkably well in every way, being again head of his form, and winning golden opinions from his masters for his industry and ability.' The school report in October 1906 read, 'Inaccurate in French grammar, Latin poor, but he prepares well. English subjects excellent. Progress good — has brains.' In fact Jawaharlal was clever and diligent, and this was his best academic phase. He never fulfilled academically, in later years at Cambridge or the Bar, the promise he showed at Harrow. The reason was that he was not very keen, did not share his father's ambition for such prizes as the senior wranglership and did well at school merely because there was at this time very little else that interested him. He carried out his fagging duties, joined the chess club, played football and cricket, ran in the half-mile and mile races and in the cross-country steeplechase and was often in the gymnasium and on the ice-rink — but all in a rather desultory way. Only the Officers Training Corps roused any enthusiasm.

Jawaharlal was not unhappy at Harrow, and when he left after two years,

[1] *Theosophy in India* (1912), p.61.
[2] Motilal to Jawaharlal, 7 December 1905.
[3] Dr Joseph Wood to Motilal, 19 March 1906, Motilal Nehru papers, Nehru Memorial Museum and Library, New Delhi, (hereafter N. M. M. L.).

on the last night, he tells us, his pillow was covered with tears. But none of his teachers had any lasting influence on him, nor did 'Joe' Nehru, while generally liked, make any deep and enduring friendships. Lord Alexander of Tunis, who was his contemporary, remembered him as merely 'an average popular boy', not outstanding in any respect, and with no close friends or enemies.[1] Sir James Butler, who was in the Headmaster's house with Jawaharlal, could only say that he had not been particularly distinguished and had made no great mark in the House.[2] Jawaharlal was a quiet and somewhat lonely boy, and though, once he had settled down, he was not particularly homesick, he never quite fitted in nor felt at ease with his schoolfellows. The English boys he found mostly immature and childish, while the few Indians, belonging to the princely families, who were there, he heartily disliked. So he looked forward eagerly to Indian visitors with whom he could talk freely and in his own language; and the nostalgia for things Indian may explain his habit in his schooldays — which he l ter discarded — of chewing betel-nut, which his mother sent him from home. In his adult years Jawaharlal was very conscious of his Harrovian connexions. While in prison in the 'thirties, he stuck pictures of Harrow in his diaries and drew up lists of poets and politicians who had been to Harrow. He even sensed a certain affinity with Byron on the ground that they had both been to Harrow and Trinity, and he used to sing the school songs with the younger members of the family. As Prime Minister he attended an old boys' dinner in London, and in 1960 visited the school and received an enthusiastic welcome. But all this did not come very naturally, and he was doubtless far happier as an old Harrovian than in his actual years at that school.

Jawaharlal's arrival at Harrow coincided with startling events in India and outside, and it was now that he began, for the first time, to take an interest in politics and world affairs. In 1904 he had attended the Congress session at Bombay with his father, an occasion that, not surprisingly, had left no impression on him; but the situation was now very different. In 1905 the Viceroy, Lord Curzon, had, by his heavy-handed partitioning of the province of Bengal, forced the transition in India from the era of supplication to that of pressure. The broad-based agitation in Bengal found vigorous support in every other part of India because the partition was regarded not as a minor administrative reform but as a deliberate attempt to weaken the growing forces of Indian nationalism. So the *Swadeshi* movement, or the insistence on the use of articles of Indian manufacture, and the boycott of British goods, inaugurated in Bengal, spread far and wide and even, to Jawaharlal's surprise, reached distant Kashmir. Motilal too, normally no admirer of the 'oily babus' of Bengal, was stirred to sympathy and appreciation, and thought that they had after all justified themselves. 'The Bengali reigns supreme throughout Bengal . . . We are passing through the most critical period of British Indian history . . . *Bande Mataram*[3] has become the common form of salutation even in Allahabad . . .

[1] Interview with the author, 30 May 1969.
[2] Interview with the author, 16 February 1969.
[3] The name of a Bengali nationalist song, 'Hail to the Motherland'.

If this movement only continues you will on your return find an India quite different to the India you left.'[1] Jawaharlal was avid for news, and asked his father to mail Indian newspapers — 'not *The Pioneer*'[2] — to him regularly Motilal's own enthusiasm was short-lived, and soon he was denouncing the movement against partition as the most stupid and dishonest thing he had ever seen;[3] but Jawaharlal was not shaken.

The course of the agitation against partition accentuated division of opinion within the Congress, between the Extremists who believed in methods of agitation and the Moderates who were committed to constitutional processes. There was no disagreement between these two groups as to the objectives. The Extremists under Tilak were not revolutionaries who sought a violent end to British rule. Even their remote ideal was only a confederacy of Indian provinces with a measure of autonomy and the reservation of all Imperial questions for the British Government. All that they wanted immediately was to impress on public opinion in England that all was not well in India, and this purpose was shared by the Moderates. The only difference was as to the way that this should be done. While Gokhale and his followers believed in speeches, meetings and deputations, the slogan of Tilak was self-reliance. Jawaharlal found himself in sympathy with the Extremists, and Tilak seemed to him the embodiment of Indian nationalism struggling for freedom.[4] But it was a vague sympathy. The ideas were unformed and the emotion imprecise, going no further than, under the influence of Trevelyan's *Garibaldi,* swashbuckling fantasies. His political enthusiasm was still a form of idealized chivalric romance.

However, it was not only developments in India that excited Jawaharlal's interest. He followed, far more closely than most of the other boys at Harrow, the general election in 1905 in Britain, which swept the Liberal Party into power and enabled Campbell-Bannerman to form his government. Even more absorbing were the changes in Asia. On the day Jawaharlal landed in Britain, news came of Japan's decisive naval victory over Russia at Tshushima. Feeling relatively a stranger in a British public school, and with his mind full of reports of the growing estrangement between the British rulers and the Indian people, he thrilled to this evidence of the new strength of an Asian nation. It was at this time that he came across Meredith Townsend's *Asia and Europe*; and his mind was particularly receptive. For the thesis of that book, shorn of its crudities such as that caste was a form of socialism and that India would gradually become a Muslim country, was that Asia and Europe were separate in every sense. Neither could conquer the other with permanence, nor would the peoples of the two continents really come together, for there was an inherent antipathy between them. Europe had never enduringly influenced Asia and was unlikely ever to do so; in fact, Europe had received from Asia far more

[1] Letter to Jawaharlal, 16 November 1905.
[2] This was an English-owned newspaper of Lucknow.
[3] Letter to Jawaharlal, 4 January 1906.
[4] See his message on Tilak, 18 June 1956.

than she had given. About India in particular, Townsend was firmly of the view that the British had won no genuine loyalty from any section of the people, and their empire, which came in a day, would disappear in a night. The effort which the British had put forward in 1857 to hold their authority could never be repeated, for the British people had lost the energy and the unscrupulousness to maintain government by slaughter; but India could not be retained in any other way. Jawaharlal was willing to be convinced.

Bored with Harrow, Jawaharlal sat for the entrance examinations to Cambridge in the spring of 1907, a year before his father and his headmaster thought he should, and went up to Trinity that October. In the intervening summer he had spent a few weeks in Ireland. He missed the rioting in Belfast and was disappointed that Dublin was quiet during his stay. But he had felt, first-hand, the force of nationalist agitation and was impressed by the Sinn Fein movement. He recommended to his father a book just then published, *The New Ireland* by Sydney Brooks, which saw in Ireland the rebirth of an ancient nation and commended the Sinn Fein movement for its revolt against 'thimble-rigging' politics and its belief that nothing could be secured from England by whining. Such gains as Ireland had made in the past had been by extortion. The only sound policy for Ireland to follow was that which caused England the greatest annoyance. But there was no need for violence; all that was required to thwart the alien ruler was to ignore him and boycott his merchandise. The parallel in India was, of course, obvious, and Jawaharlal's visit to Ireland and his understanding of her politics seem to have strengthened his Extremist sympathies. The result was that he became more critical of his father's attitude in politics. He accused Motilal of being 'immoderately moderate',[1] and a later light-hearted reference to the Government demonstrating their satisfaction with 'the insulting offer of a Rai Bahadurship'[2] hurt Motilal so deeply that Jawaharlal had to apologize.

The extremism, however, was confined to his letters to his father. Jawaharlal did not plunge into the student politics of Cambridge. He never spoke at the Union, though he was a member and used the club rooms. He joined the Magpie and Stump, the debating society of his own college, within a week of coming up, his name having been proposed by St John Philby and seconded by Charles Darwin. However, although failure to speak throughout a term meant payment of a fine, during his three years Jawaharlal spoke only once, for two minutes thirty seconds on 29 May 1908 on the motion 'This house approves of the present public school system. '[3] Unfortunately, the minutes do not disclose whether Jawaharlal spoke for or against the motion. Nor does he seem to have taken part in the debates in doggerel, mock trials and pageants and smoking concerts organized by this club.

[1] Letter, 20 December 1907, *Selected Works of Jawaharlal Nehru* (hereafter S.W.) vol. 1 (Delhi, 1972), p. 39.
[2] Letter, 30 January 1908, S.W., vol. 1, p. 44.
[3] Minutes of the Magpie and Stump Debating Society, Trinity College Library.

As for the other undergraduate societies, Jawaharlal was a member of the Majlis, the society of Indian students which he joined despite his father's disapproval. He seems to have attended many of its meetings and dinners but, again, rarely spoke. The only report we have of a speech was at an *Id* dinner, where he spoke reluctantly but when he did is said to have spoken well.[1] Palme Dutt, a schoolboy in those days, remembers Jawaharlal occasionally attending the meetings of the Majlis which used to be held in his father's house, but the impression that Jawaharlal had left on him was that of being an aesthetic rather than a political type.[2]

Therein, perhaps, lies part of the answer. Jawaharlal was wincingly shy, and public speaking must have seemed to him a nightmare. But, in addition, the passionate debates that went on among the Indian students on the relative merits of moderation and extremism must also have seemed to him rather vulgar. He had, for example, warmly defended in his letters Bepin Pal, one of the Extremist leaders, when Motilal had sneered at him as 'the great bathroom hero of Barisal';[3] but Pal's speech at Cambridge when, apart from adopting a narrowly Hindu attitude and speaking of India as God's chosen country, he had thundered to a small audience as if he were at a public meeting, embarrassed Jawaharlal acutely. So he wrote to Allahabad welcoming the split in the Congress at Surat and expressing his firm belief that in a very few years there would hardly be any Moderates left; but in Cambridge he successfully kept his opinions to himself.

These opinions, it should be added, were still not deep-seated or transforming his whole outlook. They were but a natural part of the general posture of dilettantism which Jawaharlal deliberately cultivated. Though he told no one but his father of these views, the occasional assertion doubtless gave him inner satisfaction. But that was all. There was no greater hint of the rebel about him or about his view of his own future. He showed at this time no real signs of any sort of fire or distinction, and did not stand out among his generation. He accepted the values and ambitions of his class, and was quite at ease in the vapid society of Indian middle-class convention. He did not, despite his epistolary extremism, resist the hopes which his father had nurtured from the start of entombing him in the Indian Civil Service. In fact, it was Motilal who, early in 1910, abandoned the idea of Jawaharlal sitting for the I.C.S. examination, mainly because he could not brook the prospect of his only son serving for long years in remote districts away from home, and had a growing feeling that the examiners were biased against Indian candidates. But neither father nor, more startlingly in the light of later events, son resented the thought of serving the British rulers. They had not yet recognized the necessity of freedom. In 1912, after listening to Fenner Brockway urging that India should move on

[1] Syed Mahmud, 'Jawaharlal Nehru as I knew him', Islamic Institute files. I owe this reference to Mr David Page.
[2] Interview with the author, 20 November 1969.
[3] Letter, 18 October 1907.

to independence, Jawaharlal criticized the speaker privately for his extremist speech.[1]

The impression Jawaharlal gives as an undergraduate is of a man only half-awakened and waiting for further experience and comprehension. He attended, in his first term, a lecture by Bernard Shaw on Socialism and the University Man, but more to see the speaker than to hear him. Shaw's plays, and even more his prefaces, had already begun to fill him with excitement, and to the end of his days Shaw 'occupied a niche in my mind and I have sought his company to my great advantage'.[2] But it was, one suspects, Shaw the social crusader rather than the political reformer who so appealed to Jawaharlal. Fabianism, with its hopes of reforming capitalism and imperceptibly gliding to socialism, was at this time popular in Cambridge, but it seems to have attracted Jawaharlal little, and there is no reason to believe that he was a member of the Cambridge Fabian Society. [3] Hugh Dalton, also at Cambridge at this time and prominent in the Fabian Society and the Union, knew Jawaharlal slightly but does not remember much else about him.[4] He clearly made no impact in left-wing circles. But Jawaharlal was, as we know, interested in William Morris, and bought a full set of the collected works, which began to be issued from 1910.[5] There was clearly greater affinity with Morris than with Shaw. The revolt of Morris against the ugliness of industrial capitalism and its impoverished human relationships had led on to a frontal attack on class exploitation and the evils of imperialism. The life of Morris was the story of the evolution of a revolutionary, the progress from aestheticism to the basic question of class power; and Jawaharlal may have been, in his own context, moving in the same direction. His moral sensibility and fastidiousness were beginning to develop in the social context. His awareness of the class issue is indicated by a trivial fact: his keenness to dance with a waitress to discover what she would talk about.

Looking back on these years, Jawaharlal described his primary mood as a vague kind of Cyrenaicism.[6] But even the assiduous cultivation of pleasure seems to have been only half hearted. Cambridge in those days was an exciting place, but Jawaharlal never got into its full swing. In his own college, admittedly a large one with about 600 members, he hardly seems to have been noticed. He lived the first year in lodgings, at 40 Green Street, and then in Whewell Court, in what he described as 'probably the rottenest rooms in the whole college', with the only advantage that they were near the baths. He got on well with his tutor, Sir Walter Fletcher, but neither Fletcher nor any other senior member of the university had a great influence on him. He took as his

[1]Lord Brockway in a B.B.C. broadcast. See *Personality and Power* (B.B.C. publication, 1971), p. 55.

[2]To S. S. Dhavan 15 July 1950. Nehru papers.

[3]The records of the Cambridge University Fabian Society for these years are unfortunately not available.

[4]*Call Back Yesterday* (London, 1953), p. 52.

[5]See his letter to E. P. Thompson, written in 1955. Nehru papers.

[6]*Autobiography* (Indian edition, 1962), p. 20.

subjects chemistry, geology and physics but soon gave up physics for botany, and in the final tripos was placed in the second half of the second class. This was an achievement well below the level of his talent, but Jawaharlal was not by temperament an academic, and appears to have done very little work. However, he had so diligently prepared his family for an outright failure that the result was received with champagne. The type of education provided at Cambridge and Oxford seemed to him of little value to an Indian. He was not therefore greatly concerned at the proposal to restrict the admission of Indians to Cambridge, and took no part in the controversy that raged fiercely on this issue during his years at the university. He believed that it would be an advantage if such restriction forced Indian students to go to universities in Europe and elsewhere, and thus be better fitted for the world.

Outside the laboratories and lecture rooms, Jawaharlal led a busy life, even if it was unspectacular. He played tennis, rode a great deal and applied for admission to the University Mounted Infantry. He was summoned to a riding test but did not go, ostensibly for lack of time but probably because he knew that as an Indian he would be rejected, for at that time Indians were not admitted. He joined the Trinity Boat Club and being only 8 st. 4 lb. in weight was made cox. He had not looked forward to this, but proved efficient enough. In the third-division trials his boat won easily. 'Nehru coxed well', says the record.[1] In the Lent college races in 1908, however, his boat was no great success. 'On the whole', he wrote over fifty years later,[2] 'I rather liked it though my boat . . . did not perform any wonders. All we could manage to do was to go through the races with some dignity and avoid being bumped.' Here his memory was being kind. In fact his boat was bumped thrice. He did not go on the river again.

Jawaharlal had many acquaintances but no small intimate social circle, no close friendships without reserve; nor does he seem to have known any women. His public-school background helped him to do without them. But as he confessed to his father, at times he was 'almost overpowered by the sense of my solitary condition'.[3] As for his vacations they were spent frequently in hydros, which were hotels meant mainly for invalids. Where, then, was the successful pursuit of egoistic hedonism, the deliberate achievement of sensation? It was obviously a pose to cover an emptiness in his life. Jawaharlal had opinions but needed a cause; there stretched before him a future secure but with no purpose. He accepted the *ennui* of bourgeois stability for want of anything more demanding. He went through his years at Cambridge without demur, although its attractions had little to offer him.

Even before his final tripos examination, Jawaharlal had joined the Inner Temple, and the fond father believed that the son had followed his aptitude.

---

[1] Trinity Boat Club minutes, Trinity College Library.
[2] To his nephew Harsha Hutheesing, 26 August 1959. Nehru papers.
[3] Letter, 29 October 1908. S.W., vol. 1, p. 59.

Motilal was confident of Jawaharlal's success; 'if my knowledge of human nature does not deceive me I think he is bound to rise in his father's profession. He has already begun to like it and in deciding that he should devote his energies to the study of law I have only followed the bent of his own mind.' [1] Motilal felt that he himself had but five or six years' work left in him, but in that period he intended to merge his own professional existence in that of Jawaharlal, have no clients of his own but pass them on to his son and place Jawaharlal well on the road to success.[2] He had failed to realize that Jawaharlal had no enthusiasm for the law and joining the Inner Temple was merely part of his general policy, at this time, of drift. He was bored with Cambridge, which was 'becoming too full of Indians', and wanted a change; but it was Oxford rather than London that he had preferred. When Motilal opposed this because he wanted Jawaharlal, in addition to qualifying for the Bar, to work in the chambers of a senior lawyer and attend the law courts, he at last had an inkling into his son's mind. He would much rather, wrote Jawaharlal, risk his success at the Bar than go through life as a mere lawyer with no interest in anything save the technicalities and trivialities of law.

However, as usual, Jawaharlal gave way to his father's wishes and moved to London. The only sop given him was permission to join the London School of Economics. 'Politics are inseparable from law and economics the soul of politics.'[3] But being forced to do what he disliked resulted, as was to be expected, in Jawaharlal leading a life of idleness. But before that he had nearly succeeded in killing himself. On a holiday in Norway with a friend, while trekking somewhere north of Bergen,[4] he plunged into an ice-cold fjord for a bath and became numb. His foot slipped and he was swept away by the current. His companion pulled him out on the brink of a waterfall. But Jawaharlal was always a man of physical courage, and proximity to death pleased rather than sobered him.

For the next two years Jawaharlal was caught up in the whirl of London life. Renewing contact with some old school acquaintances, he was very much the gay man of fashion — 'very well-dressed, well-mannered, almost European'.[5] Music concerts, golf at Crowborough, tennis at the Queen's Club, watching cricket at Lord's and waltzing on ice-rinks, rather than attending lectures at the L.S.E. and devilling at the law, took up his time. The pastimes seem to have been innocent but they were expensive. Never overloaded with money, Jawaharlal now found himself often in debt, was forced to pawn his watch and chain, sometimes had no money even for bus or tube fare, and more and more frequently approached his father for supplementary

[1] Motilal to his brother 30 January 1910. Motilal Nehru papers.

[2] Motilal to Jawaharlal, 1 September 1910 and 6 January 1911.

[3] Motilal to Jawaharlal, 13 October 1910. Motilal Nehru papers.

[4] Jawaharlal could not remember the exact place; letter to Judge Andren, 11 October 1954. Nehru papers.

[5] Brockway, op. cit., p. 55.

grants. He never in his life had any money sense. 'If I had £5000 a year I am sure I would spend it all with the greatest ease and then get into debt.'[1]

His expenditure in 1911 was about £800, which in those years enabled most Indian students to pay for a stay of three years in London. Motilal was alarmed. Far from carrying off the scholarships and prizes at the Bar examinations, Jawaharlal just managed to pass, and seemed more interested in concerts. 'Your papers at the last exam. must have been very musical. I hope the examiners had the sense to appreciate them. It would perhaps be an improvement in future to let the musical treat follow the exam. instead of allowing the two to overlap.'[2] And when, the next year, Jawaharlal passed the Bar finals, Motilal expressed his great relief. 'I do not look upon it as a great achievement. But you have eminently succeeded in investing the event with an importance which it did not possess.'[3]

Such heavy sarcasm irritated Jawaharlal, and when his father wrote a brusque letter demanding to see his accounts, Jawaharlal replied with such acidity that this time it was Motilal's turn to apologize. The fact was that Jawaharlal was spending much but enjoying himself little. He was bored and listless rather than immersed in extravagant dissipation, and the gaiety was very much on the surface. Never in perfect harmony with the British environment, he was quite happy to return in August 1912 to what Motilal termed 'this land of regrets'. In his *Autobiography* Jawaharlal described himself at that time, a young man of 23, as 'a bit of a prig with little to commend me'.[4] It was a harsh self-judgment. In fact he seems to have been a rather vague and unpractical person, dominated, even suppressed, by a doting and determined father. Jawaharlal had done all the things he had been told to do, but with no great enthusiasm. His deep attachment to his father had the defect that it made him almost passive. He was willing to conform and to leave the major decisions of his life to be made by his father. He had emerged from seven years in England, having passed through the mill of a traditional education, with no confidence in himself or interest in the world. But his mind and character had been trained not for a profession but for the call which was to come in the years ahead. Two stray remarks in his letters home give some indication of the future. 'I am', he wrote to his father,[5] 'an ardent believer in a child — or for the matter of that a grown up person — being endowed with a lot of imagination, and can conceive of no greater evil than for a person to be totally devoid of it. Of course too much imagination is bad for one, but I had rather suffer from that than from the other extreme.' And again, looking back on his years in England towards the end of his stay, he commented, 'To my mind education does not consist of passing examinations or knowing English or mathematics.

[1] Letter to father, 11 April 1912.
[2] Motilal to Jawaharlal, 15 June 1911.
[3] Idem, 6 June 1912.
[4] p. 26.
[5] 20 October 1911.

It is a mental state and if this is not present it matters little how many examinations a person has passed.'[1] Others might have been disappointed that he
had not fulfilled the promise of Harrow and carried off the academic spoils,
but Jawaharlal himself saw no reason to regret or repent. He returned to India
with a nurtured mind and imagination.

In addition, he brought back with him attachments to Britain, and the
values he considered British, which were never to leave him. They moulded
his outlook, sustained him in his struggles and influenced his policies in the
days of his power. Throughout his life, Britain was a country with which
Jawaharlal identified extensively in the personal sense. He himself was aware
of this.

Less than ten years ago [he told the judge at his trial in May 1922[2]] I
returned from England after a lengthy stay there. I had passed through
the usual course of public school and university. I had imbibed most
of the prejudices of Harrow and Cambridge and in my likes and dislikes
I was perhaps more an Englishman than an Indian. I looked upon the
world almost from an Englishman's standpoint. And so I returned to
India as much prejudiced in favour of England and the English as it
was possible for an Indian to be.

Indeed, he felt that his reaction to foreign rule would be that, in similar
circumstances, of any average Englishman uncontaminated by imperialism.
Addressing an audience of schoolchildren he advised them to emulate the
spirit of adventure and patriotism which inspired the English schoolboy and
impressed upon them how the ancestors of the British had risked their lives
in the past. That spirit was the possession of free nations but in India it had
died during the past one hundred and fifty years of slavery. [3]

[1] 26 April 1912.
[2] S.W., vol. 1, pp. 252-3.
[3] Address to the Tilak Vidyalaya, Allahabad, 2 April 1922, U. P. Government Intelligence
Reports for 1922.

2

Marking Time

Back in India, Jawaharlal slipped without resistance into the vacuous, parasitic life of upper-middle-class Indian society in Allahabad. He joined his father's chambers and Motilal saw to it that work came his way. 'An over-zealous client sent a money order for Rs.500 to you as your fee and it has been redirected to Mussoorie. The first fee your father got was Rs. 5 (five only). You are evidently a hundred times better than your father. I wish I were my son instead of being myself. Rao Maharajsingh has several cases pending in the High Court and I do not know in which of them he intends to retain you. But the money is yours . . .'[1] Clearly, though the father's pride forbade him to recognize it, Jawaharlal was being paid handsomely to keep Motilal happy. Jawaharlal toiled fairly hard and had the advantages of his father's sponsorship and of social contacts with judges, eminent lawyers like Sapru and Rash Behari Ghose and the leading landlords and industrialists of the U. P. But he could whip up no enthusiasm for the law, was shy of speaking, and found the work tedious.'Reading books written by great lawyers', he wrote long after, 'is apt to make one think of big and intricate cases. But the average lot of the lawyer, especially a junior one, is to deal with petty and rather dull cases.'[2] So it is doubtful whether, even if politics had not seduced him, he would have developed into one of the leading lawyers of the U.P. or India. It is more likely, as he himself thought, that if he had continued at the Bar he would have led a comfortable existence and retired as a judge, 'highly respectable and solemn looking',[3] but probably of no great distinction.

Apart from professional work, Jawaharlal continued in Allahabad the life of a man-about-town which he had led in his last years in London. He enjoyed the lavish entertainments of his father; and there are, in addition, reports of his own late-night parties and revels. The casual sympathy with Extremist

[1] Motilal to Jawaharlal, 21 October 1912.
[2] To Harsha Hutheesing, 26 August 1959. Nehru papers.
[3] ' The Mind of a Judge', *Modern Review,* September 1935, reprinted in *India and the World* (London, 1936), pp. 130-45.

politics which he had shown in Cambridge did not inhibit him from participating in the formal rounds of Anglo-Indian society. He left his cards at the homes of English judges and officials, and they in turn called on him. 'Called on 8 English families', runs the entry in his pocket diary for 27 March 1916; and again three days later,'Called on 9 English families'.

However, the great event of that year was his marriage on 8 February 1916. This question had been worrying Motilal and his wife ever since their son went to Harrow. For even though their son was then only a boy of fifteen, Motilal was concerned lest Jawaharlal begin to show interest in women, particularly in view of the entanglement of one of his friends. Writing, as he said, not as a father but as his dearest friend, Motilal invited confidences, warned against passing passions, and condemned the concept of love at first sight.[1]

Motilal had no cause for worry. His son, apart from showing little interest in women, declared that he had never been in favour of marrying a European and had, during his years in England, seen no reason to change his opinion.[2] He sometimes gave expression to idealized views about marriage.

> Would you like me to marry a girl whom I may not like for the rest of my life and who may not like me? Rather than marry in that way, I would greatly prefer to remain unmarried. After all, I have to spend my whole life with my wife. Is it surprising, then, if I wish to marry a girl whom I like? I am not obliged to like a girl of a good family, nor is it to be taken for granted that every educated girl would come up to my expectations. I accept that any girl selected by you and father would be good in all respects, but still, I may not be able to get along well with her. In my opinion, unless there is a degree of mutual understanding, marriage should not take place. I think it is unjust and cruel that a life should be wasted merely in producing children.[3]

But there is, in the number of letters he wrote on this subject, little evidence of a desire in his own life for an intense and romantic experience. Once, while still at Harrow, he evinced an upsurge of restlessness which quite surprised his father.

> The sooner it is done the better it will be. I am in no hurry to get married or even engaged but it is most tiring and annoying not to know what is going to happen. If no one had ever mentioned anything about my marriage I would have been quite contented and happy, but now that all this fuss and trouble has been taken I cannot rest till something is done.[4]

But in fact it was irritation rather than impatience. Jawaharlal was tired of

[1] Letters to Jawaharlal, 1 March 1906 and 1 September 1910.
[2] Jawaharlal to his father, 30 September 1910.
[3] Letter to his mother, 14 March 1912 (Original in Hindi). S.W., vol. 1, p. 97.
[4] Letter to his father, 21 December 1906.

the subject and wished to be done with it. With an odd detachment he wanted his father to settle his engagement so that there need be no further discussion.

This suited Motilal, who took, as of natural right and with Jawaharlal's consent, the decisions in this as in all other major matters in his son's life. 'It is all right my boy. You may leave your future happiness in my hands and rest assured that to secure that is the one object of my ambition.'[1] The conditions of Indian life, he assured Jawaharlal, were so different to those prevailing in Europe and elsewhere that Jawaharlal's happiness could not be secured by leaving him to act independently of his parents.[2] There were only two points which Jawaharlal suggested rather weakly: that he need not necessarily marry within the Kashmiri community, and that the engagement need not be fixed while he was still in England and had hardly had the chance to know the girl. 'I hope', he hastened to add,[3] 'you will take my objections into consideration before arriving at a decision, which of course lies with you.' But Kashmiri Pandits, even those who had migrated to Allahabad, had a strong sense of exclusiveness,[4] and in this respect Motilal was no more immune than the rest. So he preferred a Kashmiri if he could find a suitable one and he surveyed the Kashmiri girls everywhere, even those settled in Madras, for one who was neither an illiterate beauty nor a plain blue-stocking, but combined good looks with education. 'I asked Jawahar if he preferred books to looks or *vice versa*. His answer was that I might as well ask if he preferred a nose to eyes — they were both necessary.'[5] There was no obvious 'Blue Bird' to be found who would not require a special course of preparation and instruction before she fully qualified to be Jawaharlal's wife; but Motilal could see no far superior person outside the community either, and this strengthened his feeling akin to prejudice against it.[6] However, the lack of an obvious candidate enabled Motilal to yield to his son's second suggestion, that he should see the girl before the final selection.

After years of search, in 1912, just before Jawaharlal's return to India, Motilal chose Kamala Kaul, a young girl of thirteen belonging to a Kashmiri Brahmin middle-class family who ran a flour mill in Delhi. Jawaharlal, being nearly ten years older, thought she was too young for him. Nor did he think he could marry her for another six to seven years, till she was at least eighteen or nineteen. But this did not worry him as he was not, as he observed, 'in a matrimonial state of mind at present';[7] and it suited Motilal as it provided time to mould the young girl into a proper wife for Jawaharlal. She had been educated at home and spoke Hindi and Urdu; and after the engagement she

[1] Motilal to Jawaharlal, 21 February 1907.
[2] Idem, 9 December 1910.
[3] Letter to his father, 7 October 1910.
[4] Cf. Urmila Haksar, writing of the late 'twenties: 'For the first time, in Allahabad I became aware of the fact that we were Kashmiris and that it set us apart from the rest of Indians in the country. "We" were Kashmiris whereas everyone else was "they".' Op. cit., pp. 44-5.
[5] Motilal to his brother, 11 February (1911?). Motilal Nehru papers.
[6] Letters to Jawaharlal, 1 September and 28 October 1910.
[7] Letter to his father, 26 April 1912.

was brought to Allahabad for training in deportment. When she was seventeen the marriage was celebrated in Delhi on a munificent scale, with special trains carrying the guests to the 'Nehru marriage camp'.

That summer Jawaharlal spent in Kashmir. He went in pursuit of bear and shot one as well as a large number of pigeons and marmots. He also had his second brush with death. Trekking up to the top of the Zoji-la, a very stiff climb of about three and a half miles, he then attempted to go over the Amarnath shoulder into the head of the valley above the cave. From Matayan he and his friends moved to Gumba and went up to the Gumba ravine and glacier. After climbing a very steep gradient for miles, they arrived at the top of the glacier and then set off, at about 17,000 feet, in bad weather, to cross a large ice-field covered with fresh snow. Trying to hop across a crevasse, Jawaharlal slipped and fell in, and was pulled out by the rope. As there were many other such crevasses and it was still snowing, the party turned back.[1]

Along with high life and *shikar,* there was the usual ostentatious public service. For three or four years Jawaharlal served as one of the provincial secretaries of the St John Ambulance Association. He was also one of the joint secretaries of the U.P. South Africa Committee for the collection of funds for Gandhi's passive resisters in South Africa, but this was not an anti-Government activity, for the Government of India had frequently expressed their support for the Indian community in South Africa. He was willing to join the Indian Defence Force, constituted on the lines of the territorial army, and encourage other young Indians to do the same. It was decided to constitute a strong and representative committee in Allahabad for this purpose, and an invitation to all who were interested was published in the local newspapers.[2]

Within a week, however, the situation underwent a marked change. For many years the Indian national movement had been at a low ebb. The Congress was controlled by the Moderates who were satisfied with the annual adoption of academic resolutions. Jawaharlal and others like him in the U.P. had no great interest in such activity nor were they drawn into Extremist agitation. Tilak and Mrs Besant, failing to secure the re-admission of the Extremists into the Congress, had set up Home Rule Leagues. Mrs Besant's plan was to agitate on the lines of British radical movements in the nineteenth century, and in April 1915 she had presided over the U.P. Provincial Conference.[3] Jawaharlal had taken no interest in this. His first public speech was on 20 June 1916, to protest against the Press Act and the demand from Mrs Besant of security under that Act,[4] but this intervention would seem to have been

---

[1] Diary entries from 24 August to 7 September 1916; letter to S. S. Khera, 1 July 1958, Nehru papers.

[2] Notice signed among others by Motilal, Jawaharlal and T.B. Sapru, 13 June 1917, *The Leader,* 22 June 1917.

[3] See H.F. Owen, 'The Home Rule Leagues 1915-18', in D.A. Low (ed.), *Soundings in Modern South Asian History* (London, 1968), pp. 159-95.

[4] Report in *The Leader,* 23 June 1916.

more out of personal loyalty to Mrs Besant, whom he had known from his child-hood, than from any strong feelings about the freedom of the press. It was no sparkling performance, and all that his father could say, after reading the report in the press, was that the speech, though not very informative, had the rare merit of being free from commonplaces, which was the besetting sin of all Indian speakers, at least in the U. P.[1] He had not been anything more than a silent spectator at the Lucknow Congress in December 1916. But what Mrs Besant and Tilak had failed to achieve on their own was accomplished by the Government.

The Home Rule Leagues of Mrs Besant were intended to be primarily educative — to argue the case for Home Rule, hold classes and seminars, cir-culate literature, collect funds and organize social work. But the Government feared Mrs Besant's influence. She was first expelled from Bombay and then from the Central Provinces and finally, in June 1917, interned at a hill station by the Madras Government. This panicky step caused resentment throughout India; and among those roused to annoyance was Jawaharlal. He was, at long last, beginning to find his role. The meeting for considering the expansion of the Indian Defence Force was promptly cancelled;[2] and Jawaharlal withdrew his own application for enlistment. A Home Rule League was formed in the U. P. with Motilal as president and Jawaharlal as one of the joint secretaries. The internment of Mrs Besant seemed to him a sign of the madness which had befallen the bureaucracy and presaged its fall. 'Home Rule has come and we have but to take it if we stand up like men and falter not.' Mere protest meetings and representations were the politics of cowards and opium-eaters: what was now needed was non-co-operation with the Government till they re-versed their folly.[3]

Such vehemence showed that despite the superficiality of his way of living, his spirit was not dead and he was keen on action. He had been greatly moved by Roger Casement's speech at his trial. 'It seemed', he said years later,[4] 'to point out exactly how a subject nation should feel.' In August 1917, when Motilal called on the British public, 'the sole tribunal appointed by Providence', to mediate between the Indian people and the bureaucracy, someone from the audience shouted 'Question'. Motilal lost his temper and challenged the heckler to come out in the open. There was complete silence.[5] What is of inter-est is that we now know that the timid heckler was Jawaharlal.[6] But what action should be taken, what form non-co-operation should be given, was not clear to him. He had no startling ideas of his own. Neither the Anglo-Saxon approach

[1] Motilal to Jawaharlal, 27 June 1916.

[2] Letter to the editor, 20 June 1917, *The Leader,* 22 June 1917.

[3] Letter to the editor, *The Leader,* 21 June 1917.

[4] B. Inglis, *Roger Casement* (London, 1973), p. 346.

[5] Account of Kapil Deva Malaviya, *Pandit Motilal Nehru,* cited in B.R. Nanda, *The Nehrus* (London, 1962), p. 139.

[6] Eye-witness account of Sachidananda Sinha in his article on Motilal Nehru. Sachidananda Sinha papers at Patna.

of Mrs Besant nor the orthodox extremism of Tilak had any great appeal for him, and, while he spoke in terms of Home Rulers capturing the Congress, [1] he had given no thought as to what should be done once that organization had been taken over. In fact his mind, for lack of anything better, fell into Moderate grooves, and he objected to the refusal by the Government to permit deputations to proceed to England to plead the cause of Home Rule [2] At this time, unlike the year before, it was Motilal who was the stauncher revolutionary, and he pointed out to Jawaharlal that the work which lay before them in India was far more important than anything that deputations could achieve in England.[3]

So Jawaharlal, even in his late twenties, was a man who had yet to know his mind, discontented with his lot of comfort and affluence, dissatisfied with merely helping to run *The Independent,* the newspaper started by his father in February 1919 to give voice in the U. P. to the viewpoint of the Congress, and groping for some form of action which would provide mental and emotional satisfaction. When, therefore, the call of Gandhi came he could respond to it not merely at a political but at a human level. Long after, looking back on these fallow years, he remarked that it was the acceptance of Gandhi's leadership, and the civil disobedience and jail-going which had followed, that had made a man of him.[4] Life now had meaning in the service of a cause.

---

[1] See his letter to A.M. Khwaja, 12 December 1917.

[2] Resolution moved by Jawaharlal at the U.P. Political Conference, *The Leader,* 16 October 1918.

[3] Motilal to Jawaharlal, 16 February 1919.

[4] Narendra Deva, 'Favourite of Fortune', in *Nehru Abhinandan Granth* (New Delhi, 1949), p. 108.

3

Immersion in Politics

The Independent began its career with severe criticism of the Rowlatt Bills, whereby the Government of India established summary procedures for dealing with political agitation; and Jawaharlal did not rule out the possibility of his arrest. 'That too would be preferable to the present state of doubt and despair.'[1] This did not happen. Jawaharlal was one of the signatories of the *satyagraha* vow, formulated by Gandhi, pledging refusal to obey cer ain laws, and, a member of the committee formed at Allahabad to organize *satyagraha* in that district and to get in touch with other districts to constitute a provincial committee.[2] After the massacre at Amritsar, he assisted the Congress Inquiry Committee, and visited Amritsar and the Punjab to take depositions and collect material for the speeches in the Assembly of his father and Pandit Malaviya, a moderate Congress leader, about the actual firing, the atrocities under martial law and the 'general misbehaviour of tommies'.[3] He also helped in relief work, though the Government believed that any distinction between such humanitarian effort and political agitation was fanciful.[4] The Allahabad *Seva Samiti*, or relief organization, raised over a *lakh*[5] of rupees for the work and Jawaharlal took some volunteers with him to the Punjab to help in organizing such relief.[6] A chance encounter with General Dyer on a train led to a classic piece of description:

---

[1] To Padmaja Naidu, 22 February 1919.

[2] *The Leader*, 3 April 1919. *Satyagraha*, or 'truth-force', was Gandhi's name for his technique of passive resistance.

[3] *Notes on the Occurrences in the Punjab*, April-June 1919. S.W., vol. 1, pp. 130-40. At Amritsar, General Dyer, dealing with civil disorder, had opened fire without warning on a large crowd that had inadequate means of dispersal, ordered that Indians could only crawl on their stomachs along a street in which an English woman had been attacked and had some persons whom he suspected of defiance of this order summarily whipped.

[4] Report on the political and economic situation in the Punjab for the fortnight ending 15 September 1919. Home Dept. Political Deposit, October 1919. Proceeding 59.

[5] A *lakh* is one hundred thousand.

[6] Note of the U.P. Criminal Investigation Dept., 18 December 1919. Home Dept. Pol. A., June 1921, Proceedings 248-62.

The compartment I entered was almost full and all the berths except one upper one, were occupied by sleeping passengers. I took the vacant upper berth. In the morning I discovered that all my fellow-passengers were military officers. They conversed with each other in loud voices which I could not help overhearing. One of them was holding forth in an aggressive and triumphant tone and soon I discovered that he was Dyer, the hero of Jallianwala Bagh,[1] and he was describing his Amritsar experiences. He pointed out how he had the whole town at his mercy and he had felt like reducing the rebellious city to a heap of ashes, but he took pity on it and refrained. He was evidently coming back from Lahore after giving his evidence before the Hunter Committee of Enquiry. I was greatly shocked to hear his conversation and to observe his callous manner. He descended at Delhi station in pyjamas with bright pink stripes, and a dressing-gown.[2]

Jawaharlal wrote to the press in rather stilted language in defence of Malaviya and Motilal when the Punjab Government accused them of not substantiating their charge that some police officers had taken bribes. 'It would be weariness to the flesh to controvert all the misstatements which Mr. Thompson managed to compress in his two speeches in Council.'[3] Jawaharlal met the Deputy Commissioner of Amritsar on 5 September on his father's behalf and said the data in Motilal's possession regarding police bribery would be disclosed on condition that those who had provided the evidence would be publicly assured immunity; but the Punjab Government were willing to give no more than private assurances. Jawaharlal also challenged the official figure that only 291 persons had been killed in the Jallianwala Bagh. A few days later Jawaharlal wrote another letter to the press pointing out that the 'crawling order' was not, as Gandhi had suggested, a 'hands and knees' order; people had in fact been made to crawl 'on their bellies after the manner of snakes and worms'.[4]

Later that month, at the U.P. Political Conference at Saharanpur, Jawaharlal moved the resolution protesting against the appointment of the official Hunter Commission and urging that it be replaced by an independent Royal Commission. If the Hunter Commission were to continue, at least one member of the Congress Committee should be co-opted to it, as the Indian members of the Hunter Commission had no local knowledge. Full opportunity should also be given to the people to present their case and counsel should appear on both sides. Instead of the Commission selecting whom it would hear, counsel should have the right to present witnesses and to cross-examine, for it was the

---

[1] The garden at Amritsar which was the scene of the firing.
[2] *Autobiography*, pp. 43-4.
[3] Letter to the editor, 28 September 1919. *The Bombay Chronicle,* 2 October 1919.
[4] 1 October 1919. *The Bombay Chronicle,* 6 October 1919.

Government which was on trial. If these facilities were not granted, the Hunter Commission should be boycotted.[1]

Yet, as in the case of Mahatma Gandhi and many others in India, it was not the happenings at Amritsar and the attitude of Dyer at the time and later before the official commission of inquiry which upset Jawaharlal as much as the reaction in England to these events. 'This cold-blooded approval of that deed', he wrote many years later,[2] 'shocked me greatly. It seemed absolutely immoral, indecent; to use public school language, it was the height of bad form. I realized then, more vividly than I had ever done before, how brutal and immoral imperialism was and how it had eaten into the souls of the British upper classes.' Till now he had been in the stream of Indian moderate tradition, expecting favours from the benign British rulers; and his conversion was part of the general realization that freedom could never be a gift but only the achievement of struggle and resistance.

In February 1920 Jawaharlal participated in the Allahabad district conference at Bahadurganj, and in July he was elected vice-president of the Allahabad district congress committee. Meantime, Gandhi had taken up the cause of the Khilafat. To men like Jawaharlal, while active opposition to Government was welcome, such a *prima facie* religious issue did not fit in with their secular political attitude. So attempts were made in *The Independent* to provide political arguments for supporting the Khilafat movement. It was contended that the Caliph had been set aside because Britain and the other European powers wished to divide the Turkish Empire amongst themselves and the Khilafat movement was part of the political struggle for the freedom of Asia. The agitation in Allahabad city itself was intense. There was considerable fraternizing between Hindus and Muslims,[3] and the U.P. Government reported that 'the extremists appear to have got most of the city on their side.'[4]

Motilal, however, disliked greatly the idea of boycott of the Councils and, not expecting that the Congress would accept this programme of Gandhi for non-co-operation, planned the election campaign in the United Provinces for the Congress against the Moderates. Jawaharlal helped in drafting the election manifesto,[5] and Motilal was seriously considering the choice of a suitable constituency for his son. 'You ought to select a constituency from which you are sure to be returned. I am more keen on your going into the Council than mine [*sic*].'[6] He finally decided on Fatehpur and was disappointed that Jawaharlal turned it down, preferring to follow Gandhi's lead. 'So far as your following the request of Gandhiji is concerned, there is nothing to be said. That is

[1] *The Leader,* 22 October 1919 and *The Independent,* 24 October 1919.

[2] Article on the Quetta earthquake written in August 1935 and reprinted in *India and the World* (London, 1936), p. 147.

[3] *The Independent,* 12 October 1919.

[4] 1 December 1919. Home Dept. Pol. Deposit, June 1920, no. 44.

[5] See Motilal to Gandhi, 25 April 1920. Gandhi papers. Gandhi Smarak Sangrahalaya, Serial No. 7163.

[6] Motilal to Jawaharlal, 13 June 1920.

more or less a matter of sentiment of a kind which does not enter into my composition.'[1]

On 22 August the U.P. Congress Committee met at Motilal's residence and resolved, with not more than two or three members voting against, that the usual methods of agitation hitherto followed were wholly insufficient to meet the intolerable situation created by official policy in regard to the Punjab and the Khilafat questions, and whole-heartedly recommended the principle of non-co-operation with the Government 'at the greatest sacrifice possible'. As regards the steps to be taken in the first stage of non-co-operation, it was decided after prolonged discussion to suggest the renunciation of titles, arbitration instead of recourse to law courts, the promotion of national education by establishment of national schools and colleges and gradual withdrawal of students from Government institutions, resignation from all honorary non-elective posts in public bodies, refusal to buy government loans and attend official functions and boycott of British goods. The Committee then considered the boycott of councils. Jawaharlal pointed out that this could not mean entering the councils even to obstruct but refusal either to participate in elections or to attend the councils after the elections. He expressed his own preference for boycott of even the elections, but finally the Committee recommended, by a narrow majority of about two, the boycott of councils, thus leaving open the question of participation in elections.

Jawaharlal was satisfied. 'The real question of principle, to my mind, was that we should not enter the Councils and take the oath of allegiance. The rest was a matter of tactics.' But he regretted that the Committee had not gone further along the lines laid down by Gandhi and advocated total renunciation of legal practice, immediate withdrawal from educational institutions, and rejection even of elective places in official bodies. 'I am an ardent believer in non-co-operation with all that it implies and I am firmly convinced that non-co-operation and no other course will bring us victory. That victory will not come in a day or a year, but come it will and must, *ruat coelum.*'[2] Later, a special session of the Congress decided by an overwhelming majority in favour of complete boycott of the councils and called on voters to abstain from voting.

Motilal fell into line with no great enthusiasm. He knew that his destiny and that of his son were scrambled together, but he did not always relish it. Austerity and puritanism did not come naturally to him, and watching Jawaharlal embrace Gandhian rigours caused him intense pain. 'This is a time', he remarked with tears when he saw Jawaharlal boarding a third-class railway compartment, 'when he should be enjoying himself, but he has given up everything and has become a *sadhu.*'[3] He gave up his legal practice at a time when his services were in demand in various parts of the country, and he was concerned about the future. 'Have you had any time to attend to the poor cows in Anand Bhavan. Not that they are really cows but have been reduced to the

[1] Idem, 5 July 1920.

[2] Letter to the editor, 1 September 1920. *The Leader,* 4 September 1920.

[3] Rajendra Prasad's article in S.P. and P. Chablani (eds.), *Motilal Nehru* (Delhi, 1961), p. 7.

position of cows by nothing short of culpable negligence on your part and mine — I mean your mother, your wife, your child and your sisters? I do not know with what grace and reason we can claim to be working for the good of the masses — the country at large — when we fail egregiously to minister to the most urgent requirements of our own flesh and blood and those whose flesh and blood we are.'[1] The closing down of *The Independent* the next year became inevitable, and savings had to be counted.

> To live on public charity does not appeal to me even in the best interests of the motherland. I can easily kick away the lakhs and lakhs put before me but will die a thousand deaths before I come to the stage where I have to be supported by others. I am willing to undergo any sacrifice to be able to live within our means — but we must have some means within which to live. . . You can easily understand how I feel with all these matters troubling me and with the prospect of a beggarship after turning away from me a stream of gold flowing at my very feet. [2]

When Jawaharlal sought permission to transfer his war bonds worth Rs. 10,000 to the Tilak Swaraj fund and meantime announced it as an anonymous donation in *The Independent*, Motilal in great irritation replied that he was planning to resume practice.

> *Swaraj* or no *swaraj* the one thing which I will not willingly permit is the possibility of any child or grandchild of mine having to depend for maintenance on any other person in the world however near or dear, or that of their being a charge on the nation. If to avoid this it is necessary to make more money I would resume my practice today in spite of all that has happened . . . I do not think that a man who is capable of starving his own children can be of much good to the nation.

And he added brutally, stressing that it was his affluence that made possible Jawaharlal's political involvement: 'You cannot have it both ways: Insist on my having no money and yet expect me to pay you money.'[3]

These financial worries, however, Jawaharlal left to his father. Gandhi had at last given India a lead in action, and Jawaharlal was enthusiastic. His main preoccupation was the task of organizing non-co-operation in the U.P., and he was soon among its recognized leaders. To introduce some discipline into the movement, he organized drill for the volunteers and had plans for linking up the various local organizations. He was elected President of the Etah district Congress conference; and though the Government banned the procession and sought to prevent the conference, Jawaharlal was welcomed by large crowds

---

[1] Motilal to Jawaharlal, 16 September 1920.
[2] Idem, 19 September 1920.
[3] Motilal to Jawaharlal, 27 June 1921.

at every wayside station and he delivered his address as scheduled.[1] No report of his speech exists, but the general tenor of his advocacy can be gleaned from a speech he delivered to students at Allahabad a few weeks later. It was not, he said, a time to weigh losses and gains; to enter the movement with a mathematical mind would only be to hinder it. The existing system had to be destroyed; there was no middle course left; one was with either the country or its enemies, either with Gandhi or with the Government. If on account of their lack of enthusiasm the cause was defeated, future generations would curse them.[2]

The hold which Gandhi had acquired on Jawaharlal and which he was never to lose is, at first view, incongruous. Gandhi was Christ-like in his seizure of men; but his conversion of Jawaharlal is capable of rational explanation. What appealed to the younger man was Gandhi's strength, his rock-like commitment to India's freedom, the way in which he had perfected his character and personality so as to make himself an effective instrument of political change in India — 'Indian leadership, Indian style'. He was above all a man of action, of enormous restlessness and energy, with a will to power and a touch of ruthlessness. He functioned with a shrewd grasp of whatever context he found himself in, and was a saint who placed his halo at the service of his secular aspirations. He repeatedly stressed that God appears not in person but in action. Throughout his life he functioned primarily in politics; and if, curious about his body and his spirit, he experimented constantly, he acknowledged that it was from 'experiments in the spiritual field that I derived such power as I possess for working in the political field'.

It was this primacy of action, and successful action at that, that throughout Gandhi's life retained Jawaharlal ultimately in thrall. At this time he was quite captivated and, along with Gandhi's political leadership, willingly accepted all his other teachings. As the years passed, Jawaharlal realized that Gandhi had no use for systematic thinking on economic problems and that, while he had secured a hold on the masses by living and working among them and being absorbed by them, he made no effort to inspire and rouse them on anything other than political and social reform movements. But still he clung to Gandhi; and this one-to-one relationship, in which Gandhi specialized, was based on the call to battle with alien rule which Gandhi gave.

Jawaharlal's first direct clash with the Government, however, came about in an entirely fortuitous way and had nothing to do with Gandhi. In the summer of 1920, he had taken the family up to Mussoorie, a hill station, and was spending his time teaching his wife and sisters when, as he wrote to his father,[3] greatness was thrust on him by the Government. An Afghan delegation was staying at the same hotel and the authorities well knew that Jawaharlal had, during the period of over a fortnight when he was there, not seen anything of them.

[1] *The Independent,* 1 October 1920.
[2] Ibid., 14 November 1920.
[3] 14 May 1920. S.W., vol. 1, p. 161.

Yet suddenly the local superintendent of police called on him and asked him either to furnish a positive undertaking not to get into touch with the Afghan delegation or to leave Mussoorie on his own. The police official was, in fact, carrying out a decision of the Government of India. Alarmed by the rumours in the Punjab that the Afghan delegation had come to India to support the Khilafat movement with which the Amir was believed to be in full sympathy, suspecting even men like Rajagopalachari, an extremely conservative follower of Gandhi, of pro-Bolshevik sympathies and of clandestine contacts with *emigré* Indians in Afghanistan and the Soviet Union,[1] and disturbed by the police report that Indian malcontents were flocking to Mussoorie, the Home Department drew up a list of twenty-three persons who should be excluded from Mussoorie.[2] Jawaharlal's name was on this list, and it was then realized that he was already in Mussoorie. The police at once jumped to the conclusion that the purpose of his visit was to secure an interview with the Afghans. Hence the sudden visit of the police officer.

Jawaharlal, faced with this unnecessary provocation, refused to bind himself not to meet the Afghans or to leave Mussoorie on his own. However, he departed after an expulsion order had been served on him. He made no effort to resist expulsion, nor, on his return to the plains, did he seek to break the order and return to Mussoorie — inaction which pleased his father.

We have in all conscience suffered enough during the last six months and I would not court further trouble by a provocative act. The consequences are so obvious both from the public and private points of view that it is hardly necessary to discuss them. It will mean the final break up of the family and the upsetting of all private, public and professional work. One thing will lead to another and something is sure to turn up which will compel me to follow you to the jail or something similar. I would leave well alone. We have certainly scored so far and should wait for further developments.[3]

It is hard to believe that the Jawaharlal of later years would have so mildly complied with such an 'insensate'[4] order and been satisfied with a mere refusal to give an undertaking. Even at this time, when there was a deterioration in his mother's health, he might have returned to Mussoorie in defiance of the order and courted arrest, had not the U.P. Government, genteel as ever, withdrawn the order in view, as they said, of the health of the ladies of the family.

---

[1] Weekly Reports of the Special Bureau of Information, 1920, cited in Z. Imam, *Colonialism in East-West Relations* (New Delhi, 1969), p. 70.

[2] Note of the Home Dept.; C.I.D. report from Mussoorie, 28 April; Home Secretary to Chief Secretary U.P., telegram 1 May 1920. Home Dept. Pol. B. Confidential, June 1920, nos. 165-6.

[3] Motilal to Jawaharlal, 3 June 1920. J. Nehru, *A Bunch of Old Letters* (Delhi, 1958), p. 12.

[4] *The Independent,* 19 May 1920.

4

Among the Peasants

More crucial to Jawaharlal's development than his expulsion was his involvement in the peasant unrest in the United Provinces. The importance of bringing the peasants, with their tradition of agitation, into the national movement had been underlined by Gandhi's successful organization of resistance to the indigo planters in Champaran in Bihar in 1917; and towards the end of that year Malaviya and a few others in Allahabad established the United Provinces *Kisan Sabha* (peasant association). The sponsors are in themselves testimony to the moderate objectives of this association; and it was reported that the Home Rule League had provided Rs 4,000 for its organization.[1] Its avowed objectives were to check the growing antagonism between peasants and *zamindars* (landowners) and establish friendly relations, educate the peasants and inform them of their political and social rights, promote legislation beneficial to them and amend statutes prejudicial to their interests, protect them from unlawful actions, establish village *panchayats* (councils), further mutual trust and cordiality between the rulers and the ruled and adopt such constitutional measures as might be conducive to their welfare. Branches of the *Kisan Sabha* were set up in many villages and *tehsils* (revenue sub-divisions) and attempts were made to establish similar organizations in other provinces and link them up with the National Congress. Peasant delegates were mustered in considerable numbers at the Congress sessions of 1918 and 1919, by which time Gandhi had led another peasant campaign, this time against the Government, at Kaira in Gujarat. At the Congress session in 1919, the U.P. *Kisan Sabha* submitted a draft resolution which was surprisingly radical, urging the Government, among other things, to declare peasants all over India to be actual owners of the soil they cultivated; but the Congress did no more than direct the All-India Congress Committee (AICC) to investigate the various revenue systems and the condition of the peasantry.

The special cause of agrarian distress in Avadh (Oudh) was the inelastic

[1]Circular No. 3 of the Criminal Investigation Department, United Provinces. Home Dept. Pol. Deposit, January 1920, no. 49.

Rent Act of 1886 which forbade landlords to enhance rents by more than one anna in the rupee [1] once every seven years. Clearly, with the great rise in prices of consumer goods, landlords would try to circumvent the rigidity of the statute by demanding payment of other dues; and the lack of occupancy rights enabled them to collect these dues by holding out the threat of eviction. Actual evictions were frequent, both because landlords saw an advantage, with the rising price of foodgrains, in cultivating the land themselves and enforcing their customary right to free or ill-paid labour, and because, with the apparent imminence of an amendment of the law granting fixity of tenure, it appeared worth while to terminate tenancy of any duration. In Pratabgarh district, for example, there were 936 notices for eviction in 1906-7; this figure rose to 1,238 in 1911-12, 1,403 in 1916-17 and 2,593 in 1919-20. But more often the threat to evict was utilized to compel the tenant to pay higher cesses or *nazarana* in addition to the rent; and this had become a regular form of income to the landlords. Tenants could only secure renewals of their leases by borrowing heavily from money-lenders or from their relatives — or from the landlords themselves — in order to pay *nazarana*. 'Fathers have sold their daughters for *nazarana* money to husbands of advanced years.'[2] Sometimes the holding was divided into two parts and settled with two competitors both of whom had paid substantial *nazarana;* and frequently a lease was terminated because another bidder had made a more tempting offer.

However, these *kisans* (peasants), never wholly lacking in some form of power in at least some estates,[3] were no longer unaware of anything better; and there was a growing resentment at working for, and paying heavy cesses to, distant and unknown landowners at the bidding of foul-mouthed middlemen. Nor was there much faith left in the efficacy of the law courts as a means of obtaining redress, it being firmly believed that a poor man had no chance against a rich one in a contest in the courts; 'and who will say that there is not some truth in this under the system of civil and criminal justice as it has come to be practised in India?[4]

The situation was particularly critical in Pratabgarh district. The population here was unusually dense, being 1.82 per cultivated acre as against 1.68 in Fyzabad and 1.7 in Sultanpur; and the figure appears more striking when it is remembered that there were no towns in Pratabgarh district with a population larger than 6,000. On the other hand, large tracts of land in the district were barren, and only 53.3 per cent of the total area was under cultivation as against 55.9 per cent in Sultanpur, and 61.8 per cent in Fyzabad. So there was a keen competition for land, and this enabled the landlords, who, as the

[1] At this time there were 16 annas in the rupee.

[2] Report of V. N. Mehta, Deputy Commissioner, Pratabgarh, November 1920. Revenue Department, File 753 of 1920. U. P. archives at Lucknow.

[3] Musgrave, op. cit., p. 275.

[4] Report by a C.I.D. officer on the *kisan sabha* in Allahabad, January 1921. Home Dept. Pol., February 1921, no. 13.

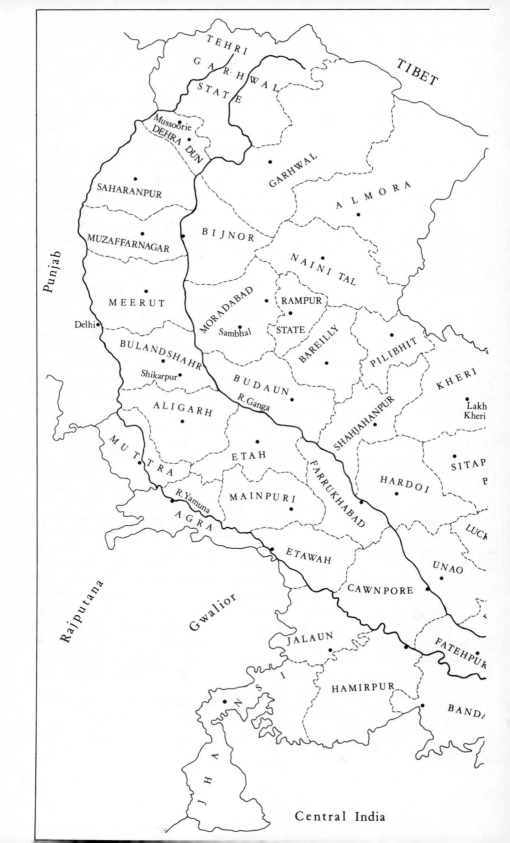

THE UNITED PROVINCES Before 1947
(Towns marked without names bear the same names as the districts)

United Provinces

NEPAL

mpur

BAHRAICH

UR

Bahadurganj

GONDA

Bihar

NOW

BARABANKI

BASTI

GORAKHPUR

FYZABAD

Tanda

Bhiti

Akbarpur

RAE BARELI

Fursatganj

SULTANPUR

Tajuddinpur

AZAMGARH

Unchahar

PARTAB GARH

BALLIA

JAUNPUR

GHAZIPUR

ALLAH

ABAD

Chheoki

BENARES

MIRZAPUR

Central India

Commissioner recognized,[1] were in this district a particularly poor lot, to demand exorbitant *nazarana*.

The social composition of Pratabgarh district was also somewhat uncommon. 11.3 per cent of the population was composed of Kurmis, a low caste who could not muster the resistance to the exactions of landlords which high-caste tenantry were generally able to do. They had to pay a higher rental than Brahmin or Kshatriya tenants.[2] Nor were there underproprietors to act as a breakwater between the landlords and these low-caste tenants. While, for example, in Sultanpur there were many ..nants of the same caste as the landlords who enjoyed a certain measure of protection from the head of the family, in Pratabgarh the Kurmis had to deal directly with the landlords.

However, if the repression of the tenants was more severe in Pratabgarh than in other districts of Avadh, there were other balancing reasons which made a peasant outbreak more probable here than elsewhere. The Kurmis had a tradition of defiance; as far back as 1867 they had risen in revolt, and they had never lost their social coherence and capacity for organization. It was of course easier to organize concerted action within a caste, however low, than to draw tenants of high and low caste together. Moreover, the Kurmi peasants of Pratabgarh could not fail to notice the occupancy rights enjoyed by the tillers, after twelve years of continuous cultivation, in the neighbouring districts of Allahabad and Jaunpur (which were part of the Agra division); and their kinsmen in these districts were reluctant to enter into marriage relations with persons who might overnight be reduced to the level of beggars at the whim of their landlord.[3] The proximity of Allahabad city was also a source of strength, for the tenants of Pratabgarh could derive leadership and advice from urban politicians, who had by now begun to realize the value to them of peasant support.

Trouble began in Pratabgarh from April 1920, the beginning of the season of notices of eviction and of ejectment. At first the leadership of the Kurmis of Pratabgarh was assumed by a millenarian figure of shadowy antecedents, Baba Ram Chandra, who addressed large crowds, calling on them to stand up for their rights and resist the landlords, to pay their rents but not illegal cesses. He then, in June 1920, led about 500 of his followers to Allahabad in the hope of meeting Gandhi. They failed to find Gandhi, but instead met Jawaharlal, who happened to be there because of his expulsion from Mussoorie, and persuaded him to return with them to Pratabgarh. So casual circumstance thrust Jawaharlal into the problem of the Indian peasantry and gave a new and permanent dimension to his outlook. The tranquil firmness of these men, living

[1] H. R. C. Hailey to M. Keane, 26 November 1920. Revenue Dept. File 753 of 1920. U.P. archives.
[2] M. H. Siddiqi, 'The Peasant Movement in Pratabgarh, 1920', *Indian Economic and Social History Review,* September 1972, pp. 316-17.
[3] Commissioner, Fyzabad division to Chief Secretary U. P., 25 November 1920. Revenue Dept. File 753 of 1920. U. P. archives.

often below the margin of subsistence but never being overcome, impressed him profoundly.

I have had the privilege of working for them, of mixing with them, of living in their mudhuts and partaking in all reverence of their lowly fare. And I, who for long believed in the doctrine of the sword, have been converted by the *kisans* to the doctrine of non-violence. I have come to believe that non-violence is ingrained in them and is part of their very nature.[1]

Jawaharlal now gave publicity to the grievances of the *kisans,* objecting even to donations to the proposed University of Lucknow by estates under the management of the Court of Wards. 'It is bad enough for illegal exactions and oppression to take place in the domains of illiterate and self-seeking talukdars who manage their own estates. It is far worse for the Government as represented by the Court of Wards to encourage such practices.'[2] But in Pratabgarh itself, where he was accompanied by Gauri Shankar Misra, a follower of Pandit Malaviya and much more conservative even than the Jawaharlal of those days, the general effect of their presence was, as the Commissioner acknowledged, 'to bring a number of vague demands into a coherent shape and to a certain extent to moderate it'.[3] They encouraged the peasants to organize themselves into village *kisan sabhas* and to formulate their demands for restrictions on evictions and forced labour, leases for fourteen years, payment of cesses at only customary rates, cessation of fines and free access to landlords — demands which could hardly be regarded as extreme. When the authorities arrested a few *kisans* for 'highhandedness', Jawaharlal and another colleague from Allahabad, Purushottam Das Tandon, met the Deputy Commissioner and, while not approving of the conduct of the men arrested, suggested that the cases be withdrawn so that the relations between *zamindars* and tenants might not worsen.[4]

By now, however, with the non-co-operation movement in full swing, Jawaharlal began to feel that some of his colleagues were taking their moderation too far. They had set up, with the blessings of the district authorities, a *Kisan Hitkarini Sabha,* ostensibly to serve as a forum for landlords and tenants to discuss and settle their problems; but Jawaharlal had no use for it. 'Its sole function appears to be to collect a few talukdars and their dependents and then to curse with bell, book and candle the irresponsible agitators who have the effrontery to visit the tenantry. I have little doubt that this must be a comforting, though somewhat fruitless, operation. Unhappily the agitators are

[1] 'The Rae Bareli Tragedy', *The Independent,* 22 January 1921.
[2] Letter to the Editor, 27 June 1920, published in *The Independent,* 3 July 1920.
[3] Hailey to Keane, 26 November 1920, Revenue Dept. File 753 of 1920 U. P. archives.
[4] Report of V. N. Mehta, ibid.

little affected by it. They continue to flourish.'[1] What, in fact, Jawaharlal hoped for was to link *kisan* discontent with nationalist politics. He had made no study of economic and land problems and he had no clear ideas about peasant participation. It was not his intention to provide a revolutionary dimension to Indian nationalism. But this contact with the *kisans* was satisfying psychologically, as it gave him the feeling that he was re-Indianizing himself and functioning in a wholly Indian situation; and politically it was important, for it provided an opportunity to do in his own province what Gandhi had done elsewhere, harnessing peasant strength in the interests of the Congress.

Pratabgarh and Rae Bareli were more suited for Jawaharlal's effort than Allahabad district itself, for there the presence of many Muslim landlords would give communal overtones to any *kisan* agitation, and this was hardly to be desired while the Khilafat agitation was at its height. At a meeting held in Pratabgarh in October to federate the numerous village *sabhas* into an *Oudh Kisan Sabha,* the objectives were defined, in a harmless enough manner, as being to improve the condition of the tenantry, to promote amity between *kisans* and *zamindars,* to do everything to advance the cause of the country and to establish *panchayats* for the settlement of all disputes between tenants. The Deputy Commissioner attended the meeting, but was obliged to walk out when Jawaharlal advised his *kisan* audience to boycott elections to the Councils and stressed that the only moral to be drawn from the Punjab and Khilafat events was that the Government was an utterly unjust one which cared little for the lives, honour and even the religion of the Indian people. The non-co-operation programme was approved by the *Sabha* and the Congress urged to 'stick to it'.[2] But this effort to associate the *kisan sabhas* with the Congress programme led to a split in the parent U.P. *Kisan Sabha* itself. At a meeting of its executive committee held on 24 October 1920 a majority of its members refused to subscribe to non-co-operation and decided to remain neutral on the issue;[3] and by February 1921 there were two U.P. *Kisan Sabhas,* each claiming to be the legitimate organization.

Throughout the winter months of 1920-21 the efforts to harness tenant power to the non-co-operation movement continued. Jawaharlal spoke to large *kisan* audiences and was struck above all by their discipline.[4] Gandhi himself visited Pratabgarh in November — though in his case the motivation on this occasion was alleged to have been not so much to draw in the peasants

---

[1] Letter to the Editor, 22 September; *The Leader,* 25 September 1920.

[2] Report in *The Independent,* 27 October 1920; P.D. Reeves, 'The Politics of Order', *Journal of Asian Studies,* February 1966, p. 263.

[3] *The Leader,* 28 October 1920, quoted in Reeves, op. cit.; letter of I. N. Dwivedi in *The Leader,* 21 February 1921.

[4] Many years later he recounted an incident that occurred at this time. While speaking, he noticed people pushing and elbowing each other, though still remaining seated. Irritated by this behaviour, he asked that section of the crowd what was worrying them and they replied, 'There is a snake here, but we dare not stand up, because the organisers have ordered us not to do so while you are speaking.' Speech at Calcutta, reported in the *Free Press Journal* (Bombay), 12 November 1956.

1   Ganga Dhar Nehru, Jawaharlal's grandfather

2   Jawaharlal as a boy, with his mother and father

3   At Harrow in 1907

4   As a member of the Harrow
     School Cadet Corps

5   As an undergraduate member of Trinity College Boat Club, at Cambridge
     (*seated on ground, right*)

6 Swaraj Bhawan, the home of the Nehrus until 1928

7 Anand Bhawan, the house built by Motilal Nehru in Allahabad

as to frighten the landlords into supporting the Congress.[1] The *Kisan* Congress, meeting at Fyzabad in December, attracted more persons from a few districts than the National Congress meeting at Nagpur attracted from the whole of India. The landlords also helped by utilizing what they believed was their last opportunity to push through a rush of enhancements. This enraged the lower tenantry, who were now joined by landless labourers, suddenly caught by the rise in prices and diminished prospects of employment.[2]

The distress which, as even discerning officials realized, was genuine and very great, began to assume political overtones.

> The Indian peasants' chief idea about the war is that they supplied the men and the money and the zamindars got the credit. Government took their money and issued them bits of paper instead. It will be noticed that these notions distinctly smack of Bolshevism, and it would be interesting to know whether they are in some way the indirect result of Bolshevik propaganda, or have arisen from the same causes as have produced them in other countries. The Bolshevik idea is also rapidly spreading . . . that it is the cultivators who plough, sow, irrigate and reap and are thus entitled to the whole of the produce of the land. There is no need of, and no right to be, such things as zamindars. Here again the contention of the cultivators is very hard to refute, as there is no denying the fact that the Indian landlord is singularly backward in the performance of his duties.[3]

It was still, however, not the Congress nor their own strength but the Government whom the *kisans* looked to for an improvement of their condition. Their discontent was entirely with the landlords and was not in any way anti-British or anti-Government. Their objectives might have seemed Bolshevik to alarmed officials; but their methods were as yet the opposite of revolutionary. 'They have their grievances and their miseries and it is up to Government to put things right. There is no other power under Heaven that can save them.'[4] The vast majority of cultivators still sought a redress of their grievances from the authorities.[5] The *kisans* did not seem to be interested in non-co-operation, and at a *kisan* meeting in Lucknow, when Jawaharlal began his speech by explaining the significance of non-co-operation, the

[1] See Weekly Report of Director, Intelligence Bureau, 11 January 1921. Home Dept. Pol. Deposit, January 1921, Proceeding no. 75.
[2] C. A. Bayly, 'The Development of Political Organization in the Allahabad Locality 1880-1925', Oxford D.Phil. thesis, 1970, pp. 369-70.
[3] Report by a C.I.D. officer on the *kisan sabha* in Allahabad, January 1921. Home Dept. Pol., February 1921, no. 13.
[4] Ibid.
[5] Report of the Director, Intelligence Bureau, 11 January 1921, Home Dept. Pol. Deposit, January 1921, no. 75; Sir H. Butler's speech to U.P. Legislative Council, *The Leader,* 24 January 1921. This is a common feature of peasant revolts. Engels noted that the Russian peasants often

audience, according to official reports,[1] melted away. The most that the *Kisan Sabhas* could do was to secure the defeat of some *zamindar* candidates in the elections of December 1920. But the U. P. Government threw away its chance and, by its reckless handling of the situation, gave a strong fillip to the movement, so that throughout the year 1921 many districts in Avadh were shaken by explosions of agrarian unrest.

Early in January local ruffians in Rae Bareli district took advantage of the tension to burn crops grown on the *sir* (personal) lands of the *zamindars* and to loot shops in the bazaars; and there was probably some ground for the belief that a few of these miscreants had been encouraged by the *zamindars* themselves in order to bring the *kisans* and their organizations into disrepute. On the 5th three of the *kisan* leaders were arrested, and a large crowd began to drift towards Rae Bareli town in the hope of seeing these leaders. Encouragement for this move was provided by the deputy commissioner's assurance to the *kisans* that he would listen at Rae Bareli to their grievances which had been heightened by the failure of the *kharif* (autumn) harvest and the holding off of the winter rains. However, on the 6th the police opened fire on a crowd at Fursatganj, ten miles to the east of Rae Bareli, killing between four and six people; and the next day there was heavy firing at Munshiganj, two miles south of the town, with at least nine dead and a large number wounded.

On both occasions the authorities had clearly panicked. At Munshiganj neither the deputy commissioner nor the superintendent of police had given the order to fire, and it was generally believed that the firing had been started by the local *talukdar*, on a crowd which was not interested in looting and had done no more than throw a few stones. Butler, the Lieutenant-Governor, reported to the Government of India that 'the Deputy Commissioner was a poet and had lost his head';[2] and to avoid his cross-examination in court the U.P. Government decided not to prosecute *The Independent* for its scathing articles on these events. It would have been difficult to explain away what even the deputy commissioner accepted, that a large proportion of the injuries received by members of the crowd were in the back.[3] But to the public it was pretended that the firings alone had saved the whole of the south of Rae Bareli district from widespread looting and the rapid attainment of a state of anarchy; and Butler sent a telegram of congratulations to the district authorities and the *talukdar*.

It was the wanton firing on the 7th near Rae Bareli which brought the *kisans* into direct collision with the authorities. Even the crowd at Fursatganj on the

revolted against the nobility but never against the Tsar. Chinese historians speak of a 'peasant monarchism', the peasants being unable to conceive of any alternative to seeking salvation from an emperor. See J. P. Harrison, *The Communists and Chinese Peasant Rebellions* (New York, 1969), pp. 184-5.

[1] Chief Secretary U. P. to Home Secretary, 2 January 1921. Home Dept. Pol. Deposit, February 1921, no. 77.

[2] Butler to Vincent, Home Member, 10 March 1921. Home Dept. Pol., July 1921, no. 3 (confidential) & K.W.

[3] Report of A. C. Shirreff, 29 January 1921. Home Dept. General File 50 of 1921, U. P. archives.

6th was not a gathering of peasants but 'a mob of rioters out for loot'.[1] A first-hand account in *The Independent* asserted that the '*kisan sabhas* are not in the least concerned with the disturbances, for which a few confirmed vagabonds and convicts are responsible'.[2] However, to many officials the differences between dacoits, *kisans* and non-co-operators were becoming increasingly blurred. 'Ignorant peasantry', alleged a Government communiqué, 'had been persuaded by perambulating agitators that not only *talukdar* but British *raj* would shortly cease to exist and that under the beneficent rule of Mr Gandhi they would enter on a golden age of prosperity in which they would be able to buy good cloth at 4 annas per yard and other necessaries of life at similar cheap rates.'[3]

This confusion in the official outlook suited the *talukdars;* but it worried the *kisan* representatives, some of whom came to see Jawaharlal at Allahabad on the 5th and requested him to visit the Rae Bareli district. Jawaharlal was reluctant, as he had just returned from the Congress session at Nagpur; nor was he willing to see the Congress and *kisan* organizations associated with the looting that had occurred. But on hearing from a well-known citizen of Rae Bareli the next day that the situation was serious, and knowing that the local *kisans* had no capable leader, Jawaharlal left by the night train, reaching Rae Bareli at 2 p.m. on the 7th. He then heard of the firing at Fursatganj the previous day, and of the confrontation between the officials and the large *kisan* crowd at Munshiganj. He promptly went to the scene with the intention of directing the crowd to disperse, and told the *kisans* he met on the way to go home. But meantime he received a pencilled note from the deputy commissioner: 'Pt Jawaharlal Nehru. You are hereby informed that your presence in this district is not desired — you are directed to leave by the next train.' Jawaharlal sent his reply on the back of the slip: 'I should like to know if this is a formal order or a mere request. If it is the former then it should be drawn up in a formal manner mentioning the section etc. Until such an order is served on me I propose to remain here.' Stopped by policemen from crossing a bridge on the other side of which the firing was taking place, Jawaharlal addressed such of the *kisans* as came across, impressing on them the need to be both non-violent and fearless. It was obviously a deep experience for Jawaharlal.

> They behaved as brave men, calm and unruffled in the face of danger. I do not know how they felt but I know what my feelings were. For a moment my blood was up, non-violence was almost forgotten — but for a moment only. The thought of the great leader, who by God's goodness

[1] Report of J. A. Farron, I.C.S. Home Dept. General, File 50/1921 K.W.S., U. P. archives.
[2] *The Independent*, 12 January 1921.
[3] Quoted in *The Bombay Chronicle*, 14 January 1921. The Lieutenant-Governor also, eager to clear the *talukdars* of responsibility for agrarian distress and the Government for their clumsy handling of the situation, encouraged this kind of sloppy thinking. 'The agrarian disturbances which were largely due to local agitators acting as non-co-operators have been firmly dealt with and order has been restored.' Butler's Minute 9 March 1921. Home Dept. Pol., July 1921, no. 3 (Confidential) and K.W.

has been sent to lead us to victory, came to me, and I saw the *kisans* seated and standing near me, less excited, more peaceful than I was — and the moment of weakness passed. I spoke to them in all humility on non-violence — I who needed the lesson more than they — and they heeded me and peacefully dispersed. On the other side of the river, however, men lay dead and dying. It was a similar crowd with a similar object. Yet they poured their hearts' blood before they would disperse.[1]

The deputy commissioner, who had by now come back across the bridge, sent for Jawaharlal and informed him that meetings were prohibited. Though aware that Jawaharlal was using his influence against violent agitation, yet the officials were unwilling to let him speak to the crowd; for as they said to him, they were not there to increase his prestige.[2] Jawaharlal, abiding by this order, dissolved the meeting after addressing it for a few minutes. The deputy commissioner thanked Jawaharlal for his talk which had had a good effect on the *kisans*, and took Jawaharlal in his car, along with the local *talukdar*, to his house, where they had a desultory, inconsequential conversation. Told that every effort to disperse the *kisans* had been in vain, Jawaharlal replied that he perhaps might have succeeded where they had failed.[3]

The Rae Bareli firing was of major significance. The sense of tenant wrong had converged with an awareness of tenant strength. 'For the first time in history, they had begun to realize the power of an united peasantry — to realize that they themselves had the remedy of the most flagrant of their wrongs, the illegal exactions of their landlords, in their own hands. If they stood together, *nazarana, begari* and other oppressive taxes would automatically cease.'[4] And in the exercise of this new-found power, they had now the leadership of the Congress, whose influence over the *kisans* had been strengthened by the Government: 'there is nothing to choose locally 'between a gathering under the auspices of the *kisan sabha* or of the Khilafat Committee. Both movements appear to have been completely captured by the non-co-operating party, and there is one movement only in progress at the present time and that is the non-co-operation movement.'[5]

Joined by his father the next day, Jawaharlal visited the wounded in hospital and then left for Allahabad. His dispatches, signed and unsigned, to *The Independent* were sharply critical of the Government and the local *talukdar*; but his conduct at Rae Bareli itself was far from being that of a 'firebrand',[6] as

[1] 'The Rae Bareli Tragedy', *The Independent,* 22 January 1921. ·
[2] See Jawaharlal's article in *The Independent,* 23 January 1921.
[3] Report of Shirreff, 29 January 1921, Home Dept. General File 50 of 1921. U. P. archives; evidence of Jawaharlal in *Pratap* defamation case, *The Independent,* 6 July 1921.
[4] Report of J. A. St John Farnon, 19 January 1921, General Dept. File 50/1921. K.W., U. P. archives. *Begari* was forced labour.
[5] Report of S. R. Mayers, District Superintendent of Police, Rae Bareli, 25 February 1921. Ibid.
[6] *The Independent,* 11 January 1921.

the deputy commissioner had expected before his arrival. This implied that Jawaharlal would stir the *kisans* to further violence and give them a wider cause. But he had at this time no economic ideology to offer, and he had certainly no intent of securing any weapons for these *kisans* to sustain their revolt. His whole influence was thrown on the side of moderation, in urging the *kisans* to be quiet and peaceful, to abide by whatever orders were issued by the local officials and to go back to their homes. A few days later, when disturbances began in Fyzabad division, where too, as in Pratabgarh, the small tenants were low-caste men employed by Brahmin *zamindars*, he went to Unchahar to call off the meeting, which had been announced long before to inform the *kisans* of the decisions of the Nagpur Congress, and persuaded the *kisans* who had collected from various parts of Avadh to disperse;[1] and the commissioner arranged for their free transport to their home by train.[2] The Finance Member of the U.P. Government noted smugly that 'it looks as if the agitators were getting cold feet'.[3]

Then, when news came in of sporadic renewal of looting, Jawaharlal was asked by local leaders to visit Fyzabad district; and he addressed large meetings exhorting *kisans*, if they were serious and earnest about *swaraj*, to take a pledge not to resort to violence or looting.[4] Often, after he had spoken, men got up to confess to looting, knowing well that this would lead to their arrest. At Akbarpur, criticizing the 'babas' or messianic leaders like Ram Chandra and his imitators who were preaching extremism, Jawaharlal warned the *kisans* not to believe that every person in coloured clothes was a real *sadhu* and a messenger of Gandhi; for Gandhi would never advise irreligious or unlawful activities. Those who had taken part in dacoities should purge themselves of their sin by expressing their sympathy with those robbed and their hatred of the robbers. Every *kisan* should take a vow not to rob anyone or abuse anybody.[5] Jawaharlal glamorized the *kisans* and saw them as brave men uncontaminated by city life or text-book education; but he was not deeply moved by their economic wretchedness. He saw in them a sturdy peasantry which would be the backbone of a successful nationalist movement, and he wished to enlist them wholly for the political struggle as it was being waged by the Congress; but he did not envisage the co-ordination of these scattered outbursts against local misery and the development of a large-scale peasant revolt and even perhaps a revolution. He agreed with Gandhi and the other leaders of the Congress that the *kisans* should pay their rents and devote their full attention to the non-violent struggle for *swaraj*. When one local agitator advised the *kisans* not to pay rent, the *kisan sabha*

---

[1] *The Independent*, 18 January 1921.
[2] Commissioner, Fyzabad to Chief Secretary, 14 January 1921. General Administration Dept. File 50/1921-K.W.S., U. P. archives.
[3] General Dept. File 50-3/1921. U. P. archives.
[4] *The Independent*, 26 January 1921.
[5] See report of Akbarpur Conference enclosed with Commissioner's letter to Chief Secretary, 27 January 1921. General Dept. File 50/1921 K.W. U. P. archives.

informed the authorities that they had nothing to do with him.[1] Indeed, later Jawaharlal even preached *kisan-zamindar* unity;[2] and on the issue of ejectment, which, more than any other, agitated the *kisans* of the U. P., all he could say was that this was but a minor part of the major issue of ejectment of the British from India.[3]

At this time Jawaharlal had not considered carefully whether economic and social change should be part of, or even parallel to, the political revolution; and he was willing to accept without thought the suggestion that economic issues should not be allowed to hinder political activity. His idea of freedom was purely political — ridding the British of their control over finance, the army and the police. Freedom was spinning, the wearing of hand-spun cloth, justice, prohibition, removal of untouchability and all such moral virtues; and foreign rule was the opposite of these.[4] There was very little economic connotation. But even this concept of 'politics in command' was narrow and limited. The *kisan sabhas* of the Congress during this period were very different from Mao's peasant associations in China a few years later. These associations did not undertake drastic land reforms but they at least organized the peasants and attacked the social domination of the landlords. Jawaharlal's political ideas in these years tended in the same direction, for they were a curious, unformed mixture of anarchism and village government, of Gandhi and Bertrand Russell. Representative institutions and democracy as found in Western countries had proved failures, and the problem was to free democracy from the malign influences of capital, property, militarism and an overgrown bureaucracy. Orthodox socialism also did not give much hope, and the war had shown that an all-powerful state was no lover of individual liberty. Life under socialism would be a joyless and a soul-less thing, regulated to the minutest detail by bureaucratic rules and orders. Jawaharlal was at this time a great believer in devolution and as little centralization as possible. *Swaraj* was to him *panchayat raj* and he favoured giving these village councils considerable powers even in civil and criminal matters.[5] But all this lay in the future. It did not strike him to take any immediate steps such as setting up village schools and co-operatives or demanding even the minimum redressal of tenant wrong.

Whether Jawaharlal was aware of it or not, his attitudes at this time implied informal collaboration with the Government in the maintenance of law and order; and the U.P. Government were shrewd enough to realize this. As they

---

[1] *The Independent,* 26 January 1921.

[2] Speech at Tanda, 5 March 1923.

[3] Speech at Pratabgarh, 22 April 1923. Cf. Fanon: 'The nationalist parties do not attempt to give definite orders to the country people, although the latter are perfectly ready to listen to them . . . the nationalist parties make no use at all of the opportunity which is offered to them to integrate the people of the countryside, to educate them politically and to raise the level of their struggle.' *The Wretched of the Earth* (Penguin edition, 1967), pp. 92.3.

[4] See his Hindi pamphlet 'Where are You?', published in 1922.

[5] Incomplete review of Russell's *Roads to Freedom,* written sometime after April 1919, and letter to Sir Sita Ram, 11 May 1920, S.W., vol. 1, pp. 140-44 and 160 respectively.

recorded, 'Serious as these [*kisan*] disturbances have been, they would undoubtedly have been far more serious, had not the leaders considered that the time had not yet come for pushing things to extremes.'[1] *The Independent* was of the same opinion. 'For our part we believe that, but for the timely appearance of Pandit Jawaharlal Nehru on the scene, the situation would have become more complicated.' Sir Lawrence Porter, the Finance Member, who was rather unperceptive, was too easily persuaded by the *talukdars* to prohibit the meetings addressed by Jawaharlal and his friends; but Butler overruled him.[2]

In February 1921, when Baba Ram Chandra was arrested, a serious riot broke out. Gandhi and Jawaharlal were then in Banaras, and Jawaharlal urged the excited crowd to obey Gandhi and allow Ram Chandra to be arrested quietly.[3] The U.P. Government now prohibited public meetings in the five districts of Avadh and decided to prosecute three local agitators and the officials of village *panchayats* — though not Jawaharlal or any other prominent leader. The situation was, from the Government's point of view, deepening into a crisis. *Kisan* unrest was widespread and, in parts of the Fyzabad district, embraced the bulk of the rural population. In the affected areas, few were now on the side of the Government. It was possible for leaders to collect at a very short notice enormous crowds who were prepared to carry out any instructions without question. Where the *kisan sabha* movement had spread, the authority of the *talukdars* had crumbled at a stroke; and very few of them did anything else but shut themselves up in their houses or leave for the nearest town. The *kisans* had to a large extent lost all fear of the police, and the efforts of the Congress had succeeded to the extent that the *kisans* were now prepared to defy not just the landlords but even the Government. It was believed by the officials that the leaders of the non-co-operation party had built up an enormous organization which they could start working whenever they pleased, and that they were steadily using their influence to instil hatred of Europeans and Indian officials. No longer could the authorities comfort themselves with the belief that the *kisans* had no grudge against them but sought redress from them.[4] In one village, Tajuddinpur, for a few weeks *swaraj* was proclaimed and a parallel government set up.[5]

The Government were baffled. 'There is undoubtedly a conspiracy behind the whole movement which we have not yet managed to unravel. The C.I.D. appear to know nothing about it.'[6] The suspicion, though baseless, made the Government all the more anxious that the leadership of this movement should remain with men like Gandhi and Jawaharlal, who advised the tenants to pay

[1] Administration Report of the United Provinces, 1920-21, supplementary chapter.
[2] General Dept. File 50-3/1921. U. P. archives.
[3] Sri Prakasa's article in *1921 Movement: Reminiscences* (Delhi, 1971) p. 199.

Note of Commissioner, Fyzabad Division, 1 February 1921. General Dept. File 50-3/1921. U. P. archives.

[5] Report of Collector, Sultanpur District, 1 April 1921. Ibid.
[6] Note of Butler, 2 April 1921. Ibid.

rents, rather than that it should pass to the itinerant *sadhus* who ordered the cultivators to pay nothing. The strengthening of the moderate Congress influence was part of the same policy as marching troops through the district; they were both intended to keep the *kisans* from passing wholly under the influence of the extremist agitators.

The arrest of these agitators cleared the way for the strengthening of Congress influence over the *kisans.* The Government were relieved to find that though the leaders of the Congress formally recorded their protest at these arrests, they placed less emphasis on inflammatory propaganda and concentrated their efforts on organization and the collection of funds. In Fyzabad division the tenants were directed to remain quiet and avoid disturbances and meetings; they should pay their subscriptions and leave it to Gandhi to win *swaraj* in a few months.[1] Motilal Nehru drafted a leaflet for distribution to the *kisans,* urging them to join the Congress, take up spinning, settle disputes in their own *panchayats* and not in the law courts, subscribe to the *swaraj* fund and promote caste and communal harmony. Nothing was said about rents or evictions, and a positive directive was given to avoid gatherings in districts where public meetings had been prohibited. 'But above all it is most necessary that all *kisans* should follow the path of righteousness, should speak the truth, should not indulge in any looting and should refrain from every violence in word and deed, and should commit no excesses of any kind.'[2]

These instructions, far from being revolutionary, were to the benefit of the authorities. Yet the Government arrested six young men who were distributing the pamphlet and sentenced them to jail for six months on the ground that the pamphlet attempted to excite disaffection and to bring the Government into hatred and contempt. The harsh action was clearly meant to proclaim that the Government had recovered their nerve, and intended no longer to tolerate intervention by Congressmen in *kisan* affairs. The pamphlet itself was later proscribed; but significantly no action was taken against its author, Motilal Nehru, or against Jawaharlal who distributed the pamphlet in the court room itself and wrote formally to the magistrate that he would continue to give the widest possible publicity to the pamphlet which gave expression to his views.[3]

The failure to be arrested, at a time when his followers were receiving savage sentences for carrying out his orders, acutely embarrassed Jawaharlal; and his predicament was not lessened by Gandhi's article in *Young India* disapproving of any radical demands by the *kisans.* 'There is little doubt that the *kisans* . . . are not making wise use of their newly found power . . . Whilst we will not hesitate to advise the *kisans* when the moment comes to suspend payment of taxes to the Government, it is not contemplated that at any stage of non-co-operation we would seek to deprive the *zamindars* of their rent. The

---

[1] Chief Secretary, U. P. to Home Secretary, 7 May 1921. Home Dept. Pol. Deposit, June 1921, no. 13.

[2] '*Kisanon ka sandesa*', English translation in *The Independent,* 3 May 1921.

[3] *The Independent,* 30 April 1921.

kisan movement must be confined to the improvement of the status of the *kisans* and the betterment of the relations between the *zamindar* and them.'[1] Nor, despite all the hopes held out, did the revision of the Oudh Rent Act improve substantially the condition of the tenantry; on the other hand, it strengthened the authority of the landlords, giving them the rights to evict 'undesirable' or non-resident tenants, to increase the area of land under their own cultivation and to acquire lands for a wide range of 'developmental' purposes. Cesses also continued to be exacted, while some landlords refused to give receipts for rents paid, as they were collecting more than was recorded in the village accounts.[2] In November 1921, the AICC permitted full civil disobedience including non-payment of taxes (but not of rents); and though the Congress had little to do with the Eka Movement in Hardoi, Sitapur and Lucknow, which was a revival of *kisan* agitation in a new form, the Eka associations soon began to pass political resolutions. But Jawaharlal himself took little part in this *kisan* resurgence, being preoccupied elsewhere.

[1] 18 May 1921.
[2] Report of Lt.-Col. J. C. Faunthorpe on the Eka Movement, 8 April 1922. U. P. Government Gazette, 13 May 1922.

5

The Moderate Disciple of Gandhi

Jawaharlal had by now begun to take an interest in all-India affairs. He planned to accompany Gandhi on his tour of the Central Provinces, and he had visited Calcutta in January 1921 to address the Postal Peons Union and advise the men as to how a labour union could be utilized as a political weapon against the Government.[1] But he gave close attention to the development of the non-co-operation campaign in his own province, and this afforded him no great satisfaction. 'I am afraid all we can do is to try to carry on. The conditions of the experiment are such that it is exceedingly difficult for the U.P. to to fulfil them.[2] The Government were of a similar opinion, and therefore complacent. It was true that there was a spirit of unruliness and unrest which had to some extent loosened authority, weakened the sense of law and order and depressed officials and loyalists. But the campaign of non-co-operation appeared to have generally failed, and the U.P. Government felt no need for special measures to control it or for the arrest of national leaders. It seemed adequate to prohibit meetings, protect loyalists from social boycott, organize propaganda against non-co-operation in every district and rely on the preventive sections of the ordinary law.[3] In fact, even these measures were not always thought to be necessary and the Government permitted the holding of a political, a Khilafat and various other conferences at Dehra Dun.[4]

Jawaharlal presided over the political conference, and urged his audience not to cease from fighting till *swaraj* had been won. There could be no half-measures, no compromise on vital issues. A new spirit of liberty, sacrifice and self-purification was abroad in the country, and the Government were in a state of 'blue funk'. Their policy of repression was a sure presage of coming victory.[5] He appealed to students to leave Government schools and colleges

[1] See extracts from the weekly report of the DIB, 17 January 1921.
[2] To Syed Mahmud, 9 April 1921.
[3] G.B. Lambert, Chief Secretary U.P. to Home Dept., 11 February 1921; minute of Butler, 9 March 1921; Butler to Vincent, Home Member, 10 March 1921. Home Dept., Pol. Deposit, July 1921, Proceeding no. 3 (Confidential).
[4] *The Independent,* 30 March 1921.
[5] Ibid., 1 April 1921.

and to serve as volunteers or go out to assist the *kisans*. 'But if the flesh is weak and the conditions appear hard, then there is one service which all can do — the turning of the spinning wheel.'[1] This sounds like comic bathos; but there was a manifold purpose behind Gandhi's emphasis on spinning. It provided an easy source of supplementary income to the starving millions in the countryside and helped to restore their self-confidence; and the use of the *charka* or spinning-wheel by all Congressmen could prove a binding link between the town-dwellers and the *kisans*. To create a market for this hand-spun yarn, Gandhi made compulsory the wearing of *khaddar*, or cloth woven of this yarn. *Khaddar*, in Jawaharlal's later phrase, became the 'livery of freedom'.

Jawaharlal organized the Allahabad district conference, presided over by Maulana Mahomed Ali and attended by Gandhi and other leaders, and proposed that at least 50,000 persons in the district should be registered as members of the Congress, special efforts being made to enlist women.[2] But Jawaharlal was not prepared to recommend a no-tax campaign in Allahabad city without consultation with their leaders until the other items in the non-co-operation campaign had been completed, as he did not believe this could be properly carried out.[3] He then undertook a tour of the districts of U.P. to strengthen the Congress and Khilafat movements. He travelled by train, car and *ekka* (horse carriage) and even on one occasion ran between two places[4] precedents for the election campaigns he was to undertake years later in all parts of India. Once he reached a railway station too late and missed the train. The stationmaster, an official but a patriot, provided him with a trolley to cover the twenty or thirty miles to the next junction, and was dismissed for his pains.[5]

Yet, despite all this energetic effort of Jawaharlal and his colleagues, the non-co-operation campaign failed to gather impetus in the United Provinces. Over 3,000 *panchayats*, encouraged to take the place of the law courts for settling disputes, were functioning, but nearly 7,000 *panchayats* in north-eastern Avadh were suppressed by the Seditious Meetings Act. District courts, which had worn a deserted appearance at the beginning of 1921, now once again were crowded, though mostly by friends and relatives of defendants. Many workers had been cowed by official displeasure and action, for the U.P. Government had recourse to both preventive and punitive measures. Official propaganda also was gaining ground.[6] So the Government could

[1] Letter to the Editor, *The Leader*, 25 April 1921.
[2] *The Independent*, 13 May 1921.
[3] Report of speech in Allahabad, *The Independent*, 7 May 1921.
[4] Jawaharlal in *The Independent*, 25 May 1921.
[5] Jawaharlal to Bhai Parmanand, 26 November 1933.
[6] Report of the Secretaries U.P.C.C. on progress of non-co-operation 20 March-20 July 1921. *The Independent*, 26 and 27 July 1921; Jawaharlal to Secretary, Aligarh District Congress Committee, 10 August 1921, Khwaja papers, N.M.M.L.

relax, and even the Congress acknowledged that a distinct change was notice-able in official policy from the end of August.[1]

Jawaharlal was now an ardent advocate of *swadeshi* and no longer the 'pink and pretty' young man who wore only silk underwear[2] and was worried as to how he would be able to move about in *swadeshi* socks.[3] From July 1921 the U.P. Congress concentrated on promoting the making of yarn by the use of the *charka* and the weaving of cloth from this yarn. Most district committees formed special *swadeshi* departments and put their best workers in charge of them. *Charkas* were distributed widely, and the weavers were encouraged to utilize the yarn spun from these *charkas.* Model weaving-schools were esta-blished, and almost every national school had its spinning and weaving depart-ment. A large amount of yarn was also sent to other provinces. The converse of this propagation of *swadeshi* was the campaign against foreign cloth. Most towns and large villages had their bonfires of such cloth. Merchants and tailors were asked to take a pledge not to sell or use it; and here again the success was considerable, even without resort to large-scale picketing.[4]

This boycott now claimed Jawaharlal's full attention. While he still demanded militant action and declared that the place of every Indian was in-side jail,[5] yet the emphasis was on boycott of foreign cloth. In Allahabad city he was one of those who went round from house to house collecting foreign clothes.[6]

At the U.P. political conference in October 1921 Jawaharlal moved the resolution on *swadeshi.* At this time an unqualified Gandhian, he argued that as the attainment of *swaraj* depended on the use of *swadeshi* cloth, the people should be asked to discard, burn or export foreign cloth and use home-made cloth instead. He was as impatient to drive out the English from India as any-one else, but he had not till now discovered any new method of doing so except *swadeshi.* He did not agree with those who advocated the use of the sword. In the last resort they would all come to the conclusion that they could win and retain *swaraj* only by the use of *swadeshi* cloth.[7]

This was indeed moderation, which the Government could not seriously quarrel with; and it was further emphasized by the resolutions passed under Jawaharlal's presidency at the Rae Bareli district conference in November. Strict non-violence, the maintenance of Hindu-Muslim unity and the removal of the evil of untouchability were stated to be the appropriate preparations for civil disobedience.

[1] Report of the U.P. Congress on Government repression in U.P., *The Independent,* 27 November 1921.
[2] Oral testimony of his brother-in-law Kailas Kaul, N.M.M.L.
[3] Padmaja Naidu's account of her conversation with Jawaharlal at Mussoorie in 1918, interview with the author, 24 December 1969.
[4] Report of U.P. Congress Committee, *The Independent,* 26 November 1921.
[5] Speech at Agra, 11 September 1921, *The Independent,* 13 September 1921.
[6] *The Independent,* 12 August 1921.
[7] *The Leader,* 26 October 1921.

As the achievement of *swaraj* is only possible if people of all professions live in union and as the tenants and zamindars can be truly happy only when independence is achieved, so this conference expresses its desire that tenants and zamindars should live in harmony through mutual goodwill and sympathy and insists that although the recent Rent Act has made their position worse, still they should patiently bear all troubles, pay their rents and keep the welfare of the country in view.

An appeal was made to *zamindars* and *talukdars* not to be led away by petty personal gains but to make every effort in helping their tenants to attain *swaraj.* The *talukdars* were also asked to boycott the visit of the Prince of Wales to Lucknow. The one non-platitudinous resolution of the conference was the insistence on the 'instant universal use' of *khaddar* and on the manufacture of *khaddar* on a considerable scale.[1]

Jawaharlal was also very careful at this time to abide by the various orders of the Government. There was little defiance in his mood. At Shikarpur, for example, when an order under S. 144 prohibiting a meeting was served on him while he was speaking, he immediately stopped and turned his attention to the collection of foreign clothes and subscriptions for the *swaraj* fund.[2] When a similar order was served on him at Bhiti, he marched with the whole audience of about a thousand to the next district four and a half miles away and held the meeting there.

However, for some time the U.P. Government had been collecting material for taking action against *The Independent* for its articles, and against Jawaharlal for seditious speeches. But as the case against the Ali brothers was thought to be the stronger one, Jawaharlal's case was held over till a decision had been taken by the Government of India on that case and that of *The Independent.* Opinion at Simla was in favour of giving *The Independent* an opportunity to express regret; and the U.P. Government, although (excepting one minister) of the view that there was no alternative to taking proceedings, decided to give a similar opportunity to Jawaharlal.[3] So, on 16 June 1921, Jawaharlal was informed that no proceedings would be taken against him if he undertook not to deliver speeches directly or indirectly inciting to violence or calculated to create an atmosphere of readiness for violence. Similar notices were sent the same day to the editor and printer of *The Independent.*

Jawaharlal promised the Collector of Allahabad, who had forwarded the Government's notice, to send a reply within a week; but his father, who was at Ramgarh near Naini Tal in the hills, telegraphed direct to the Collector that a reply would only be sent after due consideration.[4] Motilal was still inclined

[1] *The Leader,* 26 November 1921.
[2] *The Independent,* 25 September 1921.
[3] Chief Secretary U.P. to Home Secretary, Government of India, No. 1543, dated 9 July 1921, Home Dept. Pol. 1922, File 112, nos. 1-8.
[4] See telegrams exchanged between Jawaharlal and Motilal, Jawaharlal's letter to Collector, Allahabad, 30 June 1921, and Motilal's telegram to Collector.

to treat his son (who was now thirty-two years of age) as an impetuous school-boy. He decided, as he told Jawaharlal, to act the boss, as he believed he had every right to do, and rectify by his interference — 'vis major' — Jawaharlal's mistake in making promises.[1] Jawaharlal now drafted his reply with great care — at least three drafts exist — and took it to Ramgarh to have it reviewed by his father. Motilal was of course fully aware that he and Jawaharlal sooner or later would find themselves in gaol, and he was unflinching. He had spurned the suggestion that he might meet Harcourt Butler or proceed to Simla to see the Viceroy.[2] 'I would not for the life of me approach Sir H. in the interest of Jawahar or myself or for that matter any other individual . . . Jawahar and I both know what is coming and are fully prepared for it.'[3] But he saw no reason to make the Government's task easier, and tightened up his son's draft so as to make it more precise without being any the less defiant, removing any suggestion that Jawaharlal could still be regarded by anyone else but him as an 'impressionable youngster easily carried away by anything that he reads'.[4] The accuracy of police reporting of Jawaharlal's speeches was questioned, and any apology or undertaking was refused; if he had erred by saying any-thing which was untrue or exaggerated or had produced the impression that he was condemning the whole British people, he would apologize, but only to the public.[5]

The Home Member and his department agreed with the U.P. Government that Jawaharlal should now be prosecuted.[6] But the Viceroy, as Motilal had expected, viewed this in the all-India context and, as part of the delaying tactics he was employing against the Congress, decided to ignore Jawaharlal. The U.P. Government were instructed to proceed only against the editor and printer of *The Independent*. Butler now agreed.

If they start civil disobedience, they will put themselves in the wrong, whereas if we run in prominent leaders, we may drive a good deal of sympathy to their side. It is a choice of evils, and I think the lesser evil is to hold one's hand for the present.[7]

By November 1921 the Government of India were ready to take drastic action against the non-co-operation campaign, which was now developing new manifestations and frequently erupting in violence. Among other measures it was decided to strike down the volunteer movement in the

[1] Motilal to Jawaharlal, 27 and 30 June 1921.
[2] Sapru to Motilal, 5 June 1921. Sapru papers, National Library, Calcutta.
[3] Motilal to Sapru, 24 June 1921. Ibid.
[4] Motilal's note on Jawaharlal's drafts.
[5] Jawaharlal to Chief Secretary U.P., 4 July 1921.
[6] Notes of H.D. Craik, 13 July 1921. Home Dept. Pol., 1922, File 112, nos. 1-8.
[7] Butler to Reading 3 August 1921. Butler papers. India Office Library (hereafter I.O.L.), Mss. Eur.F. 116/57.

U.P.[1] There, thanks chiefly to Jawaharlal, the volunteer squads had become well-drilled units which successfully organized a complete *hartal* (strike) in Lucknow, Allahabad, Kanpur and the other principal towns and were effectively picketing shops selling foreign goods. Even the Viceroy conceded this success, particularly in Allahabad.

> The non-co-operators put forward the full strength of an undoubtedly powerful organization and yet, save in Allahabad, have really not succeeded anywhere, although, surveying the situation impartially, I am bound to admit that they have at places managed to prevent the visit [of the Prince of Wales] being the unqualified and triumphant success it would otherwise have been.[2]

The U.P. Congress had also announced its intention of preparing selected *tehsils* for civil disobedience;[3] and though the Government did not take this seriously,[4] it was obvious that, if civil disobedience were started, trained volunteers would be utilized for this purpose. Every district Congress committee had been directed to constitute a volunteer board immediately. So the volunteer organization in the U.P. was declared unlawful, and Jawaharlal, the convener and secretary of the U.P. volunteer board, and his father were arrested on 5 December for their connection with this activity. Motilal was delighted to go to jail with his son, and departed in a mood of exaltation. Jawaharlal too was happy to secure, as the accolade of patriotism, a sentence of six months' simple imprisonment and a fine of Rs 100 or a further month in jail. Father and son and a few others, who were being treated better than the rank and file of Congress prisoners, wrote to the jail superintendent declining these special privileges. 'We wish to recognize no class distinction in our army of *Swaraj*.'[5] A fellow Congressman who saw the Nehrus in jail a week after reported that 'the smiling and happy countenance of Pandit Jawaharlal Nehru stood out in relief amongst the persons in the lock-up.'[6] He continued to direct from jail the work of the U.P. Congress, and drew up plans to ensure that it did not cease to function despite official suppression and that it demonstrated its authority by filling the jails.[7]

Because of some technical defect in his sentence, Jawaharlal, to his own

[1] Home Dept. circular to local governments, 24 November 1921. Home Dept. Pol. 1921, File 303, nos. 1-48; R. D. Mathur, 'British policy towards the volunteer movement in India during the non-co-operation campaign', Indian History Congress proceedings, 1970. pp. 214-25.

[2] Reading to Montagu, 23 February 1922. Reading papers, I.O.L. Mss. Eur. E. 238, vol. 4.

[3] Report of the U.P. Congress committee, 26 November 1921; resolutions of U.P. Congress committee, 3 December 1921. *The Independent,* 6 December 1921.

[4] Viceroy's telegram to Secretary of State, 6 December 1921. Home Dept. Pol. 1921, File 18.

[5] Letter 27 December 1921, reprinted in *Young India* 19 January 1922.

[6] Pandit Gaurishankar Bhargava, reported in *The Bombay Chronicle,* 15 December 1921.

[7] See note traced by C.I.D. and said to have been written by him in jail between 9 and 12 December 1921. Home Dept. Pol. 1922, File 767.

surprise, was released in March 1922 when he had only served half his term. By now Gandhi had called off the civil disobedience campaign because of the increasing violence. Jawaharlal, like most others, was bitterly disappointed, especially as the campaign in his own province had been mùstering strength. Even the Government had been worried by the widespread tension and preparations for intensification of civil disobedience. 'The situation is rapidly deteriorating and getting more out of control. His Excellency in Council has no doubt that the deterioration will spread and have alarming developments, unless action is taken to stop the agitation at its source.'[1] Volunteer units in uniform were attempting to replace the police, while Congressmen in certain districts set up their own schools, courts and cattle pounds. The Commissioner of Allahabad reported that the establishment of Congress *thanas* (police stations) with men performing point duty and other police functions 'was not so much an organized movement run by the nominal leaders as a more or less spontaneous movement of the lower castes, Muhammadans more especially. This made it all the more likely to spread, and the Commissioner thought that there was danger of its developing into a general strike or boycott of Europeans.'[2] The U.P. Government had therefore proposed legislation to prevent usurpation of the functions of the police.

Gandhi's action enabled the Government to relax and made Jawaharlal's task in sustaining the morale of Congressmen so much the harder. 'I have only to say this — keep fighting, continue to work for independent India and do not stop. Do not abandon your creed. Do not accept false compromises. Continue to follow your great leader Mahatma Gandhi and remain true to Congress. Be efficient, be well organised and above all remember the *charka* and *ahimsa.* '[3] He attended Gandhi's trial at Ahmedabad, and then returned to organize spinning, boycott and picketing in the United Provinces. The suggestion that he should visit England as a member of the Khilafat delegation appealed to his father who was still in jail.

> I would readily welcome the opportunity of your having to spend some time on the sea and in Europe in the interest of all — yourself, myself and the country at large. As you know I am unable to follow the politic-religious philosophy of Gandhiji beyond a certain point . . . in any case some understandable service from outside is far preferable in my opinion to the very doubtful merit supposed to flow from rotting in jail to expiate the crime of Chauri Chaura. [4]

[1] Chief Secretary U.P. to Home Secretary, No. 366, dated 15 February 1922. Home Dept. Pol. 1922, File 18.
[2] Chief Secretary U.P. to Home Secretary, No. 444, dated 24 February 1922. Home Dept. Pol. 1922, File 327, Part III, nos. 1-10.
[3] Message on release from prison, *Aaj,* 10 March 1922.
[4] Motilal to Jawaharlal, sometime in April 1922. It was the incident at Chauri Chaura, a village in the United Provinces, where a mob set fire to a police station and 22 constables lost their lives, that led Gandhi to call off civil disobedience.

But the idea of leaving India at this time could not have been attractive to Jawaharlal. However much he might deplore Gandhi's latest action, he had, unlike his father, no reservations about Gandhi's leadership and believed he had enough to do even outside political action.

> You will be glad to learn that work is flourishing. We are laying sure foundations this time. God willing, our next march forward will end in victory. Rest assured that there will be no relaxation, no·lessening in our activities and above all there will be no false compromise with Government. We stand for the truth. How can we tamper with anything which has been soiled by the touch of falsehood?[1]

As the Government recognized, 'quiet propaganda work' organized by Jawaharlal from Allahabad was widespread.[2] He addressed ·public meetings in the city and elsewhere and circulated Hindi pamphlets. The voice throughout was Gandhian. The atmosphere, he said, was calm but this did not mean that non-co-operation was dead. It could never die until the goal was reached; and the great war raging in the country could have only one result — an Indian victory. So they should go forward trusting God. The practical work to be done was promotion of *swadeshi* and spinning, removal of untouchability, subscription to the Tilak fund and enrolment of volunteers and of Congress members, the age limit for which had been reduced from twenty-one to eighteen. But all violence was to be avoided and there should be no forcible closing of shops. Students should not court arrest but if arrested should gladly meet their fate.

The advice Jawaharlal gave to the students he himself for a time followed. While his activity was open and effective, he did not at first go out of his way to court arrest. He gave the lead in organizing *hartals* of mourning on 6 April, at the start of the National Week, in lament for lack of freedom, and on 13 April, to commemorate Jallianwala Bagh. But he advised the organizers of the political conference at Dehra Dun to abide by the prohibitory order of Government. However, he began to feel that concentration on constructive work was becoming almost impossible because of official oppression and terrorism. He and a colleague visited Sitapur district to inquire into one instance of such allegations,[3] and the atrocities committed there, said Jawaharlal in a public speech, were such as to make the occurrences in the Punjab pale.[4] So it might be necessary to start individual civil disobedience again of some kind.[5] The organization should therefore be perfected, tours planned and

---

[1] Jawaharlal to Syed Mahmud, 4 April 1922.
[2] Chief Secretary U.P. to Home Secretary, 3 May 1922, Home Dept. Pol. 1922, File 18.
[3] Inquiry report of Jawaharlal and M. Saxena, 27 April 1922, S.W., vol. 1, pp. 242-7.
[4] Speech at Lucknow, 26 April 1922.
[5] Circular letter of U.P. provincial Congress committee, 25 April 1922.

efforts made to visit all important towns and rouse the people. The Government reacted, and on 5 May the Congress offices and Anand Bhawan were searched. Clearly arrest was imminent, and Jawaharlal issued another circular to Congress committees, written while the search was being conducted, 'almost in the shadow of the police'. The people had shown enthusiasm and courage, and only organization was necessary to achieve success. Non-co-operation had gained India a new status in the eyes of the world. 'That has been the achievement of a few months. Truly a wonderful record for which let us, in all humility, thank the Giver of all.'[1]

A week later, on 12 May, Jawaharlal was arrested on a charge of organizing picketing and advocating it in his writings and speeches. As a non-co-operator he refused to plead, cross-examine the witnesses or offer any defence, but he made a long statement. He pointed out that though he was being tried for criminal intimidation and extortion the prosecution could not produce any witness to suggest that the picketing had not been peaceful. On the other hand, it was the Government which had, throughout the province, been guilty of intimidation and terrorism. However, he was grateful to the authorities for framing this particular charge, for it gave publicity to the boycott of foreign cloth. The people of Allahabad and the U.P. 'would know that the salvation of India and her hungry millions demanded the use of the *charka* and the weaving of *khaddar*, and they would cast out all foreign cloth and consign them to the flames or to the dustbin.'

Jawaharlal also referred to the wider issue of British rule. Fond as he was of England — and perhaps because of his fondness — he had now become a rebel and all his activities had but one end in view.

Jail has indeed become a heaven for us, a holy place of pilgrimage since our saintly and beloved leader was sentenced . . . I marvel at my good fortune. To serve India in the battle of freedom is honour enough. To serve her under a leader like Mahatma Gandhi is doubly fortunate. But to suffer for the dear country! What greater good fortune could befall an Indian, unless it be death for the cause or the full realisation of our glorious dream.

His heart-warming statement of nationalist passion, with its loyalty to Gandhi's leadership blended with romantic echoes of the Risorgimento, was heard far beyond the district court and Jawaharlal's own province. The Government were deluding themselves with the belief that, while the cloth-dealer witnesses had respectfully saluted the accused, the case had attracted little public attention.[2] Jawaharlal had in mind a wider audience, and the first of his trial statements secured for him a national audience and became the manifesto of

[1]Circular, 5 May 1922.
[2]Chief Secretary U.P. to Home Dept., 4 June 1922. Home Dept. Pol. 1922, File 18.

the educated youth of India. Motilal was delighted to find, on an all-India tour later in the year, that his son's influence was widespread; and he was much moved when a large crowd in Delhi cheered him and his wife as the father and mother of Jawaharlal. [1] As Motilal saw, the points of law in the statement were weak and could be improved upon. It was not sufficient to say that picketing had been peaceful in order to disprove the charge of extortion; an association of cotton merchants had been levying fines on those who had been selling foreign cloth, and Jawaharlal should have established that he and the Congress had nothing to do with this organization. But these deficiencies in legal argument did all the more credit to Jawaharlal's heart and to his intense patriotism and enhanced the value of the statement from the viewpoint of the Congress and non-co-operation. 'On reading your statement I felt I was the proudest father in the world. In its firm and simple dignity it would bear comparison with the best productions of the Master himself.' [2]

Jawaharlal had expected and hoped for a long sentence; [3] he had been somewhat galled by his earlier premature release, especially as his father was still in jail. 'One feels almost lonely outside the jail, and selfishness prompts a quick return.' He was not disappointed, the sentence being 18 months' rigorous imprisonment and a fine of Rs 100 and 3 months' further imprisonment in case of default. He was placed in Lucknow district jail — a fact which worried his father, who did not believe Jawaharlal could bear extreme heat and would have preferred his son to join him in Naini Tal jail or to be sent to Almora. Jawaharlal's health was at this time none too good and he continued in jail homoeopathic treatment, which consisted mainly of arsenic and sulphur. His diet was frugal and vegetarian — curds, bread and butter, milk and fruit, apart from rice, *chapatis, dal* and vegetables for lunch, which was his only substantial meal.

Because the jail superintendent and warders harassed visitors and subjected them to petty indignities, Jawaharlal and his companions for some months gave up interviews and saw no friendly face from outside. He did not even visit other barracks during this period. But on the whole Jawaharlal was content with his existence. The mere fact of being confined boosted his self-respect. He hoped too that jail life, with its deprivations, would harden him, and enjoyed his enforced leisure to the full.

It is those who work and labour outside who deserve sympathy, not we who laze and eat and sleep. Soon the pleasant autumn days will come and it will be delightful to be under the trees. And what can be pleasanter than freedom from worry? We have no appointments to keep, no piling up of work with which we cannot cope, no speechifying, no hurry. Time

[1] Motilal to Jawaharlal, 22 July 1922.
[2] Motilal to Jawaharlal, 24 May 1922.
[3] See his circular, 5 May 1922, and statement in court, 17 May 1922.

almost ceases to have significance and life moves on like a gently flow-
ing river.[1]

Apart from physical exercise — walking and running — and regular daily
spinning, he spent most of his time reading. He was allowed two daily newspapers, *The Leader* and *The Englishman*, till 15 November, when the jail
authorities discontinued them. He started learning Urdu. The journals he
received were the *Nation*, the *New Statesman* and the *Modern Review*. But
Jawaharlal was not greatly concerned with current developments outside. His
interests ranged far and wide, and he was determined to refurbish his mind
which had rusted since his return from England. He was not greatly interested
in philosophy or religious thought and his speculations in these matters never
progressed beyond the superficial. He read in jail the Koran and Arnold's *Light
of Asia* as well as the *Bhagavad Gita* in Mrs Besant's translation; but he was at
this time basically an unthinking, conventional Hindu theist. His attitude was
almost platitudinous and lacking in humour. 'It is a redeeming feature that the
jail authorities have not the power to keep God and His nature out of jail.' He
expressed his gratitude for having such parents and near relatives as held up a
lofty ideal before him and always added to his strength and spirit; and he was
sure that the life they were leading now was much better than what they had
abandoned. 'Now', he added, 'I understand a little what Jesus meant when he
asked us to forsake the world and save our soul.' He observed his birthday in
jail according to his mother's directives, even setting aside five rupees for distribution to the poor.

His special interests were history, travel and poetry. It was now that he
began to collect the facts and thoughts which later went into the making of
Glimpses of World History. Among the books he specially asked for were
Havell's *Aryan Rule in India* — which appealed to him through its idealiza-
tion of India's past — and Bryce's *Holy Roman Empire*, the memoirs of Babar
and Bernier's travels. He also read Sven Hedin's books, and, hugging to himself
a private dream-world, he drew up an itinerary of a journey he would undertake
after *swaraj* was won, via Kashmir and Ladakh to Manasarovar and Kailas and
the famous cities of central Asia, and then across Afghanistan, Iran and Arabia
to Europe.

In poetry his interests were romantic — Keats, Shelley, Swinburne, Tenny-
son's *Idylls of the King*; and his long letters to his family also bear a marked
streak of romanticism. He relished the idea of being in the thick of a nationalist
struggle, and was full of Italian precedents. 'In the golden days to come when
the history of our times and our country comes to be written the present will
occupy a glorious chapter. And shall we not think of the good old days? Shall
we not remember the great men who showed us the way and filled us with the
fire of faith?' And then he quotes Meredith, replacing 'Italia' with 'India':

[1] Jawaharlal to Motilal, 1 September 1922.

> We who have seen India in the throes,
> Half risen but to be hurled to the ground, and now,
> Like a ripe field of wheat, where once drove plough,
> All bounteous as she is fair, we think of those
> Who blew the breath of life into her frame.

This was adolescent exaltation, yet to be channelled by hard thinking. There is, in all his letters of this time, the glow of virginal suffering and a complacent absence of reflection. Jawaharlal was so excited by the situation in which he found himself, so much in love with sacrifice and hardship, so self-conscious about the immediate context that he gave no thought to the way or the goal. He had made a cradle of emotional nationalism, and rocked himself in it. The special correspondent of the *Manchester Guardian*, who was permitted by the superintendent of the jail to interview Jawaharlal, was not unfair in reporting that what had struck him most in Jawaharlal's own account of his life was the steady growth of an impulse to do something, he knew not what, for his country, and the deep satisfaction he felt when Gandhi at last showed him definite things to do; but these were acts of self-sacrifice.

> The desire to make a sacrifice had evidently been and still, I think, was very strong in him . . . But though the man's intelligence, refinement and patriotism were very apparent, I failed to get from him any clear idea of how he proposed to win *Swaraj* or what he proposed to do with it when he had won it.[1]

Selfishness, Jawaharlal had written, would hardly favour a quick discharge.[2] However, once again he was released before serving his full sentence. He was set free on 31 January 1923, as part of a general amnesty declared by the U.P. Government without consulting the Government of India,[3] in order to give effect to a resolution of the Provincial Legislative Council recommending such a measure. Welcoming the release of these 107 political prisoners, *The Leader* wrote: 'The greatest among these patriotic souls, the true disciple of Mr Gandhi, is Pandit Jawaharlal Nehru, who moves on a very high plane of thought indeed, who hates none but loves his country with the intensity of a pure nature and a feeling heart.'[4]

The Leader went on to hope that Jawaharlal would abandon the policy of useless sacrifice and suicidal courses in favour of political action. What it seems to have had in mind was that Jawaharlal should join the Moderates and help in the functioning of dyarchy.

---

[1] Report of interview in October, reprinted in *The Bombay Chronicle,* 26 December 1922.
[2] To his father, 15 November 1922.
[3] See Home Dept. Pol. 1923, File 56.
[4] 31 January 1923.

The essence of non-co-operation consists in teaching the people the lesson of self-help. Such a lesson cannot be inculcated by laying stress merely on handspinning, or by promulgating doctrines of hatred. In the field of agriculture, of industries, of co-operation, of education, of local self-government and social service, there is unlimited scope for preaching the gospel of self-help.

The same suggestion was made by the well-meaning Chief Justice of the Allahabad High Court, Sir Grimwood Mears. He wrote to Motilal three days before Jawaharlal's release that he wished to establish friendly relations with the latter 'and I honestly think I could make life happier for him if he would let me try'.[1] Then, when he met Jawaharlal, Mears hinted to him that a ministership could come his way if he wished.[2]

It seems astounding that this could even be thought of, and is of interest only as showing how, despite his two terms in jail, Jawaharlal was generally thought of, at least in his home province, as basically a moderate nationalist. It was true that Jawaharlal was by no means a revolutionary extremist, but he was not an incipient loyalist and the career of a man like Surendranath Bannerjee, who had left the Congress to become a leading Moderate and a minister in Bengal, was not likely to be his model. He had not, as yet, far-reaching ideological commitments, and violent techniques were abhorrent to him; but office under the British certainly could not lure him. Reading was shrewder in his assessment of Jawaharlal as 'fanatical in his hostility to Government'.[3]

Jawaharlal, therefore, wasted little time in politely rejecting these suggestions. What gave him greater concern was the sharp difference of opinion within the Congress itself. With Gandhi in jail, the Congress leadership was almost equally split on the issue of entry into Councils. The Civil Disobedience Inquiry Committee set up by the Congress had stated the arguments of both sides — of those who were for contesting the elections due to be held in 1923 as well as of those who opposed it. Those in favour believed that with civil disobedience called off, it would be unwise to let the Moderates have a monopoly of the Councils. The Congress should win the elections and control the working of these assemblies. 'Knock these Councils on the head, and you will achieve what millions spent in foreign propaganda cannot achieve.' But those who opposed any such step argued that it would enhance Government's prestige; any wrecking of official machinery should be done from outside. C. R. Das and Motilal were the leaders of the group favouring Council entry which they envisaged as a new form of non-co-operation — Congressmen should contest the elections and present the country's legitimate demands in the Councils; if these were not granted within a reasonable time Congressmen should adopt a policy of uniform, continuous and consistent obstruction with a view to make

---

[1] Sir G. Mears to Motilal, 28 January 1923.
[2] *Autobiography*, pp. 101-2.
[3] To Montagu, 6 July 1922. Reading papers, vol. 5.

government through Councils impossible. At the annual session of the Congress in December 1922 this policy was rejected by a considerable majority. Das, who was president of the session, was persuaded not to resign; but he and Motilal formed, within the Congress, the Swaraj Party to further their policy of Council entry. It was hoped that this would enable constitutionalists like M. A. Jinnah, who had left the Congress in 1920, to return to the fold.[1]

The predicament of Jawaharlal was that, while he was emotionally attached to the leaders of the Swaraj Party, his mind was inclined to agree with those opposed to entering the Councils. In his first speech after his release, he declared that he still stuck to his conviction that non-co-operation was the only path which could lead them to self-government. They should continue their fight and indeed further intensify it till their object had been attained. On the specific move of Council entry he declined to express his opinion on the ground that he was not in touch with current politics; but he emphasized that the destination and road of both groups were the same, though their conveyances might differ.[2] It worried him too that the differences within the Congress might weaken the organization as a whole. So he, with a few others, sought not so much a compromise — the positions were irreconcilable — as 'an atmosphere of charity and goodwill'[3] in which both sides could function. At the session of the AICC in Allahabad towards the end of February, he and Maulana Azad persuaded the two groups to suspend all propaganda till the end of April. He himself spent this period of truce touring some of the districts of the United Provinces, collecting funds for the Congress and urging discipline and the wearing of *khaddar*. But there was little heart in his speeches, and even the U.P. authorities were satisfied that his utterances were mild.[4] At Allahabad, on 6 April, addressing a meeting to inaugurate the National Week, he was reported to have said no more than that everyone should examine for himself the events of the past four years and pray for guidance. It is not surprising that his election at this time as chairman of the Allahabad Municipal Board caused no alarm in official circles. 'He is reported as inclined to be reasonable, but as insisting that his duty to the nationalist cause must precede his obligation to the ratepayers.'[5]

Jawaharlal was at this time, in fact, rudderless, with no clear ideas as to what he should do. He wrote in reply to a colleague's demand for a more revolutionary programme:

> I wholly agree. But what is it to be? Let us remember that most people like to talk of revolution and direct action but they have no desire to participate in it. Those of us who really believe in direct action must stick to

[1]M.R. Jayakar, *The Story of My Life,* vol. 2, 1922-1925 (Bombay, 1959), pp. 81, 84-5.
[2]Speech at Allahabad, 1 February 1923, reported in *The Leader,* 4 February 1923.
[3]Jawaharlal's telegram to 'Swarajya', Madras, *The Bombay Chronicle,* 24 February 1923.
[4]See, for example, U.P. Intelligence reports on his speeches at Sitapur, 18 March, and Gorakhpur towards the end of March 1923.
[5]Chief Secretary to Home Secretary, 19 April 1923. Home Dept. Pol. 1923, File 25.

it and keep the ideal before the public. If you have any specific notions, do write to me.[1]

He himself, he wrote in a public letter, was a bit of a missionary in his own way;[2] but he was a missionary without a mission. Congress politics too were once again heading to a collision; the truce was over, and in the first days of May both Motilal and Rajagopalachari, the leader of the no-changers, as they were called, issued manifestos drawing up the lines of battle. Jawaharlal was concerned to avoid this clash, if only to save the Congress, which seemed to him to have practically ceased, during the past four months, to function. "Effective political work has ceased in every province and if this state of affairs is prolonged for some time the Congress would cease to exist. It is undeniable that the most imperative necessity at the present time is to restore the Congress to its original prestige.'[3] Jawaharlal's opinion was shared by the Viceroy, who reported smugly at about the same time that non-co-operation as an effective force was practically dead.[4]

The solution favoured by Jawaharlal was one which would give the Swaraj Party the substance and its opponents only the shadow. The decision taken by the Congress in December 1922 against Council entry would still hold, but no propaganda should be done in its favour; in other words, its operation would be suspended, and those who wished to contest the elections would be free to do so. This formula deceived nobody; but it was accepted by the U.P. Congress committee,[5] and then by the AICC at Bombay in the last week of May. Six members of the Working Committee who were opposed to Council entry promptly resigned. Jawaharlal, whose purpose was to fend off final decisions while allowing the Swarajists to have their way, suggested that these resignations be not accepted; his resolution was carried by a large majority but the no-changers were firm. In the circumstances, it was agreed that Das also should resign the presidency, and the party executive be manned by those uncommitted to either side, such as Jawaharlal.

This was Jawaharlal's achievement — one which even he had not expected.[6] It was the first time he had functioned decisively on the national plane, and we have an interesting first-hand account of the impact he made on his audience.

He is no orator, has no tricks of manner of speech. He is sparing in the use of words, but the words are carefully chosen, for which his Harrow and Cambridge education are perhaps responsible. His voice is feeble

[1]An intercepted letter to Sampurnanand dated 25 April 1923, quoted in C. Kaye's confidential publication *Communism in India* (Delhi, 1926).
[2]*The Leader*, 13 May 1923.
[3]Circular letter of Jawaharlal, Dr M.A. Ansari and others, 11 May 1923.
[4]Reading to Peel, 10 May 1923. Reading papers, vol. 6.
[5]*The Leader*, 16 May 1923.
[6]See Jawaharlal to A.M. Khwaja, 6 June 1923. S.W., vol. 1, pp. 358-60.

and low, and he should make an effort to raise it, for it is possible, and should not expect his audience to do the impossible and intensify their power of hearing. When he speaks, sincerity exudes from him as perspiration from the body in the month of May in Bombay. He succeeds in impressing his audience probably because he does not consciously try to do so. His anxiety is merely to explain his attitude and to lay bare the processes of the working of his mind and he sometimes overdoes it. He should remember that people are mostly interested in the finished article and not in the processes of its manufacture. His modesty is a virtue; he should be careful not to convert it into a vice. He is sometimes impatient when the audience does not rise to his intellectual level but let him remember there are hordes of people in this world who have to manage with a lower level of mental equipment than himself and he should sympathize with them.[1]

No polished orator, but one thinking on his feet; modest, stumbling along, but with sincerity intense and transparent — these remained his characteristics as a public speaker through the years. The only respect in which he did change, and for the better, was that incessant contact with the masses rid him of the early trait of talking down to his audience. In later years his hearers could follow him effortlessly, step by step, in the argument, and never felt that he was preaching to them.

However, the hollow compromise fashioned by Jawaharlal soon crumbled. Rajagopalachari repudiated it while Das toured southern India, Rajagopalachari's home ground, campaigning for Swarajist policy. Jawaharlal did not believe that entry into Councils would achieve anything substantial or important, but he blamed Rajagopalachari for violating the arrangement.[2] Vallabhbhai Patel, one of the no-changers, pointed out the contradiction of Jawaharlal's position in agreeing with them but sympathizing with the Das party: 'I wonder why you would not allow those who are in the right to have their own way and prefer to allow those who are in the wrong to do so . . . How do you expect us to quickly reach [sic] with equanimity the rapid demolition of the magnificent edifice that had been erected by the combined sacrifice of so many in this land.'[3] In Nagpur in July the AICC rejected by a majority of two votes Jawaharlal's resolution advocating disciplinary action against those provincial Congress committees which had defied the compromise resolution of May. Thereupon Jawaharlal, along with his colleagues, resigned from the Working Committee and is reported to have expressed a desire to retire from the AICC as well.[4] 'I wish', he remarked to a friend, 'we would not hurt each other's hearts so easily and so constantly.'[5] He had already, on 30 June, resigned his secretaryship of the U.P. provincial Congress committee.

[1] 'Simplex' in The Bombay Chronicle, 30 May 1923.
[2] Interview in Aaj, 19 June 1923.
[3] 24 June 1923.
[4] The Leader, 14 July 1923.
[5] Sri Prakasa's oral testimony, N.M.M.L.

6

In Nabha Jail

Jawaharlal was now, therefore, a free man, relieved of the tussles within the party which had filled him with such distaste. As irksome to him as the lack of discipline of the no-changers was the resistance of the Swarajists to working through the Congress machinery. 'Are you going to keep the Congress intact or let it go to pieces?'[1] At the Congress session in Delhi in September the no-changers conceded defeat by agreeing to the entry into Councils of such Congressmen 'as have no religious or other conscientious objection' to it; but Jawaharlal took little part in arriving at this decision. His attention was given wholly to such opportunities for 'cold-blooded action'[2] as came his way. 'I am weary', he wrote to a friend in August,[3] 'and sick at heart. Nagpur has been a most painful experience for me. I came here with the intention of wandering about in the interior for a while away from the haunts of man.' Strengthening of the party organization and extension of its network, the training and discipline of volunteers and the creation in the country of a general atmosphere of resistance and of indifference to the Government — these were to him the important tasks. He recognized that mass civil disobedience was out of the question for the time being, but he helped to organize the *satyagraha* campaign that developed in Nagpur over the refusal of the district magistrate to allow a Congress procession to carry the national flag. Volunteer squads from different parts of the country were sent to reinforce the local workers till the authorities gave way and permitted a Congress procession with the flag to pass. Again in need of some issue to occupy him, Jawaharlal went to Nabha for a first-hand view of the Akali agitation.

The Sikhs had for long been a group favoured by the British Government. They were encouraged to remain a separate community and not to merge in the general Hindu fold. Sikh soldiers were required to keep the five distinctive symbols, and the premium placed on Sikh recruitment led many Hindus to

[1] Report in *The Bombay Chronicle*, 10 July 1923.
[2] Interview in *Aaj*, 19 June 1923.
[3] To Mahadeva Desai.

become Sikhs.[1] The 1919 reforms extended separate representation to Sikhs. However, at the end of the First World War, certain sections of the Sikh community wished to reform the management of the Sikh temples (*gurdwaras*), which were believed to have become 'dens of drunken vice and debauchery',[2] and the reformers sought to take over the shrines. The Punjab Government saw in this Akali movement a threat to law and order, and the resistance that the Akalis encountered led to their efforts developing into a widespread mass movement. A plan for religious reform had been converted, despite itself, into a political campaign. A semi-military organization, the Akali Dal, was formed, not merely to evict the corrupt managers of the Sikh shrines but also to accept the challenge of the Government.

It was natural that the Akali movement should, at this stage, evoke the interest of the National Congress. This was not because, as Sir Malcolm Hailey later suggested, the Congress had always been looking for a party of physical force to replace their own 'somewhat backboneless agitation', and it would be a godsend to them to secure the Akalis 'as a kind of spearhead to their very wobbly staff'.[3] Rather, influenced by Gandhi's leadership of the non-co-operation campaign, the Sikhs had pledged themselves to non-violence; and they abode by their pledge despite severe provocation. In February 1921, the authorities of Nankana, the shrine at Guru Nanak's birthplace, were alleged to have poured oil on about two hundred Sikh pilgrims and burned them alive, and officials near by had not intervened. But this did not stop the volunteers of the Akali Dal from proceeding to this and other shrines in protest at mismanagement. In 1922 a *jatha* (squad) of 100 Sikh dissenters proceeded daily to the Guru-ka-bagh temple, there to be beaten up by the police; and this continued for about three weeks, resulting in about 2,000 Sikhs being beaten without their attempting to defend themselves. Thereafter the police, tired of *lathi* charges, summarily arrested the volunteers, and in time about 6,000 found themselves in jail.

So, whatever the original motivation, the Akalis were now acting in the spirit of the Congress campaign, and the Congress in turn took an interest in them. The movement was of special interest to Jawaharlal, for he attached importance to discipline, and was impressed by the organization of the Akali Dal, which maintained order among its recruits and provided for the upkeep of the families of those injured or arrested. He attended conferences, at Lahore and Amritsar in June and July 1923, of Congress, Khilafat and Sikh League workers, and urged them not to be distracted by such sterile issues as communal representation on district boards and municipalities. The Congress regarded the principle as essentially evil, and local bodies were not of any importance;

[1] 'It was almost a daily occurrence for—say—Ram Chand to enter our office and leave it as Ram Singh—Sikh recruit.' H. L. O. Garrett in Census Report of 1921, quoted in B. R. Nayar, *Minority Politics in the Punjab* (Princeton, 1966), p. 65.
[2] Sardar Didar Singh's telegram to Ramsay MacDonald, 15 February 1924. AICC File 4(1)/1924, N.M.M.L.
[3] Hailey to E. Howard, 15 July 1924. Hailey Papers, I.O.L. Mss. Eur. E. 220, vol. 6.

but if agreement could be reached on the basis of such a principle in the Punjab, the Congress might be prepared to approve it so as to enable the immediate success of the struggle against the bureaucracy.[1] And in September, when in Delhi for the special Congress session, Jawaharlal heard that Sikh *jathas* were daily proceeding to Nabha state, the deposition of whose maharaja in July for maladministration was strongly resented by the Sikhs; and he decided to go there to see for himself the Akalis in action.

On the night of the 19th September, Jawaharlal, with two companions, Gidwani and Santanam, left Delhi for Muktesar, an Akali centre, and after addressing a meeting there on the 20th, commending the Akali struggle,[2] he entered Nabha state on the morning of the 21st, along with a Sikh *jatha*, at Jaito. There he and his two friends sat down under a tree to watch proceedings and intended to return to Delhi by the evening train. Wilson Johnston, the British official who was serving as the administrator of the state, on hearing that Jawaharlal had set out for Nabha, had obtained the permission of the Viceroy and the Home Member to serve an order on Jawaharlal at the frontier of Nabha state forbidding him to enter the state for two months;[3] but he had not anticipated that Jawaharlal would come by road on horseback. The result was that Jawaharlal was well within the state before the order was served on him not to enter Nabha on the ground that he and some of his companions were members of the AICC and their presence was likely to lead to a disturbance of the peace. Jawaharlal replied that he had already entered Nabha and could not vanish into thin air, but that he had no intention of leaving the state; and he and his two friends, on whom an oral order had been served, sat down in a rest-house near by. A prohibitory order incapable of enforcement was *ipso facto* invalid, and an oral order was of no worth at all; but clearly the Nabha Government, even though now headed by a British official, attached no importance to legality. Although the presence of Jawaharlal had led to no disturbance, he and his companions were arrested, handcuffed and chained together, and marched to the railway station. They were brought by the night train, in a crowded third-class compartment, to Nabha town, and the chains and handcuffs were only removed twenty hours after, by noon the next day, after they were locked up in Nabha jail.

The conditions in this jail were, even by official admission, 'horrible';[4] and Wilson Johnston reported that though the jail department left much to be desired any immediate improvement was out of the question as the Akali agitation was keeping their hands full.[5] The prisoners were prevented from seeing or communicating with persons outside, denied all books and papers, and for two days not even allowed to bathe or change. Their trial was held *in camera* by a

[1] Report of Jawaharlal's speech in *The Tribune*, 4 July 1923.
[2] Home Dept. Pol. 1924, File 1.K.W.
[3] See Home Dept. Pol. File 401 of 1924.
[4] Note of Special Commissioner on conditions in Nabha jails, 14 June 1923. Home Dept. Pol. File 401 of 1924.
[5] 24 September 1923. Ibid.

magistrate who knew no English and openly referred every issue for decision to Wilson Johnston. The latter had by now realized that, even in Nabha, Jawaharlal could not be convicted for entering the state before he had been prohibited from doing so, and decided to alter the charge to one of being in the company of an Akali *jatha* and therefore of being a member of an unlawful assembly.[1] On the 24th fresh proceedings were casually started before another magistrate, and Jawaharlal and the others were charged with being members of the *jatha* and forcibly resisting dispersal. 'The straight thing to do', wrote Jawaharlal in his draft statement[2] which was later revised by his father and these sentences excised, 'is to run me in for sedition and I shall gladly and joyfully admit the charge. But the ways of the Nabha administration are not straight. They are crooked.'

As soon as Motilal heard of his son's arrest he left for Nabha and informed the Viceroy that his sole object was to see Jawaharlal. He had so far taken no part in the Akali agitation and expected that there would be no interference in the exercise of his 'natural right'.[3] The Administrator of Nabha gave orders forbidding Motilal's entry but was overruled by the Government of India, who ordered that Motilal should be permitted to enter Nabha provided he undertook not to engage in political activities in the state and to leave it immediately after his interview with his son.[4] Even this was an indefensible attitude and demonstrates that Wilson Johnston was not wholly responsible for all the arbitrary actions of the Nabha administration. Motilal naturally refused to give any such undertakings and, on being ordered to leave the state, did so without meeting Jawaharlal. Wilson Johnston described Motilal's reaction as one of 'veiled insolence', but the Secretary of State, Lord Olivier, later remarked that this was what any self-respecting professional man in his position in any other civilized country would have done.[5] In fact, the Government of India realized immediately that they had overreached themselves, and modified the conditions; Motilal was now required not to engage in any political activity in Nabha and to leave immediately after the conclusion of the trial.[6] This was still much to demand, but so intense was Motilal's anxiety, especially as he had heard of the unhealthy conditions in Nabha jail, that he agreed to abide by these restrictions and returned to Nabha.

On the 27th Motilal saw his son in jail. The interview, lasting over two hours, was not a success. The officials at Nabha flattered themselves that both father and son looked dejected because Motilal had concluded that Jawaharlal's action had put him legally in the wrong and there was little hope of his escaping conviction.[7] In fact, the reasons for the unsatisfactory nature of the interview were

---

[1] Administrator Nabha state to Agent, Governor-General Punjab, 22 September 1923. Ibid.

[2] 25 September 1923.

[3] *The Bombay Chronicle*, 24 September 1923.

[4] Telegram of Administrator, 23 September and telegram of Home Dept., 24 September, Home Dept. Pol. 1924, File 401.

[5] To Reading, 20 March and 26 June 1924. Reading Papers, vol. 7.

[6] *The Bombay Chronicle*, 27 September 1923.

[7] Administrator to Agent, Gov.-Gen. Punjab, 27 September 1923. Home Dept. Pol. File 401 of 1924.

very different. Jawaharlal had shown his irritation at his father's intervention, and this had deeply upset Motilal. So Motilal left Nabha.

> I was pained to find that instead of affording you any relief my visit of yesterday only had the effect of disturbing the even tenor of your happy jail life. After much anxious thinking I have come to the conclusion that I can do no good either to you or to myself by repeating my visits. I can stand with a clear conscience before God and man for what I have done so far after your arrest but as you think differently it is no use trying to make opposites meet . . . please do not bother about me at all. I am as happy outside the jail as you are in it . . . I do not wish you to have the impression that you have offended me in the least. I believe honestly that the position has been forced upon us both by circumstances over which neither has any control.[1]

Jawaharlal was now deeply sorry. 'I confess that the idea of causing you any pain is most distressful to me and I am haunted by the thought. It is a dearly cherished desire of mine to serve you and to lighten if possible the heavy burden you carry.'[2] But he was quite reconciled to a term in Nabha jail. 'It will be a new experience and in this blasé world, it is something to have a new experience.'[3] However, Motilal sent his son, through his secretary, a drastically altered statement to be read by him in court. Jawaharlal had written an emotionally worded text, criticizing the Nabha administration and eulogizing the Akali movement.

> I rejoice that I am being tried for a cause which the Sikhs have made their own. I was in jail when the Guru-Ka-Bagh struggle was gallantly fought and won by the Sikhs. I marvelled at the courage and sacrifice of the Akalis and wished that I could be given an opportunity of showing my deep admiration of them by some form of service. That opportunity has now been given to me and I earnestly hope that I shall prove worthy of their high tradition and fair courage. *Sat Sri Akal.*[4]

Motilal replaced these paragraphs with a closely argued statement written with the cold pen of a lawyer, and it was this which Jawaharlal read.

Meantime, the case dragged on. The Government of India directed that sentence should be passed on Jawaharlal but it should be announced at the same time that the Nabha Government had suspended its execution without

---

[1] Motilal to Jawaharlal, 28 September 1923.

[2] Jawaharlal to Motilal from Nabha jail, 30 September 1923.

[3] Jawaharlal to Kapil Deva Malaviya and Mahadeva Desai, undated but clearly written from Nabha jail.

[4] Draft statement, 25 September 1923. *Sat Sri Akal* is a Sikh form of greeting, meaning "True is the Immortal God."

condition, and Jawaharlal should be expelled from the state. This would meet the probable contingency of the convicted persons declining to accept any conditions; but if they returned to the state the suspension would be cancelled. This did not please Wilson Johnston, who wished Jawaharlal to serve his sentence, and argued that mere expulsion would severely shake the confidence of loyalists by establishing that there was one law for Akalis and another for Congressmen. But the Government of India believed that such discrimination would in itself be of advantage in that it would loosen the alliance between the Akalis and the Congress.[1] So Jawaharlal and his two companions were each sentenced to 30 months' rigorous imprisonment; but these sentences were suspended and they were ordered to leave the state and not to return. They all left Nabha the same night.

It was not, however, disclosed that the sentences would be operative if they returned to Nabha; and Jawaharlal had no reason to believe that the suspension was conditional. So he later challenged the statement of the Administrator that if they had refused to leave they would have had to undergo the sentence, and he added the hope that if it was necessary in the interests of their cause to return to Nabha, he and his companions would do so.[2] In fact, the next year, when Gidwani returned to Nabha he was thrown into prison, and Jawaharlal challenged the Administrator to let him have a copy of the suspension order and to inform him as to whether he too would be arrested if he returned to Nabha.[3] The Administrator replied that the sentence had only been suspended and not remitted, to which Jawaharlal retorted that the suspension had been unconditional.[4]

As Jawaharlal recognized years later in his *Autobiography,* probably the bold step to have taken, especially as Gidwani had been imprisoned again, would have been for him to return to Nabha. 'As often with us all, discretion was preferred to valour.'[5] On his return to Allahabad, where he received a hero's welcome, he had developed typhoid with high fever and confessed that he had not felt quite so feeble physically for a long time.[6] Gandhi dissuaded him from returning to Nabha,[7] and his father too made sure that he did not involve himself in Nabha affairs again. He would not even permit Jawaharlal to meet the Maharaja of Nabha. 'Having once burnt your fingers over Nabha

[1] Home Dept. to Administrator Nabha, 25 September 1923; Administrator Nabha to Agent to Gov.-Gen., 25 September 1923; Home Dept. to Administrator Nabha, 26 September 1923. Home Dept. Pol. 1924, File 401.

[2] Jawaharlal's letter in *The Tribune*, 11 October 1923.

[3] Jawaharlal's letters to the Administrator, 24 May and 19 June 1924, reprinted in *The Leader,* 29 May and 23 June 1924, respectively.

[4] Administrator Nabha to Jawaharlal, 25 June, and his reply, reproduced in *The Leader,* 27 July 1924.

[5] p. 116.

[6] To Sri Prakasa, 7 October 1923.

[7] Gandhi to Jawaharlal, 6 September 1924, *Collected Works*, vol. 25 (Delhi, 1967) p. 98; Jawaharlal's speech at Allahabad, 20 September 1924.

I do not wish you to take any more risks.'[1] So the Government of India, who had encouraged the Administrator of Nabha to act arbitrarily, were not embarrassed by any further challenge. Both the Secretary of State[2] and Lord Curzon, who was by no means dominated by a commitment to the rule of law and spoke for the opposition in the House of Lords, felt that the situation had not been handled quite so well as it possibly might have been. But the Government were enabled to congratulate themselves on an easy if undeserved victory. 'There is no doubt that Nehru and his son were substantially defeated over the Nabha affair and they know this full well.'[3]

[1] Motilal to Jawaharlal, 29 August 1925.
[2] Olivier to Reading, 20 March 1924. Reading papers, vol. 7.
[3] Home Dept. to Administrator Nabha, 9 October 1923. Home Dept. Pol. 1924, File 401.

7

Escape into Administration

Free again after a fortnight in jail, but now a sick man, Jawaharlal could do little more for a while than write speeches. In his presidential address to the U.P. provincial conference in October, which was read in his absence, he deplored the loss of the faith and confidence which had inspired the Congress in 1920 and 1921. 'We did not sit down to debate and argue, we *knew* we were right and we marched on from victory to victory. We felt the truth in us and every fibre of our being thrilled at the idea of our fighting for the right, and fighting in a manner unique and glorious.' But now pro-changer and no-changer 'went for each other, and the average no-changer was not behind the pro-changer in forgetting the basic lesson of non-violence and charity and in imputing the basest of motives to persons of a different way of thinking.' These two viewpoints being fundamentally different, there could be no real or stable compromise between them; and the result was that a noble movement had been converted into two caucuses, concerned only with securing support against each other.

The Congress session at Delhi, said Jawaharlal, had marked a retreat from direct action. But non-violent non-co-operation could not die, and it was the duty of those like him to fight on while the main army rested or was engaged in peaceful pursuits. Till the time came for launching another mighty campaign of civil disobedience, they should keep the practice and ideal of direct action and peaceful revolution before the people. He was still very much a Gandhian.

I believe that the salvation of India, and indeed of the rest of the world, will come through non-violent non-co-operation. Violence has had a long enough career in the world, it has been weighed repeatedly and found wanting. The present condition of Europe is eloquent testimony of the inefficacy of violence to settle anything. I believe that violence in Europe will go from excess to excess and will perish in the flames it has itself kindled and be reduced to ashes.

Bolshevism and Fascism were the ways of the West; they were really alike and represented different phases of insensate violence and intolerance. 'The choice for us is between Lenin and Mussolini on the one side and Gandhi on the other. Can there be any doubt as to who represents the soul of India today?' Non-violence was not weakness but required courage; better the honest man of evil and violence than the non-violent coward. However, no circumstance could justify terrorism or secret violence, the dagger of the assassin or the stab in the dark.

Besides extolling non-violence Jawaharlal expounded in Gandhian terms the merits of non-co-operation.

> Evil flourishes only because we tolerate it and assist in it. The most despotic and tyrannical government can only carry on because the people it misgoverns themselves submit to it. England holds India in bondage because Indians co-operate with Englishmen and thereby strengthen British rule. Withdraw that co-operation and the fabric of foreign rule collapses.

Political freedom was bound to come before long, if not entirely through their strength then through the weakness of Europe and England. Europe was in the melting pot, and England, with all her seeming might, could not but be affected by the collapse of the continent. But by then, feared Jawaharlal, once again reflecting an unqualifiedly Gandhian viewpoint, India, instead of being a shining example to the rest of the world, might have become but a cheap and inefficient replica of the countries of the West. 'Let us take the longer view from now and try to avoid this, and build up a great and strong India worthy of the great leader whom God has blessed us with.'

Two months later, at the Kakinada session of the Congress, he again emphasized, in Gandhian terms, that there was not really much in common between Indian volunteers and any Western counterparts, and an Indian volunteer organization must have non-violence as its basic principle. What India needed was non-violent, disciplined soldiers. 'We meet as soldiers of freedom and must be men of action rather than of words.' They should have little to do with the wordy warfare that was going on and devote themselves to training as many as possible for effective action; for without such training strength would be wasted and courage bear little fruit. But much as Jawaharlal desired action, he never doubted that such action should be controlled and encompassed by the Gandhian doctrine. Indeed, there was frequently a clear suggestion in his speeches that the sterile debate in the Congress had only been made possible by the absence of Gandhi in jail. To Jawaharlal non-violent non-co-operation was a positive programme, and its exponent above all a man of action.

Jawaharlal himself, however, could at this stage engage in no thrilling action and had to consume his energies in a variety of administrative duties. 'I am developing into a kind of Pooh-Bah.'[1] He was already president of the Allahabad town Congress committee and heavily involved in provincial Congress work, and at Kakinada the President, Maulana Mohamed Ali, insisted on Jawaharlal becoming one of the general secretaries of the Congress. This added considerably to Jawaharlal's work, he being the most active of the three secretaries. He tried to introduce method and procedure into Congress administration, which had till then been rather *ad hoc* and haphazard. This meant that he had to give considerable attention to matters of detail. He also checked the office accounts carefully, demanded that everyone, from the President downwards, should submit detailed accounts, and issued regular statements on Congress finances. He kept in touch with committees abroad — in Britain, Japan and the United States — that sought affiliation to the Congress. He toured the province widely on a fund-collecting mission for the U.P. Congress which, in January 1924, had only twenty rupees in the bank.[2]

Because of the direct interest which Jawaharlal had shown in the Akali campaign and his excursion to Nabha, the Congress had appointed him one of the liaison officers to keep in touch with the defiant Sikhs; and as general secretary it was his responsibility to implement the Congress resolution to render all possible assistance, including the dispatch of men and money. An Akali Sahayak (assistance) Bureau was set up at Amritsar, and though Jawaharlal was in no position to act on Rajagopalachari's suggestion[3] that he should take charge of this office, he kept in close touch with Gidwani, who was appointed to this post, and, after Gidwani's arrest, with his successor, K.M. Panikkar. The Congress had little money to provide, and Jawaharlal thought that the best assistance it could render was to perfect its own organization and throw in its whole weight at the moment of crisis, and till then to give full publicity to Akali activities, keeping the political side of it and the side affecting other communities well in the forefront.[4] Jawaharlal felt that the Congress could also help in rallying Hindus and Muslims behind the campaign, which should be regarded as part of the general movement for freedom. Shaukat Ali, for example, had pledged the full support of the Muslims. 'To the Akalis I will declare that the warfare they have engaged in is like the Khilafat question taken up by the Muslims and the Swaraj problem by the Hindus . . . So long as this war shall last Hindus and Mussalmans will be ready to participate in it in lakhs and lakhs.'[5] But the Sikhs themselves did not seem anxious

[1] To A.M. Khwaja, 6 June 1923. S.W., vol. 1, p. 359.
[2] Jawaharlal to A.T. Gidwani, 25 January 1924, AICC File 4(1) of 1924.
[3] See Jawaharlal to Rajagopalachari, 12 March 1924, AICC File 4(1) KW(II) of 1924.
[4] To Gidwani, 25 January 1924; to Panikkar, 27 March 1924, AICC File 4 of 1924.
[5] Speech at a public meeting in Delhi, 27 February 1924.

to receive such support even from the Hindus, let alone the Muslims, or from the Congress.[1] Clearly their hope now was to secure concessions from the Government, as in fact they did in 1925. Nor were Jawaharlal's efforts to improve relations between the Hindus and the Sikhs acceptable even to the Hindus of Amritsar because on his visit to that place he had stayed in a hotel where the cooks were Muslims.[2]

All these activities kept Jawaharlal busy, and enabled him to ignore the malaise afflicting Congress. He had even hoped to return to jail, even though on a false issue, for at one time it seemed probable that the Government would arrest him for defying, along with Pandit Malaviya, the injunction against bathing in the Sangam at Allahabad during the Kumbh Mela festival in January. That year the Ganga had somewhat changed its course, and the current was so strong near the Sangam that bathing without proper precautions became dangerous. So, with financial assistance from Government, volunteers prepared a suitable bathing place, but the district authorities refused all access to the Sangam. 'The question of danger receded into the background and the whole issue became one of prestige. Danger can be discussed and overcome, prestige cannot.'[3] So Malaviya, Jawaharlal and a few others courted imprisonment by jumping over the barrier and bathing in the Sangam. But the Government refrained from action. 'There appears to be little chance of my arrest for the Kumbh Mela affray. Worse luck!'[4]

However, he was soon glad to be unconfined, for on 5 February 1924 Gandhi was released on grounds of health. After seeing Gandhi at Poona, Jawaharlal spent a few weeks at Juhu, where Gandhi was having talks with the Swarajist leaders Motilal and Das. In the elections in November 1923 they had achieved a considerable triumph, and they now sought Gandhi's approval of their policy. This they could not secure, and it looked as if the Congress would break under the strain. Everything, wrote Gandhi to Jawaharlal,[5] was in the melting pot including himself; and Jawaharlal felt it might become necessary for him to resign the secretaryship. 'Surely you can imagine a situation when it may be impossible for me as well as others to continue in office. When everything is in the melting pot, as you put it, why should I be impervious to heat or refuse to melt?'[6]

At the meeting of the AICC in Ahmadabad in June 1924, Gandhi moved a resolution requiring all Congressmen to spin. This was challenged by Motilal and Das, and the resolution was finally carried with the omission of the clause depriving of Congress offices those failing to spin sufficient yarn. Gandhi

[1] See Jawaharlal to Panikkar 2 April and to Dr Kitchlew 27 April 1924, AICC File 4 of 1924.
[2] Panikkar to Mahatma Gandhi 1 April 1924. Home Dept. Pol. 1924, File 67, Part B.
[3] Jawaharlal's note, 15 January 1924. Allahabad municipality file 17.
[4] To Gidwani, 25 January 1924.
[5] 6 June 1924.
[6] To Shankarlal Banker, 14 June 1924, S.W., vol. 2 (Delhi, 1972), p. 106. In fact, it was Gandhi who had said it.

regarded himself as defeated and humbled, and, recognizing the support which the Swarajists enjoyed in the party and the country, decided to leave the field to them. The British Government, however, spurned their offers of co-operation. Motilal had expected that the first Labour Government would invite him and Das to London,[1] and Das, it is said, made a generous donation to Labour Party funds. Motilal's hopes were disappointed; but then Das expected much from Birkenhead. This too fizzled out. The policy, wrote Birkenhead confidentially to Reading,[2] that he would recommend to the Cabinet over the next four years would be politically one of negation. So the Swaraj party lost all purpose and could achieve little. Deprived in June 1925 of the leadership of Das, they were further weakened by the hankering for office shown by an increasing number of their members.

Meantime, the growing tension between Hindus and Muslims seized Gandhi's attention. The Muslims, who, according to the 1921 census, formed nearly a quarter of India's population had, before the advent of the British, lived in social harmony with the other communities. This is not surprising, for most Muslims in India were converts from Hinduism and had much in common with their Hindu neighbours. Under the East India Company, however, regional imbalance in economic and social development led to the classes who gained most from British rule being predominantly Hindu; and by the time the interior areas of India caught up with westernization, national consciousness, particularly in Bombay but also in Bengal, increasingly spoke in a Hindu idiom. The British were not slow to take political advantage of this. Gandhi, in his search for mass support, also expressed himself in Hindu terms and, rather than strengthen the national identity, drew up a programme which took for granted the divergence between the two communities but was acceptable to both. So the official policy symbolized by separate electorates, or constituencies where the essential qualification for candidates and voters was a particular religion, and the response of the Congress with such activities as the Khilafat campaign combined with the lag in development between the two communities, the decline of the Muslim upper class and the failure to offset this (as in the case of the Hindus) by the rise of new classes, to strengthen the religious element in Indian politics. This was reflected in communal rioting. During the years 1900 to 1922 there were sixteen such riots; for the three years from 1923 to 1926 the number was seventy-two.

In September 1924, to check the growing communal rancour, Gandhi began a fast for twenty-one days. He termed it both a penance and a prayer; but its objective on this occasion was to blackmail the conscience of his countrymen. When Jawaharlal, who had been visiting the riot-stricken area of Sambhal, received 'the shattering news whose consequences are terrible to contemplate', he called upon each town and village in the United Provinces to hold immediately

---

[1] Motilal to Das, 27 July 1924, Motilal Nehru papers.
[2] 29 January 1925, Reading papers, vol. 8.

its conference of leaders of all communities and parties to find means of unity. 'Leaders of all communities are meeting at Delhi on the 23rd and, God willing, will find a way out of the impasse. But time passes and daily the danger increases.'[1]

A day after commencing the fast, Gandhi had written to Jawaharlal:[2]

My dear Jawarlal [sic], You must not be stunned. Rather rejoice that God gives strength and direction to do my duty. I could not do otherwise. As the author of non-co-operation, a heavy responsibility lies on my shoulders. Do give me in writing your impressions of Lucknow and Cawnpore. Let me drink the cup to the full. I am quite at peace with myself.

Jawaharlal, on his return from the Unity Conference which had passed a series of platitudinous resolutions but could not persuade Gandhi to terminate his fast earlier than scheduled, himself went down with fever; but he sent Gandhi long reports on the disturbances in Allahabad itself. Speaking with this first-hand knowledge of communal animosity, he told the U.P. Political Conference that whatever pride he had had in the national strength and awakening had been shattered, and he was now not only humiliated but ashamed. They themselves had done more harm to their country than any foreigner.[3] An All-Parties Conference, meeting in January 1925, proved a failure, and Jawaharlal found its discussions painful to listen to.[4] All that there was to do, therefore, seemed to be the preaching of unity and of non-violence, spinning and the wearing of khaddar. When a young man came to him in search of national work, the only possible activity Jawaharlal could think of was khaddar work.[5]

It is surprising that Jawaharlal did not think of utilizing the services of such young men for promoting communal harmony. Gandhi had suggested the formation of a flying column of Hindu and Muslim workers who would at a moment's notice be ready to go to riot areas for investigation and relief.[6] But Jawaharlal seems to have been too dispirited to act on this suggestion. This communal problem was such a wasteful diversion from the main campaign against the British, and it revolved round what seemed to him such unreal issues that he could not bring himself to take energetic measures to deal with it. In his own city of Allahabad, there was a revival of aggressiveness of Hindu communalists, inspired, according to the local magistrate, largely

[1] Letter to the Editor, The Leader, 22 September 1924.
[2] 19 September 1924. Facsimile in Tendulkar, Mahatma (1961 edition), vol. 2, between pp. 160-61.
[3] The Leader, 6 November 1924.
[4] To Syed Mahmud, 3 February 1925.
[5] See his letter to Shankarlal Banker, 28 July 1925. AICC File G. 60/1925, Part II.
[6] Letter to Jawaharlal, 12 November 1924.

by the desire to show the Nehru family that they had little influence with the Hindus.[1] 'As for our politics and public life,' Jawaharlal wrote,[2] 'I am sick and weary of them.'

These were also to Jawaharlal months of great personal stress and depression. In November 1924 his wife lost a child after premature birth and soon after began to show signs of tuberculosis. Then, in March 1925, he himself had to undergo a minor operation, performed by Dr Ansari at Delhi. The deep commitment to Gandhi and known dislike of Swarajist policy had caused friction in his relations with his father, and Gandhi had sought to intervene.

This letter like the former is meant to be a plea for Jawaharlal. He is one of the loneliest young men of my acquaintance in India. The idea of your mental desertion of him hurts me. Physical desertion I hold to be impossible. Needless to say Manzar Ali and I often talked of the Nehrus whilst we were together at Yeravda. He said once that if there was one thing for which you lived more than any other, it was for Jawahar. His remark seemed to be so true. I don't want to be the cause direct or indirect of the slightest breach in that wonderful affection.[3]

These differences with Motilal made Jawaharlal acutely conscious of his dependence on his father for money. Gandhi had offered to arrange for some remunerative work, either as a press correspondent or as a college professor,[4] but nothing had come of this. Gandhi later suggested that Jawaharlal be paid as general secretary by the Congress or that personal friends be permitted to find funds for retaining his services. 'I will not mind even if you decided to do some business. I want your mental peace. I know that you will serve the country even as manager of a business.'[5] The Bombay firm of Tata's offered to employ him, and Motilal strongly recommended to his son that he proceed to Bombay and call on Tata.[6] But this again did not materialize, probably because Jawaharlal showed no keenness to serve in a commercial firm. Finally, to earn the money required to pay for the trip to Europe which he and Kamala were planning, he had to return to the distasteful practice of law; and for preparing a brief Motilal secured for him the large fee of Rs 10,000 — an amount which the client doubtless paid to ensure that Motilal would handle the case.

However, there was one sphere of activity which in these years provided

[1] Report on the political situation in the U.P. for the first half of September 1925. Home Dept. Pol. 1925, File 112.

[2] To Gidwani, 3 November 1925, AICC File G21 (ii) of 1925.

[3] To Motilal, 2 September 1924, *Collected Works,* vol. 25, p. 65. Manzar Ali Sokhta was a Congressman from the U.P. and a friend of the Nehru family.

[4] Letter to Jawaharlal, 15 September 1924, *Collected Works*, vol. 25, pp. 148-9.

[5] Idem, 30 September 1925.

[6] Motilal to Jawaharlal, 9 November 1925.

Jawaharlal with some satisfaction. For two years, from April 1923 to April 1925, he was chairman of the Allahabad Municipal Board; and this phase in his life is of interest as marking his first experience of official administration. It is also of some significance, because many of the traits which marked his prime ministership can be discerned here in embryo — his domination of his colleagues, his desire for efficiency, his loyalty to his competent subordinates, his efforts to push forward in all directions with new ideas. Even officials had to recognize that he had brought a fresh impetus to municipal administration and that his management of Allahabad affairs was marked by both constructiveness and competence.

In 1923 the United Provinces Congress committee decided to contest the municipal elections on the Congress and Khilafat programme, and to enter these local bodies not to obstruct but to direct their affairs honestly and efficiently. Jawaharlal was, much against his will, persuaded to stand as one of the Congress candidates from Allahabad, and as the Congress had a majority, soon found himself elected chairman for three years. It had earlier been thought that Purushottam Das Tandon would be chairman, but he decided to stand down in favour of a Muslim Congressman, as some loyalist Muslims had objected to a Hindu chairman. However, when it became clear that the loyalist Muslims wished to have not so much a Muslim as a loyalist, and as the Muslim Congressman was unwell, Jawaharlal's name was suddenly put forward and he was elected by 20 votes as against 11 secured by the candidate sponsored by the officials.[1]

Jawaharlal was a most unwilling chairman. To him the primary task was the fight for *swaraj,* and he decided to continue as secretary of the provincial Congress committee, a post which he regarded as more important than the chairmanship of the municipal board and which, he declared, he was prouder to hold.

> The day I am satisfied that the municipal chairmanship is injuring my Congress work that day I shall submit my resignation of the chairmanship. For the chairmanship is to me only the means for serving the nation for hastening *swaraj.* The best method is to go straight ahead on the lines chalked out by our leaders and not to wander in the shady alleys and lanes of constitutional activity. My mentality is revolutionary. I believe in revolution and in direct action and in battle. I know that many times we shall have to advance and engage the enemy and offer the inevitable price of freedom before we finally carry the citadel . . . I do not forget the history and agony of India during the last few years and I am not going to spend most of my time in any office while my beloved leader lies in jail. I shall give battle whenever I can. I shall fight and hit hard whenever

[1] See account in *The Leader,* 6 April 1923, and Jawaharlal's letter in the same issue.

I may. That is my main function till *swaraj* is attained. All else is training and preparation.[1]

Invited by the Collector of Allahabad to come and discuss the possibility of keeping general politics outside the municipal sphere, he replied that he would try to carry out the policies of the Congress, and would resign if he disagreed with the Board on any matter of principle or if the Congress committee so desired it. 'I regret that I cannot split myself up into various compartments — one for "general politics", another for "municipal affairs", and so on.'[2] Repeatedly during the next two years, till his resignation was finally accepted by the Government, Jawaharlal offered to relinquish office, and he never allowed it to hamper his activities in the wider world and even courted arrest as at Nabha.

However, though Jawaharlal's priorities never wavered, his distaste for municipal affairs gradually weakened, and he found himself enjoying the work. 'What I feared and disliked I have begun to like, and municipal work has begun to have some fascination for me. I feel that it is in the power of our board to make life a little more bearable, a little less painful to the inhabitants of Allahabad.'[3] And he always retained this interest in his home town, continued to keep an eye on its development and, even when engrossed in later years in national work, could find time to protest against vulgar posters or noisy brass bands.[4]

Once he had assumed this responsibility of the chairmanship, Jawaharlal worked hard. Himself regular in attendance, whenever he was in Allahabad, at meetings which were held at least twice a week, he deplored the tendency of the members to look to their own convenience and urged them to sacrifice their own professional work, if need be, for the sake of the municipality.[5] Indeed, he almost coerced his colleagues to work as hard as he did, and rather than adjourn meetings for lack of a quorum, he directed members to wait so that they were driven to send for their truant colleagues. Soon after taking over as Chairman, he issued a public statement rebuking some members for idleness;[6] this had its effect, so that later he could agree to refrain from such public criticism. Chairmen and members of standing committees were told that, in addition to their routine work, they should inspect their departments periodically and introduce efficiency. Public grievances should be removed and,

[1] Circular letter of Jawaharlal as secretary, prov. cong. committee to all district, town and *tebsil* Congress committees and members of prov. Cong. committee, 5 April 1923.

[2] To Collector of Allahabad, 4 April 1923, Allahabad Municipality File 13.

[3] Letter to the Executive Officer, Allahabad Municipality, written from Nabha jail, 26 September 1923, *The Leader*, 6 October 1923.

[4] See, for example, his letters to the Chairman, Allahabad Municipal Board, 24 September 1936 and 11 July 1939.

[5] Meeting of 26 April 1923, reported in *The Leader*, 28 April 1923.

[6] *The Leader*, 16 June 1923.

where this was not possible, satisfactory explanations should be provided.
'Members have not been put on committees for show purposes but for hard
work. It will perhaps be better for any member who finds it difficult to give
enough time to his committee work to resign and make room for another
who can give the necessary time.'[1] He also forbade members to exercise
patronage in appointments or to secure municipal contracts or any other
favours from the Board.[2] But he soon won the confidence of all groups on the
Board and was able to direct the proceedings on the lines he desired. It was
the nominated Anglo-Indian member who, but two months after voting
against Jawaharlal, sought an assurance from him that there was no truth
in the rumour of his resignation;[3] and in 1924 the Board unanimously requested the Government not to accept Jawaharlal's resignation and, if this
were not feasible, to permit the Board to re-elect him.[4]

The secret of Jawaharlal's influence was his manifest integrity. On one
occasion, one of the vice-chairmen, Zahur Ahmed, offered his resignation
orally but retracted it after its acceptance by Jawaharlal. Realizing that he
had erred in acting on an oral resignation, Jawaharlal requested the Board to
censure him. 'I think that the Board would be justified in expressing its displeasure of this action and I can assure the Board that I will appreciate this.
I believe in discipline and no one should be above it.[5] The Board declined
and stood by Jawaharlal's action, but was persuaded by him to cancel its vote
of confidence and permit Zahur Ahmed to continue in office.[6] While he did
not conceal his views on major issues, he never permitted the Congress
majority to push matters to extremes, and in minor matters he voted, as was
expected from a chairman, against any change. He turned down the request
of the municipal employees that they be allowed to suspend work on Jallianwala Bagh day, for he knew that they were only interested in a holiday. He
secured the rejection of the proposal of a member belonging to the Congress
party that the Board dispense with chairs and conduct proceedings while
sitting on the floor, by pointing out that this had nothing to do with *swadeshi*.[7]
He encouraged the wearing of *khaddar* by municipality employees and the use
of Hindi or Urdu in official transactions but rejected suggestions that these
be made obligatory.[8] He supported the passing of a resolution deploring the
treatment of Indians in the United States and the British colonies, but rejected
as impractical suggestions for retaliation such as doubling municipal taxes
on Englishmen and Americans or debarring them from buying land.[9]

[1] Chairman's circular, 13 April 1923, Allahabad Municipality File 4. Serial 1.
[2] *The Leader,* 16 November 1923.
[3] *The Leader,* 13 June 1923.
[4] Proceedings of 29 April 1924, reported in *The Allahabad Municipal Gazette,* 1 May 1924.
[5] Note 19 July 1924, Allahabad Municipality File 6.
[6] Proceedings of the Board, 23, 24, 25, 28 and 31 July 1924.
[7] Report in *The Leader,* 3 May 1923.
[8] Report in *The Leader,* 7 July 1923: *The Allahabad Municipal Gazette,* 16 December 1923.
[9] Proceedings of the Board, 9 October 1923.

From the municipal officials he expected efficiency but was loyal to those who served him well — and those who were surprised by his support of members of the Indian Civil Service after 1947 would have done well to study his attitude years earlier as municipal chairman. He had no illusions about civil servants. 'Permanent officials who are not under popular control, as we know to our cost, are a danger against which we must guard. They are too wooden, and utterly out of touch with the people, and have no sense of proportion or vision. They always tend to make a close corporation of themselves, indulge in mutual praise and are wholly intolerant of people who differ from them.'[1] But he was willing, in the conduct of municipal affairs, to co-operate with Government servants so long as the public interests and the principles of the Congress were not jeopardized.[2] As he told the Collector, he and his fellow Congressmen had not sought election purely for discovering opportunities of friction, with the Government. 'Mr. Knox and I agreed that it was hardly possible for us to convince each other of the correctness of the other's viewpoint on wider issues. That difference must be faced, but in the routine work of the Board this will hardly trouble anyone.'[3] He instructed the heads of departments to get rid of incompetent subordinates with all speed and without mercy.[4] Within a week of taking charge of his office, he suspended a dispatcher and a messenger for delay in delivering a letter. 'I shall be obliged if you will make it clear to every member of the staff that if there is one thing which will not be tolerated it is incompetence and slackness and any instance of this will be severely dealt with . . . no kind of effective work is possible unless our office is run on business lines.'[5] Informed that the engineering staff was efficient in its work but slack in sending reports, he recorded, 'I am afraid the staff will have to get over this aversion to pen and paper. Any slackness of this kind is most objectionable and is own brother to incompetence. It is impossible for a person who is slack to be efficient and I desire no slackness in the municipal employ.'[6] Delay, he informed the Board,[7] might be excused but it was seldom justifiable; and he expected prompt results. 'Success and failure will be the tests applied. In case of the latter excuses will not find favour with the board, and immediate and drastic action will be taken. Only such officers will be employed who are prepared for this responsibility.'[8] But those officials who worked well received the chairman's full support even in face of public criticism and *satyagraha*;[9] and no bureaucrat could have

[1] Note of 24 July 1923, Allahabad Municipality File 26.
[2] Speech at Ballia, 9 April, reported in *The Leader,* 11 April 1924.
[3] Note on interview with Collector, 6 April 1923, Allahabad Municipality File 13.
[4] Jawaharlal's note on municipal work, April-May 1923, dated 10 June 1923. *The Leader,* 16 June 1923.
[5] Note to Executive Officer, 6 April 1923, Allahabad Municipality File 13.
[6] 17 December 1923. *The Allahabad Municipal Gazette Extraordinary,* 21 December 1923.
[7] Proceedings of the meeting of the Board, 16 January 1925.
[8] Note on the Water-Works Dept., *The Leader,* 30 April 1923.
[9] Jawaharlal's letter to the editor, 18 April, published in *The Leader,* 21 April 1924.

improved on his rebuke to the Public Health Committee: 'Has the Committee ever heard of discipline? What does it think will be the effect of the Committee siding with some employees of the Board as against a high officer . . . It is difficult for officers to carry on their work properly if they are censured and condemned in this manner for trivial details.'[1]

Most important of all, Jawaharlal was clearly above sectarian prejudices. His guidance enabled the Board unanimously to reject the suggestion to prohibit the slaughter of cattle;[2] and the next week he reminded the members that while Christian missionaries had originally certainly come to India to convert Indians, at the same time their object was also to benefit India as far as possible.[3]

Such moderation and impartiality gave Jawaharlal a commanding influence. He first turned his attention to formulating a scheme for widening the municipal franchise and ensuring fair elections. He desired the abolition of plural constituencies and the replacement of communal by proportional representation. He also suggested, to avoid impersonation, smaller constituencies and personal registration of voters.[4] But electoral reform was beyond the purview of the Municipal Board. Jawaharlal had to content himself with introducing, whenever possible, the spirit of nationalism in municipal administration and implementing the constructive, nation-building programme of the Congress. The singing of Iqbal's *Hindustan Hamara* (Our Hindustan) was made a part of the school curriculum. Tilak Day (1 August), the anniversary of the death of Tilak, and Gandhi Day (18 March), the anniversary of the day when Gandhi was sentenced to jail, were added to the list of public holidays, while Empire Day was omitted. The release of Gandhi in February 1924 was celebrated by the illumination of municipal buildings. Civic addresses were presented to the Congress leaders Das, Ajmal Khan and Shaukat Ali. The United Provinces Government sought to prevent such defiance by directing that civic addresses should be presented only to the Viceroy and the Governor of the province, but Jawaharlal secured the unanimous rejection by the Board of this directive, which he termed 'an insult and impertinence'. In other words, even the nominated and non-Congress members supported his assertion of the Board's independence on such matters.[5] Jawaharlal made it clear to his colleagues that they should be prepared for the consequences of their disobedience; but in fact it was the Provincial Government which had to withdraw from their position.[6]

This was soon followed by the Board's decision to ignore a viceregal visit to Allahabad. Jawaharlal was ill at the time of Reading's arrival, but he circulated a note to the members of the Board emphatically objecting to the

---

[1]Note, 4 April 1924, Allahabad Municipality File 16.
[2]Proceedings, 29 June 1923, reported in *The Leader,* 2 July 1923.
[3]Proceedings, 3 July 1923, reported in *The Leader,* 7 July 1923.
[4]Note, 10 May 1923, Allahabad Municipality File 5.
[5]*The Leader,* 29 June 1923.
[6]*The Leader,* 2 July and 10 September 1923.

presentation of an address to the Viceroy, who had ordered the arrest of Gandhi and many others, and was suppressing the Sikh agitation in the Punjab.

> I feel that a public reception to the Viceroy is a shameful thing for any one to whom the honour of India is dear and precious. I wish no personal discourtesy to Lord Reading. But we are human beings with eyes to see and, sometimes, to weep and ears to hear and hearts to feel — and feel the more because our arms are weak and there is no strength in us to stand upright and protect our own . . . Lord Reading, secure in his strength and proud of his might, has flung this challenge to the Sikhs and the Indian people and he would have us applaud him for it and thus complete our degradation. I am weak and powerless but I too have a little pride — the pride of the weak, perhaps, it may be, but I would sooner be trampled by Lord Reading's soldiery than bow down to welcome a person who was responsible for so much sorrow to my country and countrymen.[1]

Jawaharlal also secured the introduction of spinning and weaving in schools, and rejected the objection of the Commissioner of Allahabad Division to what seemed to the latter to be a Congress measure.

> We have laid great stress on spinning in our schools because we believe in its economic value. I have little doubt that if you considered the question on its merits and without the prejudices born of political opinions you will appreciate the attempts to revive spinning and put it on a firm basis. If you will take the trouble to learn spinning yourself you will after a few days feel its charm and delight in the music of the wheel. Spinning is not a party matter confined to a particular group.[2]

Most of the teachers and the boys and girls dressed in *khaddar*.

Jawaharlal was eager to improve the quality of instruction imparted in the municipal schools, to raise the salaries of teachers, to make education compulsory and to train children to be good citizens who neither cringed nor boasted. 'I have felt that the physical and mental development of the young should be the special care of the state and the municipality and in this respect we might well take a leaf out of the book of Soviet Russia.'[3] Scouting was introduced for boys and a day's outing was arranged every month for all children for nature study. But as Government declined to give further grants for education which was directed to encouraging the 'new spirit', it could only be given low priority by the Board, after the maintenance of the basic municipal services — sanitation, water supply and the upkeep of roads. The staff of sanitary inspectors was in-

[1] *The Bombay Chronicle*, 27 October 1923.
[2] *The Tribune*, 27 August 1924.
[3] A note on municipal work during December 1923 and January and February 1924, *Allahabad Municipal Gazette*, 1 April 1924.

creased, and better arrangements made for the disposal of refuse. As the water-works plant was worn out, there could be no marked improvement in water supply; but even so, many new water connections were provided. As for roads, Jawaharlal observed that although more was being spent on roads than ever before, many roads in the city had so deteriorated that soon it would be impossible for vehicles to use them.[1] 'In some places it is difficult to get any medical advice as no vehicle can safely go there and doctors refuse to walk the distance especially when this will involve wallowing in the mud.'[2] Jawaharlal thought the reason for this was that a great part of the municipal funds allotted for roads was being utilized to improve and beautify the Civil Station where Europeans and the richer class of Indians lived. This led him to suggest a tax on large compounds, which were to be found mostly in the Civil Station, for he thought that this area should be more built up and the compounds become smaller and better looked after. The income of the Board would also be raised and the general appearance of Allahabad would improve. He also wished to tax open sites whose owners, interested in land speculation, had failed to build on. There should be a tax both on land value and on improvements and houses, but in such a way that the latter were encouraged.[3] But nothing came of these suggestions. Nor, because of the recalcitrant attitude of the Allahabad Town Improvement Trust, dominated by civil servants and loyalists, was he able to implement any of his ideas on town planning.

However, Jawaharlal could show more substantial results in the matter of improvement of municipal finances. He was convinced that the rates would have to be increased, but in such a way as to limit the increase's incidence to the rich. Unwilling to raise money at the expense of the poorer classes, he rejected the suggestion of an octroi duty on cycles[4] and exempted houses with a low rental value from payment of water rates.[5] He also terminated the practice whereby octroi was levied on foreign goods at the 'invoice' rate, while Indian goods were charged at the market rate which often was higher, with the sult that Indian goods paid more. It was laid down that the market rate should be the wholesale and not the retail rate, although this meant a loss in income. Jawaharlal urged that a heavier rate be charged on foreign goods so as to encourage Indian manufacturers,[6] but the Board resolved on a complete boycott of British goods unless they were not manufactured elsewhere in the world or were not available in India.[7]

[1]Proceedings of Board meeting, 28 May 1924, *The Leader,* 2 June 1924.

[2]Jawaharlal's note on municipal work, June-August, 1923, *Allahabad Municipal Gazette Extraordinary,* 15 September 1923.

[3]Note on municipal work, December 1923-February 1924, *Allahabad Municipal Gazette,* 1 April 1924; Jawaharlal's note on taxation, 28 August 1924, *The Leader,* 6 September 1924.

[4]*The Leader,* 7 July 1923.

[5]Annual Administration Report of the Allahabad Municipal Board, 30 May 1924.

[6]Jawaharlal's notes on municipal work, June-August 1923 and September-November 1923, *Allahabad Municipal Gazettes Extraordinary,* 15 September 1923 and 21 December 1923, respectively.

[7]Proceedings of the meeting, 25 October 1923, reported in *The Leader,* 27 October 1923.

Yet, despite these decisions, the Municipal Board under Jawaharlal's guidance, by more efficient collection of taxes, increased levy on railways passing through the city, and the imposition of a new tax on passengers, improved its financial position, paid back, for the first time for years, a part of the loan received from the Government, and set self-sufficiency as its objective.

Jawaharlal's work attracted wide public attention because, apart from his general standing, he issued a fortnightly municipal gazette reporting the proceedings of the Board and its committees and, in addition to the annual report, gave a detailed account of municipal activities once every three months. There were also Hindi and Urdu editions of the gazette. For the first time, too, the average citizen of Allahabad felt that he had a municipal chairman who was accessible and concerned with his welfare. The *ekkawalas* (drivers of horse carriages), for example, approached him with their grievances and on investigation Jawaharlal was astounded to find that in three months about 1,400 prosecutions had been initiated against them by the police. This was not the direct concern of the Municipal Board, but it convinced Jawaharlal that something was very wrong somewhere, and he induced the Board to do what it could to make the life of the *ekkawalas* more tolerable.[1]

Jawaharlal had also, from the start, kept in close touch and exchanged ideas with the ten other Congress chairmen of municipal boards in the United Provinces,[2] and he was elected Chairman of the United Provinces Municipal Conference that met at Aligarh in December 1924. This provincial conference accepted Jawaharlal's proposals that training as scouts should be made part of physical education in schools, adult franchise introduced for municipal elections and the autonomy of municipal boards protected. These recommendations were in line with his view that municipalities could become minor arenas for national education and for constructive national and political work. He also, however, knew that the real arena for national advance lay elsewhere. In February 1924 he was dissuaded by Gandhi from resigning the chairmanship;[3] but at the Congress session in December presided over by Gandhi he opposed a resolution advocating the capture by Congressmen, whenever possible, of local boards and municipalities. His own experience, he said, had convinced him that Congressmen in these boards were so restricted that the effort was futile; and on his return from the Belgaum Congress he resigned both his chairmanship and membership of the Board, ostensibly on the ground that he had little time to devote to municipal work. Three years later, in 1928, he allowed himself to be dragged again into municipal politics and even, despite Gandhi's advice,[4] permitted his name to be put forward for the chairmanship; but on this occasion he was, surprisingly, defeated by one vote by the loyalist candidate.[5]

[1] Jawaharlal's note on municipal work, June-August 1923, op. cit.
[2] See Allahabad Municipality File 22.
[3] Mahadeva Desai, *Day to Day with Gandhi* (Banaras, 1970), vol. 4, p. 22.
[4] 'My conviction is that you cannot combine all India work with solid municipal work.' Gandhi to Jawaharlal, 28 November 1928.
[5] *The Leader,* 20 and 21 December 1928.

His two years in municipal office could not have given Jawaharlal much cause for satisfaction. For a man who believed that a municipality should not confine itself to such matters as housing and sanitation but should regard social welfare in its widest sense as its primary concern, the disappointment could not be glossed over. But it was astonishing how much he had succeeded in achieving, despite the inherent limitations of the post and the demands of his wider interests. Even the Commissioner was compelled to record reluctantly his impression that 'the improvement in the administration was largely due to the chairman, Pandit Jawaharlal Nehru, and a few public spirited members of the Board.'[1] The comment of the U.P. Government at the time of Jawaharlal's relinquishment of the chairmanship is also worth mention. 'Pandit Kapildeo Malaviya', they wrote in April 1925, 'was elected chairman of the Allahabad Municipal Board by (a majority of) two votes, in succession to Jawaharlal Nehru, who strove to show that a swarajist could be an administrator and a gentleman, and the Commissioner thinks that the newcomer's position will be very difficult.'[2]

[1] *The Tribune,* 24 August 1924.
[2] Fortnightly report on the political situation in the United Provinces for the second half of March 1925. Home Dept. Pol. 1925, File 112.

8

Europe 1926-1927

On 1 March 1926 Jawaharlal sailed with his wife and child for Europe. The trip was undertaken primarily in the cause of his wife's health. It was hoped that a long stay in Switzerland would help her to shake off the tuberculosis that was still in an incipient stage, while her husband would spend his time in study and travel. But these two years, while they did Kamala little good, were to have a profound effect on Jawaharlal's mental development. Till now he had been one of the ordinary run of conforming nationalists, an unquestioning follower of the Mahatma. The Government of the United Provinces, reporting their decision to give him a passport, summed up his position: 'He is a devoted follower of Gandhi, is much respected and carries great influence with his party.'[1] An over-enthusiastic district magistrate had suggested to Jawaharlal that he should facilitate the issue of a passport by giving an assurance that he was not visiting Europe for political purposes; but neither at Lucknow nor at Simla did Jawaharlal's refusal to give any such assurance cause any hesitation in permitting him to leave. He was not regarded as particularly dangerous, and it seemed worth while to keep his father in good humour. But it was this spell in Europe, and not the earlier years at Harrow and Cambridge, that was to provide Jawaharlal with his real political education; and here again it was Gandhi who was the most perceptive. 'I expect', he wrote to Motilal on the eve of the family's departure, 'great results from this trip, not only for Kamla [sic] but also for Jawaharlal.'[2]

In leaving India, Jawaharlal felt somewhat of a deserter.

I am certainly looking forward to the visit to Europe but I am full of apprehension. It is quite likely that when I get there I shall be looking backward to India! It is good to have a change and a holiday but this should rest on the solid foundation of something accomplished. The idea of going away just at present with your mother as president of the

[1] Letter of Chief Secretary to Government, United Provinces, to Home Secretary, Government of India, 6 February 1926. Home Dept. Pol. File 23 of 1926.
[2] 17 February 1926, *Collected Works*, vol. 30 (Delhi, 1968), p. 20.

Congress and Gandhiji toiling away as ever is not particularly gratifying. On the whole perhaps it is as well that I am going but I doubt if I shall be very happy there. India is so like a woman — she attracts and repels.[1]

It was the sense of relief, however, which grew as the months passed. Indian politics at this time were in a low and grim condition. The Congress was riven with dissension, and even within the Swaraj Party Motilal was fighting a losing battle against opportunism. Communal tension was rising, and many old Congressmen were reacting to events more as Hindus and Muslims than as nationalists. Gandhi had not lost heart, but even he was reconciled to the situation getting much worse before it began to improve. 'I must confess', wrote Jawaharlal to his father later in the year,[2] 'to a feeling of satisfaction at not being in India just at present. Indeed the whole future outlook is so gloomy that, from the political viewpoint, a return to India is far from agreeable.' Settled in Geneva in cheap lodgings, his principal occupations now, besides nursing his wife and escorting his daughter to school and back, were learning French, reading widely and attending various courses and lectures.

The older I grow the more I feel that there is so much to be learnt and studied and so little time to do it in. Most of us after a very perfunctory education imagine that we have learnt as much as is necessary and do not even attempt to increase our knowledge. This is sad for progress can only come with knowledge and the few years that we spend at school and college teach us precious little.[3]

Bertrand Russell's books, particularly *On Education* and *What I Believe,* made a deep impact.

I think what is required in India most is a course of study of Bertrand Russell's books, or at any rate some of them. No country or people who are slaves to dogma and the dogmatic mentality can progress, and unhappily our country and people have become extraordinarily dogmatic and little-minded. Generosity of heart is a good thing but what is wanted is not an emotional outburst of generosity but coldly reasoned tolerance.[4]

Like Gandhi he was a long-term, far-seeing optimist about India: 'The outlook in India is dark enough but somehow I do not feel as pessimistic as the news would warrant. Do not get down-hearted. We shall still see *Swaraj*. Whatever

[1] To Padmaja Naidu, 29 January 1926, S.W., vol. 2, p. 226. In December 1925, Sarojini Naidu had taken over as President of the Congress.
[2] 6 October 1926, S.W., vol. 2, p. 244.
[3] To Syed Mahmud, 22 March 1927, S.W., vol. 2, p. 314.
[4] Idem, 12 September 1926, S.W., vol. 2, p. 242.

India might or might not do, I am fairly sure that England cannot hold on to India for long.'[1] The news from India of communal rioting depressed him, but he was convinced that the only remedy was to scotch this so-called religion, secularize the intelligentsia at least and proceed on secular lines in politics. 'How long that will take I cannot say but religion in India will kill that country and its peoples if it is not subdued.' Europe, as Jawaharlal saw it, had got rid of religion by mass education which had followed industrialism, with the result that conflicts were now not religious but economic; and the same process was bound to be repeated in India.[2] This was, of course, too easy and hopeful a solution, based on a somewhat simplistic understanding of European developments. But Jawaharlal was still optimist enough to believe that religious differences in India would be automatically dissolved by economic advance, and therefore gave no serious thought to it.

By the end of the year it was clear that Kamala had benefited little from the treatment of Spahlinger's vaccine injections; so Jawaharlal decided to shift her from Geneva to Dr Stephani's clinic in the more bracing climate of Montana (Valais). The move to the mountains enabled Jawaharlal to take lessons in skiing and ice-skating; but he was beginning to feel restive, for the wider world and for India. He could not as yet return to India; his wife was still far from well and Motilal was planning a trip to the West. So the family started their wanderings round Europe. There were visits to the museums of London, Paris, Berlin and Heidelberg, tours of factories and interviews with Indian exiles and revolutionaries. Jawaharlal was at Paris airport, with his daughter perched on his shoulder,[3] waiting for Lindbergh to complete his lone journey across the Atlantic — an achievement which greatly impressed him for its human daring and resolution. Always keen on flying, and having himself done two short hops at this time from London, once to Paris and once to Ostend, Jawaharlal urged his countrymen to become more air-minded.[4]

However, the real significance of these travels was that Jawaharlal now came into contact with European political workers and movements, and these gave a new depth to his thinking and activities. The discursive reading undertaken in Switzerland had ploughed up his mind; it was ready for new seeds but had not yet received them. A letter published in the *Journal de Genève* was staunchly nationalist in tone and expounded the standard arguments about the traditional unity of India and the impoverishments and divisions brought about by British rule;[5] but there was no glimmer of any fresh effort at interpretation. In an article published in India, he advocated complete independence

[1] Idem, 11 August 1926, S.W., vol. 2, p. 241.
[2] Idem, 24 May, 15 July and 11 August 1926 and 14 July 1927, S.W., vol. 2, pp. 232-6, 240-41 and 328-9.
[3] Mrs Gandhi's broadcast reported in the *Hindustan Times*, 24 July 1969.
[4] Letter to his father, 16 November 1926, and 'Victory over the Air', article in *Aaj*, 28 September 1927, S.W., vol. 2, pp. 250-51 and 364-7, respectively.
[5] 3 August 1926, S.W., vol. 2, pp. 236-240.

in the sense of full freedom in both external and internal affairs and favoured the formation of an extremist pressure-group within the Congress to counter the activities of those who tried to hold the organization back.[1] This received wide publicity and, as Motilal complained, was generally interpreted as a criticism of the Swaraj Party and of its leadership: 'it is the most famous document in India at the present moment and is being used for a variety of purposes not even dreamt of by you.'[2] Jawaharlal was irritated equally by the Liberals, the Swarajists, and the no-changers, all of whom seemed to have more or less the same moderate mentality.

> The mention of Independence frightens them and every effort is made to dissociate oneself from the idea or from its implications. The Indian States and foreign policy are taboo and not to be discussed; the army and problems of defence are beyond us, and so we spend all our energy in protesting, with varying degrees of emphasis, against internments and imprisonments and regulations etc. I am afraid this very tame and constitutional and legal and proper and reasonable activity raises no enthusiasm in me.[3]

But while there was commitment and impatience, there was no fresh line of analysis.

The turning-point in Jawaharlal's mental development was the invitation to help in organizing — and to participate as the representative of the Indian National Congress in — the International Congress against Colonial Oppression and Imperialism to be held at Brussels in February 1927. The chief organizer of the conference was Willi Muenzenberg, who 'really invented the fellow-traveller'.[4] The Soviet Union kept severely aloof and no one from that country attended the conference, though, as Jawaharlal realized even at the time,[5] the objectives of the conference were wholly in accordance with Soviet foreign policy and were intended to bring together the forces of anti-colonialism and organized labour as against imperialism, especially British imperialism. This did not frighten Jawaharlal and he suggested that a large delegation, including an economist and an expert on military matters, be sent from India by the Congress,[6] but in fact he was the only delegate.

Clearly, at such a conference where the prime target was British imperialism, the official representative of the Indian Congress would be an important

[1] Article in *Pratap,* December 1926.
[2] 13 January 1927.
[3] To A. Rangaswamy Iyengar, general secretary of the Congress, 25 January 1927, S.W., vol. 2, pp. 258-9.
[4] Hugh Thomas, *The Spanish Civil War* (Pelican edition, 1968), footnote on pp. 285-6.
[5] See his confidential report to the Working Committee, 19 February 1927, S.W., vol. 2, pp. 278-97.
[6] To his father, 16 November 1926, S. W., vol.2, pp. 250-51.

figure; and Jawaharlal was appointed one of the members of the Presidium. He arrived at Brussels on 6 February, took part in all the informal meetings, presided over one of the formal sessions and played a leading role in the drafting of many of the resolutions. 'I am dead tired', he wrote from Brussels on the 16th,[1] 'after 8 or 9 days of the Congress here. I have not had a good night's sleep and hardly a decent meal since I came here.' It was a strange medley of delegates — European Communists, trade unionists and pacifists, nationalists from Asia, Africa and Latin America, and secret service agents — with many delegates doubling the roles. However, Jawaharlal could not but be influenced by some of the men and women he met here — Henri Barbusse, George Lansbury, Ellen Wilkinson, Fenner Brockway, Harry Pollitt, Reginald Bridgman, Edo Fimmen, Willi Muenzenburg, Ernst Toller, Mohammed Hatta and Roger Baldwin, apart from a large number of delegates from China, Africa, Mexico and Latin America — and his fallow mind was receptive to Marxist and radical ideas.

In his first statement to the press, Jawaharlal merely emphasized the common element in the struggles against imperialism in various parts of the world; the fabric of imperialism looked imposing and appeared to hold together, but any rent in it would automatically lead to its total destruction. Indian nationalism was based on the most intense internationalism, just as the problem of Indian freedom was a world problem; as in the past, so in the future, other countries and peoples would be vitally affected by the condition of India. But his speech at the inaugural session of the conference was at a deeper level. Jawaharlal pointed out that India was the prime example of imperialism. She had been continuously exploited and terrorized by the British, and her workers and peasants had been systematically crushed. 'It does not require statistics, facts or figures to convince you that India in the course of the last few generations had terribly deteriorated, and is in such a bad way that if something drastic is not done to stop this process India may even cease to exist as a nation.' It was the policy of the British to create differences among Indians or, where they already existed, to increase them, to maintain the feudal princes in power, to support the rich landowners and to promote an unholy alliance of British and Indian capitalists. 'Naturally, therefore,' concluded Jawaharlal, introducing into his articulated thought a consciousness of the interlinking of economics and politics, 'from their capitalist and imperialist point of view they wanted to do everything in their power to hold on to India.' For the first time, instead of merely condemning British imperialism, Jawaharlal had tried to understand the motives, manner and methods of its functioning. His mind had taken a big step forward.

The resolution on India, drafted by Jawaharlal, accorded the warm support of the conference to the liberation of India from foreign domination and all

[1] To A. Rangaswamy Iyengar, 16 February 1927, S.W., vol. 2, p. 277.

kinds of exploitation as an essential step in the full emancipation of the peoples of the world. The peoples and workers of other countries should fully co-operate in this task and in particular take effective steps to prevent the dispatch of foreign troops to India and the retention of an army of occupation in India. This was really meant by Jawaharlal for his audience in India, to weaken 'the extraordinary mentality which clings on to the British connection in spite of everything' and took the presence of British troops for granted. Similarly, to goad the Indian National Congress into looking beyond political freedom, Jawaharlal, in the last paragraph of the resolution, expressed the hope of the conference that the Indian national movement would base its programme on the full emancipation of the peasants and workers of India, 'without which there can be no real freedom', and would co-operate with the movements for emancipation in other parts of the world.

Apart from India, the chief planks of the conference were China and Mexico. At this time in China the Kuomintang, in short-lived alliance with the Communists, was riding on a wave of nationalism and seeking to unite the country; and the Chinese delegation to the Brussels conference, to a large extent official, was hoping to enlist the sympathy, if not support, of public opinion and labour organizations in other countries. A joint declaration of the Indian and Chinese delegations, clearly drafted by Jawaharlal, bears the marks of an outlook which was to remain unchanged for over thirty years. Friendship with China was the core of his pan-Asian feeling. The declaration, in line with the prevalent attitude of cultural nationalism in India and its stress on the ancient civilizations of the East, recalled the close cultural ties between the peoples of India and China for over three thousand years and blamed the British for fostering ill-will against India in China by utilizing Indian merce-nary troops 'in support of British capitalist brigandage'. It was therefore urgent and essential that the Indian people should be educated regarding China, and British imperialism should be simultaneously engaged on two of its most vital fronts. 'We must now resume the ancient personal, cultural and political rela-tions between the two peoples. British imperialism which in the past has kept us apart and done us so much injury, is now the very force that is uniting us in a common endeavour to overthrow it.' The Indian and Chinese delegations thereafter persuaded the British delegation, representative of the British Com-munist Party, the Independent Labour Party and certain sections of the Labour Party, to commit themselves to support the oppressed countries in their fight for 'full independence' (a phrase preferred by the British to 'severance of the British connexion'), to oppose all forms of coercion against colonial peoples, to vote against all credits for the maintenance of armed forces to be used against oppressed nations and to carry on propaganda among British troops. In parti-cular, the British delegation promised to advocate direct action, including strikes and embargoes, to prevent the movement of munitions and troops to China, and demanded unconditional recognition of the nationalist Government, abolition of unequal treaties and of extraterritorial rights and surrender of foreign concessions.

The Chinese delegation was keen on promoting contacts between the Kuomintang and the Indian Congress and on educating Indian opinion on the Chinese question. Jawaharlal realized that the British Government could prevent exchange of visits at any level, but he felt that the effort should be made. 'It is up to us in India to do something practical for China. Vague resolutions of sympathy do not carry one far.' What he had in mind was the dispatch of an ambulance unit of twenty to twenty-five volunteers.[1] This was intended not only to encourage cordial relations between India and China; Jawaharlal was also anxious to widen the vision of Indian nationalism. He saw too the importance to the world of the future of China, especially as at this time the Kuomintang and the Chinese Communist Party were acting in alliance. What was happening in China, therefore, was not merely an assault on foreign imperialism but a direct attack on the capitalist system.

A victory for the Chinese means the creation of a great Soviet republic in the East closely allied with Russia and together with it gradually dominating the whole of Asia and Europe. This does not mean that the Chinese Republic will be fashioned wholly on the lines laid down by Marx. Even Soviet Russia, owing to the pressure of the peasantry, has had to give up part of its communism, and in China where the small peasant is the deciding factor, the departure from pure communism will be all the greater.[2]

This prescience, the realization that if the alliance of Chinese parties held it would be the Communists and not the much larger Kuomintang who would determine the lines of the future, and the recognition that there would be a large indigenous element in Chinese communism, can only be regarded as astounding — especially as at this time Stalin's agents were dominating the Chinese Communist Party. But this was not all. Jawaharlal proceeded to point out that Britain, even with the aid of other European countries, would be unable to do much injury to the great continental bloc of Russia and China. 'What is more likely is that England in order to save herself from extinction will become a satellite of the United States and incite the imperialism and capitalism of America to fight by her side.' It was at Brussels that Jawaharlal for the first time, perhaps because of his meeting with the delegates from Mexico and other countries of America, discerned that Britain was fast losing its leadership to the United States.

Most of us, specially from Asia, were wholly ignorant of the problems of South America, and of how the rising imperialism of the United States,

---

[1] Letter to N.S. Hardikar, 8 March 1927, S.W., vol. 2, p. 304. See also his article in *The Volunteer*, April 1927, on 'The Situation in China and India's Duty', ibid., pp. 326-8.
[2] Confidential report to the Working Committee, 19 February 1927, S.W., vol. 2, p. 281.

with its tremendous resources and its immunity from outside attack, is gradually taking a stranglehold of central and south America. But we are not at liberty to remain ignorant much longer, for the great problem of the near future will be American imperialism, even more than British imperialism. Or it may be, and all indications point to it, that the two will join together to create a powerful Anglo-Saxon bloc to dominate the world.

Jawaharlal expected, in face of the Chinese threat to imperialism, a world war in five years if not earlier. In any such war the North-West Frontier area of India would naturally be a principal battleground, and it was thought that the British were planning with this in view. Again, under the guise of encouraging Indian industries, the British were seeking to make India a self-sufficient country in munitions and other sinews of war. Jawaharlal wished the Indian Congress to take cognizance of these developments and formulate its own policy and programme on that basis. There should be a strong agitation against British intervention in China and the utilization of Indian troops for this purpose.

Jawaharlal's forecasts did not come immediately true, if only because the Kuomintang fell out with its Communist partner. But more than twenty years after this report was written, with the triumph of the Communists in China, the conclusion of a Sino-Soviet alliance, the formulation of a Chinese pattern of Communism and the evolution of Britain's 'special relationship' with the United States, Jawaharlal was to be proved one of the most far-seeing prophets in world affairs in our age.

The Brussels conference concluded with the issue of a manifesto based on the Marxist-Leninist theory of imperialism. It was asserted that European capitalism had battened on the exploitation of countries in Asia, Africa and America. In its latest phase of finance capitalism a few countries, and in them a few individuals, controlled the world. But the world war and its consequences had clearly shown that imperialist capitalism was its own grave-digger. A huge wave of the movement for national emancipation was passing over the world, and had received a mighty push forward from the Russian revolution and the formation of the Soviet Union. But the imperialists would not easily give up their booty, as was proved by the activities of 'the worst adventurer of our time', Winston Churchill. So the Brussels Conference decided to found the League against Imperialism and for National Independence, to organize co-operation between nationalist movements in the colonial countries and labour and anti-imperialist movements in the exploiting countries.

Jawaharlal does not seem to have taken an active part in drafting this manifesto, originally written in French, and resented the way in which it was rushed through the conference. But by this time he had no very great objection to its sentiments. He had come round to the Marxist viewpoint in its broad essentials. He agreed that imperialism and capitalism went hand in hand and neither would disappear until both were put down. As against this, the forces opposing imperialism and capitalism should be co-ordinated so as to strengthen each other. In colonial countries, nationalism automatically and rightly took precedence over all other ideologies, but such nationalism should have a broad basis, derive its strength from the masses and work specially for them.

Jawaharlal was appointed an honorary president of the League as well as a member of the Executive Committee, though he declined appointment as one of the secretaries on the grounds that he would be away in India. But during his stay in Europe for the rest of the year he attended regularly the meetings of the Executive Committee. Though the Communists were only a minority in this body, they sought to dominate it, and Jawaharlal was one of the leaders of an effective resistance. Often irritated, but never angry,[1] he made it clear that while he accepted in its fundamentals the socialist theory of the state, he had 'the strongest objection to being led by the nose by the Russians or by anybody else'.[2] But he did not think there was much danger of this, and, so long as the Soviet Union tried to utilize the League on unobjectionable lines, he saw no harm in co-operating with her against British imperialism. So he recommended to the Working Committee that the Congress might become an associate member of the League. It was possible that the League might develop, in contrast to the ineffective League of Nations, into a powerful League of Peoples; but this was not the reason why Jawaharlal advocated association of the Congress. He was enough of a realist not to place faith in such fantasies. Nor did he trust much to the support of British and other foreign working-class movements; 'almost every Englishman, however advanced he may be politically, is a bit of an imperialist in matters relating to India.'[3] He would have agreed broadly with Gandhi that India had little to expect from such bodies as this League, because most of the European states were partners in the exploitation of India, and their sympathy could not be expected in the final heat of the struggle.[4] He wrote to Gandhi:[5]

I do not expect much from it and indeed I am quite sure that none of the members of the so-called imperialist or oppressing nations will help us in the least whenever their interests conflict with ours. I have no illusions about their altruism. But I welcome all legitimate methods of getting into touch with other countries and peoples so that we may be able to understand their viewpoint and world politics generally. I do not

[1] Roger Baldwin's recollections recorded in 1967, N.M.M.L.

[2] Confidential report to the Working Committee, S.W., vol. 2, p. 289.

[3] Note for the Working Committee on a proposal to prepare a Parliamentary bill for India, 10 March 1927, S.W., vol. 2, pp. 306-7.

[4] See, for example, Gandhi to Motilal, 14 May 1927, *Collected Works,* vol. 33 (New Delhi, 1969), p. 321.

[5] 22 April 1927, S.W., vol. 2, p. 326.

think it is desirable, nor indeed is it possible for India to plough a lonely furrow now or in the future. It is solely with a view to self-education and self-improvement that I desire external contacts. I am afraid we are terribly narrow in our outlook and the sooner we get out of this narrowness the better. Our salvation can of course come only from the internal strength that we may evolve but one of the methods of evolving such strength should be study of other people and their ideas.

Association would also enable the Congress to utilize the League as its vehicle for propaganda abroad without committing it to the adoption of a socialist programme or limiting its freedom of action in India or elsewhere. Moreover, the League could be used by the Asian members to keep in close touch. At Brussels many delegates from Asia, despite discouragement from the organizers, had met informally and talked in terms of forming an 'Asiatic federation.' But this was thought to be premature and it was decided, for the time being, to concentrate efforts on strengthening the League and promoting bilateral relations.

However, it was the Soviet Union that now dominated Jawaharlal's mind, just as it had, an unseen presence, dominated the Brussels conference. He read all that he could lay hands on, books both by partisans and by critics, about developments and conditions in that country, and found much to admire. He believed that whatever the tradition of hostility between Britain and Russia, to a free India she would be no threat; and even if India were wholly opposed to Communism she could have friendly relations with Russia. Jawaharlal, far-seeing as ever, recognized that as she grew in power Soviet Russia might develop a new type of imperialism; but he thought there was little chance of this for a long time to come, and for the moment, for reasons of self-interest, Russia was befriending all oppressed nationalities.[1] It seemed logical, therefore, that he should visit the Soviet Union before returning to India; and the opportunity came, after Motilal's arrival in Europe in the autumn, when father and son were invited to the decennial celebrations of the 1917 revolution. When they were at Berlin the Soviet ambassador conveyed the invitation to them; and though this was short notice they decided, after some hesitation, to accept it.[2]

The invitation came in the last phase of the Soviet policy of support for national liberation movements in Asia, regardless of their ideology. This was a heritage from Lenin, who had believed that colonial countries like India should have their bourgeois, democratic revolution before they could think of proletarian rule, and that therefore it was the duty of Communists to work at this stage in co-operation with the leadership of the bourgeoisie. So to Lenin Gandhi was a revolutionary, and he rejected the argument of M.N. Roy that

[1]A Note on Foreign Policy for India, 13 September 1927, S.W., vol. 2, pp. 348-64.
[2]Nehru to Amal Home, 20 October 1959, Nehru papers.

the Indian bourgeoisie was no different from the traditional feudal classes. The thesis of Lenin became the official policy of the Soviet Union and the Comintern, and although by the end of 1922 there were the beginnings of Communist party organization in India, the general plan was for the Communists to infiltrate the Congress rather than promote a revolutionary mass party of their own. It was true that in May 1925 Stalin had accepted the position of Roy and advocated the formation of a revolutionary bloc in India led by the proletariat in general and the Communists in particular, and including the revolutionary section of the bourgeoisie.[1] But the other line of working with bourgeois leadership still held the field till the end of 1927. The Brussels Congress testified to the importance the Soviet Union still attached to bourgeois nationalist movements; and the severance of diplomatic relations by Britain in 1927 followed by strong rumours of British preparations for military invasion, with Peshawar as a base,[2] led to a war scare in the Soviet Union. Now more than ever it seemed invaluable to have the sympathy, if not the active support, of the Congress Party.

A change in Soviet attitude came towards the end of 1927. The setbacks in China and the failure of the efforts to reach a *rapprochement* with the Western Powers unnerved the makers of Soviet and Comintern policy; and Stalin, who was now finally emerging as the victor in his rivalry with Trotsky, viewed the colonial question only against the background of European events and had a more limited idea of the security of the Soviet Union. At the Fifteenth Party Congress, Bukharin made it clear that the bourgeoisie in India could no longer be supported. The Sixth Congress of the Third International formally abandoned in 1928 the policy of a united front against imperialism and directed the Indian Communist Party to act in isolation and work for an armed insurrection, for the bourgeois nationalist parties had become supporters of imperialism and, having assumed 'a reformist and class-collaborationist character', could not be expected to lead the revolution.

So November 1927 was the last occasion, for many years at any rate, when the Nehrus could expect an official invitation to Moscow. They were in Russia for only a few days, but the articles which Jawaharlal wrote for *The Hindu* covering this visit and which were later published as a book,[3] show the deep impression made on him by 'this strange Eurasian country of the hammer and sickle, where workers and peasants sit on the thrones of the mighty and upset the best-laid schemes of mice and men'.[4] They were, he wrote to his sister from Moscow,[5] 'in topsy turvy land. All one's old values get upset and life wears a strange aspect here.' He knew that they were on a conducted tour, seeing only what they were allowed to see; he knew too that conditions in the

[1] D.N. Druhe, *Soviet Russia and Indian Communism* (New York, 1959), p. 93.
[2] *New York Times*, 30 June 1927.
[3] *Soviet Russia, some random sketches and impressions* (Allahabad, 1928).
[4] Ibid.
[5] 10 November 1927, S.W., vol. 2, p. 369.

sprawling provinces hardly came up to what was to be found in Moscow and its environs. Yet he was convinced that the Soviet Union had made rapid progress in agriculture, prison reform, the eradication of illiteracy, the treatment of women, the handling of the problem of minorities and the removal of the sharp contrasts between luxury and poverty and of the hierarchy of class. He was sure too that the Soviet Union had much to teach India, which also was a large agricultural country with a poor and illiterate population. His mood was defined by the lines which he put on the title-page of his book:

> 'Bliss was it in that dawn to be alive,
> But to be young was very heaven.'

Starry-eyed? Perhaps; but it is well to remember that the Russia which Jawaharlal visited was still very much the Russia of Lenin, even though Lenin had been dead for over three years. Stalin had not yet become the undisputed dictator, and there was a considerable amount of mass support for the Soviet regime. The New Economic Policy was still in effect. 'Get rich', Bukharin had advised the peasants in 1925; and the peasants still dominated the countryside and brought about a strong recovery in food production. This was to them the 'golden era of Soviet rule'. The number of family holdings rose to 25 millions in 1927, and comprised $98 \cdot 3$ per cent of the sown area.[1] Stalin, like Lenin, was still speaking in terms of voluntary collectivization of agriculture. It was only after 1927 that it was felt that 'Bolshevism in alliance with the peasants', apart from being ideologically untenable, was also impracticable. The food shortages in large cities in the summer of 1927, despite a good harvest, showed that, without mass production of consumer goods, the peasants could not be induced to sell their grain. The percentage of the crops being sent to the urban markets was even less than that in the years before the war. On the other hand, industrial production, which till 1927 had shown a rapid rise because of the reactivation of productive capacity of the years before 1917, now began to slacken. If industrialization — and specially heavy industrialization, thought to be so necessary with the imminent prospect of war — were to be maintained, it was necessary to insist on the peasants disgorging their supplies; and this meant rapid and enforced collectivization. In December 1927, therefore — a month after the visit of the Nehrus — the Party Congress decided on an offensive against the *kulak*, opening a new chapter in Soviet history.

So Jawaharlal saw the Soviet Union in the last days of its first, halcyon period. If his reaction was idealistic, it was partly because there was still some idealism in the air. The grounding in Marxism, which he had received at the Brussels conference and after, was followed by a near-conversion to communism by practical testimony. Jawaharlal had been particularly impressed by Lenin's leadership, by his realism and resilience, and above all by his insistence

[1] A. Nove, *An Economic History of the U.S.S.R.* (London, 1969), p. 106.

on professional, full-time revolutionaries. The need for such workers in India was obviously even greater, and it was as one such that Jawaharlal now doubtless saw himself. He who had sailed from India as a dedicated disciple of Gandhi returned a self-conscious revolutionary radical. Although always to be deeply influenced by Gandhi, he was never again to be wholly a prisoner in the Gandhian mould. But it is significant that the change was wrought not by the revolutionary situation in India but by what he saw and heard and read in Europe. Jawaharlal was always a radical in the European tradition, seeking to apply and adapt its doctrine to his own country. This could be both a strength and a weakness.

9

The Campaign for Independence

ONE

It was in this mood, not as before of novelettish romanticism but of thoughtful commitment to revolutionary change, that Jawaharlal returned to India. The British Government, too, had noticed this change of outlook, and, as Jawaharlal knew, shadowed his activities in Europe during 1927, while at Simla the Home Member had warned his father that 'Jawahar was sailing too near the wind'.[1] In fact, it was after this friendly caution that Motilal decided to sail for Europe to keep an eye on his son and escort him safely home.

However, Jawaharlal, his wife and daughter came back ahead and reached Madras in time for the Congress session in December 1927. He was itching for action. For this, the first step seemed to him to be the acceptance of full independence as the objective. Jawaharlal had been thinking about this for a long time and had now finally come round to the view that the Congress should commit itself firmly to the goal of independence. He could not accept the usual argument that there was no real difference between Dominion Status and independence because the former carried with it the right to secede. Theoretically this was so, but in fact Dominion Status implied the maintenance of a connection with Britain and allowing her dominance in every major field. This might be suited to countries like Australia and Canada, but was meaningless for India. Either India left the empire or she stayed as a dependent, under whatever guise, within it; there was no third alternative. Co-operation between the lamb and the lion always resulted in the lamb being inside the lion. But this need not mean enmity with Britain. Though there could be no friendship within the empire, once India was out of the imperial stranglehold, she could co-operate with Britain as an equal.

Even more important to Jawaharlal than the political and economic implications of independence were the psychological consequences of a commitment to such an uncompromising policy. The assent to Dominion Status

[1]Motilal to Gandhi, 6 May 1927. Gandhi Smarak Sangrahalaya, vol. 32, no. 12576.

as the objective was in itself an indication of India's mental degradation, for behind it lay an unquestioning acceptance of the inevitability of a British presence in India. That the Congress should adhere to it revealed a craven fear of being declared an unlawful assembly if it claimed anything more, and the preponderance within it of elements which on the whole profited by the British connection. The spider's web of imperialism had obviously caught even Congressmen. But once the Congress made independence its goal, it would shake off the defeatism and weariness that had followed the non-co-operation movement, sweep away Swarajist temporizings, gain a new strength and again pull in the masses. Jawaharlal's stay in Europe had confirmed him in the resolve that India should look for no favours from Britain. Relatively and potentially Indian nationalism was not weak, while England was daily losing ground despite her apparent strength. It made no difference which party was in office. His first-hand contacts with British Labour leaders had filled him with particular contempt for these 'sanctimonious and canting humbugs'.[1]

Jawaharlal, therefore, was eager for wholehearted combat, with no quarter sought or given. His new radical ideas affirmed rather than diverted his enthusiasm for political action. Even the arrest of capitalist exploitation and a lightening of India's poverty required the termination of imperialist rule. But the mirage of Dominion Status weakened resistance in India to the British and generally strengthened reformist as against revolutionary forces. The real strength of the British in India lay in the submissive attitude of Indians to the *status quo* — to the *raj,* to established ideas, to old customs and traditions. So, as he complained to Gandhi, 'it passes my comprehension how a national organization can have as its ideal and goal dominion status. The very idea suffocates and strangles me.'[2]

It was Gandhi, of course, who was the main hurdle. He was not present at the sessions of the Madras Congress when Jawaharlal secured the passage of a resolution committing the Congress to independence. But the followers of Gandhi had been there in sufficient numbers to secure the removal of the parts of the resolution which clarified independence to mean full control of defence, finance and economic and foreign policy and demanded that this be implemented immediately, in particular by the complete withdrawal of the British army of occupation. So all that the party accepted was a general adherence to the goal of complete national independence; and even this was not incorporated into the constitution of the Congress. That still proclaimed the objective to be *swaraj,* and thus enabled those who did not believe in independence and a total severance from Britain, and had no wish to see the British army withdraw at once, continue to be members of the party.

So Jawaharlal's resolution, as he himself recognized,[3] was not really taken

[1] Speech at the All-Parties Conference, 29 August 1928, S.W., vol. 3 (Delhi, 1972), p. 59.
[2] 11 January 1928.
[3] *Autobiography*, p. 167.

seriously and was meant primarily to humour him. But Gandhi did not conceal his disdain for what seemed to him mock heroics. He described the resolution in *Young India* as 'hastily conceived' and 'thoughtlessly passed', and the Congress as a whole as having descended to the level of a schoolboy debating society.[1] He also warned Jawaharlal privately that he was proceeding too fast.[2] When Jawaharlal replied stiffly that he had a large measure of support, that Gandhi's leadership was now hesitant and ineffective, and that their ideals were very different,[3] Gandhi offered to publish the correspondence. In other words, he was prepared for an open break. The relationship had not yet developed to the extent that to the older man it was in any way indispensable. But Jawaharlal drew back. The firmness of his views was not to him incompatible with emotional dependence, and he was eager to remain, in Gandhi's phrase, 'under stupefaction'.[4] He recoiled from further publicity being given to their differences which, he assured Gandhi, were only on a few points and need not spread to the many other issues on which they agreed. His regard and affection for Gandhi were personal, but they were also something more; 'even in the wider sphere am I not your child in politics, though perhaps a truant and errant child?'[5]

So, without breaking away completely from Gandhi and the old leadership, Jawaharlal campaigned for independence as the ultimate objective. It was a circumscribed revolt. The issue came up again at the All-Parties Conference and at the proceedings of the committee set up by it, with Motilal Nehru as the chairman, to draw up a constitution for India as an answer to the challenge of the Secretary of State, Lord Birkenhead, that Indian politicians were capable of no constructive suggestions. Though Jawaharlal was not a member of this committee, he took an active part in its meetings and helped his father with the secretarial work. But he was thoroughly ill at ease in an atmosphere of haggling and compromise. 'The fault must be mine but anyway it results in my feeling always that I do not fit in with anything. I am always the square peg and the holes are all round. I feel very lonely.'[6] His suggestions that the constitution should establish a democratic socialist republic and a beginning be made in elections by economic units[7] were not given even a moment's consideration. To secure the broadest level of agreement in a body many of whose members were not Congressmen, Motilal favoured Dominion Status and gave his attention mostly to finding a possible solution of the communal problem. In this he was successful, and the Nehru Report recommended, as concessions to the

[1] 5 January 1928.
[2] 4 January 1928. *A Bunch of Old Letters*, pp. 55-6.
[3] 11 January 1928.
[4] 17 January 1928, *Collected Works*. vol. 32 (New Delhi. 1969), pp. 468-9.
[5] 23 January 1928.
[6] To Gandhi, 30 June 1928.
[7] Note, 8 March 1928, Report of the Committee to the All-Parties Conference.

Muslims, not separate electorates but reservations of seats, the constitution of Sind as a separate province and the introduction of the reforms of 1919 in the North-West Frontier Province (NWFP) and Baluchistan. The hope of Jawaharlal and many others that reservation of seats should be terminated after ten years or earlier with the consent of the parties concerned[1] could not be incorporated into the report. But even this measure of consensus was a notable achievement and Jawaharlal was not alone in expecting that the report might provide the finishing kick to communalism.[2] But the acceptance of Dominion Status went against the grain. He spoke repeatedly against it and often had to engage in public debate with his father. He knew, however, that he had no chance of getting the decision reversed, and fell back on keeping alive the commitment of the Congress to independence. The fact that it was a party to the Nehru Report need not mean that it had abandoned its own preference.

It was for this purpose that he organized the Independence for India League as, in the first instance, a pressure group within the Congress. Knowing that Gandhi and other leading Congressmen disapproved of independence and all that it implied, Jawaharlal resigned the general secretaryship; but the Working Committee declined to accept it.[3] Ostensibly this was because the resolution of the Madras Congress gave legitimacy to propaganda for independence; but in fact it was because the general run of Congressmen attached little importance to Jawaharlal's efforts. To them the only value which the demand for independence now had was that it enabled them to bargain for Dominion Status. Had there been any danger of the Independence for India League altering the general direction of the Congress, it would doubtless have been hastily stifled. For the League was intended to keep alive not only the objective of political independence but also the concomitant ideals of republicanism and socialism. To Jawaharlal independence was not a purely political issue. Severance of the British connection implied also an attack on the vested interests supported by the British in India; indeed, the basis of the struggle was economic. The future republican government of India would be based not on the exploitation of the masses but on social equality.[4] The object of the Independence for India League was therefore both to achieve independence and to reconstruct Indian society by changing its capitalist and feudal basis. 'It means that the League aims at the socialist democratic State in which every person has the fullest opportunities of development and the State control of the means of production and distribution.'[5] Instead of a few individuals amassing huge fortunes by the exploitation

[1]Note, 7 July 1928.

[2]Interview to the press, 4 September. *The Tribune*, 9 September 1928.

[3]*The Bombay Chronicle*, 4 Septmber 1928

[4]Presidential address at the first session of the Republican Congress, *The Hindu*, 29 December 1927.

[5]Programme of the Independence for India League, U. P. Branch, April 1929, S.W., vol. 3, p. 287.

of others, the state should be organized on a vast co-operative basis for the benefit of all, and this in turn should lead on to 'a great world co-operative commonwealth'.[1]

Independence, therefore, was a composite ideal, and for its attainment Jawaharlal looked far beyond the Congress. The League should be both an active element within the parent party and a general catalyst in the nation. The Congress might head the political campaign and take the lead in drafting constitutions, but economic and social changes could be effected only by the sanction provided by the exploited classes. For this a revolutionary atmosphere would have to be created in the country and the people organized on a large scale.[2] But this required an economic programme. Gandhi had drawn the masses into the political struggle in a way in which no one else could have done, and this to Jawaharlal made his leadership indispensable. But they could only be kept in this struggle by providing an economic content to *swaraj* — something which Gandhi had never done. Gandhi claimed not to object to this on principle, but thought the effort was premature. 'I am quite of your opinion that some day we shall have to start an intensive movement without the rich people and without the vocal educated class. But that time is not yet.'[3] However, Jawaharlal went ahead and formulated a precise programme. Though he had a grand design of socialism, he wanted a very modest beginning. In the U.P. in particular there seemed to be no alternative to the abolition of landlordism, but this should be done with the payment of partial compensation and replaced by smallholdings owned by individual peasant proprietors with no right of alienation. There would be not nationalization but socialization of land, and the most that the State would manage would be model farms. Agricultural debts should be written off but after part payment. The State should gradually acquire key industries, ensure a minimum living wage and impose sharply graduated direct taxes, an inheritance tax and a tax on agricultural income.[4]

Jawaharlal was aware that such a programme would inevitably, at some stage or other, raise issues of the class struggle and bring about clashes of interests between labour and capitalists and between landlords and tenants; but these could not be shirked. It was no wisdom to refuse to recognize or face conflict where it existed. Such conflicts would have to be fought and overcome. Pushed to it, Jawaharlal was willing to concede both that violence was not objectionable in itself and that the final goal, the resolution of the struggle, might well be communism. If India were convinced that she could become free through violence, she would undoubtedly have the right to indulge in it as other countries had done. He stood for intensive non-violent non-co-operation, only

[1]Circular letter to Congressmen, 5 April 1928, S.W., vol. 3, p. 184.

[2]See speech at Banaras, 17 January, *The Bombay Chronicle,* 18 January 1928.

[3]To Jawaharlal, 1 April 1928, *Collected Works,* vol. 36, p. 174.

Presidential address to the U. P. Provincial Conference, 27 October 1928, S. W., vol. 3, pp. 255-63; Programme of the Independence for India League, U. P. Branch, op. cit.

because in India's condition mass violence was impracticable while individual acts of terrorism had a counter-revolutionary effect and injured the national cause.[1] Violence was contrary to the logic of politics and not of ethics; and terrorism was a tactic of defeat. As for the ultimate objective, addressing a students' conference in Calcutta, he publicly accepted that though he personally did not agree with many of the methods of the Communists and was by no means sure to what extent Communism would suit conditions in India, yet he did believe in Communism as an ideal of society. For essentially it was socialism, and to him socialism was the only way if the world was to escape disaster.[2]

For the work of organization Jawaharlal looked to the young men and women of India. Impressed by what he had seen in the Soviet Union and read about the achievements of Lenin and the Bolsheviks, Jawaharlal was thinking in terms of youth cadres in India. He did not fancy Communist workers, if only because there appeared to him to be no trained Marxists in India, and he certainly did not consider himself as one. Moreover, the strongest appeal in India inevitably came from nationalism, and any programme for economic and social reforms would have to be linked to that. So, while he continued to promote the work of the Hindustani Seva Dal, he also looked further afield. Within a few months of his return, he wrote to the press calling on those who were for independence, detested the growing influence of religion in politics and desired the removal of inequalities of class and caste and wealth to get in touch with each other and with him.[3] But revolutionary battalions do not spring into existence on the mere writing of letters to the editor, and Jawaharlal's appeal was significant only as indicative of his own aspirations. Throughout the year he gave the greatest importance to youth leagues and conferences, and was prepared to sacrifice all other work to the organization of youth. But an all-India corps dedicated to 'full-blooded socialism' and carrying the fight to various parts of the country never came into being.

Nor did the Independence for India League, as Jawaharlal sadly recognized soon enough, fulfil the hopes of its creator. It consisted of a few politicians who either were disgruntled with Gandhi and Motilal or hoped to draw on the growing popularity of Jawaharlal for their own advantage. Indeed, often people joined the League with the intention of smothering it.[4] Jawaharlal was too honest himself to realize in time the machinations of others; and it has been suggested that he was by now increasingly the victim of flattery.[5] The charge

---

[1] See addresses to Punjab Provincial Conference, 11 April, *The Tribune*, 18 April 1928, and to Delhi Political Conference, 15 October, *The Bombay Chronicle*, 20 October 1928.

[2] Address to the Bengal Students Conference, 22 September 1928, S.W., vol. 3, p. 193.

[3] Letter to the press, 20 March 1928.

[4] See Jawaharlal's letter to G. S. Vidyarthi, 2 October 1928.

[5] 'As for Pandit Jawaharlal I love and admire few men as I do him, but I also feel that he is getting too fond of clap-trap, too eager to receive idolatrous homage from people around him. This weakness he must have imbibed recently.' Kapil Deva Malaviya, an old friend of the family, in *The Leader*, 30 November 1928.

is unjustified; Jawaharlal was more the victim of innocence. But the result was that the Independence for India League never became the spearhead of revolution, well-knit in its organization and clear-cut in its ideology. Rather, for a year it struggled on in a state of suspended animation till it ceased to have a *raison d'être* in the beginning of 1929, with the Congress as a whole committed, in certain circumstances, to the goal of independence. Its significance in history is its testimony to the unalloyed idealism of Jawaharlal. But his enthusiasm for action in a noble cause was not matched by a capacity for organization.

TWO

However, if at this time Jawaharlal failed to create an instrument to mobilize the country for a long-term revolution, he was more successful in helping to plan demonstrations all over the country as a reply to the insult proffered to it by the announcement in 1927 of a Commission consisting solely of British members of Parliament to consider whether India was ready for a further instalment of constitutional reforms. The mistake was primarily that of the Viceroy, Lord Irwin, and his officials. They soon realized that they had blundered, but convinced themselves that a boycott of the Commission was not a serious threat. It was thought that the Congress was weak and divided, and dominated by the Swarajists who were moving more and more towards constitutional opposition;[1] and with the Congress lukewarm in its boycott of the Commission, other parties need not be expected to be rigid in their hostility. So things might right themselves in the course of a few months, especially if some small sops could be found.[2] Various concessions were suggested by the Government of India and by Sir John Simon, the chairman of the Commission, to make it easier for the Indian political parties to abandon the boycott and co-operate with the Commission. Gandhi thought this might well happen;[3] and Motilal, who shared this fear, was, by the summer, planning to visit Canada rather than waste his time in India.[4]

However, the boycott held. Liberals like Sapru, who relied heavily on British goodwill, resented the jilting so deeply that for once they refused to behave like moderates. Jinnah also could not be won over by the Government, with the result that the Muslim leaders who were willing to collaborate could not claim to represent all Muslims. To Jawaharlal the failure to nominate any Indian to membership of the Commission seemed but a minor incident of

[1] See letters of Home Dept. to India Office, 13 January and 2 June 1927, Home Dept. Pol. File 6 of 1927.
[2] See Crerar to Hailey, 14 November and Hailey to Frank Brown, 14 December 1927. Hailey papers, vol. 11.
[3] Gandhi to Motilal, 29 February 1928, *Collected Works,* vol. 36, pp. 67-8.
[4] Motilal to Jawaharlal, 22 March, and to Gandhi, 27 June 1928. Motilal Nehru papers.

Imperial rule; what should be boycotted was not only the Simon Commission but the whole conception behind it, that India would be for ever a part of the British Empire and the British Parliament had the right to give India what it wished and deny her what it liked.[1] Freedom was India's fundamental right, and as all commissions sent out from England denied that right they could receive no quarter in India. 'Our aim is a completely free India and we have nothing to discuss except on this basis.'[2] But at least the affront of the Simon Commission could be used as an occasion for united action, to bring together members of various parties in a common cause. The boycott might not lead India far on the path of independence, but it would certainly help to create a healthy atmosphere in which work of national organization could be expedited.[3] The chance of hitting back had almost a therapeutic effect on Jawaharlal, and he set about, as general secretary of the Congress, organizing the boycott on a countrywide scale. February 3rd, the day the Commission was to land in India, was to be treated as a day not of mourning but of rejoicing, for on that day would commence afresh the war for independence.[4]

The national *hartal* was a greater success than Jawaharlal had anticipated,[5] and thereafter, throughout the year, wherever the Commission went, demonstrations ending in police charges and firing took place. At Lahore the leading Congressman of the Punjab, Lajpat Rai, was severely beaten. Jawaharlal and his colleagues now awaited the arrival of the Commission in the United Provinces. The Provincial Government at first decided to adopt an accommodating attitude and to allow processions, provided the organizers asked for permission and agreed to follow the route laid down by the police. This moderation was believed to have been based on the assumption that the demonstrations would not amount to much, as the Muslims would not participate in it. The local organizers of the boycott also decided to abide by these conditions, as they had no desire to have a conflict with the police; and processions were taken out with permission on 23 and 24 November. Jawaharlal arrived in Lucknow on the 25th and the tempo immediately rose. He had little enthusiasm for law-abiding processions. 'I shall only stay on till the 28th if there is much doing. Otherwise I do not propose to waste good time in waving a little flag.'[6] News of the death of Lajpat Rai on 18 November had already inflamed tempers throughout India, and Jawaharlal called on the youth of Lucknow to answer this challenge.[7] A procession on the 26th, permitted by the authorities, was so vast that there could be no doubt of the tremendous strength of feeling

[1] Speech at Allahabad, 10 January, *The Leader,* 12 January 1928.
[2] Message to the press, *The Bombay Chronicle,* 25 January 1928.
[3] Speech at Lucknow, 25 January, *The Leader,* 27 January 1928.
[4] Speech at Allahabad, 19 January, *The Leader,* 21 January 1928.
[5] See his letter to the editor, 3 February, *The Leader,* 6 February 1928, and interview at Bombay, *The Bombay Chronicle,* 7 February 1928.
[6] To M. Saxena, 14 November 1928, AICC File G 73 of 1928.
[7] See his circular 'They have dared!', ibid.

against the Commission; and though the procession proceeded without incident, the officials realized that such demonstrations were serving to organize
and rehearse what was planned to take place on the arrival of the Commission.

When the boycott committee sought permission for a procession on the
28th, it was granted on condition that the route was changed to avoid the
European shopping area, where the Governor was that day attending a garden
party.[1] The organizers of the procession replied that it was too late to alter
the route, and when the procession started to move it was *lathi*-charged by
mounted police. Jawaharlal had by this time, probably expecting no major
confrontation, left Lucknow; but on hearing of the *lathi* charge he returned
to the city on the 29th. The police, who believed that the defiance of the boycott
committee on the 28th had been on Jawaharlal's orders,[2] refused to permit
any more processions. They stopped a small group of twelve led by Jawaharlal
and Govind Ballabh Pant, which was on its way to a public meeting, and asked
them if they had secured a licence for a procession. Jawaharlal replied that in
view of the behaviour of the police the previous day he was not prepared to
have any further dealings with them, and the police thereupon broke up the
group with *lathis*. Jawaharlal himself received two blows. Despite this, the
group refused to disperse. Meantime a large crowd had gathered, and the
officials were compelled to permit Jawaharlal and his companions to proceed
along their chosen route to the meeting with, in fact, the police riding in front
as a vanguard.[3]

The next morning the Commission arrived in Lucknow. The Congress,
which had sought permission to hold a black flag demonstration, was allotted
a site nearly 500 yards from the station, so that Simon and his colleagues would
hardly notice it. A large procession, led by Jawaharlal — Motilal, who had come
from Allahabad, was prevented by his son from joining them — reached the
station, and sought to take up a position nearer to the route of the Commission
than the one allotted to them. This was near an open space, and the police carried
out a cavalry charge, using both *lathis* and spears, on a crowd of over thirty
thousand for two or three furlongs. Though hundreds were beaten and many
trampled down, the large crowd generally stood its ground, neither retreating
nor retaliating, till the police, once the Commission had passed, fell back.
Jawaharlal, after receiving half a dozen *lathi* blows on his back, shoulders and
legs, was surrounded by students who shielded him from further attack.[4] Just
then a young man, ostensibly a student but later discovered to be a police agent,
offered to provide Jawaharlal with two revolvers.[5] The offer was politely

[1] Report of Deputy Commr Lucknow, 5 December 1928. Home Dept. Pol. File 130 of 1929.
[2] Ibid.
[3] Report in *The Tribune*, 1 December 1928; press statements of Jawaharlal, 1 and 4 December
1928, S.W., vol. 3, pp. 108-15 and 119.
[4] Press statements of Jawaharlal, 30 November and 1 December 1928; report in *The Tribune*,
2 December 1928; Gandhi in *Navajivan*, 9 December 1928. *Collected Works*, vol. 38, p. 184.
[5] Jawaharlal's letter to Gandhi, quoted by him in *Young India*, 13 December 1928. *Collected
Works*, vol. 38, p. 209.

declined, but the incident is suggestive of an effort to aggravate the situation and seriously incriminate Jawaharlal. It strengthens Jawaharlal's accusation that the police, angry at their loss of prestige on the two previous days, were out on this occasion for vengeance, and primarily against Jawaharlal.

The news of the *lathi* charges on the 29th and 30th and of the injuries inflicted on Jawaharlal roused widespread anger in India. The deputy commissioner of Lucknow sought to play it down. Of the clash on the 29th he reported that if Pant and Jawaharlal were beaten it was very slightly indeed; and as for the confrontation the next day at the station he remarked that the 'actual occurrence was rather like the clearing of a football ground in England when the crowd have broken loose. There have been gross exaggerations in the press, and Jawaharlal's report is so ludicrous and overstated as to carry its own refutation.'[1] In fact, it was Jawaharlal's statements, fortified by other eye-witness accounts in the press, that were believed. The *raj* was thought to have bared its teeth, and its actions, born of bloodlust and cracking of nerve, evoked memories of Amritsar in 1919. Jawaharlal was not slow to draw the parallel.

The events of Lucknow make it clear that the authorities in the United Provinces at least are modelling themselves on the old Punjab model and Haileyism is coming to mean much the same thing as O'Dwyerism. O'Dwyerism was followed by non-co-operation and the greatest national awakening of modern times in India. That awakening shook the fabric of British rule. India is different today from what it was nine years ago and Haileyism is likely to lead to an even greater national response which may carry us to our goal.[2]

THREE

Apart from the impact on the development of the national resistance to British rule, the police actions at Lucknow confirmed Jawaharlal's national standing. He was no longer merely a politician of the United Provinces; throughout India his popularity leapt, and he was firmly established as one of the frontrunners of his generation. Gandhi realized and welcomed this. 'My love to you. It was all done bravely. You have braver things to do. May God spare you for many a long year to come and make you his chosen instrument for freeing India from [the] yoke.'[3]

The Government's reaction to the growing popularity of Jawaharlal was to consider his arrest. As early as September, when Jawaharlal founded the Independence for India League, there was a rumour that he was soon to be

[1]Home Dept. Pol. File No. 130 of 1929.
[2]Annual Report of the General Secretaries of the Congress (drafted by Jawaharlal). See AICC File G 80 of 1929.
[3]3 December 1928, *A Bunch of Old Letters*, p. 68.

imprisoned,[1] though Jawaharlal himself attached no importance to it.[2] But in October the Viceroy directed that his speeches be scanned carefully,[3] and in December, when Jawaharlal came to Poona, after the Lucknow *lathi* charges, to address the Bombay Presidency Youth Conference, he was received with a rapturous enthusiasm which alarmed the Government. 'From start to finish', reported the Bombay police, 'the prevalent note of the conference was frankly communistic and revolutionary;'[4] and Jawaharlal's speech itself was described by the Home Secretary as no casual utterance but a deliberate preaching of violent revolt with the intention to follow it up by organization.[5] In fact, the speech was in Jawaharlal's usual vein, a castigation of British imperialism as an aspect of the world phenomenon of capitalism, a vivid description of India's low condition and a call to revolt against evil and the establishment of a co-operative socialist commonwealth in a world federation of socialist states. As suited an address to students, it was more academic than his other speeches of the time. Yet the jittery Government of India asked the Bombay Government to consider prosecution, and were brought back to reality only by that Government's comment that everyone must agree with much of what Jawaharlal had said, and it would be difficult to prove that communism and revolution, and not merely socialism, were being advocated.[6]

The Government acquired another opportunity to proceed against Jawaharlal at Jharia, where the annual session of the All-India Trade Union Congress was being held. The League against Imperialism had deputed W.J. Johnston as a fraternal delegate, and the police walked into the meeting to arrest him. Jawaharlal had the police turned out, made a fiery speech and led the infuriated delegates in affiliating the Trade Union Congress to the League. When, the next day, Johnston was arrested outside the conference *pandal,* Jawaharlal delivered yet another vehement denunciation of imperialism and called for united action against the British.[7] But, rather than arrest Jawaharlal, the Government preferred to await the decisions of the National Congress which was to meet in its annual session in a few days at Calcutta.

The hope of Motilal at Calcutta was to secure the adoption by the Congress of the Nehru Report and the acceptance of Dominion Status without prejudice to the ultimate goal of complete independence. In this way he expected to hold the line, and to retain moderate support without losing that of his son and the other members of the Independence for India League. Gandhi came to Calcutta

[1] Statement of Maulana Zafar Ali, *The Tribune,* 12 September 1928.
[2] To Syed Mahmud, 14 September 1928.
[3] Note of Home Secretary, 18 October 1928. Home Dept. File 179/29-Pol. of 1929.
[4] Note, 15 December 1928, ibid.
[5] Note of Home Secretary, 27 December 1928, ibid.
[6] Telegram to Bombay Government, 29 December 1928 and Bombay Government's reply, 11 January 1929, ibid.
[7] G. Chattopadhyay, *Communism and Bengal's Freedom Movement,* vol. 1 (Delhi, 1970), pp. 115-16 and 141.

especially to ensure this. Jawaharlal was in a difficult position. The psychology behind the Nehru Report was alien to him. 'It is obvious that the Congress contains at least two if not more groups which have nothing in common between them and the sooner they break apart the better.'[1] But if such a break occurred, Gandhi and his father would be on the other side; and, as so often in his public life, affection prevailed over logic. He opposed Dominion Status in the severest terms. To accept it, as Gandhi suggested, was to declare that the Congress was prepared to allow India to be exploited by British imperialism. All energy oozed out of him at the very thought of Dominion Status.[2] But he toned down independence to mean severance of all connection not with the British but only with British imperialism; and he commended the Nehru Report without prejudice to the independence resolution of the Madras Congress. This suggested both a desire to find common ground and a willingness to face both ways.

Gandhi was as anxious to avoid a break. He, of course, preferred Dominion Status to independence, but he was not enamoured of the Nehru Report. 'The way to constitutional *swaraj* may lie through Lucknow; the way to organic *swaraj*, which is synonymous with Ramarajya, lies through Bardoli.'[3] If he supported the Report it was primarily out of loyalty to Motilal. But in the effort to hold the party together, he was not prepared to discard all consistency. The final sentence in Jawaharlal's speech probably gave him the clue: 'Prepared as this House should be for any compromise on any lines, it should not be prepared to give up its definite real goal of independence for any length of time.' This hinted that Jawaharlal was willing to shelve temporarily the demand for independence. So Gandhi recommended that if the Government did not accept and act upon the Nehru Report within two years, the Congress should revert to full independence. Such flexibility of approach involved no long-term compromise on ideals and, especially as no one seriously expected the Government to accept the Nehru Report, made a concession only to the ear. As a further step to placate Jawaharlal, the time-limit was reduced in discussions to one year. So Jawaharlal and his friends could accept the resolution; but to mark his disapproval of even the paper concession, Jawaharlal stayed away from the final session when the resolution was passed. Gandhi explained his absence.

> He thinks this resolution itself falls far short of what he wants but, a high-souled man as he is, he does not want to create unnecessary bitterness . . . how can he help feeling disatisfied? He would not be Jawaharlal if he did not strike out for himself an absolutely unique and original

[1] To Ansari, 21 September 1928.
[2] Speech 27 December 1928, S.W., vol. 3, pp. 270-74.
[3] To B.G. Horniman, 28 August 1928, *Collected Works,* vol. 37, p. 212. Ramarajya is the Hindu ideal of the golden age. Bardoli, in Gujarat, had been the scene of a peasant no-tax campaign in 1928.

line in pursuance of his path. He considers nobody, not even his father,
nor wife, nor child. His own country and his duty to his own country
he considers and nothing else.[1]

FOUR

So the Congress gave its support to the Nehru Report and the demand for
Dominion Status for one year, after which it would again resort to non-co-
operation as the means for securing independence. As there was obviously
no chance of the Government responding to this resolution in any satisfactory
way, 1929 was clearly to be a year of preparation. It was in that spirit that
Jawaharlal carried out his duties as general secretary of the Congress, and he
was encouraged in this by Gandhi. 'I wish that Jawahar could travel throughout all the provinces and see that the Congress organizations become living
bodies.'[2] He asked Jawaharlal to reorganize the provincial Congress committees, compel obedience to instructions from the Working Committee and
direct them to implement fully the constructive programme.[3] Jawaharlal
had also been directed by the AICC to prepare, with Subhas Bose, a scheme
to train volunteers to work in the villages and among the city labourers. So
Jawaharlal set out to revitalize the Congress and run it on proper lines.

> It seems to be the general opinion that everything connected with the
> Congress can be done in an unbusinesslike way. Certainly no business
> could have survived the want of method which the poor Congress has
> had to put up with. My own personal bent is all for method and thorough-
> ness. The less I see of these in Congress offices the more I get put out.[4]

He himself was short of money, but spent as much as he could out of his own
pocket on Congress work.[5] He secured authorization from the Working Committee to inspect, personally or by representatives chosen by him, the offices
of the provincial committees and to make recommendation for their improved
working. He also arranged for auditors to visit these offices and examine the
accounts. Almost all the provincial headquarters were inspected and suggestions made for their improvement, and their finances were put in order.

Jawaharlal also, while he sought to avoid public speaking as far as possible
and was not greatly excited by the constructive programme of spinning and
boycott, gave considerable attention to the Congress volunteer corps, the
Hindustani Seva Dal, youth leagues and student organizations. What he
wanted was dedicated young men and women who would organize the peasants and workers and create a mass consciousness in preparation for the

---

[1] 28 December 1928, *Collected Works,* vol. 38, pp. 284-5.
[2] Gandhi to Motilal, 1 February 1929, *Collected Works,* vol. 38, p. 426.
[3] 12 January and 1 February 1929, Ibid., pp. 337 and 423-4.
[4] To Lala Shankarlal, 2 May 1929.
[5] See Sri Prakasa's article in R. Zakaria, *A Study of Nehru* (Bombay, 1959), pp. 328-9.

coming struggle. The main question before the people was that of bread, and when the driving forces of hunger led the poor into the struggle for freedom, then *swaraj* wold be attained.[1] He planned an Indian National Service, at both all-India and provincial levels, and collected funds for building up a cadre of whole-time workers in the United Provinces. He also sought to reactivate the Independence for India League and provide it with an economic and social programme, even though the League had never shown much sign of life and, by the end of the year, there would be no need for a separate pressure group to champion the cause of independence as the whole Congress would be committed to it.

These activities of Jawaharlal alarmed the Government. They regarded the Calcutta resolution, passed primarily to accommodate Jawaharlal and those of his way of thinking, as a clear triumph for extremism. As the ultimatum presented to the British Government was not expected to be complied with, the resolution was a definite declaration that civil disobedience would be started a year later. 'If the experience of the Calcutta Congress is any guide, the decision of future policy appears to be almost entirely with the younger men notably Pandit Jawaharlal Nehru and Babu Subhas Chandra Bose, and on their intentions and activities future developments may be expected largely to depend.'[2] The Government attached greater significance at this time to these efforts of Jawaharlal and his colleagues to rouse the masses and particularly, as they thought, the peasants and the students, to destroy the *raj*, than to the Communist programme to stir up a movement, chiefly among industrial labour, to attack the economic organization of society and aimed directly against employers and only indirectly against imperialism. The Government recognized that the two movements had points of contact and in some respects were closely linked. 'There is a tendency for the political and the Communist revolutionaries to join hands, and Pandit Jawahar Lal Nehru, an extreme nationalist who is at the same time genuinely attracted by some of the Communist doctrines, stands about at the meeting point.'[3] But the tacticians of the Home Department felt that it would be advantageous from their point of view to stress the différences between the Communists and the nationalists.

Communism contains grave dangers for the very classes who support the extreme nationalist movement, and our aim should be to do nothing which will produce an artificial union between the two movements which, if left to themselves, may tend to diverge. This suggests the conclusion that we should be very cautious in taking action against Communism which may rouse for the Communists any general sympathy among the nationalists or provide the nationalists with what they are searching

[1]Speeches-at Delhi, 5 February, and at Lahore, 8 February 1929, S.W., vol. 4, (Delhi, 1973), pp. 1-4.
[2]Home Secretary to all Local Govts., 21 February 1929, Home Dept. Pol. File No. 168 of 1929.
[3]Ibid.

for at the moment, namely a good rallying-cry for an intensive anti-Government agitation.[1]

At first, it was intended merely to prosecute Jawaharlal;[2] but then the Government decided to move on the other front and deal first with the Communists. But rather than try and uproot Communism by attacking Communist organizations throughout India and seeking special powers for this purpose, the Government preferred to arrest the leading Communists in various parts of India and to prosecute them for conspiracy to overthrow British rule. It was hoped to secure a judicial pronouncement which would enable the Government to deal with the further spread of Communism and to prevent the movement recovering from the blow which it had been dealt by the arrest of its leaders; and there might also be the political advantage of convincing the general public that Communism was not the kind of movement that should receive the sympathy of nationalists.[3] Meantime, no action was contemplated against the latter.

The trial of the Communist leaders was staged at Meerut, chosen as the venue in order to avoid a jury, who might jeopardize the chance of a conviction. The Congress, though on principle it did not believe in defence in British courts, promptly formed a defence committee, of which Jawaharlal was a member; and this committee engaged lawyers to appear for the defence. For the first time, and as a very special case, the Congress sanctioned Rs 1,500 for the defence, while Jawaharlal sought financial and other assistance from abroad. Indeed for months there was a widespread belief among the public, shared by both Motilal and Jawaharlal, that Jawaharlal himself would soon be arrested.[4] In the long indictment of Communist activities made by the prosecution, the League against Imperialism was specially mentioned as one of the organizations inspired by the Communists; Jawaharlal's correspondence with Virendranath Chattopadhyaya and others in Europe was regularly intercepted;[5] and the Intelligence Bureau and the Home Department attached great importance to a faked letter from M. N. Roy, in which Jawaharlal was described as the 'liaison agent between Moscow and India'.[6] But after a careful examination of his dossier, the prosecution concluded that there was insufficient evidence against him.[7] A number of letters received by Jawaharlal from abroad were cited by the procecution, but they could find no letters written by him; and though his book on Soviet Russia was placed before the

---

[1] Note of H.G. Haig, Home Secretary, and J. Crerar, Home Member, 4 January 1929, Home Dept. File 18/XVI Pol. and K.W. of 1928.

[2] Note of Haig, 4 January 1929, Home Dept. Pol. File 179/29 of 1929.

[3] See Haig to J.W.A. Langford James, chief prosecution counsel, 29 April 1929, Home Dept. 10/IV/29 Pol. of 1929.

[4] See Jawaharlal to A.C.N. Nambiar, 11 July 1929, AICC File FD 20, part II, 1929.

[5] Home Dept. Pol. File 20/XI of 1929.

[6] Home Dept. Pol. File 18/VII/28, Appendix III to Notes.

[7] J.P. Mitter, junior prosecution counsel in the Meerut case, in *The Sunday Standard,* 21 December 1969.

court, it was realized that a charge based on that alone could hardly stand. The magistrate trying the case served notice on Jawaharlal to produce all the letters received by him from certain persons abroad. Jawaharlal's first reaction, approved by Gandhi, was to refuse, on the principle that the prosecution should not be helped in any way. However, on second thoughts which were clearly encouraged by his father, he replied that he had thrown away or destroyed those letters which he had received in his personal capacity; his correspondence as general secretary of the Congress was to be found in the official files, but these he could disclose only with the permission of the Congress. Motilal was concerned that a further order would follow which would result in a search of the Congress offices and the court securing the papers it wanted, and the locking up of Jawaharlal for six months. 'To my mind Jawahar will only make himself ridiculous by both helping the govt to the fullest extent he can and going to jail for it.'[1] But, in the event, Jawaharlal was only asked to certify that he had no personal correspondence in his possession. Jawaharlal did so, and to avoid his being cited as a witness by the prosecution, Motilal advised the lawyers for the defence not to object to secondary evidence of those letters being produced.[2] Later, when the prosecution wished to call Jawaharlal as a court witness, the magistrate agreed that Jawaharlal seemed to be the representative in India of the League against Imperialism, and his evidence would probably be illuminating; but calling him would not be worth while as it would mean unreasonable delay, and he was anxious that the arguments should begin.[3] So Jawaharlal did not appear in the case, either as witness or as accused.

The lack of direct evidence and the desire to isolate the Communists from the general nationalist movement and not Motilal's alleged influence with the authorities, though he was doubtless greatly relieved, would seem to be the real reasons for the Government's obvious reluctance to drag Jawaharlal into the net. Gandhi, perceptive as usual, saw this from the start. 'It is quite like Jawahar', he wrote to the worried father, 'that he should give up smoking, a fine preparation to face Hailey. I do not know that Hailey will lay his hands upon Jawahar quite so easily as you think.'[4] Though attracted by the ideology of Communism, Jawaharlal was not involved in the activities of the Communist Party. Not, as was clear from the names of quite a few who had been arrested, that the Government had any qualms about involving the innocent. As Jawaharlal is reported to have remarked on his first visit to Meerut jail, 'How little do these accused persons know about the Communist International. I know a lot more than they.'[5] But the Government could secure little direct evidence implicating him, while the Communists themselves felt little accord

[1] Motilal to Gandhi, 4 September 1929, Motilal Nehru papers.
[2] Motilal to K.C. Chakravarty, 10 September 1929, Motilal Nehru papers.
[3] *The Bombay Chronicle,* 13 November 1929.
[4] To Motilal, 17 January 1929, *Collected Works,* vol. 38, p. 361.
[5] Muzaffar Ahmad's introduction in *Communists Challenge Imperialism from the Dock* (Calcutta, 1967).

with one whom they regarded as 'a timid reformist'.[1] The Communist assessment of Jawaharlal at this time was not left in doubt. A writer in the Comintern journal condemned the Independence for India League as 'a superficial intelligentsia organization which in parts had already fascist tendencies' and described Jawaharlal as a person 'who promises all the blessings of socialism without a revolutionary struggle'.[2] Jawaharlal, wrote a British Communist, had

> formed an Independence of India League: and at the same time he is president of the Socialist League of Youth. The Independence of India League is a complete sham. The Socialist League of Youth is a more complete sham; it puts forward most wonderful slogans for Communism and the Dictatorship of the Proletariat and takes no steps to achieve them. They are merely a means for getting support from the proletariat and for stemming the tide of the onward movement . . . It is clear that the British Government knows the difference between young Nehru and the Workers' and Peasants' party, and that the latter cannot look over the hedge, where Jawahar Lal Nehru can steal a horse.[3]

FIVE

It was in this context that Jawaharlal found himself pitchforked by Gandhi and his father into the presidency of the Congress. Motilal had for long wanted his son to secure this high honour, and had discussed it with Gandhi even two years earlier. In 1927 Gandhi had not been enthusiastic and, after consulting Jawaharlal who was then in Europe, had decided in favour of Ansari, in the hope that the latter would improve relations between Hindus and Muslims.

> Things, as they are shaping in the Congress, confirm the opinion that it is not yet time for Jawaharlal to shoulder the burden. He is too high-souled to stand the anarchy and hooliganism that seem to be growing in the Congress, and it would be cruel to expect him to evolve order all of a sudden out of chaos. I am confident, however, that the anarchy will spend itself before long and the hooligans will themselves want a disciplinarian. Jawaharlal will come in then.[4]

The next year Motilal renewed his suggestion and Gandhi was agreeable, but on this occasion the leaders of the Congress in Bengal, where the session was to

[1] Muzaffar Ahmed to P.C. Joshi, 9 March 1929, Meerut Conspiracy Case, Exhibit No. P. 304.
[2] Communist International, May 1929.
[3] R. Page Arnot, How Britain Rules India (London, 1929), pp. 29, 30.
[4] Gandhi to Motilal, 19 June 1927, Collected Works, vol. 34, p. 31.

be held, successfully insisted that Motilal himself should preside. Though the reasons given were local, the real objection, as Jawaharlal saw it, was not youth or jealousy but fear of his radical ideas.[1] In 1929, ten Congress committees voted for Gandhi, five for Vallabhbhai Patel and only three for Jawaharlal.[2] The general feeling was that he was still unseasoned for the presidency. Jawaharlal himself was unwilling.

My own personal inclination always is not to be shackled down to any office. I prefer to be free and to have the time to act according to my own inclinations . . . I represent nobody but myself. I have not the politician's flair for forming groups and parties. My one attempt in this direction — the formation of the Independence for India League last year — was a hopeless failure so far as I was concerned . . . Most people who put me forward for the Presidentship do so because they want to keep someone else out. I am the lesser evil. This kind of negative backing is hardly good enough . . . If I have the misfortune to be president you will see that the very people who put me there, or many of them, will be prepared to cast me to the wolves.[3]

But Gandhi wrung consent out of him and then announced that the crown should be worn by Jawaharlal. Older men had had their innings, and it was but right that the young should be led into battle by one of themselves. Gandhi added, with a candour that was not flattering to his victim, that his relations with the younger man were such that the latter's being in the chair was as good as he himself being in it.[4] Again Jawaharlal begged Gandhi not to press his name,[5] while Motilal, much as he desired his son's election, pointed out to Gandhi that forcing Jawaharlal on the country against its will was unfair to both Jawaharlal and the country.[6] But Gandhi had made up his mind, and on 29 September 1929 the AICC reluctantly elected Jawaharlal to preside over the next session at Lahore in December.

So circumstances, and Gandhi's will, were too strong for Jawaharlal. 'I have been quite clear in my own mind that my election as President would reduce my effectiveness in many directions. But fate has willed it otherwise and I feel in spite of my scientific spirit and outlook that after all we are to some extent playthings of fate.'[7] From the viewpoint of the older leaders, there was a great advantage in having in the chair the malleable founder of the independence movement; his opinions underwrote the genuineness of their inten-

[1] To Syed Mahmud, 30 June 1928.
[2] See AICC File G 100 for 1929-30.
[3] Jawaharlal to Gandhi, 13 July 1929.
[4] Article in *Young India*, 1 August 1929, reprinted in *Collected Works*, vol. 41, pp. 239-41.
[5] Telegram to Gandhi, 21 August 1929. Gandhi Smarak Sangrahalaya P.S. 15496.
[6] 21 August 1929, *Collected Works*, vol. 41, p. 305n.
[7] To S.A. Brelvi, 7 October 1929, AICC File G 40(ii), Part III, 1929.

tion to start civil disobedience, even while they could be confident that he would be amenable, if need be, to Gandhi's persuasion. On the other hand, Jawaharlal's colleagues in the League against Imperialism expected that he would use his position to split the Congress and carry the country with a fully revolutionary programme.[1] Only Jawaharlal knew his predicament, that he would be torn between his loyalty to Gandhi and the Congress organization on the one side, and his ideological leanings on the other. As he wrote to an old friend, 'I am afraid I shall have my work cut out for me to avoid losing all my cheerfulness and light-heartedness.'[2]

The testing-time was not long in coming. Jawaharlal was getting ready for civil disobedience. 'Already the blood tingles in the veins and the call to the field of action becomes louder and louder.'[3] But the lines of battle were suddenly blurred by the Viceroy's statement, on his return from Britain at the end of October, that the British Government would meet representatives of British India and the Indian States for securing the greatest possible measure of agreement for the final proposals to be submitted to Parliament and that the natural issue of India's constitutional progress was the attainment of Dominion Status. This in itself meant nothing, but Gandhi was convinced of Lord Irwin's sincerity[4] and associated the Congress with the Liberals and others in what he regarded as a reciprocation of this sincerity. The Delhi manifesto offered co-operation to the British provided the Government adopted a policy of general conciliation, political prisoners were granted a general amnesty, progressive political organizations were adequately represented at the conference with the Congress being given predominance, and it was understood that the conference was not for discussing when Dominion Status was to be established but to frame a scheme of a Dominion constitution suitable for India's needs.

Despite these provisos, however, the manifesto marked a retreat by the Congress. Far from preparing for a struggle for independence, or even from insisting on a full acceptance of the Nehru Report, it was, under Gandhi's guidance, thinking in terms of negotiations with the British Government without the latter making any precise commitments beforehand. Jawaharlal fought hard, if he could not secure rejection of the Viceroy's proposals, at least to stiffen the terms offered by the Congress: but he failed, and then, to the surprise of his friends, signed the manifesto. Subhas Bose, who had refused to sign, saw in this the triumph of Gandhi's personality over Jawaharlal's principles. 'Jawaharlal has now given up Independence at the instance of the Mahatma.'[5] In fact, Jawaharlal had not changed his views but was persuaded to sign by appeals to his sense of discipline. It was urged that as a member of the Working Committee

[1] See, e.g., V. Chattopadhyaya to Jawaharlal, 28 August 1929, AICC File F.D. 1(ii), Part I, 1929.
[2] To Shivaprasad Gupta, 1 October 1929, AICC File F.D. 1 (ii), Part III, 1929.
[3] To Master Tara Singh, 10 October 1929, AICC File G 93 of 1929.
[4] Article in *Young India,* 7 November 1929.
[5] To Mrs C.R. Das, 5 November 1929, S.C. Bose, *Correspondence 1924-32* (Calcutta, 1967), p. 403.

Arrests after the massacre at Amritsar, 1919

9 Jawaharlal, aged 32, as leader of the peasants, 1921

10 Edward, Prince of Wales, aged 28, during his tour to India, 1922

British rule in India: the Prince of Wales receiving gifts from the Maharajah of Kolhapur, 1921

The Prince of Wales visiting Malakand Pass, 1922

13 Gandhi spinning at a demonstration in Calcutta, 1925

14 Rioting in Bombay, 1929

and general secretary he was bound to carry out the wishes of the majority of the members. But having done so, he resigned both his membership and the secretaryship,[1] and seriously considered abdicating from the presidency. 'I am myself a believer in discipline. And yet I suppose there can be too much of discipline. Something seems to have snapped inside me evening before last and I am unable to piece it together.'[2]

However, Gandhi, Motilal, Ansari and others persuaded Jawaharlal to hold his hand, mainly on the ground that he could rely on the British not to accept the four provisos stipulated by the Congress;[3] and on 19 November the Working Committee, while confirming the Delhi manifesto, revised Gandhi's draft resolution to say, obviously to placate Jawaharlal, that it should be clearly understood that this confirmation would only hold till the next session of the Congress.[4] Jawaharlal was greatly relieved. 'It is clear enough that there is not an outside chance of the British Government acceding to the four conditions laid down, so that even moderate Congressmen will have no alternative left except to stick to independence.'[5] By giving some rope to those who favoured a compromise, the ground for the coming struggle was being better prepared. The Government, even if they could not accept the Nehru Report, could still perhaps have retained Gandhi's co-operation by some gesture such as the release of prisoners;[6] for to Gandhi, as Hailey observed,[7] Dominion Status was not a constitutional objective but a frame of mind, 'a general kind of political kiss-in-the ring'. But imagination was not among the virtues of Irwin's Government, and by the middle of December Gandhi was thinking in terms of being in prison by January.[8] When he and Motilal met the Viceroy along with Sapru, Jinnah and Vithalbhai Patel on 23 December, the break was clear. Gandhi announced that unless the establishment of Dominion Status could be presumed as an immediate result of the conference he could not attend; not Parliament but India ought to frame India's future. He added that he doubted the sincerity of British purpose broadly, though he recognized that of individuals; and the Viceroy replied that there was obviously no common ground.[9] The focus of attention now shifted to Lahore.

[1] To President AICC 4 November 1929, AICC File G-117 of 1929.

[2] To Gandhi, 4 November 1929, reprinted in Collected Works, vol. 42, Appendix II, p. 516.

[3] Gandhi's telegram 6 November and letter, 18 November 1929, Collected Works, vol. 42, pp. 101 and 181, respectively; Ansari to Jawaharlal, 7 November 1929, Ansari papers, Jamia Millia; Motilal to Jawaharlal, 7 November 1929, Motilal Nehru papers.

[4] The Leader, 20 November 1929.

[5] To S. Srinivasa Iyengar, 20 November 1929, AICC File G 117 of 1929.

[6] Sapru to Irwin, 25 November (after meeting Gandhi) and Hailey to Irwin 4 December 1929. Halifax papers, I.O.L. Mss.Eur C 152, vol. 23.

[7] Hailey to Irwin, 4 December 1929, Halifax papers, vol. 23.

[8] See his letter to Ramanand Chatterjee, 16 December 1929, Collected Works, vol. 42, p. 285.

[9] Minutes of conversations drafted by Private Secretary to Viceroy, Sapru papers, I 19.

SIX

Jawaharlal had, therefore, been vindicated. He had had his way by yielding in the first instance. The hope of the officials that the Viceroy's statement might split the Congress[1] had been defeated. But though Jawaharlal's nationalist followers in India now had no grievance, he had still to contend with his radical friends abroad. Convinced by the frequent references to the League against Imperialism in the Central Assembly during the debates on the Public Safety Bill and by the proceedings at Meerut that the Government was making a dead set against the League, Jawaharlal took much trouble during the summer of 1929 to prove to the public that the League was not a Communist organization, even though many Communists belonged to it, but rather an association to establish contacts between all movements throughout the world which supported the struggle against imperialism. If a broader and more international vision was gradually animating the Congress, this was the direct consequence of its association with the League. Communists were undoubtedly the strongest opponents of imperialism and as such their co-operation was welcome to all nationalists. They need not be treated as untouchables. Co-operation with them — as with imperialist powers other than the British like the United States — was possible when interests coincided, though this co-operation should be on one's own terms. But Jawaharlal was certain that in no sense did Communists dominate the League. Nor was the Congress, which was merely associated with the League, bound by every resolution or programme of that organization.

This confidence of Jawaharlal was shaken by the end of the year when he heard that the Communists had taken over the central apparatus of the League and muzzled non-Communists like James Maxton. Clearly he himself would have no place in the League, and the organization as he had conceived it, the grand all-party alliance between the forces of national freedom and social equality, had collapsed. So it caused him no great concern that those now in charge of the League disapproved of his acceptance of the Delhi manifesto.

> It is a fundamental political error to think that unity in the Congress is more important than the vital interests of the masses. After having risen to be the undoubted leader of the youth of the country and to enjoy even the confidence of the working masses, you seem in a moment of inexplicable weakness and mental confusion to have left your followers in the lurch.[2]

Possibly Jawaharlal was rationalizing his weakness and proneness to what Subhas Bose termed 'sentimental politics' into a claim to superior tactics and

[1] See, for example, Hailey to O'Dwyer, 4 October and 15 December and to Irwin, 7 October and 18 November 1929, Hailey papers, vol. 16.
[2] V. Chattopadhyaya to Jawaharlal, 4 December 1929.

to permitting events so to develop as to stress the unavoidability of a clash with the Government; but in doing so he was certainly not distressed by the rebukes of the Communists. Rather, he would seem to have been reinforced in his conviction that the political struggle for freedom demanded the first priority, and that in this the leadership of Gandhi was the most powerful individual factor. Future success seemed to him to lie in acceptance of this rather than in co-operation with the Communists. And his first ill-fated experiment of working with the Communists suggested to him that equal co-operation with them was not to be too easily taken for granted.

So the decks were clear, and Jawaharlal was free to act as he chose, neither held back by his moderate colleagues nor pushed off course by his erstwhile friends of the left. In the last week of November, before his gamble had paid off, he presided at Nagpur over the annual session of the All-India Trade Union Congress. Elected the previous year in his absence, Jawaharlal had agreed to serve because, although he had no experience of trade unionism, he realized the importance of awakening industrial labour to the national cause. But during his year in office he could hardly devote himself to this effort in education. While the Government, by their legislation and summary arrests and trials, mounted a massive attack against the whole labour movement, the latter was riven by sharp differences between the Communists and the rest; and Jawaharlal had to toil hard — and, as it proved, in vain — merely to hold the movement together. The moderates in the Trade Union Congress, led by the general secretary, N. M. Joshi, were anxious to isolate labour from political currents in India and abroad and to improve working conditions in industry by co-operating with the Government. Jawaharlal, of course, reacted instinctively against this, and in consequence was regarded as acting in accord with the Communists. Jawaharlal feared that a split was inevitable, but sought not to precipitate it.[1] However, the advent to office of the British Labour Party in the summer of 1929 strengthened the moderate trade unionists in their eagerness to co-operate, and increased the differences within the movement. Jawaharlal was requested by the radicals to accept the presidentcy of the largest railway trade union, that of the Great Indian Peninsular in Bombay, which was dominated by the Communists, and although he already had as much work as he could manage he was willing to consider acceptance if it would help in securing a compromise.[2] The fact that the Communists were criticizing Jawaharlal as one of the 'dangerous enemies of labour'[3] might have been expected to make his name acceptable to conservative trade unionists; but in fact the suggestion fell through.

The criticism itself was obviously unjustified. Jawaharlal was primarily involved in politics, and his basic loyalty was to the Congress; and that was, of

[1] Jawaharlal to C.B. Johri, 12 July 1929, AICC File P/20 of 1929.
[2] To Johri, 25 August 1929, AICC File G 40, Part III of 1929 and to D.B. Kulkarni, 10 September 1929, AICC File 16 of 1929.
[3] Article in *G.I.P. Railwayman,* see Jawaharlal's letter to Kulkarni, 10 September 1929.

course, far from being a purely labour organization. But in problems concerning the workers, there was no doubt as to where his sympathies lay; and in the struggle for trade union leadership, he threw his weight against the moderates. To the chagrin of these men, who wished to co-operate with the Royal Commission on Labour appointed by the Government, Jawaharlal publicly called for a boycott.[1] There was such acrimony that Jawaharlal thought of resigning the presidency, but decided that, with the year drawing to its close, it was not worth while.[2]

It was in this atmosphere of dissension, with both sides so suspicious of each other that they sparred fiercely even on such trivial issues as the dates of meetings, that the Trade Union Congress met for its annual session. Jawaharlal's address was wholly acceptable to neither faction, but true to himself. He placed the responsibility for the miserable condition of the Indian worker on the system which was the natural outcome of capitalism and imperialism, and called on labour to join the national movement in its fight against imperialism even while it sought to recruit nationalists in its own struggle against capitalism. The real problem was the conquest of power, the overthrow of both the foreign ruler and the exploiting employer, and the goal was a socialist order of society in which the interests of the workers were supreme and the sources of wealth were owned by the community and not by individuals.

All this was most pleasing to the Communists in his audience, but then Jawaharlal concluded with the suggestion that the Trade Union Congress should affiliate itself to neither the Second nor the Third International. The Second International was disliked by Jawaharlal because it was mainly preoccupied with the fight not against capitalism but against Communism; but the Third International had for Jawaharlal its own drawbacks. Personally he was a staunch admirer of the general trend of policy in the Soviet Union; that country, despite all its heavy blunders and many sins, still held out, more than any other country, the bright promise of a better day to the world at large and to the worker especially.

> With all my sympathy for the Communist view point, however, I must confess that I do not appreciate many of their methods. The history of the past few years in China and elsewhere has shown that these methods have failed and often brought reaction in their train. To affiliate with the Third International must mean an adoption of their methods in their entirety. I do not think this is desirable for us.

These sentences the moderates applauded. But if they saw in this rejection of the leadership of Moscow an indication that the president would support them in the wrangles of detail, they were soon disillusioned. Indeed, his only positive

[1] Statement, 20 September 1929, S.W., vol. 3, pp. 41-2.
[2] To Bakhale, 24 September 1929, AICC File 16 of 1929.

act shifted the bias of the whole session. For by his casting vote Jawaharlal recognized the Girni Kamgar (Red Flag) Union of the textile workers in Bombay as having a membership of 40,000, thus giving it and the G.I.P. Railway Union, both controlled by the Communists, a majority, under the constitution of the Trade Union Congress, in the open sessions. Otherwise, he sat silent at the meetings of the Executive Committee while resolutions were passed rejecting the Nehru Report, condemning the Delhi manifesto, favouring independence as against Dominion Status, demanding the establishment of a workers' republic and calling for affiliation with the League against Imperialism. The fact that he and the Congress were still committed to negotiations for Dominion Status does not seem to have bothered him, while his inner hesitations about the League found no expression. It was not so much that Jawaharlal saw his role as president to be akin to that of a figurehead as that, whatever his public posture, he privately approved of most of these decisions. He also made no strong effort to prevent the secession of the moderates and the formation of a separate All-India Trade Union Federation.

If at Nagpur Jawaharlal had to connive at the rejection of policies to which he was still officially committed, at Lahore at the end of the year he was utterly unshackled. Riding, with his sense of theatre, on a white charger in the Congress procession, he fitted to perfection, as Gandhi had prophesied, the role of the young Galahad of revolt. The Congress was by now committed to independence and to civil disobedience. The Viceroy, it is said,[1] had at one stage considered banning the session, but finally decided not to interfere. Such action, even if ostensibly in the interests of maintaining law and order in the city, would have been foolhardy. There was, as an impartial eye-witness noted, no spirit of animosity to the British but a love of India. confidence in their leaders 'and a new spirit of sacrifice dominant in their thought even to the point of suffering and loss'.[2] The same conclusion was reached by an English observer who was normally an ardent Imperialist: 'The present movement is a deep all-India affair. It's no use pretending that it is the concern of the Indian "Intelligentsia" ... Time and education can only intensify the feeling of thinking Indians for India: and the love for the *idea of India* is one of the finest, and also one of the most incalculable forces in the country.'[3] Jawaharlal's speech was attuned to this atmosphere of defiance and rebellion. He had begun to draft his presidential address about the tenth of December,[4] but even then he could write with the full knowledge that the talks with the Viceroy had no prospect of success.

Jawaharlal put the Indian problem in its international context. The whole world was one vast question-mark, and every country and every people were in

[1] A. Campbell Johnson, *Viscount Halifax* (London, 1941). p. 241.

[2] Report of Emily Kinnaird, 8 January 1930, enclosure to Wedgwood Benn's letter, 5 March 1930, Halifax papers, vol. 6.

[3] J.L.Morison from Lahore to Dr Norman Leys, 11 January 1930. T. Jones, *Whitehall Diary*, vol. 2 (London, 1969), pp. 238-40.

[4] See letters to Dr Gopichand, 6, 10 and 14 December 1929, AICC File G 100 of 1929-30.

the melting-pot. It appeared to be a dissolving period of history, when the world was in labour, and out of her travail would give birth to a new order. In this Asia and even India would play a determining part, for the brief day of European domination was already approaching its end and the future lay with America and Asia. But if India had a message to give to the world, she had also much to learn and receive from other peoples.

Then, reverting to India, Jawaharlal pointed out that though her social structure had proved to be wonderfully stable, it had failed in one vital particular: it had found no solution for the problem of equality and in fact had deliberately based itself on inequality. But a solution based on the genius of the Indian people and on India's thought and culture had to be found if the political and social structure was to have any stability and the discords between the various communities were to disappear. And this led Jawaharlal to plead for the faith and generosity which would remove fear and suspicion between the communities. ' . . . by right of birth I shall venture to submit to the leaders of the Hindus that it should be their privilege to take the lead in generosity.' That was not only good morals but often good politics and sound expediency. The time was coming soon when such labels as Hindus, Muslims and Sikhs would have little meaning, and when struggles would be on an economic basis. Till then it mattered little what mutual arrangements were made, provided only that barriers in the way of future progress were not built up.

The British army of occupation, Jawaharlal went on, held India in its iron grip, and the whip of the master was ever ready to come down on the best of them who raised their heads. The answer to the Calcutta resolution had been clear and definite. Only by the greatest stretch of imagination could the Viceroy's statement be interpreted as a possible response, but he and others like him had signed the Delhi manifesto because even an outside chance of honourable peace had to be taken before launching on a national struggle. But now they had but one goal — independence, complete freedom from British domination, which alone could lead to world co-operation and an international community of equals. The British Empire was certainly not such a group; it could not be a true commonwealth so long as imperialism was its basis and the exploitation of other races its chief means of sustenance. In any such group, India's position was bound to be one of subservience. Out of imperialism and capitalism peace could never come, and because the British Empire stood for these and based itself on the exploitation of the masses India could find no willing place in it. Many of the problems India had to face were the problems of vested interests, mostly created or encouraged by the British Government; and so long as the British Empire continued, in whatever shape, in India it would strengthen these vested interests and create more.

The controversy about the relative merits of independence and Dominion Status was to Jawaharlal really a question about the conquest of power, and he did not think that any form of Dominion Status applicable to India would transfer real power. A test of this power would be the entire withdrawal of the alien army of occupation and of its economic control. India demanded the fullest freedom. They were very conscious of their weakness, but let no one underrate the strength of their resolve. There would be no turning back. A great nation could not be thwarted for long when once its mind was made up.

'I must frankly confess', Jawaharlal continued, 'that I am a Socialist and a republican, and am no believer in kings and princes, or in the order which produces the modern kings of industry, who have greater power over the lives and fortunes of men than even the kings of old, and whose methods are as predatory as those of the old feudal aristocracy.' He acknowledged that the Congress, as it was then constituted, might not be able to adopt a full socialistic programme, but the philosophy of socialism had gradually permeated the entire structure of society the world over, and almost the only points in dispute were the pace and the methods of advance. India too would have to go that way if she wished to end poverty and inequality, though she might evolve her own methods and adapt the ideal to her own genius.

On the two particular problems of India, the minorities and the states, Jawaharlal had little that was startlingly new to say. He wanted the minorities to be given the fullest assurances that their culture and traditions would be safe. The princes were the products of a vicious system which would ultimately have to go. Only the people of the states could determine the future of those areas, and while the Congress was perfectly willing to confer with such rulers as were prepared to do so and to devise means for smoothing the transition, in no event could the people of the states be ignored. But, as regards the problem of peasantry and labour, Jawaharlal asked the Congress to commit itself to ending the domination of any one class over another, and to draw up a programme of such changes as could be immediately put into operation. Paternalism and trusteeship were both equally barren theories. The least that every worker in field or factory was entitled to was a minimum wage and humane hours of labour; and in the long term the Congress should strive for workers' control of industry on a co-operative basis and for a system of peasant proprietorship.

The immediate problem, however, was the conquest of power, and the forging of sanctions to enforce the national will. The Congress had not the material or the training for organized violence, and individual and sporadic violence was a confession of despair.

> The great majority of us, I take it, judge the issue not on moral but on practical grounds, and if we reject the way of violence it is because it promises no substantial results. But if this Congress or the nation at any future time comes to the conclusion that methods of violence will rid us of slavery then I have no doubt that it will adopt them. Violence is bad, but slavery is far worse.

Gandhi himself had said that it was better to fight than to refuse to fight out of cowardice. But except in times of organized revolt, all mass movements must necessarily be peaceful. The basic idea of non-co-operation must remain, but

Jawaharlal did not think it wise to declare a boycott of schools and law courts at the very start. The programme should be one of political and economic boycott, the reduction of all points of contact with the British Government. This would release energy and direct attention to the real struggle, which should take the shape of non-payment of taxes and, where possible, general strikes. It was now an Open Conspiracy, which everyone should join, to free the country from foreign rule.

The presidential address shows both the strength and the weakness of Jawaharlal at this stage. His impatient and full-blooded eagerness for freedom was manifest. He had no use for political compromise. He wished to eject the British from India and thereafter cut his country off from the British Empire. In the campaign of civil disobedience which was to begin he accepted the leadership of Gandhi, but made it clear that he accepted non-violence as a technique rather than as a moral end in itself, and did not rule out the adoption of violent methods at any future time. There was still very much of the romantic in Jawaharlal; he was still, beneath the added maturity and sophistication, the emotional nationalist of the early twenties. The impact of ideology to which he had been exposed during his stay in Europe in 1926 and 1927 could be clearly seen, but it was not deep absorption. With courage he announced that he was a socialist and a republican, but it was courage tinged with apology. The socialism which he envisaged was clearly of a mild and timid variety, and he spoke of India evolving her own methods and adjusting it to her traditions. There was little here of forthright Marxism or of the scientific socialism of which he had heard so much in Europe. He was groping more in the direction of Utopian, Gandhian socialism, though he went on to criticize the concepts of trusteeship. Similarly, while he realized that the basic problem in India was an economic one and communal troubles were artificial, he spoke of finding an interim solution which would be typically Indian. The confusion of thought was probably the result of a dislike of precise choice, an instinctive reluctance to abandon Indian ways even while his mind turned away from them, and the feeling of a lack of immediacy about these matters. They all had to give way to the conquest of power, and for this the Congress was the obvious instrument. He added almost in the same breath as his assertion of his personal credo that he did not expect the Congress, with its predominantly middle-class composition, to agree with him or to adopt a revolutionary programme. His loyalty to the Congress being unreserved, this could only mean that, while he would not abandon his principles, he would be willing to keep them in abeyance. His extremism in objectives did not carry with it an intensity of purpose and method. So, while the leader-writers of the British and the Indian press threw up their hands in horror at this enthronement by the sedate Congress of a seeming revolutionary, for Gandhi there was no dismay. He did not forget that the author of this radical address was also a signatory of the Delhi manifesto and that to Jawaharlal discipline was more important than revolution and political freedom took priority over economic and social change. There was little to fear from a man whom Gandhi described as a confirmed socialist who wanted for his country only what it could manage, a practical statesman who tempered his ideals to suit his surroundings.[1] On the other hand, it was worth having in the chair a figure of glamour and integrity who would keep captive within the Congress his wide following among the students and the intelligentsia. During the next ten years, no single individual did more to build in the Congress an awareness of economic issues; but Jawaharlal was also the best shield of the Congress against left-wing groups and organizations.

[1] *Young India,* 9 January 1930.

10

Action — and Anti-Climax

After the Lahore Congress, however, Jawaharlal could push aside these nagging problems of the gap between thought and practice and devote himself happily to action. He had, at a moving ceremony on the banks of the Ravi, unfurled the flag of independence; and on New Year's Eve he danced round the flagpole.[1] The Congress now urged its members to work exclusively towards the attainment of independence. It also authorized the AICC, whenever it deemed fit, to start a programme of civil disobedience, including the non-payment of taxes, in selected areas or all over the country and under whatever safeguards it considered necessary; but in fact this meant that full direction in the tactics of struggle was left to Gandhi.

While Gandhi brooded over the best means of initiating the battle, Jawaharlal, as president, was engrossed in mobilizing the forces, though he expected to be arrested at any moment. In fact, the Punjab Government had suggested prosecuting Jawaharlal for his Lahore address, but the Government of India preferred to wait and watch developments, leaving the initiative to the Congress.[2] So Jawaharlal was free to organize the celebration throughout India of 26 January as Independence Day, when everyone was called upon to take the independence pledge drafted by Gandhi and Jawaharlal. The latter had directed that this should be done in the morning, at the time of the unfurling of the national flag, with a procession and a public meeting later in the day;[3] but Gandhi vetoed processions and speeches. He was anxious not to precipitate a crisis till he was ready to commence civil disobedience.[4] The Government, on their part, as anxious to avoid a clinch, did not prohibit the meetings. On the actual day, the response seemed to the Congress spectacular, while the Government preferred to believe that outside the

[1] To A. C. Bombwal, 5 June 1963, Nehru papers.
[2] Chief Secretary Punjab Government to Home Secretary, 3 January 1930, and Home Secretary to all Local Governments, 30 January 1930. Home Dept. Pol. File 98 of 1930; Note of Home Secretary, 27 January 1930, and Home Secretary to Chief Secretary, Punjab, 30 January 1930. Home Dept. Pol. File 65 of 1930.
[3] Statement, 6 January, *The Tribune*, 8 January 1930.
[4] Gandhi to Jawaharlal, 12 January 1930, AICC File 26 of 1930.

Punjab, the United Provinces, Bombay and Delhi there had been little enthusiasm. [1]

With the Government refusing to act on their own, with Gandhi still inert, and with both sides satisfied with the result, Jawaharlal was free to continue the work of consolidation in anticipation of the big struggle. The incident at Bombay on the 26th, when some mill-workers sought to displace the national tricolour with the red flag, coming in the wake of continuous efforts by the League against Imperialism to ridicule the Congress and its leadership, clearly infuriated Jawaharlal. 'It seems to be a deliberate policy of Communists to be offensive. As a matter of fact there are very few real Communists in India. Many people who pose as such are British agents.'[2] He informed the League and its supporters in India in no uncertain terms that the Congress would not allow its ranks to be weakened by the Communists. While the Congress was willing to co-operate with Communists or to be associated with any anti-imperialist organization, in no event would it take orders from the League or be associated with it if that were going to function as a purely Communist organization. Never had the Congress been more advanced in its views, both political and social, and to attack its leaders without the least knowledge of conditions in India at a moment when they had begun a great revolutionary struggle was in effect to help the British Government. Jawaharlal also requested the League to accept his resignation from its Executive Council if the position of non-Communists in the League were not clarified.[3]

Having done what he could to answer the Communist critics, Jawaharlal sought to ensure the support of the minorities, and especially the Muslims, for the Congress cause. Leading Muslim Congressmen, including Ansari, Tassaduq Sherwani and Khaliquzzaman (but with the honourable exception of Azad), disliked the non-co-operation campaign,[4] and gave priority to the building of communal harmony. In the Working Committee, which met on 15 February, Syed Mahmud asserted that the Muslims as a whole were indifferent to the struggle and he feared that civil disobedience would rapidly, with official encouragement, degenerate into Hindu-Muslim riots. Gandhi was reported to have replied that he realized this danger but it could not be helped. They had to march ahead, as there was no other alternative.[5] Till now they had failed in achieving Hindu-Muslim unity because they had been working on

---

[1] Statement of Jawaharlal, 28 January, *The Tribune,* 30 January 1930; Home Department's telegram to Secretary of State, 5 February 1930, cited in S. Gopal, *The Viceroyalty of Lord Irwin* (Oxford, 1957), p. 55.

[2] To Edo Fimmen, 4 March 1930.

[3] To Secretaries, League against Imperialism, 30 January 1930.

[4] See Ansari to Sherwani, 6 January, and to Gandhi, 10 and 13 February 1930; Khaliquzzaman to Ansari, 1 March 1930; and Sherwani to Ansari, 3 March 1930, Ansari papers; M. Desai, *Maulana Abul Kalam Azad* (Indian edition, 1945), p. 60.

[5] Mahmud to Ansari, undated but written after meeting of Working Committee, Ansari papers.

wrong lines; they should seek it on an economic basis and in the course of the fight for freedom. This would also sterilize the third party, the British.[1] But Jawaharlal was more sensitive than Gandhi or his father to the fears of the minorities and recommended assurances that under no circumstances would any coercion or repression of these communities be tolerated and, in fact, favoured treatment in economic matters would be guaranteed. Political representation should also be on economic lines, as this would fit in far more with modern conditions and do away automatically with communal electorates. The Nehru Report had lapsed, but its non-controversial parts were still binding on the Congress; and Jawaharlal hoped that its role in the fight for freedom would convince all of its *bona fides*.[2]

Meanwhile, the Working Committee authorized Gandhi to start civil disobedience as and when he desired, and advocated, once the mass movement had started, a boycott of law courts and schools. By now Gandhi had at last seen his way ahead, and decided to march to the sea and violate the salt laws. Jawaharlal had not been enamoured of the eleven points earlier put forward by Gandhi. Prohibition, reduction of land revenue, military expenditure and high salaries, abolition of the salt tax, lowering of the exchange ratio of the rupee, licences for firearms, tariffs on foreign textiles, reservation of coastal shipping, a political amnesty and abolition of the secret police had seemed to him to comprise a tame definition of independence. He himself had been thinking in terms of public ownership of the principal industries, peasant proprietorship, annulment of agricultural indebtedness, a minimum wage, a steeply graduated income tax, high death duties, and no indirect taxation.[3] But law-breaking was invigorating in itself, and his support for Gandhi now was without any mental reservation. 'How I wish I could join your gallant band or at least could see it start off bravely on the morning of the 12th.'[4] Gandhi's march to the sea at Dandi, with a small group of tough and disciplined men and women, has a high place, as fact and as legend, in the history of the Indian freedom movement and, indeed, of freedom in the world. The challenge gripped the imagination in India and beyond, and the refusal of Irwin's Government to arrest Gandhi in the belief that the march would evoke no response showed how little they were aware of the true situation. Thousands lined the route, large meetings were held at every halting-place, and many village and district officials resigned, while the rest of India was enthralled by every detail of Gandhi's progress. Jawaharlal with a few friends went down to Gujarat and marched with Gandhi for one stage, and the impression left on him was profound and permanent. Over twenty years later he wrote:[5]

[1] Gandhi to Ansari, 16 February, and Motilal to Ansari, 17 February 1930, Ansari papers.
[2] The Problem of Minorities', 14 March 1930, reprinted in *Young India*, 15 May 1930.
[3] Resolution at meeting of U.P. Congress Committee, 26 February 1930, *The Leader*, 1 March 1930.
[4] Jawaharlal to Gandhi, 7 March 1930.
[5] 30 June 1951. Foreword to Tendulkar, *Mahatma*, vol. 1 (Bombay, 1951).

Many pictures rise in my mind of this man, whose eyes were often full of laughter and yet were pools of infinite sadness. But the picture that is dominant and most significant is as I saw him marching, staff in hand, to Dandi on the Salt March in 1930. He was the pilgrim on his quest of truth, quiet, peaceful, determined and fearless, who would continue that quiet pilgrimage regardless of consequences.

After this experience it was not perhaps to be expected that, whatever the ideological and temperamental strains, Jawaharlal would ever completely break away from his leader.

As the Government had not arrested Gandhi, Jawaharlal and other Congressmen could only wait impatiently till he reached the sea and collected salt before themselves launching a mass campaign of civil disobedience by violating the salt laws. Jawaharlal appealed especially to the young to be ready to jump into the fray,[1] and persuaded the Congress committee in his own province to look ahead and organize wherever possible a campaign for non-payment of land revenue or rent.[2] He toured intensively in the villages and was filled with confidence by the spirit among the peasants.

There is no doubt that India is awake and astir and we are going to give a good fight to the British Government. The Government will no doubt try its utmost to break us. But it is quite likely that in attempting to crack the nut the cracker itself may break. Somehow I cannot help thinking that the days of the British Empire are numbered now and that it is going to be our privilege and good fortune to help to end it.[3]

On 6 April, Jallianwala Bagh Day, Gandhi manufactured salt and Jawaharlal called on the country to go ahead with mass civil disobedience. He himself took charge of the campaign in Allahabad district. As there was no possibility here of manufacturing salt, technical breaches were organized for inviting arrest. On the 9th he sold packets of contraband salt in the city, and the next day he and his wife led a large procession and collected salt from a special kind of earth brought in for the purpose. 'I have never seen Allahabad quite so excited.'[4] But the U.P. Government, though authorized by the Government of India to arrest Jawaharlal if need be,[5] declined to do so on this occasion because, in what Jawaharlal termed 'an amazingly idiotic'[6] communiqué, it concluded that salt had not been manufactured but brought in bottles. There-

[1] 'Inquilab Zindabad', 24 March 1930, published in *Young India*, 3 April 1930; 'The AICC', 23 March 1930, published in *Young India*, 27 March 1930.
[2] *The Leader*, 19 March 1930.
[3] To Roger Baldwin, 4 April 1930.
[4] To Sitla Sahai, 11 April 1930.
[5] Home Department telegram to Governor U.P., 4 April 1930. Home Dept. Pol. File 249 and KW of 1930.
[6] To Syed Mahmud, 11 April 1930.

after Jawaharlal organized the collection of salt in various parts of the city as well as in vehicles, making salt in them and selling it with appropriate songs. More worrying to the Government was his activity in the Rae Bareli district and the formation of associations among the tenants for non-payment of rent.[1] On the 14th, while on his way to Raipur to attend a local Congress conference, Jawaharlal was arrested at Cheoki, a few miles outside Allahabad, tried in Naini jail and sentenced to six months' simple imprisonment for assisting in the manufacture of salt on 11 April.

'Great Day!' Jawaharlal wrote in his pocket diary the day the prison gates shut on him. He was placed in solitary confinement in a barrack reserved for dangerous prisoners and surrounded by a circular wall nearly fifteen feet high. To Jawaharlal this gave a greater sense of captivity than any rectangular enclosure; for, apart from creating a feeling of being closed in, it cut off a good bit of the sky in the day and the stars at night — the sight of which was one of Jawaharlal's chief pleasures in prison. 'What a terrible waste of brick and mortar,' he wrote in his diary,[2] 'just to deprive people of their liberty! A very decent, large-sized house could be built out of the materials of my particular wall only.'

Jawaharlal had been placed in the 'A' class, which meant that once a fortnight he could have one interview, write one letter and receive one. As a special concession, he was allowed to sleep outside his cell, but his bed was chained to the wall to prevent it being used for scaling the wall. He could also receive two weeklies, one in English and the other in Hindi, but no daily newspapers. A fellow-prisoner was deputed to cook for him, and he was in addition permitted to receive food and fruit from home. He was also allotted some servants to work the *punkha* fan. But Jawaharlal chafed at these privileges, especially as news reached him that others in prison for salt *satyagraha* were being treated harshly. So he dispensed with the *punkha* boys, and wrote to the jail superintendent, much against his father's wishes, that he did not desire any special treatment.[3] Told in reply that it was always open to him not to utilize these privileges, he returned some sweets sent from home and asked that no more fruit be sent.

Even the weekly budget of news that trickles through the massive walls and iron gates of Naini prison, by means of the Hindi *Bharat,* is enough to give some idea of happenings outside. Frequent firings, assaults, martial law, flogging of boys, imprisonment of women and so on and so forth denote a state of affairs that is very far from normal, and in this state it is difficult for me to accept with pleasure dainty articles of food. The very sight of these dainties has the reverse of an agreeable effect on me. If Naini prison prevents me from doing something when barbarities are

[1] Hailey to Hirtzel, 8 May 1930, Hailey papers, vol. 19.
[2] Entry 16 April 1930.
[3] 4 May 1930.

being committed all over the country, at least I cannot hold high festival here.[1]

He decided to have two light, simple meals and no more, and as a result often went hungry.

Worse than the hunger, however, was the boredom. Life in prison was about as uneventful as that of the average turnip.

The object of jail appears to be first to remove such traces of humanity as a man might possess, and then to subdue even the animal element in him so that ultimately he might become the perfect vegetable! Soil-bound, cut off from the world and its activity, nothing to look forward to, blind obedience the only 'virtue' that is instilled, and spirit considered the great sin — is it any wonder that the prisoner approximates to the plant?[2]

To evade this ennui, Jawaharlal organized his life to a rigorous schedule. Up with the dawn, after a run of about a mile beside the main prison wall and a brisk walk for the same distance, Jawaharlal spent the remainder of the day mostly in spinning, weaving and reading. Since at first he was not allowed a *charka*, Jawaharlal, keen on some form of manual labour, took up *newar* weaving and continued it even later. But as a disciplined Congressman his main interest was in hand-spinning.[3]

Jawaharlal was allowed only six books at a time, and there was some uncertainty as to whether this included reference works and dictionaries and whether a multi-volume work counted as one book or more. So Jawaharlal had to give up the idea of continuing his letters to Indira, tracing the history of man. In 1928, when she was in Mussoorie and he was wandering in the plains, he had written to her giving in brief outline the origins of the earth, the beginnings of life and human prehistory. He had got as far as the formation of classes, the development of organized religion and the coming of the Aryans, when he had been forced by the stress of public affairs to discontinue.[4] Now, in prison, though time was not lacking, he needed more books and probably even missed the inspiration: 'my mind was too full of the making of history, as it was being made from day to day in India, for me to think of the dead past.'[5] But he read much and made copious notes; and the books he read disclose the spreading range of his interests. Spengler, Bukharin and

[1] To his father, 28 May 1930.

[2] To Vijayalakshmi Pandit, 25 June 1930.

[3] During this term of six months he spun over 30,000 yards of yarn on the *charka* and nearly 750 yards on the *takli* (a hand spindle).

[4] *Letters from a Father to his Daughter* (Allahabad, 1929).

[5] Preface to second edition, October 1931.

Russell's *ABC of Relativity* were gutted, with Maurois's *Ariel* and *Disraeli* and Romain Rolland's *Jean-Christophe* (all in French), Lloyd George's speeches, Shakespeare and an anthology of French poetry as light relief; and the interest in Indian and Asian history was maintained. "I seldom read the notes again but I had a substance of that book in my memory. I had to think of what the book meant, put it down and that became for me a library of reference.'[1]

Jawaharlal's isolation was never complete. It was broken from the start by the presence of numerous convict warders and orderlies, ostensibly intended to attend on him but also used to keep a watch on him, and not allowed to mix with other prisoners lest they carry messages. But in fact a large number of other warders and servants also came daily for *darshan* and to discuss *swaraj*. Convicts smuggled in flowers, and his *punkha* coolie, who was not a convict, brought him a few little mangoes almost daily. 'They are not up to much,' wrote Jawaharlal, much moved, 'but the gift is worthy of the Gods. The man is very poor.'[2] Officials of the jail and the town also called on him frequently. A month after his arrest, another Congressman arrested for civil disobedience was placed in the same barrack. But it was the arrival of Motilal Nehru and Syed Mahmud on 30 June that disrupted the placid routine of Jawaharlal's life. Looking after his father became now his main preoccupation, till both father and son were soon drawn, even from within jail, into political negotiations.

Jawaharlal, despite the taboo on discussion of politics at interviews and the denial of newspapers, had been kept fairly well and quickly informed of events outside by the warders and later arrivals in prison. *'Peshawar occurrences'* runs the entry in the pocket diary for 23 April, revealing that the solitary prisoner had heard and been thrilled by the knowledge that the Government had virtually lost control of that city. What particularly delighted Jawaharlal was the fact that the inhabitants of the N.W.F.P. were predominantly Muslim, and by their revolt had belied the foreboding that the Muslims would keep aloof from the movement. The news of the spread and intensification of civil disobedience was indeed so exciting that Jawaharlal fretted in his idleness and could not sleep. On 5 May he heard that Gandhi had been arrested in far-off Bombay a few hours earlier, and was well pleased. 'Ça marche bien. It is full-blooded war to the bitter end. Good.'[3] Nothing, he thought, would be more unfortunate than any premature compromise.

This attitude ensured from the start that the effort of the professional mediators, Sapru and Jayakar, to negotiate a settlement between the Government and the Congress was bound to fail. Jawaharlal held all Liberals in contempt and minced no words in his diary:[4]

[1] Speech to the Foreign Press Association, New Delhi, 20 March 1956.
[2] Diary entry 2 May 1930.
[3] Diary entry, 5 May 1930.
[4] 31 May 1930.

Some of the moderates are waking up, but some behave like old women — weeping and howling and feeling terribly oppressed about everything! The *Leader* is evidently among the weeping widows. If they have not got gumption enough to do anything why do they not shut up? It is enough to sicken one to hear them sing the praises of Irwin and Benn and co! It is difficult to imagine a greater dope at the political game than the moderate in India. Nothing could condemn British rule in India more than the amazing product of it!

So he was taken aback when some slack statements to a British journalist by Gandhi and Motilal were picked up by the two leading Liberals as a basis for a settlement at a time when both civil disobedience and the Government's attempts to crush it were in full fury. Armed with some general platitudes from the Viceroy, they saw Gandhi in Yeravda jail and found him in what they felt to be a co-operative mood. In fact, however, while Gandhi sounded accommodating on the constitutional issue, he had clearly not given his whole mind to it and insisted that Jawaharlal's should be the final voice.[1] So the peacemakers proceeded to Naini prison to interview the Nehrus.

Lot of time was wasted in listening to what Irwin said and Jinnah did and Fazl-i Husain intrigued. Nothing important or hopeful. Bapu's[2] note disappointing although it is clear that even that will not be acceptable to the Viceroy. We have not suggested anything. Have said that without full consultation with colleagues, especially Gandhiji, we cannot make any suggestion. We have not committed ourselves in any way although we have hinted at a stiff attitude. I have been worried however for last two or three days. I wish we had definitely stopped all talk of 'peace'. It is harmful and diverts attention. There is no peace anywhere in sight.[3]

However, the impression of the over-optimistic negotiators was very different. Sapru reported to the Viceroy:[4]

Much to our agreeable surprise we found Pandit Jawaharlal Nehru in quite a reasonable frame of mind yesterday. Both he and his father gave us a very patient and courteous hearing. On the constitutional issue however we did not find our task with them so easy as we had found with Mr. Gandhi, whereas on the question of salt and the 11 points of Mr. Gandhi on which he had laid so much stress at Poona we did not find them in complete agreement with Mr. Gandhi.

[1] Gandhi to Motilal, 23 July 1930, *The Bombay Chronicle,* 6 September 1930.
[2] Gandhi was addressed as 'Bapu' or 'father' by Jawaharlal and many others.
[3] Diary entry, 1 August 1930. Fazl-i Husain, leader of the Unionist party in the Punjab and at this time member of the Viceroy's council, was a frank protagonist of Muslim communalism.
[4] 28 July 1930, Sapru papers I 47.

So, despite a letter[1] from Jawaharlal to Gandhi given them to deliver, in which Jawaharlal made clear that he and his father had not been persuaded by Gandhi's approach to the constitutional issue and that he himself wished to continue the campaign, Sapru persuaded the Viceroy to transport the Nehrus to Yeravda for consultations with Gandhi. Though Jawaharlal had not been very keen, Motilal had said that they had no objection,[2] and a special train sped them across the country to see Gandhi. Meanwhile, Jayakar, who had taken the letter to Gandhi and seen him alone, was confident that Gandhi was anxious for a settlement.[3]

But the talks of Gandhi and the Nehrus with Sapru and Jayakar came to nothing. The Congress stated its terms precisely and stiffly to be a complete national government with the right of secession and reference of all British claims to an independent tribunal. These terms would obviously not be acceptable to the Government; and though the indefatigable Sapru and Jayakar continued their 'silly peace negotiations'[4] and shuttled between Simla, Naini and Poona, no one shared their illusory hopes of a compromise. What, indeed, struck the Secretary of State was 'Gandhi's deference to Jawaharlal and Jawaharlal's pride in what had been achieved as well as his declaration of belief in non-violence. It was the apparent pride which depressed me, because it did not show the spirit of a beaten man.'[5]

A few days later, Motilal was released on grounds of ill-health, and Jawaharlal's own term of six months was drawing to a close. But the U.P. Government had no intention of leaving him at large for long.[6] Nor did Jawaharlal expect it. Released on 11 October, he promptly resumed the Congress presidency, thereby, as the organization had been outlawed; rendering himself liable to arrest, and he then directed all the provincial committees to launch a fresh offensive. The manufacture of salt and the boycott of British goods, especially cloth, which formed the backbone of the movement, should be vigorously sustained, and in addition efforts should be made to initiate no-tax campaigns as in Gujarat.[7]

> It is clear that India, big as it is, is not big enough to contain both the Indian people and the British Government. One of the two has to go and there can be little doubt as to which this is going to be . . . we are in deadly earnest, we have burnt our boats, we have taken the great resolve and there is no going back for us.[8]

[1] 28 July 1930.
[2] Sapru to Jayakar, 8 August 1930, Sapru papers J 16.
[3] Jayakar to Sapru, 4 August 1930, Sapru papers J 15.
[4] Hailey to General Shea, 15 August 1930, Hailey papers, vol. 19.
[5] Wedgwood Benn to Irwin, 3 September 1930, Halifax papers, vol. 6.
[6] Hailey, Governor, to Crerar, Home Member, 2 October 1930, Home Dept. Pol File 257/III of 1930.
[7] Circular to provincial Congress committees, 14 October 1930.
[8] Speech at Allahabad, 12 October 1930.

In his own province, where agricultural prices had been on a steep decline throughout the year, a no-tax campaign would obviously meet with a favourable response; and Jawaharlal announced that the district and town Congress committees would shortly organize non-payment of land revenue, rent and income-tax.[1] Though, on the face of it, this involved all sections of society, landowners, tenants and professional classes, in the political struggle against the Government, basically it was a call to the peasant tillers not to pay rent to the landlords; and its explosive nature lay in its rousing class conflict and spreading it to the countryside. The next day he was arrested, tried for sedition and incitement to manufacture of salt and non-payment of taxes, and sentenced to two years' rigorous imprisonment plus five months in default of fines. He had been out of prison for less than ten days.

Denied the artistry of action,[2] Jawaharlal reverted to the regular tenor of Naini life. A pain in the shoulder prevented him from much spinning and *newar* weaving. But the insatiable reading was taken up again. He re-read Radhakrishnan's *Hindu View of Life*, and made notes from, among others, Trotsky, Shaw, Maeterlinck, Kropotkin and Keyserling. He also recommenced his letters to his daughter, basing himself on his memory and his notebooks, for by now it was clear that ahead lay many years in prison — indeed he would only be able to write in prison — and if he hoped for the help of reference books he would never write at all. But his sense of wonder had led him to amass a great deal of odd information. Over these letters Jawaharlal took much trouble, collecting his thoughts on paper and then organizing them lucidly to suit a girl of thirteen. The handling of the language was easy, but his style had not quite settled down and occasionally there was a trace of affectation. The letters dealt with the history of man. Like Raleigh and Condorcet, Jawaharlal wrote a history of the world while sitting in prison. Each letter was devoted to one theme or development; and the whole, starting with Mohenjo-Daro and ancient Greece and ending with the writer's own times, was spread over nearly three years. The letters showed, when published as *Glimpses of World History*, a unity of outlook and a command of fact which would have done credit to any professional writer; and that they were written with no research assistance of any kind and as an escape from the monotony of jail made the work an astonishing achievement.

The news of the celebration of his forty-first birthday all over the country on 16 November thrilled him. 'Jawahar Day! Arrests — convictions — *lathi* charges all over the country!'[3] About twenty million people had participated in 384 cities and villages (including Colombo); the police had opened fire in one place and carried out *lathi* charges in 26 others; one person was killed, about 1,500 were wounded and 1,679 were arrested. So the morale of the movement

[1] Speech at Lucknow, 18 October 1930, *The Tribune,* 21 October 1930.
[2] See letter to Dhan Gopal Mukherji, 17 October 1930.
[3] Diary entry, 16 November 1930.

was obviously still high, and Jawaharlal gave some thought to its future. A revolutionary dynamic, even in politics, could only be maintained by the goal of an economic revolution and by the rousing of a mass revolt.

> Ultimately, that is the only thing that will tell. In spite of the great success of our movement we have not yet come within reasonable distance of moving the masses in a revolutionary sense. There is sympathy but no more. Gradually, if we do not look out, even this sympathy will get less and less.[1]

From this point of view, a no-tax campaign was vital and some attention should be given to defining its objective. The battle-cry of an economic programme was a far more powerful one for the peasant than that of political *swaraj* alone, and the object of a no-tax movement should be economic advance and not the release of a few leaders. Even the idea of a Constituent Assembly to settle the political future of India, which struck Jawaharlal at this time, could not be expected to rouse the *kisans*. In May 1929 the national body, following in the steps of the U.P. Congress, had accepted that the poverty and misery of the Indian people was due not only to foreign exploitation but also to the economic structure of society which required 'revolutionary changes'. Thanks to Jawaharlal the Congress was acquiring, if not a socialist viewpoint, at least an economic dimension. But no thought had been given to these 'revolutionary changes'. The Congress, in the middle of a war, could not be expected to draw up a definite economic and agrarian programme, but it should at least formulate some tentative ideas. Jawaharlal thought of some, '*not*', as he said, 'from a purely socialistic standpoint, but from a Congress viewpoint with some leanings towards socialism'. Big *zamindaris* should be acquired by the State, with compensation to all except those who had sided with the British and against the national movement, and replaced by peasant proprietorship and large state farms, where major experiments could be tried by the cultivators to whom they would be jointly leased. There should be also an inheritance tax and a land tax which would be at a flat rate of 25 per cent of the agricultural income above a certain minimum and up to a certain limit, and beyond that graduated like the income tax. Tenants should have rights of occupancy, purchase, transfer, improvement and inheritance, and a ceiling should be placed on rent. The time might not be ripe for a radical agrarian programme for the whole of India, and leading Congressmen would not agree to it; but the U.P. could take the lead. While there was no point in needlessly irritating the *zamindars* and the capitalists and adding to one's enemies in the middle of a great fight, where a choice had to be made between two positions the Congress should without fear back the masses — the *kisans*, the landless people and the petty *zamindars* — for they were the vital groups. The Congress was wise in avoiding precipitation

[1] Notes probably written in October-November 1930.

of the class conflict, but it should always be remembered that such a conflict was there and could not be wholly ignored. The ultimate ideal should be clear-cut in their minds; it need not be advertised but it need not be kept secret either.

These ideas, very similar to the U.P. manifesto of 1928, were, as Jawaharlal was well aware, by no means revolutionary; but even their attainment was poised in his eyes on the continuance of a revolutionary struggle, and to that extent he was racing far ahead of reality. Even from within prison he and his companions sought to resist, and for the first time Jawaharlal contravened the jail rules by organizing a three-day fast in protest against the flogging of political prisoners and their harsh treatment in other jails. He was vastly delighted, too, by the news of his wife's arrest on New Year's Day and by her message on that occasion: 'I am happy beyond measure and proud to follow in the footsteps of my husband. I hope the people will keep the flag flying.' But generally, as Jawaharlal was compelled angrily to recognize, spirits were flagging and there was a mood for compromise.

Unhappily the *hartal* age inaugurated by the Mahatma and the Congress has had some evil effects. It has resulted in continuous *hartals* in the heads and brains of some people. The upper storey has been locked up and the key is missing. It is a sad and deplorable result, but I suppose we must all bear up with this additional affliction.[1]

It was in this context of fatigue that the British Government sent out seductive messages suggesting a settlement. The first session of the Round Table Conference had made clear that it was futile to discuss Indian problems with anyone except the Congress: 'no Indian delegation', wrote the correspondent in India of *The Times*, 'without a three-quarter line composed of Gandhi on one wing, the two Nehrus in the centre, and Malaviya or Patel on the other, can possibly be looked on as representative.'[2] The Viceroy also came round to the recognition that logically there were only two alternatives: to govern without consent or to make terms with Gandhi. The concept of the knock-out blow being futile, there had to be some settlement.[3] On 17 January 1931 the Viceroy, in the new, Christian style of imperialism, appealed to Gandhi for co-operation on a basis of mutual trust; and two days later the Prime Minister, Ramsay MacDonald, offered provincial autonomy, responsibility of the central executive to a federal legislature with some safeguards for minorities during a period of transition, and reforms in the existing constitution pending final decision on permanent changes. The thought that these siren voices might strike a response in the Congress drove Jawaharlal almost frantic. All such statements, he pleaded with his father, even if they offered full independence,

[1] To his father, 28 December 1930.
[2] Letter to his editor, 12 September 1930, *The History of the Times, 1912-1948*, pt. ii (New York, 1952), p. 877.
[3] Irwin to Wedgwood Benn, 5 September and 3 November 1930, Halifax papers, vol. 6.

should be ignored and the fight carried on; but, in fact, MacDonald's statement amounted to nothing. 'The British Government are past masters in the art of political chicanery and fraud, and we are babes at their game.' In even dreaming of a compromise the Working Committee would be playing with fire — fire which might consume the country at no distant date — and lowering the morale of the people. 'Some people may be tired. There are also some people who have got the iron into their souls and who will go through hell if necessary before giving in to an ignoble compromise.' The Government should be made to realize that the fight would go on not for months but for years if necessary and the Congress would not give in except on its own terms. 'The day we convince the enemy that we are immovable like the Himalayas and as difficult to crush, that nothing in the world can make us bend — that we shall put up with all that they may inflict on us — that day the enemy will crumple up.' The larger world-situation also demanded that Britain make peace with India.[1]

Motilal, however, was dying, and could give no guidance to the Working Committee, whose members had now been released. Gandhi was unwilling to reject the Government's overtures out of hand both because he sensed a kindred spirit in the Viceroy, and because he believed that the war-weariness was more widespread than Jawaharlal was willing to recognize. The latter was prepared to overcome the staleness in the towns by stirring up the rural areas, but this did not appeal to Gandhi. Out of tune, therefore, with the mood of his leader, and deeply stricken by his father's death on 6 February, Jawaharlal made no decisive contribution to the discussions. Trained to conceal his emotions, he continued to attend all the meetings of the Working Committee. But the undemonstrativeness could not hide the depth of his grief. Jawaharlal's personality was still incomplete and lacking in an assured centre. He was a man in the process of becoming, and therefore greatly dependent on his strong family background and on the support of a powerful father. His mother had no influence over him. The differing attitudes of father and son on many political issues, the gradual shift of Motilal to a viewpoint closer to Jawaharlal's and the many legends woven round his ambitious and spoiling love for his son, cannot detract from the fact that his was the weightier influence. For long after Motilal's death, Jawaharlal felt the lack of his sheltering wisdom, and doubtless this deprivation did much to reinforce his dependence on Gandhi.

Just at this moment, however, Gandhi's ways were wholly alien to him. The negotiations with the Viceroy, carried out by Gandhi on his own, and the settlement which resulted, seemed to Jawaharlal a total and unwarranted surrender. He still had not understood that Gandhi was no different from the Moderates in his basic strategy of negotiating with the British for concessions; he only sought to build up greater mass pressures in his favour.[2] 'All these

---

[1] Two undated letters to his father, clearly written in January 1931.

[2] For an analysis of this, see Bipan Chandra, 'Elements of Continuity and Change in Early Nationalist Activity', paper read at the Indian History Congress, December 1972.

forms of action', in Fanon's words,[1] 'serve at one and the same time to bring pressure to bear on the forces of colonialism, and to allow the people to work off their energy.' Assuming that the Congress was committed to the position Gandhi and the others had taken up at Yeravda the year before,[2] and expecting, till almost the very end,[3] the talks to break down, the actual terms came to Jawaharlal as a severe jolt. Gandhi had agreed to discontinue civil disobedience in return for a partial amnesty limited to those not charged with violence, and permission to picket peacefully and to manufacture salt under certain conditions; and he committed Congress to take part in the Round Table Conference to consider a scheme of federation and responsibility with safeguards 'in the interests of India' for such matters as defence, external affairs, the position of minorities, financial credit and the discharge of obligations. This was a far cry from the demand for independence and the right to secede, and even from the position taken up by the Congress in the talks with Sapru and Jayakar in the summer of 1930. Nor had Gandhi stood firm on the demands for a general amnesty, an inquiry into police excesses, which to Jawaharlal was preliminary to any participation in the Round Table Conference,[4] the return of all immovable property which had been attached, and the unlimited right to collect salt.

> Thousands of poor people are pledged to eat only tax-free salt or salt manufactured by themselves. Hundreds have during the past eight months bled for vindicating the right. The leaders are involved in the pledge taken by the people. Humiliation of the people and their leaders and invitation to break their pledge is hardly the way to approach peace.[5]

It appeared to most members of the Working Committee, and above all to Jawaharlal, that Gandhi had been outwitted and, in return for some empty phrases which recognized the indispensability of Congress in any Indian settlement, had yielded on every crucial issue and ignored the long-term objectives. But Gandhi threatened to retire if his settlement were repudiated and demanded personal loyalty even if not approval. Jawaharlal was in tears and more aware than ever that the loss of his father was more than a personal one. Never had Motilal's clear-sightedness and ruthlessness in negotiation been more needed. 'Always', he recorded in jail a year later, 'when thinking of the truce people start guessing what might have happened if father had been there and there appears to be a general consensus that events would have taken a very different turn. Foolishly I said so in Delhi a few hours after the truce. How Bapu was pained at my remark!'[6]

[1] Op. cit., p. 52.
[2] See his comments to a journalist, 18 February, *The Tribune,* 22 February 1931.
[3] 'The long conversations are at last drawing to a close and we have to prepare again for jail or worse! This is all to the good.' Jawaharlal to Vijayalakshmi Pandit, 28 February 1931.
[4] See his undated note which clearly was written at this time, AICC File G 6(KW)(i) 1931.
[5] Ibid.
[6] Prison diary, 4 March 1932.

However, despite his disappointment, at the Congress session at Karachi Jawaharlal moved the resolution ratifying this settlement. It has frequently been suggested that Gandhi secured this by agreeing, in turn, to a resolution, drafted by Jawaharlal and revised by him, committing the organization to provide in any future constitution for not only the basic civil liberties, adult suffrage and free primary education, but also 'real economic freedom'. But the argument that in return for his acceptance of the political compromise Jawaharlal was given a recognition of socialist objectives is defeated by the list of fundamental rights incorporated in the resolution. In industry, economic freedom meant only a living wage and proper conditions of work, liberation from serfdom or conditions bordering on serfdom, decent treatment of women workers, prohibition against the employment of school-going children, the right to form trade unions and the establishment of machinery for settling disputes by arbitration. The state should control mineral resources and the key industries. These could not constitute part of the 'revolutionary changes' which the Congress had accepted in 1929 as being necessary. But in agriculture the position was even worse. The Karachi resolution stipulated no more than a substantial reduction of land revenue and rent with total exemption only for necessary periods in the case of uneconomic holdings, a progressive tax on agricultural income above a certain level and a graduated inheritance tax. There was no reference to the abolition of landlordism or the socialization of land or even the annulment of at least a portion of the rural debt. On the other hand, much of Gandhi's eleven points of 1930 was included — reduction of civil and military expenditure, exclusion of foreign cloth and yarn, prohibition, abolition of the salt tax and lowering of the exchange ratio of the rupee.

Obviously, therefore, this resolution was no sugar on the political pill. There was nothing socialistic about it. Only the secret police could have believed that M. N. Roy, who was present at Karachi, had helped in drafting this resolution, which he later denounced as confused, compromising with foreign imperialism and native feudalism and 'an instrument of deception'.[1] Jawaharlal too was aware that this resolution did not go even as far as his earlier efforts, from 1928 onwards, at drafting an economic programme which would have some meaning for the peasants and workers of India. But he sponsored it as it formed at least one more step taken by the Congress, however haltingly, not on the road to socialism but towards the recognition of the need for an economic policy. It indicated 'that our national movement is gradually turning towards the left. I think this is a desirable development and that this in itself will help the fuller development of an advanced ideology in groups. It will provide the background out of which that ideology can develop.'[2]

So the resolution on fundamental rights in itself did not compensate for the loss of ground suffered because of the political settlement; and if Jawaharlal

[1] J.P. Haithcox, *Communism and Nationalism in India* (Princeton, 1971), pp. 190-91.
[2] To Onkar Nath Verma, 2 December 1933.

publicly supported the latter, it was because such conduct was in consonance with both his policy and his character. Once the settlement had been reached, Jawaharlal, 'lonely and almost uninterested' as Gandhi described him,[1] informed his colleagues that he was unable to accept or reconcile himself to the references to safeguards and reservations. But he added: 'I do not desire, however, that any impediment should be placed in the way of those who interpret the words differently from me and who propose to extract independence out of them. Truce having been proclaimed by the Working Committee, I trust all of us will honour it and carry out the directions of the W.C. in regard to it.'[2] In other words, Jawaharlal resented the conclusion of this agreement but was not going even to offer to resign, as he had done in 1929, and intended to abide by the settlement. But the contradiction between his mental attitude and his decision to conform was not complete. It was not the case of a middle-aged fledgling who believed in extremism and acted in moderation. As Jawaharlal saw it, the settlement was undoubtedly a self-inflicted defeat. But he would not have agreed with Irwin's claim, at a private meeting of the Conservative Party after his return to London, that he had built a breakwater against the great agrarian forces which were being harnessed by Jawaharlal by ensuring the loyalty of the older politicians who were on the side of 'conservatism'.[3] No permanent damage had been done to Indian nationalism. Gandhi had not broken, but only ignored, the logic of the struggle for freedom; that struggle, in fact, could only end with the attainment of independence. So this was no peace but only a truce. The temporary phase was bound to pass sooner rather than later, and the fight recommence; and then once again the nation would require the leadership of the man who had called a depressed people to life and action. Till then, in the period of neither peace nor war, it was Jawaharlal's duty to keep the spirit of battle alive, to respect the cohesion of the party and to abide by the leadership of Gandhi. The fears of the British Government[4] that he might split with Gandhi and carry on civil disobedience on his own showed how little they knew him. As he advised a young Congressman:

> We cannot afford to get excited in politics. We must preserve our balance and not rush into any action without proper consideration. Such action as we take should not be individual as far as possible. If we do so we lose the benefit of collective action and of an organization.[5]

---

[1]See Gandhi's handwritten note to Jawaharlal, AICC File G 6(KW)(i) 1931.
[2]Undated note, AICC File G 6(KW)(i) 1931.
[3]Lord Butler, *The Art of the Possible* (London, 1971), p. 41.
[4]Wedgwood Benn to Irwin, 25 March 1931, Halitax papers, vol. 6.
[5]To Anjani Kumar, 21 July 1931, AICC File G 59 of 1931.

11

Agrarian Crisis
in the United Provinces

Jawaharlal's speeches, immediately after the announcement of the settlement, were, somewhat to Gandhi's embarrassment,[1] bellicose. He called on Congressmen to retain the war mentality, for the time was sure to come when they would have to fight again; meanwhile, they should abide by the agreement which their leader had reached, and exploit it fully in such matters as picketing of liquor shops, manufacture of salt, boycott of foreign cloth and preaching of *swadeshi*.[2] There was also scope for more important activity in the sensitive areas of Gujarat and the United Provinces, where the movement of 1930 had developed into rural no-rent campaigns. That in Gujarat had been the more successful, but it was also the more easily called off, for it had been primarily a political effort in a small area no larger than half a district in the U.P., with relatively well-to-do cultivators responding to the call of Gandhi and Vallabhbhai Patel to pay nothing until the Government cancelled a summary enhancement of the revenue. The authorities were forced to acknowledge that the assessment had been carelessly arrived at, and, after the settlement, the chief issues were the restoration of lands which had been confiscated and the reinstatement of officials who had been dismissed. But the situation was very different in the United Provinces. Here, between the Government and the cultivators, there was an intermediate class of about 160,000 landlords, but the fragmentation of land was such that the vast majority of these landholders paid less than Rs 100 a year in land revenue. But if the landlords were for the most part impoverished, the condition of the tenants was relatively much worse. Pressure on land was continuously increasing, and rents paid by the tenants were enhanced far more rapidly than the revenue payable by the landowners to

[1] See the Viceroy's record of interview with Gandhi, 19 March 1931, *Collected Works*, vol. 45 (Delhi, 1971), p. 315.
[2] Speeches at Lucknow, 8 March, *The Leader*, 11 March 1931; Allahabad 9 March, *The Leader*, 12 March 1931; Bombay 15 March, *The Bombay Chronicle*, 16 March 1931.

the Government. Between 1900 and 1931 rents had increased by Rs 669 lakhs while land revenue had increased by only Rs 75 lakhs. Agricultural prices, already low by January 1930, fell by December by about 50 per cent and were lower than at any time since 1901; and the yield was not sufficient even to cover the rising costs of production, let alone to enable payment of rent. Added to this was a series of bad harvests since 1927. Nearly 40 per cent of the peasants and the poorer *zamindars* were sunk in debt. Two years after the agrarian riots of 1921, life tenure was given statutory recognition in Avadh (Oudh), and a similar statute was passed in 1926 in Agra. But this acceptance of tenancy right had its darker side, in that rents were stabilized at a time when they were high. But there were no occupancy rights in Avadh; conditions were slightly better in the Agra districts, but evictions were widespread throughout the province, the landlords being eager to evict occupancy tenants.

The agrarian question, therefore, in the United Provinces was much more an economic than a political one; and even after the truce of March 1931 there were many instances of landlords and the police acting together in evicting and harassing tenants in order to extract rents. Some villages were even reported to have been deserted by the inhabitants out of fear.[1] Jawaharlal was under the impression that while Gandhi had assured Irwin that even if he did not attend the Round Table Conference he would not resume civil disobedience so long as the Conference was sitting, he had made it clear that this assurance did not apply to any local economic struggle that might be forced upon the Congress.[2] There is nothing to this effect in the official record but it is confirmed by implication; and it was explicitly stated in Gandhi's later correspondence, in August, with the Government. So in March 1931, as the slump in prices continued and even the *rabi* (spring) crop was a failure, the whole scope of the movement in the United Provinces was changed, as Gandhi described it,[3] from one for non-payment of rent to one purely for seeking economic relief. Tenants were advised to pay what was possible, which in general appeared to be 50 per cent by occupancy tenants and 40 per cent by statutory tenants, provided the landlords gave receipts for the full amount. The Congress organizations in the *tehsils* acted as agents of the peasants in negotiations with the landlords, and Jawaharlal met some senior officials of the U.P. Government, while the provincial Congress committee opened an office at Lucknow to deal with the Government and deputed Govind Ballabh Pant to be in charge.[4]

The Government, however, though they recognized the economic distress and realized that there was nothing objectionable in the attitude of the Congress, feared that its mediation would strengthen its hold in the rural areas and refused

[1] Jawaharlal to Jagdish Prasad, Chief Secretary U.P., 11 March and to Maharaj Singh, Commissioner, Allahabad division, 9 April 1931. Home Dept. Pol. File 33/XVI and K.W. of 1931.

[2] *Autobiography,* p. 299.

[3] Letter to Emerson, Home Secretary, 23 March 1931, *Collected Works,* vol. 45, pp. 334-5.

[4] *Agrarian Distress in the United Provinces,* report of the U.P. Congress Sub-Committee (Lucknow, 1931), p. 46.

to recognize that the Congress had any role in this matter. It seemed to them more than a matter of prestige.

> Jawaharlal and his school have of course a great influence locally, and there is no doubt that they have for a long time been bitten with the idea of making a kind of Soviet organization of peasant workers, which will first of all abolish the landlord and then possibly Sovietize Government. The procedure now adopted is well chosen and difficult to meet. Congress announces that it is really a peasant trades union and cannot desert the tenant in his hour of stress. It no longer pursues the no-rent campaign as a political measure, but it demands the right to judge as between landlord and tenant and to decide what rent the latter can pay. The landlords are thoroughly unhappy, and we ourselves find it difficult to meet the new position without recourse to ordinances, which might break up the Delhi settlement. [1]

Knowing Gandhi's keen desire to make the settlement a success, they sought to drive a wedge between him and Jawaharlal. In this they were not wholly unsuccessful. Emerson reported that Gandhi fully accepted the position that it was wrong to refer to the settlement as a truce, to talk about a future war, to refer to Government as an enemy and to exploit the settlement as a victory for Congress. 'He was very loyal to Pandit Jawaharlal, but, I gathered, did not regard it as altogether improbable that he would take his own line sooner or later.' [2] Gandhi, in fact, was frightened by the officials with the bogy of a class war being let loose by Jawaharlal. He liked the idea of Congress *tehsil* committees acting on behalf of the tenants, but disapproved of advice to withhold payment of rent even in part, the appointment of Congress *tehsildars* and attacks by tenants on *zamindars*. [3] He even, to the Government's delight, practically withdrew the claim of the Congress to be an intermediary between the Government and the people.[4]

Jawaharlal's health at this time being on the verge of collapse, he had to take a holiday, and while he was in Sri Lanka and southern India, Gandhi was in charge of the U.P. problem. This appeared to be the chance for the Government to press home their advantage, and to get Gandhi to throw in his weight against his 'wild men'.[5] Hailey, back as Governor by the end of April after being present

[1] To Sir Findlater Stewart of the Indian Office, 25 April 1931, Hailey papers, vol. 20.
[2] Emerson's report of his interview with Gandhi, 19 March 1931, *Collected Works,* vol. 45, Appendix IX.
[3] Emerson's report of his interview with Gandhi on 6 April 1931, Home Dept. Pol. File 33/XI of 1931.
[4] Crerar, Home Member, to Hailey, 6 May 1931, Hailey papers, vol. 20.
[5] The phrase was that of Willingdon, the new Viceroy; letter to Hailey, 29 April 1931, Hailey papers, vol. 20.

in London for the Round Table Conference, was wiser than most other officials in Lucknow, and realized that the economic crisis was real and it would not do merely to coerce and harass the tenants to pay rents. Remissions of revenue of about Rs 67 lakhs were announced, with parallel reductions of rent for the *rabi* harvest of about Rs 220 lakhs. But, though in remitting revenue the Government went back to the level of 1901, rents were taken back only to the level of 1915-16, and the remission amounted to only about two annas in the rupee. If rents also had been pushed back to 1901, the *talukdars*, the traditional allies of the Government, would have lost heavily and the Government were not willing to contemplate this. This was hardly adequate remission even for current rents — nothing was said about arrears or the *kharif* (autumn) harvest — and many district officers and most of the *zamindars* pointed this out.[1] Landlords were practically unable to collect any rent at all in Barabanki, Rae Bareli and parts of Lucknow and Pratabgarh districts; and the situation was not much better in parts of Agra, Meerut and Allahabad districts. But the U.P. Government were prepared at this stage to do no more. On the other hand, the Divisional Commissioners were ordered to provide police assistance to landlords in carrying out the ordinary processes of eviction and distraint.[2] This seemed the only way of smashing the almost total hold which the Congress had acquired in some districts, and of retaining the loyalty of the *talukdars*. And the pretence of conciliation, however minimal, seemed a sufficient backdrop for talks with Gandhi.

The Home Secretary, Emerson, met Gandhi at Simla in the middle of May. Gandhi was not prepared to accept that the Congress had no right to intervene at all in the relations between the Government and the tax-payer; even if it was not a recognized intermediary, it had a role to play as the poor man's friend in advising him on rent matters. But he roundly condemned pressure being brought on landlords, direct appeals not to pay, the proposal of a general 50 per cent reduction of rent and any refusal to pay less than what was within the individual's capacity. He was then invited to meet Hailey at Naini Tal to discuss details, and the spectre was presented to him of tenants refusing to pay any rent and resorting to violence if pressed by landlords. When he suggested an inquiry into the exact pitch of rents so as to ascertain if payment was practical, Hailey replied that this would involve such a delay in collections that Government could not agree.[3] The Governor was too shrewd to press Gandhi to any precise commitment, but that Gandhi had been sufficiently won over was shown by the manifesto he issued immediately after the interview. Ignoring the resolution of the U.P. Political Conference passed a few weeks earlier that the rents should on no account exceed those prevailing at a time when agricultural prices were

[1] Hailey to Crerar, 8 May 1931. Home Dept. Pol. File 33/XI of 1931.

[2] Chief Secretary's circular to Commissioners, 7 May 1931, ibid.

[3] Emerson's note of discussions with Gandhi, 13, 14, 15 and 16 May 1931, Home Dept. Pol. 33/IX of 1931; Hailey's note of discussions, 20 May 1931, Home Dept. Pol. 33/XI of 1931.

what they were at this time, Gandhi called upon the tenants to pay all the rent they could as early as possible, and in no case less than 8 annas in the rupee in the case of statutory and non-occupancy tenants and 12 annas in the case of occupancy tenants — more than what the U.P. Congress had recommended. He added that the tenants should certainly not listen to advice to pay no rent at all or resort to violence. [1]

Fortified by Gandhi's half-hearted support of the *kisans*, the Government now forced the pace and, without openly denouncing the settlement, set about breaking up the alliance of the U.P. Congress and the tenantry as well as the Congress organization in the countryside. If the Congress built up an influence in the rural areas such as they already had in the towns, in any future campaign of civil disobedience they would have the whole population behind them; and serious as Bardoli had been, it would appear insignificant compared to any no-rent campaign which might develop, encompassing the whole of the United Provinces. Administration would practically come to an end, it would be impossible to maintain law and order or even a semblance of government, and right in the heart of India 49 million people would be entirely out of hand. That was why it seemed important to Hailey and other perceptive officials not only to destroy the potential of the Congress in the countryside but to ride Gandhi off the United Provinces. This was doubtless one major reason why the Government were anxious that Gandhi should have no opportunity for reconsidering his position and should be encouraged to attend the Round Table Conference in London.

It is, I think, the mercy of Heaven that they have concentrated on a *tehsil* in Bombay when they might have been playing havoc with six or seven million tenants in the United Provinces. I do not mean that all of them are thoroughly discontented, but there is quite enough rack-renting and bullying by landlords in some of the districts to make a very fine field for agitation. Jawahar Lal and his friends have done and are doing their best, but of course they lack the halo which surrounds the unprepossessing poll of the Mahatma. [2]

So when Jawaharlal came back to the U.P. in the middle of June, he found the situation and atmosphere much worse than in March. The *talukdars* were terrorizing the peasants with the help of the police, Congress volunteers were being beaten up in many places, and even activity such as peaceful picketing, permitted by the settlement, was in places banned by overenthusiastic district authorities. Jawaharlal had no intention of submitting meekly to this, despite letters from Gandhi,[3] seen in the mail by the authorities, deploring the element

[1] Manifesto, 23 May 1931.
[2] Hailey to Haig, 10 October 1931, Hailey papers, vol. 22.
[3] 20 and 24 June 1931.

of violence in the Congress ranks and urging him not to break any law himself but to seek an interview with the Governor or with Emerson. 'On your side', Gandhi wrote to a U.P. Congressman,[1] 'it is all well, so long as you hold the *kisans* in check. But Jawaharlal's presence must now ease the situation. He has no difficulty in dealing with the *kisans* and restraining them.' As much in reply to Gandhi as to the Government, Jawaharlal said that the Government were breaking the truce and using the *zamindars* to crush the *kisans*, and the Congress would have to take drastic action in reply. *Talukdars* who preferred to bask in official sunshine rather than to be on friendly terms with their tenants had no place in India, and those who were guilty of oppression would have to answer for it before the nation.[2]

Jawaharlal was too loyal to Gandhi to accept, even to himself, that his leader was weakening their case, and he dutifully sought an interview with Hailey, which, however, was not granted. But he took the view that what Gandhi had asked the tenants to pay was not the minimum but the maximum and this need not be paid if it entailed debt and sale of cattle and ploughs, or if the *kisans* were ill-treated.[3] The U.P. Congress set up commissions of inquiry to visit the districts and ascertain details of official and *zamindari* repression. For their part, the U.P. Government claimed that they were prepared to grant no further remissions and were even willing to consider the arrest and prosecution of Jawaharlal for his support of the tenants or even for organization of peaceful picketing in Allahabad.[4] It is difficult to believe that Hailey, who was perhaps the shrewdest of his generation of civil servants in India, was serious about this, and it was probably intended to keep the Government of India, of which in Willingdon's time he had no high opinion,[5] from making any concession on the U.P. to Gandhi. For such a stupid step as the arrest of Jawaharlal would clearly have served to push Gandhi too far. However keen he might have been, as the authorities at Simla thought, to maintain the settlement and proceed to London he could hardly have done so with one of his chief lieutenants in prison; and an open war with the Congress at this stage could hardly have been of advantage to the Government. But fortunately, from their viewpoint, Jawaharlal left the U.P. to attend a meeting of the Working Committee and then accompanied Gandhi to Simla. There Gandhi suggested to the Viceroy and his officials that the district authorities should fix the amount of revenue and rent to be collected after consultation with Congress workers, but if this were not acceptable to the Government, at least a detailed inquiry to enable temporary adjustments should be ordered. The Government of India were willing to consider this, but it was veoted by the U.P. Government. Jawaharlal also, on this occasion, met a number

[1] To Mohanlal Saxena, 15 June 1931, *Collected Works,* vol. 46 (Delhi, 1971), p. 384.
[2] Speeches at Delhi, 22 June, *The Bombay Chronicle,* 29 June 1931 and at Lucknow 26 June 1931.
[3] Speeches at Rae Bareli, 25 June, *The Leader,* 3 July and Soram 5 July, *The Pioneer,* 8 July 1931.
[4] Chief Secretary U.P. to Home Secretary, 30 June and 2 July, and Governor's telegram to Home Member, 20 July 1931. Home Dept. Pol. 33/XVI and K.W. 1931.
[5] See Hailey to Dawson, 7 June, and to Findlater Stewart, 15 June 1931, Hailey papers, vol. 21.

of official including the Viceroy. 'Jawaralalal [*sic*] I also saw for a short time, quite a nice man to talk to, much more practical than G.', recorded Willingdon with silly condescension. [1]

Jawaharlal's serious conversations were with Emerson, who was impressed by his genuine concern about the economic depression, which was limiting opportunities for constructive work and social reform. He made no secret of the fact that landlords had no place in his scheme of things, but he intended to buy them out rather than confiscate their estates, and even this only when the Congress party came constitutionally into power, and not as the result of a peasants' revolt. In the U.P., he said, the Congress was acting merely as the organization of the *kisans* and advising them on what rents they should pay or none at all. Indeed, according to Emerson himself, it was he who took the offensive in these discussions and Jawaharlal who was moderate. Emerson contended that the Government would never have concluded the settlement if they had had any idea of the agrarian programme which the Congress would undertake in the U.P. and, when asked by Jawaharlal what the Congress should do if the *kisans* came to them with their grievances, replied naïvely that the Congress should refuse to intervene. Pressed by Jawaharlal as to what he would say if a peasant who had been evicted wished to till his land rather than leave it fallow, Emerson seems to have replied that he would simply refuse to answer him. Obviously this was not going to convince Jawaharlal or deflect him from his line of action, but it was clear that he was no hot-headed revolutionary.

> He was not prepared to admit that Congress activities had generally been objectionable, but was less uncompromising in this matter than Mr. Gandhi. . . The Pandit seemed to me to appreciate more clearly than Mr. Gandhi the complexity of the problem, and while of course he was naturally anxious to get from the local Government some concession in regard to existing collections, he probably realised that this was impracticable. He was more concerned with a permanent solution or, at any rate, alleviation. [2]

In a sense, of course, these conversations were unreal, because both Jawaharlal and Emerson were perceptive enough to see that, whatever the short-term bargains and haggles, there could be no final settlement between an imperialist Government and a Congress committed to independence. As Emerson recognized, even if Gandhi gave a hint to Jawaharlal to slow down Congress activities in the U.P. and even if Jawaharlal wished to do so, circumstances would

[1] To Hailey, 22 July 1931, Hailey papers, vol. 21. That Willingdon could often (and not just on this occasion) get Jawaharlal's name wrong is but one indication of his general flippancy and light-heartedness in public affairs.

[2] Emerson's note on discussions with Jawaharlal, 19 and 20 July 1931, Home Dept., Pol. 33/23 of 1931. Jawaharlal's account (though the officials are not named) is to be found in *Autobiography*, pp. 284 and 305.

15 Jawaharlal, 1929

16 A procession in Madras,
1928, supporting a boycott
of the Simon Commission

17 Jawaharlal and Kamala leading a procession against the Salt Tax in Allahabad 1930

18 Police disperse crowds on the Wadala Salt Pans, 1930

19 Followers of Gandhi in prison at Yeravda, near Poona, 1930

20 An election in Bombay, 1930; some of the demonstrators clashing with police

21   Jawaharlal, after his committal to prison, with his father
      outside Naini Jail, 1930

22   Jawaharlal in prison, 1932   23   Kamala Nehru

probably prove too strong for him. On return to Lucknow Jawaharlal met the Chief Secretary and urged that as the season for collection of rents was over and tenants had already paid 9 to 12 annas or more in the rupee, further collections should be suspended and coercive processes stopped. This would immediately relieve the tension and produce the proper atmosphere for an inquiry into future adjustments. But the Government, on the plea that rents had earlier been deliberately withheld, insisted that the process of collection should continue longer than in normal years. So evictions continued, and attempts were made to secure new tenants for these holdings. Congressmen in particular were penalized for taking an interest in these matters, and such tenants as declared themselves against the Congress were given special remissions.[1]

Jawaharlal, supported by Tassaduq Sherwani, himself a *zamindar* and president of the U.P. Congress committee, and Pandit Malaviya, by no stretch of the imagination a radical, reported all this to Gandhi, who sought clarification from Hailey and received a soft but evasive answer. Gandhi made no specific demands, Hailey was only too anxious to keep the U.P. in the background of controversy, and the Working Committee was not keen to have a breakdown of the settlement and the cancellation of Gandhi's journey to London on such an explosive, class-ridden issue.[2] It was Bardoli and coercive processes there which the Committee put in the forefront, and Jawaharlal did not embarrass it by making the U.P. crisis a test case. Asked by Gandhi for a definite answer as to whether he should decline to attend the Conference because of the U.P., Jawaharlal and his colleagues from the province replied that although there were sufficient instances in the U.P. of a breach of the truce, they would try to see that conditions improved and they did not want the U.P. to stand in the way of Gandhi going to London.[3] For Jawaharlal realized that though he himself favoured the abolition of landlordism, his colleagues in the Working Committee (not excluding Gandhi) were unwilling to recognize, whatever their theoretical commitments in earlier resolutions, even the possibility of marked social and economic change. The crisis in the U.P. was real enough, and conservatives like Sherwani and Malaviya could not shut their eyes to it; but the Congress leaders from other parts of India had no wish to take up a problem which might open the door to unpredictable forces, and preferred to confront the Government on the safer ground of Gujarat. On this, however, a last-minute agreement was reached, and Gandhi sailed for England, leaving Jawaharlal to deal with the U.P.

Indeed, even before Gandhi's departure, Jawaharlal appears to have decided that on the U.P. problem his guidance was unsafe. The U.P. Government set

[1] Jawaharlal's letters to Jagdish Prasad, 29 and 30 July and 1 August 1931, AICC File G. 118 of 1931 and 31 July 1931, AICC File G 40(KW)(iii) of 1931; report of U.P. Government for the second half of July 1931, Home Dept. Pol. 18/7/31.

[2] See Purushottam Das Tandon's comments on the Working Committee meeting, *The Leader*, 9 August 1931.

[3] Jawaharlal's speech at Allahabad, 20 August, *The Leader*, 22 August 1931.

up a committee to consider future agrarian policy and invited Govind Ballabh Pant to serve on it. Gandhi, when consulted, advised that Pant should agree, but his advice was ignored and Pant declined to serve till he had received the approval of the U.P. Congress committee.[1] Clearly Jawaharlal's normal and ostentatious loyalty to his leader did not now exclude an occasional exercise of quiet defiance. The official committee recommended a complicated system of reduction of rents on the basis of the fall in prices, but never more than 50 per cent and never below the average rentals for 1901-05. They would also not be reduced if their rise could be shown to be the result of causes other than the rise in prices, such as irrigation or the use of improved seeds.[2] The Government accepted this recommendation, which would result in a reduction of Rs 4.1 crores[3] out of a total cash rental of Rs 18 crores. But the actual implementation of this cumbrous scheme depended on a host of minor revenue officials, susceptible to local pressures and the influence of *zamindars*. Evictions, issue of processes and arrests of Congressmen continued as before, though 'more quietly and without fuss'.[4] There were about 5,000 evictions in Allahabad district alone, while in Muttra district over 2,000 processes were issued in August. There were more ejectments, sales of property and cases and convictions of ejected tenants for trespass in the ten months from October 1930 to July 1931 than in the twelve months of the previous revenue years 1928-29 and 1929-30.[5] Officials both at Simla and at Naini Tal counselled Jawaharlal to be patient and give them time to reinstate the tenants,[6] but in fact there was never any intention of doing so. The argument that there should be no evictions for non-payment of rent was regarded by the U.P. Government as untenable and tantamount to granting proprietary rights to the tenants.[7] They were prepared, on the other hand, for any organization by Jawaharlal of defensive direct action — that is, civil disobedience — in the last resort, a course which the Congress had made known to the Government that it kept open to itself.[8] So, although at this time the Central Government adopted a posture of friendliness and seemed to wish to strengthen the efforts of the Congress to maintain the settlement,[9] the U.P. Government did not even pretend to do so. Gandhi's suggestion[10] to

[1] See Jawaharlal's telegram to Gandhi and Gandhi's reply, 15 August 1931.

[2] Letter of Revenue Secretary U.P. to district officers, 24 August 1931, *The Leader,* 12 October 1931.

[3] A crore is ten millions, or one hundred lakhs.

[4] Jawaharlal to Gandhi, 1 September 1931.

[5] See table on p. 163: enclosure to letter from Chief Secretary, U.P. to Home Secretary, Government of India, 26 October 1931, Home Dept. Pol. File 33/36 of 1931.

[6] See Jawaharlal to Jagdish Prasad, 5 September 1931.

[7] Fortnightly report of the U.P. Government for the second half of August 1931, Home Dept. Pol 18/8/31.

[8] Jawaharlal's interview in *The Bombay Chronicle,* 31 August 1931, and circular to provincial Congress committees, 31 August 1931, AICC File P-1/1931.

[9] E.C. Miéville, Private Secretary to Viceroy, to Jawaharlal, 28 August 1931, AICC File G-7/1931.

[10] Letter, 28 August 1931.

Statement showing ejectments etc. in the United Provinces

	Revenue year 1928-29 (1 October 1928 to 30 September 1929)	Revenue year 1929-30 (1 October 1929 to 30 September 1930)	Revenue year 1930-31 (1 October 1930 to 31 July 1931)
(1) Number of arrears of rent suits	271,919	340,249	288,465
(2) Number of ejectments ordered for arrears	42,280	53,421	64,076
(3) Area from which ejectment actually took place (in acres)	117,517.874	149,071.254	189,362.960
(4) Number of applications for surrender or relinquishment	25,182	26,188	94,800
(5) Number of cases in which property was actually sold after distraint	8,880	10,897	13,337
(6) Number of cases under Section 447, Indian Penal Code, against ejected tenants for re-entering or attempting to re-enter their holdings, and number of convictions, *vide* Section 95 of the Agra Tenancy Act			
Cases	818	982	1,054
Convictions	284	267	345

Hailey to send for Jawaharlal was coldly ignored. It was not that an open confrontation with the Congress was desired, but the hope was that if Jawaharlal and the U.P. Congress were pushed to extreme courses, in Gandhi's absence Jawaharlal's rivals, who had no wish to revive civil disobedience, might gain the upper hand, and the organization itself might split up.[1]

Sensing that the Government of India were, at least as far as the U.P. was concerned, at this time less belligerent than the Local Government, Jawaharlal

[1] Hailey to Frank Brown, 9 August, and to Gen. Shea, 29 August 1931, Hailey papers, vol. 21.

got Patel, as president of the Congress, to write to them to intervene.[1] But nothing happened, and meantime the general attitude of the Government of India also stiffened. There were shooting outrages at Hijli detention camp in Bengal, the salt concession in the whole area covered by the Salt Range in Shahpur district in the Punjab was withdrawn, and Congressmen were arrested in large numbers in that province. In the U.P. itself, evictions and harassments continued, and men and women were beaten up for the recovery of such petty arrears as two or five rupees.[2] Yet, under Jawaharlal's guidance, the U.P. Congress committee did not consider the request of the Rae Bareli district committee for permission to start civil disobedience, but instead called on all its branches to refrain from any such action for the time being.[3] The committee appointed by the U.P. Congress to inquire into the agrarian situation, which also reported at this time, publicly denied that the Congress was opposed to the *zamindars* or wished to countenance a class war.[4] Jawaharlal had no wish to embarrass Gandhi in London or his colleagues in the Working Committee; nor was the organization on a war footing.

Touring the district, Jawaharlal found the conditions varied, depending on the particular attitudes of the local officials. He was more interested in ascertaining the facts than in exploiting them. Even the U.P. Government conceded that his speeches were 'less open to objection than usual'.[5] But, on the whole, the situation was grim. The *kisans,* losing all hope of redress from the Government or the Congress, were desperately raising money to avoid eviction and the loss of their crops. They sold their cattle, dumped their grain on the markets thus further reducing its price, and borrowed from moneylenders and paid not only the current rent in full but often some arrears and heavy costs. Those who had been evicted paid very much more to recover their land than if they had paid the full rent without any remission at the start, and in the process they lost their occupancy rights and became life tenants.[6] Moreover, these direct transactions were regarded by the authorities as mutual arrangements between the landlords and the tenants which dispensed with the need for remissions. To deter Jawaharlal from visiting villages in Gonda district, where there were serious allegations of harassment, ditches were dug across the road; and in Bahraich district, to prevent attendance at Jawaharlal's meetings, the *kisans* were directed to stay in their villages on the particular dates to receive their remission slips.[7] In many districts the peasants were informed that these remissions

[1] Patel to Emerson, 15 September 1931, Home Dept. Pol. File 33/36 of 1931.

[2] Jawaharlal to V.N. Mehta, Commissioner, Allahabad Division, 23 September 1931, AICC File G 40(KW)(iii)/1931.

[3] *The Leader,* 23 September 1931.

[4] *Agrarian Distress in the United Provinces,* pp. 49-50.

[5] Fortnightly report of U.P. Government for the first half of October 1931, Home Dept. Pol. 18/10/31.

[6] Jawaharlal to Gandhi, 16 October 1931.

[7] *The Leader,* 14 October 1931.

would be cancelled if the rent for the current *kharif* crop was withheld for over a month. It was only when rent had been fully paid, moreover, that any objections of the tenant regarding the rent would be considered. But it was obvious that money once paid would never be returned, and clearly the purpose was to terrorize the peasant into paying all he could. In Allahabad district, the population had increased over the years, while the cultivated area had declined, so that the pressure on holdings, already uneconomic, was acute. The *kharif* crop was also well below average because of untimely rains. But heedless of these considerations, as well as of the public opinion to which the district was exposed, the Collector, R.F. Mudie, granted remissions for 1931 of only Rs 9.5 lakhs, out of a total cash rental of Rs 57 lakhs for both the *kharif* and *rabi* crops, as against Rs 11 lakhs in 1930 for the *rabi* crop only,[1] on the ground that there were a large number of occupancy tenants whose rents had not been raised in recent years. The Collector also contended that the rental demand in 1915-16 had been the same as in 1901, the base year selected by the U.P. Government, and on this wrong premiss, assumed without checking or publishing the figures, further reduced the remissions.[2] So the remissions were only 17 per cent or 2 annas 7 pies[3] in the rupee, although the prices of cereals had fallen by 55 per cent, and grain formerly worth a rupee was now worth only seven annas.

Jawaharlal was at last forced to contemplate a no-rent campaign. 'Thus the outlook for the tenant', he wrote to the Chief Secretary, 'is about as black as it could well be and there seems no way out. If the Government policy is enforced he is doomed to even greater suffering than he has passed through. We have been anxiously considering this and the Allahabad District Congress Committee have felt that they can be no parties to this continuous oppression of the kisan leading to his economic death.' So it might become necessary to advise the tenantry to withhold payment of rent till a satisfactory solution was found. Though they did not wish to take any decision, involving such far-reaching consequences, without the fullest consultation, there seemed no other way. But they were convening a representative *kisan* conference to consider this question, and also communicating with the provincial and the All-India Congress.

I regret greatly that such a step should be contemplated by them, specially at a time when Gandhiji is attending the Round Table Conference. But the question of payment or non-payment is an urgent issue and cannot await the deliberations of the Round Table Conference or the return of Gandhiji. We have tried to avoid raising any issue which might lead to

[1] Though for 1930 the U.P. Government had sanctioned remissions of Rs 12.3 lakhs, the Collector granted only Rs 11 lakhs.
[2] Press interview of Collector of Allahabad, 14 October, *The Leader,* 16 October 1931; Jawaharlal to Jagdish Prasad, 15 October 1931 (two letters), AICC File 54, Part III/1931.
[3] A pie was one-twelfth of an anna.

friction and we shall continue to do so. But the fates seem to be against this.[1]

Jawaharlal also brought the crisis to the notice of the Viceroy and of Gandhi. The Government of India merely referred his letter to the U.P. Government, while Gandhi authorized Jawaharlal to do as he thought fit.[2] Both the Allahabad district committee and the *kisan* conference recommended the cessation of payment of rents,[3] 'It is war,' Jawaharlal was reported as having said, 'war now and ever till the end of our lives.'[4] What exasperated him as much as tenancy wrong in the U.P. was the shabby treatment to which Gandhi was being exposed in London.

By now the Government of India were prepared for a fight. 'Jawarlalal [*sic*] seems to be on the warpath again and Gandhi's last speech when he evidently lost his temper and let himself go makes one feel one will be busy again ere long'.[5] But at this stage it was the U.P. Government that hung back. Hailey felt that Jawaharlal was bluffing, and that the telegraphic correspondence with Gandhi was as much meant for the official censor as for themselves.[6] Yet the Governor was not willing to call the bluff. Mudie was transferred from Allahabad, an error in his calculation of the remissions was acknowledged and a further one lakh was sanctioned, and the Congress leaders were invited to a discussion with the officials concerned. This enabled the Working Committee to postpone a firm decision and refer the recommendation of the district committee to the U.P. committee, with the final approval or veto of a no-rent campaign vesting in the president. Patel.[7]

The talks, however, came to nothing, the official side refusing to discuss the proposals of the Congress for further rental reductions, cancellation of arrears, revocation of ejectments and lowering of interest on money owed to moneylenders. Any modifications of the decisions already announced were regarded as impracticable, and nothing more than further information about present policy was offered.[8] The U.P. Congress committee, still reluctant to have a confrontation in which the tenants would obviously suffer most, offered to renew negotiations.[9] But there was not even a remote chance of these succeeding, for the authorities were determined to yield no ground; the only question for them

[1] Jawaharlal to Jagdish Prasad, 15 October 1931, AICC File 54, Part III/1931.

[2] Jawaharlal to E. C. Miéville, P.S.V., 16 October 1931 and Emerson to Jagdish Prasad, 21 October 1931, Home Dept. Pol. 33/36 of 1931; Jawaharlal's cable to Gandhi, 16 October 1931, and Gandhi's reply, 19 October 1931.

[3] *The Leader*, 19 and 25 October 1931.

[4] *The Tribune*, 25 October 1931.

[5] Willingdon to Hailey, 22 October 1931, Hailey papers, vol. 22.

[6] Hailey to Crerar, 24 October, and to Stewart, 28 October 1931, Hailey papers, vol. 22; Jagdish Prasad to Emerson, 26 October 1931. Home Dept. Pol. 33/36 of 1931.

[7] 29 October 1931, *The Leader*, 31 October 1931.

[8] Jawaharlal to Jagdish Prasad, 3 November 1931, AICC File G/25 of 1931; Hailey to Crerar, 9 November 1931, Home Dept. Pol. File 33/36 of 1931.

[9] T. A. K. Sherwani to Chief Secretary, 3 November 1931, Home Dept. Pol. File 33/36 of 1931.

was whether the charade of discussion should be gone through. The Central and Local Governments believed that this would have the advantage of strengthening the forces within the Congress against Jawaharlal.

> As you say in your letter, Jawaharlal himself is probably in favour of an immediate declaration of Civil Disobedience if he can get sufficient support from other Congress leaders. He has always objected to the Delhi pact; he is clearly disgusted that Congress ever consented to appear at the Round Table Conference; and he is of course inordinately vain and desirous of attracting to himself the limelight which has hitherto shone on Gandhi and to a certain extent on Patel.[1]

In fact, this assessment was inaccurate as well as prejudiced. Jawaharlal was as disinclined as any other Congress leader to start a no-rent movement, primarily because of the absence of Gandhi. He now, unlike in 1921, understood the basic nature of the peasant problem; he knew that it was a part of the class war; but he preferred to project it as an aspect of the struggle against the British, and even in this he sought to avoid battle. But the option was being gradually removed. The Government expressed their willingness to parley, but made it clear that there would be no reconsideration of principles. Meantime, collections for the current season were due to commence on 15 November, and the U.P. Congress committee, with the authorization of Patel, directed the *kisans* of Allahabad district to withhold payment of rent and revenue while negotiations were pending.[2]

There was logic in this, for it was pointless to pay rent and revenue while the whole question of the quantum was under discussion. But the Government utilized this resolution to call off the discussions. Indeed, the Government of India, in Hailey's words, 'took fire'[3] and wanted him to move against the Congress with all his forces and without delay. The Congress and its affiliated bodies should be outlawed, the Instigation Ordinance re-promulgated and the leaders arrested.[4] With the Conservatives back in power in Britain and the second Round Table Conference a failure, the Government of India had clearly decided to turn their backs on Irwin's settlement; and the harsh Bengal Ordinance and the drastic policy favoured in the U.P. were both parts of a general return to a policy of repression. Willingdon and Emerson went to Lucknow to speed up matters, but Hailey refused to be hustled. The Round Table Conference had still a fortnight to run, the payment of rents had been delayed by late rains and would not start on any large scale until 1 December, and the Congress had served no clear-cut challenge. So, in the U.P. at any rate, there continued

[1]Hailey to Crerar, 9 November 1931, ibid.
[2]*The Leader*, 18 November 1931.
[3]To de Montmorency, 3 December 1931, Hailey papers, vol. 22.
[4]Crerar to Hailey, 16 November 1931, Home Dept. Pol. File 33/36 of 1931.

what Jawaharlal described as an impossible situation. 'Peace we can understand and war we are not unused to, but this hybrid state we cannot understand.'[1] The Congress had received private information from Delhi that the Government of India were spoiling for a fight,[2] but yet there was no action in the U.P.

Clearly, however, this was only a temporary lull. The days of the truce were obviously numbered, and Jawaharlal and his colleagues braced themselves for the struggle which they had sought so hard to postpone. 'If we are to die, we shall die after a fight. I do not want a half-way settlement or a half-way fight.'[3] He expected to be arrested within a few days, and had no hope of seeing Gandhi on his return.[4] Indeed, the *Pioneer,* which had access to official sources, referred to the possibility of deportations,[5] and Willingdon would certainly have done this if he could. 'One thing I do regret very much in all this business and that is we have no power of deportation out of India. It would be an enormous advantage if we can take hold of 15 or 20 of these leaders, send them right away to the West Indies or somewhere instead of having to keep them under surveillance in some Province or other.'[6]

On 6 December the district Congress committees in Rae Bareli, Etawah, Kanpur and Unao, in addition to Allahabad, were authorized to commence their no-rent campaigns.[7] Payment of rent in these districts came to an almost complete standstill,[8] other districts were also lining up, and it was clear that once the movement started it would spread throughout the province. The U.P. Government secured the permission of the Government of India to arrest Jawaharlal if he toured any of these districts.[9] However, though Jawaharlal did visit some of these districts, nothing was done. Hailey knew that his case was weak and, despite the impatience of the authorities at Simla, remained 'cold-footed'.[10] Unlike in the previous year, this no-rent campaign had no obvious political overtones and was motivated, and justified, by economic causes. In many European countries there would have been hesitation in penalizing such agitation, and repressive action would alienate moderate opinion in India and abroad. Nor, unlike the Government of India, did he now believe that the Congress under Jawaharlal was determined to force the issue in Gandhi's absence. 'It is not unlikely that the Congress really desire to wait till

[1] Speech at Calcutta, 17 November, *The Tribune,* 19 November 1931.

[2] *Autobiography,* p. 309.

[3] Speech at the *kisan* conference at Allahabad, 25 November, *The Leader,* 27 November 1931.

[4] To Patel, 26 November 1931, AICC File G 60 of 1931; to Syed Mahmud, 27 November 1931.

[5] 27 November 1931.

[6] Willingdon to Sir Samuel Hoare, Secretary of State, 13 December 1931, Templewood papers, I.O.L. Mss, Eur. E. 240, vol. 5.

[7] *The Bombay Chronicle,* 7 December 1931.

[8] Fortnightly Report of U.P. Government for the first half of December 1931, Home Dept. Pol. 18/12/31.

[9] U. P. Government's telegram and reply of Government of India, 7 December 1931, Home Dept. Pol. File 33/36 of 1931.

[10] To de Montmorency, 3 December 1931, Hailey papers, vol. 22.

Gandhi's return before precipitating matters.'[1] So, to strengthen their case, the U. P. Government lowered the water rates, introduced a bill to secure tenants from eviction if they paid two-thirds of the arrears due for the previous four years, and offered to consider immediate measures to protect tenants against debts which had become overdue owing to the fall in prices.

Then, at last, Hailey decided to strike. What ultimately determined his action was not so much the spurring from Simla as the fear that the situation might slip out of control and if Gandhi, on his return, decided to support the agitation, no rent or revenue at all could be collected.[2] Even then, he toned down the Ordinance drafted by the Government of India[3] and issued it together with what was really a long apologia. It was contended that the Congress had utilized the economic crisis to increase its following among the *kisans*, that the spirit of the truce had never been respected and that Jawaharlal had preached class warfare.[4] Under the Ordinance which, even as modified, was drastic enough, action was now taken against Congressmen. Notices were served on Jawaharlal and other leaders prohibiting them from speaking or writing in support of the campaign; and Anand Bhawan, along with many Congress offices, was searched. Jawaharlal's own arrest was delayed because he was away on tour in Bombay and the Karnatak.

Even at this stage, the Congress was in no mood for a general campaign of civil disobedience. The Secretary of State, Sir Samuel Hoare, found Gandhi in London as well disposed as could be expected. He contemplated no immediate general renewal of civil disobedience, and promised before taking any such step to communicate with Hoare and Willingdon — 'the satisfactory part about the interview was the genuine friendliness of the old man.'[5] In Bombay, Patel, the Congress president, publicly offered to let any impartial judge, or even Irwin, decide as to which party had broken the settlement, and Jawaharlal suggested an inquiry by any Indian or European judge appointed by the Government.[6] On his return to Allahabad Jawaharlal was served with a notice not to leave the city without official permission and the U. P. Provincial Conference, scheduled to be held on 26 December, was banned. Still the Congress struggled to avoid battle, and postponed the conference.[7] But Jawaharlal himself was arrested on 26 December for violating the order restricting him to Allahabad. The local magistrate had thought that this restriction had merely been to

---

[1]Fortnightly report of U.P. Government for the second half of November 1931, Home Dept. Pol. File 18/11/31.

[2]Hailey to Verney Lovett, 14 December 1931, and to Irwin, 2 January 1932, Hailey papers, vols. 22 and 23, respectively.

[3]Hailey to Emerson, 11 December 1931, Home Dept. Pol. File 33/36 of 1931.

[4]Statement issued by the U.P. Government, 14 December 1931.

[5]Hoare to Willingdon, telegram 7 December and letter, 10 December 1931, Templewood papers, Box 11 and vol. 1, respectively.

[6]Speeches at Bombay, 15 December, *The Bombay Chronicle*, 16 December 1931.

[7]*The Leader*, 25 December 1931.

prevent Jawaharlal's furtherance of the no-tax agitation in his home province, and had informed the Government that he was willing to allow Jawaharlal to proceed to Bombay if informed of this by Jawaharlal.[1] Though Jawaharlal gave no formal notice of this, it was known that he was leaving Allahabad in order to welcome Gandhi on his return from London and not to promote the no-rent campaign; but the U.P. Government ordered his arrest. He was arrested and taken off the train at Iradatnagar station, and sentenced a week later to two years' imprisonment. He was also fined Rs 500, and for realizing this amount a car registered in the name of his daughter was attached.

The arrest of Jawaharlal soon appeared as not just a provincial matter but part of a general offensive against the Congress. Willingdon and his Government believed that Irwin had made an error in negotiating with the Congress and signing a truce, and they had no intention of repeating it. The Viceroy was 'perfectly clear as I have always been that Gandhi is a sort of Jekyll and Hyde, and while he may possibly have his saint-like side, on the other he is the most Machiavellian bargaining little political humbug I have ever come across.'[2] When Gandhi sought an interview with the Viceroy, he was asked first to repudiate his colleagues and to agree not to discuss Bengal, the U. P. and the North-West Frontier, where also a number of stern ordinances had been imposed and Abdul Gaffar Khan arrested. These were terms which Gandhi obviously could not, and was not expected to, accept; and when the Working Committee decided on a resumption of civil disobedience, Gandhi, Patel and other leading Congressmen were arrested. The 'shock tactics'[3] of the Government of India surprised almost everybody. The Secretary of State was not too happy but supported the man on the spot,[4] who, on his own admission, was 'becoming a sort of Mussolini in India'.[5] This time, however long it might take, the back of the Congress was to be broken. 'We can, in my opinion,' wrote the Home Member after twelve months of repression,' do without the goodwill of Congress, and in fact I do not believe for a moment that we shall ever have it, but we cannot afford to do without the confidence of those who have supported us during the long struggle against the Congress.'[6] So the policy of seeking to destroy the nationalist movement was to be continued, and Jawaharlal would obviously remain one of its prime targets. His ambition

[1] Fortnightly report of the U.P. Government for the second half of December 1931, Home Dept. File No. 18/12/31 Poll.

[2] Willingdon to Hoare, 10 January 1932, Templewood papers, vol. 5.

[3] Hailey to de Montmorency, 17 January 1932, Hailey papers, vol. 23. Surprisingly, however, even a friend of the Congress like Edward Thompson at this time supported Government policy. 'But Congress last December was an insolent and intolerant faction.' A Letter from India (London, 1932), p. 41.

[4] Hoare to Willingdon, 31 December 1931 and 8 January 1932, Templewood papers vol. 1.

[5] Willingdon to Hoare, 26 December 1931, Templewood papers, vol. 5.

[6] Note of H. G. Haig, Home Member, 28 December 1932, Home Dept. Pol. File 31/97/32.

was believed to be some form of Leninism, the establishment of a Leninite directorate.[1] 'Jawahar Lal is a fanatic. There are threatenings of an attempt to revive a no-rent campaign in the U.P. Jawahar Lal Nehru is the author of that policy and his release would obviously give it a definite stimulus.'[2]

[1] Hailey to Hoare, 28 February, and to C.S. Newham, 20 October 1932, Hailey papers, vols. 23 and 25, respectively.
[2] Haig, op. cit.

12

In and Out of Prison

Clearly, therefore, this was going to be a long spell in jail for Jawaharlal and now, for the first time, prison life began to tell on him. He had trouble with his teeth, and his general condition was poor. He began to run a temperature in the evenings, but for months the jail superintendent would neither try to diagnose the cause nor permit examination by other doctors. Ultimately, after Jawaharlal's transfer to another jail, Dr Bidhan Roy and Dr Ansari were permitted to see him and it was found to be a recurrence of pleurisy on the right side. Gradually Jawaharlal shook it off, but meanwhile had to forgo his running and exercises and even walks, and content himself with sunbaths.

His living conditions too were, at the start, such as made for relative discomfort. He was first placed in Naini jail, and then, after a few weeks, transferred to Bareilly where both environment and men were vile. His barracks were at least six feet below ground level, which meant that the surrounding walls were over twenty-four feet. 'The wall which faces me', he wrote to his daughter,[1] 'must bear some relation, in height at least, to the Great Wall of China!' Further, for the first time since Nabha, not only the ward but the barracks also were locked at night. The fortnightly interview with his family was spoilt by the close supervision of not only the jailor, but of a policeman who took notes. His companions also, with the exception of Govind Ballabh Pant, took notes. His companions also, with the exception of Govind Vallabh Pant, irritated him. So generally Jawaharlal fretted. 'On the whole I have not been able to settle down this time as I have done in the past. Perhaps a slight touch of ill-health — perhaps my transfer — perhaps my missing my old companions — perhaps a certain want of satisfaction with things, and happenings in general — perhaps so many other things!'[2]

This malaise was worsened by other events. In April his mother was beaten in a *lathi* charge and badly injured. The old lady was full of courage and spirit. 'I am proud to have been beaten with sticks for the cause of my motherland . . . While being beaten I thought of you and your father and did not utter

[1] Letter, 26 March 1932, *Glimpses of World History* (Bombay, 1967 ed.), p. 58.
[2] Diary entry, 4 March 1932.

a sigh . . . The mother of a brave son is also somewhat like him. It was only a *lathi* — had it been a gun I would have bared my chest.'[1] But it added to the intense despair of Jawaharlal. Then, because, at an interview in jail with Ranjit Pandit, Indira had shown him a school report of his children, the jailor insulted Jawaharlal's mother and wife who were also present, and the Government ordered that they could not interview Jawaharlal for a month. This roused Jawaharlal to bitter anger, and he declined to have any interviews even after the month was over; for on no account, as he put it, was he prepared to take the slightest risk of further insult to his mother and wife.[2] It was not till early in 1933, after a break of eight months, that he began, on Gandhi's persuasion, to see visitors again.

The self-denial of interviews, which formed the sole relief in the boredom of prison, robbed life of the excitement of anticipation.

The days and the weeks and the months pass by one after the other, merging into each other, and there is little to distinguish one from the other. And the past looks like a blurred picture with nothing standing out. Yesterday takes one back to the day of one's arrest, for in between is a blank with little to impress the mind. It is the life of a vegetable rooted to one place, growing there without comment or argument, silent, motionless. And sometimes the activities of the outside world appear strange and a little bewildering to one in prison; they seem distant and unreal — a phantom show. So we develop two natures, the active and the passive, two ways of living, two personalities, like Dr. Jekyll and Mr. Hyde.[3]

In June 1932 Jawaharlal was transferred to Dehra Dun jail. Here the climate was pleasant and the jail buildings not severe. The superintendent, an Irishman whose name deserves to be remembered, Captain Falvey, had been a pupil of de Valera, and he did what he could to alleviate conditions. Jawaharlal was even permitted to take his walks outside the prison gates. But all this could not diminish the inner turmoil. Indeed, on hearing of the savage treatment of political prisoners in other jails in the United Provinces, Jawaharlal felt ashamed of the better conditions of his own prison life, and he invited the Government to give him the same treatment as the others.[4]

Jawaharlal was concerned, too, about his wife and mother roughing it out on their own and his two sisters languishing in jail; but it was the thought of his growing daughter that frequently came strongly to him and filled his mind. It was because letters to her brought her image close to him that he continued writing his neat little essays, taking her stage by stage through the human past, even though they could not be sent to her and had to be kept aside for a later date.

[1] Letter (in Hindi) to Jawaharlal, 16 April 1932.
[2] To the Superintendent, District Jail, Dehra Dun, 11 July 1932.
[3] Letter to Indira, New Year's Day 1933, *Glimpses*, p. 491.
[4] Letter to the Superintendent, District Jail, Dehra Dun, 16 November 1932.

Jawaharlal was no professional scholar writing within a clearly defined and balanced framework. Taking, as he described it, centuries at a stride and seeing continents at a glance, he rushed past what he found dull and lingered at points where his interest was aroused. He was, for instance, fascinated by the great men of history — and not necessarily the men of virtue and idealism. Genghis Khan and Napoleon take up as much space as Asoka, Leonardo or Lenin. Strength, even in cruelty, commanded his attention. This was to be expected of someone who was never happier than when under the influence of stronger characters. But it was also the product of a temporary sense of loss. Jawaharlal himself throve on action, and, forced in jail to .action, he glamorized the vigorous performances of others whatever their results.

In the preface written on 1 January 1934, he commented that 'even as I was writing the letters my outlook on life changed gradually. Today if I had to rewrite them, I would write differently or with a different emphasis.' He would probably have qualified the ultimate belief that history tells of growth and progress and of the possibility of an infinite advance for man.

> History is not pleasant. Man, in spite of his great and vaunted progress, is still a very unpleasant and selfish animal. And yet perhaps it is possible to see the silver lining of progress right through the long and dismal record of selfishness and quarrelsomeness and inhumanity of man.[1]

He might have toned down too his glorification of certain individuals. But otherwise he retained all his life the half-liberal, half-Marxist view of history which holds the book together. The story of man was one connected whole, and the only history that could be properly written was the history of the world. It was the product not of individuals or national peculiarities but of world forces, and developments in different countries told basically the same tale. Even the 'superficial sketches' which he had 'joined together by a thin thread'[2] and which dealt mostly with Europe and Asia were intended to establish that history was not what was achieved by leaders or governments but what happened to peoples, and this was the result of the interplay of ideas, economic interests and social relations. Though he made no deep analysis, he broadly believed that the class which controlled the means of production was the class that ruled, and that the history of man was the history of class conflicts and social struggles. To grasp this was to secure the ability both to understand the past and to face the future with confidence and to be prepared for effective action.

The intellectual acceptance of history as the result of impersonal world forces for which no individual could be blamed or applauded, led Jawaharlal to criticize the imperialist system rather than the British and to strive to consider even issues pertaining to India impartially as a scientist examining facts. Jawaharlal could not jump out of his skin. He was a sensitive Asian nationalist, and

---

[1] Letter, 1 January 1933, *Glimpses,* p. 491.
[2] Letter, 9 August 1933, *Glimpses,* p. 985.

hard as he tried to be fair to the British, a certain impression of 'nagging' crept in,[1] especially when he was dealing with matters that had nothing to do with India. But he was wary of nationalism as 'an unreliable friend and an unsafe historian',[2] and dwelt on the shortcomings of his own people as much as those of their rulers. He had, since his return from Europe in 1927, shown an acute distaste for institutional worship. He continued to admire the great Hindu scriptures. The *Bhagavad Gita* was 'that jewel of a poem'; and as for the *Ramayana* and the *Mahabharata* — 'Who but the greatest of men could have written them?'[3] But they impressed him more as literature and historical testimony than as revelation. He disliked temple-going, was scornful of ritual and regarded prayers as morbid. But, writing in the early 'thirties when the memory of the Kanpur riots in which his friend Ganesh Shankar Vidyarthi had lost his life was still fresh, he was particularly concerned with the savagery committed in the name of religion. It was important to release India from the chains of the complex ideology of custom, convention and superstition. He was at pains to tell his fellow-countrymen that Islam did not believe in religious persecution and a man like Mahmud of Ghazni, whom most Indians regarded as an arch-iconoclast, was in fact no more than a successful soldier. He had come to India to conquer and loot, and would have done so whatever religion he had belonged to. The best of Indian culture was a synthesis; this had badly frayed and should be rebuilt on the securer foundations of freedom and social equality and in consonance with a better world order.

When Jawaharlal was too tired to write, there were always books. Fortunately there was no restriction this time on the number he could read and keep, and he was also allowed newspapers and journals without restriction. So apart from *The Statesman* and the *Pioneer*, he read the *Living Age*, the *Manchester Guardian Weekly*, the *New Leader,* the *New Republic*, the *Modern Review*, the *New Statesman*, the *Nation* and the *Spectator*; and his reading lists show that he was as well read and up-to-date as any leisurely person of cultivated tastes in London or New York. For the authors include Toynbee, Maurice Dobb, Leonard Woolf, Tawney, Laski, Louis Fischer, Julian Huxley and H. G. Wells as well as Sven Hedin, Tagore, Charles Morgan, Maurois, Lowes Dickinson and L.A.G. Strong. They not only, as Jawaharlal said, saved him from tedium and depression; they also kept him intellectually sensitive and vigorous.

So Jawaharlal settled down to jail routine and was irritated by talk of the release of all political prisoners. He even turned roundly on a fellow-prisoner who talked of parole for medical treatment. 'I have almost brought myself to the frame of mind when a ten year sentence of imprisonment will make little difference! Life outside under present circumstances has little attraction, so why should jail frighten?'[4] The occasional nostalgia for *la douceur du vivre* —

---

[1] E. Thompson's letter to Jawaharlal, 3 May 1937, *A Bunch of Old Letters*, pp. 233-40.
[2] Letter, 14 December 1932, *Glimpses*, p. 457.
[3] *Letters from a Father to his Daughter* (1972 ed.), p. 80.
[4] Jail diary, 10 March 1933.

pleasant surroundings, good friends, agreeable women, interesting conversation — was quickly smothered by the distaste for the bickerings in the family
and the petty rivalries in the Congress and its downhill slide and, above all, by
the growing alienation from Gandhi and his methods. The problem of the
Harijans and the question of their entry into temples engrossed Gandhi to the
extent that he pushed the main issue of British rule to the background. Gandhi's
fast in 1932 in protest against the Communal Award treating the Scheduled
Castes as a separate community for purposes of elections was a sharp shock.
The thought that Gandhi might die, and for such a minor reason, and that the
only remaining protective force in his life might be removed, knocked Jawaharlal
for a time off balance. 'My little world in which he has occupied such a big place,
shakes and totters, and there seems to be darkness and emptiness everywhere
. . . Shall I not see him again? And whom shall I go to when I am in doubt and
require wise counsel, or am afflicted and in sorrow and need loving comfort?'[1]
He wept, with mixed anguish of anger and love for a man who could precipitate
such a crisis so wantonly, and with bitterness towards a people who could let
their heroes risk death in such a way. Gandhi, amid his own travail, sensed this
reaction and sent Jawaharlal a reassuring telegram which helped, along with
the news of the fast having been broken, to restore Jawaharlal's stability. However, the whole episode drove him further on his inner resources. His existence
was based wholly on mind, emotion and memory. Sitting alone for hours that
seemed unimaginably long, he was frequently immersed in nostalgia. His father
he missed deeply and, as his mind went back to him again and again, he felt
shelterless.

> If father had been alive! How my mind wanders unconsciously and dwells
> on him and how empty I feel at the thought that he is not there. For months
> and years we lived far from each other — when I was in Europe — but it
> did not matter so much. Always one had the feeling that he was there and
> one could always go to him for help and counsel. Now there is an
> emptiness . . . [2]

And in another moving and candid entry he reveals how close to the surface
was this ache for his father:

> I was reading the newspaper — There was an account of a ceremony of
> unveiling a bust or statue of father's at the Hindu Boarding House in
> Allahabad. Hirday Nath Kunzru did the unveiling. I glanced casually at
> what he said, but I did not see anything. To my surprise, and quite un-
> awares, my eyes were full of tears.[3]

[1] Letter, 15 September 1932, *Glimpses*, pp. 337-8.
[2] Diary entry, 4 March 1932.
[3] Diary entry, 18 August 1932.

The next year, Gandhi undertook a purificatory fast and again plunged Jawaharlal, along with millions of his countrymen, into an emotional crisis. Gandhi realized this from afar, and wrote a chatty letter which was meant to soothe. The two telegrams Jawaharlal sent in reply indicate his bewilderment and dread of personal loss. 'What', wired Jawaharlal in his first mood of petulance, 'can I say about matters I do not understand. I feel lost in strange country where you are only familiar landmark and I try to grope my way in dark but I stumble. Whatever happens my love and thoughts will be with you.' But as the hours passed, he felt that he owed Gandhi a more cheerful message, and that evening he wired again: 'Now that you are launched on your great enterprise may I send you again love and greetings and assure you that I feel more clearly now that whatever happens it is well and whatever happens you win.'[1]

At the commencement of the fast the Government released Gandhi, who suspended civil disobedience for six weeks. This was a shock to Jawaharlal, but his mind, still numbed by the fear of Gandhi's death, accepted it. However, once the ordeal was over, Jawaharlal was able to see Gandhi with a much clearer vision than at any time before or since. For a short while the blinkers fell. He realized that Gandhi's attitude was sheer revivalism against which cool thinking had no chance. Gandhi's political actions were often guided by an unerring instinct, and, fortified by this, he did not encourage others to think. He himself, as he frequently asserted with pride, was satisfied with the next step and had given no precise thought to the long-term objective. The emphasis on God and faith, the acceptance of the existing social order, the stress on compromise, the reliance on lieutenants who were proclaimed reactionaries — all these jarred on Jawaharlal, and his love for Gandhi could not conceal from him that he was drifting further and further away from his leader. 'I am getting more and more certain that there can be no further political co-operation between Bapu and me. At least not of the kind that has existed. We had better go our different ways. My way will keep me in jail. That is dull work and depressing, but perhaps it is as well.'[2] Obviously a stiff battle between rival loyalties awaited him outside, and, not relishing this prospect, he did not look forward to his release. But coincidentally, just as he had finished the last of his letters to his daughter, he was transferred to Naini jail and, a week later, on 30 August, twelve days before he was due to be out of prison, he was released. His mother was seriously ill, the province was quiet, the Congress, with Gandhi's assistance, had seemed to have succeeded in tying itself into knots, and Jawaharlal himself was (erroneously) believed by the Government to be in favour of giving up civil disobedience. From his letters, read by the censors, it was gathered that he had no clear plan as to what he intended to do, and the world history he was writing was expected to keep him busy for some time. So, all points considered, the U.P. Government

[1] Telegrams, 8 May 1933.
[2] Diary entry, 18 July 1933.

(in Hailey's absence, since he was in London) felt it could take the risk of releasing him; and the Government of India approved.[1]

Jawaharlal's comment, on emerging from jail, that he attached little importance to the *swadeshi* and Harijan movements, the reports of his talks with his colleagues in the U.P. and his statements to the press that India's primary problem was economic and a new structure of society was inevitable raised expectations that he would formally break away from Gandhi and the old Congress and form a new party with independence as its goal.[2] There was certainly little in common between the public attitudes of Jawaharlal and of Gandhi. The younger man, while in jail, had made a wide study of international affairs, and saw India as a part of the pattern of world forces — the failure of capitalism, the rise of Nazism, the growth of dictatorial tendencies even in England[3] and the United States, and the shaping struggle between fascism and communism. There was, as Jawaharlal saw it, an inevitable, universal swing, not necessarily to the Soviet model but towards the general lines of the Soviet conception. Fundamentally the choice before the world was between some form of communism and some form of fascism, and he was all for the former. There was no middle road; one had to choose between the two, and Jawaharlal unhesitatingly chose the communist ideal. From this time dates the intense dislike of fascism, which was never to leave him, and the conviction that, while communism would have to adapt itself to changing conditions and different countries, its basic ideology, general outlook and scientific interpretation of history were sound. The affinity to the left, born of the visit to Europe in the 'twenties and nourished by reading, was confirmed by the rival philosophies that had spawned in Italy and Germany.[4]

In India, the effort of the British to protect not merely their own vested interests but also those of their allies, the *zamindars*, the princes and the capitalists, had not to Jawaharlal a chance of success because it went against the broad economic forces determining the future of the world. But nationalists, on their part, could not possibly hope to confine themselves to a replacement of foreign by home interests and seek to avoid the disturbance of class divisions and the social *status quo*. A socialist state was a concomitant of independence, and if an Indian Government took the place of the British and kept all the vested interests intact, this would not even be the shadow of freedom. The Congress, as the spearhead of the Indian nationalist movement, needed a new ideology which was

[1] Miéville, P. S. V., to Hailey, 29 June 1933, Blunt, Finance Member, to Hailey, 13 August 1933, Nawab of Chhatari, acting Governor, to Hailey, 26 August 1933, Hailey papers, vol. 26.

[2] Statement at Kanpur, 1 September, *The Leader*, 3 September 1933; interview in the *Pioneer* 1 September 1933; statement to the press, 4 September, *The Leader*, 6 September 1933; report of Banaras correspondent, 11 September, *The Leader*, 13 September 1933.

[3] Jawaharlal was apparently not alone in thinking this. 'I believe', wrote Hoare to Willingdon of Winston Churchill, 'that at the back of his mind he thinks that he will not only smash the Government but that England is going Fascist and that he, or someone like him, will eventually be able to rule India as Mussolini governs North Africa.' 6 April 1933, Templewood papers, vol. 3.

[4] To J. T. Gwynn, 2 November and 27 December 1933; statement to the press, 17 December 1933.

oriented to economic priorities and world conditions. This was an urgent task, for the impoverished peasants, whose drill-sergeant was hunger, were being driven to seek immediate relief.

> Roast lamb and mint sauce may be a tasty dish for those who eat it, but the poor lamb is not likely to appreciate the force of the best of arguments which point out the beauty of sacrifice for the good of the elect and the joys of close communion, even though dead, with mint sauce.[1]

There had to be a fundamental change of regime, politically, economically and socially, and the three were inextricably linked. British imperial rule had to be destroyed, the autocracy of the Indian states had to be ended, the whole land system had to be changed, industry brought under public control and all wealth shared. Each was a part of a total problem.

These ideas were all far removed from the outlook of Gandhi, who was seeking to renew peace negotiations with the British and to convert his countrymen, through fasts, to better social behaviour. His were the politics of intuition, requiring no argument or logic; Jawaharlal followed the path of reason, applying the laws of history and change. The break seemed inevitable, and as Jawaharlal went to Poona to confront his leader, also just released from prison, even he probably prepared himself for it. But he could not forget that, intermeshed as was the crisis, the most important front was the political one; and till the British had been expelled there could be little advance towards socialism. To combat economic wretchedness with the State power obstructing them was a hopeless waste of energy. But in this political struggle, Gandhi's leadership, however wayward, still seemed indispensable; and Congress was still the most militant organization in India. He himself was the quintessential upper-class figure, and even his radicalism, modelled on European example, seemed at times to him no more than a product of his deep-seated class sense, a *de haut en bas* posture. So both leader and party were necessary to him, and it was not just the springs of personal loyalty and affection which proved once again too deep to permit release. Jawaharlal, face to face with Gandhi after two years, publicly affirmed his continuing acceptance of Gandhi's leadership, and letters were exchanged in which Jawaharlal stated his position in terms which were easy for Gandhi to approve. The objective of independence included full control of the army and of foreign relations as well as financial and economic control, vested interests had to be 'devested' as gently and as rapidly as possible. the Round Table Conference was a futile effort, and the problem of Indian freedom could not be separated from vital international issues. Indeed, the clash of viewpoint was reduced almost to the ridiculous by Jawaharlal laying emphasis on his divergence from Gandhi on such paltry issues as to whether individual civil disobedience

---

[1] *Whither India?* These three articles, written in October 1933, provide the clearest exposition of Jawaharlal's views at this time.

was different in kind from mass civil disobedience, and secrecy in action was never desirable; and Gandhi closed the discussion by declaring that the differences were only temperamental and confusion had been created by Jawaharlal's tendency to be repetitive.[1] A few months later, Gandhi confidently gave Jawaharlal 'power of attorney' to state the policy of the Congress and was frank in his justification.

> I do not think that Jawaharlal's own views are yet sufficiently crystallized to make any fundamental departure from Congress policy likely. He is a firm believer in socialism, but his ideas on how best the socialist principles can be applied to Indian conditions are still in the melting pot. His communist views need not, therefore, frighten anyone.[2]

This failure to break with Gandhi was, of course, a disappointment to Jawaharlal's radical supporters, and when he followed up his correspondence with Gandhi by stating that he was perfectly happy with the way in which the struggle was being conducted and saw no need to summon a meeting of the AICC,[3] even his friends were driven to protest. For all his rhetoric he had no new policy and, seemingly, no use for democracy either, for he refused to consult other Congressmen.

> The fact is that Pandit Jawaharlal and his friends are themselves completely out of touch with the realities of the situation. Alternatively, we should have to suppose that they are purposely deluding themselves into the belief that the present policy has succeeded, which, of course, is unthinkable . . . No useful purpose is served by putting before Indians a radical economic policy, without telling them how to implement it . . . If Pandit Jawaharlal, in the face of the present appalling situation, has nothing better to offer us but the repetition of old shibboleths and the assertion that he, and he alone, is in touch with Congressmen and the masses it is clear that the reins of leadership, however regretfully, will have to be taken up by others, who will restore the Congress to its pristine power as the premier political influence in the country.[4]

What Jawaharlal's critics had failed to understand was that once he had decided not to break with Gandhi and the Congress, it was out of character for him to lead a rebellion from within. However sharp his expression of disagreement in private conversation, to the outside world he was determined to accept Con-

---

[1] Jawaharlal's statement to the press, 11 September, *The Leader*, 16 September 1933; Jawaharlal's letter, 13 September and Gandhi's reply, 14 September 1933.

[2] Interview in the *Madras Mail*, 22 December 1933.

[3] Interview in *The Bombay Chronicle*, 18 September 1933.

[4] Editorial, 'Save the Congress', in *The Bombay Chronicle*, 19 September 1933.

gress policy and decisions and interpret them in as favourable a manner as possible.[1] His loyalty might at some time snap; but while it lasted it was firm. Ups and downs were inevitable in a broad national movement and the lull to which he was now committed could best be used in hard thinking about methods and objectives. It was idle to expect the Congress as constituted to become a full-fledged socialist organization, but there was every hope of its becoming more and more socialistic. 'I do not see why I should walk out of the Congress leaving the field clear to the social reactionaries. Therefore, I think it is up to us to remain there and try to force the pace, thereby either converting others or making them depart.' A time might come, sooner rather than later, when the new ideas might cause a split in the Congress; but till then advantage should be taken of the national movement and it should be pushed as far as it could go. The Congress should be led out of the backwaters of pure politics by socialist elements who, rather than forming independent and sterile study centres, could exploit the Congress programme of mass action. For although ideologically backward, the Congress was still the most advanced revolutionary organization in the country and what was required was to give it a new orientation rather than to abandon it. Separate organizations for promoting the interests of workers or peasants were desirable, but not political organizations counter or parallel to the Congress. 'There is a great talk of the socialist party or the like but I am convinced that much of this talk is merely meant to cover ineffective action and also as a means of self-aggrandisement.'[2]

The plan to give Congressmen courses of instruction in ideology assumed that he would remain out of jail, and about this Jawaharlal was rightly not optimistic. Within a week of his release he was expecting to return. Prison was a part of the day's work, and he would clearly be back soon 'to muse on the earthly paradise and the various bars, of iron and of the spirit, which prevent us from reaching it'.[3] In fact, as time passed, he longed for prison. Life outside, in an atmosphere of repression, was suffocating. Conditions, in some places like Bengal, were more humiliating than elsewhere, but in fact all Indians were caught and being crushed in the mill. Indeed, suggested Jawaharlal, it would be simpler, instead of a variety of ordinances and orders and rules, to have a comprehensive enactment abolishing all schools and colleges and suppressing all newspapers and books, and laying down that every Indian must consider himself in prison ('C' Class), salute the Union Jack every morning and sing the British national anthem at divine service twice a day; 'and the afternoons might be profitably devoted to listening to an inspiring address on the virtues of British rule'.[4]

---

[1] See, for example, letter to Kapil Deva Malaviya, 10 September 1933.
[2] To Abdur Rahim, 30 October and C. Mascarenas, 10 November 1933; to M. R. Masani, 19 December 1933, Maharashtra Government file of intercepted letters.
[3] To Aldous Huxley, 3 September 1933.
[4] 'Earthquakes — natural and political', statement to the press, 31 January 1934.

So throughout the country the choice was becoming clear, and it was not possible to opt out. 'I am quite clear as to what I should do and this gives me peace of mind. I have been perfectly prepared to go back to prison from the day of my discharge. Now, I am not only prepared but I am eager to do so. My instinct tells me that I must take a step forward and instinct in this matter is a safe guide for me.'[1] The seizure of his shares worth about Rs 20,000 by the Government rid him of what he regarded as a liability and he followed it up by selling the family jewellery at a nominal price. Jawaharlal, unlike Gandhi, was encumbered by complex thought, but in the matter of worldly goods he was becoming as much of a political ascetic.

But while he was out, he sought to keep up the struggle, even if at a lower pitch, for the only alternative was a compromise with imperialism, and this was unacceptable not only to him personally but manifestly to the Indian people. Travelling round the country, Jawaharlal was convinced that never, at any rate since 1857, had there been such extraordinary bitterness against the Government and such a passionate desire to be rid of it.[2] So he concentrated on the sustenance of the struggle, and declined to be distracted by such side-shows as village uplift and the Harijan movement. 'This kind of safe and pious activity can well be left to old ladies.'[3] It was a question not merely of time and energy but of creating a psychological atmosphere. The national fight had to continue, and it would be strengthened by making it a social and economic fight for the masses and purging it of Hindu and Muslim communalism.

Jawaharlal had till now deliberately ignored the growth of the communal evil in Indian politics in the hope that public attention could be diverted from it by emphasis on the positive aspects of the national struggle. Hunger, poverty and exploitation had nothing to do with religion. But the time now appeared to have come for a frontal attack on communalism as a cover for political reaction.[4] In language which even Gandhi regarded as too fierce,[5] he condemned the Hindu Mahasabha for its reactionary and anti-national policy of co-operation with the Government and support of vested interests.[6] The Hindu communalists wanted no basic change of the political and economic structure, and sought official favours to augment their own position. This criticism applied equally, of course, to Muslim communal organizations, and Jawaharlal recognized that they were as anti-national and reactionary in every sense of the word.[7] But he rebuked them in milder terms. Fear was justified, or at least understandable, in a minority community which was economically and educationally backward; and communalism born of fear had to be exorcized and not just brushed aside. 'Honest com-

[1] To Sri Prakasa, 11 January 1934, Sri Prakasa papers. N.M.M.L.
[2] To H. K. Hales, M. P., 9 November 1933.
[3] Statement to the press, 12 January 1934.
[4] Interview in *The Leader*, 21 November 1933; to S. A. Brelvi, 3 December 1933.
[5] To Jawaharlal, 27 November 1933.
[6] Speech at Banaras, 13 November, *The Hindu*, 14 November 1933; statement at Allahabad, 22 November, *The Tribune*, 24 November 1933.
[7] Interview in the *Pioneer*, 18 November 1933.

munalism is fear; false communalism is political reaction.' In Jawaharlal's understanding, there were shades of both in Muslim communalism. Moreover, while the Congress had drawn into its ranks most of the vital elements of Hindu society, the communalists were the dominant and politically clamorous group among the Muslims. No other organization had so far arisen which could successfully challenge their claim to speak for the Muslims, and their aggressively communal character gave them an advantage over the large number of nationalist Muslims in the Congress.[1]

Obviously Jawaharlal had no illusions about organizations which worked under the leadership of so feudal and reactionary a figure as the Aga Khan. Their activities at the Round Table Conference, where they stymied all efforts by Gandhi to confront the British Government with an agreed solution on the communal problem, were but the latest testimony to their narrow upper-class base and commitment to subordinate collaboration with the Imperial power. The only way to ascertain the wishes of the Muslims was to ask them to elect representatives to a Constituent Assembly on the widest possible franchise but, if necessary, on the basis of separate electorates. Then economic demands would undoubtedly get their rightful priority and the communal problem would be found to be an insubstantial ghost. But, in the meantime, in what could be interpreted as an apologia for Muslim communalism, he came close to recognizing the hold of communal parties on the Muslim community and justifying their attitudes. He always, like Gandhi, took the line that it was for the Hindus, as the majority community, to make concessions while the communal problem lasted. This in itself, despite the call to magnanimity, assumes a communal approach, however subconscious. The argument is based on the belief that the majority community is a privileged one, and the minority community has reason to be communal. It was true that Jawaharlal had not carefully probed this issue, and was irritated by the Mahasabha's criticisms of Gandhi and the Congress and its open wooing of the Government. But even so, the implication that there was something to choose between Hindu and Muslim communalism was dangerous in its possibilities.

However, all these public activities were not to be for long. The Government were as anxious as Jawaharlal to get him back in prison as soon as possible. They saw in the conversations with Gandhi not the dialogue between master and disciple, which it was, but a Machiavellian attempt to organize forces to greater effect against the British. Gandhi, it was believed, would tour the country, ostensibly to promote his Harijan schemes but really to sow the seed of further activities in regard to civil disobedience, while Jawaharlal, whose socialism had become 'redder', would seek to strengthen peasant support, particularly in the United Provinces, with a programme of expropriation of the landlords. 'The one real danger that we have at the present moment in regard to our political future', reported the Viceroy, 'is the fear lest Jawaharlal Nehru should start a

[1] Interview, 29 November, *The Bombay Chronicle,* 2 December 1933.

secretive propaganda in the villages on purely socialistic and communistic lines, for this might be a very troublesome thing to deal with.' The U.P. Government had little doubt that Jawaharlal's main object was to organize the masses and 'inoculate them with the virus of Communism'. The result would be, according to the Director of the Intelligence Bureau, that for the next civil disobedience campaign Gandhi would have raised a huge Harijan army and Jawaharlal a host of stalwart agriculturists.[1] The Bengal Government went further, and publicly stated that Jawaharlal was carrying on his revolutionary agitation under the guise of anti-untouchability activities and with the money collected for Harijan work.[2]

All this was beside the mark, for Gandhi made it clear that only those Congressmen who were too weak to court arrest or had lost faith in civil disobedience should join the Harijan movement, and forbade its use to strengthen the political activities of the Congress or its hold on the people. As for Gandhi and Jawaharlal acting in concert, Andrews called on the Home Member and assured him that Gandhi was not in sympathy with Jawaharlal's views.[3] Regarding the allegation about Jawaharlal's duplicity, he, a year later, while in England, sharply protested, and the Bengal Government were forced, with 'an ignominious crawl',[4] to withdraw it. 'British officialdom in India', commented the *Manchester Guardian*,[5] 'seems to be suffering from a bad attack of stupidity . . . The charge to anyone who knew anything of Nehru was ridiculous; one might as easily imagine Savonarola robbing a till.' But talk about a two-pronged offensive by the Congress was wishful, for it justified the attitude of unqualified hostility to the party which the Government had adopted since 1932 and had no desire to change.[6]

Jawaharlal's activities in particular were made to sound dangerous enough to require his speedy return to prison. All Local Governments were authorized to arrest him if opportunity arose not on some minor issue but on a serious charge which would involve a substantial sentence.[7] 'My one hope is that Jawaharlal is such a temperamental person that he may go off the deep end before long and we shall be able to get him back into jail, which is really the safest place for a person with his political views.'[8] What worried the Govern-

---

[1] Willingdon to Hoare, 18, 24 and 29 September 1933, Templewood papers, vol. 6; Hailey to Chhatari, 26 September and to Clay, 29 September 1933, Hailey papers, vol. 26; notes of Home Department in Home Dept. Pol. File 4/8/33; note of D.I.B., 16 February 1934, Home Dept. Pol. File 4/4/34. Appendix to Notes I, *India and Communism* (compiled in the I.B. 1933), pp. 218-19.

[2] Bengal Administration Report for 1934-5.

[3] Haig's record of interview with Andrews, 26 October 1933, Home Dept. Pol. File 169 of 1933.

[4] Ellen Wilkinson to Jawaharlal, January 1936.

[5] 9 January 1936.

[6] Haig's note, 15 November 1933, Home Dept. Pol. File 169 of 1933.

[7] Home Secretary to all Local Governments, 26 September 1933, reprinted in *The Civil Disobedience Movement 1930-1934* (Govt. of India confidential publication, 1936), pp. 88-9.

[8] Willingdon to Hoare, 29 September 1933, Templewood papers, vol. 6.

ment now was not so much Jawaharlal's efforts in the rural areas as the impact of his writings and speeches on the lower middle classes. These were in grave economic distress and might well respond to his call for a new revolutionary ideology. 'You can never tell how far an emotional people will be captured by programmes of this nature; your own De Valera seems to me a man somewhat like J. L. N. I certainly see no other leader at the moment who is likely to have an equal following, for the rest of India will never follow a Bengali.'[1] If he broke the Congress and led a movement of his own it would be serious enough; but even more menacing was the possibility that, as Gandhi had hinted,[2] he might cease to stress his leanings towards communism and merely call upon the Congress to give attention to economic problems. His open renunciation of the no-rent campaign[3] suggested that this was likely; and this spurred the Government to action. 'Honestly, I think he is much better put out of the way, and I only hope that the Courts will convict him and give him a satisfactory sentence.'[4] In December the Chief Commissioner of Delhi was asked to consider if Jawaharlal could be arrested for a speech denouncing British exploitation and the feudal autocracy of the Princes. But, while the Delhi authorities agreed that the speech was most objectionable, they had no great hopes of a successful prosecution.[5] All Local Governments were then ordered once again to examine Jawaharlal's speeches carefully with a view to prosecution on some serious charge involving a substantial sentence of imprisonment.[6] The speech to the Trade Union Congress at Kanpur in December calling for the overthrow of British imperialism· seemed to the Home and Law Members to be as strong a case as they were ever likely to get, and the U.P. Government were pressed to prosecute. 'The Government of India regard him as by far the most dangerous element at large in India, and their view is that the time has come, in accordance with their general policy of taking steps at an early stage to prevent attempts to work up mass agitation, to take action against him.'[7] Hailey, however, though he was keenly aware of Jawaharlal's growing influence, was hesitant to act, and ultimately it was the Bengal Government which agreed to bell the cat. On his visit to Calcutta in January, Jawaharlal had in forthright terms condemned the vulgarity of imperialism and stressed that there was no half-way house between nationalism and imperialism. He had also sharply rebuked the terrorists for adopting a futile and out-of-date policy. But the Government had no use for such an ally against terrorism. Jawaharlal was arrested at Allahabad on 12

[1] Hailey to J. T. Gwynn, 6 November 1933, Hailey papers, vol. 26.

[2] Gandhi's interview in *Madras Mail*, 22 December 1933; see also Hailey to Irwin, 19 January 1934, Hailey papers, vol. 27.

[3] Statement at Allahabad, 26 December, *The Tribune,* 29 December 1933.

[4] Willingdon to Hoare, 30 January 1934, Templewood papers, vol. 7.

[5] Notes of Home Secretary and Home Member, 15 December 1933 and letter of Chief Commissioner, 18 December 1933. Home Dept. Pol. 4/1/34.

[6] Home Secretary to all Local Governments, 22 December 1933, ibid.

[7] Home Secretary to Chief Secretary U. P., 19 January and Home Member to Governor U. P. 21 January 1934, ibid.

February and brought down to Calcutta, tried for sedition and sentenced on 16 February to two years' simple imprisonment.

'Individuals', said Jawaharlal in court before he was silenced, 'sometimes misbehave in this imperfect world of ours; so also officials and those in power. Crowds and mobs of people also lose control of themselves sometimes and misbehave. That is regrettable. But it is a terrible thing when an organized Government begins to behave like an excited mob; when brutal and vengeful and uncivilized behaviour becomes the normal temper of a Government.' Undoubtedly the Government of India at this time, believing that it had the Congress by the throat, was out for a kill. Repression and savagery were un-abashed and believed to be successful. As the one man among the leaders who was neither cowed nor shaken in nerve was Jawaharlal, the authorities stalked him till they once more had him behind bars. Back for a 'rest cure' in his 'other home',[1] this time the central jail at Alipore in Calcutta, he reverted to the routine of prison life and adjusted himself to living in a small cell and bare barrack yard, with a clerk sentenced for embezzlement as his only com-panion. 'The days pass, and so do the nights, and so we carry on. How soon one gets used to a particular mode of life!'[2] The Bengal authorities did not encourage reading and writing, and for some time, after he had exhausted the novels in the prison library, the only book Jawaharlal had was a German grammar. This was later set right. But he never settled down in Alipore and was relieved when, early in May, he was transferred to the familiar barrack in Dehra Dun jail.

Throughout these months, the news from outside was depressing. The ill-health of his mother and wife was a constant source of worry; and political news was no more cheerful. Gandhi's statement in April withdrawing civil disobedience was a heavy blow. 'It marks an epoch not only in our freedom struggle but in my personal life. After 15 years I go my way, perhaps a solitary way leading not far. But meanwhile there is prison and its lonely existence.'[3] An undated, incomplete note obviously written at this time indicates that Jawaharlal was being driven once more to the recognition that he had come to a parting of the ways. There was hardly any common ground between him-self and Gandhi, and he had been wrong in subordinating their differences in a larger loyalty to the cause of national freedom. 'Our objectives are different, our ideals are different, our spiritual outlook is different and our methods are likely to be different.' The Congress was now aggressively anti-socialist and, in its acceptance of constitutionalism, politically more backward than it had been even in the heyday of the Swarajist party. Gandhi's statement withdrawing civil disobedience, the reasons given and the general outlook displayed 'seemed to me to be an insult to the nation, to the Congress and to any person with a grain of intelligence. I felt with a stab of pain that the

[1] See telegrams to Gandhi and to his daughter, 13 February 1934.
[2] To Vijayalakshmi Pandit, 1 March 1934.
[3] Diary entry, 13 April 1934.

cords of allegiance that had bound me to him for many years had snapped.'
The concentration on non-political issues and the personal and self-created
entanglements which led Gandhi to desert his comrades in the middle of
the struggle were amazingly casual and likely to be fatal to the movement.

In August, when Kamala's condition took a turn for the worse, the U. P.
Government let Jawaharlal out of prison, and he took this opportunity, in
what even Willingdon, who had seen a copy made by the police, described
as 'this very human document',[1] to pour out his heart to Gandhi. The abandonment of civil disobedience had been bad enough, but the reasons given by
Gandhi and his suggestions for future work had astonished him.

> I had a sudden and intense feeling that something broke inside me, a bond
> that I had valued very greatly had snapped. I felt terribly lonely in this wide
> world. I have always felt a little lonely almost from childhood up. But
> a few bonds strengthened me, a few strong supports held me up. That
> loneliness never went, but it was lessened. But now I felt absolutely alone,
> left high and dry on a desert island.

The decisions that followed the termination of civil disobedience, such as
the approval of the formation of a parliamentary party and the contesting of
elections, had been shock after shock, allowing his mind and feelings no peace
or rest and making prison life a greater ordeal for his nerves than at any time
before. What was happening was not a setback, common enough in all great
struggles, but a spiritual defeat and surrender of ideals. The Congress had
become a caucus where opportunism flourished and the Working Committee's
resolution condemning socialism showed such astounding ignorance of even
the elements of the subject that it was painful to read it and realize that it
might be read outside India. 'It seemed that the overmastering desire of the
Committee was somehow to assure various vested interests even at the risk
of talking nonsense.'[2]

Apart from this private letter, which Gandhi did not take seriously,[3] Jawaharlal responded to the Government's gesture and took care to keep away
from political activity. However much he might have sympathized in private
with the criticism made by his follower, Rafi Ahmad Kidwai, of the Congress
leadership, he publicly dissociated himself from it. The proclaimed socialists
in the Congress, who in May, as a counter-blast to the milk-and-water programmes of the parent body, had formed the Congress Socialist Party, had
not concealed that they sought and drew inspiration from him. They believed
that they were echoing his ideas in hailing the Congress as potentially the

[1] To Hoare, 24 September 1934, Templewood papers, vol. 7.

[2] To Gandhi, 13 August 1934. The resolution had denounced confiscation and class war as
contrary to the creed of non-violence and committed the Congress to no more than a 'wiser and
juster use of private property' and 'a healthier relationship between capital and labour'

[3] 'Jawaharlal's explosion is not so dangerous as it sounds. He only exercised his right to let off
steam. I believe he is now quiet.' Gandhi to Patel, 19 August 1934, quoted in K. Dwarkadas,
India's Fight for Freedom (Bombay, 1966), p. 444.

greatest revolutionary force in the country and seeking to combine the national struggle with socialism.[1] The decision to keep the Socialist Party within the Congress was also modelled on Jawaharlal's precedent of the Independence for India League. Yet Jawaharlal refused, while out of prison, to give them any encouragement.[2] He shared the socialist outlook; but there was no truth in the claim[3] that he was fully in agreement with the decision to form the party. He considered the step premature and likely to divert attention from the immediate issue of political independence. The socialists had no support among the people, and it was more important to push the Congress as a whole, however slowly, towards acceptance of economic objectives than to nurture the doctrinaire views of a handful of individuals. Jawaharlal had a radical rather than an ideological mind. The precedent of the Independence for India League was not a happy one. It can be argued that Jawaharlal was giving up too easily, that while he had a socialist vision derived from Europe he lacked the stamina to formulate specific programmes suited to India and promote the strenuous work of forming cadres and establishing an organization — in other words, that he lacked a 'revolutionary perspective'.[4] Such criticism is balanced by the fact that, however disappointed with Gandhi and the Congress, Jawaharlal was still certain of their indispensability in the struggle to expel the British; nor could he regard the motley crowd of Marxists, Fabians, Gandhians and orthodox Hindus who led the Congress Socialist Party with anything but 'amused contempt'.[5]

The U.P. authorities, however, feared that the Socialist Party, which was the 'greatest menace to peace in the rural areas', had about fifteen centres in the province, very few of which were really active; but they would all receive a tremendous fillip when Jawaharlal came out of jail.[6] The Government of India feared the release, especially on the eve of the elections to the Central Assembly, of the one person they had cause to worry about and of whom they had made a bogy man — 'the high priest of Communism'.[7] So it was made clear that no remission of his sentence could be considered,[8] and after eleven days, when his wife's health slightly improved, he was taken back to prison. But this time he

[1] Acharya Narendra Deva's presidential address at the first session of The Socialist Party Conference, reprinted in *Socialism and the National Revolution* (Bombay, 1946), pp. 5-29.

[2] To Sampurnanand, 22 August 1934, Sampurnanand papers, National Archives of India.

[3] Jayaprakash Narayan to Rajendra Prasad, 25 July 1934, U.P. C.I.D. File PPF-J 25.

[4] Subhas Bose, *The Indian Struggle* (Calcutta, 1964), p. 336.

[5] Sampurnanand, *Memories and Reflections* (Bombay, 1962), p. 72. It might be added that M. N. Roy was also against the formation of a separate socialist party within the Congress because it would exclude the left wing from leadership and continue the dominance of the conservative elements in the party.

[6] Note of the U.P. C.I.D. on revolutionary affairs in the province 1934, U.P. C.I.D. File No. PPF N.26.

[7] See U.P. Government's publicity pamphlet 'Communistic Likes and Dislikes', Home Dept. Pol. File 7/13/34.

[8] Answer of Secretary of State in House of Commons, 16 July 1934. Hoare had wished to say there could be no remission 'at the present time' but deleted the proviso at the instance of the Government of India, Home Dept. Pol. File 27/19/34.

was lodged in Naini jail, and allowed out once or twice a week to see Kamala. Then, in October, when she was moved to a sanatorium at Bhowali, Jawaharlal was transferred to the nearby jail at Almora.

The illness of his wife pushed all else to the background. Over the years their relationship had matured from indifference to a deep attachment. Often in jail his mind wandered to her, and he sat waiting for her letters and looking forward to her interviews. 'Felt greatly cheered', runs a characteristic diary entry, 'at seeing her. I am much too fond of her!' [1] Now, with her at death's door, he became a bundle of nerves, and more to take his mind off the crisis than anything else, he set to work feverishly drafting the work which was to be his greatest literary achievement. He began in June 1934 the writing of his life story and finished it on 14 February 1935. So a massive manuscript of 976 pages was dashed off in less than nine months. First called *In and Out of Prison*, it was later published with the bare title, *An Autobiography*.

Tagore, Andrews, Sapru and a host of lesser men, as well as the nationalist press as a whole, and Attlee, Lansbury and other leaders of the Labour Party in Britain, none of whom had any sympathy with Jawaharlal's political views, pleaded for magnanimity and a full release. But to set him free in India seemed to the Government of India out of the question, for they saw no reason to believe that Jawaharlal would 'behave well', that is, refrain from political activity. Jawaharlal himself was too proud a man and too committed a nationalist to ask for special favours. Even when let out of prison in August, he had declined to give any undertaking to the Government. [2] Now, while thanking the U.P. Government for the various courtesies being shown to him, he asked for no more.

Quite frankly I feel that the U.P. Government has gone very much out of its way to meet an individual case and I am somewhat embarrassed by this special consideration. It would be wrong and absurd to expect the Government to vary State policy because of individual cases. Personal reasons cannot and should not interfere with principles and larger issues. I have myself endeavoured to act in that way, and if I may say so without impropriety, I thoroughly appreciate that Government cannot do so. [3]

When an advocate of Allahabad petitioned the High Court for his release and followed it up with a memorial to the Government, Jawaharlal promptly repudiated this unauthorized intervention in his personal affairs. He had told Kamala in August that he might be released in December, after the elections.[4] Disappointed in that, he counted the days and weeks till the end of his sentence but sought no concessions.

[1] 9 April 1934.
[2] Letter to District Magistrate, 12 August 1934.
[3] To Jagdish Prasad, Home Member, U. P., 5 November 1934.
[4] Diary entry, 30 April 1935.

"Sad winds where your voice was;
"Tears, tears where my heart was;
And even with me,
Child ever with me
Silence where hope was."

Part of a page from Jawaharlal's prison diary

The treatment at Bhowali did Kamala little good and it was decided that she should go to Europe. For the first time, Jawaharlal had to worry about money. He had an annual income, derived from book royalties and such shares as were still left to him, of about nine thousand rupees, and with this he had to run a large establishment at Anand Bhawan, pay heavy medical bills and arrange for the passages by sea and the stay in Europe.[1] It was probably at this time that a member of the Birla family, the wealthy financiers, hearing of his difficulties, offered to pay him a fairly substantial monthly allowance, such as they provided to many leading Congressmen; but Jawaharlal expressed his surprise at the suggestion and sharply declined the offer.[2] He mustered such savings as he had and made the arrangements, and Kamala sailed, with Indira and a doctor in attendance, in May. The Government of India were unwilling to remit Jawaharlal's sentence on condition that he left India with his wife for Switzerland, for that in itself would encourage the socialist wing in the Congress and dispirit officials and loyalists.[3] The hope was that, with the official retirement of Gandhi from the Congress in September, the party would become moderate and constitutional under the leadership of Patel and Rajagopalachari. For this the socialists would have to be kept under, and nothing would facilitate this more than the retention of Jawaharlal in prison.[4]

In a way, this was not unacceptable. Kamala was anxious to brave the journey, not only for a change of climate and in hopes of a cure, but because close proximity to Jawaharlal was at this time jarring on the nerves of both. Mutual dependence caused its own frictions. In 1933, while on a visit to Jawaharlal in Dehra Dun jail, Kamala had called on a Bengali lady *sanyasini*. They had not

[1] See note on income and expenditure, 14 May 1935.
[2] Letter to U. N. Dhebar, 7 June 1957, Nehru papers.
[3] Telegram to Secretary of State, 10 November 1934, Home Dept. Pol. File 38/7/34.
[4] See Willingdon to Hoare, 22 October 1934 and 5 May 1935, Templewood papers, volumes 7 and 8, respectively.

talked much, but Kamala felt a profound sense of peace. She later visited this lady several times and her influence grew. [1] Jawaharlal pretended not to mind, but such a development was alien to his own nature; and he also resented the intrusion of another.

> What a child K is! That irritates me often enough and yet I think that is partly her charm. How my moods change when I think of her. How much she means to me and yet how little she fits in or tries to fit in with my ideas. That is really the irritating part, that she does not try, and so she drifts apart. [2]

With Kamala and his daughter in Europe, Jawaharlal felt lonelier than ever in jail. He had now no major writing task to divert his mind, and though he set himself to writing articles in English and Hindi and reading a large variety of books, these could not subdue his emotional tension. He became a prey to nightmares and tears and, what was so rare with him, began to lose his very interest in life. All these years, his dedication to India's freedom had kept him going even when his personal affairs had been a shambles. As he had once told a senior British official in the halcyon 'twenties, his only ambition had been to be buried in the foundations of free India. [3] But now he despaired even of that. The Congress had become a cautious, almost loyalist body, more frightened of communism and a class struggle than inimical to the British; Subhas Bose, in exile abroad, fancied himself as a future fascist dictator, and Gandhi gave all his attention to such problems as the relative merits of cow's milk and buffalo's milk. 'Even Bapu', wrote Jawaharlal perceptively in his diary, 'he is either a non-co-operator or a full-blooded co-operator. The fire or a sofa — though a sofa is hardly the correct place for him. He can think only in extremes — either extreme eroticism or asceticism. Was it not Aldous Huxley who said that the ascetic was the counterpart of Don Juan?' [4] Nor did the masses of India, indulging in wild communal rioting, seem to deserve better. 'What a disgusting, savage people we are. Politics, progress, socialism, communism, science — where are they before this black religious savagery?' [5] There were very few oases of intellect and character in the arid waste of Indian humanity, and doubts arose in his mind as to whether anything could be done with this material. To crown it all, the news from Europe of Kamala was depressing. She had stood well a complicated operation in Berlin for the removal of lung adhesions but, far from

---

[1] Draft Second Volume of Autobiography (hereafter DSVA) written in Dehra Dun jail 1941. This draft was later rejected by him as not suited for publication; but parts of it were incorporated in The Discovery of India.

[2] Diary entry, 19 March 1935.

[3] Sir William Duke to Motilal, quoted in Motilal to Jawaharlal, 18 March 1928, Motilal Nehru papers.

[4] 30 April 1935.

[5] Diary entry, 17 April 1935.

recuperating, was losing heart. 'She is slipping away and the thought of it is unbearable, hellish.'[1] A verse jotted down in his diary[2] sums up his heartbreak and loneliness:

> Sad winds where your voice was;
> Tears, tears where my heart was;
>   And ever with me
>   Child, ever with me
> Silence where hope was.

[1] Diary entry, 28 August 1935.
[2] 9 June 1935.

13

Death of Kamala Nehru

On 2 September the doctor cabled Jawaharlal as well as the Government that Kamala's condition was critical, and his sentence was suspended to enable him to proceed at once to her bedside. 'So this is the end' he wrote in his diary; but even at this moment his dignity did not fail him. He asked for clarifications, and was told that his movements would be unrestricted in India till his departure as well as in Europe, but if he returned before his sentence expired in February 1936 he would be imprisoned again.[1] He was also requested not to make any political speeches before departure. On these terms, which did not infringe his honour, Jawaharlal left Almora for Allahabad and took the first available flight to Europe.

Kamala was in a clinic in Badenweiler in the Black Forest in Germany, and Jawaharlal found her condition changed very much for the worse. However, he still thought there was an even chance of a slow recovery. Keeping away from the Nazis and only asserting his viewpoint by patronizing Jewish shops, Jawaharlal spent his time nursing his wife, correcting the proofs of the *Autobiography* and meeting the odd visitor — Andrews, Subhas Bose, Raja Rao. But the long hours in hospital were oppressive, and as he observed long after, 'I found that life affecting me powerfully, as it was affecting much more the patients themselves. Since then I have never advised anyone to stay too long in a clinic.'[2] Kamala too, in addition to the physical ravages of her illness, was giving way to the psychological strain. She was anxious to get back to Switzerland and Jawaharlal therefore moved her early in 1936 to a clinic in Lausanne. 'There is no immediate crisis', he reported in January, 'but there is a kind of continuing semi-crisis and certain complications appear to have set in due largely to extreme weakness. Her heart is not as good as it was. This present state cannot continue for long. It will either grow worse or better within the next three or four weeks at most.'[3] Her condition fluctuated daily, and

[1] Press statement, *The Bombay Chronicle*, 5 September 1935.
[2] To Jayaprakash Narayan, 28 July 1952, Nehru papers.
[3] To Rajendra Prasad, 23 January 1936, AICC file G 43 (KW)(i) 1935.

Jawaharlal clutched at momentary glimmers of recovery. But there was really no hope, and at 5 a.m. on 28 February she died.

Kamala's short life — she was not thirty-seven when she died — was overcast with acute pain and suffering. Born in a social milieu much humbler than that of the Nehrus, she was faced from the start with the resistance of some of her husband's family, who treated her as an intruder from the outside world into their exclusive relations with Jawaharlal. Smart, snobbish and insensitive, they led her to feel that she did not belong, made Jawaharlal a poor wife — and was plain and dowdy into the bargain. Fine-grained and high-spirited, Kamala was continually humiliated in her deepest feminine instincts, and consequently developed a growing sense of futility.

Nor, in these early years of tension and repression, were Kamala's relations with Jawaharlal cloudless. Theirs was not love in spring. He did not suspect her distress and fear of inadequacy, and after 1920 was so engrossed in public affairs that the result was emotional reluctance. It is curious how little she figures in his jail diaries of the 'twenties. Different in temperament and upbringing, deliberate adjustment was required from both sides and a special effort from Kamala to raise her personality to his level, if their marriage was to succeed. But from the start she was dogged with sickness. Their daughter, Indira, was born in November 1917; but thereafter her health slowly slid downhill. Tuberculosis was first diagnosed in 1919 and, despite varied treatment and a long stay in Europe, took firm root. In 1925 a son was born prematurely and died after two days; and three years later she suffered a miscarriage.

Added to this were the strains of national politics, with the family often scattered, Jawaharlal for long stretches in prison and the house frequently searched and property attached. It was no wonder that not only did her health sharply deteriorate, from about 1932, but she became increasingly neurotic.[1]

Yet, despite all these stresses and disadvantages, Kamala's life was, in its own way, one of happiness and achievement. Never a simpering consort, she slowly rose above her surroundings and grew in mind and character till she could derive joy and companionship from her married life. The moody self-pity and death-wish, induced by being bedridden for months at a time, were shaken off. Illness was no longer stagnation but an impetus to energy. That she had not received a regular education was a handicap she felt sorely. 'Today in this world only the educated are honoured. People do not want to talk to those who are uneducated; indeed close relatives and even husbands do not wish to talk to them. Under such conditions the lives of the girls become unbearable; and then will it be a life or a curse?'[2] This disadvantage too she surmounted in her own life; but the education of women became to her a part of the struggle for freedom.

[1] The facts about Kamala Nehru's health are derived from Jawaharlal's note on the subject written for the doctors in May 1935.
[2] To Syed Mahmud from Geneva, 4 November 1926, original in Urdu.

'Daily I grow more determined that on my return, taking your wife along with me, I shall urge Indian women to have faith in God and fight for their own freedom — and educate their daughters so that they may not be in trouble like us and may be able to win independence for their country and end Hindu-Muslim conflict.'[1]

It was more than mere faith in God and works of charity in the Ramakrishna Mission and similar institutions which gave her strength and scope for service. She was formally enrolled into the Mission as a lay follower,[2] but did not adopt the life of a recluse. Social action of a more exciting kind called her, and she trained herself not only to endure the separations from Jawaharlal but to participate in the struggle. Though ill, her courage never failed. One of Jawaharlal's keenest experiences of satisfaction was when she was arrested in 1931 and went to jail with a statement which was an unconscious blend of self-confidence and commitment to him. Even during her last months, the impression she left on Palme Dutt was of a woman of strength and perception: 'a wonderful person', with enormous directness, clarity of political vision and burning desire to serve — and with such influence over her husband that Palme Dutt was convinced that 'with her death some of his backbone went out of him.'[3]

Gradually, as time passed, their relationship had matured. His early lack of serious interest was replaced first by a light-hearted, protective loyalty and then by a commitment which was stronger than passion and warmer than consideration. In Sri Lanka in 1931 they had discovered each other again, and realized that their marriage had neither broken nor tarnished. Stricken by his past neglect, he allowed Kamala to move slowly from the fringes towards the centre of his life, till, by the end, as even the unimaginative police department recognized, he was a 'devoted husband'.[4] Many women, drawn by his charm or driven by snobbery, made claims on him and, especially after Kamala's death, sought to thrust themselves into his life; and he did not always firmly resist their gross ardours. Yet, despite occasional dalliances, Kamala was the only woman who ever meant anything to him; and he kept her image unsullied. 'Kamala five years' runs the single-line entry in his pocket diary on 28 February 1941. He kept in his bedroom or his jail cell, along with her photograph, a small portion of her ashes, and requested that they be mingled with his own after his death. As far as he was concerned, the wound of her death never healed; but, of course, the wounds which do not heal are usually those which have remorse festering in them.

So, over the years, Kamala had evolved an equal human relationship with her husband. Writing two years after her death, Jawaharlal acknowledged that she,

[1] To Syed Mahmud from Brighton, June 1927, original in Urdu.
[2] P. Kalhan, *Kamala Nehru* (Delhi, 1973), p. 85.
[3] Interview with the author, 20 November 1969.
[4] Note of H. Williamson, Director, Intelligence Bureau, 27 September 1935, Home Dept. Pol. 4/7/35.

his father and Gandhi were the major personal influences in his life. 'My wife influenced me considerably in many ways, though unobtrusively.'[1] A serious, deeply moral, intense figure, she was a champion of Women's Lib long before that became a slogan and a movement,[2] and had she lived might well have had a career akin to that of Eleanor Roosevelt. If a successful struggle for self-awareness and self-emancipation is the true test of greatness, then Kamala ranks among the greatest of the Nehrus.

Messages of condolence swamped him, from the Secretary of State and the Viceroy as well as from humble Congress workers and friends in various parts of the world. 'How shall I console you', wired Gandhi, 'all our hearts with you. God give you peace love Bapu'. Another message is also worthy of remembrance. 'You will not', wrote Naomi Mitchison, 'have made the mistake of importing human qualities like justice and mercy into the universe: one has to go to deeper principles less easy to understand.' These were no routine messages, for to Jawaharlal the loss was severe. The child-wife he had married on his father's directive had become in twenty years a brave and true comrade whose death left him lonely and desolate.[3]

The publication of Jawaharlal's *Autobiography* in the spring of 1936, only a few weeks after the death of Kamala, gave the world an inkling of his nature and enabled it to share his sorrow. All the reviews in Britain, including those in Conservative journals, immediately recognized the book's importance and quality. It was not surprising that friends like Ellen Wilkinson, Edward Thompson and H. N. Brailsford hailed it as a basic utterance of one of the few great men of the time; but even those who disapproved of Jawaharlal's politics commended it. The life, the man, the witness, all seem to have imposed a paralysing humility on the critics. Any understanding, wrote *The Economist*,[4] of the last fifteen years in India was incomplete without reading it; Sir Stanley Reed thought it an exceptional book;[5] 'a book to read', said *The Times*,[6] 'however much one may disagree with the outlook of the author.' It was an essential document of the period, a key to the ideas and politics of a whole new world. Here was a man who spoke and thought in the language of modernity and reason, whom, unlike Gandhi, the West could understand, a man like themselves who happened to find himself on the other side. His individual vision was of general interest and universal value. In this, the first important first-hand account of the modern phase of Asian nationalism, Jawaharlal showed that in India it was a civilized, responsible movement that owed as much to the principles of European revolution and the liberalism and nonconformity of Britain as to the Indian context.

---

[1] Note for John Gunther, 16 March 1938.

[2] On this point she was clear-sighted even about Gandhi: 'there is no one else like Gandhi in the world, but as regards women's rights he is no better than other men.' Letter to Jawaharlal (in Hindi), 9 October 1932.

[3] See his statement to the press, 17 March 1936; *The Discovery of India* (Calcutta, 1946), p. 40.

[4] 11 July 1936.

[5] *The Spectator*, 15 May 1936.

[6] 28 April 1936.

So the *Autobiography,* despite being a long and serious book, became a best-seller and within weeks ran into many editions — though unfortunately for Jawaharlal his publisher, The Bodley Head, soon after went into liquidation. [1]

The book was characteristic of Jawaharlal. It was honest and introspective. Standing almost outside himself he commented frankly on the society and age in which he lived, on the people he had known and on his own mental development. The book is not a wooden narrative of events; nor is it, like Gandhi's autobiography, a part of confessional literature. Jawaharlal was too undemonstrative, too repelled by any trace of exhibitionism, to interest the world primarily in himself. Indeed the *Autobiography* is in one sense a *tour de force* in that, after over 600 close-knit pages, his privacy remains unbroken. It is a reverie on the context into which he had been thrown, and of his reactions to it. If a portrait of a personality, wistful, complex and of indrawn tension, caught in its own integrity, is gradually built up, it is almost as a by-product. But what Jawaharlal did set out to tell was of the Indian condition and of British rule, which hurt both his feelings and his intelligence by forcing the large majority of his countrymen to live in sordid and brutal circumstances. The reader found himself in the presence of great moral and historical issues as seen through the eyes of a refined and humane man.

What further helped to gain a wide audience for the *Autobiography* was its prose style. It was a clear, fluent book, 'an excellent substitute for a novel', [2] written with terse, nervous elegance and control of phrase and with a wide knowledge of English writing, old and new. It showed a mind of intellectual and moral quality, free of cliché emotions, but attractively replete with half-tones, subtleties and diffidences. In later years, Jawaharlal often spoke of the *Autobiography* as having 'dated'. It has, of course, 'dated' in the sense that it deals with a period that is dead. But the book has not lost its freshness as a piece of craftsmanship and as the expression of a sensitive human being.

Moreover, Jawaharlal wrote with detachment. There was self-scrutiny and self-criticism but no self-pity. The hardships he had opted for were taken for granted. The attempt was not at self-justification but at justification to himself. Estranged from his own people by being soaked in the exploiter's culture, he was a mixed-up being, yearning for roots and struggling to work out his own destiny. Tortured by doubt, impressive in his indecision, agonizing over all sides of every question, always asking to what end was the long, wearying struggle, he provided a picture of warm and vulnerable humanity. Jawaharlal made no claim to be exceptional; rather, he was a natural disciple with a taste for heroes. He clung to those who would determine his intellectual uncertainties. Motilal and Gandhi are the chief characters in the book, and he recognized how much he owed to them and depended on them, even while he was clear-sighted, especially about

---

[1] Soon after liquidation, a new administration took over The Bodley Head, and from then on regular royalty payments were made to Nehru's account.

[2] *The Statesman* (Calcutta), 10 May 1936.

Gandhi's limitations. The bond of mutual confidence between him and Gandhi was also seen as an iron corset, supporting but confining. He confessed to his repeated display of weakness at critical moments, to his frequent surrender of judgment to personal loyalties, to his dedication to purpose and principle rather than to doctrine and definition.

Jawaharlal was not strong in analytic thought and the book provides no profound ideas or philosophy. Such ideas as he had were intellectual impulses rather than logical constructions. Even his Marxism was vague and confused, for his ideology was to a large extent based more on sympathy than on conviction. But he bore witness to a passionate commitment to nationalism, though in no narrow sense, to an awareness of world forces, and to a total personal integrity. Born to wealth and an easy life, he had been forced by the situation into the world outside. A heterogeneous character with great inner resources and of infinite mood, aware of natural beauty and in love with mountains, capable of responding to every side of life, yet he had preferred to spend years in prison. Fastidious and lonely by instinct, he had taken to politics and become indifferent to all else because he cared about the human scene and was disturbed by the ugliness and stupidity of the world. The deep personal affections he could give he had almost stifled. His sense of the essential pushed private life to the background, and led to a conscious withholding of emotion. Out of the pages of the *Autobiography* rises, almost, it would seem, against Jawaharlal's will, the story of the slow development of what was by the end a happy marriage; and its tragic close was revealed in the six brief words of the dedication, 'To Kamala, who is no more'.

The whole book was written in jail at a time when writing was at once a discipline, an indulgence and a solace. But there is no bitterness against the British. The book was not abrasive; it had no rant or claptrap. Jawaharlal's quarrel was not with the foreign ruler but with systems — with imperialism, with capitalism, with the social evils of religion. Such bitterness and contemptuous wit as he does disclose he reserves for some of his fellow-Indians. The Liberals who, as he thought, concealed behind platitudes and compromises a low-minded opportunism, came in for sharp derision. Gandhi, who read the book in manuscript, suggested that these portions be revised;[1] but Jawaharlal left them as they were. The Liberals were naturally resentful. 'It is an insufferable book', wrote Jayakar to Sapru,[2] 'full of self-laudation . . . There is nothing in that book which is illuminating or exalting . . . the vapourings of a half-baked politician.' Right-wing Congressmen, whose thinking and attitudes were alien to him, Jawaharlal had tended to ignore. There is no mention, for example, throughout the book, of Rajagopalachari. Their reaction was summed up in the review by K. M. Munshi, who described Jawaharlal as being scarcely in tune with the 'soul of India' (whatever that might be) and criticized him for having time and again destroyed the possibility of immediate gains by insisting on independence and socialism. [3]

[1]Mahadeva Desai to Jawaharlal, 11 December 1935.
[2]21 May 1936. Sapru papers.
[3]*The Hindu*, 21 June 1936.

But most Indian readers, drawn from the middle classes, were able to identify themselves with Jawaharlal in his expression of the hopes and obstacles of a whole generation.

After his wife's death, Jawaharlal returned to India, resisting, on the way, the blandishments of Mussolini who sent a personal message of sympathy and sought to inveigle Jawaharlal into an interview while in transit at Rome airport. 'It was a most embarrassing and ticklish affair but I survived it with a display of extreme tact and firmness.'[1] He brought back Kamala's ashes and immersed all — but the few he retained — at the Sangam in Allahabad. 'Despite his courage, Pandit Jawaharlal was visibly moved as he immersed the ashes in the waters of the two mighty rivers.'[2]

Jawaharlal sought to smother the inner emptiness in work. Many years later he wrote to a friend who had suffered a like bereavement, 'those who have had similar experiences, and I am one of them, can understand to some extent the sorrow that comes to one. The only way to deal with it, so I found, is to apply oneself with greater earnestness to the causes for which one has stood.'[3] But the emotional strain was never far below the surface.[4]

---

[1] Letter to Krishna Menon, quoted in Marie Seton, *Panditji* (London, 1967), p. 88.

[2] AICC letter No. 40, dated 12 March 1936.

[3] To Keith Marvin, New York, 24 February 1962, Nehru papers.

[4] There is a moving description of Jawaharlal at the end of the Lucknow session of the Congress in April 1936, which gives some idea of the stress. 'While speaking in Hindi, tears appeared in the eyes of Pandit Jawaharlal, who sat down immediately. He wiped the tears, but the colour of his face did not change for some minutes and he was not aware that two or three people were addressing him. He did not seem to be aware that he was replying to questions put to him. He rushed to his tent and fell asleep a few seconds later.' *The Bombay Chronicle*, 15 April 1936.

14

Leading the Party

During Jawaharlal's absence in Europe he had been elected president of the Congress for 1936. The decision was, as usual, primarily that of Gandhi. The main issue before the Congress was whether they should contest the elections and accept office in the provinces under the new Government of India Act. Jawaharlal's views on the subject were well known. He regarded the Act as deliberately designed to strengthen all the vested and reactionary elements in India, and acceptance of office under this Act would be a retrograde step which might well lead to the disintegration of the Congress and obstruction of a civil disobedience campaign at any early date. Gandhi too seems to have been of this view, despite the persuasion of Rajagopalachari and Ansari, and therefore was keen that Jawaharlal should once again accept the responsibility, even if it meant that many senior leaders would feel unable to follow his leadership. 'Your presidency is the rightest thing that could have happened for the country.'[1] The Working Committee accepted Gandhi's suggestion as the only way of avoiding bitter controversy. The new constitution of the Congress would enable Jawaharlal to pick his own committee, and even those who could not support him agreed to stand by and give his policies a fair and unobstructed trial.[2]

In Europe, Jawaharlal's hostility to the Act and his radical tendencies had been strengthened. He paid short visits to England in November 1935 and January 1936, when temporary improvements in Kamala's condition permitted him to leave her bedside. He had not wanted to do so, for his mind rebelled against social relations with those responsible for the nightmare years of oppression in India.[3] But Gandhi encouraged him to go.[4]

Unlike in Paris, where he happily discussed Hinduism with Malraux and conditions in Russia with Gide, in London he could not avoid politics. He declined to meet any member of the British Government and took no initiative in

[1] Gandhi to Jawaharlal, 3 October 1935.
[2] Gandhi to Jawaharlal, 22 September and 15 October 1935; Mahadeva Desai to Jawaharlal 6 September 1935.
[3] See his letter to Agatha Harrison, 25 September 1935.
[4] Gandhi to Jawaharlal, early in 1936

meeting anyone other than a few personal friends. Even so, his few days in London were crowded with talks with politicians of every variety. What impressed Jawaharlal was the personal friendliness[1] as well as the general boredom over the Indian question. The presence of a representative from Scotland Yard by his side from the moment he landed at Dover constantly reminded Jawaharlal, even if he were inclined to forget, that he was in a sense a ticket-of-leave man with part of a sentence still hanging over him. But the British public gave him a warm welcome. There was general and great appreciation of him as a man. The reporter for *The Tribune* was lyrical.

> When the man stepped out of the train there was almost a hush. I saw a beautifully featured pale face, cast in a classic mould; certainly one of the most dignified and truly aristocratic faces I have ever seen. I heard a soft and mellow voice. I felt, as everybody who has ever met him must feel, that Jawaharlal is a Presence and in an immeasurable degree much more than a politician.[2]

The modesty of Jawaharlal, his lack of bitterness and his commitment to ideals, the sadness of mien born of imminent sorrow and past suffering, the difficulty he experienced in even articulating his speeches after nearly four years in jail, the dazzlement by the light after long darkness, made a deep impact. 'Few in the House of Commons seemed to care', wrote Hannen Swaffer in *John Bull*, 'but when you went there the other day, one of the world's bravest spirits — one embodied in your slight retiring frame — was within the walls of the Palace of Westminster . . . Although you were heard by only a few people in England, you left behind you a great inspiration. If all the reformers in this country were as calmly valiant as you, a new hope would dawn in the minds of oppressed millions.' But Jawaharlal knew that smiles, good humour and personal approval did not carry far. Even the members of the Labour Party, by and large, with all their theoretical dislike of imperialism, moved in its orbit and felt powerless to step out of it. It did not therefore seem possible to avoid conflict with the British, and all one could hope for was a little more civility in ordinary life and less brutality in battle.[3] So he was more at ease talking to intellectuals and literary figures than to politicians. The discerning account of Jawaharlal in London, provided by Leonard Woolf, makes this clear.

> I liked Nehru very much as a man; he was an intellectual of the intel-
> lectuals, on the surface gentle and sad. He had great charm and, though

[1] Even to this, however, there were exceptions. A. G. Fraser, principal of the Achimota College in what was then the Gold Coast, invited Jawaharlal to dinner at his club. The secretary of the club objected to Jawaharlal appearing in the public dining room. Fraser resigned from the club and arranged the dinner in a private room in a hotel. See Jawaharlal's note to Secretary-General, Ministry of External Affairs, 29 May 1954, Nehru papers.

[2] 16 November 1935.

[3] Note on a visit to England, 22 February 1936.

there was a congenital aloofness about him, I had no difficulty in talking
to him. It was a rather strange and inconclusive conversation. I had
thought and still think that he had intended to discuss politics and, in
particular, Imperial politics from the Labour angle with me. And in a
vague way we did talk politics, the problems of India and Ceylon;
but it was pretty vague and somehow or other we slipped into talking
about life and books rather than the fall of empire or empires . . .[1]

The most lasting impression on Jawaharlal was made not by any Englishman
but by Krishna Menon, whom he then met for the first time. 'He is very able
and energetic and is highly thought of in intellectual, journalistic and left wing
labour circles. He has the virtues and failings of the intellectual.'[2]

However, it so happened that at Lausanne Jawaharlal met by chance Ben
Bradley, who was also a patient at the clinic, and Palme Dutt who had come
to see Bradley. Palme Dutt and Jawaharlal spent three days together, and the
British Communist found the 'Professor', as Jawaharlal was known in Comintern circles, very receptive. He agreed that the Congress was, on the whole,
moving towards the right, but was himself willing to work in close collaboration with the communists. He was not well read in Marxism but was persuaded
of its validity and emotionally inclined toward it. He also had a deep admiration
for the achievements of the Soviet Union. Russia was the land of the future.
'With all its defects and mistakes and ruthlessness, it is taking visible, vital
shape there, stumbling occasionally but ever marching forward.'[3] He hoped
that some variation of the political and economic systems prevalent in Russia
would extend to India, but he was not prepared to have this by coercive methods.
'I do not want India to be drilled and forced into a certain position, because
the costs of such drilling are too great; it is not worth while; it is not desirable
from many points of view.'[4] Civil liberties were to Jawaharlal of absolute value,
and the communists had to reckon with this. Jawaharlal was not a Marxist in
the normal sense of the word. He accepted the Marxist interpretation of history
and its vision of a classless society, but he certainly did not believe in revolutionary dictatorship. Conditioned under Gandhi, he hated violence even if he
did not in theory reject it, and stood for democratic and peaceful though not for
constitutional means. But with these reservations, Jawaharlal, according to
Palme Dutt, promised that he would, as president of the Congress, do all he
could to promote the Communist Party in India, and he even gave a series of
specific undertakings as to what he would try to do.[5]

---

[1]*Downhill All the Way* (London, 1967), pp. 230-32.
[2]To Rajendra Prasad, 22 November 1935, Home Dept. Pol. File 1/2/36.
[3]Foreword to M. R. Masani's book *Soviet Sidelights*, 25 February 1936.
[4] Talk to the Indian Conciliation Group in London, 4 February 1936, reprinted in *India and the World* (London, 1936), p. 259.
[5]Palme Dutt's interview with the author, 20 November 1969.

The communists, of course, were now in a mood to co-operate with the Congress. In 1931 Jawaharlal, 'a candidate well placed for becoming the Indian Kerensky',[1] had been expelled from the League against Imperialism. 'Jawaharlal Nehru', ran the resolution, 'has become traitor to the cause of the emancipation of the people of India from the British imperialist yoke; it [the League] stigmatises his desertion to the camp of counter-revolution before the broad masses of India and expels him from its ranks,' In subsequent years, as part of the policy of refusing to work with bourgeois nationalist parties, the communists had condemned him vehemently for his 'left reformism' and as one of 'the most dangerous enemies in the struggle for independence'. Bradley himself had criticized Jawaharlal for trying to stem the rising peasant movement with vague talk of socialism and communism.[2] But by the summer of 1935 there had been a shift in Soviet and international communist policy. The call was now for popular fronts. In India, said Dimitrov, speaking at the seventh congress of the Third International, the communists had to support, extend and participate in all anti-imperialist mass activities, not excluding those under national reformist leadership. The interview given by Jawaharlal over two years before, declaring that the choice lay between communism and fascism and he preferred the former, was now reported with approval.[3]

The details of what the communists hoped for from Jawaharlal in India can be discerned in an article by Palme Dutt and Bradley.[4] It was conceded that the Congress was the principal mass organization of diverse elements seeking national liberation in India: but it was not yet the united front of the Indian people. To achieve this, its constitution, programme and leadership would all have to be revised and strengthened. Workers' and peasants' unions and other such organizations should be brought into the joint struggle either in a united front or by collective affiliation to the Congress. The constitution of the Congress should be amended to permit such collective affiliation at the local, district, provincial and national levels, and joint bodies should be set up immediately. There should also be provision for greater initiative of the rank and file within the Congress in place of the hierarchical structure dominated by the Working Committee. Centralized direction was of course vital in a struggle; but it ought to be based not on personal dictatorship but on democratic centralism. The dogma of non-violence was a weakness which should be omitted from the Congress creed; but while a sharp ideological struggle should be conducted on this question, it was not so important that it should be allowed to split the national front. The elections should be fought jointly by the front in such a way as to provide sufficient representation for the left-wing elements and to enable the demands of the masses to be clearly expressed. The chief demand, the positive

[1] Saperov in the *Bolshevik* in 1930, quoted in Druhe, op. cit., p. 305.
[2] 'The Background in India', *Labour Monthly*, March 1934.
[3] International Press Correspondence, 4 January 1936.
[4] Palme Dutt and Bradley, 'The Anti-Imperialist People's Front in India', *Labour Monthly*, March 1936.

slogan of the front, would be for a Constituent Assembly freely elected by universal suffrage.

It is clear that this article was written after the talks with Jawaharlal at Lausanne, and stated what Palme Dutt and Bradley believed to have been accepted by Jawaharlal as the common programme for which he would strive. He was for a joint front against imperialism; indeed, he regarded the Congress under Gandhi as already in essence such a front which only required to be widened. He also continued to favour a Constituent Assembly;[1] and the communists, reversing their earlier condemnation of this idea,[2] now accepted this. But he was not ready to abandon Gandhi's leadership or the method of non-violence. Quite apart from its ethical aspect, non-violence had helped to preserve India from civil conflict and to tone down indigenous opposition to the national movement. The concession in the article of Dutt and Bradley that, though non-violence was outmoded, its rejection was not a fundamental issue, was obviously made with Jawaharlal's attitude in mind. As for Gandhi, as Palme Dutt reports it,[3] Jawaharlal had confessed that he felt in his nature an aristocrat; he was sorry for the Indian people, it moved his heart to see them turn to him for guidance, but he lacked the common touch and could not get as close to them as Gandhi did, though even Gandhi was not of the masses. This, according to Jawaharlal, was the source of his tremendous deference to Gandhi; and his audience doubtless recognized that. by its very nature, it could not be set aside for intellectual reasons. There is corroborative evidence of this overwhelmingly emotional mood of Jawaharlal at this time. He condemned imperialism for its horrors, its indecency and vulgarity as much as for its exploitation, and appreciated Gandhi above all for the psychological transformation he had wrought in the Indian people.[4] In an article written at about this time in answer to Indian left-wing criticism of Gandhi, Jawaharlal contended that Gandhi had played a revolutionary role in India because he had reached the heart of the masses while groups with a more advanced ideology had functioned largely in the air.[5]

Now the Congress awaited Jawaharlal's guidance. Till his return to India, no major decisions had been taken, and the party, as Gandhi described it, was 'literally tacking'.[6] It was for Jawaharlal to end this policy of 'non-action and non-thought'.[7] Meeting Gandhi and senior Congressmen before the session at Lucknow, Jawaharlal found considerable support for office acceptance; and he was isolated in the Working Committee.[8] But embarrassment to him was avoided by shelving any firm decision on an issue which would only arise after

[1] Note on a Constituent Assembly for India, 25 February 1936.
[2] See Adhikari's thesis February 1934, *Imprecor,* vol. 14, no. 40, 20 July 1934.
[3] Interview with the author, 20 November 1969.
[4] See his letters to Lord Lothian, 9 December 1935 and 17 January 1936.
[5] *Mahatma Gandhi,* 20 January 1936.
[6] To Jawaharlal, 22 September 1935.
[7] To Rajendra Prasad, 20 November 1935, Home Dept. Pol. 1/2/36.
[8] To Syed Mahmud, 5 May 1936.

the elections. Meantime, reflecting Jawaharlal's new ideas derived in Europe, the Working Committee agreed that it was desirable to develop closer association between the masses and the Congress organization so that they might take their full share in the shaping of Congress policy. It was also decided that the Congress constitution should be revised to make it a joint front of all anti-imperialist elements and enable closer co-operation with organizations of peasants and others.[1] These resolutions, along with that opposing India's participation in any imperialist war, were drafted by Jawaharlal and, as he wrote later, increased his confidence in himself. There was nothing very new in substance, but they hinted a new orientation, and generally a more emphatic and radical tone was adopted.[2] They also delighted the socialists; and the fact that Jawaharlal, though he abstained from formally joining the Congress Socialist Party, was 'now a socialist in the full sense of the term,'[3] gave the socialists great hopes of increasing their influence in the Congress. Jawaharlal might think that they themselves had not adequate support among the masses to take over the Congress organization, but he would certainly not allow the Congress to become a mere parliamentary body. The Congress was 'in a rut due to idiotic ideas of certain people', and it should be given a new direction by socialist permeation.[4]

However, it soon became clear that the socialists had overestimated both Jawaharlal's influence as president and his commitment to them. There was not the faintest suspicion of socialism in any of the resolutions. Despite Jawaharlal's open opposition the Subjects Committee approved of the Working Committee's resolution discarding proportional representation in elections to Congress offices, thus eliminating any chances the socialists might have; and this was only set right by the full session of the Congress.[5] He spoke in favour of non-acceptance of office, for the revolutionary as against the reformist mentality, but would not support the socialist amendments committing the Congress to this position because of his desire to prevent a split.[6] Jawaharlal clutched at the avoidance of a decision in his own mind and in the party. He believed that, while making his own position clear, he should not push the issue to breaking-point. He had been long away. either in prison or abroad; the hunger for office had grown among his colleagues and could not be just wished off the scene; and Gandhi, though out of tune with this mood, was unwilling to battle with it. Jawaharlal could, in the future, use the office of president to

[1] Resolutions to be placed before the Lucknow Congress, *The Bombay Chronicle*, 26 March and 8 April 1936.

[2] DSVA, pp. 40-41.

[3] Message to the All-India Socialist Conference at Meerut, *The Bombay Chronicle*, 16 January 1936.

[4] See the report of the viewpoint of socialist leaders at Lucknow, *The Bombay Chronicle*, 6 April 1936.

[5] *The Bombay Chronicle*, 11 and 14 April 1936.

[6] *The Tribune*, 12 April 1936.

strengthen the radical forces and win the party round, but a direct collision at this stage held no hope of success. To seek satisfaction merely in brave ideas was the way of facile intellectual opportunism. The true socialist was no armchair politician but a man of action, utilizing his philosophy and scientific outlook for achievement. The immediate task was the elections, and this could be used to widen the base of the national movement and develop mass contacts. Indeed, the only thing to be said in favour of the 1935 Act was that it created a wider electorate. To divide the Congress at this stage on a remote issue and weaken its prospects at the polls seemed foolish tactics. Jawaharlal did not face up to the fact that electoral success and the opportunity of forming ministries would in themselves further weaken the position of those in the party of his way of thinking. It would have been far easier to secure a commitment to non-acceptance when the lure of office was not immediate. Postponement, by the very nature of the situation, transferred the advantage to the other side.

In his presidential address Jawaharlal, as was now to be expected of him, analysed the world situation and India's place in it. Two vast groups faced each other; decaying capitalism, imperialist and fascist, on the one hand and the progressive forces, socialist and nationalist, on the other. British imperialism in India also, though still powerful, was showing signs of decay and, in its desire to hold on, was developing an increasingly fascist mentality. The growing intensity of repression required no elaboration, but worthy of special mention was the tremendous deprivation of civil liberties. All this only steeled Jawaharlal to a greater resolve to end this infamy and to have nothing to do with those willing to compromise with such a rule. But in the national movement itself there was a spirit of disunion, a malaise, a stress on petty, internal conflicts. Middle-class leadership was inevitable, but it easily tired if it did not draw strength and inspiration from the masses. The Congress should be not only for the masses but of the masses; only then would it really be for the masses.

So Jawaharlal argued for the forming of new links which would permit the growth of mass consciousness within the Congress, and the revision of the party constitution for this purpose. The real problem was to join together all the anti-imperialist forces in the country, to forge a broad front comprising the mass elements as well as the great majority of the middle classes. The primary committees should be made living organizations, as in the account of Soviet Russia given by the Webbs, and organizations of producers such as trade unions and peasant associations should be affiliated to the Congress or brought into full co-operation with it. The Congress could have a corporate as well as an individual membership. There was no near prospect of direct action or civil disobedience, and the elections could be used to carry the message of the Congress to the people. The removal of social and economic burdens and the convening of a Constituent Assembly to frame a constitution formed the minimum programme, and these could not come through the Government of India Act or the legislatures constituted under it. To accept office under the Act which they had rejected was to stand self-condemned, to slide back to static futility and revive the old sterile creed of reformism. National honour and self-respect could not accept this position, for it would inevitably mean co-operation in some measure with the repressive apparatus of imperialism and partnership in the exploitation of the Indian people. The price of office acceptance was surrender. It would be a descent into a pit from which the Congress would find it difficult to come out. The sole purpose of entering the provincial assemblies should be to create deadlocks so as to kill the proposals for federation and make the working of the Act impossible.

The address had been written on 31 March, when Jawaharlal had not known for certain the strength of feeling in the party in favour of office acceptance. That he should have stuck to the written text even after he had virtually been voted down showed courage; but it also made clear how wide a gulf stretched between the president and his followers. The speech, as a whole, mirrored the contradictions in Jawaharlal's outlook and the weaknesses of his political position. He affirmed his Marxist approach, his recognition of the Indian problem as a part of the world problem of capitalist imperialism. The laws of historical development had to be grasped to realize the organic connection of events and changes. "Let us try to develop the historic sense so that we can view current events in proper perspective and understand their real significance.' The only key to the solution of the world's problems, and of India's problems, lay in socialism, 'and when I use this word I do so not in a vague humanitarian way but in the scientific, economic sense.' But immediately, in the very next sentence, he moved away from the precise Marxist attitude. 'Socialism is, however, something even more than an economic doctrine; it is a philosophy of life and as such also it appeals to me.' It was not merely the ending of poverty, of vested interests and private property, but a change in instincts and habits and desires, a new civilization such as was being fashioned in Soviet Russia. But it was not just a communist utopia, modelled on the Russian example and to be achieved by any means. The socialist approach in India would have to be adapted to the Indian conditions and speak in the language of the country. Socialism was to Jawaharlal more a tendency than a definable body of doctrine. He was always critical of the Indian communists for their imprisonment within the walls of dogma and for their rigid adherence to the Soviet example. 'For you,' he frequently told them, 'history begins with 1917.' There was much that had happened in the Soviet Union which pained Jawaharlal greatly and he avoided the word communism because in the general understanding it signified Soviet Russia. He was a libertarian Marxist, whose idea of socialism encompassed at every stage a large and irreducible measure of civil liberty. A belief in democracy was the core of his socialist attitude. He rejected any mechanical view of human nature and looked forward to a socialist society which, by removing economic and social inhibitions and obstacles, would provide greater scope for individuality. It was this understanding of socialism which underlay his presidential address; and immediately after the Congress session he established an Indian Civil Liberties Union on non-party lines, with members of all shades of political opinion and even from outside politics. What was happening in many parts of India was beyond the limits of 'common decency' and it was the duty of every public-spirited citizen to protest. For when civil liberties were suppressed a nation lost all vitality and became impotent for anything substantial.[1]

The details of his programme for action were also not framed wholly to please the socialists, let alone the Marxists and communists. He made it clear that he would not, as president, seek to impose socialism on the Congress, even though it 'is a vital creed which I hold with all my head and heart'. He would like the Congress to become a socialist organization but he accepted that the majority in the party were not prepared to go that far; and he would not force the issue on what was basically a nationalist organization and thereby create difficulties in the struggle for independence. Socialism was to him a personal matter; he therefore saw no role for himself in the Congress Socialist Party; and as president of the Congress Party he would, without compromising his beliefs, function as a political leader, leading the majority the way it wanted to go. He cast himself in the mould of Blanqui: 'I am their leader, therefore I must follow them.' And, above all, he had no intention, as he had made clear in Europe to Bradley and Palme Dutt, of moving away from Gandhi; and the address ended with the customary paean to him.

It is true that Jawaharlal advocated the two chief proposals now being commended by the communists — the formation of a joint anti-imperialist front, and the affiliation to the Congress of trade and peasant unions. This gave the Communist Party much satisfaction. 'In his presidential address Nehru's anti-imperialist voice stammered on some vital points yet it was full-throated on several others, it was a clearer anti-imperialist call than had ever been made from the Congress chair.'[2] But even here the implementation was to be very different from what the communists expected. Jawaharlal's idea of a joint front was not solely an alliance of the Congress with political organizations ideologically to the left of it. He was thinking as much of the Congress drawing to its side groups which were more conservatively inclined, as at the time of the boycott of the Simon Commission in 1928, and spoke of it as seeking to become 'an All-Parties Conference in permanent session'.[3] He was willing to co-operate with anybody, irrespective of ideology, who was opposed to imperialism; and within a few days of the Lucknow session he began negotiations with Pandit Malaviya, whose

[1] Speech at Allahabad, 11 May, *The Bombay Chronicle*, 12 May and talk in Bombay, *The Bombay Chronicle*, 18 May 1936.

[2] Statement of the Politbureau of the Central Committee of the Communist Party of India, 24 July 1936.

[3] Speech at Bombay, *The Bombay Chronicle*, 19 May 1936.

outlook in politics was frankly communal, for an electoral alliance with his Nationalist Party.[1] Jawaharlal's general indifference to communal issues and his belief that they would be submerged once the emphasis was shifted to economic matters affecting the common people enabled him to ignore the communal tinge in organizations which were otherwise opposed to the British and were prepared to join him in the campaign for civil liberties. As for the affiliation of peasant and worker associations, this was watered down by the Working Committee to the constitution of a small committee to consider the promotion of closer contacts between the Congress and the masses; and this in turn became the need to grant greater responsibilities to the primary committees of the Congress so as to make them living bodies.[2]

So left-wing forces had cause to be disappointed with the Lucknow Congress. Jawaharlal's speech was heart-warming, and his personal standing in the party and the country was second only to that of Gandhi. But he had not even sought to assert the strength of his position. He had, at the end of the session, considered resignation and informed the delegates that having sat on a high pedestal for three days he was now going back to oblivion. But he later decided not to precipitate matters. So it was the 'old guard' which had been successful. It had been, as Satyamurti, the Congressman from Madras, gloated, the triumph of Gandhism over socialism.[3] G. D. Birla crowed:[4]

Mahatmaji kept his promise and without his uttering a word, he saw that *no new commitments were made.* Jawaharlalji's speech in a way was thrown into the waste paper basket because all the resolutions that were passed were against the spirit of his speech . . . He could have caused a split by resigning but he did not . . . Jawaharlalji seems to be like a typical English democrat who takes defeat in a sporting spirit. He seems to be out for giving expression to his ideology, but he realises that action is impossible and so does not press for it.

As Gandhi himself observed in a letter[5] which was seen by Jawaharlal, their ways were different and Gandhi accepted hardly any of Jawaharlal's methods. He would strain every nerve to avoid a class war; so perhaps would Jawaharlal but he did not think it possible to avoid it. 'But though he is extreme in his presentation of his methods, he is sober in action . . . Whatever he does, he will do it nobly. Though the gulf between us as to the outlook upon life has undoubtedly widened, we have never been so near each other in hearts as perhaps we are today.'

[1] Letter to M. M. Malaviya, 20 April, and statement to the press, 22 June 1936.
[2] Circular to prov. cong. Committees, 14 May 1936.
[3] *The Bombay Chronicle*, 16 April 1936.
[4] To Purushottamdas Thakurdas, 20 April 1936. Purushottamdas Thakurdas papers, File 177. N.M.M.L. Emphasis in original.
[5] To Agatha Harrison, 30 April 1936.

Jawaharlal consolidated the victory of his opponents by selecting, out of fourteen members of the Working Committee, no less than ten who disagreed with him, disapproved of socialism and were inclined towards office acceptance. Subhas Bose was in prison; and only three members, Narendra Deva, Jayaprakash Narayan and Achyut Patwardhan, were socialists. Even they owed their appointment not to Jawaharlal but to Gandhi, who thought these socialists would be useful in weakening the support which the terrorists commanded among the younger generation; and these three were selected on the ground that they were socially acceptable.[1] Jawaharlal thought it vulgar and inappropriate to thrust his views, however deeply held, on a party in which he and his followers were in a minority, and created for himself what was in many ways the role of an ineffective president. Rafi Ahmad Kidwai, devoted to Jawaharlal and sharing his views but not a member of the Socialist Party, was expected to replace Acharya Kripalani of the right wing as general secretary; he was not even included in the Committee. Pattabhi Sitaramayya, the only member of the old Working Committee who had on occasions joined Jawaharlal in opposing office acceptance, was now dropped. Nor, surprisingly, was any woman included. The three socialist members realized that they would have little influence in the Committee, but agreed to serve out of personal loyalty to Jawaharlal.[2]

Powerful as the presidential address was as an attack on imperialism, the Government felt that they would be unable to sustain a prosecution on it. In the months that followed, while Jawaharlal toured the country addressing scores of meetings and 'simultaneously carrying on war at various fronts', [3] the authorities, regarding him as 'a potential danger of the first magnitude',[4] followed him round with their notebooks seeking carefully but in vain for any statement that would justify his arrest and ensure a long sentence. Instead, they had to console themselves with the thought that his preaching of socialism was weakening the Congress and this would be reflected in the elections.[5] 'Indeed we should keep him in cotton wool and pamper him, for he is unwittingly smashing the Congress organization from the inside.'[6] This hope was again to be belied. But the Government were right to the extent that his speeches frightened many in the Congress and outside. He started what was virtually a country-wide election campaign in Bombay with a bang. The Congress was contesting the elections and entering the assemblies in order to combat the Act and render it unworkable. As to how this should be done, there was as yet no agreement; but he himself was convinced that acceptance of office would weaken their movement. The first and immediate issue was political, the

[1] Author's interview with Achyut Patwardhan, 3 April 1970.
[2] See statement of the executive committee of the Congress Socialist Party, 16 April, *The Bombay Chronicle*, 17 April 1936.
[3] To Ellen Wilkinson, 15 June 1936.
[4] Home Secretary to all Local Govts., 19 August 1936, Home Dept. Pol File 4/15/36.
[5] Home Dept. Pol. Files 4/4, 4/6, 4/14, 4/15, 4/23, 4/32 and 4/34 to 4/38 of 1936.
[6] Governor of Madras to Home Member, 20 April 1936, Home Dept. Pol. File 4/6/36.

development of a revolutionary mentality for the attainment of independence. He believed that socialism was inevitable for the solution of India's prime problem of poverty and degradation but he had no wish to force the issue. If he talked about it now, it was solely to educate the people so that they would be in a better position to decide when the issue came up. Socialism — and here Jawaharlal's divergence from the communists was clear — could not be imposed on India. Violence was abominable to him and he hoped that socialism would be attained with the support of the vast majority and the least harm to anyone. Compensation should be paid, though not in full, at least partially, to propertied and vested interests. However, there might be upheavals if resistance to economic progress developed, and he doubted if the rich in India were wise enough to avoid this.[1]

Such unhesitant exposition of his intellectual and emotional commitment to the socialist ideal naturally roused resentment. Bombay was the heart of 'big business' and there were reactive tremors to 'the storm of communism'[2] that was passing over the city. Twenty-one leading businessmen issued a manifesto condemning Jawaharlal's 'destructive and subversive programme' which, according to them, would create disorders and impede the achievement of self-government.[3] Jawaharlal's reply was vigorous.

I have hardly mentioned socialism except incidentally, but I have laid stress on the amazing poverty of our people, the vast unemployment of our peasants and workers and middle class, on the progressive deterioration of all classes except the handful at the top. That has been my sin in the eyes of that handful. But that is the only future that comes before my eyes when I think of India. I cannot rid myself of it, try as I may. It is not a pleasant picture. I do not like it, and as I see it, sometimes my blood freezes within me and sometimes it boils with indignation that such things should be.[4]

He accused Indian capitalists of creating Indian fascism, which was the ally of British imperialism. Their attack on his socialist views was merely a façade for attacking the Congress and the national movement. As the Congress became increasingly a lower-middle-class and mass organization, the upper strata of Indian society were drawing closer to the foreign rulers. As the struggle for freedom grew more intense, one was either for or against; there was no room for third parties or a middle course. Indian capitalists had supported the Government in seeking to repress civil disobedience and break the boycott. They had defended the ordinances, they had reached agreements with foreign textile interests and they had sent their representatives to those sessions of the Round

[1] Speeches and statements at Bombay, *The Bombay Chronicle,* 16 and 18 May 1936.
[2] Sir Cowasji Jehangir in *The Bombay Chronicle,* 28 May 1936.
[3] Manifesto of the 21', *The Tribune,* 20 May 1936.
[4] Reply to Critics', *The Tribune,* 9 June 1936.

Table Conference which had been shunned by the Congress. For them to speak now of their share in the national movement and of his weakening it was therefore an impertinence.[1]

The more intelligent among the businessmen realized that to promote a public debate with Jawaharlal was to invite humiliation. 'You have rendered no service to your caste men. It is curious how we businessmen are so short-sighted . . . It looks very crude for a man with property to say that he is opposed to expropriation in the wider interest of the country.'[2] It would be obviously far more effective to strengthen the opposition to Jawaharlal within the Congress. Jawaharlal had been unfair to the Indian capitalist class in castigating them as allies of the British imperialists. Though heavily dependent on them, the Indian capitalists had not been their junior partners. They had, on the other hand, supported the non-revolutionary, right-wing elements in the anti-imperialist camp;[3] and they now looked to these men to deal with Jawaharlal. They left it to Vallabhbhai Patel and others to remind the president of the party that he represented a very small section of minority opinion and had no mandate to make such a severe onslaught on the ideological hegemony of propertied interests. Patel, Rajendra Prasad and Rajagopalachari objected as strongly to Jawaharlal's speeches in Bombay as any of the capitalists,[4] and appealed to the grand master Gandhi, who called on Jawaharlal for an explanation. They could not openly object to his crusade for socialism, but they criticized his under-rating of *khaddar* and his suggestion that the responsibility for not including women in the Working Committee was not his. Jawaharlal replied that, though technically he was responsible for the decision, the Committee as it took shape was not of his making; and Gandhi retorted that he was not satisfied with the answer.[5] Yet, on the main issue, Jawaharlal was unrepentant; and he toured the Punjab making the same points with equal vehemence. The political battle for independence was the first priority, but after freedom was won, socialism was bound to come. 'The whole economic structure will crash and there will be upheavals which no human power can avert, the capitalist system will go and along with it the British Empire, this is how I visualise the happenings of the next ten years.'[6]

The public response was enthusiastic. 'I am being attacked and criticized', wrote Jawaharlal to Krishna Menon,[7] 'by a variety of people, Big Business, Liberals, Responsivists, some Congressmen and of course our beloved Government.

---

[1] Speeches and interviews, *The Bombay Chronicle*, 19, 20, 21 and 23 May 1936.

[2] G. D. Birla to Walchand Hirachand, one of the signatories of the manifesto, 26 May 1936. Purushottamdas Thakurdas papers, File 177.

[3] See Bipan Chandra, 'The Indian capitalist class and imperialism before 1947" (1972).

[4] See Vallabhbhai Patel to Rajendra Prasad, 29 May 1936, Maharashtra Govt. records—intercepted letters.

[5] Jawaharlal to Gandhi, 25 May and Gandhi to Jawaharlal, 29 May 1936.

[6] Speech at Lahore, 2 June, *The Tribune*, 3 June 1936.

[7] 18 June 1936.

And yet behind all this lies the fact that wherever I go I get a prodigious welcome and the response is such that it puts out the critics. It is a tiring business to carry on wars on numerous fronts and there are few to help. But I carry on. The process is not without its exhilaration.' But at Wardha, when the Working Committee met in the first week of July, Jawaharlal was plainly rebuked by Gandhi and the others. Rajendra Prasad, on behalf of the right wing, wrote to Jawaharlal criticizing him severely and the latter offered to resign and submit the dispute to the AICC for discussion. 'Today there is no loyalty of the spirit which binds our group together. It is a mechanical group and on either side there is a sense of suppression and that, as every student of psychology knows, results in all manner of undesirable complexes, both individual and social.' But Gandhi pulled him up for arrogance, intolerance and lack of a sense of humour. 'You are in office by their unanimous choice but you are not in power yet. To put you in office was an attempt to find you in power quicker than you would otherwise have been.' Jawaharlal should therefore cease wrangling and the 'tragi-comedy' he was playing and not destroy himself by moving openly into opposition. [1]

Jawaharlal meekly submitted and publicly acknowledged his responsibility for the exclusion of women from the Committee. [2] Objection having also been taken to his appointment of young socialists in the AICC office, his enthusiasm for building up the central office was checked. His speeches also were thereafter all in a lower key, and lacked, as Jayakar gleefully reported to Sapru, 'the triumphant freshness'[3] of his earlier performances. He now gave greater emphasis to the part which the Congress had played in involving the peasants in the national movement, and made claims for the party and its leader which he himself could not have seriously believed. The Congress was not, of course, socialistic, but it no longer ignored economic issues; and whenever a conflict of interests emerged it was always willing to sacrifice the interests which clashed with those of the masses. The socialist outlook, which the Congress had been stressing since Gandhi took it over, helped in the political struggle by clearing the issues and strengthening the role of the masses. These bore reserves of power and a deep unrest, a hunger that gnawed and required satisfaction; and it was because the Congress promised to provide the satisfaction that the people came in their thousands to hear its leaders. No socialist imagined that socialism could have any place in India before political freedom had been established. Indeed, no longer stressing the inevitability of socialism, Jawaharlal accepted that after independence socialism could come only if India were ripe for it and the great majority of people desired it. Those who believed in socialism could not assume an attitude of superior knowledge and make of themselves a sect apart. Their correct understanding of history and of social change was not

---

[1] Jawaharlal to Gandhi, 5 July 1936; Gandhi to Jawaharlal, 8 July, 15 July and 30 July 1936.
[2] *The Bombay Chronicle*, 7 July 1936.
[3] 8 July 1936, Sapru papers.

enough; they had to justify themselves in other ways and seek to win over to their way of thinking others in the Congress and the country at large.[1]

If Jawaharlal gave way to the pressure of the right wing, it could not have been for the personal reasons which Gandhi elaborated. By now Jawaharlal was as indispensable to the Congress as the party was to him. He commanded, even before his election tours gave him a wide popular appeal, the support of large sections of radical youth who, but for him, would have left the Congress for left-wing parties. Even the Congress Socialist Party might have broken away from the parent body. Throughout India there were men and women who, along with nationalist feeling, had developed a conscience on economic matters, who saw in Jawaharlal the spokesman of their viewpoint, and who, because of him, followed the lead of the Congress even if they did not belong to it. He was, too, the only Indian politician who had an international audience, and it was he who secured for the party recognition on the world stage. Had Jawaharlal, therefore, insisted in the summer of 1936 on resigning the presidency, it is difficult to believe that Gandhi and his followers would have been short-sighted enough to let him do so. But it was not just that it did not lie in Jawaharlal's nature to precipitate such a conflict and to safeguard his political chastity at the price of weakening the nationalist organization. The psychological hankering to follow Gandhi and the ingrained loyalty to the party were only part of the explanation. Jawaharlal knew that there was no working-class leadership or even an alternative elite leadership available; and so long as this was the case, it would be disastrous to weaken the Congress. And, as ever, his colleagues took advantage of this.

Meantime, as the mimic war of the elections drew nearer, Jawaharlal gave it increasing attention. The election manifesto of the Congress, largely drafted by him,[2] rejected the Act of 1935 and the Communal Award that went with it. The only purpose of sending Congressmen to the legislatures was to seek to end the Act; but how this was to be done, and whether office should be accepted or not, would be considered after the elections. The economic programme of the Congress remained in essence the resolution on fundamental rights passed at Karachi: land reforms, reduction of rent and revenue and an equitable adjustment of the burden on agricultural land, and reasonable standards of living and of working conditions for industrial labour. Jawaharlal excluded any reflection in the manifesto of socialist doctrine. His weakness he justified to himself by the outbreak of the Spanish Civil War and the rapid drive to a world war which made it all the more necessary to see the Indian problem in perspective as part of the world struggle and concentrate on the fight against imperialism. Before criticizing him, it should be remembered that the socialist members of the Working Committee also raised no objection to the manifesto and did not seek to include in it such objectives as the abolition of landlordism or the

[1] Articles on 'Congress and Socialism', *The Bombay Chronicle*, 20 and 31 July 1936; statement on the Punjab peasantry, 12 August, *The Tribune*, 13 August 1936.

[2] See AICC File G 71 of 1936.

nationalization of key industries. On the other hand, Narendra Deva was delighted with the manifesto, which had been revised overnight by Jawaharlal as desired by Narendra Deva himself,[1] and he commended it to the AICC as a revolutionary and not a reformist document.[2]

Jawaharlal's right-wing colleagues were naturally elated. 'I was charmed', wrote Rajagopalachari to Gandhi, who had not been present at the Working Committee session which ratified this document, 'with the manner in which Jawaharlalji got through the Working Committee. All the business was done exceedingly well and everyone was pleased.' Vallabhbhai Patel was equally satisfied.

> We have been getting on beautifully this time. The smooth and harmonious working reminds me most forcibly of the Working Committee meetings before 1932. It has been more like a gathering of family members than a formal committee meeting. We have just finished and within half an hour the AICC will meet. The manifesto was prepared and passed almost unanimously all co-operating with the utmost confidence and trust. I cannot speak too highly of Jawaharlal. He has done wonderful work, and has been burning the candle at both ends. We found not the slightest difficulty in co-operating with him and adjusting ourselves to his views on certain points. I have an impression that he is also satisfied.[3]

Whether, as claimed, Jawaharlal was equally satisfied is doubtful. But he made no public grievance of the clipping of his wings. If he realized that, though he was president, he was being steadily forced to continue the retreat which had begun at Lucknow, he did not disclose it even to his closest friends and threw all his energies into the winning of the elections. This was the first of his national campaigns, covering the Indian village network by train, plane, car, bicycle, cart and steamer, on horse, elephant and camel, and on foot. Once he even ran for half a mile to reach a meeting-place, the crowd following him.[4] On another occasion the audience was so packed that he had to walk on their shoulders, and later felt ashamed for having done so with his shoes on.[5] But such actions had little effect on his popularity. His frequent losses of temper were short-lived and patently without malice.[6] There was a degree of spontaneity and aggressive vitality in his behaviour which, combined with his 'actor's presence', endeared him to the people.

[1] See his article, 'Favourite of Fortune', in *Nehru Abhinandan Granth*, pp. 108-9.
[2] *The Tribune*, 23 August 1936.
[3] Letters to Gandhi communicated to Jawaharlal by Mahadeva Desai, 26 August 1936, AICC File G 85(1) of 1936.
[4] *The Bombay Chronicle*, 26 January 1937.
[5] Lal Bahadur Shastri's article in Zakaria, *A Study of Nehru*, pp. 150-51.
[6] Francis Watson provides an eye-witness account of such an occasion at the Congress session in 1939. 'As though to ensure that I should not overlook the item, my neighbour in one of the preliminary sessions, some three or four rows from the front, heckled the platform in a crescendo of

Day, after day the programme began at dawn and went on till late at night, and on one occasion without a break for twenty-four hours. He drew strength from the *bain de multitude,* made himself receptive to the impressions and thoughts roused by the thousands he met as well as by the diverse contexts in India, and yet snatched the odd hour to read Huxley's *Eyeless in Gaza* and live for a while another life. 'It is an exhausting business and yet I find a strange relief in it from the politics of committees and individuals. I seem to feel a little nearer to reality and I suppose the enthusiasm and the crowds cheer me up.'[1] His speeches were impersonal, with little reference to individual candidates. He talked about the common problems of the Indian people — poverty, debt, foreign rule — made them think of India as a whole, explained the party manifesto, and promised nothing except unceasing struggle till freedom was won. He spoke in simple terms but treated his audience as mature. Many of them were little interested in all this, and came merely to see for themselves the god-like figure of whom they had heard so much. Gandhi was one of them, but Jawaharlal was the glamorous prince. Yet in the eyes of a few there was a responsive gleam. A British official, reporting to his superiors, has given a vivid description of Jawaharlal on these tours.

> In spite of his unattractive Congress dress and cap the Pandit looked a thorough gentleman and an impressive figure. He is about the only good-looking Indian as I have seen in a Congress cap and appears sturdy and vigorous. He used no notes whilst he was talking and did not wear spectacles. He has a good deep voice and rams home his arguments merely by working his right forearm. He does not 'intone' like so many Indian public speakers, but at the same time addresses his audience in rather a scolding manner. He certainly does not go out of his way to flatter them. It is easy for a European to follow his Hindustani, partly because he uses simple words and phrases, and partly because he talks it with what I can only describe as an English accent . . . The Pandit is by far the most attractive public speaker whom I have heard in India, and there is no doubt that his manliness, frankness and reputation for sacrifice attracts a large public.[2]

It was obviously senseless to make a change in the Congress presidency

---

Panditji-baiting questions until Panditji, projecting himself from the dais like a rocket and landing more or less in my lap, shrivelled the offender with his wrath, demanded his pass, tore it up and in seconds cast the whole meeting into uproar. When I crawled out under a collapsed corner of the canvas, the Congress volunteers in their blue shorts were still trying to tranquillize the shouting tangle of patriots. It was some hours later that I had a chance of talking to Nehru alone and enquired the cause of the disturbance. He gave me a puzzled frown, "What disturbance?" he asked, and we passed to other matters.' *The Trial of Mr. Gandhi* (London, 1969), p. 21.

[1] To Agatha Harrison, 3 September 1936.

[2] Report of the District Magistrate, Multan, after hearing Jawaharlal on 28 July 1936, Home Dept. Pol. File 4/14/36.

in the middle of the campaign, and Jawaharlal was re-elected to preside over the Congress session at Faizpur in December 1936. He reiterated in his address what were by now familiar views — that the primary issue was political freedom, that socialism helped to analyse the situation and provided the only future solution to economic problems, and that the Indian struggle was but part of a titanic conflict which gripped the world. He felt the latter even more strongly than before, for the civil war in Spain, which had broken out since the Congress last met, was to Jawaharlal, as to so many intellectuals in the West, a matter of personal involvement. But on the other hand, deep in the throes of election-eering, he tended to give less urgency to socialism. It was world peace and free democracy in India which were now the prime objectives.[1] But his colleagues in the Congress had little time for these visions. They were concerned solely with the polls and what would follow. Jawaharlal repeated that the Congress was contesting the elections in order to rally the masses and not in search of con-stitutionalism or a barren reformism; to him the cornerstone of Congress policy was still the demand for a Constituent Assembly. The Act had to be wrecked so that they could write on a clean slate, but this could be done not so much by action within the assemblies as by mass struggle.

The long tirade against office acceptance, however, was not taken seriously by the audience. Jawaharlal was a useful standard-bearer, whose energy, eloqu-ence and popularity were assets in winning votes. These the Congress party-managers exploited, without paying much heed to his ideas, which could be defeated after the polling was over. The token protest of a *hartal* on 1 April, when the new Act would come into force, had little meaning. More signi-ficant was the decision to summon a convention of all Congressmen who had been elected. Jawaharlal might regard it as a preparation for a Constituent Assembly,[2] while the Viceroy was convinced that the object was to improve Congress discipline as a prelude to refusal of office and preparation for civil disobedience.[3] Both were credulous. Though called ostensibly to consider how to refuse to work the Act, any such convention of legislators could be expected to display an eagerness for office; and to summon such a meeting was to promote a decision to that effect. Indeed, the magnitude of the triumph of the Congress at the polls, a victory for which no single individual had been more responsible than Jawaharlal, strengthened the forces against him. The Congress had con-tested 1,161 of the 1,585 seats and won 716. It had a clear majority in 6 of the 11 provinces and was the largest single party in three others.

Jawaharlal believed that there had been a change in Congress thinking since the Lucknow session. Then, acceptance of office was a dead certainty: now, it

[1] Presidential address at Faizpur, December 1936, reprinted in *Eighteen Months in India*, pp. 72-98.

[2] President's circular to all provincial Congress committees, 2 January 1937.

[3] Linlithgow to Zetland, 15 February 1937, Zetland papers. I.O.L. Mss. Eur. D 609, vol. 14.

seemed a very doubtful proposition. 'Try to imagine', he wrote to Krishna Menon,[1] who, living in London, was critical of Jawaharlal's failure to suppress the 'hobnobbing with ministerialism'. 'what the human material is in India. How they think, how they act, what moves them, what does not affect them. It is easy enough to take up a theoretically correct attitude which has little effect on anybody. We have to do something much more important and difficult, and that is to move large numbers of people, to make them act, and to do all this without breaking up the Congress. I must say that the results of the last six months have been quite extraordinary.' But to his chagrin, immediately after the declaration of the results many Congressmen thought and spoke in terms of ministries. The ostensible objective of contesting the elections, wrecking the Act, was hardly remembered, lost in arguments about the spoils of office. Such behaviour seemed to him not merely an abdication of purpose but so foolish and lacking in self-respect and political sense that he took hold of the debate in the U.P. and forced through a resolution in the provincial Congress committee against acceptance of office. Then, moving to Delhi for the crucial meetings of the Working Committee and the convention of legislators, he asserted that what the electors had said was in effect, 'To hell with this Constitution.'[2] In the presidential speech for the convention, drafted and made public well in advance, he argued that the electors had given notice to British imperialism to quit, and the Act should therefore 'go, lock, stock and barrel, and leave the field clear for our Constituent Assembly'. Till such an Assembly met there could be nothing but conflict and struggle, and the narrow issue of office acceptance hardly arose. To co-operate was to submit to imperialist dictation and to share the odium of exploitation.[3]

Gandhi's own inclination was to support Jawaharlal, but he responded to the overwhelming mood of the party. The Working Committee described the results of the elections as a condemnation and rejection of the Act, impressed on all Congressmen that the fundamental policy of the party was to combat and seek to end the Act, and then, without a trace of logic or embarrassment, authorized acceptance of office if the leaders of the party in the assemblies were satisfied that while the ministries acted within the constitution the Governors would not interfere. M. N. Roy was at this time Jawaharlal's neighbour in Delhi, and his record of Jawaharlal's reaction has the ring of truth.

> On the third day, late in the afternoon, he walked in and threw himself on the bed, a broken man, nearly on the point of crying. 'I must resign' he said. I enquired, 'Why? Have they rejected your draft?' 'No,' he exclaimed in impotent rage; 'they have accepted the whole damn thing, supple-

[1] 28 September 1936.

[2] Speech at Delhi, *The Bombay Chronicle*, 15 March 1937.

[3] Presidential address at All-India Congress legislators convention, March 1937, *Eighteen Months in India*, pp. 111-24.

mented by a short paragraph dictated by Gandhiji, which invalidates the rest of the resolution'.[1]

He did not, it is needless to say, resign, but with his firm sense of discipline, accepted defeat. While he had not changed his views he would, 'like a humble soldier', loyally abide by the resolution which had been adopted. The time might come when he would wish to resign, for no man could lead an army who did not know the way; but that time was not yet, and till then the Congress should 'hold together, push together, fight together and win together'.[2] It was theoretically feasible to accept office not in order to co-operate but to work for revolutionary change. However, Jawaharlal still thought it possible that the assurances sought from the Governors would not be given, and, therefore, Congress ministries might not be formed.[3] At first, this was the case. The Governors ignored the Congress majorities and called on men defeated in the elections to take office. Jawaharlal denounced this as the culmination of the growth of the fascist spirit in the British Government in India,[4] and the Viceroy seriously considered his arrest.[5] Jawaharlal could see no room for compromise and was confident that even the moderate elements in the Congress would be forced to recognize that the conflict inherent in the Act had taken immediate shape.[6] But the Congress resolution had left the initiative for securing assurances to the leaders of the provincial parties; and Rajagopalachari, the leader of the Congress party in Madras, exploited the opportunity. A self-proclaimed political ascetic who, in the 'twenties, had led the opposition to Das, Motilal Nehru and the Swarajists, Rajagopalachari had now quietly put himself in line for the Chief Ministership in Madras and was determined to take office. Enjoying Gandhi's confidence and ignoring Jawaharlal, who was first put out of action by a mild attack of typhoid and was then away in Burma and Malaya, Rajagopalachari negotiated with Lord Erskine, the Governor of Madras. While he had commended office acceptance to the convention of legislators as a means of wrecking the Act,[7] he assured Erskine that 'there was a real chance to get rid of the Civil Disobedience mentality for good, and that it would be a thousand pities if the chance was missed'.[8] In London, Halifax in the Cabinet was in favour of some gesture which would help Rajagopalachari and others of his way of thinking;[9] but Zetland and Linlithgow saw no need for it. They made speeches which sounded accommodating

[1] M. N. Roy, 'Jawaharlal Nehru', *Twentieth Century*, February 1952.
[2] Speeches at the convention of legislators, 19 March, *The Bombay Chronicle*, 20 March 1937.
[3] Letter to K. T. Shah, 27 March 1937.
[4] Statement to the press, 28 March 1937.
[5] Linlithgow to Zetland, 2 April 1937, Zetland papers, vol. 14.
[6] To Agatha Harrison, 18 April, to H. G. Alexander, 21 April, to H. N. Brailsford, 22 April, and to Stafford Cripps, 28 April 1937.
[7] *The Bombay Chronicle*, 20 March 1937.
[8] Erskine's telegram to Viceroy, 11 June 1937, Erskine papers I.O.L. Mss. Eur. D. 596, vol. 8.
[9] Zetland to Linlithgow, 3 and 9 May 1937, reprinted in Zetland, *Essayez* (London, 1956) pp. 220-22.

without conceding anything of substance. However, alarmed by Jawaharlal's repeated assertions, both abroad and on his return to India, that the fundamental struggle between nationalism and imperialism could not be submerged and an Act which protected imperial and other vested interests and petrified the misery of millions would have to go, they kept ready an ordinance in the improbable circumstance of the Congress breaking off negotiations and starting civil disobedience.[1] But, in fact, they had assessed their counterplayers correctly. The Working Committee, overruling Jawaharlal, decided that even though no assurances had been given the Congress should accept office. The majority were so anxious for a quick decision that they were unwilling even to refer the matter to the AICC. As Jawaharlal ruefully commented, the question was being considered the wrong way; not what are the reasons for accepting office, but office must be taken and therefore reasons have to be found for it.[2] But in sight of the prize, Rajagopalachari and the right wing were not to be diverted by such arguments. A few days later, Congress ministries were formed in six provinces.

[1]Zetland to Linlithgow, 5 July 1937, Zetland papers, vol. 8.
[2]Proceedings of the Working Committee, 5 to 9 July 1937, AICC File 42 of 1936.

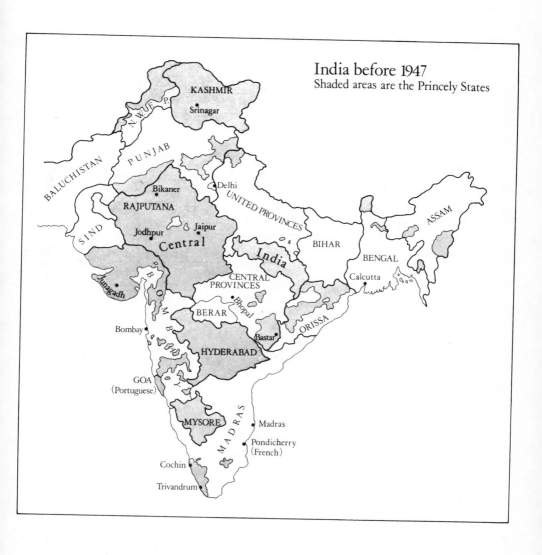

India before 1947
Shaded areas are the Princely States

KASHMIR
Srinagar

N.W.F.P.

BALUCHISTAN

PUNJAB

SIND

RAJPUTANA
Bikaner
Jodhpur
Jaipur

Delhi

UNITED PROVINCES

Central

India

BIHAR

ASSAM

BENGAL

Calcutta

Junagadh

B
O
M
B
A
Y

CENTRAL
PROVINCES

Bhopal

BERAR

Bastar

ORISSA

Bombay

HYDERABAD

GOA
(Portuguese)

M
A
D
R
A
S

MYSORE

Madras

Pondicherry
(French)

Cochin

Trivandrum

15

Out of Tune with the Congress

Again, Jawaharlal loyally accepted the decision. 'Every decision of the Working Committee is the right one. Just as the King can do no wrong, the Working Committee also can do no wrong.'[1] Acceptance of office, he announced, seemingly more to convince himself than others, did not mean acceptance of the slave constitution, but was primarily a means to fight the imposition of federation. If they remembered this, the risk of getting involved in petty, reformist activities would be lessened. So, to be loyal to the spirit underlying the decision, Congressmen should not lose their sense of perspective and should carry on their work outside the legislatures with even greater energy.[2] But such loyalty could not conceal that in his heart Jawaharlal hated it all. The Congress had moved away from almost everything that it had stood for in his eyes, and had become a responsivist, constitutional organization, avid for the minor loaves and fishes of office. So Jawaharlal virtually went into retreat. Though still the president of the party, he did not serve on the parliamentary board which sought to guide and co-ordinate the working of the ministries. He took no serious interest in the composition of the Governments, not even that in his home state, the United Provinces. It is necessary to state this, because years later the charge was made by Maulana Azad that the leaders of the Muslim League in the U.P. had agreed to co-operate with the Congress in return for two seats in the Cabinet, but Jawaharlal had whittled down the number to one and thereby destroyed the agreement reached by Azad. 'Jawaharlal's action gave the Muslim League in the U.P. a new lease of life. All students of Indian politics know that it was from the U.P. that the League was reorganized. Mr Jinnah took full advantage of the situation and started an offensive which ultimately led to Pakistan.'[3]

Such severe criticism from so authoritative a quarter cannot lightly be set aside. Even if Jawaharlal had been responsible for the decision to exclude the representatives of the League in 1937, it is obviously too superficial to trace

[1] Message to the Associated Press, *The Bombay Chronicle,* 8 July 1937.
[2] The Decision to Accept Office', 10 and 20 July 1937 *Eighteen Months in India*, pp. 248-54.
[3] Maulana Azad, *India Wins Freedom* (Calcutta, 1967 edition), pp. 143-5.

the growing influence of Muslim communalism to one such single event. But did Jawaharlal in fact decide in this manner? Azad's memoirs, prepared under his instructions by Humayun Kabir, were published in January 1959 after his death. The manuscript was shown to Jawaharlal, who asked Kabir not to make any changes.[1] He also referred to the criticism at a press conference but in very general terms, merely remarking that Azad had thought too much sometimes in individual terms and not in terms of the historical forces at work.[2] His loyalty to the memory of an old colleague was too strong to permit him to rebut the charge in detail. The result has been the entrenchment of a myth, and its frequent repetition even in scholarly accounts of this period.

However, the facts are very different. When Jinnah took up again in 1936 the leadership of the Muslim League, he was still a nationalist who had no wish to support, or rely on, foreign rule. Indeed his aloofness, brittle ability and anti-imperial attitude made him as disliked by the British as any Congressman. 'Of all the Indians I have met', Hoare wrote to Willingdon, 'I think I have disliked Jinnah the most. Throughout the Round Table discussions he invariably behaved like a snake, and no one seemed to trust him. I greatly hope that he is not getting a following among the Muslims.'[3] But Jinnah had no use for mass politics. His idea was to revert to the pre-Gandhian period and to form once more an alliance of élite politicians acting together to wrest concessions from the British. He had been the chief architect of the Lucknow Pact of 1916 between the Congress and the League,[4] and his hope now was for another similar understanding. He therefore secured the election as president of the League not of a loyalist contender but of Sir Wazir Hasan, a retired judge of Lucknow whose family had close links with the Congress leadership in the U.P. The election manifesto of the League drafted by Jinnah was very similar to that of the Congress, and in the League parliamentary board there were representatives of Muslim organizations, such as the *Jamiat-ul-Ulema,* which supported the Congress. In all his speeches in 1936 Jinnah stressed his nationalism and commitment to freedom;[5] and in August he and Jawaharlal spoke from the same platform at the All-India Students Conference in an atmosphere of personal cordiality.

Yet Jinnah's tactics had never a chance of success. The Congress, and Indian politics as a whole, had moved far since the nascent days of 1916. The premiss of the Lucknow Pact, that the Congress and the League were two communal

---

[1] Letter to Humayun Kabir, 1 April 1958, Nehru papers.

[2] Report of press conference, *The Hindu,* 8 February 1959.

[3] 5 April 1934, Templewood papers, vol. 4.

[4] H. F. Owen, 'Negotiating the Lucknow Pact', *Journal of Asian Studies,* May 1972, pp. 561-87.

[5] For example: 'Whatever I have done, let me assure you there has been no change in me, not the slightest, since the day when I joined the Indian National Congress. It may be I have been wrong on some occasions. But it has never been done in a partisan spirit. My sole and only object has been the welfare of my country. I assure you that India's interest is and will be sacred to me and nothing will make me budge an inch from that position.' Speech at Lahore, reported in the *Civil and Military Gazette,* 3 March 1936.

parties with political objectives and that they could form an equal partnership, was long dead. Certainly the Congress, which had mobilized the masses in a series of campaigns and established itself as a broad nationalist front, could not now be expected to agree that it was primarily a Hindu organization and would not seek to enlist the Muslim and other religious minorities in India. To Jawaharlal in particular, critical of vested interests and emphasizing the basic problems of poverty and hunger from which the vast majority of the Indian people, whatever their religion, suffered, the religious élitism of Jinnah appeared medieval and obscurantist. Throughout the early months of 1937 he and Jinnah attacked each other in the press. When Jawaharlal stated that there were only two forces which mattered in India, British imperialism and nationalism represented by the Congress, Jinnah replied that there was a third party, the Muslims. Jawaharlal brushed this aside as communalism raised to the nth power. Muslims could not be regarded as 'a nation apart'; and the Muslim League represented a small group functioning in the higher regions of the upper middle classes and having no contacts with the Muslim masses and few even with the Muslim lower middle class. The controversy soon descended to verbal slanging. Jinnah spoke of the Peter Pan who refused to grow up, 'the busybody President' who seemed 'to carry the responsibility of the whole world on his shoulders and must poke his nose in everything except his own business'.[1] On his part, Jawaharlal declared that there were Muslims in the Congress 'who could provide inspiration to a thousand Jinnahs'.[2] He had no use for secret pacts with anybody, much less with Jinnah.[3] It is at this time that Jinnah seems to have developed a particular allergy to Jawaharlal, his exuberance and his socialist ideas. He even appealed over Jawaharlal's head to Gandhi for an understanding on Hindu-Muslim relations, but was firmly rebuffed. [4]

The election results had their own lessons for both Jawaharlal and Jinnah. While the Congress had done spectacularly well in the general constituencies, in the 482 seats reserved for Muslims it had put up only 58 candidates and won in 26. In eight provinces it had not put up candidates for these special seats at all, and most of its victories in such constituencies were in the NWFP, where Abdul Gaffar Khan had given the Congress a decisive hold. On the other hand, the Muslim League had not contested all these 482 seats, and had won only 109 of them. It could not gain a majority even in the Muslim-majority provinces of the Punjab and Bengal. In the former, it was the Unionist Party, dominated by landlords, which won a majority, while in Bengal the single largest parties were the Congress and the peasants' party led by Fazlul Haq. To Jawaharlal this suggested that the Congress had not done enough work among the Muslims, and that in the new 'mass contact' programme a special effort should be made to reach the Muslims. There was a widespread anti-imperialist spirit in the country

---

[1] *The Bombay Chronicle*, 19 January and 26 July 1937.
[2] Ibid., 10 February 1937.
[3] Ibid., 16 February 1937.
[4] Gandhi's letter to Jinnah, 22 May 1937, cited by Jinnah, *The Bombay Chronicle*, 26 July 1937.

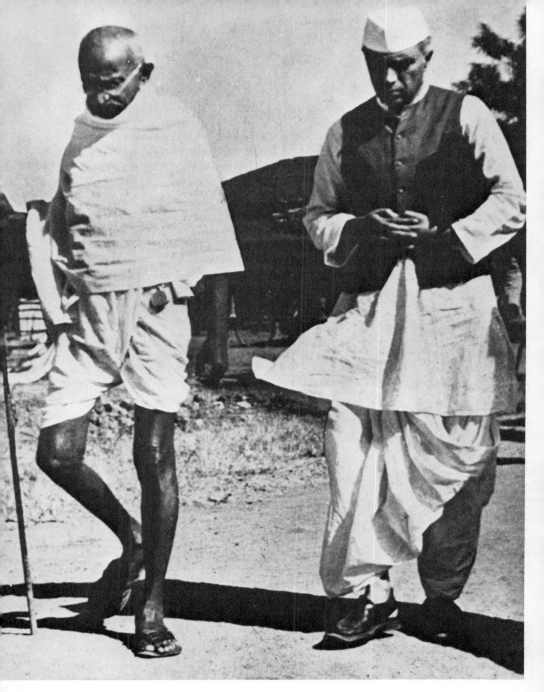

With Gandhi, 1938

25   Jawaharlal presents a signed copy of his *Autobiography* to his daughter

26   An election speech in 1936

Speaking on 'Aid to Spain' in Trafalgar Square, 1938

Jawaharlal and Krishna Menon with General Lister, at Lister's headquarters in Spain, 1938

29   With his daughter and grandson, 1946

and, apart from a microscopic handful at the top who were fearful of social changes, the Indian people as a whole were with the Congress. The party had therefore erred in not setting up more Muslim candidates. The younger generation of Muslims and the Muslim peasants and workers were getting out of the rut of communalism and thinking along economic lines, and the Congress should set about organizing this latent support. 'The Congress is supreme to-day so far as the masses and the lower middle classes are concerned. Even the Muslim masses look up to it for relief. It has hardly ever been in such a strong position.'[1] The elections had gone some way to lay the ghost of communalism, and the Congress should follow this up by working among the Muslim intelligentsia and masses and rid India of communalism in every shape and form. Each provincial Congress committee should set up a special committee to increase contacts with Muslims and enrol more Muslim members. The central office of the Congress would also set up a separate department for this purpose. Notices should be issued in Urdu as well as in other local languages and wide circulation should be given to a new Congress journal being published in that language.[2] Gandhi disapproved of this 'mass contact' programme and preferred to proceed cautiously through constructive work among the Muslim masses by both Hindu and Muslim workers, but the Working Committee preferred Jawaharlal's scheme. For it recognized that the Gandhian constructive programme no longer evoked enthusiasm, and Muslims had absolutely no trust in Gandhi and considered him their enemy.[3]

Jinnah's diagnosis was very similar, but the lesson he drew was the opposite. The Muslim League had made a mistake in not organizing itself better for the elections and contesting all the seats reserved for the Muslim electorate. The Congress was becoming increasingly a mass party and striking out in new directions. Were its approaches to the Muslim masses to prove effective, Jinnah and the League would be left high and dry. So, if the Congress were to take him seriously, it would be necessary to strengthen the communal feelings among the Muslims. The only possible answer to the Congress 'mass contact' programme was to make the Muslims submerge their economic interests in religious zeal. Then the Congress would be forced to deal with the League. The hold of Islam on the Muslim masses should be strengthened to provide the sanction for the demand of the Muslim upper and middle classes for jobs and security.

It is against this general background that developments in the U.P. fall into place. In the elections, the chief opponent of the Congress was not the Muslim League but the National Agriculturist Party, an organization of landlords promoted by the Government to challenge the influence which the Congress had gained over the tenants.[4] The British attached greater importance to this party

---

[1] Jawaharlal to Stafford Cripps, 22 February 1937.

[2] Circulars to provincial Congress committee: 31 March and 10 July 1937.

[3] Proceedings of the Working Committee, April 1937, AICC File 42 of 1936.

[4] P. D. Reeves, 'Landlords and Party Politics in the United Provinces, 1934-7', in Low, *Soundings in Modern South Asian History*, pp. 261-82.

than to the Muslim League and did not hesitate to coerce Muslim *talukdars* to transfer their allegiance from Jinnah, 'the arch enemy of the British raj', to loyalists like the Nawab of Chhatari.[1] So the Congress and the League reached an informal, unspoken understanding in this province and avoided a conflict as much as possible. The question of Hindu-Muslim relations and of the recognition of Muslims as a separate third party, raised by Jinnah on an all-India level, did not apply in the U.P. Here the main issue was authority, landlordism and reaction on the one hand and tenant right on the other. In this contest, the Congress and the League made a joint effort to defeat the Government and their puppets. The parliamentary board of the League in the U.P. was an odd assortment of reactionaries, leaders of the *Jamiat* who supported the Congress, ex-Congressmen with personal affiliations to the Nehru family like Chaudhuri Khaliquzzaman, and many with no fixed attachments. The most energetic campaigner for the League was a leader of the *Jamiat,* Maulana Husain Ahmad, who was very close to the Congress. Some candidates of the League would probably have stood as Congressmen if requested, and during his election tours Jawaharlal supported the League candidates if they were not obvious reactionaries and the Congress was not contesting the seats.

After the elections, the various elements in the parliamentary board of the League fell out. When in March the Congress refused to take office and a loyalist 'interim' ministry was set up by the Government, Khaliquzzaman was asked to join it but refused.[2] However, another member of the League joined, and, though he was expelled from the board, some other members, including Maulana Husain Ahmad, resigned. At this stage Govind Ballabh Pant and Mohanlal Saxena, leading members of the U.P. Congress, not expecting their own party to take office in the near future, approached Khaliquzzaman to reinforcè his decision not to join the 'interim' government and pressed him to return to the Congress.[3] It is possible, though they did not admit this, that they went even further and offered to form a pact with the League. The atmosphere then, born of a collective triumph over the Government and the latter's efforts to thwart the decision of the elections, was conducive to this. Jawaharlal got wind of these overtures and warned Pant against any such agreement. 'I am personally convinced that any kind of pact or coalition between us and the Muslim League will be highly injurious. It will mean many other things also which are equally undesirable.'[4] It is worth adding that Azad, who was staying with Jawaharlal at this time, was equally opposed to any such pact.[5]

Faced with this reprimand, the U.P. Congress abandoned any idea it might

[1] The Raja of Mahmudabad's account of his interview with the governor of U.P. in 1936, 'Some Memories', in C. H. Philips and M. D. Wainwright (eds.), *The Partition of India* (London, 1970), p. 384.

[2] C. Khaliquzzaman, *Pathway to Pakistan* (Lahore, 1961), pp. 154-5.

[3] Pant to Jawaharlal, 2 April 1937.

[4] Jawaharlal to Pant, 30 March 1937.

[5] Jawaharlal to Abdul Walli, 30 March 1937.

have had of a pact with the League; but relations between the two parties continued to be cordial. In a vacancy which arose in a Muslim constituency which had been held by the League, the board of that party in the U.P., despite Jinnah's announcement that it should be retained by the League and warning the Congress not to claim it,[1] decided to leave it to a leading Congressman, Rafi Ahmad Kidwai. Jinnah himself, however, was in favour of a coalition with the Congress, or, as he termed it, 'a united front'. Now that the Congress was willing to accept office if it were satisfied on certain points, there seemed to him to be no substantial difference between the two parties. He was right to the extent that the Congress no longer even claimed to be a revolutionary organization and there was no difference on that score between it and the League. But the main hitch still remained, that any coalition with the League implied the Congress accepting a Hindu orientation and renouncing the right to speak for all Indians. For fear that Khaliquzzaman might go further than a coalition and agree to merge the League in the Congress, Jinnah came to Lucknow and authorized the continuance of negotiations on the basis of the maintenance of separate identities.[2] But this the Congress was not prepared to grant. When, towards the end of June, it became clear that the Congress would take office, Khaliquzzaman and Nawab Ismail Khan again suggested a coalition. Khaliquzzaman seems to have gone even further and informed Azad that the League would accept any terms provided he and Ismail Khan were included in the Ministry.[3] Jawaharlal was not enthusiastic, for a Congress ministry should undertake land reforms and he did not wish this to be precluded by any agreement with the League, which was influenced by *zamindari* interests. But Azad was attracted by the possibility of the League ceasing in the U.P. to exist as a separate group. He was in charge of the negotiations, being authorized by the Working Committee to deal both with Congress affairs in the U.P. and Bihar and with Muslim representation in all the provincial ministries. He consulted Jawaharlal, Pant, Kripalani and Narendra Deva and it was decided to offer ministerships to Khaliquzzaman and Nawab Ismail Khan in return for acceptance of the Congress programme and the winding up of the Muslim League group and the U.P. parliamentary board. All Muslim League legislators should become full members of the Congress party and abide by its discipline; no Muslim League candidates should be set up in by-elections, and they should resign their offices or vacate their seats whenever the Congress decided to do so.[4]

These were stringent conditions which, if accepted, would have seriously

---

[1] *The Bombay Chronicle*, 19 March 1937.

[2] Z. H. Zaidi, 'Aspects of Muslim League Policy 1937-47', *The Partition of India*, p. 256.

[3] Jawaharlal to Rajendra Prasad, 21 July 1937. In Khaliquzzaman's account of his meeting with Azad, he states that discussion centred only on two points: whether the League would resign office along with the Congress if at any time the Congress resigned (to which he agreed), and whether he would agree to another Muslim in place of Nawab Ismail Khan (which he refused) *Pathway to Pakistan*, p. 160.

[4] Jawaharlal to Rajendra Prasad, 21 July 1937; Khaliquzzaman, op. cit., p. 161.

weakened the Muslim League in the U.P., although Khaliquzzaman and others were not asked to sever all connection with the parent Muslim League or specifically to take the Congress pledge. Khaliquzzaman agreed to all conditions except two: the winding up of the parliamentary board and the injunction against contesting by-elections. He himself was willing to accept even these but was not authorized to do so. However, he added, this might happen in any case. In fact, so eager was he to reach an agreement and take office that he offered to call a special meeting of the executive committee of the U.P. Muslim League to consider the question of by-elections. He also suggested that members of the League be given freedom of vote on communal matters. But Azad and Jawaharlal insisted on full acceptance of the original conditions, and the negotiations broke down. Neither at the time, nor even later during his life did Azad voice any regrets, either to Jawaharlal or in public.[1]

This account makes clear that while Jawaharlal was never happy about these opportunist, unprincipled bargainings with the League which had now, in the U.P., become a narrow upper-class organization, he had allowed Azad, Pant and Rafi Kidwai to do what they thought best. Certainly the discussions had not broken down on the question of one or two representatives of the League in the ministry, nor had Jawaharlal decided unilaterally that it should be one and not two. Whether, if the negotiations had succeeded, the country and the Congress would have benefited in the long run is debatable. Any agreement would in effect have accepted that politics were a matter of alliances between upper-class groups, betrayed all Muslims who thought in non-communal terms and abandoned the economic programme on which Jawaharlal had been laying so much stress. No such agreement could have endured, for the League had no long-term economic or social objectives. The only incentive where its leaders were concerned was the hope of office, and once this was fulfilled the cracks were bound to widen. Indeed, the negotiations were throughout hollow and unreal, for alongside the parleys of Azad and Khaliquzzaman a by-election was being fought in a Muslim constituency where the new strategy of Jinnah was finding full play. Both the Congress and the League set up candidates, converting it into a test election. Jawaharlal himself spent two full days in the constituency, speaking as usual of economic and national interests, while the League raised the cry of 'Islam in danger'. Jinnah issued an appeal in the name of Allah and the Koran, and Maulana Shaukat Ali spoke of civil war and called on the voters 'to crush the swollen head of Jawaharlal'.[2] Money and bearded maulanas were in great demand.[3] Supporters of the League gave large donations to mos-

---

[1] In fact, he seems to have expressed his satisfaction. Edward Thompson reported a conversation in October 1939: 'We will not have in the Cabinet' said one leader who had a lot to say in what happened (and he was a Moslem), 'a man who was our comrade for twenty years and then ratted because he thought we were going to be beaten!' *Enlist India for Freedom* (London, 1940), p.56. The reference is clearly to Azad speaking about Khaliquzzaman.

[2] Fida Sherwani to Jawaharlal, 30 June 1937.

[3] Assistant Secretary U.P.P.C.C. to Rafi Kidwai, 6 July 1937, AICC File G. 61/1937.

ques and *madrasas,* while the 'interim' government assisted the League by arresting Muslim workers of the Congress. [1] The League's candidate was helped by the fact that he was a Malkani Rajput (a sect of Rajputs converted to Islam), and the caste *panchayat* decided to penalize any member who voted against him. This, along with the bigotry that had been aroused, ensured the defeat of the Congress candidate. It was the beginning of a new phase of Indian politics, in which communal rancour was to spread and embitter all relations. For the first time in his career, Jawaharlal was the object of a hostile demonstration. On his way to a meeting in the constituency, his car was pelted with stones. [2] In these circumstances, little importance can be attached to the talks with Khaliquzzaman, and no weighty consequences followed their failure.

A few months after the formation of the first Congress ministries, the party also took office in Assam and the North-West Frontier, and all these ministries functioned for over two years. The eight ministries had to their credit considerable achievements. Conciliation machinery was established in labour disputes, though in Bombay the effect was nullified by banning strikes and obstructing the growth of a genuine labour movement by the encouragement of unions promoted by employers and of occupational unions. In a few districts prohibition was introduced, there was some improvement in the condition of Harijans, mass literacy campaigns were promoted, and steps were taken to spread primary education. The sight of men and women in *khadi* exercising authority also served to lift the morale not just of the party but of ordinary people. This was a particularly exhilarating experience in the North-West Frontier, home of the conservative Pathan, with its large Muslim majority, and which the British had for so long sought to seal off. But, on the whole, the record of the Congress ministries was, as Jawaharlal realized soon enough, static if not counter-revolutionary. [3] The worst cases were Bombay and Madras. There was no question now of taking office to combat the new Act; [4] the ministers worked in close co-operation with the Governors, and in carrying out minor reforms forgot the major issues. Soon after they took office, Jawaharlal, as Congress president, directed them to release all political prisoners. [5] Govind Ballabh Pant's first act on taking charge in the U.P. was to sit down at his office table to write the order for their discharge. But K.M. Munshi, the Home Minister of Bombay, 'if anything more royalist than the king,' [6] ignored this directive, Keen to detain communist and left-wing leaders, he asked a surprised Viceroy to put the C.I.D. of Bengal in touch with his own C.I.D. to deal with communists in and around Bombay. [7] When Jawaharlal rebuked Munshi for his zeal in this

[1] Jawaharlal's statement to the press, 10 July, *The Bombay Chronicle,* 11 July 1937.
[2] *The Bombay Chronicle,* 14 July 1937.
[3] To Govind Ballabh Pant, 25 November 1937. *A Bunch of Old Letters,* pp. 256-7.
[4] K. M. Munshi, *Pilgrimage to Freedom* (Bombay, 1967), vol. 1, p. 44.
[5] President's circular to Congress committees, 16 July 1937.
[6] Note of R. M. Maxwell, Home Secretary, on Home Ministers Conference, 31 May 1939, forwarded to Governors by Viceroy, 15 June 1939, Erskine papers, vol. 16.
[7] Linlithgow to Zetland, 16 December 1937, Zetland papers, vol. 14.

matter — 'You have already become a police officer'[1] — Munshi appealed to the higher authority of Gandhi and continued as before. Jawaharlal protested in the Working Committee that Congress ministers appeared more concerned about the effect their actions would have upon the British Government than upon their own people;[2] but his arguments had no effect. The reliance which B.G. Kher, the Chief Minister, and Munshi placed on the Viceroy and the Governor, and the full reports they provided to the British of discussions and differences within the Congress, encouraged Linlithgow to promote the restiveness of the Bombay ministry against central control. 'My advice to you, for what it is worth,' he wrote to Lord Brabourne, the Governor,[3] 'would be, here as elsewhere, to play for time and to miss no chance of impressing Kher and his colleagues with a sense of their own importance and of the necessity for standing on their own feet. This sort of pressure from the Centre cannot last for ever.' But Kher and Munshi were basically weak men who, however much they might ignore Jawaharlal, did not dare to defy Patel, who was responsible in the Working Committee for Bombay. If they were able to adhere to a right-wing policy, it was because this suited Patel.

In Madras, however, Rajagopalachari was a law unto himself. He was too senior in the Congress hierarchy and too close to Gandhi to be answerable to anybody. He combined a contempt for his colleagues in the ministry and the Working Committee with an undue deference to the British Governor — a man of very average ability — and senior British officials. The result was 'a negation and a reversal of fundamental Congress principles and policy'.[4] Rajagopalachari ordered the police to shadow Congressmen, arrested Congress socialists, continued the ban on the Independence pledge and demanded security from a socialist journal. When these matters were considered in the Working Committee, Rajagopalachari stayed away and left it to Gandhi to defeat Jawaharlal's proposal that the Congress ministries should secure the Committee's approval before initiating such arrests and prosecutions. He invoked the Criminal Law Amendment Act, which the Congress had sharply denounced in earlier years, against anti-Hindi pickets; strong action, he told Erskine, paid in India and the British had been far too weak during the civil disobedience campaigns.[5] He intrigued with the Governor against his own party to prevent the formation of an Andhra province,[6] and when he took a month's leave requested the Governor to take over much of his work as he trusted Erskine more than any of his colleagues.[7] He wished to recommend some of his supporters for knight-

---

[1] *Pilgrimage to Freedom*, vol. 1, p. 49.
[2] Proceedings of the Working Committee, 14 to17 August 1937, AICC File 42 of 1936.
[3] 25 August 1937, Brabourne papers. I.O.L. Mss. Eur. F 97, vol. 8.
[4] Jawaharlal to P. Subbarayan, 21 November 1937.
[5] Erskine to Brabourne, 23 June 1938, Erskine papers, vol. 13.
[6] Erskine to Linlithgow, 4 April 1938, Erskine paper's, vol. 13.
[7] Erskine to Linlithgow, 24 April 1939, Erskine papers, vol. 13.

hoods and other titles, [1] and was 'out-heroding Herod as a defender of the rights of the Services'. [2] Asked at a press conference about a proposed Coronation durbar, Jawaharlal replied that if the Government wished to avoid a clash between the Congress ministers and the Governors, the best way they could do it was to keep the King in England. [3] A few weeks later, Rajagopalachari assured the British that there would be no Congress boycott of a durbar or disturbance of any kind. [4] The conduct of Rajagopalachari, in short, was the epitome of all that Jawaharlal had feared would be the result of office acceptance. 'In fact,' summed up Erskine, a diehard Tory himself, 'he is even too much of a Tory for me, for though I may want to go back twenty years, he wishes to go back two thousand and to run India as it was run in the time of King Asoka.' [5]

Jawaharlal's general attitude, to the great disappointment of the left wing,[6] was to stand up loyally for the ministries in public and protect them from petty and petulant criticism; 'we cannot agitate against ourselves.'[7] But though he tried consistently to develop an atmosphere of friendliness towards the ministries, he made it clear to them privately how much he disapproved of their conformism.[8] 'It is all very well to prevent one's enemies getting dug in but the alternative of getting buried oneself is equally unpleasant.'[9] In the U.P. itself he assisted Pant in dealing with labour troubles in Kanpur, controlling the students and facing the criticism of the provincial Congress committee that Pant was becoming 'a second Chhatari'[10] So vigorous was his support that both Gandhi and the British toyed with the hope of his taking over from Pant as chief minister. This only shows how little they had understood his mind and sentiment. The whole atmosphere in India was alien to him — the semi-loyalist activities of the ministries, the quarrels for jobs, the refusal to handle agrarian problems boldly, the suggestion that British troops might be

[1] Lumley, Governor of Bombay, to Erskine, 4 October 1938, reporting Kher's account of conversation with Rajagopalachari, Erskine papers, vol. 20.

[2] Brabourne, acting Viceroy, to Erskine, 2 July 1938, Erskine papers, vol. 13.

[3] The Bombay Chronicle, 13 August 1937.

[4] Erskine to Linlithgow, 25 September 1937, sent by Linlithgow to Zetland, 30 September 1937, Zetland papers, vol. 14.

[5] Erskine to Sir Geoffrey Bracken, 30 January 1939, Erskine papers, vol. 21.

[6] 'I should confess moreover that his role in future cannot be of any decisive revolutionary importance. Things are moving too fast for him and you should not be surprised if within a year or two instead of a United front we in India prepare for a civil war and like so many liberal intellectuals Nehru disappears from the scene. For the present, however, even parlour socialists have a contribution to make. I may add in passing that Nehru is easily one of the finest types of a gentleman one meets in any part of the world. He means well and wants to help us all.' K. M. Ashraf to Phyllis Kemp, 9 August 1938, U.P. Govt. C.I.D. File P/M-83.

[7] Note on The AICC and Congress Ministries, 4 November, The Bombay Chronicle, 11 November 1937.

[8] See, for example, his letters to Rajagopalachari, 1 October and 4 November, to Subbarayan, 21 November and to Pant, 25 November 1937.

[9] To Edward Thompson, 11 November 1937.

[10] Report of the Governor, Sir Harry Haig, of conversation with Vijayalakshmi Pandit in letter to Linlithgow, 23 November 1938, Haig papers, I.O.L. Mss. Eur. F115, vol. 7.

necessary for the maintenance of internal security,[1] the justification by Congress members of the Central Assembly of the dispatch of Indian troops to China.[2] His main objection to federation as envisaged in the Act of 1935 was the inclusion of the feudal and autocratic elements in the Indian States, and he wished the Congress to support the popular movements in the States. But Gandhi himself objected to this and pulled up Jawaharlal in public for permitting a resolution in the AICC criticizing the Government in Mysore. Jawaharlal drafted a sharp rejoinder but refrained from publishing it. All this, however, jarred. So he virtually opted out of the day-to-day activities of domestic politics and was happier visiting the remote areas of Assam or the Frontier Province, writing a long tract on the language problem or indulging in a narcissist *jeu d'esprit:* an anonymous attack on the latent dictatorial tendencies in himself.[3] 'This is', he wrote to a friend, urging him to prolong his stay in Europe,[4] 'a dull country.'

Jawaharlal was more at ease and fully integrated in dealing with developments outside India. The growing tension in the world sharpened his views. Fascism and imperialism were blood brothers and the freedom struggle in India was part of the general confrontation in the world. Freedom, like peace, was indivisible. 'The frontiers of our struggle lie not only in our own country but in Spain and China also.'[5] Even in the stress of the election campaign he did not forsake the international aspect of the Indian problem. In the final analysis, it did not matter much where fate had pitched one's tent. His own lot was cast in India, and he could work most effectively there; but he always thought in terms of the larger world issues, tried to fit India into them and taught his audiences to do the same. Such interest and commitment would also enable the Indian people to play a part, however small, in international affairs and give them a voice in the councils of the world. When Italy attacked Ethiopia, he called for demonstrations throughout the country as an expression of sympathy and solidarity with the Ethiopians. The people of India could give no substantial assistance, but they should at least express their determination to stand together with victims of imperialism elsewhere, especially as the British were making clear their support of Mussolini.[6] Similarly, with all his sympathy for the Jews, he believed that the Arabs were fighting British imperialism in Palestine. The Jews should not rely on British support but reach an agreement with the Arabs to safeguard their position in an independent Arab country. To Jawaharlal the British appeared to be exploiting the differences between Jews and Arabs in the same manner as they were promoting

[1] See Jawaharlal's letter to Asaf Ali, 5 August 1937.
[2] Statement to the press, 25 August 1937; Jawaharlal to Bhulabhai Desai, 12 September 1937.
[3] 'The Rashtrapati' by Chanakya, *Modern Review*, November 1937.
[4] To Jal Naoroji, 30 August 1937.
[5] Article in *National Herald*, 24 January 1939. This newspaper was started by Jawaharlal at Lucknow in the summer of 1938.
[6] Statements to the press, 5 and 8 May, and speech at Allahabad, 9 May 1936.

communal tension in India.[1] But imperialism had to be challenged wherever it appeared, and Jawaharlal organized a boycott of Japanese goods, a China relief fund and a medical unit for service in that country.

However, it was the Spanish Civil War which dominated his attention. He felt, like every other sensitive liberal of the time, a personal commitment in this fighting. 'From day to day I watch with almost painful anguish the development of the trouble in Spain.'[2] For to him it was a battle not just between the Spanish Government and some rebel generals or even between fascism and democracy in Europe; the conflict was a much wider one, between the forces of progress and of reaction throughout the world, and the result would be of enormous consequence to men and women everywhere. The gates of Madrid had become 'the symbols of human liberty',[3] and Jawaharlal organized the collection of funds for the dispatch from India of foodgrains and an ambulance unit.

With this deep involvement in world issues, it was natural for Jawaharlal to think of a trip abroad in the summer of 1938. His mother had died, after a long illness, in January 1938; and, with his daughter at Oxford, he had no strong domestic attachment to hold him to India. The national movement was in reverse gear and at Haripura Subhas Bose had taken over the Congress presidency. Jawaharlal was pressed hard to become the general secretary but refused. He had even wished to step out of the Working Committee. He had been prevailed upon not to do so, but his interest was elsewhere, and in June, gleefully turning his back on India, he sailed for what to him were the vital centres of activity in Europe. 'It is a curious puzzling world but I get on with it to some extent because I like unusual things happening and rather enjoy taking part in them.'[4]

His own attitudes to the European crisis were clear. He felt that the dictators would have to be halted in their aggression and a world war was inevitable; but on no account would India help in such a war even against the fascist powers. The policy of appeasement was less of a surprise to him than to his friends abroad, for India saw more of the imperialist than of the democratic face of the British Government. Though baffled and concerned, like any other left-wing sympathizer, by the trials in Russia,[5] he declined to lend his name to an appeal for an inquiry. He had close links in Britain with Stafford Cripps and his Socialist League and the Left Book Club and approved of their programme of popular fronts and an alliance with Russia. Collective security was the answer, though, presumably as a sop to the method of non-violence which he supported in India, he declared that it was quite possible to control the aggres-

---

[1] Statement to the press, 21 September and speech at Allahabad, 27 September 1936; letter to A. E. Shohet, 26 August 1937.
[2] To Ernst Toller, 10 August 1936.
[3] Statement to the press, 20 February 1937.
[4] To Rabindranath Tagore, 2 June 1938.
[5] See letters to Krishna Menon, 22 May and 11 November 1937.

sors by economic sanctions alone. [1] When, in February 1937, at the Left Book Club rally for world peace and against fascism at the Albert Hall, Victor Gollancz read out an unexpected telegram from Jawaharlal as a message from the people of India, there was deafening and repeated applause. [2] Though the Indian Government banned the entry of Left Book Club books into India, a few managed to get through and were eagerly read. Jawaharlal thought of circumventing this ban by reprinting some of the books in India, but nothing came of the idea. [3] In the circumstances, it is incredible, if characteristic, to find Lord Lothian, who had corresponded at length with Jawaharlal and reviewed the *Autobiography*, writing to the Aga Khan in the summer of 1937 that Germany should be appeased; for otherwise Germany would try to make alliances with Italy and Japan directed against the Empire. 'That will exactly suit Jawaharlal Nehru.' [4] But no man of normal intelligence could have had any doubt as to Jawaharlal's total commitment to the fight against fascism. For him the Left meant the struggle for freedom in India, a commitment to the traditions and aspirations of his own people, resistance to Nazism and fascism and a faith in the Russian revolution despite all its crimes and inadequacies. He was anti-totalitarian as well as anti-fascist and hoped to blend civil liberties and the parliamentary system with economic progress such as Russia had achieved.

En route to Europe Jawaharlal met Nahas Pasha and the leaders of the Wafd party at Alexandria, and then, on landing in Italy, set off immediately on the pilgrimage to Spain as the guest of the Republican Government. He spent five days at Barcelona on the eve of the Battle of the Ebro. He had his first experience of air raids, visited the front and was captivated by the charm and self-confidence of General Lister. Success, he thought, was bound to attend the armies of the Republic, created in the stress of war, with their informality, comradeship and dedication. They would triumph over the professionals and experts of the rebel troops, despite German and Italian support and superiority in heavy armaments and aircraft, if only the British and French Governments did not deny the Republic food and munitions. An afternoon with the British and American battalions of the International Brigade filled him with longing to join them: 'something in me wanted to stay on this inhospitable looking hill-side which sheltered so much human courage, so much of what was worth while in life.' [5] Meetings with President Azaña, Alvarez del Vayo, the Foreign

[1] Foreword to *Foreign Policies of the Indian National Congress and the British Labour Party*, by R. M. Lohia (AICC, 1938).

[2] V. Gollancz to Jawaharlal, 8 February 1937, *A Bunch of Old Letters*, p. 215; John Lewis, *The Left Book Club* (London, 1970), p. 40.

[3] Lewis, op. cit., p. 75; correspondence between Mahmuduzzafar, secretary to Jawaharlal, and Gollancz, Home Dept. Pol. File 4/13/38.

[4] Lothian to the Aga Khan, 19 May 1937, Lothian papers, Edinburgh. I owe this reference to Mr Martin Gilbert.

[5] Article in the *National Herald*, 7 July 1939, reprinted in *China, Spain and the War* (Allahabad, 1940), p. 78.

Minister, and 'La Pasionaria' rounded off the trip. Influenced by his own attitude in India, he was unhappy that the political revolution was being merged with drastic efforts at social change;[1] but this did not cloud his ardent desire that the Republican government should win. Jawaharlal returned from Spain convinced that the chief responsibility for the course of the war lay not with the rebels or even with the dictators but with the British Government, the French being completely under British influence.[2] As Zetland ruefully reported after talking to him on the subject, 'when I referred to the trouble there as a civil war he dissented and rather suggested that he regarded Franco as being supported almost entirely by foreign countries and having little Spanish following. He clearly takes a very biased view of the present situation in Europe and I do not think that any amount of reasoning would cause him to change his view.'[3]

In England this time, Jawaharlal was, thanks to the *Autobiography* and the success of the Congress in the elections, an even better-known figure than before. He attributed the greater interest in him to the importance that attached to what India might do in a world crisis; she had a tremendous nuisance value.[4] But the fact was that he now commanded greater stature in the world. He was accepted as the true representative of the Indian people and he moved in the mainstream of world opinion. He spoke at the Albert Hall and at Trafalgar Square under the auspices of the 'Aid to Spain' committee, and at a Left Book Club rally organized especially in his honour. There were lunches at the *New Statesman* (where Attlee was present but unnoticed)[5] and at the House of Commons, long conversations with Robert Vansittart and Tom Jones, and an afternoon with the Webbs.

As a contrast[6] Nehru, the leader of the Indian Congress and his lovely daughter spent some hours here on Saturday with Ponsonby[7] to meet them. I had read and admired his autobiography and welcomed him warmly. He is the last word of aristocratic refinement and culture dedicated to the salvation of the underdog whether in race or class; but I doubt whether he has the hard stuff of a revolutionary leader. He is in theory a communist; but doubts the possibility of the complicated Soviet organization among the mixed races of the Indian continent. 'Between two worlds, one dead and one powerless to be born' is a quotation which he recognized but did not agree with. He believes with fervour that a united

---

[1] Lord Brockway's oral testimony, 24 July 1967, N.M.M.L.

[2] This account of Jawaharlal's visit to Spain is based on his confidential note written for the Working Committee, and the articles written a year later and reprinted in *China, Spain and the War*.

[3] Zetland to Brabourne, acting Viceroy, 5 July 1938, Zetland papers, vol. 10.

[4] Note to the Working Committee, 30 July 1938.

[5] Kingsley Martin, *Editor* (London, 1968), p. 10.

[6] To a visiting American professor.

[7] Arthur, first Lord Ponsonby, Minister in the Labour governments and a specialist in foreign affairs.

India can be born, is, in fact being born, largely owing to the teaching of
Gandhi — whose power as a saint and a missionary he realizes and
admires — but whose economic proposals he dismisses as romantic rem-
nants of the past. Nehru is convinced that the freedom of the individual,
as manifested in the presence of opportunity to live the good life, cannot be secured without the organization of the principal services and
main industries deliberately for communal consumption and without
the profit-making motive. Today the Indian people are too primitive for
Soviet Communism. But they have been roused, not only by internal
conditions of India but by the horror of the invasion of China by Japan
and by their sympathy with other oppressed races. [1]

And recalling this meeting over two years later, Beatrice Webb recorded that
they had been 'struck more by his charm than by his force — he seemed too
ultra refined to influence English official or politician! He is a subtle thinker;
an agnostic, in respect of man's relation to the universe and, through the study
of the capitalist system, a convert to communism for India and in the western
world . . .'[2]

Jawaharlal also met the executives of the Labour Party, the Communist
Party and the National Council for Civil Liberties. He even spent a weekend
with Lothian and the 'Cliveden Set', and listened in silence to a tirade against
socialism by Nancy Astor. George Padmore saw him to explain the problems
of Africa. Jewish leaders called on him and put forward their side of the case,
and Jawaharlal arranged for the settling in India of some Jewish refugees from
Germany. The principal difficulty was the attitude of the Government of India,
which insisted on guarantees of employment for life, which no provincial
government or industrial firm was in a position to give.

This time Jawaharlal, unlike on his previous visit to Britain, was willing to
meet figures in the Government. Apart from talks with Halifax and Zetland,
he met Linlithgow, then on leave in England. The Viceroy had, especially after
the acceptance of office by the Congress, been anxious to meet him, and Gandhi
had tried to arrange it. But Jawaharlal had had no wish to have any contact with
the leading instrument of British imperialism in India, especially at a time
when prisoners in the Andaman Islands were on hunger-strike.[3] Now the strike
was over and Jawaharlal saw no objection to talking to the Viceroy on leave
outside India. The conversation was general and there was no detailed
discussion of Indian politics.[4] But as Jawaharlal recorded later, he told

[1] Entry for 3 July 1938, Beatrice Webb's diaries. Passfield papers, London School of Economics
Library, vol. 52, pp. 78-9.
[2] 24 September 1940. Beatrice Webb's diaries, vol. 54, pp. 175-6.
[3] Viceroy's report on interview with Gandhi, 4 August 1937, Haig papers, vol. 13; Gandhi to
Jawaharlal, 4 August 1937, *A Bunch of Old Letters*, p. 240; proceedings of the Working Committee, 14-17 August 1937, AICC File 42 of 1936; Linlithgow to Zetland, 4 February 1938,
Zetland papers, vol. 15.
[4] Glendevon, *The Viceroy at Bay* (London, 1971), p. 101; Jawaharlal's note for the Working
Committee, 30 July 1938.

Linlithgow then 'that I gave England at the outside ten years before India was independent. I was not so far out.'[1] All that the Viceroy could retort, as they parted, was that a wide gap separated them and they would look at each other across it.[2]

From London Jawaharlal went to Paris to address an international conference on the bombing of civilian populations. Speaking after Lord Cecil, who had referred to the recent visit to France of the King and Queen of England, Jawaharlal said he spoke not in the name of kings or queens or princes but on behalf of hundreds of millions of down-trodden Indians. Fascism was a recent growth in the west, but they in India had known it for long under the different name of imperialism. If the aggressors of the day had to be checked, the aggressors of yesterday had also to be called to account. They were all deeply moved by the aerial bombing in Spain and China, but this was really no different from the British bombing on the North-West Frontier.[3]

The organizers of the conference forbade 'La Pasionaria' from speaking on the ground that she was a communist. When the delegates insisted on hearing her, the chairman adjourned the meeting. Ellen Wilkinson reconvened the meeting unofficially and called on 'La Pasionaria' to speak. She took the floor but two attendants seized her and carried her off behind the platform.

> Then Nehru walked on. Nobody would dare touch him. He was oriental dignity itself, olive-skin face, dream eyes, thin grey hair. But he was angry. Viscount Cecil wished to demonstrate that the Communists did not dominate the peace movement. Nehru wished to assert the right of free speech for Communists fighting Fascism ... Nehru is not a Communist but in my many years in Russia and Europe I have rarely seen a truer revolutionary.[4]

The Nazi Government made informal approaches to Jawaharlal in the hope of inducing him to visit Germany as their guest.[5] In fact, Jawaharlal spent two days in Munich but as a private tourist and declined to meet any Nazi officials. He then went on to Prague, met Dr Ripka, the communist leader Clementis and, accompanied by Werzel Jaksch of the German Social Democrat Party, visited the border areas. All his sympathies were with the Czech Government in their resistance to Hitler; and the encouragement given to him by the British Government, with its own class sympathies and leaning towards fascism, nauseated Jawaharlal. 'The perfect description has been given by someone. It was the rape of Czechoslovakia by Germany with England and France hold-

[1] Note written on 24 October 1955, Nehru papers.
[2] Jawaharlal to J. B. Kripalani, 27 July 1938.
[3] Report in *The Bombay Chronicle*, 8 August 1938.
[4] Louis Fischer, *Men and Politics* (London, 1941), pp. 506-7.
[5] Message of German Consul in Bombay conveyed through Shankar Rao Deo, see Jawaharlal to Shankar Rao Deo, 26 May 1938; J. G. Studnitz, German newspaper correspondent, to Jawaharlal, 25 June and 5 September 1938.

ing her forcibly down!' [1] Jawaharlal made it clear that when war came, as it was bound to, the Indian people would not allow the British Government, whom they utterly distrusted, to take any decision for them. India would willingly throw her entire weight on the side of democracy and freedom; but Britain should first establish her *bona fides* by eliminating empire from India. [2] To add weight to his opinion, he urged the Working Committee to pass a resolution condemning Nazi attempts at aggression and stating emphatically that in event of war India could only be committed by a decision of her people. [3]

In September, at the height of the crisis, Jawaharlal was at Geneva, and was caught up in the tension. While the Lea ·e of Nations was meeting peacefully and discussing every question but that of war and peace, the air was full of rumours; and Jawaharlal was swept to and fro, to cafés and press conferences, through the night. 'Hello Prague? Hello Paris? Hello London? Is it peace or war?' [4] Back in London he was fitted with a gas mask which he later presented to the Allahabad municipal museum, heard and was sickened by Neville Chamberlain's broadcast, and was present in the House of Commons to hear Chamberlain announce that he was flying the next day to meet Hitler and Mussolini at Munich. Jawaharlal shared the general relief that war had been postponed. But he had no illusions about the attitude of the British Government, their anxiety to abandon Czechoslovakia and isolate Russia, their fear not of defeat but of victory, for that would have been a victory of real democracy. The weakness of England and France was their imperialism, and so the ending of imperialism was necessary even from the wider international viewpoint. Collective security could not function effectively so long as it had an imperialist base; and this made the freedom of India a vital factor in world politics.

Unable to secure in time a visa to visit Russia, which might have enabled him to fulfil an old desire to take the overland route via the Central Asian republics, Jawaharlal returned to India by the end of the year, and was drawn again into domestic politics. No one in Britain, even when discussing India, had referred to Hindu-Muslim relations or regarded it as of great importance. But in India it could not be ignored. The refusal of the Congress to form coalitions with the League seemed to Jinnah to be a betrayal born of arrogance, and since then his policy had been clear. Acceptance of office by the Congress made it an easy target. He attacked it as a Hindu fascist body which was out, with the assistance of a few Muslim 'traitors', to destroy the Muslim minority. When Jawaharlal and other Congress leaders asked him repeatedly to specify instances, Jinnah, now fast beginning to show the mastery of obstructive tactics and skill in avoidance which were to dominate Indian politics for the next ten

[1] Article in *National Herald*, 5 October 1938.
[2] Letter to the *Manchester Guardian*, 8 September 1938.
[3] To J.B. Kripalani, Secretary, AICC, 30 August 1938; note for Working Committee, 7 September 1938; cable to Kripalani, 26 September 1938.
[4] Article dated 21 September 1938 in the *National Herald*, reproduced in *China, Spain and the War*, p. 102.

years, steadily refused. He talked of the suppression of Urdu although Urdu was not the language only of the Muslims and Jawaharlal had clearly reiterated the Congress policy of developing Hindustani in both Urdu and Devanagari scripts as the national language.[1] He objected to the singing of *Bande Mataram*, ignoring the facts that that song had long rid itself of its Hindu antecedents and that the Congress, on Gandhi's initiative, had decided that only the first two stanzas, which had no religious overtones, should be sung at public gatherings.[2] But otherwise Jinnah would mention no particular grievances. It would indeed have been difficult for him to do so; for, as even the British Viceroy and Governors conceded, the Congress ministries took special care to avoid harming Muslim interests. The documentary record of complaints published later by the League carried little conviction and explains why the League would not agree to the Congress proposal for an impartial inquiry. Sir Sikandar Hyat Khan, the premier of the Punjab and the most cool-headed of the League leaders, later toned down the charge of 'atrocities' committed by Congress governments to high-handedness of the majority community in some Congress provinces.[3] When Linlithgow informed Jinnah that he had examined the position and could find no specific instances of oppression, all that Jinnah could say in reply was that the Hindus had 'a subtle intention' of undermining the Muslim position.[4] But this did not mean that Jinnah's effort to create a legend of the Muslim community being trampled on by the Hindus was a failure. As the majority of Indians happened to be Hindu by religion, it was an easy slide from the fact of Congress ministries representing majority opinion to the suggestion of these ministries representing Hindu majority opinion. That the Congress was in office put it on the defensive, and the League's successful myth-making was not the least of the unhappy consequences of office acceptance. Jinnah went round the country denouncing the Congress as anti-Islamic and promoted a drive to build up the organization of the League at the provincial and district level. The League was as committed on paper as the Congress to economic and social reforms and proclaimed the objective of full independence in the form of a federation of free democratic states. But the decision to convert the League into a mass party and the resentment of the 'mass contact' campaign of the Congress did not mean the overthrow of the League's reliance on the upper classes. Indeed, the tenancy reforms proposed by the Congress brought many Muslim *talukdars* in the U.P. from the National Agriculturist Party into the League, and in the Punjab the link between the League and the Unionist Party was facilitated by support to rich agricultural producers.[5] 'What', Sikandar

---

[1] *The Question of Language,* August 1937.
[2] Statement of the Working Committee, 28 October, *The Bombay Chronicle,* 30 October 1937.
[3] Letter to Jawaharlal, 14 February 1939.
[4] Glendevon, op. cit., p. 157.
[5] For Jinnah's assurances to Muslim landlords in the Punjab, see K.B. Sayeed, *Pakistan,The Formative Phase* (London, 1968), p. 95.

Hyat Khan said to Jawaharlal sometime in 1938, 'have I got in common with Jinnah? Nothing except' (pointing dramatically at Jawaharlal) 'common opposition to you!'[1]

Jinnah, in fact, was prepared to use every influence and interest to strengthen Muslim communalism, He frightened the wealthy by prophesying that one result of Congress policy would be class bitterness.[2] On the other hand, he encouraged Fazlul Haq of Bengal to support the peasants of that province against the *zamindars* not on an economic but on a communal basis; and Fazlul Haq agreed to this after failing to secure a coalition with the Congress. Jinnah also made overtures to the British, warning them that if they did not devote more attention to the Muslims there was a real risk that these would be driven into the arms of the Congress. However, if the British 'protected' the Muslims in the Congress provinces, the Muslims in return would 'protect' the British at the Centre.[3] But at this period the British were having a semi-honeymoon with the right wing of the Congress, and paid little heed to Jinnah. Linlithgow, in particular, had a poor opinion of Jinnah as a leader.[4] Jawaharlal's talks in London with Zetland and Linlithgow made the League suspicious,[5] and in desperation Jinnah sent A. R. Siddiqi and Khaliquzzaman to Europe in 1939 to contact the German and Italian Governments.[6]

The Government of India ignored these efforts and set aside the Muslim mood of frustration to be exploited in any change of circumstance. But the Congress was baffled. Jawaharlal was willing to go so far as to consider, in any scheme of provincial redistribution, the grant to important groups and minorities of territories within which they could feel that they had full opportunities of self-development, without which a creative life was hardly possible.[7] He disliked the term 'communal provinces' but his scheme contained the germ of territorial redistribution on the basis of religion. But to concede Jinnah's main demands, that the Congress should not approach the Muslim masses but should recognize the League as representative of Muslim opinion, was unthinkable. However, so long as the Congress was in office it could not ignore even uncorroborated allegations of partisanship. One way out of this dilemma was to approach the Muslim peasantry over the heads of the leaders of the League with a programme of economic change; but here Jawaharlal found that, with the Congress ministries not proceeding fast enough, the communal approach, however

---

[1] DSVA, p. 164.

[2] Presidential address at the Lucknow session of the Muslim League, October 1937.

[3] Reports of Jinnah's interviews, with Linlithgow in Linlithgow to Zetland, 9 September 1937, Zetland papers, vol. 14, and with Brabourne in Brabourne to Zetland, 19 August 1938, Brabourne papers, vol. 61.

[4] See, for example, Linlithgow to Haig, 17 April 1939, Haig papers, vol. 3.

[5] Brabourne to Zetland, 21 July 1938, Zetland papers, vol. 16.

[6] Linlithgow to Zetland, 12 April 1939 and Zetland to Linlithgow 2 May 1939, Zetland papers, vols. 17 and 11, respectively.

[7] See his draft concluding chapter written on 23 August 1937 for K.T. Shah's book *Federal Government*.

'hysterical' and 'medievalist',[1] was successfully hampering efforts to draw the Muslim masses into the Congress. The other alternative was to take advantage of the League's decision to widen its base and precipitate a conflict between the reactionary outlook of its leaders and the needs of the Muslim masses. So Jawaharlal encouraged the holding of Muslim mass meetings demanding debt relief and abolition of the *talukdari* system in the interests of the Muslim *kisans*.[2] But these were long-term projects which hardly gathered any momentum in the context of extreme communal propaganda and violence. The League, which was promoting this activity, understandably rejected all suggestions by the Congress for consultation to promote communal harmony. The British police and magistrates also often did little to curb religious riots in order presumably to discredit the Congress ministries. If this were their objective they gained considerable success, for Hindu-Muslim rioting strengthened the anti-Congress feeling among the Muslim masses. Jawaharlal realized what this might finally mean.

> As you know I am overwhelmed with this sense of impending catastrophe. I find that few persons even among our leading politicians have this sense of tension and this premonition of approaching disaster. I fear we are rapidly heading for what might be called civil war in the real sense of the word in India. Our future conflicts are never going to be on the straight issue of Indian nationalism versus British imperialism. British imperialism in future is certainly going to play an important part in opposing us. But it will do so more from behind the scenes exploiting all manner of other groups to this end.[3]

Weakened by office and punched continuously by an enemy on whom it could get no hold, the Congress was now stricken by in-fighting at its highest level. Subhas Bose had, through long years of prison and exile, earned the succession to Jawaharlal as president of the Congress in 1938. But, during his year of office, he took hardly any interest in problems of organization and gave no clear lead in many matters that came up before the Working Committee. More important, he could not get on with Gandhi. This was not just difference of viewpoint. Jawaharlal differed with Gandhi just as much, but 'we know that neither of us can do without the other, for there is a heart union between us which no intellectual differences can break'.[4] With Bose there was no such affinity, and when he announced early in 1939 that he would seek re-election, Gandhi encouraged the right wing of the Congress to set up its own candidate. But Bose won decisively and Gandhi acknowledged it to be his own defeat.

However, this was only the beginning of the crisis. With his re-election Bose

[1] Jawaharlal's comments on the Muslim League session October 1937, *The Bombay Chronicle*, 19 October 1937.
[2] Jawaharlal's letter to Siddiq Ahmed Siddiqui, 8 September 1937.
[3] To Sri Prakasa, 15 August 1939.
[4] Gandhi in May 1939, quoted in Tendulkar, *Mahatma*, vol. 5, p. 95.

believed that his hour as a charismatic leader had arrived. Impatient, wilful and endlessly ambitious, he decided to press home his victory. He ignored the fact that many local and regional factors for which he could take no credit had played a part in the election. He stressed only that there was widespread dissatisfaction with the older leaders and believed that he had been chosen to replace them. Incapable of the wider view, he tended to see most events in relation to his own career. A dedicated yet egotistic, complicated, ill-fated being, he lived out the fantasy of his life which ended in premature death; and there was something almost natural and inevitable in his loss of life in an air accident. The elements of tragedy were never absent from Bose's destiny.

Now, in 1939, riding on the crest of a wave, Bose launched a fierce struggle of will. He insinuated that the 'old guard' were conspiring with the Government to establish federation, announced that the 'Right' and the 'Left' were in confrontation and demanded the immediate issue of an ultimatum to the Government and the launching of a struggle. This was heady stuff. But Bose, though an instinctive fighter, had no ring-craft and he had underestimated Gandhi and his followers. They welcomed a break, and brought it about in their own way. Realizing that, despite Bose's electoral victory, the majority in the Congress still preferred Gandhi's leadership with its moderation, twelve leading supporters of Gandhi resigned from the Working Committee and then carried a resolution at the Congress session in Tripuri that Bose should nominate the new Committee in consultation with Gandhi and accept his advice. Gandhi, however, declined to co-operate, with the result that Bose had to resign the presidency. Then followed, step by step, his ostracism, his setting up of a new party, and his lone path, away from the Congress, during the war.

In all this, Jawaharlal's attitude was individualistic and unwelcome to both sides. He disapproved of the manner in which Bose was being hounded out after winning an election, but he could not bring himself to support Bose. So he declined to sign the letter of resignation of the twelve members of the Working Committee, but resigned on his own. Although some of his statements tended to be critical of Bose, at Tripuri he remained almost silent, tried in private discussions to patch up a compromise and urged Bose not to resign. When Bose insisted, Jawaharlal, while making clear his dislike of Bose's action, declined to serve in the reconstituted Working Committee till the outbreak of war changed the situation. Such ambivalence Bose could not understand and this, more than the direct offensive of Gandhi and the others which drove him out of the fold, he found most difficult to forgive. 'Nobody has done more harm to me personally, and to our cause in this crisis, than Pandit Nehru. If he had been with us, we would have had a majority. Even his neutrality would have probably given us a majority. But he was with the Old Guard at Tripuri. His open propaganda against me also has done me more harm than the activities of the twelve stalwarts. What a pity!'[1]

[1] Bose to his nephew, 17 April 1939, quoted in N.G. Jog, *In Freedom's Quest* (Delhi, 1969), p. 158.

To suggest that Jawaharlal had allowed Bose to be destroyed is, of course, to exaggerate absurdly. Bose had really destroyed himself. The logic of his attitude demanded his expulsion from the movement, and there was no way back. But Jawaharlal's seemingly erratic attitude certainly cries out for explanation. Some have hinted the simple, personal, petty answer of consistent opportunism. Jawaharlal, said Rajagopalachari long after these events, [1] had always been a worshipper of success. Applying this yardstick his behaviour in this crisis is easily understood; for Bose was a born loser. In Gandhian India, leadership could come only by gift, never by seizure. So Jawaharlal, it is alleged, preferred to remain in the Congress and by Gandhi's side, a 'safe' militant who occupied as much of the central ground as possible while he awaited his destiny. Happy on the inside track, he allowed his only rival, on the outer rails, to be pushed off the course.

This explanation is too easy. Personalizing clouds and distorts the issues. The quarrel between Bose and Gandhi was not, as Bose sought to make out, [2] a straight fight between the Left and the Right. He had been tardy in condemning Germany, Italy and Japan, had in December 1938 met the German Consul in Bombay, [3] had criticized Jawaharlal for supporting all lost causes such as China and Spain and was not enthusiastic about welcoming Jewish refugees from Europe. While his willingness to exploit the world situation to India's benefit was not wrong in itself, he had, despite long years in Europe, no acute international sense. In India, while clamouring for struggle with the British and condemning office acceptance, he attempted to establish a coalition ministry in Bengal and sought the Governor's assistance in this. [4] This again could be justified on pragmatic grounds as strengthening the prospects of a *satyagraha* campaign, [5] but it weakened Bose's ideological crusade. In fact, Jawaharlal was right in suspecting a weakness in commitment to anything broader than nationalism; nor could one have confidence in Bose's judgment even in this narrow field. He viewed most problems in too finite, clear-cut and limited a way. This distrust on Jawaharlal's part of Bose's approach strengthened the temperamental dissimilarity which undoubtedly existed. The autobiographies of the two men, published within a few months of each other, drive home the contrast. Bose's book [6] lacks the intellectual grace and stature of Jawaharlal's; the ideas are jejune and the prose without flavour. The book also shows a matter-of-fact

---

[1] See N. Majumdar, ' C.R. The Unfinished Century ', *The Statesman,* 27 December 1972.

[2] Curiously, this idea is still prevalent, even among left-wing writers. Hiren Mukerjee describes Jawaharlal's failure to heal the breach as 'a major blemish on Jawaharlal's record' and thinks history might have been different and brighter if Jawaharlal and Bose had, at this stage, together led left-wing forces. (*The Gentle Colossus,* Calcutta, 1964, p. 80). Mohit Sen regards it as a tragedy that the 'left nationalists', Jawaharlal and Bose, could not unite. (*The Indian Revolution,* New Delhi, 1970, p. 35.

[3] I owe this information to Dr M. Hauner who has found evidence in Nazi records.

[4] Brabourne to Linlithgow, 19 December 1938, Brabourne papers, vol. 56.

[5] Bose to Gandhi, 21 December 1938.

[6] *The Indian Struggle* (London, 1935).

mind, and a muscular, sanguinary temperament, totally different to Jawaharlal's highly strung personality, plagued by introspection.

Jawaharlal, therefore, could not be expected to side with Bose when battle was joined. He was particularly put off by the fact that Bose had desired re-election and had induced even Rabindranath Tagore to lobby for him.[1] Bose's eagerness, after the election, to precipitate a conflict also repelled him. With the world on the brink of war and a crisis in India impending, it was foolish to divide the Congress. The left-wing forces within the Congress were not strong enough to act on their own, and the party still needed Gandhi's leadership. The socialists and the communists, who at first supported the challenge of Bose, were soon disheartened to find themselves in alliance with adventurist elements out for selfish advantage; and Bose himself reduced the differences to a conspiracy against Bengal. 'For the moment Subhas has become a kind of a symbol of Bengal and it is quite impossible to argue with or about symbols.'[2] Jawaharlal, with his image of the Congress as a broad anti-imperialist front, had never been in favour of homogeneous committees in a sectarian sense; his idea of the Working Committee was of men with different views working together with mutual confidence. So he resented Bose's aspersions against his colleagues, but he also disliked the efforts to displace Bose, and in consequence refused to attach himself to either side. To the end he stood out of the intrigues of both groups and sought a settlement by dealing with the crisis as differences among comrades within a movement. He tried to explain to Bose that any rebellion such as his could only be successful if it was rebellion within a discipline; and he pleaded with Gandhi to make a friendly approach to Bose.[3] But Gandhi was tougher than Jawaharlal and Bose less accommodating.

In this cheerless atmosphere two developments gave Jawaharlal comfort. The problem of the Indian States had thrust itself into the forefront of Indian politics and the Congress had decided to support the growing movement for civil liberties and responsible government. Gandhi himself went to Rajkot and forced concessions and British intervention by undertaking a fast. Jawaharlal was president for this year of the All-India States Peoples Conference, and he planned to co-ordinate the agitation in the various States and involve the rest of India as well. This should become the major issue in the struggle against the British, transcending the wrangles in the Congress and the controversy with the League, underlining the total unacceptability of federation as envisaged in the Act of 1935 and perhaps even leading to the resignation of the Congress ministries.[4] Though he was considerably hampered by Gandhi's very different

[1] See A.K. Chanda, Tagore's secretary, to Jawaharlal, 28 November 1938, *A Bunch of Old Letters,* pp. 299-300; and Jawaharlal to Chanda, 1 December 1938.

[2] To Krishna Menon, 4 April 1939.

[3] For the important letters between Bose, Gandhi and Jawaharlal, see *A Bunch of Old Letters,* pp. 307-75; Jawaharlal's general attitude on the crisis is explained in his articles in *National Herald,* later reprinted as a pamphlet, *Where are we?* (April, 1939).

[4] Message to the 'States People', 3 February 1939; speech at Allahabad, 9 February, *The Bombay Chronicle,* 10 and 11 February 1939; presidential address at the All-India States Peoples Conference, 15 February 1939.

approach of overtures to the rulers and acceptance of British arbitration, yet this was a field of action which Jawaharlal welcomed.

The second congenial task was national planning. The concept of a planned economy was, even in Europe in the late thirties, still vague and ambiguous. But it was felt that only in Soviet Russia was there national planning in the real sense, with the whole economy geared to the production of plenty for human welfare and not driven by the profit motive or intended for efficiency in war. In other words, planning was a part of socialism.[1] Jawaharlal agreed with this. However critical he might be of the political aspects of the Stalin regime, he had been deeply impressed by the economic progress achieved by the Soviet Union.

> The argument about the success or otherwise of the Five Year Plan is rather a pointless one. The answer to it is really the present state of the Soviet Union. And a further answer is the fact that this Plan has impressed itself on the imagination of the world. Everybody talks of 'planning' now, and of Five-Year and Ten-Year and Three-Year Plans. The Soviets have put magic into the word.[2]

He believed that India too had much to learn from the Soviet example. But to apply these lessons in a colonial economy and to consider planning in a country which was not yet free showed a bold and pioneering mind. This was the kind of work, long-term, adventurous and leading to socialism, which excited him. The fact that the Congress was in charge of many provincial administrations, whatever its political drawbacks, could be utilized for planning. Jawaharlal encouraged the Bihar and U.P. Governments, the two ministries with whom he exercised the greatest influence, to recruit experts from Europe and to get in touch with the League of Nations and the International Labour Organisation for the kind of assistance they had given to China.[3] Meantime, at a meeting of ministers of industry from the Congress provinces, it was decided to set up a National Planning Committee with Jawaharlal as its chairman. Jawaharlal took up the work with enthusiasm and constituted a committee with not only Congressmen but scientists, economists, businessmen and industrialists as well. The Congress ministries were represented; in addition Punjab, Baroda and Mysore agreed to send representatives, and contacts were established with the departments of the Government of India. A long questionnaire was drafted and widely distributed and nearly thirty sub-committees were constituted to make detailed recommendations on specific subjects.

Jawaharlal's own contribution, apart from holding the assorted crowd of planners together, was a clear statement of the general objectives of planning in India. To him planning was inevitably connected with a socialist economy within a democratic structure, but he had no wish to frighten away people by stressing the socialist aspect. The Congress had taken up planning because any

[1]See G.D.H. Cole, *Practical Economics* (Pelican, May 1937).
[2]Letter to Indira, 9 July 1933, *Glimpses*, p. 887.
[3]To Syed Mahmud and to G. B. Pant, 1 October 1938.

vital national movement was bound to interest itself in all aspects of national life, but the Congress itself was not committed to socialism. So what Jawaharlal hoped to do was to lead his party and the Indian middle classes generally to socialism without their knowing it. Any attempt to dispense with the middle classes and bring about a premature conflict on class lines would lead to chaos and possibly to prolonged inability to build anything. 'The disruptive forces in the country seem to be growing in strength and it almost seems that we are going the way of China.'[1] Jawaharlal had moved even further away from the doctrinal positions of the left wing and preferred a pragmatic, undefined approach.

He was, therefore, deliberately imprecise in formulating the aim of planning. 'The ideal of the Congress is the establishment of a free and democratic state in India. Such a free democratic state involves an egalitarian society in which equal opportunities are provided for every member for self-expression and self-fulfilment, and an adequate minimum of a civilised standard of life is assured to each member so as to make the attainment of this equal opportunity a reality. This should be the background or foundation of our Plan.'[2] A year later he was more forthcoming and acknowledged that the over-all objective was to socialize national life in all its many sectors.[3] Advantage could be taken of the Congress resolution of May 1929 that revolutionary changes, economic and social, were essential in India and of the clause in the 1931 resolution on fundamental rights that the state should own or control key industries and services, to start planning in the socialist direction. Private enterprise was not ruled out but it would have to be strictly controlled and co-ordinated to the general plan. The emphasis placed by the Congress on cottage industries did not exclude large-scale industries and any plan should provide for both; and increasingly the Congress would realize the importance of the latter. He rejected the Gandhian viewpoint that machinery was evil in itself and resigned from the executive committee of the All-India Spinners Association.[4] For a country to turn its face against industrialization was to render itself a prey to the industrialized countries. Even the development of cottage industries required the control of political and economic power, and this could not be secured by a people dependent wholly on cottage industries. It was not large-scale industry that brought injustice and violence but its misuse by capitalists. Private ownership and the acquisitive society encouraged competitive violence, and when replaced by a socialist society the advantages of large-scale industrialization and its co-ordination with cottage industries could be realized. The Congress had devoted more attention to small-scale industries not merely because all its members accepted Gandhi's views on the subject. Large-scale industries were strong enough to look after themselves, and were also often in the grip of foreign vested interests. The *charka* and *khaddar* on the other hand

[1] To K.T. Shah, Secretary, National Planning Committee, 13 May 1939.
[2] Memorandum to National Planning Committee, 4 June 1939.
[3] Note to National Planning Committee, 30 August 1940.
[4] To Shankarlal Banker, 24 February 1940.

created self-reliance and utilized the wasted man-power of India.[1] This made sense at a time when the Congress was a party of challenge, but it obviously would have to shift its approaches when it planned for a free India.

The lack of sovereign authority was another road-block which on first sight was insuperable, for planning assumed independence and freedom from imperialist control. Land reforms, for example, were urgently required, but neither peasant proprietorship nor co-operative or collective farming could be introduced so long as British rule prevailed. But while planning, in its full dimension, should be for a free India, steps could be taken immediately to develop national resources, increase the national wealth between two and three times within ten years, raise the standards of the Indian people and prevent the creation of fresh vested interests. This emphasis on concrete short-term steps such as improved nutrition, more clothing and better housing for every Indian over the next ten years had the further advantage of by-passing the theoretical and ideological differences among the planners. The immediate national objective was stated to be self-sufficiency, planning for which might, apart from other benefits, help to weaken economic imperialism even before the British left India.

The work of the National Planning Committee alarmed not so much the Government of India as the right wing of the Congress itself. The detailed explanations provided by Jawaharlal that planning did not mean the abandonment of *khaddar* and the destruction of cottage industries[2] carried hardly any conviction. The agreement which was gradually developing in the Planning Committee in favour of at least state control of industry and agriculture also roused opposition. Gandhi himself called on his followers to stay away from the Planning Committee. 'I have advised you about Jawaharlal's invitation. In my opinion, the whole of his planning is a waste of effort. But he cannot be satisfied with anything that is not big.'[3] He also wrote to Jawaharlal to complain.

I have never been able to understand or appreciate the labours of the Committee. I do not know that it is working within the four corners of the resolution creating the committee. I do not know that the W. C. is being kept informed of its doings. I have not understood the purpose of the numerous sub-committees. It has appeared to me that much money and labour are being wasted on an effort which will bring forth little or no fruit. These are my doubts. I seek light.[4]

What saved Jawaharlal from having to fight last-ditch actions was the outbreak of war. The fall in imports of textiles and the boycott of goods from both Britain and Japan increased the demand for hand-spun cloth. The war also gave a boost to industrial and other forms of economic development and

---

[1]To Krishna Kripalani, 29 September 1939.
[2]Proceedings of the Working Committee reported in *The Bombay Chronicle,* 28 June 1939.
[3]To Amrit Kaur, 29 June 1939, quoted in A.H. Hanson, *The Process of Planning* (Oxford, 1966), p. 28n.
[4]Gandhi to Jawaharlal, 11 August 1939 *A Bunch of Old Letters,* pp. 378-9.

made planning seem all the more necessary. 'If we had not had a planning committee already we ought to have formed one.'[1] A special sub-committee was created to consider the war situation and its repercussions on the Indian economy. There was scope now, even from the point of view of war production, for promoting industrial development, while the impact of war on agriculture emphasized the need for planning and state control on a countrywide scale. The over-production of sugar cane in the U.P., for example, could be dealt with, according to Jawaharlal, on the lines of Roosevelt's New Deal, by the Government stabilizing prices and buying up surplus stock for distribution gratis to the poor.[2] But the Government of India refused to adapt themselves to the changing context. They were still anxious to assist foreign industrial interests and to leave agricultural problems to *laissez-faire* and cut-throat competition.

By the summer of 1940, despite the tremendous disadvantages of lack of a common viewpoint among the planners, paucity of statistics and other data, and no immediate likelihood of implementation, seventeen sub-committees had presented final or interim reports. These covered not only technical programmes of production but also wider issues of distribution, social justice and social welfare. The sub-committee to which Jawaharlal probably attached the most importance was that on the condition and rights of women. The second stage of planning had now been reached. A comprehensive report, based on the suggestions of the various sub-committees, was taking shape. The Committee met daily for a fortnight in May 1940 and again in June, under Jawaharlal's presidency and approved the general framework. Though there were various inconsistencies and frequent ambiguities of phrasing, the broad trend was in favour of state ownership or state control or a blend of the two. However, political developments now took command. The Congress ministries, which had given the Planning Committee a purchase on the State, were gone. Jawaharlal himself was removed from the scene in October 1940 and the Government refused to permit him to deal with matters concerning the Planning Committee while in jail. To keep the concept of planning before the public eye, Jawaharlal suggested publication of the reports of the sub-committees; but some other members of the Committee were not in favour. The matter was referred to Gandhi who vetoed publication.[3]

Jawaharlal's contribution to planning before 1947 has, therefore, to be considered a mere torso. Even so, it was path-breaking. The plethora of plans drawn up in various quarters during the war years and the setting up by the Government of India in rivalry of a department of planning with an industrialist from Bombay in charge all had their genesis in the work of the National Planning Committee. Jawaharlal had made India plan-conscious.

[1] Jawaharlal to K.T. Shah, 18 September 1939.
[2] To Rajendra Prasad, 4 August 1940.
[3] K.T. Shah to P. Thakurdas, 21 April, A.D. Shroff to K.T. Shah, 25 April, and K.T. Shah to P. Thakurdas, 30 April 1941. Purshotamdas Thakurdas papers, File 220/1938-1949.

16

The War Crisis

When the war broke out, Jawaharlal was in China. Few people in India had approved of his going at a time when Europe was again approaching a crisis, and he himself had been reluctant to leave India just then. But all plans had been made and it was difficult to back out. So he went to Kunming, Chungking and Chengtu but, before he could go to the north-west and meet Mao and the communists, he had to cut short his visit and return hurriedly to India. He liked the Chinese, who struck him 'as a singularly grown-up people', and he established a personal friendship with Chiang Kai-shek and his wife. He was much moved by the idea of visiting another Asian country with an old civilization and with which India had had centuries of contact; and as a result of the visit, 'China has grown very near to me, and all my thoughts are mixed up with her.'[1] In the new world order that was emerging, he was determined that India and China should work together; and this idea did not leave him till 1962. In fact, he thought in terms of an eastern federation in which India and China would be the senior partners, and called on his countrymen to plan and work for it.[2]

However, throughout the fortnight in China, he kept his sense of humour and balance. He did not fail to notice that the Kuomintang was not a very democratic body though it called itself such, and was unfavourably struck by the fact that every time the name of Chiang was mentioned at a public meeting the audience had to stand up in respect.[3] But the problems faced by India and China were so similar, since both were striving to build national power in order to gain national freedom, that he left a note with Chiang suggesting closer contacts between the two national movements and the development of a common outlook and policy on major international issues.[4]

On his return from China on 9 September, Jawaharlal found that Gandhi's immediate reaction to the war had been, apart from abhorrence at the

[1] To Madame Chiang Kai-shek, 17 December 1940.
[2] The Eastern Federation', article in *National Herald*, 28 October 1940.
[3] See 'Diary of a Journey', reprinted in *China, Spain and the War*.
[4] A note on the development of contacts between India and China, written at Chungking, 29 August 1939.

triumph of violence, a spontaneous support of Britain. He had told the Viceroy that he viewed the war 'with an English heart' and, while he could not speak for his colleagues, personally was for full and unquestioning co-operation. At the thought of the possible destruction of the Houses of Parliament and West-minster Abbey, he had broken down. 'I could not', reported the Viceroy, 'help myself being profoundly moved by the emotion which he showed during a con-siderable part of it [the interview] . . . His whole attitude could not have been better, and in his conversation he showed the same breadth of approach and the same disinclination to trouble about minor or subsidiary issues as I have always noticed in him.'[1] In the U.P. the ministers seemed willing to give full co-operation in prosecution of the war, while in Madras the Governor had to restrain Rajagopalachari, on the outbreak of hostilities, from detaining all Germans and seizing their bank balances, 'whereupon he commented that the English seemed to want to wage war according to High Court rules'.[2]

However, the Congress attitude to the war was formulated not by Gandhi or Rajagopalachari but by Jawaharlal, and his approach was less emotional. This was to be expected and should have been no surprise to the Government. For years Jawaharlal had been stating his viewpoint on the European crisis and by periodical resolutions had been committing the Congress to it; and the mere involvement of Britain in war was not going to change it. He had been consist-ently opposed to fascism and Nazism and believed in some form of collective security to curb their continual aggression. If other Powers co-operated with the Soviet Union, the policy of peace would become unassailable. Neville Cham-berlain's policy of appeasement, therefore, had filled him with disgust, and he held Britain primarily responsible for the collapse of Spain and the destruction of Czechoslovakia. India would be no party to this policy, which was an addi-tional and unanswerable argument for complete independence. His writings and speeches to this effect in Britain in 1938 seem to have evoked Winston Churchill's approval, for though Jawaharlal did not meet him, Churchill sent him a message of goodwill through a mutual friend a year later, on the eve of Jawaharlal's departure to China.[3]

Jawaharlal's analysis of appeasement was that the British Government were inspired by class interests and were more hostile to Soviet Russia than to Nazi Germany. While Britain had been the leader in introducing political democracy, she was socially backward and the strain of social conflict had been only lessened by the exploitation of her colonies. She was anxious to protect her own empire and for this purpose connived at Nazi aggrandizement. Even when British imperial interests had been threatened by the dictators and there was growing criticism of their foreign policy, the British Government, the most reactionary

[1]Glendevon, op. cit., p. 136; Linlithgow to Zetland, 5 September 1939, Zetland papers, vol. 18; Tendulkar, Mahatma, vol. 5, p. 197.
[2]Haig's telegram to Viceroy, 17 September 1939, Haig papers, vol. 7; Erskine's telegram to Viceroy, 3 September 1939, Erskine papers, vol. 17.
[3]The Discovery of India, p. 439.

for generations, had continued to support Hitler and Mussolini, for their dislike of democracy and socialism was greater even than their attachment to empire. Even within Britain a fascist outlook was developing, and Jawaharlal believed that Chamberlain was following the road to internal fascism under cover of war preparations.[1] As for the opposition, the Labour Party did not seem to know its own mind and played an ineffective role, the pacifists in their eagerness to avoid war supported Hitler while the Independent Labour Party behaved worst of all and praised Chamberlain as a man of peace.

The hope of the Chamberlain Government of protecting vested interests at home and abroad while Germany fell on Russia had been defeated by Russia's understanding with Germany. Even though Jawaharlal deplored the cynical opportunism which underlay it, he recognized the diplomatic reasons which had led Stalin to veer his policy. But the fact that Britain and Germany were at war with each other while Russia stood apart did not alter Jawaharlal's general analysis of the situation and strengthened his attitude on non-participation by India. He had no trust in a Britain which still had Neville Chamberlain as Prime Minister. Fascism and imperialism were both parts of the same reactionary complex, and India was opposed to both. Jawaharlal's views on this point had never been in doubt. In London in 1938, he had emphasized that the Indian people should themselves decide on participation in any war, and so long as they did not have independence they would regard any war in which Britain was involved as an imperialist war and an occasion to intensify their own national struggle. The fact that the British Labour Party found this difficult to understand only showed how a dormant imperialism coloured even its outlook.[2] He wrote a few months later:

> We want to combat Fascism. But we will not permit ourselves to be exploited by imperialism, we will not have war imposed upon us by outside authority, we will not sacrifice to preserve the old injustices or to maintain an order that is based on them. We will not and cannot forget our own struggle for freedom for slogans which may sound pleasant to the ear but have little reality behind them or vague promises which have been broken often.[3]

It was for India to decide whether she would go to war. The Viceroy had now, without consulting representative opinion, taken that decision. But it was

[1] See his articles 'The Hoax' and 'England's Dilemma', in the *National Herald*, 25 October 1938 and 31 May 1939, respectively.

[2] F. Brockway, 'A Talk with Jawaharlal Nehru', *The New Leader*, 1 July 1938.

[3] 'The Choice Before Us', article in the *National Herald*, 5 October 1938.

absurd for a subject India to fight for the freedom of Poland. If India were to participate enthusiastically in the war, she would have to be granted freedom. One had to be free and democratic to fight for freedom and democracy. If Britain fought for democracy, her first task was to eliminate empire from India. The Indian people would not bargain or seek to take advantage of Britain's difficulty; but whatever they did would have to be in accord with India's freedom and dignity.

The resolution of the Working Committee was on these lines. On the train to Wardha, Jawaharlal had prepared two drafts, and the Committee accepted a merged version after merely toning down criticisms of the British and tightening the prose. It rejected both Gandhi's advice that there should be no demand for a statement of war aims and the suggestion of Subhas Bose that civil disobedience should be launched immediately. While condemning the Nazi attack on Poland, the Committee reaffirmed that India could not associate herself in a war said to be for democratic freedom when that freedom was denied to her and such limited freedom as she possessed had been taken away from her. The word of the British and French Governments, that they were fighting for democracy and freedom, was not enough. If Britain fought for democracy, she should necessarily end imperialism in her own possessions and establish full democracy in India. A free democratic India would gladly associate herself with other free nations for mutual defence against aggression and for economic co-operation. The British Government were, therefore, invited to declare their war aims clearly and state how these would be applied to India and given effect to immediately, so that India could assume her proper role in the emergence of the new world order.

The author of the resolution, commented Gandhi,[1] was an artist, an ardent patriot who was also a humanitarian and an internationalist. Jawaharlal made clear the commitment of the Congress to an anti-fascist position and to national freedom in the larger world context. The years of continuing Nazi aggression in Europe were to him the basic cause of the war, and this knowledge was never clouded in his mind by the intensity of his dislike of British imperialism. Even after the Government had rejected the Congress offer, he rebuked the editor of the *National Herald* for pro-German headlines and ordered the dismissal of the sub-editor responsible.[2] He wrote to Edward Thompson:[3]

Some Congressmen tell you that it is not possible to make India enthusiastic on your side. But I know that they are wrong — I would guarantee to do it myself. In the last war there was a doubt about your cause, and whenever you had a defeat there was rejoicing in the bazaars. In this war you will no doubt have setbacks, and some of them may be serious, and

[1] Tendulkar, *Mahatma*, vol. 5, p. 204.
[2] Private letter to the editor, *National Herald*, 27 October 1939.
[3] Cited in E. Thompson, *Enlist India for Freedom!* p. 48.

there will be the old temptation to rejoice. But everyone knows your cause is 'just'.

However, Jawaharlal was unwilling to be stampeded by sentiment as Gandhi had been. The war was clearly going to be a long one which in time would probably extend beyond Europe and involve the United States. So what was required of the Congress was to state the general attitude not only of the Indian nationalist movement but of all colonial peoples, and wait for the British Government to clarify their cause by appropriate action. His lack of faith in Neville Chamberlain's Government was, it should be remembered, widely shared in Britain. The *Manchester Guardian* approved of the resolution. 'Nehru', recorded Beatrice Webb in her diary,[1] 'has called the British bluff, the pretence of fighting for political democracy and the rights of man.' Stafford Cripps urged Jawaharlal not to accept anything short of conclusive action and to see to it that the Congress stood firm as a rock,[2] while Attlee counselled the British Cabinet to respond to the demand of the Congress with 'imaginative insight'.[3] Even a considerable number of Conservative back-benchers pressed Zetland to reach an agreement with the Congress.[4] But the Viceroy had made up his mind that his present duty was neither to move even at snail's pace along the path of constitutional progress nor to seek ways of harnessing India's enthusiasm for democratic principles. He had no commitment to the Indian people, and even the tragedy of famine in Bengal caused him no concern. He was now a war Viceroy,[5] whose first objective was to make India a safe base for the mechanical prosecution of the war, and to provide men and money. Every decision had to be judged soley by the extent to which it would promote an Allied victory; and Linlithgow lacked the imagination to see that wars are not won by guns and soldiers alone. In this projection the Congress, as guided by 'a doctrinaire like Nehru with his amateur knowledge of foreign politics and of the international stage',[6] had no place. On the other hand, more importance should be given to the Muslim League; and the Viceroy thought that this would have the added advantages of appeasing the army, which was largely Muslim, and the tribal elements on the North-West Frontier. Linlithgow decided, therefore, to ignore Jawaharlal and to break with the Congress; 'the present is probably a better opportunity than may present itself later'.[7] Sikandar Hyat Khan, though nominally a member of the League, had no wish to see Jinnah break up the Unionist Party in the Punjab, which was a party mainly of rural landed interests

[1] 5 October 1939, Beatrice Webb diaries, vol. 53. p. 143.
[2] Letter to Jawaharlal, 11 October 1939.
[3] Zetland to Linlithgow, 16 October 1939, Zetland papers, vol. 11.
[4] Idem, 20 December 1939, Zetland papers, vol. 11.
[5] Linlithgow's report of his conversation with W. Phillips, President Roosevelt's personal representative, 19 February 1943. *Transfer of Power* (H.M.S.O. 1971) vol. 3, p. 689.
[6] Linlithgow to Zetland, 18 September 1939, Zetland papers, vol. 18.
[7] Idem, 21 September 1939, Zetland papers, vol. 18.

held together by economic and not communal considerations. He therefore advised the Viceroy that nothing should be done to inflate Jinnah or make him more difficult to deal with.[1] But, despite this warning, Linlithgow sent for Jinnah; and Jinnah asked that the Congress ministries be dismissed.[2]

The Congress, in fact, at this time, despite the insistence in the resolution for some action by the Government to establish its *bona fides*, conveyed to the Viceroy that it would be satisfied with a declaration clearly stating that India would be free to determine her own destinies after the war. Jawaharlal was less impulsive on this occasion than Gandhi; but his preference for the Allies was no weaker. He made clear, even if only indirectly, his anxiety to assist personally to the full in the war effort, and wanted the association of persons like himself, who were representative of public opinion, with some form of a National War Council. If India and Britain waged war together as equal partners, with no formal legal changes, but with Indian leaders being taken into confidence and associated with decisions on such matters as the extent of India's war effort, the raising of armies and industrial mobilization, this in itself would have removed most of the constitutional difficulties by the time the war had been successfully concluded. But it was hinted that Jawaharlal would not insist on even this.[3]

Zetland, the Secretary of State, approved of Jawaharlal's proposals,[4] but by then it was too late. Desmond Young, the editor of the *Pioneer*, had rushed to Delhi carrying Jawaharlal's message; Linlithgow was half-convinced but Sir Gilbert Laithwaite, the Viceroy's private secretary, brushed it off.[5] Gandhi himself was told, unbelievably, that the British Government would be most unwilling to define their war aims at this stage and had never committed themselves in the least degree to fighting for democracy.[6] Jawaharlal began to lose hope of any reasonable arrangement, and his interview, along with Rajendra Prasad, with the Viceroy on 3 October confirmed his fears. The Viceroy made no secret of his 'rather negative' conclusions. The British Government could not ignore the Muslims and the Princes, and could make no specific commitment about Dominion Status till federation had been introduced. There could be no extensive expansion of the Executive Council or sharing of power with political parties in the central government. All he was prepared to do was to form a group consisting of a few members from the two houses of the central legislature with whom the Government would keep in touch on defence matters.[7]

[1] Linlithgow to Zetland, 5 September 1939, Zetland papers, vol. 18.

[2] Linlithgow's record of interview with Jinnah, 4 September 1939, Zetland papers, vol. 18.

[3] Haig's telegram to Viceroy reporting conversation with Mrs Pandit, 19 September, and Desmond Young's report of conversation with Jawaharlal, 21 September 1939, Haig papers, vol. 7; Viceroy's note on interview with Gandhi, 26 September 1939, Zetland papers, vol. 18.

[4] Zetland to Linlithgow, 9 October 1939, Zetland papers, vol. 11.

[5] D. Young, *Try Anything Twice* (London, 1963), pp. 245-6.

[6] Viceroy's note on interview with Gandhi, 26 September 1939, Zetland papers, vol. 18.

[7] Jawaharlal's note on interview with Viceroy, 3 October 1939.

Yet Jawaharlal continued to pine for a gesture which would enable India to end a hundred years of hostility to Britain and 'join in a struggle for freedom'.[1] He even took the step, unusual for him, considering that he viewed events in an impersonal framework, of making a private appeal to Linlithgow. Ignoring the disappointing trend of his interview with the Viceroy, he acted on Gandhi's suggestion that he explain developments in the U.P. and used the opportunity to touch on wider issues.

This letter, written in the train to Wardha, has grown long. But I want to add a few words to it and to tell you how much I desire that the long conflict of India and England should be ended and that they should cooperate together. I have felt that this war, with all its horrors, has brought this opportunity to our respective countries and it would be sad and tragic if we are unable to take advantage of it. None of us, in India or England, dare remain in the old grooves or think in terms of past conditions. But events are moving so fast that sometimes I fear that they will overtake our slow moving minds. There are all the elements of a Greek tragedy in the world situation today and we seem to be pushed along inevitably to a predestined end. You told me that I moved too much in the air. Probably you are right. But it is often possible to get a better view of the lie of the land from the heights than from the valleys. And I have wandered sufficiently on the solid earth of India and mixed with the people who labour there to think of India in earthly terms.

May I say how much I appreciate your friendly courtesy to me? It was a pleasure to meet you for a second time, and whenever chance offers an opportunity for this again, I shall avail myself of it. But whether we meet or, as you once said, look at each other from a distance over a gulf that has not been bridged, we shall do so, I earnestly trust, with no trace of unfriendliness, and realizing the difficulties which encompass us and which compel us to pursue different paths.[2]

The two paragraphs justify full quotation, for they mark the only occasion, at any time from the Amritsar tragedy in April 1919 till Lord Mountbatten's arrival in India in March 1947, when Jawaharlal broke through to a human level in his dealings with British officials. It is curious that the recipient of such warmth should have been Linlithgow, the least emotional of men, 'heavy of body and slow of mind, solid as a rock and with almost a rock's lack of awareness,'[3] as Jawaharlal later bitterly described him. It is not so much that there was in Linlithgow a hidden vein of a finer quality that had struck a chord in Jawaharlal as that Jawaharlal was desperately anxious to find a way which would

[1]Message to *News Chronicle*, 5 October 1939.
[2]To Linlithgow, 6 October 1939.
[3]*The Discovery of India*, p. 437.

enable the Congress to co-operate with the Government. So, though all reason weighed against it, he sought to reach out to the Viceroy. Awaiting a response, he pushed through, to the annoyance of the socialists, a resolution at the AICC meeting, endorsing the stand taken by the Working Committee. India should for the present stand aloof, but if given the opportunity she should join the war. It was an imperialist war but might not continue as such; it would certainly create a new world order and if India played her part in the right direction she could influence this change for the better. But if the response were not forthcoming, there was no alternative to conflict with the British. 'The next few weeks will probably make a big difference in India, this way or that.'[1]

Within not weeks but days, however, there came the stinging British reply. Linlithgow had sent a friendly but non-committal answer to Jawaharlal's letter,[2] and his public statement left no doubt that the Government had not revised their policy in the context of the war situation. The Viceroy stressed the differences among the Indian political parties, contended that no precise definition of war aims was as yet practicable, and was ready to say no more than that Britain was fighting to resist aggression. As for India's future, attention was gravely drawn to the preamble of the Act of 1919, to the statement on Dominion Status in 1929 and to the virtues of the Act of 1935. At the end of the war, the British Government would be very willing to enter into consultations as to any modifications of that Act that might be made with the agreement of all the vested interests in India; and in the meantime, a consultative group for war activities could be set up.[3]

Though Jawaharlal knew that his hope had been faint, yet his disappointment was intense. It had been made clear that Britain clung to her imperialism and was fighting to preserve it; and Indians were asked to shed their blood in order to strengthen their shackles. The statement showed the most amazing ignorance of India and of the temper of the Indian people. The Congress in turn could only say 'an emphatic no' to this and once more prepare to go into the wilderness. If one door, that of co-operation, was barred to them, they would open other doors.[4] Jawaharlal was for the Congress declining to assist in the war effort and preparing for the resignation or dismissal of the provincial ministries, but the Working Committee went further and directed the Congress ministries to resign as a first step.[5] There had never been so much unanimity in all Congress circles.[6] But the Government were still incapable of grasping the consequences of their mulishness, and sought to evade the conflict by relying on Gandhi's

---

[1] To Frances Gunther, 13 October 1939.

[2] 15 October 1939.

[3] Speech, 17 October 1929, *Indian Annual Register*, 1939, vol. 2, pp. 384-9.

[4] 'The Answer', 'What Britain Fights For' and 'Twenty Years', articles written for the *National Herald* 17, 18 and 19 October 1939; message to the *News Chronicle,* 18 October 1939.

[5] Jawaharlal's draft resolution, 21 October and Working Committee's resolution, 22 October 1939.

[6] To Krishna Menon, 21 October 1939.

30 Jawaharlal with M. A. Jinnah, 1946

31 With Lord Mountbatten in Singapore, 1946

32   The Naval mutiny, 1946

33   Jawaharlal defends the leaders of the I.N.A., 1946

34 With Lord Pethick-
Lawrence, 1946

35 With Lord Wavell, 1946

36 The Constituent Assembly, New Delhi, 8 February 1947: Jawaharlal moves the resolution for an independent sovereign republic

37 Independence Day celebrations below the Red Fort, Delhi, 15 August 1947

preference for unconditional co-operation. The subtlety of Gandhi's reactions, and his placing of this offer in the context of total non-violence, were beyond their comprehension. The Congress leaders were summoned to Delhi again and asked to reach an agreement with the League in the provinces, in which case the Government would be willing to create two or three more seats in the central Executive Council. To ensure that Gandhi accepted and was satisfied with this trivial change, the Government manoeuvred to secure Rajagopala-chari's presence in Delhi to advise Gandhi.[1] But Gandhi, to the surprise of no one except the Government of India, refused to abandon the Working Committee, and merely assured the Viceroy that he was anxious to avoid civil disobedience. The sentence in Rajendra Prasad's official letter to the Viceroy of 3 November, that till 'the main and moral issue' about clarification of war aims had been dealt with the Congress could not consider any subsidiary proposal was, in fact, drafted by Gandhi.[2]

From the start of the war crisis, the Congress had hoped for a joint approach with the League to the British Government. Jinnah had been invited to the meeting of the Working Committee in September, but had declined. However, the Congress thought the idea worth pursuing. The League was also committed to independence, and it was this demand which the Government had spurned. So the Congress might utilize the urgency of the situation to secure priority for the political issue over communal differences. Jawaharlal met Jinnah informally early in October and thought the latter had not been totally immune to this suggestion. To humour Jinnah's vanity, Azad stayed away from the talks with the Viceroy.[3] Sikandar Hyat Khan rang up Azad to say that a compromise might be reached if the Congress recognized the League as an 'important' organization even if not the sole organization representing Muslim opinion.[4] This was unobjectionable, and made an agreement seem possible. The day after Linlithgow's statement, Jawaharlal wrote a friendly letter to Jinnah, offering to meet him again wherever it suited him to come to closer grips with their differences.

> I entirely agree with you that it is a tragedy that the Hindu-Muslim pro-
> blem has not so far been settled in a friendly way. I feel terribly distressed
> about it and ashamed of myself in so far as I have not been able to con-
> tribute anything substantial towards its solution . . . With your goodwill
> and commanding position in the Muslim League that should not be so
> difficult as people imagine . . . The Viceroy's statement has been asto-
> nishing in its imperialist challenge to all of us . . . I earnestly trust that

[1] See Viceroy's telegram to Erskine, 28 October, and Erskine's telegram to Viceroy, 29 October, and telephone message, 31 October 1939, Erskine papers, vol. 17.
[2] See the draft of the letter in Rajendra Prasad papers, National Archives of India.
[3] See Linlithgow to Zetland, 4 October 1939, Zetland papers, vol. 18.
[4] Jawaharlal to Rajendra Prasad, 17 October 1939.

you will also express your strong disapproval of the Viceroy's statement and refuse to co-operate with him on the lines he has suggested. I feel strongly that our dignity and self-respect as Indians have been insulted by the British Government. They take us for granted as hangers-on of their system, to be ordered about when and where they will.[1]

At the end of the month, Gandhi, Jawaharlal and Rajendra Prasad met Jinnah again. He was assured that the Constituent Assembly would be formed on the widest possible franchise and by agreement on communal representation, and that Assembly would frame full protection for the rights and interests of all minorities. Jawaharlal thought this had satisfied Jinnah. 'And so the whole fabric of communal disunion as a bar to India's progress, conjured up by the Viceroy, fades away and vanishes at the touch of reason and reality.'[2] He had found, he said later,[3] that he and Jinnah had a great deal in common in regard to the objective and this had brought them much nearer than they had been for years.

These efforts worried the Government, who were relying heavily on the antagonism of the League to the Congress. The nationalist leaven·was bound to work in that body, particularly among its younger members,[4] while Jinnah was unpredictable, 'and I had one or two rather anxious moments during the period when he, Jawaharlal and Gandhi were discussing the situation together'.[5] But the Viceroy's fear was short-lived. A Constituent Assembly elected on adult franchise and framing a constitution after the British had left held no appeal for Jinnah, because the Muslim masses might well smother communal tendencies even in separate electorates. But Jawaharlal might have been led to believe that in their talks Jinnah had agreed to this, by Jinnah's lack of real interest in this subject. He was still thinking in terms not of the future but of the immediate present, and trying to force the Congress to form coalition ministries with the League. In the talks, communal matters were only raised by him casually, but he was very keen on the Congress reversing its general policy and becoming again a liberal and moderate party.[6] Jawaharlal and the Congress may have temporarily forgotten that the League's chief interest was jobs for the upper classes and felt confident that it would not oppose the freedom movement. But Jinnah's premiss throughout was that no alliance was possible with a politically advanced party. When, therefore, the Congress announced that its ministries would resign, he lost interest in these conversations. He had

[1] Jawaharlal to Jinnah, 18 October 1939.
[2] 'The Right and the Wrong of It', editorial in the *National Herald*, written by Jawaharlal, 6 November 1939.
[3] Statement to the press, 6 November, *The Bombay Chronicle*, 7 November 1939.
[4] Linlithgow to Zetland, 23 October 1939, Zetland papers, vol. 18.
[5] Idem, 18 November 1939, Zetland papers, vol. 18.
[6] Note on Jinnah's talks with Viceroy, 13 January 1940, Linlithgow to Zetland, 16 January 1940, Zetland papers, vol. 19; Jawaharlal to Zakir Hussain, 25 November 1939.

no wish to be involved in any agitation which the Congress might launch and was prepared to fall in line with the Government in order to secure concessions from them. To the Congress resolutions in the provincial assemblies on India's attitude to the war, the members of the League were directed to move amendments asserting that democracy was unsuited to India. Fazlul Haq, the premier of Bengal, a volatile politician who at this time was passing through a phase of devotion to the League, challenged Jawaharlal to join him in a joint inquiry into atrocities committed by the Congress against the Muslims. Jinnah himself declined to sign a communiqué, drafted by Jawaharlal, stating that the Congress and the League had much in common on the political issue and the general objective; and, soon after the Congress ministries resigned in the first week of November, he called on all Muslims to celebrate a 'deliverance day'. The challenge of Fazlul Haq, which Jawaharlal had promptly accepted, was conveniently submerged in the demand for a Royal Commission which obviously the Congress could not accept as it implied acquiescence in British intervention in Indian affairs. Their suggestion of a reference to Sir Maurice Gwyer, the chief Justice of the Federal Court, held to interest for Jinnah.

There was clearly no scope for further talks with Jinnah, and Jawaharlal called them off. Though he had, in the first shock of anger at the British attitude, made overtures to Jinnah, the failure of these efforts now caused him little concern. The 'deliverance day' celebrations had been no great success, and the League seemed to be visibly weakening. The Muslim peasantry, particularly in the U. P., and industrial workers did not support it, and Jinnah was relying on the feudal and upper middle classes.[1] There was also no room for further negotiations with the Government. Zetland's reference to the Congress as a Hindu organization which should reach a settlement with the Muslim League put a lid on all talks.[2] 'Lord Zetland and his Government have put the final seal on this bill of divorce, and the gulf that separates us is wider than the many oceans that intervene between his country and ours.'[3] The Congress would go its own way with no turning back or regrets. But that way was not clear. The resignation of the ministries was the beginning of 'partial non-co-operation',[4] but the next step was uncertain. Gandhi was firm that while the Congress could not co-operate with the British, it should not embarrass them in the prosecution of the war. Civil disobedience should be begun only when it became inevitable because of some aggressive action by the Government, and the people were strong and prepared for struggle. As it was, in view of the hostility of the League, any such campaign would almost certainly deteriorate into communal rioting. The Working Committee decided that the

[1] To Stafford Cripps, 17 January 1940.
[2] Jawaharlal to Gandhi, 8 November 1939, on Zetland's speech of 2 November.
[3] Lord Zetland's Apologia', editorial in the *National Herald,* written by Jawaharlal, 19 November 1939.
[4] Jawaharlal to E.M.S. Namboodripad, 22 December 1939.

policy of non-co-operation should continue till the Government ceased to maintain their imperialist domination in alliance with the reactionary elements in the country. But, after slight wavering, the Committee returned to the Gandhian path. Stress was laid on non-violence and on the constructive programme as the only ways of preparing the country for civil resistance; and the Committee reaffirmed that it was inherent in every form of *satyagraha* that no effort should be spared to achieve an honourable settlement. [1]

For the present, wrote Jawaharlal,[2] all of us have to go through the valley of the shadow. But in some ways the darkness was much greater for him. He had never been happy about Stalin's alliance with Hitler, and did not expect it to last long. There had been some justification for it in Russia's need to protect her own interests; it had strengthened Russia's whip hand in Europe, kept her out of war, and halted Germany's eastward drive. However, the partition of Poland had been bad enough; and now Russia had gone to war with Finland. This again, as Jawaharlal saw, could be justified as intended to stave off the possibility of Finland being used by other powers as a platform for attacking Russia.[3] Nevertheless, he did not conceal that the invasion had been a great shock to him.[4] Russia's strength in the outside world lay in her principles and her idealism. The principles, for all he knew, might still be there, but the idealism was wearing thin. Russia, the symbol to all progressive forces of hope and fulfilment, had descended from the pedestal on which her ardent champions had placed her, and bartered away her moral prestige and the support of so many of her friends for seeming political advantage. In a signed article, intended to correct the pro-Soviet bias of some editorials in the *National Herald*, Jawaharlal recounted the gloom which had been cast on him by the purges within Russia and the too facile opportunism of Soviet foreign policy. By lining herself with the aggressor nations, and attacking a small democratic country, she was paying heavily and 'in a coin which cannot be counted, for it is made up of the wishes and ideals of innumerable human beings'. Stalin's government had dealt themselves a severer blow than any combination of enemies could have done and in the process injured the cause of socialism itself.[5]

In these circumstances, Jawaharlal looked to the United States. He had admired Roosevelt's attitude in the Czech crisis, and what now gave him confidence was the belief that the burden of the future would ultimately fall on the United States. 'India is far from America, but more and more our thoughts go to this great democratic country, which seems, almost alone, to keep the torch of democratic freedom alight, in a world given over to imperialism and fascism,

---

[1] Working Committee resolutions, 23 November and 22 December 1939.

[2] To Madame Chiang Kai-shek, 25 December 1939.

[3] See his editorials in *National Herald*, 'What is Stalin aiming at?' and 'Russia and Finland', 14 November and 3 December 1939, respectively.

[4] Press conference at Bombay, 15 December, reported in *The Bombay Chronicle*, 16 December 1939.

[5] 'What of Russia now?', article written on 16 January 1940 for the *National Herald*.

and violence and aggression, and opportunism of the worst type.'[1] But Soviet policy and action strengthened his acceptance of the Gandhian method. It was Russia's failure to keep her means above reproach that had led to the ends being twisted to fit in with these means. This example of violence and opportunism distorting objective impressed on him the necessity of relying on non-violence and ethical action in achieving a free India. It is difficult otherwise to comprehend his meek acceptance of the constructive programme as the next step to be taken after the abandonment of provincial office. He himself resumed regular spinning after a break of nearly four years.

So, if Jawaharlal had laid down the Congress policy of non-co-operation, it was for Gandhi to implement it. His mind was preparing for a struggle, and he continually laid stress on discipline and non-violence. But he could not see his way ahead. Having said 'nothing doing',[2] the Congress could do little more. There was no question of any compromise or manoeuvring, but there was also no desire to precipitate a conflict. Jawaharlal does not seem to have expected anything much to happen immediately, and was almost in a relaxed mood. He took slow trains as a diversion and was considering a trip in the summer first to Switzerland to see his daughter and then perhaps even to the United States.[3]

The world is in a curious muddle and we in India are also tied up in many knots. But there is no need to worry overmuch either about our personal affairs or about national affairs. When there is so much that is bad taking place in the world, we can shoulder our own burdens, which are relatively light, more easily.[4]

The Government thought they were better placed. They had no intention of breaking the stalemate they had created. But they fancied, perhaps because Gandhi was guiding the Congress again and was reluctant to resort to civil disobedience, that a settlement on their terms was feasible. Linlithgow felt that despite Jawaharlal's irreconcilable attitude, the general atmosphere was a good deal more conducive to an agreement than one could have hoped, while Harold Laski, with his access to official quarters, reported that India 'is a brighter spot. I think there is a good chance of Congress settling on the basis of Dominion Status at the close of the war plus representation in the Viceroy's Council now. There is a long story behind this, but I feel better about the Indian prospect than for years.'[5] The Viceroy reverted to his old, foredoomed policy of seeking to detach Gandhi from Jawaharlal. When he saw Gandhi early in

[1] 'India's Demand and England's Answer', article written on 6 January 1940 and published in the *Atlantic Monthly,* April 1940.
[2] Jawaharlal to the press at Bombay, 10 February, *The Hindustan Times,* 11 February 1940.
[3] To Madame Chiang Kai-shek, 20 February 1940.
[4] To Syed Mahmud, 21 February 1940.
[5] Linlithgow to Erskine, 22 January 1940, Erskine papers, vol. 16; Laski to Felix Frankfurter, 30 January 1940, Laski papers.

February, he flattered him, declared that Jawaharlal lacked Gandhi's experience, steady vision and control of utterance and said that he could not accept responsibility for his share of any agreement unless he had a firm assurance that Gandhi would direct the Congress.[1] This ridiculous attempt at low cunning came, of course, to nothing, for beneath Gandhi's courtesy and attachment to Britain lay a steely determination to press for India's freedom. There was a shift in emphasis, in the resolution of 1 March of the Working Committee, from the importance of preparing for civil disobedience to the inevitability of such action as soon as organization permitted or circumstances demanded it. To avoid any blurring of issues, the paragraph in Jawaharlal's draft condemning Soviet action in Finland was omitted; and Jawaharlal himself seems to have been converted to the view that Russia's error in attacking Finland should not divert attention from the actions of Britain and France, who were exploiting the Finnish war to weaken Russia, seeking to entangle her in a war in West Asia and converting the war in Europe into a side-show of the real battle against Russia, who was the one irreconcilable opponent of all forms of imperialism.[2] The option of restricted or mass civil disobedience, suggested by Jawaharlal, was also deleted by the Committee; and to dispel suggestions that the Congress was prepared to compromise, the Committee reaffirmed that nothing short of complete independence — not even Dominion Status — and a constituent assembly would be acceptable. Only then would a permanent solution of the communal problem be possible, and the difficulty of the States, which was of British creation, disappear.[3] Gandhi and Jawaharlal favoured the issue of another resolution defining the content of *swaraj* — deepening, as it were, the Karachi resolution on fundamental rights. They thought this would strengthen the Congress in the coming struggle; but as Patel, Azad and Rajendra Prasad disapproved, the idea was dropped.

Jawaharlal, with the support of Azad, was for the early, if not immediate, commencement of civil disobedience. The question of preparation did not arise for it was not a matter of taking the offensive but of repelling the Government's attack. They could not avoid the struggle by sitting still. In Bengal the press was being stifled by censorship and demands for security, and large numbers of Congress workers were being arrested in various parts of the country. The Government seemed to be trying to see how much goading the Congress could bear. The possible hostility of the Muslim League should not be a deterrent to mass action. The Pakistan resolution passed by the League was a 'mad scheme' which could not last a day and was beyond discussion. To consider it seriously would be to encourage diverse separatist and disruptive forces.

[1] Linlithgow to Zetland, 24 January, and note of conversation with Gandhi, 5 February 1940, Zetland papers, vol. 19.

[2] 'On the Eve of Ramgarh', editorial written by Jawaharlal for the *National Herald,* 11 March, and published 14 March 1940.

[3] Jawaharlal's two drafts of 29 February 1940, and final resolution of 1 March 1940.

The communal problem was best shelved till the British left India, because not only would the British base of that problem drop out but, if there were civil war, Jawaharlal could not envisage utilizing British assistance to suppress the Muslims.[1]

Gandhi was not convinced. He dare not, he said, start civil disobedience, because if he did, disobedience would remain and civil would disappear. Even in the Frontier Province discipline had cracked. The Congress should form *satyagraha* committees and prepare the people, but there was no hurry to launch the movement. Once it started, the Government would probably take no action and allow the League and other anti-Congress forces to complicate the situation. Patel agreed but suggested individual civil disobedience to avoid demoralization, and Gandhi was willing to consider this either on a large scale or restricted to a few or confined only to him.[2]

Aware of the general trend of these discussions, the Government showed no concern. They did not take the demand for Pakistan seriously, but saw no reason to throw too much cold water on it, for it weakened the position of the Congress. On learning that Sikandar Hyat Khan was trying to get in touch with moderate Congress leaders so as to bring the Congress and the League together, Linlithgow cracked the whip and called him off.[3] The widening gulf between the two parties enabled the Government to abandon all efforts to reach a settlement. Nothing more seemed to be required than preparations to deal firmly and promptly with any form of civil disobedience.[4] I am not too keen to start talking', commented the Viceroy,[5] 'about a period after which British rule will have ceased in India. I suspect that that day is very remote and I feel the least we say about it in all probability the better.' There could be no more revealing gloss on all the statements made by British authorities over the years on their determination to leave India.

In contrast, Jawaharlal thought that the British empire was doomed, and the war had made this more certain than ever. But his enthusiasm for action was now dimmed by his sense of chivalry. Events in Europe took charge of developments in India. The Nazi *Blitzkrieg* brought him in line with Gandhi. He had surmised that the war could not continue for long in its 'phoney' phase and the German advance did not rattle him. Rajendra Prasad, the Congress president, and Asaf Ali, a member of the Working Committee, issued hasty

[1] Discussions in the Working Committee, 16 to 19 March 1940, Anand Bhavan papers, and 16 to 19 April 1940, AICC File G 32 of 1940; Jawaharlal's speeches at Allahabad, 13 April and at Poona 18 April 1940, *The Hindustan Times*, 15 and 20 April 1940, respectively.

[2] Discussions in the Working Committee, op. cit., Jawaharlal's note of discussions, 15 April 1940, Anand Bhavan papers; Gandhi's article in *Harijan* cited in Tendulkar, *Mahatma*, vol. 5. p. 341.

[3] P. Moon, 'May God be with you always', *The Round Table*, July 1971, p. 418.

[4] Linlithgow to Zetland, 5 April, 26 April and 3 May 1940, Zetland papers, vol. 19; Zetland's report to War Cabinet, 14 April 1940, Glendevon, op. cit. pp. 168-9.

[5] To Zetland, 5 April 1940, Zetland papers, vol. 19.

statements pledging support to the British; but Jawaharlal recognized that from India's viewpoint there had been no real change. Neville Chamberlain's Government had gone, but a Cabinet with Winston Churchill and Leopold Amery determining Indian policy was not likely to be more sympathetic to the nationalist viewpoint;[1] nor, despite its earlier attitude, could much be hoped for from the Labour Party. Therefore, while India had no wish to see the triumph of Nazism, she could not be expected to rally to the cause of a tottering imperialism which spoke with arrogance and in terms of domination. To contend that British rule was preferable to that of the Nazis was to accept that Indians were a helpless people whose only choice was between masters. The Congress should adhere to its policy and add to its strength by preparing for *satyagraha* but take no action so long as Britain was in peril. [2]

It was decided, as a demonstration of coolness, not to summon an emergency meeting of the Working Committee; but the policy as formulated by Gandhi and Jawaharlal was stated in a resolution, drafted by Jawaharlal, of the United Provinces Congress committee. As the British Government still thought in terms of empire and the picture of India was still one of British imperialism in action, so, whatever might happen in Europe and however deep the sympathy of India for the victims of aggression, there could be no change in India's attitude towards Britain. [3] But Jawaharlal opposed an amendment that civil disobedience should be started immediately on the ground that it was not worthy of the Congress to take advantage of Britain's difficulties.

'It is heartening', wrote the *Manchester Guardian,*[4] 'at this grave moment to have this knowledge, but since common danger has evoked this response, the Government of India should take advantage of it.' But the authorities were unequal to this level of honour. Amery wrote of a possible partnership with Jawaharlal. 'The new War Cabinet seems to be working well and the whole machine has been speeded up beyond recognition. Bevin is making an admirable driver of the working man. I suppose there is no chance of enlisting Nehru as recruiter-in-chief?'[5] But his first speech on policy was still in terms of possible revision of the Act of 1935. The Government were incapable of the magnanimity of the Congress, which with every reverse suffered by the British became more generous and accommodating. In June the Working Committee announced its disagreement with Gandhi's faith in non-violence in all circumstances. While the struggle for freedom should remain non-violent, the Committee felt unable to apply the creed to national defence and absolved Gandhi from

[1] 'Even as late as 1940 when I ventured to urge on L. S. Amery, who had just become Secretary of State for India, the need, as a pledge of our sincerity, to fix the latest date — one or two years after the end of the war, I suggested — for our leaving India, he refused even to discuss it.' Malcolm Darling, *Apprentice to Power* (London, 1966), p. 128.

[2] Statement to the press, 10 May, *The Hindustan Times,* 11 May 1940; letters to Rajendra Prasad and Maulana Azad, 16 May 1940.

[3] Resolution, 19 May 1940, U.P. P.C.C. papers, Lucknow.

[4] 22 May 1940.

[5] To Linlithgow, 30 May 1940, Linlithgow papers, I.O.L. Mss. Eur. F. 125, vol. 9.

responsibility for the programme and activity of the Congress. In other words, if the British made it possible, the Congress was willing to join in the fight in India's defence. Meeting again in the first week of July, the Working Committee went even further. Setting aside on this occasion not only Gandhi but even Jawaharlal, the majority in the Committee did not insist on a declaration about independence by the British but offered to assist in defence if a fully national government were established. Jawaharlal argued that to reduce acquisition of power to assumption of office and to seek to worm into it was to move along constitutional lines. Real power was the hold on the people, and this would be lessened by 'office power'. This form of power, secured on terms different from those laid down in earlier resolutions, would prove disastrous. But Rajagopalachari, the author of the proposal, won over Patel and Azad, and Jawaharlal agreed to abide by it. He was not convinced that this was the best way of serving India, but his concern for Britain swung him into acceptance.[1]

It had not been easy for Jawaharlal to keep his emotions out of the way, to differentiate persistently between the British people and British imperialism and think clear-sightedly about India's own problem. He had always seen it in the context of world affairs and argued that an acceptance of India's freedom was not only right and just in itself but would strengthen the Allied cause immeasurably. Even so, the skittling of the European countries by the German war machine had depressed him intensely. On the fall of France, he wrote one of his most moving articles, looking beyond Petain and Laval to another France:

> there must be one, for the heritage of a thousand years does not vanish in a night. That other France will rise again and assert the invincible spirit of freedom which made her great . . . let us pay homage to the France of the Revolution, the breaker of the Bastille and of all the bonds that hold the human body and spirit captive.[2]

And so, though he believed that his colleagues were hustling themselves, he was willing not to assert his dissent. At the Working Committee he had declared that, considering the mentality of the British Government, he would welcome chaos if the alternative was association with that Government; but at Poona towards the end of the month, commending the resolution to the AICC, he acknowledged the merit of its offer. 'It may be that the dancing star of independence may emerge out of chaos, but it may also be that nothing but black clouds may emerge out of chaos.'[3]

The Congress, having offered a way out of the stalemate without compromising its basic position, awaited official reaction. The situation was bringing

---

[1] Discussions in the Working Committee, July 1940, Anand Bhawan papers.
[2] Quatorze Juillet', article published in *National Herald*, 16 July 1940.
[3] Report in *The Hindustan Times*, 29 July 1940.

matters to a head, and either the Government accepted the co-operation of the Congress or the conflict would be intensified, In their eagerness for a solution Azad and Rajagopalachari stretched the resolution beyond warrant and interpreted it as an offer to assist not only in defence but in the war effort as a whole. But the Government persisted in refusing to accept this opportunity. It was sad, as Jawaharlal wrote, to see a great people so blind to everything except the narrow interests of a class, and risking everything but not taking the step which would put them right with the world and with the historic processes that were marching on with giant strides. Even now the independence of India stuck in the throat of the British Government, and they continued in the old lordly way, threatening their penalties and preaching their homilies.[1] They were still placing their faith in the League as the prop of empire. The section of the Urdu press which was controlled by the League fed the Muslim masses with abusive misrepresentation of the Congress.[2] Such propaganda was not without effect, enabling the British to rely on the communal problem and charge the Congress with being unrepresentative of total Indian opinion. The response of the Government therefore, when it came at last, was the usual stale anti-climax. They offered to appoint a few 'representative Indians' to the Executive Council and set up a War Advisory Council. The future constitution of India should be framed by a small body 'representative of the principal elements in India's national life' — and these elements included the Princes and British commercial interests; and any decision of that body would be subject to the fulfilment of Britain's obligations in India. 'The whole thing', commented Jawaharlal,[3] 'is fantastic and absurd and has not even the merit of decent phraseology about it.'

This 'offer', which was made almost simultaneously with the publication of an ordinance banning all volunteer organizations, left no doubt that the British attitude remained unchanged. As a result, the Congress resolutions died a natural death and there was no further need for intellectual debate as to when non-violence was obligatory and when it was not feasible. The Congress had been driven from its moorings by emotional reaction to Britain's distress and the Nazi victories in Europe, but the British Government restored the old position. The travail of spirit and mental conflict was ended.

There was a fear in some people's minds that the British Government might be clever enough to take advantage of the situation. But they gave

---

[1] 'A Crumbling World' and 'What of Us?', articles in *National Herald*, 17 and 18 July 1940.

[2] e. g. *Maulvi*, an Urdu monthly published from Delhi, wrote (July 1940): 'Atheists like Pandit Jawaharlal Nehru who do not like even to swear in the name of God are placed in the forefront Jawaharlal Nehru wo do not like even to swear in the name of God are placed in the forefront when the issue is the construction of a slaughter house in Lahore, but when there is any question relating to a mandir, or the language and customs of the Hindus, the same Pandit reveals himself in his true colours as a staunch Hindu. He can, however, never tolerate that the Muslims shall also remain staunch Muslims. It is people of such low mentality who have disgraced the Congress and who are responsible for the separation of the Muslims from it.'

[3] Press Conference at Bombay 27 August, *The Hindustan Times* 28 August 1940.

credit for intelligence where it was not due . . . Nothing is more astonishing than the ineptitude of the British ruling class in England during the last few years, nothing with one notable exception. That exception is the Government of India.[1]

Despite all the resistance and suspicion that had been built up over a long period, the Congress had sought to work with the British in their crisis of survival; and the offer had been contemptuously rejected. It was 'the final breaking of such slender bonds as held our minds together, it means the ending of all hope that we shall ever march together'.[2]

The Congress had, therefore, been pushed back into the mood of civil disobedience. It accepted again the leadership of Gandhi and prepared for conflict. The Government of India, on their part, decided to strike at once and with the utmost vigour if faced by a challenge from the Congress and to destroy it as a political party. On the very day that the constitutional proposals were announced, the Viceroy wrote to the Governors that he felt very strongly that the only possible answer to a 'declaration of war' by any section of the Congress should be a proclaimed determination to crush that organization as a whole.[3] They believed that the Congress was losing its grip and had little support among the Muslims. The British Government agreed that immediate action to paralyse the movement was preferable to a policy of waiting to see how the movement developed and only wished to be consulted before any action was taken.[4] The Labour Party, which was now in the coalition government, supported this policy and disapproved of the attitude of the Congress.[5]

The Government, therefore, went ahead with the arrests of Congressmen and Jawaharlal expected to return at any moment to prison. As he cabled to his daughter in Switzerland,[6] an early resumption of the old pilgrimage was likely. He even courted it by wandering about the U.P. in the uniform of a Congress volunteer and advising the volunteer corps to continue its activities. But again Gandhi moved away from a head-on collision, because it was not in his nature to press the British Government at a time when they were themselves threatened in their home. All that he committed the Congress to was non-violence and a demand for freedom of speech to preach against participation in the war; self-imposed restraint could not be taken to the extent of self-extinction. The demand would be expressed by individual civil disobedience. The first to court arrest by making a public speech against support of the war would be Vinoba Bhave, and the second Jawaharlal.

[1] 'India in Travail', Jawaharlal's article in *National Herald*, 9 August 1940.

[2] 'The parting of the ways', article written by Jawaharlal on 10 August 1940.

[3] Letter of 8 August 1940, Home Dept. File 6/13/40-Pol. (I); History of the Civil Disobedience Movement 1940-41, Home Dept. File 3/6/42. Pol. (I).

[4] Viceroy's telegram to Secretary of State, 11 September 1940, and Secretary of State's telegrams, 13 and 17 September 1940. Home Dept. File 3/13/40. Pol. (I).

[5] Krishna Menon's telegram to Jawaharlal on interview with Attlee, ibid.

[6] 10 September 1940.

Even the Government of India could not argue that individual civil disobedience for asserting the right to free speech could justify drastic action. But they decided to arrest Jawaharlal even before he offered *satyagraha*. He was thought to be going faster than Gandhi, and to be one step ahead of him. Gandhi appeared to be determined to carry on with civil disobedience at a low temperature and in very small doses, but Jawaharlal seemed eager to push things to extremes. He had been touring the United Provinces drawing attention once more to agrarian grievances. His arrest might well upset whatever long-term plans Gandhi might have. The War Cabinet approved and, on its own, suggested that Jawaharlal be prosecuted on a substantive charge rather than merely kept in detention.[1]

Jawaharlal himself probably preferred this, for while he loyally accepted Gandhi's decision about the manner and object of civil disobedience he could not have been greatly excited by individual *satyagraha*. The issue remained that of India and the war, and the goal was still independence; but the fight was being waged for the moment on a very narrow front. Jawaharlal was in an almost tranquil mood. His life was wrapped up in public affairs, and he had hardly any private life. An attractive personality brought him a large circle of friends and he had, when he cared to make the effort, a 'knock-down' charm. But throughout his life none of these friendships, with either men or women, impinged deeply on him; and his was a life of crowded loneliness. He could, as we have seen, be an emotional client; but he would seem to have been normally incapable of an equal relationship. This probably explains why in these years the men whom he allowed to get close to him were those, like Syed Mahmud and Sri Prakasa, who really had nothing to offer. His only deep attachment was to his daughter, and to her he was the ideal of perfection. His name for her, 'Indu-boy', makes clear the effort at compensation for lack of a son, and he probably thought of her as carrying on his work. But he never forced his affection or his will on her and, while always willing to give advice when sought, never imposed his directives. So the thought of going under completely or at least for years did not worry him.[2] There were, to him, no separate causes left in the world, as all of them ran into one another, but his primary commitment was to India's freedom and on that he was not prepared to compromise. His speeches to the peasants of his province were clear and calm.

He was evidently moved. There was a sense of vast issues, of great decisions, of the call which might come to anyone at any moment. The multitude of listeners seemed to be in tune with the speaker and seemed to rise above themselves for the moment. There was a hush and a solemnity which pervaded the atmosphere . . . And then he spoke, with a

[1] Viceroy's telegrams to Secretary of State, 21 and 22 October 1940. Home Dept. Files 3/3/40 and 3/13/40 Pol. (I), respectively; Amery to Linlithgow, 23 October 1940, Linlithgow papers, vol. 9; Viceroy's telegram to Governor of U.P., 31 October 1940, Home Dept. File 3/18/40 Pol. (I).

[2] To Syed Mahmud, 12 October 1940 and to Mrs Dorothy Enge, 27 October 1940.

quiver in his voice, of the dream that had made life worthwhile for him — the dream of the India of tomorrow. He developed this theme and the picture became a living and a glowing one. And then, suddenly, he grew sad. For twenty years and more, he said, he had seen this vision and sought to make it a reality. And yet when he saw the condition of the people round about him, their appalling poverty, their miserable environment, his heart misgave him. Was this all the result they had obtained after twenty years travail and labour? Then again, he changed his mood and spoke triumphantly of the vast inner changes that had come over the people. They were poor still, and over-burdened with care and sorrow, but they had got rid of the fear that oppressed them and the hopelessness that enveloped their lives from birth to death. That was a mighty change which had brought them near to *Swaraj*. And now they stood on the threshold of the future, a future which would mean a changed world and a new India. What this new India would be he could not say. That would depend on their stout hearts and strong arms. Fate, Destiny, *Karma*! We were not going to be their slaves, but we would bend them to our will and make India after the picture in our own hearts.[1]

Hastening to Wardha to dissuade Gandhi from undertaking a fast unto death in protest against British obduracy,[2] Jawaharlal was arrested on 30 October at Cheoki station on his way back to Allahabad and taken to Gorakhpur for trial. He declined to plead, stating merely that it was his particular function and privilege to spread disaffection against the British Government in India.[3] But he read a long statement which, over twenty years later, still gave him satisfaction.[4] He pointed out that the reports of his speeches at Gorakhpur earlier in the month were scrappy, incomplete and often distorted; but this was not of importance. He stood by the policy of the Congress on the war and had in fact been chosen to give expression to it. It was monstrous that the Indian people should be thrust into a war without their consent; but the Congress had sought a way out which would be honourable to all parties concerned. There were very few persons in India, whether Indians or Englishmen, who had so consistently raised their voices against fascism and Nazism as he had done; but the actions of the British Government compelled the Indian people to resist to the uttermost. They had therefore decided to be no parties to this war and to declare this to the world.

It is not me that you are seeking to judge and condemn, but rather the hundreds of millions of the people of India, and that is a large task even for a proud Empire. Perhaps it may be that, though I am standing before

[1] 'Jawaharlal reports himself', *National Herald*, 23 October 1940.
[2] B. V. Keskar. 'Alone with Gandhiji and Nehru', *Illustrated Weekly of India*, 30 May 1971.
[3] Report of trial in *The Hindustan Times*, 4 November 1940.
[4] See letter to Mrs Dorothy Norman, 19 January 1962, Nehru papers.

you on my trial, it is the British Empire itself that is on its trial before the bar of the world . . . Individuals count for little, they come and go, as I shall go when my time is up. Seven times I have been tried and convicted by British authority in India, and many years of my life lie buried within prison walls. An eighth time or a ninth, and a few more years, make little difference. But it is no small matter what happens to India and her millions of sons and daughters. That is the issue before me, and that ultimately is the issue before you, Sir.[1]

The district judge gave Jawaharlal what was intended to be a deterrent sentence of four years. The savagery surprised Whitehall and New Delhi as well as Sir Maurice Hallett, the Governor at Lucknow; but Hallett vetoed any change in the terms. However, Churchill directed Amery to telegraph at once to the Viceroy expressing the hope that the actual rigour of the sentence would be modified and Jawaharlal not treated like a common criminal.[2] Even this hope was unanswered. After a week in Gorakhpur jail, Jawaharlal was moved by stealth and under cover of night, in a railway compartment with shutters down and a car with curtains drawn, to his old quarters in Dehra Dun jail. There he remained, except for a week in Lucknow prison in April 1941, till his release at the end of the year. This time the Government had no intention of easing in any way the harshness of jail life. The Viceroy even reprimanded the superintendent of police who had arrested Jawaharlal at Cheoki for giving him dinner at his house before having him driven down to Gorakhpur. It was made explicit that no personal friendliness was to be shown or social relations developed.[3] In jail he was allowed one weekly newspaper and six books at any one time, and he could have one interview, send one letter without enclosures and receive one every fortnight. There were also many petty harassments. He was not for some time permitted a washerman or a barber, a warder was fined for allowing a prisoner who had been discharged to say good-bye to Jawaharlal, and the prisoner himself was not allowed to collect ten rupees which Jawaharlal had given him for his fare home. Friends from outside were not allowed to send Jawaharlal packed lunches, and he could only receive fruit if he happened to know the sender. On one occasion, fruit sent by an unknown well-wisher from Rawalpindi was sent back at Jawaharlal's expense. When Jawaharlal wrote home asking his secretary to make a public announcement that no parcels or letters should be sent to him, this passage was blotted out by the censor. As he was to buy everything he needed through the jail staff (who were not known for promptitude) and get nothing from home, he was sometimes short even of toothpaste. He was directed, for the first time in his prison career, to give his thumb impression and he refused. He was, after a while, given all the letters

[1] Statement of 4 November 1940, reprinted in J. Nehru, *The Unity of India* (London, 1941), pp. 395-400.

[2] Amery to Linlithgow, 14 November 1940, Linlithgow papers, vol. 9.

[3] P. S. V. to Home Member, 19 November 1940, Home Dept. File 3/16/40/Pol. (I).

received from his daughter abroad, but the others were piled up in the office for weeks before Jawaharlal was told of them and asked to pick one. Permission to deal with the business of the National Planning Committee was refused. Papers pertaining to the Kamala Nehru Memorial Hospital were, after many months, exempted, but this delay had so held up work that Jawaharlal resigned the chairmanship.[1] His plan for sorting out his father's letters was defeated by the authorities insisting that they would first have to go through these letters before sending them to him; for as they obviously would be unable to understand the significance of these letters, Jawaharlal dropped the proposal. The limit on the number of letters he could write was later withdrawn, but on condition that none of these was published in the press — which was absurd because, apart from Jawaharlal's known aversion to giving any kind of undertaking, he was obviously in no position to give assurances about the behaviour of the recipients of his letters. In fact, Jawaharlal virtually gave up letter-writing and depended on interviews for keeping in touch with the outside world. Indira, who returned to India in May, took a cottage near Mussoorie; and this in itself made life a little pleasanter for Jawaharlal.

He had sought no favours. On the other hand, after hearing reports of ill-treatment of political prisoners in the camp jail in Lucknow, he wrote to the jail authorities that even the few privileges he was receiving had become hateful to him and he might defy jail discipline and invite the consequences.[2] A lesser man might have become personally embittered. But Jawaharlal accepted all this as part of his life and work without worrying about it. A sentence which he jotted down in his notebook at this time and was fond of quoting was that one could enjoy life perfectly only after resolving not to count the cost. What he understood by this was something very close to the teaching of the *Gita*; one should face the risks and perils of the adventure of life without calculating either what it involved or what might be its results. By enjoyment he meant something much more than a round of eating and sleeping and amusing oneself; it was doing what one had to. 'All we can do', he advised his daughter,[3] 'is to face our job and do it as well as we can and to remain tranquil in spite of shock and disaster.' The certainties of moral and ethical values which he had built around himself gave him serenity and strength. It is not surprising that though he had long ago moved away from the simple religious faith of the 'twenties and had now no anchorage of scriptural or secular dogma, he carried about with him a tiny edition of the *Gita*.

In this spirit, as soon as he found himself again in prison, he closed the various drawers of his mind which related to his activities outside and fell into the rhythm of jail life. The purpose was to prepare himself in body and mind

[1] See letters to the jail superintendent, 2 January, 4 February, 24 February, 19 March, 29 July and 5 August 1941; to the Inspector-General of Prisons, 16 February and 10 March 1941; Padmaja Naidu to Frances Gunther, 13 March 1941, Home Dept. File 3/31/40 Pol. (I).
[2] To the Inspector-General of Prisons, 23 August 1941.
[3] Letter, 18 November 1940.

for his work on release and to store energy so that he might be able to squander it later. Spinning, reading, regular exercise and plenty of sleep formed the main planks of his existence. He spent considerable time in cleaning and washing up and even — though food never greatly interested him — helped in the cooking. But the chief physical activity was gardening. On arrival in Dehra Dun, for about a week he did nothing all day long but dig the rather stony ground.[1] He then planted some seedlings but seems to have over-watered them, for the results were not very successful. But he was joined in his cell in January by Ranjit Pandit, who brought a more expert touch to this effort; and soon the barrack garden, despite the high walls and lack of sun, could boast of a few dahlias and sunflowers.

It was not, however, easy to forget about events in the world and only cultivate his garden. Jawaharlal might ignore the unexciting progress of individual civil disobedience, but he could not shut out the war in Europe which was destroying the old order. Especially after the Nazi attack on the Soviet Union, he was infuriated by the British ineptitude which excluded him and his countrymen from participation in these developments. Though he had almost no private correspondence, he sent what were virtually long articles to British acquaintances, and in these his pent-up bitterness exploded. A perceptive mind like Beatrice Webb's, unswayed by passing winds, could grasp the quality of India's leaders.

> What is outstanding in the leadership of Gandhi and Nehru is the keenness and subtlety of intellect, the depth and refinement of the emotional life of these two men, compared not only to the brutality and ultra coarseness of Mussolini and Hitler, but even to the conventional outfit, in thought and feeling, of Churchill and Roosevelt.[2]

But most well-meaning British individuals and groups felt that the Congress had acted in a huff and forgotten the larger issues of the war in a narrow nationalism. They showed no real understanding of the Indian problem, and they certainly had no influence on the policy of their Government. But Jawaharlal had never been surer of the rightness of any decision and, though he did not share Gandhi's total pacifism, was entirely at one with him in the political decisions about the war crisis.[3]

Half-relaxed and half-resentful, determined not to worry and yet driven to exasperation by inactivity in a cataclysmic situation, Jawaharlal frequently set aside the present for thoughts of the future. But even more often his mind wandered back into the past. It was during this spell in jail that he began his

[1] See H. C. Bajpai, 'In the same cell with Jawaharlal Nehru', *National Herald*, 11 December 1940.

[2] 24 September 1940, Beatrice Webb diaries, vol. 54, p. 176.

[3] To Col. Wedgwood 23 April and 21 November 1941; to Eleanor Rathbone, 22 June and 9 November 1941; and to Sir George Schuster, 2 December 1941.

journey into the five thousand years of India's history. 'We have undertaken many a voyage in time and space, as well as geographically in the present, for the discovery of India.'[1] His election tours had woken him to the myriad aspects of India's diverse unity; and to this was added an increasing appreciation of India's thought and culture. Earlier he had wanted to change his country and bring her abreast of the twentieth century. This aspiration never left him. But with it was now blended a pride in India's achievement and a firm sense of his own basic Indian-ness. 'It is a debt I can never repay; but it is an obligation that I cannot forget and which I shall seek to discharge to the end of my days.'[2]

A further element in his mental ferment was the conscious increase in the intellectual influence of Gandhi and Tagore. The horrors of war drove him to a deeper acceptance of non-violence not merely as a political weapon for India but as perhaps the only promise for the future of man. There was a reversion in this respect to his attitude in the early 'twenties. Tagore, who died that August, had been very different from Gandhi, but he had also been basically of India's soil, the inheritor and expositor of her wisdom. 'Again I think of the richness of India's agelong cultural genius which can throw up in the same generation two such master-types, typical of her in every way, yet representing different aspects of her many-sided personality.'[3]

The result of these varied yet converging impacts could be seen when Jawaharlal, in the latter half of 1941, again took up serious writing. In 1940 he had sent to the American publishers of his *Autobiography* a hurriedly written postscript, 'Five Years After'. Now he set out to write a fuller version of a second volume of his autobiography. He drafted a few chapters but rejected them, using some of the material in the long work which he completed when again in prison. But he was more interested in the making of India than in his personal development. Even in his first draft he was often tugged for long stretches by the pull of the past from an account of himself into flashbacks into India's history, and the factors which moulded her personality. This tendency became more pronounced in the second, larger effort which was published as *The Discovery of India.*

Towards the end of the year the Government of India came round to the view that all Congressmen in jail, including Jawaharlal, could be released. Hallett, the Governor of the U.P., opposed Jawaharlal's release because he thought it would demoralize the civil services and the Muslim League, while Winston Churchill thought any such general release would be 'surrender at the moment of success'. But the War Cabinet supported the Government of India, with Churchill muttering something to the effect, 'when you lose India, don't blame me.'[4] So Jawaharlal was out again on 4 December.

[1] To Col. Wedgwood, 23 April 1941.
[2] To Eleanor Rathbone, 22 June 1941.
[3] To Krishna Kripalani, 27 August 1941.
[4] Glendevon, op. cit., pp. 208-12.

His personal mood of bitterness against British policy seemed but a reflection of the general hardening of Indian public opinion. There was a widespread conviction that the British were not only alien oppressors but the greatest disruptive force in India and the champion of all reactionary elements. Professor Coupland, visiting India at this time, thought that one particular incident, Churchill's categorical announcement in September 1941 that the Atlantic Charter would not apply to India, had led to a spreading of a new and uncomfortable suspicion of British intent even beyond nationalist circles.[1] On the other hand, the involvement of Russia and the United States and the spread of the war in Asia had altered the nature of the conflict. Jawaharlal had no hesitation in expressing publicly his hope that the progressive forces, as represented by Russia, the United States, Britain and China, would emerge victorious. But the Government of India continued their Rip Van Winkle policy. 'It is very difficult', commented Jawaharlal in exasperation, 'for intelligent people to submit to the decisions of unintelligent people.'[2] What was required to enable India to do what it wanted to do, join the war wholeheartedly on the side of the Allies, was 'a pleasant psychological shock'[3] establishing that the old order had changed in India as well; but of any such imaginative action the Government of India were wholly incapable. They were Asia's men of Vichy, living in the past and looking backwards, clinging to their interests and afraid of the people.

Jawaharlal was, therefore, keen that the Congress should not waver in its refusal to change its policy so long as the British gave no indication of anything more than remote assurances. Just as the British Labour Party had been in favour of the war but had declined to join Chamberlain's cabinet, so the Congress, while expressing its support for the Allies, should not offer any positive collaboration. The offers of 1940, to assist in defence on certain conditions, should not be resurrected. 'I am not a believer in revivalism either in religion or politics.'[4] The party should hold together under Gandhi's leadership and present an unshakeable front to the British while keeping in line with international events.[5] But at Bardoli in Christmas week Rajagopalachari once again persuaded the Working Committee to set aside Gandhi and ignore Jawaharlal and offer the co-operation of a free India in the defence of the country on a national basis. Civil disobedience seemed to Rajagopalachari to have served its purpose; the people were exhausted and unless Congress did something definite in this crisis its cause would suffer. Wisdom lay in making as much political progress as possible during the war.[6]

Jawaharlal attached hardly any importance to this resolution. As the British showed no sign of responding to the demand of the Congress, this was

---

[1] *The Cripps Mission* (Oxford, 1942), p. 22.
[2] Press conference at Lucknow, *The Hindustan Times*, 10 December 1941.
[3] Message to the *News Chronicle*, 11 December 1941.
[4] Statement at Bombay, 17 December, *The Hindustan Times*, 18 December 1941.
[5] To Sampurnanand, 14 December 1941.
[6] Jawaharlal's notes of Working Committee meetings, 22 to 24 December 1941.

a mere theoretical exercise. No compromise was possible between imperialism and nationalism, and Rajagopalachari's persistent suggestions of a settlement only added to the confusion. Gandhi, unwilling even to consider freedom at the cost of non-violence, formally withdrew from the organization. But he commended the resolution to the AICC and utilized the occasion to designate Jawaharlal formally as his chosen successor.

Somebody suggested that Pandit Jawaharlal and I were estranged. It will require much more than differences of opinion to estrange us. We have had differences from the moment we became co-workers, and yet I have said for some years and say now that not Rajaji [Rajagopalachari] but Jawaharlal will be my successor. He says that he does not understand my language, and that he speaks a language foreign to me. This may or may not be true. But language is no bar to a union of hearts. And I know this—that when I am gone he will speak my language.[1]

[1] 15 January 1942, Tendulkar, *Mahatma,* vol. 6, p. 43.

17

The Cripps Mission

The Viceroy, having no wish to co-operate with the Congress, disliked the Bardoli resolution. He, therefore, saw to it that Reuters cabled the full text of Jinnah's statement criticizing the resolution and urged Amery to give it the fullest weight in Britain and use it in the United States. 'If, under pressure from liberal quarters in the United Kingdom, Rajagopalachari and his friends were able to stifle me in their close embrace, I feel quite sure that the Mahatma would emerge once again upon the stage to give the *coup de grâce* to British influence in India.'[1] Meantime, the Japanese sweep drew closer to India's shores. Early in the year, Franklin Roosevelt thought that India was as good as gone.[2] In February Winston Churchill told the King that Burma, Ceylon, Calcutta and Madras as well as a part of Australia might fall into enemy hands.[3] Jawaharlal also realized that the British refusal to part with power was unrealistic in the face of the imminent fall of their empire in India. Whatever happened, British imperialism was doomed to collapse. It was more urgent, therefore, to plan for the confrontation of events than to hope for negotiations with the British. 'This war is our war. But you don't understand; in this war *Britain is on the other side.*[4] *Satyagraha* had been called off because of the desire not to embarrass the British, whose allies were Russia, China and the United States; but there was no question of being merely passive if the Japanese stepped into India. Congress workers should spread out into the countryside and organize towns, wards and villages for every eventuality. Small units of about fifty houses each should be formed, and the residents mobilized to prevent panic, prepare for air raids, maintain law and order when control slipped from British hands, set up local co-operatives to ensure food supplies, encourage *khadi,* cottage industries and village handicrafts to enable local self-sufficiency,

[1] Linlithgow to Amery, 30 December 1941, Linlithgow papers, vol. 10.
[2] W.D. Hassett, *Off the Record with F.D.R.* (New Brunswick, 1958), p. 28.
[3] J. W. Wheeler-Bennett, *King George VI* (London, 1958), p. 538.
[4] To Eve Curie, 22 March 1942, quoted in E. Curie, *Journey among Warriors* (London, 1943), p. 440. Emphasis in original.

and resist the Japanese as best they could. What Jawaharlal appears to have had in mind was a fragmented war of attrition such as was taking place in China. The British had spurned the offer of the Congress to co-operate in the war, but in no case would the Congress bow before a foreign invader. They might not be able to push back armies but these armies would have to pass over their dead bodies. India would never accept the fate of France.

The U.P. Government, oblivious to all that was happening, considered arresting Jawaharlal for his bitter references to the blindness and incompetence of the *raj* and his prophecy that the empire in India might not last six months.[1] But even Linlithgow realized that there could not be a worse moment for taking such a step.[2] It was not Jawaharlal but the Japanese who were destroying British prestige, and his repeated calls to resist any invasion could hardly be resented. In Calcutta he sought to allay fright and exodus, and in Allahabad he discarded his car for a bicycle to get in closer touch with the people. The elaborate black-outs and air raid precautions ordered by the Government were not only out of date but likely to increase panic: 'it does no good to worry. That is the lesson which our people should be taught.'[3] Marshal Chiang and his wife came to India, met Jawaharlal and Gandhi and, while unable to change Jawaharlal's thinking, seemingly toned down his hostility to the British. The best comment on that visit was provided by Gandhi.

> He [Chiang] came and went without creating any impression, but fun was had by all. I would not say that I learnt anything, and there was nothing that we could teach him. All that he had to say was this: Be as it may, help the British. They are better than others and they will now become still better.[4]

The general alienation from the British bureaucracy increased when, after the fall of Rangoon on 7 March, reports came in of discrimination against Indian refugees on the long trek from Burma. At last the British Cabinet woke up to the urgency of the situation. For long, even with the enemy approaching the gates, Churchill, Amery and Linlithgow had had, as Jawaharlal expected, no intention of making any move to secure popular Indian support for the war. The very danger seemed to them an argument for doing nothing, for it was contended that this was no time for long-term objectives and that the introduction of a hostile political element into the defence machine would paralyse action.[5] But there were other forces at work. Roosevelt told his wife that he

[1]Hallett to Linlithgow, 17 February 1942, Home Dept. File 3/48/41-Pol (I), vol. 5, and 21 February 1942; *Transfer of Power*, vol. 1 (H.M.S.O., 1970), pp. 219-22.

[2]Linlithgow to Hallett, 24 February 1942, Home Dept. File 3/48/41-Pol. (I), vol. 5.

[3] To G.P. Hutheesing, 28 February 1942.

[4]To Vallabhbhai Patel. Tendulkar, *Mahatma*, vol. 6, p. 62.

[5]Amery to Linlithgow, 7 January, Churchill to Attlee, 7 January and Linlithgow to Amery, 21 January 1942, *Transfer of Power*, vol. 1, pp. 13, 14 and 46, respectively.

would have to compel the British to give Dominion Status to India,[1] and he urged Churchill with tact to do so. Chiang, after his visit to India, informed Roosevelt that if the British did not fundamentally change their policy it would be like presenting India to the enemy.'[2] In Britain itself, the crisis had created a sudden interest in India among the back-benchers of Parliament, and Attlee, condemning the 'crude imperialism' of the Viceroy, called for an immediate act of statesmanship. 'To mark time is to lose India.'[3] The War Cabinet listened to Attlee rather than to Amery, and Churchill, characteristically, if only temporarily, getting into the swing of it, formulated a scheme for expanding the defence council in India, offered to broadcast to India recommending it, and even planned to fly out to Delhi. His ardour was dampened by Amery and Linlithgow, who protested that Churchill's scheme was weighted against the League and in favour of the Congress; but the idea of seeking a settlement in India had been accepted. 'We have resigned ourselves', as Churchill commented,[4] 'to fighting our utmost to defend India in order, if successful, to be turned out.' Attlee, strengthened by the entry of Cripps into the War Cabinet on 19 February, drafted the British proposals. Their main points were the convening after the war of a constituent assembly elected on a system of proportional representation by freshly elected provincial assemblies, the recognition of the possibility of Pakistan by conceding the right of any province that was not prepared to accept the new Dominion constitution to retain its existing constitutional position, and the request for the collaboration, while the war lasted, of Indian parties with the British Government, who would continue to bear the full responsibility for India's defence.

Armed with this Declaration, Cripps flew to India to secure its acceptance by the Indian leaders. It was, as Amery explained to the less percipient Viceroy,[5] in essence a conservative, reactionary and limited offer. There would be for the time being only collaboration in defence, and in the future a Dominion constitution with possibly a partition of India. Nor had Cripps any authority to alter the text of the Declaration approved by the Cabinet. Yet he was hopeful of success. There was nothing in the Declaration to which the Congress could heartily respond. The idea of Dominion Status made men like Jawaharlal 'slightly seasick'[6] while the suggestion of Pakistan was bound to cause alarm. But Cripps relied on his persuasive ability, his known goodwill for the cause of Indian freedom and, above all, his close friendship with Jawaharlal. In the winter of 1939 he had come to India 'as a self-appointed Ambassador to treat with the Congress'[7] and had been Jawaharlal's guest; now, as the emissary

[1] 26 December 1941, J. P. Lash, *Eleanor and Franklin* (London, 1972), p. 669.

[2] 24 February 1942, *Foreign Relations of the United States 1942,* vol. 1, pp. 605-06.

[3] Memorandum to War Cabinet, 2 February 1942, *Transfer of Power,* vol. 1, p. 111.

[4] To Mackenzie King, 18 March 1942, *Transfer of Power,* vol. 1, p. 440.

[5] Amery's telegram and letter to Linlithgow, 10 March 1942, *Transfer of Power,* vol. 1, pp. 396 and 403.

[6] Jawaharlal quoted in Curie, op. cit., p. 441.

[7] Laski to Mr and Mrs Frankfurter, 7 December 1939, Laski papers.

of the War Cabinet, he was confident of an agreement. What he failed to understand was that Jawaharlal liked him but had no high opinion of his judgment[1] and that the fate of India was not an issue which Jawaharlal would be willing to determine at a personal level.

From the start, Cripps's negotiations in Delhi centred on the immediate transitory arrangements during the war, the Declaration being, in the phrase of the Viceroy's entourage, 'the wrapper round a pound of tea', which was the control of the Government of India. The Viceroy insisted that this was a matter of which only he should decide the details, and he would be unwilling to alter the composition of his Executive Council if only one of the parties (i.e. the Congress) agreed to join. He feared that if the Congress secured official influence, the Muslims and other minorities would be antagonized, the war effort would be impeded and the 'Pétainism' of Gandhi and other elements in the Congress would gain ground.[2] Jinnah, however, surprised by the extent to which the notion of Pakistan had been conceded, was willing to accept the proposals and saw no great difficulty in the interim arrangements.[3] There was no discussion throughout Cripps's stay in India as to how many representatives in the Government each party should be allotted. Jinnah has been so often criticized in this book that it is a pleasure to record that, on this critical occasion, he was guided by partiotism.

The Congress disliked the provisions about a Dominion constitution rather than full independence, the representation of the Indian States in a constituent assembly by their rulers rather than popular representatives and, above all, the recognition of the idea of a partition. It was for the last reason that Gandhi opposed the Declaration and urged the Working Committee to reject 'the post-dated cheque'.[4] In an undated letter to Jawaharlal, written at 2 a.m., and which we can place because it was written on the back of a dentist's bill dated 27 March 1942. Gandhi declared that he was convinced that the offer could not be accepted. 'It will ruin the country. If you hold the same opinion, have a talk with Rajaji and take the final decision. If you and Rajaji think alike, then let us act accordingly.' The wording shows Gandhi's intense dislike of the proposals, but it also makes clear that he did not expect the final word to be his. Both before and after March 1942, the Congress had frequently not hesitated to set aside Gandhi's opinion, and on this occasion too they would have done so if necessary. Rajagopalachari was for such a step. He believed that the Congress should accept office without even examining the details of the Declaration. Jawaharlal was away in Allahabad for the wedding of his daughter

1 See Jawaharlal to Mahadeva Desai, 9 December 1939, *A Bunch of Old Letters*, pp. 402-03.

2 Note by L. G. Pinnell, acting P.S.V., of conversation with F. F. Turnbull, an official who accompanied Cripps, on 23 March 1942, Linlithgow papers, vol. 141, diary of the Cripps Mission.

3 Cripps's account of interview with Jinnah, 25 March 1942, *Transfer of Power*, vol. 1, p. 480.

4 The phrase has gone down into history as 'a post-dated cheque on a crashing bank'; but it is now known that the second part, 'on a crashing bank', was the addition of an enterprising journalist. See J. Hennessy's letter in *The Spectator*, 11 October 1969.

on 26 March; but Azad, speaking for the Congress, emphasized the importance of effective control of defence by Indian representatives. He stated that this was far more important than the provision for non-accession of provinces.[1] It was therefore clear that, however disappointed the Congress might have been with the long-term proposals and whatever Gandhi might think, its attention was concentrated on the need to mobilize the forces of the Indian people to meet the immediate crisis.

However, as Rajagopalachari told Cripps,[2] all depended on Jawaharlal. The latter was anxious to collaborate in the defence of India and if he were satisfied that the Declaration enabled this, Gandhi could not have pressed his objection. So, on the eve of meeting Jawaharlal, Cripps secured Churchill's approval for rewording the paragraph on defence arrangements, and it was now affirmed that the task of organizing the defence of India must be the responsibility of the Government of India with the co-operation of the peoples of India. However, when he met Cripps Jawaharlal made no commitment, and Cripps concluded that Jawaharlal was willing to accept the Declaration but was beaten by Gandhi who was prepared to use any means to thwart the organization of India for war.

This was a total misreading of the situation. Repeatedly in the years since the outbreak of war, the Congress had, despite Gandhi, offered its co-operation in defence. The very fact that discussions with Cripps were continued even after Gandhi had made his attitude clear establishes beyond doubt the *bona fides* of the Congress. Indeed Gandhi left Delhi on 4 April in an almost sulky mood.[3] The Congress would have reached a settlement with Cripps if the arrangements for defence had been satisfactory. But the Viceroy stepped in, and toned down the co-operation in the military effort to mean merely the designation of an Indian to some office connected with the defence responsibilities of the Government of India without in any way impinging upon the functions and duties of the Commander-in-Chief.[4] This was obviously inadequate and Cripps concluded that his mission had failed. As a final effort he suggested that Azad and Jawaharlal should meet the Commander-in-Chief, Wavell.[5] The Congress had already reached a decision rejecting the proposals not merely because of the objectionable nature of the long-term arrangements but for the failure to transfer responsibility for defence, to which the Working Committee attached the greatest importance; but Azad agreed that he and Jawaharlal would meet Wavell and the Congress refrained from publishing its resolution.

[1] Cripps's account of interviews with Azad, 25 and 28 March 1942, *Transfer of Power*, vol. 1, pp. 479 and 514.

[2] Cripps's account of interview with Rajagopalachari, 28 March 1942, *Transfer of Power*, vol. 1, p. 512.

[3] Cf. his statement at a press conference before leaving Delhi: 'I must now live my message of non-violence. What is the use of my speaking when I cannot enforce my message in my own little way?' Quoted by B. Shiva Rao, 'India, 1935-47', in *The Partition of India*, p. 432.

[4] Cripps to Azad, 30 March 1942, *Transfer of Power*, vol. 1, p. 563.

[5] Idem, 1 April 1942, *Transfer of Power*, vol. 1, p. 598.

On this basis, the talks continued. The War Cabinet was not in favour of associating a Congressman with defence responsibilities, but a more precise interpretation of the association of an Indian with defence could be considered if the Congress desired it and the Viceroy could select 'some suitable Indian' — presumably a loyalist.[1] Cripps, eager for an agreement and now realizing that if he could satisfy Jawaharlal, Azad and Rajagopalachari on defence the opposition of Gandhi would not prevail, sought to interpret the Declaration to meet the requirements of the Congress. He himself preferred to transfer the defence ministry to an Indian, subject to a written convention that nothing would be done contrary to British policy; but knowing the opposition this would arouse in Delhi and London, he suggested the transfer to an Indian of such functions of the defence ministry as the Commander-in-Chief considered could be handed over safely and practically. A further safeguard was that 'under the new arrangement whereby the Executive Council will approximate to a Cabinet' all important matters would be decided by the Council as a whole and not by any individual member.[2] It is clear from this letter that Cripps was thinking in terms of cabinet government in India as generally understood. He had also obviously spoken in these terms to Indian leaders. There is no reason to doubt Azad's statement that at the very first interview Cripps had talked of a National Government functioning as a Cabinet, and the Viceroy's position becoming analogous to that of the King of England[3] — a statement which Cripps never contradicted. In fact, at his first press conference on 20 March, he had recognized that the Executive Council could be turned into a Cabinet;[4] and on 4 April Azad wrote to Cripps that 'the effectual control of the defence of India should rest with the Indian National Government'[5] — the first time that the phrase was used in the correspondence. Linlithgow now saw another opportunity to intervene. He secured authority to write direct to the British Government on these matters, and made sure that Wavell would stand firm.[6] Wavell claimed to be working out details on the lines of Cripps's proposal.[7] There is nothing in the published British documents to show what took place at Wavell's interview with Jawaharlal and Azad, and the Congress leaders also refrained from talking about it. But in fact it was a disaster.

When tea was cleared away, Wavell asked the Indian leaders to open proceedings, and Pandit Nehru spoke for some time. Briefly he wanted the

[1] Minute of War Cabinet discussion and Churchill's draft telegram to Cripps, 2 April 1942, *Transfer of Power*, vol. 1, pp. 612-14.

[2] Cripps to Churchill, 4 April 1942, *Transfer of Power*, vol. 1, pp. 636-9.

[3] Azad to Cripps, 11 April 1942, *Transfer of Power*, vol. 1, pp. 743-5.

[4] *Transfer of Power*, vol. 1, p. 547.

[5] Azad to Cripps, 4 April 1942, *Transfer of Power*, vol. 1, p. 640.

[6] Viceroy's telegram to Amery and Amery's reply 2 April, and note of Viceroy's Secretary, 3 April 1942, *Transfer of Power*, vol. 1, pp. 614-15 and 623.

[7] Telegram to Churchill, 6 April 1942, *Transfer of Power*, vol. 1, p. 655.

Defence Member of Council to be an Indian in place of the Commander-in-Chief, who would become an executive adviser. He was asking for hundred per cent on Defence. When he had finished I imagined that some discussions, and, perhaps, bargaining would take place; Wavell perhaps offering something, Nehru conceding something until some sort of compromise might be reached to form the basis of further discussions at a higher level. How far Wavell would go I did not know. To my intense astonishment Wavell said, 'If that is your case there is nothing more to be said.' There was dead silence. After a pause Wavell stood up and the Indian leaders rose to take their leave. [1]

The Cripps mission was by now beyond redemption, and the Congress had nothing to do with its failure. Cripps had got out of his depth, and Churchill, Amery, Linlithgow and Wavell made sure that he could not scramble back to land. The War Cabinet informed him that the character of the Viceroy's Council could not be changed, and Cripps was obliged to agree with Linlithgow and Wavell that nothing more would be done but transfer some non-essential functions of the Commander-in-Chief to an Indian Member. [2] But, in his letter to the Congress enumerating the nondescript defence matters which would be transferred to an Indian, he used the phrase 'National Government'. [3] Considering that he knew by now that the Cabinet in London had rejected any such change, one can only conclude that he hoped that once the Congress came in without insisting on its understanding of what a National Government meant, he could use his authority in Britain to permit the Executive Council to function as a Cabinet and that he could even, if need be, secure the replacement of the Viceroy. The standing of Cripps at this time in Britain was high; he was regarded almost as the alternative Prime Minister. With an Indian settlement under his belt, he could have overborne any resistance to its working. He wanted such a settlement for its own sake, for India was always dear to him. India was his second country, and even on his death-bed his thoughts were of her. [4] Here was an occasion when his conscience and his career were not at war. [5] But there was naïvety in his arrogance and a streak of innocence in his brilliance; and this enabled his adversaries to outmanoeuvre him.

The final agony was drawn out by the eagerness of the Congress to find some way of reaching a settlement and the arrival of Louis Johnson, Roosevelt's personal representative in India. Johnson, apparently with Cripps's

---

[1] General G. N. Molesworth, *Curfew on Olympus* (London, 1965), p. 220.

[2] Linlithgow to Amery, Amery memorandum, minute of India Committee, Cripps to Churchill and Amery to Cripps, all of 6 April, *Transfer of Power,* vol. 1, pp. 653-63.

[3] Cripps to Azad, 7 April 1942, *Transfer of Power,* vol. 1 p. 683.

[4] Dame Isobel Cripps to the author, 2 December 1969.

[5] 'The trouble is, his chest is a cage in which two squirrels are at war, his conscience and his career.' Churchill to Stalin on Cripps, cited in Lord Moran, *Winston Churchill : The Struggle for Survival* (London, 1966), p. 74.

approval, asked Roosevelt to intercede with Churchill and, on Roosevelt declining to do so, himself began to mediate.[1] A defence formula was drawn up dividing the functions of the Indian Member and the Commander-in-Chief. Wavell first refused even to consider any such formula 'because he is tired, discouraged and depressed and hates and distrusts Nehru'.[2] Later, Wavell and Linlithgow agreed to a demarcation which gave the Commander-in-Chief residuary powers. At the suggestion of Jawaharlal, Johnson and Cripps revised the formula to leave the residuary powers with the Indian Member and authorizing the British Government and not the Viceroy to allot any new function or settle any dispute regarding the allotment.[3] This approach recognized that the National Government would be responsible for the entire government of the country including its defence but, in view of the war, would delegate full control of military operations to the Commander-in-Chief. Linlithgow objected to the Congress being shown by an American any formula of which he was unaware, and regarded arbitration by the British Government as a serious invasion of his own powers.[4] Cripps's justification was that the situation was getting hot and something had to be done; and Johnson thought that with these minor amendments the Congress would settle. In fact, the Working Committee asked for illustrative lists of the functions of the Defence Minister and the Commander-in-Chief and, to avoid delay, authorized Azad and Jawaharlal to discuss these matters with Cripps.[5] There was now general expectation of a settlement.[6] Jawaharlal himself said later that he at this time estimated the chances of success at 75 per cent.[7]

Had Churchill and the War Cabinet backed Cripps, the Viceroy's tantrums could have been ignored. But the Cabinet, fortified by Hopkins's virtual disowning of Johnson and assurance to Churchill that Roosevelt would not interfere,[8] directed Cripps to bring the whole matter back to its Declaration with only agreed amplifications and wanted a precise definition of the term 'National Government'.[9] They had no intention, as suggested by Cripps in one of his letters to Azad, of transferring the Home Department to Indian hands. When Cripps told officials in Delhi soon after his arrival that the Cabinet had quite made up its mind that India should have de facto Dominion Status and complete Indianization of the Executive Council except for defence,[10] he was guilty either of misunderstanding or, what was more likely,

---

[1] Johnson to State Department, 4 April, State Department to Johnson, 5 April and Johnson to Roosevelt, 7 April 1942, Foreign Relations of the U.S. 1942, vol. 1, pp. 626-9.

[2] Johnson to State Department, 9 April 1942, ibid,, p. 630.

[3] Ibid. For texts of formulae, see Transfer of Power, vol. 1, pp. 699-700.

[4] Note by the Viceroy, 8 April 1942, Transfer of Power, vol. 1, pp. 694-6.

[5] See Jawaharlal's note, AICC File G. 26 (Part I) of 1942.

[6] The Hindustan Times, 9 April 1942.

[7] Press Conference 12 April, National Herald, 13 April 1942.

[8] R. E. Sherwood, Roosevelt and Hopkins (New York, 1950), vol. 2, p. 102.

[9] Telegram, 9 April, Transfer of Power, vol. 1, pp. 707-08.

[10] H. V. Hodson, The Great Divide (London, 1969), p. 103.

of self-deception. His threat to hand the matter over if he were not trusted was sharply repelled by Churchill, and Linlithgow was directly informed that there was no question of any convention limiting in any way his powers under the existing constitution.[1]

The luckless Cripps now quibbled. He drew a distinction between national government and cabinet government, assuring the War Cabinet that he had throughout emphasized that the existing legal and constitutional position must remain unchanged, and described a National Government loosely as one 'mainly composed of representative Indians together with Viceroy and Commander-in-Chief'.[2] On the other hand, he informed the Congress that the Viceroy would doubtless do all he could by means of appropriate conventions. With a co-operative Viceroy this might have worked. Indeed, Jawaharlal thought that if Linlithgow had talked to the Congress leaders and discussed with them how the Executive Council worked, a settlement might have been reached.[3] But Linlithgow had no desire to see Cripps succeed.

In despair, Cripps appealed to Jawaharlal, as an old friend, to save him:

Personal and private

My dear Jawaharlal,

Let me make a final appeal to you, upon whom rests the great burden of decision — a decision so far-reaching in its bearing upon the future relations of our two peoples that its magnitude is indeed portentous.

We can and must carry our people through to friendship and co-operation — I in my sphere, you in yours.

The chance which now offers cannot recur. Other ways may come if this fails but never so good a chance to cement the friendship of our people.

Leadership — the sort of leadership you have — can alone accomplish the result. It is the moment for the supreme courage of a great leader to face all the risks and difficulties — and I know they are there — to drive through to the desired end.

I know your qualities and your capacity and I beg you to make use of them now.

Yours always
affectionately,

STAFFORD[4]

[1] Cripps to War Cabinet, War Cabinet to Viceroy and Churchill to Cripps, all of 10 April, *Transfer of Power*, vol. 1, pp. 717, 720 and 721.

[2] To War Cabinet, 10 April 1942, *Transfer of Power*, vol. 1, p. 716.

[3] Report of Sir E. Villiers of conversation with Jawaharlal, 5 July 1942, *Transfer of Power*, vol. 2 (H.M.S.O., 1971), p. 690.

[4] *A Bunch of Old Letters*, p. 468.

But Jawaharlal's hands were bound — not by Gandhi or his colleagues in the Working Committee but by Cripps's own shifts of position. He told Cripps that there were limits beyond which he could not carry the Congress and the Congress could not carry the country; but Cripps would not believe him.[1]

TRAPEZE TRAGEDY ?   —*Copyright*

Comment by Shankar, the cartoonist, on the Cripps Mission

At this stage, a weaker man would have resigned. It is no discredit to Cripps that he did not. He was a minister in a war-time government when his country was in extreme crisis. Burma and the Andaman Islands were lost; the Indian Ocean was in enemy hands; the loss of the Calcutta area and the Orissa coast was probable; and a Japanese landing in south India as part of a pincer operation against Ceylon could not be ruled out. In such a context, Cripps's attitude was in line with that of another great British socialist, Robert Blatchford: 'When England is at war, I'm English. I have no politics and no party. I am English.'[2] So patriotic motives doubtless led Cripps to stick to his post and to retract his commitments. He informed Johnson with embarrassment that he had to revert to the text of the original Declaration; and Jawaharlal and Azad were amazed, at their final interview with Cripps on 9 April, to find that all the searching for new formulae had been a waste of time and the phrase 'National

[1] Jawaharlal to Evelyn Wood, 5 June 1942.
[2] Quoted in B. Semmel, *Imperialism and Social Reform* (London, 1960), p. 226.

Government 'now meant nothing at all. It was to be neither a free nor a cabinet government.[1] Ignoring all his earlier suggestions of a National Government and constitutional conventions, Cripps now stated that there could be no joint responsibility or any assurances that the Viceroy would not exercise his powers of intervention or veto. All that he now proposed was a slight variation of the offer of August 1940. Some popular representatives could be added to the Executive Council, and if its members resented the Viceroy's attitude, it was always open to them to resign

The failure of the Cripps mission is not surprising. Both the War Cabinet (barring Attlee) and Linlithgow's Government had no wish to see it succeed. Cripps's method of negotiation was also not suited to this situation. He was a lawyer who stated his case powerfully and expected it to prevail. On this occasion, having handed over the Declaration, he could only urge the Congress to accept it. Both his technique and his brief left him no room for manoeuvre. His friends in the Congress were alienated.

> I was surprised at his woodenness and insensitiveness, in spite of his public smiles. He was all the time the formal representative of the War Cabinet, in fact he was the War Cabinet speaking to us with a 'take it or leave it' attitude. Always he seemed to impress upon us that he knew the Indian problem in and out and he had found the only solution for it. Anyone who did not agree with it was to say the least of it utterly misguided. [2]

On the other hand, his tendency to slur over differences in his anxiety to win over the Congress was exploited by his antagonists. What is clear is that the Working Committee, despite the attitude of Gandhi and its own dislike of the provisions for India's future, took the stand that it was the present that counted and was willing to co-operate in defence if given the full opportunity. But Cripps, intensely disappointed at this setback to his hopes and his career, most unfairly made the Congress the scapegoat; and it is for this that he has to be severely faulted. He accused the Congress of suggesting a change in the constitution for the first time nearly three weeks after it had received the proposals and described the working by a convention of a nominated cabinet as a constitutional government as 'an absolute dictatorship of a majority'. This was the first suggestion of any differences between the Congress and the League on this matter; for throughout the discussions there was no hint by any of the parties of any difficulty on this issue. For Cripps to allege at the end that, with deep communal divisions, 'an irresponsible majority government' would be rejected by all minorities and was not possible,[3] was incredible and mischievous.

[1] Johnson to State Department, 11 April 1942, op. cit., p. 631; Azad to Cripps, 10 April 1942, *Transfer of Power*, vol. 1, pp. 726-30.

[2] Jawaharlal to Evelyn Wood, 5 June 1942.

[3] Cripps to Azad, 10 April 1942, op. cit.

After his return from India, Cripps reported to the War Cabinet that Gandhi was determined to prevent an agreement at all costs not merely because of his devotion to non-violence but also because he feared loss of his leadership to Jawaharlal or some other supporter of the war effort. He had, therefore, in a two-hour telephone conversation from Wardha on the afternoon of 9 April, ordered the Congress leaders to break off negotiations, and Jawaharlal and Azad had come to Cripps that evening and chosen the question of a National Government as a better ground on which to do so than the defence question, which had been successfully settled.[1] Some sentences which Cripps drafted and later omitted from his broadcast to the United States on 27 July confirm how completely he had convinced himself that a fair offer had been rejected by an over-reaching Congress. Gandhi, he thought, was 'being led on by the shadow of his visions rather than by the substantial facts of the world situation', and was threatening the extremes of pressure not only against Great Britain but against the Indian minorities as well to win political power for his own party. As for the Congress, it was 'a religious party' representing not a political majority but a permanent religious and racial majority to which the minorities had no wish to be subjected.[2] 'Had Congress accepted,' Cripps wrote later to a Chinese friend,[3] 'which but for Mr. Gandhi they would have done, the Indian question would have been well on the way to settlement.' Thanks to Cripps, this interpretation has now become a part of conventional history.[4] It was this effort, so discordant with both his intellectual sharpness and his general character, to attribute petty motives to Gandhi and to prove the Congress, as Jawaharlal said, 'not only wrong but damnably wrong'[5] that poisoned for a long time Cripps's personal relations with Jawaharlal and, what was perhaps more important, made it more difficult for Jawaharlal in the coming months to prevent a direct collision between the Congress and the Government.

---

[1] Report to War Cabinet, 6 July 1942, *Transfer of Power,* vol. 2, p. 318.

[2] See the first draft of his broadcast in the Cripps papers, Nuffield College Library, File 1143.

[3] To Professor Tuan Sheng-chien, 19 February 1943, Cripps papers, File 690.

[4] For example, Roy Jenkins: 'Nehru, even Jinnah, were tempted. But Gandhi, who cared little about the threat of the new invaders, moved in and snatched the prospect of achievement away from Cripps.' *The Times,* 27 November 1972.

[5] Press Conference, 12 April, *National Herald,* 13 April 1942.

18

Collision Course

Denied the chance to form a representative government which could, in Jawaharlal's words, light a spark in millions of hearts and offer unbroken resistance to the Japanese, Jawaharlal set about the second-best task of unofficial organization for self-reliance. There was no prospect of further negotiations with the British. The debris of the Cripps mission stood in the way of both parties, and neither was prepared to make a fresh move. But Jawaharlal announced that the Congress would continue its policy of non-embarrassment to the British. War production should not be impeded. He was dissuaded by Azad from broadcasting over All-India Radio on these lines,[1] but he promised Johnson that he would proceed to Calcutta to secure the termination of industrial strikes. 'I shall have', reported Johnson,[2] 'his complete help; he is our hope here. I trust him.' On the other hand, if the Japanese invaded India they would be met not only with non-violent non-co-operation, but even, if necessary, with guerrilla warfare and a scorched-earth policy. Jawaharlal made these suggestions knowing that they did not meet with Gandhi's approval and that a large sector of nationalist opinion was so embittered by British attitudes that it was ready to stand aside if the Japanese moved into the country.

> Some people say Jawaharlal is a fool. He is unnecessarily antagonising the Japanese and the Germans. The Japanese will wreak vengeance on him when they come to this country. It is wiser for him to keep silent if he cannot actually speak well of the Japanese. I want to tell those who give me this advice that Jawaharlal is not the man who will keep quiet when he ought to speak. On the other hand, I can only reject such advice, which is essentially based on fear, with contempt.[3]

[1] Azad, op. cit., p. 58.
[2] Johnson to State Department, 11 April 1942, *Foreign Relations of the United States, 1942,* vol. 1, p. 631.
[3] Speech at Delhi, 7 April, *The Hindustan Times,* 8 April 1942.

In fact, he went further than merely demanding resistance to the Japanese, and declared that he would oppose even Subhas Bose (who had gone over to the Axis powers) and the Indian troops he had mustered, for this army was really no more than 'a dummy force under Japanese control'.[1]

Gandhi warned Jawaharlal that his attitude was likely to break up the Congress leadership. 'If your policy is accepted, then the Committee should not remain as it is today.'[2] He even forced Jawaharlal to withdraw his suggestion about guerrilla warfare and publicly exulted over it.[3] Unable to attend the Congress meetings at the end of the month, he sent a draft resolution and threatened to withdraw with his followers if his draft were not accepted. 'The time has come when everyone of us has to choose his own course.'[4] The failure of the Cripps mission had by itself restored the influence of Gandhi in the Congress command, and he was now convinced that the immediate step should be the withdrawal of the British from India. There was no purpose in even holding discussions with a Government which was willing to think in terms of a division of India. His draft resolution stated that Japan's quarrel was not with India but with the British Empire. Britain was incapable of defending India and should withdraw. India would then be able to defend herself against Japan or any other aggressor, but the first step of a free India would probably be to negotiate with Japan. The Japanese should be assured that India bore no enmity to Japan or any other nation. But if Japan attacked India and the British had not withdrawn, the Indian people should offer complete non-violent non-co-operation to the Japanese and not place any obstacles in the way of the British forces. However, a scorched-earth policy should not go beyond the destruction of war material.

This draft clearly moved away from the whole trend of Congress policy, since the beginning of the war, of sympathy with the Allies, and made the Indian people a passive partner of the Axis powers. His disgust with the Cripps Declaration blinded Gandhi to the grand design of Japanese imperialism. He assumed that the Axis powers would win the war and that a victorious Japan would make no demands on India. All this was too much for Jawaharlal and he made his opposition clear. Even a toned-down version of Gandhi's draft, produced by his followers, was unacceptable to Jawaharlal, who resisted not an odd detail or assertion but the whole attitude of defeatism and sympathy with Japan which underlay this resolution. His own draft asserted, in consistency with the earlier position of the Congress, that while India had no quarrel with the people of any country, she was opposed to Nazism and fascism as well as to imperialism. If India were free she might have kept out of the war but her sym-

---

[1] Press Conference at Delhi, 12 April, *National Herald*, 13 April 1942.

[2] Gandhi to Jawaharlal, 15 April 1942, *A Bunch of Old Letters*, pp. 470-71.

[3] Jawaharlal's speech at Calcutta, 19 April, *The Hindustan Times*, 21 April 1942; Gandhi in *Harijan*, 26 April 1942.

[4] Gandhi to Jawaharlal, 24 April, *A Bunch of Old Letters*, p. 474.

pathies would have been with the victims of aggression. Britain should abandon her hold on India, but the Congress repudiated the idea that freedom could come to India through foreign interference or invasion. Any attack on India should be resisted by non-violent non-co-operation, for the British had prevented the organization of national defence by the people in any other way. 'If he [the Japanese enemy] wishes to take possession of our houses and our fields we will refuse to give them up even if we have to die in the effort.' A scorched-earth policy was not affirmed, but was implicit in the intention to fight to the last.

There was a majority of 11 to 6 in the Working Committee for the revised Gandhi draft; but a few hours later, with the illogicality that lies at the heart of most democratic bodies, the Committee unanimously accepted Jawaharlal's draft.[1] So Jawaharlal had had his way. One can only assume that he had persuaded his colleagues to give one more chance to his policy of support to the Allies. Nothing could be expected directly from the British; but Jawaharlal placed his faith in the United States and China. In February 1942, Roosevelt had sent Jawaharlal a friendly message through Edgar Snow and invited Jawaharlal to write to him.[2] When the negotiations with Cripps broke down, Jawaharlal wrote directly to Roosevelt in the hope of involving him in the Indian problem, and stated that there could be no further talks with the British 'for the present'[3] — thus hinting that the door was not completely closed. Jawaharlal's hand, cabled Johnson to Roosevelt on the eve of the Congress meetings,[4] would be immensely strengthened if Britain, China and the United States could issue a joint statement on Pacific war aims assuring freedom and self-determination to India and resolving to defend India at all costs. Two days later, Madame Chiang forwarded to the President Jawaharlal's views on the importance for defence of real identity between the state and the people.[5] After the Working Committee had accepted Jawaharlal's draft, Johnson drew up one more formula, by which the Viceroy would have to do his utmost to persuade his Council before exercising his veto, and pleaded with his Government to secure its acceptance by the British.[6]

Roosevelt, however, refused to intervene.[7] Public opinion in the United States was, on the whole, satisfied that the British Government had done all they could to secure Indian support for the war effort, and that it was Indian

---

[1] For the various drafts and the discussions in the Working Committee, see *transfer of Power*, vol. 2, pp. 66-70 and 158-64.

[2] 'When you get there and see Nehru, say hallo for me. I wish you would ask Nehru to write me a letter and tell me exactly what he wants me to do for India. You can send it through our diplomatic pouch!' E. Snow, *Journey to the Beginning* (London, 1959), p. 257.

[3] 12 April 1942, *A Bunch of Old Letters*, pp. 469-70.

[4] *Foreign Relations of the United States 1942*, vol. 1, pp. 638-9.

[5] Ibid., vol. 1, p. 639.

[6] Ibid., vol. 1, pp. 649-50.

[7] Cable to Johnson, 8 May 1942, ibid., vol. 1, p. 650.

politicians who were intransigent.[1] Fortified by this attitude, the Government of India became even more aggressive. A ban was placed on the publication by newspapers of the Congress resolutions on the summary evacuation of areas, instances of misconduct of soldiers and the panicky and discriminatory behaviour of officials in Burma and some parts of India. These developments strengthened Gandhi's position, and he could with much justice contend, in the sharp and prolonged private debate that now went on between him and Jawaharlal, that the latter's support for the Allies evoked no effective response in any quarter and served only to expose the Indian people to the assaults of the British. With war lapping India's shores and the British administration both incompetent to defend India and preferring to lose India rather than mobilize popular support, the case for demanding British withdrawal became vastly stronger. When Jawaharlal returned after a fortnight in the mountains, he found the situation had so deteriorated that it would be difficult to abide by the policy of subordinating anti-British sentiment to the general policy of support to the Allies and resistance to the Japanese. Gandhi's programme reflected widespread Indian bitterness against the British; and the fact that Gandhi took this line was in itself an objective factor in the situation which could not be ignored. As even the Viceroy recognized, 'Gandhi is the biggest thing in India.'[2] With the United States declining to interest herself directly in Indian affairs, China helpless and the British mounting a new offensive against not the Japanese enemy but Indian nationalism, Jawaharlal had only his world outlook to justify the resolution which he had prevailed upon the Working Committee to accept. His supporters were those whom he would rather have done without — the Communists, now a semi-loyalist party supporting a 'people's war', and Rajagopalachari, strengthening the Muslim League by his willingness to accept the principle of Pakistan and weakening the Congress by seeking to form a provincial government in Madras.

So, when Jawaharlal met Gandhi at the end of May, he was in no position to withstand a policy for which he had no enthusiasm. It was, of course, still important to him not to harm the cause of Russia, China and the United States, and he argued for this, as Gandhi later told the Viceroy, with 'a passion which I have no words to describe'.[3] But he could invoke no argument more substantial than passion. Once Gandhi abandoned his pro-Japanese stance and conceded that after the British administration was withdrawn the Allied armies could remain in India and the first act of a national government should be the conclusion of a defence treaty with the Allies, there was no reason for Jawaharlal not

---

[1] One could say that as regards American opinion Cripps could not have done better.' S. K. Ratcliffe from New York to Kingsley Martin, 4 April 1942, Kingsley Martin papers; M. S. Venkatramani and B. K. Shrivastava, 'The United States and the Cripps Mission', *India Quarterly,* July-September 1963, pp. 258-9.

[2] Author's note in L. Fischer, *A Week with Gandhi* (London, 1943).

[3] Letter of 14 August 1942, *Transfer of Power,* vol. 2, p. 705.

to acquiesce in Gandhi's policy. Even from the international viewpoint, help to China and advancement of the Allied cause, a total withdrawal of British power was necessary, for only then could the Indian people shake off their passivity and be totally involved in the war effort. As it was, there was too much indifference to British defeats to enable whole-hearted resistance to Japanese invasion if it came; nor could British authority be relied upon to push back the aggressor on its own. It was known that plans had been made for retreating from Bengal and Madras. A British withdrawal from India before the Japanese came was the only way to rouse the Indian people and prevent India going the way of Burma. Jawaharlal, more than most Congressmen, was guided by his antipathy to Nazi Germany, Japan and fascism, and sympathy for Russia and China; but even his attitude was, in the ultimate analysis, dictated by a strong sense of India's survival.

> It is a hateful notion that after five years of war, China should be defeated; it is a hateful notion that Russia, which represents certain human values, which means a great deal to human civilization, should be defeated. But, ultimately, naturally I have to judge every question from the Indian view-point. If India perishes, I must say — selfishly, if you like to call it — it does not do me any good if other nations survive.[1]

British presence implied not so much serious defence against the Japanese as the building up of forces working for the division of India. Jawaharlal was reluctantly dragged to the conclusion that the ending of British rule was the primary issue. If the Congress continued its policy of doing nothing to embarrass the British, the popular will against the Government would be broken and that would break the popular will to resistance of the Japanese. On the other hand, if a spirit of resistance was built up against the British, that could be turned against the Japanese. 'Personally', he told the Congress committee of his province, 'I am so sick of slavery that I am even prepared to take the risk of anarchy.'[2] Gandhi could not have phrased it better.

Gandhi, as usual, had no clear ideas as to the way in which the British could be induced to quit India. Jawaharlal was against a mass civil disobedience movement, but Gandhi thought in terms of such direct action after the public mind had been prepared for it and in such a manner as not to aid the Japanese. 'If you won't join', Gandhi is reported to have told Jawaharlal, 'I'll do it without you.' It was also possible that out of local opposition in various places to official harassments, a major conflict might take shape. But he had no wish to act precipitately and hoped for an interview with the Viceroy before taking any

[1] Press conference, 12 April, *National Herald*, 13 April 1942.
[2] *National Herald*, 2 June 1942.

firm decisions.[1] In the meantime, Gandhi assured Chiang Kai-shek,[2] in a letter drafted by Jawaharlal, that the plan to secure British withdrawal was intended to enable India to look after herself and to help China to the best of her ability. Thanks to Jawaharlal, 'whose love of China is only excelled, if at all, by his love of his country', the Indian people were deeply committed to the Chinese cause, and an independent India would immediately sign an alliance with the Allies. A copy of this letter was forwarded by Jawaharlal to the United States Government. He added:

> It has been my earnest desire that India should cooperate to the fullest extent with China and America. Asia, or any other large part of the world, dominated by fascism or nazism is an intolerable thought to me, and I should like India to do her utmost to combat this. But the blindness and obstinacy of the British Government have created a situation of extreme gravity in India and I do not see wisdom dawning upon them in the near future. It would appear that they are determined to bring about a conflict with the Congress and nationalist elements in India. Already many of my closest colleagues have been arrested and this process is continuing. It is possible that I might be arrested. It is possible also that the Congress might be temporarily crushed by severe repression. But the Indian people are not going to be coerced, much less won over, by these methods, and the price to be paid by all concerned will be a heavy one. I have endeavoured with all my strength to avoid this conflict and this price. But the future appears to be dark.[3]

However, influenced probably by a message from Chiang Kai-shek,[4] who had prevented the publication of Gandhi's letter to him and now requested the Congress to refrain from drastic action in view of the Allied reverses in Libya, the Working Committee adopted a resolution which surprised the Government by its mildness. The Congress pleaded with the British to relinquish their political power because India's freedom was essential not only to India but to the security of the world. Resistance to aggression could only be built up in India if her people felt the glow of freedom. If such a withdrawal took place with goodwill, a stable provisional government could be established which would permit the stationing of Allied armies in India and co-operate with these powers in resisting aggression. The Congress wished to take no hasty step or

[1] Jawaharlal to Louis Johnson, 4 June 1942, *Foreign Relations of the United States 1942*, vol. 1, pp. 667-9; Fischer, *A Week with Gandhi*, pp. 78-9, 105 and 109-10; Jawaharlal's confidential note on talks with Gandhi, June 1942.
[2] 14 June 1942, *Transfer of Power*, vol. 2, p. 346.
[3] To Lampton Berry of the U.S. Mission in Delhi, 14 June 1942.
[4] S. H. Shen, Chinese Consul in Delhi, to Jawaharlal, 8 July 1942.

embarrass the Allies in any way; but some risks had to be taken to avoid far greater risks, and if Britain rejected this appeal, the Congress would be reluctantly compelled to resort to a non-violent struggle under Gandhi's leadership. Obviously to give time to the British Government to respond, the AICC was convened three weeks later, on 7 August 1942, to take a final decision.

Both Gandhi and Jawaharlal stated publicly that there was no room left for further discussion. The Cripps proposals were outdated, and the British should recognize India's independence and transfer complete power. The Viceroy and some senior officials would have to go, but the provisional Indian government would co-operate with the Allies and give the Commander-in-Chief full discretion in military strategy and dispositions.[1] But, in contrast to the public postures, in private the Congress leaders still hoped for intervention by Roosevelt. Jawaharlal's remark in his letter of 12 April to the President, that there would be no negotiations with the British 'for the present', still held the field; and there seems no doubt that if Roosevelt had requested the Congress to renew talks with the British they would have done so. Jawaharlal informed a Chinese diplomat that he would accept the promise of Dominion Status on condition of a Chinese-American guarantee.[2] Maulana Azad, the president of the party, proposed discussions as to the arrangements for the duration of the war with Roosevelt as arbiter, provided the Allies as a whole recognized India's right to independence.[3] This was very different to the proclaimed inflexibility of Gandhi and Jawaharlal, and was a virtual offer to renew talks on the basis of those with Cripps. Gandhi was at this time bitter with Azad,[4] presumably for thinking on these lines, and wanted him to be removed from the presidency; but if Azad's offer had led to anything, Jawaharlal would certainly, despite Gandhi, have followed it up.[5] So hopeful was the United States mission in Delhi that, in Johnson's absence, the officer in charge drafted a statement for Roosevelt's approval guaranteeing India's independence 'without prejudice to the principal elements in the national life of the country' and offering to draw up an arrangement for an interim Government.[6] But nothing came of this, and so the Congress had, in Jawaharlal's phrase, to plunge deliberately into the stormy ocean. The British Empire was a castle of cards, but its rulers would rather be knocked down, as in Burma, than allow their peoples to fight for their own freedom as well as that of others. India had no wish to be kicked about by either of the imperialist powers, Britain and Japan, and to be able to deal effectively with the

[1]Report of Jawaharlal's interviews with Berry, 16 and 18 July 1942, *Foreign Relations of the United States 1942*, vol. I, pp. 685-9.

[2]T. V. Soong's conversation in State Department, reported by Sir R. Campbell to Foreign Office, 12 August 1942, *Transfer of Power*, vol. 2, p. 674.

[3]Report of the U.S. Mission in Delhi, 21 July 1942. *Foreign Relations of the United States 1942*, vol. 1, p. 690.

[4]Gandhi to Jawaharlal, 13 July 1942.

[5]See his letter to Sampurnanand, 28 July 1942, Sampurnanand papers.

[6]21 July 1942, *Foreign Relations of the United States 1942*, vol. 1, pp. 690-94.

latter one had to begin by getting rid of the former.[1] At Bombay the AICC again appealed to Britain and the United Nations to end British rule in India and promised explicitly to throw all the resources of a free India into the war. This freedom should be the prelude to the freedom of all other dependent peoples, and countries occupied by Japan should not be restored to their former masters. Gandhi was authorized to start a non-violent mass struggle on the widest possible scale, a fight to the finish, but not immediately; and he announced that he would make every effort to see the Viceroy.

The War Cabinet had, even in June, authorized the Viceroy to take quick and decisive action whenever it seemed necessary;[2] and in July Amery wanted to arrest Gandhi and the Working Committee as soon as its resolution had been passed.[3] However, the Government of India decided that the best moment to strike would be immediately after the AICC had ratified the resolution.[4] The Congress should then be decapitated by the arrest of its leaders and denial to them of access to their followers. The Cabinet wished Gandhi to be deported to Aden and the Working Committee to Nyasaland, and a warship stood by at Bombay for this purpose. But in India wiser counsel prevailed. Deportation would be an unnecessary provocation of Indian opinion, and it would be sufficient to intern Gandhi at the Aga Khan's Palace in Poona, and the Working Committee in Ahmadnagar fort. This place had been used previously for State prisoners, was approachable only by a drawbridge and was surrounded by a moat.

At 5 a.m. on 9 August, the police rounded up the leaders of the Congress in their homes. A special train took them first to a station outside Poona where Gandhi and his entourage were asked to alight. Just when the Working Committee had agreed that the British knew how to do this sort of thing well,[5] there was a hitch. At Poona itself, where the train stopped contrary to schedule because a signal was against it, the crowd on the platform recognized Jawaharlal and ran towards him. When the police tried to stop them with a lathi-charge, Jawaharlal, 'with remarkable agility', jumped through the corridor window on to the platform. At least four policemen were required to overpower him and get him back into the train. When they reached Ahmadnagar, the police officer apologized for what had happened and hoped that, as he had only been carrying out orders, Jawaharlal bore him no personal animosity. Jawaharlal assured him that he did not, but was still very angry over the lathi-charge.[6]

This was Jawaharlal's longest term in prison, for 1,040 days or over 34 months, from 9 August 1942 to 15 June 1945. The twelve members lived together till March 1945, when the Working Committee was split up and the

[1] Speech at Bombay, 5 August, *The Hindustan Times*, 6 August 1942.

[2] Discussion in War Cabinet, 15 June 1942, *Transfer of Power*, vol. 2, p. 208.

[3] Amery to Churchill, 13 July 1942, ibid., vol. 2, p. 376.

[4] Telegram to Secretary of State, 16 July 1942, ibid., vol. 2, pp. 394-5.

[5] Mira Behn, *The Spirit's Pilgrimage* (London, 1960), p. 240.

[6] Report of F.E. Sharp, Dy. I. G. of Police, Bombay, 10 August 1942, Home Dept. Pol. (I) File 3/21/42, vol. 42.

members sent to jails in their own provinces. Jawaharlal, with Pant and Narendra Deva, was moved to Naini, then to Bareilly and then again to Almora. For the first few days after their arrest, Gandhi and the Working Committee were cut off from any form of communication with the outside world. No letters, newspapers or interviews were permitted, and the public did not even know where these leaders had been interned. This policy was later relaxed to the extent of allowing newspapers and two letters to, and four letters from, members of their families per week on strictly personal matters. This latter concession did not benefit Jawaharlal much, at the start, because his daughter and sister Vijayalakshmi were both in U.P. prisons, and the U.P. Government, out of step with the central government for months, refused either to deliver letters from Jawaharlal which had been cleared by the Government of India or to forward letters which Jawaharlal was entitled to receive.[1] Later, the prisoners were allowed books, but, for fear that uncensored information would reach them, these books were scanned for invisible writing.[2] After Jawaharlal and his colleagues had been for over two years in jail, in October 1944 the Government considered allowing interviews, but the prisoners of Ahmadnagar firmly refused them. After so many months of isolation, no interview for a few minutes could be satisfactory; and there was also a question of pride involved.

> I do not fancy being treated like a wild beast in a cage with occasional rope allowed so that I can move a few feet if I behave myself. I dislike being the plaything of others and to have my movements and my emotional life regulated by others. Where force prevents me from acting as I wish, I have to accept it, but I prefer to retain such freedom of mind and action as I possess. If it has been thought fit and proper to prevent us from seeing even those one cares for during these 2¼ years or so, well and good; anyway perforce I had to adapt myself to it. But I see no reason why I should adapt myself to all the new vagaries of those who keep us in prison or stabilize myself in new positions.[3]

So they met no one except the prison officials.

> The other day, reading some of the old letters of Charles Lamb . . . I came across a couple of lines. We have yet the sight, he said:

> > Of Sun and Moon and star, throughout the year, and man and woman.

[1] Home Department Pol. (I) File 3/21/42, vol. 42.

[2] See Under Secretary, Home Dept. Govt. of India to Additional Home Secretary, Bombay Govt., 29/30 September 1943, Home Dept. Pol. 3/21/42 Pol. I 1942-3, vol. 2.

[3] To Vijayalakshmi Pandit, 23 October 1944.

Yes, I thought, we have yet the sight of the sun and the moon and stars, and yesterday was *sharad purnima*. In the early dawn, when I wake up, I see Jupiter peeping over the roof of a building. It is still dark then but it is the signal for getting up. In the evening Venus appears as the Evening Star. The night sky is slowly changing over and putting on its winter appearance. We have sight of all these and they never lost their freshness. But of the men we see the range is limited and I fear we grow less and less fresh to each other. And women? It struck me as an odd and arresting fact that for nearly 26 months — for 785 days to be exact — I had not seen a woman even from a distance. Previously it was not so for even in prison we had interviews occasionally. And I began to wonder — what are women like? How do they look — how do they talk and sit and walk?[1]

There was little to do or look forward to. Jawaharlal's diary entries abound with trivia:

11 January 1943	Felt unwell
30 January 1943	Sowed carnation seeds in box. New canvas shoes
12 April 1943	New canvas shoes
13 April 1943	Rain — rain — continuous rain! The monsoon
5 May 1944	The cat tragedy! Poor Chando hit inadvertently over head by cook — concussion of the brain. Hovering between life and death
14 May 1944	Cat Chando died in hospital
20 June 1944	New canvas shoes

Forced into close companionship, these Congress leaders, who had in common only dedication to a common cause and acceptance of Gandhi's leadership, frequently found themselves in heated discussion, and by the time of their release some were hardly on speaking terms. Isolation for so long a period, punctuated with reports of the deaths of those dear to them — Ranjit Pandit, Azad's wife — added to the normal rigours of imprisonment. To tone down these frictions and fraying of nerves, Jawaharlal organized a regular community life. Duties were allotted to each person and rotated every week. He himself did more than his share, supervising the cooking, preparing salads, nursing the sick, organizing badminton and volley-ball and taking charge of the gardening. To the latter in particular he devoted, especially in the early months, a great deal of time, for it gave him a certain psychological satisfaction by providing activity for his hands and body at a time when his mind had of necessity to lie fallow. 'Before you rise, he is in the garden — sowing, digging and planting and pruning, watering and weeding. In the hot sun with his hat on and in the

[1] To Krishna Hutheesing, 3 October 1944, K. N. Hutheesing, *Nehru's Letters to his Sister* (London, 1963), pp. 166-7. *Sharad purnima* is the night of the full moon in October.

pouring rain with his raincoat, he is here, there and elsewhere.'[1] Towards the end of their term Patel collected seeds from the flowers and Jawaharlal sorted them out and presented a box containing a packet of each to every prisoner.

Of those with him in Ahmadnagar, Jawaharlal was closest to Azad, Asaf Ali, Syed Mahmud and Narendra Deva; but even from these he kept his distance. With Mahmud he for some time shared a cell and nursed him when he was ill; but Jawaharlal was as startled as the rest when Mahmud secured his release by writing to the Viceroy disowning the Congress resolution. This no doubt drove Jawaharlal even more into himself; but with this inner solitude there came tranquillity. The dull routine of prison life became unimportant; the deprivations, though felt, were placed in perspective. When books and journals were allowed in, he had a fresh source of comfort, and on 13 April 1944 he took up again the writing of the book which he had begun at Dehra Dun jail in 1941. Less than five months later, on 7 September 1944, *The Discovery of India*, running into a thousand hand-written pages, was finished.

This is a great jumble of a book which bears the marks of haste and tension. It is repetitive, has many long quotations and, if Jawaharlal had had time to revise it on his release, would probably have been reduced to nearly half its length. There are some autobiographical chapters, written mostly in 1941. The account of Kamala's death is moving in its subdued yet intense sense of loss, but this section as a whole does not rise to the level of the *Autobiography*, if only because it is more impersonal, and weak in the attractively self-conscious nature of the earlier work. The chapters on the war years blend into a general, scathing account of British rule in India. The severe criticism is not so much unfair as uncharacteristic of Jawaharlal; but, as he acknowledged, he could not, for the time at least, take a detached view of British imperialism and was filled with repugnance for England.

> I have looked into my own mind from time to time and examined its almost involuntary reaction to events. I had always looked forward in the past to a visit to England, because I have many friends there and old memories draw me. But now I found that there was no such desire and the idea was distasteful. I wanted to keep as far away from England as possible, and I had no wish even to discuss India's problems with Englishmen. And then I remembered some friends and softened a little, and I told myself how wrong it was to judge a whole people in this way. I thought also of the terrible experiences that the English people had gone through in this war, of the continuous strain in which they had lived, of the loss of so many of their loved ones. All this helped to tone down my feelings, but that basic reaction remained.[2]

[1] B. P. Sitaramayya, *Feathers and Stones* (Bombay, 1946), pp. 392-3. Sitaramayya was one of the prisoners at Ahmednagar.

[2] *The Discovery of India*, p. 495.

However, the core of the book is a long survey of India's culture before the coming of the British. The contrast with the *Glimpses* is striking. Jawaharlal is no longer primarily interested in social and economic change, in action and great men, or in Marxist analysis of class struggles. 'I have grown more contemplative. There is perhaps a little more poise and equilibrium, some sense of detachment, a greater calmness of spirit.'[1] He had not sloughed off his Marxism but there was now in his thinking an appreciation of the Vedanta, its idealism and its ethics. India's culture in particular engrossed him. He was fascinated by its continuity and seeming vitality and staying power. There appeared to him to be an unbroken chain from Mohenjo-Daro, which political fortunes could not destroy, and the result was a mellowness and a gentleness of the Indian spirit, a desire and a capacity to live and let live, an absorption of every fresh intrusion of foreign elements to form a new synthesis, a unity and stability which could only be explained by India's 'depth of soul'. So, in an astonishingly narrow nationalist tradition, he put together a version of India's cultural history derived from secondary sources and studded with testimonials from European observers. It was not just the hurry and the atmosphere in which the book was written but the theme itself which led to woolly writing. All his ideas about race, for example, make little sense.[2] 'We are an old race, or rather an odd mixture of many races, and our racial memories go back to the dawn of history'[3] — just one of many meaningless sentences of which Jawaharlal himself would later have been ashamed.

Yet, if the book is lacking in analysis, elegance and clear thinking, it had a purpose. It sought to portray an emotional comprehension of Indian nationalism and to stress the necessity of revitalizing the Indian people. India's past could be so depicted as to draw lessons for its future. Its continuity could only be explained by the fact that while the form often remained, the inner content was always changing. However, these social forms, like caste, had a limit of expansion and the result was a growing, strangling rigidity. Social conservatism and poverty had been encouraged by alien rule and were the chief characteristics of contemporary India; but if India became free and was true to herself, there was no cause for despair. *The Discovery of India*, written in the dark years of Indian nationalism, carried not a precise, scientific argument but a buoyant message.

[1] Ibid., p. 24.
[2] See D. D. Kosambi's review in *Science and Society*, 1946, pp. 392-8.
[3] *The Discovery of India* p. 55.

19

Post-War Prelude

Though the leaders of the Congress were aware, thanks to a leakage from official sources,[1] that the Government planned to arrest them immediately upon the passage of the resolution in Bombay, they made no arrangements for the functioning of the Congress after they had been removed from the scene. Gandhi was thinking vaguely in terms of a one-day general strike as a first step, and it was suggested that to avoid weakening of the war effort any such *hartal* should not apply to government offices and factories;[2] but no decision was taken. It was almost as if the Working Committee wished to escape to prison and to avoid decision at what Jawaharlal described as 'the zero hour of the world'. Leaderless and unorganized, the sympathizers of the Congress rose in revolt in various parts of the country. The events of 1942 showed the depth of the national will. Communications, particularly in the United Provinces and Bihar, were cut and the war effort seriously impeded. The Government struck hard to crush this resistance. In August and September, 57½ battalions were employed in this activity, and there were killings in Bihar and eastern U.P. on a scale greater than even that in the Punjab in 1919.[3] In other parts of the country also there were instances of military and police savagery. The Whipping Act was revived and over 5,000 persons detained without trial. Even suspected sympathizing with the Congress was dealt with ruthlessly. Considered as the most serious threat to the *raj* since the revolt of 1858, it was handled with the same severity. Efforts were made to establish the responsibility of the Congress and, in particular, of Gandhi for these disturbances, and considerable publicity material along these lines was issued. In fact, nothing could be proved. Hallett thought there had been a preconcerted central plan and oral instructions, and the intelligence system had definitely failed in not finding out the Congress plan of campaign.[4]

[1] F. G. Hutchins, *Spontaneous Revolution* (Delhi, 1971), pp. 269-70.

[2] Confidential note (in Hindi) for Working Committee, 4 August 1942. The authorship of the note is not clear.

[3] D. A. Low, *Lion Rampant* (London, 1973), p. 164.

[4] Hallett to Linlithgow, 9 September 1942, Hallett collection, I.O.L. Mss. Eur. E.251, No. 38.

But if nothing was found it was because there was nothing to find. Linlithgow himself acknowledged this in private.

> My own judgement is that few things are more important in this country than that we should show to India, and to the world, that Congress was responsible for the rebellion. The weight of evidence is steadily growing, though it is true that we have not yet got the link between the campaign of violence and the Working Committee — though we have very nearly got it in the case of Patel. What I do feel is that the outside world is not getting the facts, and that it is essential that we should take steps to publicize the best case we can put together . . .[1]

Neither the lack of firm proof nor the denials of Gandhi and Azad[2] curbed the Government's smear campaign.

By October 1943 the back of the popular revolt had been broken. Gandhi was released the next summer on grounds of health; but Jawaharlal and the other members of the Working Committee were kept in custody, as Amery had suggested on the morrow of their arrest,[3] till the end of the war. Meantime, the British consolidated their position in India. Amery thought in racist terms which would have done credit to Goebbels and Rosenberg.

> If India is to be really capable of holding its own in the future without direct British control from outside, I am not sure that it will not need an increasing infusion of stronger Nordic blood, whether by settlement or intermarriage or otherwise. Possibly it has been a real mistake of ours in the past not to encourage Indian Princes to marry English wives for a succession of generations and so breed a more virile type of native ruler. Perhaps all that may yet come about.[4]

This was too much even for Linlithgow, who preferred to ensure British rule for very many years to come by strengthening the Muslim League. Attempts within that party to weaken Jinnah's leadership continued to be discouraged. In 1941 the Viceroy directed the Governor of the Punjab to dissuade Sikandar Hyat Khan from resigning from the League, and rejected Zafrulla Khan's advice to split the League by appointing to the Executive Council Muslims who were unacceptable to Jinnah.[5] With this support, and with the Congress out

[1] Linlithgow to Hallett, 24 January 1943, Linlithgow papers, vol. 106, quoted in *Transfer of Power,* vol. 3, (H.M.S.O., 1971), p. 547n.
[2] For example Gandhi to Linlithgow, 29 January 1943, *Transfer of Power*, vol. 3, pp. 558-9; Azad to Linlithgow, 13 February 1943, Linlithgow papers, vol. 125.
[3] To Linlithgow, 10 August 1942, *Transfer of Power*, vol. 2, p. 632.
[4] Amery to Linlithgow, 1 October 1943, Linlithgow papers, vol. 12.
[5] Linlithgow to Amery, 1 March and 15 May 1941, Linlithgow papers, vol. 10. Zafrulla Khan was at that time a member of the Viceroy's council.

of the way from 1942, Jinnah strengthened both his stature within the League and the League's command of the Muslim masses. He was helped too by Raja-gopalachari, who canvassed for an agreement between the Congress and the League, and by Gandhi, who, after his release, gave Jinnah recognition by deal-ing with him on equal terms. Their talks came to nothing but enhanced Jinnah's status.

More disturbing than the shortsightedness of these Congress leaders was the attitude of the Communist Party. After having supported the war effort from 1941 in defiance of the nationalist tide, it was now willing to concede Pakistan. In contrast to Jawaharlal's interpretation of the growing influence of the League as a reflection of the backwardness of the Muslim masses and their acceptance of feudal leadership, the Communists regarded the communal problem as one of multi-national consciousness. It was to them in essence a problem of the innumerable nationalities of India coming to life 'with the further course of bourgeois development', and they discerned a democratic core in the demand for Pakistan.[1]

Jawaharlal and his companions, therefore, after they emerged from prison in June 1945, were naturally in a bitter mood. India had for nearly three years lain under virtually military rule. Collaborators, loyalist, communal and left-wing, had had their heyday at the expense of the national movement. Deep famine in Bengal had been regarded as low priority. Wavell, who had succeeded Linlithgow as Viceroy in October 1943, himself noted that the British Govern-ment's attitude to India was 'negligent, hostile and contemptuous to a degree I had not anticipated'.[2] Lord Mountbatten, in command in South-East Asia, diverted 10 per cent of the shipping at his disposal for import of foodgrains into India, but Churchill, who seemed to regard famine relief as 'appeasement' of the Congress, vetoed this, and reduced his shipping by 10 per cent. Mountbatten on his own transferred 10 per cent of his reduced shipping to food imports.[3] Corruption and blackmarketing ravaged the land. All this infuriated Jawahar-lal, and his speeches and interviews on release reflect this. India was to him comparable to the European countries freed from Nazi rule, with resistance movements emerging to the surface.[4] Though the Congress had not organized the 1942 rebellion, it delighted him that the people had not miserably submitted to repression but had, on their own, struck back. He demanded stern action against blackmarketeers and trials in open court of those guilty of atrocities against the people.[5] A statement of October 1945 charging members of the Executive Council with corruption and bribery led the Government of India

---

[1] See G. Adhikari, *Pakistan and Indian National Unity* (Bombay, 1942).

[2] Entry for 20 October 1944, Wavell, *The Viceroy's Journal,* ed. P. Moon (Oxford, 1973), p 93.

[3] Wavell, op. cit., p. 89; Mountbatten's interview with the author, 28 May 1970.

[4] Interview to the United Press of America, 21 June, *The Hindustan Times,* 23 June 1945.

[5] Press conference, 23 June, *The Hindustan Times,* 24 June 1945.

to consider his prosecution, and only the caution of their legal adviser prevented them.[1] This was after Attlee had taken office as Prime Minister; but Jawaharlal would not have been surprised at the Government of India paying no heed to the proclaimed objectives of the Labour Party's India policy. In 1942 the war against the Congress had been accepted by almost the entire British nation, and Jawaharlal saw nothing to choose between the Churchill Government and its successor.

> In our own day that curious group which has no fixed standards or principles or much knowledge of the outside world, the leaders of the British Labour Party, have usually been the staunchest supporters of the existing order in India. Sometimes a vague sense of uneasiness fills them at a seeming contradiction between their domestic and colonial policy, between their professions and practice, but, considering themselves above all as practical men of common sense, they sternly repress all these stirrings of conscience.[2]

Cripps in particular he could not forgive, and a welcoming cable went unanswered.

Gandhi was at this time thinking in terms of another campaign of civil disobedience.[3] However, the Working Committee decided to permit its representatives to attend the conference summoned by Wavell at Simla to consider the formation of an interim government. Jawaharlal was not one of the invitees but was present at Simla, a town which he hated for its atmosphere of officialdom, for part of the time; and there is a perceptive account of him at Viceregal Lodge.

> I felt he was gnawing some sorrow inside him. He seemed to me a seeking soul, happy to follow a track if he could conscientiously do so; and now by fate, or our unamiability perhaps, is made to oppose so that our unpleasantness and all must make it worse. He never relaxed the defensive for a minute.[4]

The outcome of the conference confirmed Jawaharlal's suspicions of British motives, for Wavell acted as a total partisan of the Muslim League. The Congress, though it disliked the parity proposed by the Viceroy between the 'Caste Hindus' and the Muslims, accepted it as a temporary formula for the formation of an interim government at the Centre. So it submitted a panel of fifteen names, consisting of both Congressmen and non-Congressmen and

---

[1] Home Dept. File 33/26/45 — Poll (I).
[2] *The Discovery of India*, p. 293.
[3] J. B. Kripalani, *Gandhi His Life and Thought* (New Delhi, 1970), p. 224.
[4] Freya Stark, *Dust in the Lion's Paw* (London, 1961), p. 248.

including three members of the League, from whom the Viceroy could make his selection for membership of his Executive Council. But the Congress could not expect fair play from Wavell, who never concealed his leanings towards the League. As he later told A. V. Alexander, he 'had no conscious feeling that he had been partisan in favour of the Muslim League, but I could understand that as he had been Commander-in-Chief in India in 1942, he was bound to remember that whilst the Muslim League were not politically active in his support, they did not, as the Congress Party had, organise the sabotage and destruction of his communications whilst he was trying to keep the Japs out of India. Congress had in fact acted as our enemies.'[1] So in the summer of 1945, when the immediate fortunes of the League were unpromising and it could not control the ministries in any of the provinces where Muslims were in a majority — the Punjab, NWFP, Sind, Bengal and Assam — Wavell assisted the League by the first of his many acts of partiality. He not only conceded parity between 'Caste Hindus' and Muslims and between the Congress and the League but, going back on his word to Gandhi,[2] agreed not to select a Muslim belonging to the Congress. His offer to Jinnah was that, of the five Muslims chosen, four should be from the League and one from the Punjab Unionist Party.[3] This was virtual refusal to regard the Congress as a non-Hindu, secular organization, and acceptance of Jinnah's contention that it was as much a communal party as the League. But Wavell was unwilling to let down the loyalist Muslims outside the League and particularly those who had helped so greatly in the recruitment of soldiers in the Punjab.

However, this was not acceptable to Jinnah, who insisted that all Muslim members should belong to the League and that, in an Executive Council so formed, the Muslim members should have a veto on all important decisions. These were demands which even Wavell could not accept; and, had he chosen, he could at this stage have deflated the League to manageable proportions. Jinnah was aware of this. 'I am at the end of my tether', he told the Viceroy;[4] 'I ask you not to wreck the League.' Wavell, instead of seizing this occasion to restore Indian politics to an even keel, enabled Jinnah to gain the full advantage of his obduracy by promptly abandoning his own proposals and dissolving the Conference. The offer of the Congress to join the Executive Council while leaving it open to the League to come in later [5] was ignored. Nothing could have made clearer that it was Jinnah's wishes that mattered above all else.

The League derived the fullest benefit of this in the elections for the central and provincial assemblies that were held at the end of the year. The Congress

[1] Alexander's diary of his visit to India, entry for 26 June 1946. A. V. Alexander papers, Churchill College Library, Cambridge.

[2] Wavell's account of interview with Gandhi, 24 June 1945, Wavell, op. cit., p. 145.

[3] V. P. Menon, *The Transfer of Power in India* (paperback, Madras, 1968), p. 206; Wavell, op. cit., p. 154.

[4] Viceroy's account of interview with Jinnah, 9 July 1945, Wavell, op. cit., pp. 152-3.

[5] Jawaharlal's interview to the press, 11 July, *The Hindustan Times,* 12 July 1945.

was ill prepared for these elections. Its popularity among the masses was greater than ever, but its party machinery was out of gear, many of its supporters among the narrow electorate—about 30 per cent of the adult population—had not been registered, and its leaders at every level were tired, unenthusiastic and pulling in contrary directions. Jawaharlal did a little campaigning, but nothing like his effort of ten years before. The contrast with the vigour and dash of 1936-7 was complete. Indeed, the elections of 1945 were in a sense unreal, for they could not reflect the despair and intense dislike of the Government among the people. On the other hand, the League improved its position as a result of the assiduous nursing of the separate electorates in the years when the Congress was outlawed, the ill-timed tactics of Rajagopalachari and Gandhi, the partisanship of Linlithgow and Wavell, and the support of the Communist Party. It was the last which distressed Jawaharlal the most.

> You must realise that it pains me to see the gulf that has arisen between the Congress and Communists in India. That gulf at present is wide and deep and has all the passions of three years behind it. That has nothing to do with communism and socialism, in favour of which there is considerable though rather vague sentiment. Still less has it to do with Russia for which there is great admiration, though no doubt tempered in many places by certain fears of present and future Soviet policy. The gulf has arisen because of internal policy in India and the fact that the Communists ran down popular leaders in India and, at a time when there was bitter conflict between nationalism and the imperialist structure, they appeared before the people as acting on the side of the latter. Whatever the inner motives and reasons, this public reaction is easy to understand. Politically the fact that has gone most against them and aroused the greatest resentment is their attitude on the communal question. They have become full-blooded supporters of Jinnah's demands (unspecified and vague as they are) and in the name of Congress-League unity they demand a complete surrender by Congress to Jinnah. I have no doubt that they have worsened the communal problem by their attitude. Communists who have joined the Muslim League appear to be more rabid Leaguers than others. All this has been greatly resented. I hope that changed circumstances will gradually tone down these differences.[1]

In the provinces where Muslims formed a majority, the League did not secure a majority of votes. For instance, its vote in the Punjab was 46.56 per cent, in Sind 45·75 per cent, and in the NWFP 37·19 per cent. But the seats gained by

---

[1] Jawaharlal to Palme Dutt from Gulmarg, 12 August 1945, Palme Dutt papers. There is no copy of this hand-written letter in the Nehru papers and I am grateful to Mr Palme Dutt for permission to consult his file.

the League were far more than were warranted by its vote. Except in the NWFP, where the Congress had a clear majority of 30 seats, including 19 Muslim seats, and the League only 17, the League secured all or most of the reserved Muslim seats. In the central assembly too it won every Muslim constituency with 86·6 per cent of the vote. Particularly striking was its success in provinces like Bombay and Madras, which till now had been relatively free of the communal fever but where now the League captured all the reserved seats. But it suffered from a tactical disadvantage in that in no province with a Muslim majority was it able to form a ministry with unquestioned backing in the assembly. In Assam, as in the NWFP, it was a Congress ministry which was sworn in; in the Punjab a coalition of Congress, the Unionists and the Akalis took office; in Bengal, the League ministry was dependent on European support; and in Sind the League was outnumbered by the Congress and its sympathizers and formed the government only because the Governor, with unconcealed partiality, called upon it to do so.

Yet the League had cause to rejoice. It had demonstrated that it had a considerable following, especially in the urban areas. However unpractical the concept of partition and imprecise the notion of Pakistan, they had struck a response in the minds of many middle-class Muslims. Jawaharlal was still of the view that the League had not gathered real strength and was the creation of the wishful thinking of elderly British governors. When a test came, all Muslims would come flocking back to the Congress. 'We will all march together and ask for independence together and there will be a united India and there will be no problem at all.'[1] There could be no solution of the communal problem so long as the British were in India; but once alien authority and intervention were excluded circumstances would force an agreement, because the only other alternative was large-scale fighting. But this was an ideal which neither the British nor the Muslim League would help to realize; and the Congress had to take into account the fact of the League's electoral gains and work out its ideas of a constitutional settlement on this basis. There was no time any longer for 'mass contacts'; nor, even if feasible, would the Government of India provide scope for them. Even before the elections. Wavell had been anxious not to rule out partition. He asked Attlee to alter a sentence, in his broadcast of 19 September 1945, which read 'to work out a constitution which majority and minority communities will accept' into 'to join in a settlement which majority and minority communities . . . ' Attlee refused.[2] But the results of the elections greatly strengthened the arguments for pandering to the League. Therefore, while insisting on the departure of the British and the summoning of a constituent assembly for free India, the Congress reluctantly recognized the right of any area to secede provided this was the clearly established will of

[1] Mr Woodrow Wyatt's account of a conversation with Jawaharlal in January 1946, recorded in his oral testimony, N.M.M.L.

[2] See correspondence between Prime Minister and Viceroy in Attlee papers. University College Library, Oxford, Box 18.

the inhabitants of that area and it did not result in the compulsion of any group or community in that area. Jawaharlal hoped that, granted the right to secede, the Muslims would not exercise it but rather use it to shed their fears.[1] Given a sense of freedom, the Muslim masses, at any rate, would realize the absurdity of Pakistan. A plebiscite should be held after British authority was withdrawn from India and the Muslims would either not want to secede or, if they did, would quickly retract their decision.[2] But, especially after the elections, this was a forlorn thought. It is possible that to Jinnah himself Pakistan had never been more than a battle-cry. He never expected the British to leave[3] and exploited the demand for a separate state to secure leverage against the Congress. But his followers, eager for power and excited by the prospect of a new state of their own, believed that it might now be theirs for the repeated asking and, far from subduing their demand, inflamed opinion in its favour. It was not possible to have a sovereign Pakistan which consisted of more than a part of the Punjab and a part of Bengal, and even this seemed to be ruled out by the demands of defence. So an independent Pakistan appeared a fantasy; but the problem, as Jawaharlal reluctantly acknowledged, was one not so much of logical analysis as of psychological appreciation.[4] By the spring of 1946, with the Government of India encouraging the League and the Congress reconciled to the principle of secession, the frost had settled on all hopes of a free and united India.

So, with the emphasis now on tactics, pace and procedure rather than on principles, events gathered momentum. The air was full of hate and passion, negotiations were the continuation of civil war by other means, and killing and rioting became the accepted instruments of political manoeuvre. It was a sad finale to a nationalist movement which had prided itself on its methods of peaceful struggle, and there was probably a touch of escapism in Jawaharlal's concentration at this time on two other issues outside the mainstream: the Indian National Army (I.N.A.) and relations with the neighbouring countries of Asia.

The story of the I.N.A. has been told often and at length. About 20,000 Indian officers and men taken prisoner by the Japanese had responded to Subhas Bose's call to form an army to wage war, alongside the Japanese, in the cause of India's freedom. When the war ended, Bose had died in an aircraft accident, and the British intended to treat the captured I.N.A. men as guilty of treason. Jawaharlal himself had no doubt that the action of these men had been an error of judgment. Freedom could not be secured with the assistance of any foreign nation, and certainly not Japan, which had an inglorious record of aggressive imperialism. However, the soldiers of the I.N.A., some of whom he

---

[1] See his draft note written at Gulmarg, 17 August 1945.

[2] Interviews to the press, *The Hindustan Times*, 4 and 7 April 1946.

[3] Even in January 1946, Liaqat Ali Khan told the Viceroy that the British would have to stay in India for many years, and the Muslims were not at all anxious that they should go. Wavell, op. cit., pp. 206-7.

[4] Jawaharlal to Stafford Cripps, 27 January 1946.

met, seemed to him the pick of the Indian army, who had, for the most part, been inspired by the noblest motives. They had done the wrong thing for the right reason, and it was absurd for the British to charge them as traitors. There is always a case to be made for not putting on trial soldiers who collaborate with the enemy,[1] and the case is even stronger when the soldiers are colonial recruits, the best of whom believe that they have been given an opportunity to fight for national freedom. When, in an insensate mood, explicable only by the mental decadence which comes over an imperial government in its last throes, the Government of India decided to stage a public trial, at the Red Fort in Delhi, of three I.N.A. officers, Indian public opinion was deeply stirred to an extent that surprised even Jawaharlal. It dramatized the old contest, England v. India, and all the major political parties, including the League, expressed themselves on the side of the National Army. Even serving soldiers of the Indian Army felt a wave of interest and sympathy.[2] As General Tuker wrote soon after, the I.N.A. affair, at its most acute, was 'threatening to tumble down the whole edifice of the Indian Army'.[3] Jawaharlal organized relief for the I.N.A. men and their dependants, harried eminent men and women who did not normally take an interest in politics to express their concern, set up an I.N.A. Defence Committee of lawyers and himself put on once more, after over twenty-five years, his barrister's gown and appeared in court.

The other issue, always important to Jawaharlal and in which his interest had not been dimmed by the years of isolation in prison and the tragic situation in his own country, was the condition of Asia. With the defeat of Japan, the pressure on China had been relieved; and in the civil war which followed, Jawaharlal, despite old friendships, strictly refrained from taking sides. Of more direct concern was the question whether the old imperialist powers — the British in Burma and Malaya, the Dutch in Indonesia and the French in Indo-China — would be able to restore their former dominance. This was a general problem and Jawaharlal was keen that the Asian countries should help each other. He welcomed the idea of an Asian conference suggested by Aung San of Burma,[4] and was infuriated by the British use of Indian troops to support the French and the Dutch. Even worse was the attitude of the United States, which apparently, for its own purposes, was underwriting European imperial-

---

[1] Cf. Mr Bernard Levin on American collaborators in Vietnam: 'What, after all, will be gained by putting the alleged collaborators on trial and, if they are convicted, punishing them? The demands of strict justice will have been met; those who suffered will be able to see that those who evaded their own share of the suffering have not been allowed to get away with it; and a warning will have been given to any who might be inclined to do the same in future. I have to say that it is not an impressive list . . . And it surely is possible, and it is even more surely right, to avoid the recriminations and the shame, the anguish and the echoes, that such trials as are envisaged will cause.' *The Times*, 31 May 1973.

[2] See Sir Claude Auchinleck, C-in-C, to Wavell, 26 November 1945, J. Connell, *Auchinleck* (London, 1959), p. 806.

[3] Francis Tuker, *While Memory Serves* (London, 1950), p. 43.

[4] Letter from Aung San, 13 December 1945, and Jawaharlal's telegram, 26 December, and reply to Aung San, 27 December 1945.

ism in Asia. This could only ensure a continuing revolt of millions with a passion which even the atom bomb could not suppress, and end in a third world war. [1]

Jawaharlal himself wished to visit Burma, Malaya and Indonesia, to meet the nationalist leaders of these countries, plan co-operative endeavour and inquire into the conditions of the Indians settled there. During the years of war these communities had been cut off from India; and now many of their leaders connected with the Indian Independence League and the I.N.A. had been thrown into prison. The Indian Congress had wished to send its representatives to these countries to make a first-hand report but the Government refused permission. The authorities in Burma and Java refused to let Jawaharlal visit these countries. The British Military Administration in Malaya was willing to receive him, but even this permission was couched in humiliating terms. Jawaharlal was told that there would be

> no objection to your entry into Malaya provided that your visit concerns the relief of distress among Indians and is not for political purposes. The British Military Administration desire you to be informed that an official organisation for dealing with distress among all races in Malaya has been set up and state that you will be expected to co-ordinate your efforts with those of the Military Administration. They also wish you to know that transport facilities in Malaya at present are such that they will be unable to provide you with a car during your visit. [2]

Jawaharlal, as was to be expected, refused to go merely to function according to the will of the Military Administration. His main purpose was to alleviate the distress and sense of fear among the Indians in Malaya, and he was not prepared to abandon it if the authorities regarded it as political. [3] At this stage Lord Mountbatten, the Supreme Allied Commander stationed at Singapore, intervened. Cancelling the previous directive, he arranged for all facilities for Jawaharlal's visit, and requested him to call on him at Singapore before starting his tour of Malaya. [4] Jawaharlal agreed, while making it clear that his stay and programme in Malaya would be organized by his Indian hosts. He refused to oblige the Government of India and ask the Indian community not to arrange a guard of honour of former I.N.A. soldiers on his arrival at Singapore, and went no further than suggesting that there be no procession or strikes of workers during his visit. [5]

[1] Statement to the press, 15 October, *The Hindustan Times*, 16 October 1945; and presidential address to the All-India States Peoples Conference, 31 December 1945, *National Herald*, 1 January 1946.

[2] Letter from Secretary, External Affairs Department, to Jawaharlal, 25 January 1946.

[3] Jawaharlal to Secretary, External Affairs Department, 31 January 1946.

[4] Secretary, Commonwealth Relations Department, to Jawaharlal, 28 February 1946.

[5] Sri Prakasa's telegram to Jawaharlal, 13 March 1946; Jawaharlal's telegrams to Sri Prakasa and N. Raghavan, 14 March 1946.

On arrival at Singapore, Jawaharlal met Mountbatten, who, with anticipation and a sense of drama, had arranged for Jawaharlal's reception at the airport with all the courtesies due to a prime minister-designate. He received Jawaharlal at Government House and drove with him to a canteen for Indian soldiers, where Jawaharlal had his first encounter, a startling and unexpected one, with Lady Mountbatten.

> We arrived at the canteen and l met Lady Mountbatten there. We then moved in from the porch or portico to a room inside. Just then there was a wild rush of Indian soldiers, presumably wanting to see me. When we reached the room inside, Edwina Mountbatten was nowhere to be seen. I think I got up on a chair to have a look around. Soon Lady Mountbatten crawled out of the milling crowd. She had evidently been knocked down by the soldiers rushing in. That was an unusual introduction for us.[1]

There was at Singapore a small memorial to the I.N.A., built in a prominent place by the I.N.A. personnel. This had been repeatedly destroyed by the British authorities and repeatedly rebuilt. Mountbatten was anxious that Jawaharlal should not visit this memorial, not merely because it would give recognition to the I.N.A., but also for fear that a big function which attracted large crowds might give rise to a certain resentment among the Chinese and others. It has been suggested that Jawaharlal was so bewitched by Mountbatten on his first meeting that he abandoned his principles and his integrity and did not lay a wreath at the memorial.[2] In fact, Jawaharlal did not agree with Mountbatten that the Chinese would be annoyed by any tribute he paid to the I.N.A. Indeed, he had been pleasantly surprised to find that there had been some underground contacts between the Chinese resistance movement and the I.N.A. during the war years, the Chinese having recognized that the Indians, like themselves, were working for national freedom and co-operation with the Japanese was only incidental.[3] The only concession Jawaharlal made to Mountbatten was to avoid a public function. But he visited the memorial quietly and without announcement and placed some flowers there,[4] and this was immediately known to the local population.

Mountbatten's other request was that when Jawaharlal addressed the I.N.A. personnel, who were about 3,000, they should not parade as a regular army in uniform and with badges of rank, and the general public should not be present. Jawaharlal replied that nothing could be done about uniforms, as often this was

---

[1] Jawaharlal to Dorothy Norman, 12 October 1963. D. Norman, *Nehru: The First Sixty Years* (London, 1965), vol. 2, p. 221.

[2] Mountbatten, *Reflections on the Transfer of Power and Jawaharlal Nehru* (Cambridge, 1968), p. 5; Hodson, op. cit., p. 205.

[3] Statement to the press on return to India, 30 March, *National Herald*, 31 March 1946.

[4] Jawaharlal's report to President AICC on visit to Malaya, 28 March 1946.

the only set of clothes these men possessed. As for badges, generally they would not be worn but if they were, no objection could be taken. The function would also, as far as possible, be kept private though it was not practical wholly to prevent others from coming. In fact, as almost all the former members of the Indian army had been repatriated to India, only the civilian personnel of the I.N.A. were present and the problem of badges did not arise; but considerable numbers of the general public did attend.
INA were present and the problem of badges did not arise; but considerable numbers of the general public did attend.

In his tour of Malaya, Jawaharlal was accompanied by two senior military officers attached to him by Mountbatten. Jawaharlal was not particularly anxious to have them but did not wish to appear discourteous by objecting to their presence. He told the local Indian population, who were attached to India and anxious to retain their Indian nationality, that those who had made their permanent residence in Malaya should adopt Malayan nationality, till, as Jawaharlal optimistically hoped, the time came when there would be a common nationality for India and all these regions of South-East Asia. His own visit, he felt, had had a good effect in cheering up the Indian community, improving their organization, drawing the Malayans, Indians and Chinese closer, toning down any political action that might be envisaged against Indians and opening up scope for an improvement of their economic prospects.

Back in India after an enforced night's halt in Rangoon, so that the weather thwarted the British and enabled him to meet Aung San, Jawaharlal was plunged back into discussion as to the political future. The 'stay-put attitude'[1] of the British Government, their refusal to come to terms with the demand of the Congress for independence by relying on the intransigence of Jinnah, and the League in turn assuming that intransigence was justified by the permanence of British rule in India — all these calculations had been blown sky-high by the rumblings within the military base of imperialism. Early in 1946, the R.A.F. mutinied at several stations in India and refused to obey orders because of their grievances about such matters as rate of demobilization and pay; and this was followed by a hunger-strike of some members of the R.I.A.F. More serious was the naval mutiny in Bombay. On 19 February, about 3,000 ratings in the Royal Indian Navy hoisted the national flag on their ships and marched through the streets of Bombay. The result was that many industrial workers went on strike in sympathy. There was exchange of fire between British troops and the mutineers and disturbances which, according to the official report, were without parallel in the history of Bombay city.[2] While the Communists and the Congress Socialists encouraged the mutineers to keep up their resistance, Patel and the 'old guard' of the Congress at Bombay, acting in concert with the Government, sought to persuade the sailors to lay down arms. Jawaharlal came to Bombay. Patel was thought to be none too pleased about this,

[1] Jawaharlal to Krishna Menon, 2 December 1945.
[2] Report of Home Dept. Bombay Govt., 6 March 1946. Home Dept. Pol. 18/2/46-Pol. (I) of 1946.

but the Government lifted the ban on meetings to enable Patel and Jawaharlal to condemn the outbreak of mob violence. Both leaders, though with differing emphasis, urged the ratings to call off the mutiny, if only because they could not possibly hope to succeed; and within a week it was all over. [1]

Short-lived as were the mutinies of 1946, they finally convinced the British Government that the spring of the empire was broken. *Satyagraha* may have harried the British conscience, the Labour Government may have believed as an article of faith that the British should withdraw from India, but it was the non-political events of early 1946 that made clear that the end of the *raj* was near. It was the irreversible loss of imperial power that provided the rationale for the decision of Attlee's Government to send out a special mission of three Cabinet Ministers to seek an agreement on the constitutional issue. How closely this decision to send a Mission was tied up with problems of military capacity and defence is shown by the fact that, at a meeting of the Prime Minister with the Cabinet Mission before its departure for India, it was resolved to make it a condition precedent to independence that India should, in addition to undertaking her own defence, assist in the defence of the 'South East Asia area'. [2] But the occasion when this point could be put to Indian politicians never arose.

[1] Patel to Jawaharlal, 22 February 1946; report of Bombay police, 25 February 1946, Home Dept. Pol. 5/21/46-Pol. (I) of 1946; report of Home Dept. Bombay Govt., 6 March 1946, Home Dept. Pol. 18/2/46-Pol. (I) of 1946.
[2] Auchinleck to Wavell, 9 March 1946, Connell, op. cit., pp. 830-32.

20

The Cabinet Mission

On 24 March 1946 the Cabinet Mission arrived in Delhi. It was not a happy team. Cripps was easily the ablest of the three, had long experience of the Indian problem and a commitment to the future, while Pethick-Lawrence, though old, was, as even Wavell described him, 'a sort of saint'[1] with a sentimental attachment to India. But the third member, A. V. Alexander, found himself in deep waters. He was basically imperialistic in outlook, detested the idea of losing India, and was irritated by the feeling that he was being ignored by Cripps and not taken seriously by the Indian public. In consequence, he tended to oppose his two colleagues and to support Wavell, whose anti-Congress attitude had become even more pronounced after the Simla Conference. The Viceroy had expected the Congress to launch another mass struggle and had prepared for its violent suppression. He disliked and distrusted Gandhi who was beyond his comprehension; he could not help liking Jawaharlal, but could find no level of understanding.

At the start, the Mission found that the leaders of the Muslim League, while insisting on the creation of Pakistan, had no clear idea as to what this involved. M. A. Ispahani and the Raja of Mahmudabad, who were the first to meet the Mission, broke down under Cripps's cross-examination and could not explain how they could do without a central government for at least a small list of reserved subjects such as external affairs, defence, communications and customs. Two days later Jinnah himself was unable to give a precise answer as to what he meant by Pakistan;[3] and all that his supporters in Bombay, U.P., C.P., and Madras — provinces where Muslims were in a minority — could say in favour of Pakistan was that they would then be treated better in India because of Hindu fear of reprisals on Hindu minorities in Pakistan.[4] The Mission, therefore, was

---

[1] *Chips*, the diaries of Sir Henry Channon (Penguin edition, 1970), entry on 5 September 1945, p. 502.

[2] Alexander diary, 2 April 1946.

[3] Ibid., 4 April 1946.

[4] Ibid., 8 April 1946.

not impressed by Jinnah's repeated assertions in public that there could be no compromise on the fundamentals of a sovereign Pakistan. They confronted him with the alternatives of a sovereign Pakistan with a reduced area or a non-sovereign federation of six provinces within the Indian Union; and even Alexander, friendly to the League's viewpoint, noticed that Jinnah's reaction was evasive.

> I have never seen a man with such a mind twisting and turning to avoid as far as possible direct answers. I came to the conclusion that he is playing this game, which is one of life and death for millions of people, very largely from the point of view of scoring a triumph in a legal negotiation by first making large demands and secondly insisting that he should make no offer reducing that demand but should wait for the other side always to say how much they would advance towards granting that demand. [1]

However, if Jinnah and his followers were hazy in outlook, the leaders of the Congress declined to face up to the issue. The Mission invited Gandhi to come up from Poona to meet them, and asked the Congress to depute its representatives. Azad, as president, proposed to see them alone and convene the Working Committee only if he considered it necessary. This dismayed Patel, who felt that Gandhi was out of touch with Congress policy and Azad could not be trusted to convey Congress opinion. So hope was placed in Jawaharlal, just back from Malaya. 'I am afraid that things will go wrong if you do not find some way to meet at least Cripps in time and set the train on rails.' [2]

Jawaharlal's own mind was clear on the objective. The basis of negotiations with the Cabinet Mission should be the independence of India. These talks were not a continuation of those with Cripps in April 1942, nor would the Congress accept Dominion Status with power to secede later. The exact relationship between India and Britain could be left over for future settlement, but it should be clearly understood that all such problems could only be considered on the present basis of independence. 'In effect the British Government should pass some kind of an Act of Abdication.' The final authority to determine the constitution would be a Constituent Assembly, composed of delegates elected by the provincial assemblies according to proportional representation. If any province refused to participate or to elect delegates, it could be by-passed and left out for the time being; there should be no compulsion. This Constituent Assembly would draft an all-India constitution, but such questions as Pakistan would be settled either by the consent of the parties or by a plebiscite, on a precise and defined issue, of all the inhabitants of the area concerned. 'It should be made clear that the question of Pakistan (whatever precisely it might signify) will not be decided by a mere majority of votes in the Constituent Assembly.' But time was the essence

[1] Ibid., 16 April 1946.
[2] Patel to Jawaharlal, 27 March 1946.

of the whole problem, and there should be no delay in convening a Constituent Assembly and forming a provisional Central Government acting freely as a Cabinet with no obstruction from the Viceroy or the India Office. The Congress should not get entangled in long discussions about details.[1]

When Gandhi met the Mission he pressed, as a test of its sincerity, for the release of all political prisoners and the immediate repeal of the salt tax, and suggested that Jinnah be invited to form an interim government.[2] Such suggestions which had no practical bearing on the immediate issue were regarded as characteristic of Gandhi; but more surprisingly, Rajagopalachari urged the Mission to insist on the adoption of democratic constitutions by the Indian States and advised the British Government not to impose a settlement on the Indian parties but to refer the issue of Pakistan to an international arbitration committee on which the Soviet Union was represented.[3] Neither Gandhi nor Rajagopalachari claimed to speak for the Congress; but even Azad, in his talks with the Mission, laid emphasis not on constitution-making but on the transfer of real power to an interim government.[4]

This refusal on the part of the Congress to discuss any long-term plan was probably deliberate. Immediately after the elections, Rajagopalachari had suggested that it would be wise to devolve the initiative to the provinces. A resolution should be tabled in each of the eleven provincial assemblies that the province was willing to join an Indian federation on certain basic principles and a minimum federal list. The positive answer of the NWFP and Assam would unsettle the League's position; and if Bengal also agreed, that would finish the battle.[5] Jawaharlal's mind was working on the same lines. He had advised Cripps that both the Constituent Assembly and the provisional Central Government should be formed in accordance with the suggestions of the elected Provincial Governments.[6] He now instructed the Congress premiers to get together and appoint a small committee of constitutional experts to draft the general principles of a permanent constitution. The same, or another, committee should consider the general problem of realignment of provincial boundaries. By separating from the Punjab the areas where the Hindus and Sikhs were in a majority and divesting Bengal of Burdwan and parts of the Presidency division, four provinces would be created — NWFP, West Punjab, Sind and East Bengal — where Muslims would be in a definite majority; and this might placate Muslim opinion to a considerable extent.[7]

[1] Jawaharlal's confidential note on impending conversations with Cabinet Mission, 15 March 1946.

[2] Alexander diary, 3 April 1946.

[3] Ibid., 12 April 1946.

[4] Ibid. , 17 April 1946.

[5] Rajagopalachari to Jawaharlal, 28 February 1946.

[6] 27 January 1946.

[7] Jawaharlal's note of instructions to Congress leaders in provinces, written sometime in April 1946.

With the two main parties unable or unwilling to make constructive sugges-tions on the future of India, the Cabinet Mission put forward proposals of its own. The scheme of Cripps to ask the Muslim members of the assemblies of Sind, NWFP, Punjab and Bengal to vote on separation was rejected by both Jinnah and Jawaharlal. However, on 26 April, Jinnah expressed a preference for a three-tier federal union rather than a sovereign Pakistan with a reduced area;[1] and Azad repeatedly hinted at the possibility of some provinces coming together for certain subjects provided the compulsory link with the centre was not severed.[2] This encouraged the Mission to formulate a plan suggesting the establishment of a Union Government dealing with foreign affairs, defence and communications; two groups of provinces, one predominantly Hindu and the other predominantly Muslim, which would deal with all other subjects which the provinces desired should be dealt with in common; and the vesting of all residuary powers in the provinces.[3] To consider this plan, a conference of the leaders of the two parties was convened at Simla. When Dr Ambedkar, the leader of the Scheduled Castes Federation, which had, in the elections, won only 2 out of 151 seats, objected to his exclusion, Alexander advised him to become a Christian.[4] However, the Cabinet Mission left a memorandum to be passed on to the Constituent Assembly without disclosing its origin, suggesting that of the six Scheduled Castes representatives, two should be drawn from Ambedkar's organization.[5]

The conference did not get off to a good start. Jinnah, while still harping on Pakistan — 'surely the poor Mohammedans were entitled to one quarter of India'[6] — attended. He shook hands with Jawaharlal and Patel but turned scorn-fully away from the proferred hands of Azad and Abdul Gaffar Khan. However, prospects soon brightened. It was implicit in Jinnah's arguments that he was not thinking in terms of a sovereign state. He recognized that the Union execu-tive could deal with most matters referred to it though he felt there was no need for a Union legislature; and he inquired whether the constitution of the Union would be permanent or provision would be made for revision after a set period. Even before the conference met, the Congress had objected to compulsory groupings or sub-federations, and felt it would be wholly wrong to compel a province to function against its own wish.[7] There were Congress ministries in Assam and NWFP and the Congress could not possibly agree to the one being linked to Bengal and the other to the Punjab and Sind. This would virtually mean abandoning their supporters and handing these provinces over

[1] Alexander diary, 26 April 1946.

[2] Menon, op. cit., pp. 238 and 254.

[3] Pethick-Lawrence to Azad and Jinnah, 27 April 1946, *Papers relating to the Cabinet Mission to India* (New Delhi, 1946), p. 9.

[4] Alexander diary, 15 April 1946.

[5] Note of India Office, 24 October 1946, Attlee papers, Box 4.

[6] To Alexander, 29 April 1946, Alexander diary.

[7] Azad to Pethick-Lawrence, 28 April 1946, *Papers relating to Cabinet Mission*, pp. 9-10.

to the League. But at the conference, Jawaharlal pledged the Congress not to exercise compulsion on the units to stay in an all-India federation. Jinnah stated that if the Congress would accept the groups, the League would accept the Union. Jawaharlal said that while his position came near to that of Jinnah, any Union would be futile without a legislature and the provinces must decide for themselves about groupings; and to this Jinnah replied that he had fought for freedom equally with Jawaharlal and would be very glad to sit with him to discuss matters.

Encouraged by this, the Cabinet Mission drew up on 8 May 'Suggested Points for Agreement' between the two parties. There should be an all-India government and legislature, both composed of equal proportions from the Muslim-majority and Hindu-majority provinces, and dealing with foreign affairs, defence, communications and fundamental rights. Residuary powers would vest with the provinces. 'Groups of provinces may be formed', and such groups could determine the provincial subjects they desired to take in common and set up their own executives and legislatures. Any province could after ten years call for a reconsideration of the terms of the constitutions of the Union and the groups. The Constituent Assembly would be elected by the provincial assemblies. The Assembly 'will divide into three sections', representing the Hindu-majority provinces, the Muslim-majority provinces and the States. The first two sections would meet separately to decide the provincial constitutions for their group, and if they wished, a group constitution; and thereafter it would be open to any province to change its group or remain outside any group. The three sections would then rejoin to draft a Union constitution, but every major point affecting the communal issue would require a majority of each of the two communities.

That the Mission no longer insisted on groupings was clear. The Constituent Assembly should divide into sections, but provinces might form groups. The Viceroy recognized this concession to the Congress.[1] Jinnah, too, understood this clearly and promptly protested. 'In the new "suggestions" the question of grouping of provinces is left exactly as the Congress spokesmen desired in the course of discussions that have taken place hitherto, and is totally different from your original formula.'[2] Pethick-Lawrence rejected this interpretation, and contended that the Mission had done no more than slightly simplify the original formula as a reasonable compromise.[3] This was quibbling; in fact the Mission, eager for agreement, made concessions to the Congress while pretending to the League that they had not. This equivocation only served to build up trouble for the future.

---

[1] 'I went to bed unhappy all the same. I sympathise with the Muslims rather than with Congress, and I am not convinced that our document is quite fair to them.' Diary entry, 7 May 1946, Wavell, op. cit., pp. 260-61.
[2] Jinnah to Pethick-Lawrence, 8 May 1946, *Papers relating to Cabinet Mission*, pp. 15-16.
[3] Pethick-Lawrence to Jinnah, 9 May 1946, ibid., pp. 16-17.

The Congress, of course, reiterated its position. All groupings should be optional, and this subject should be left open to decision by the Constituent Assembly. Constitution-making should begin with the Federal Union. If an agreement with the League favourable to the growth of a free and united India could not be achieved, an interim government should be formed at once and matters in dispute referred to an independent tribunal.[1] Immediately, Jawaharlal suggested an umpire, and he and Jinnah retired to consider the proposal. Cripps was enthusiastic.

> I felt inordinately proud of my friendship with you yesterday afternoon and I do congratulate you and your colleagues upon their most statesman-like attitude. I pray that success may come to your labours and that you two may be hailed as the Saviours of India as indeed you will be if you succeed in coming to an agreement.[2]

The Congress prepared a list of possible umpires who were neither English nor Indian, and Cripps made various proposals: the selection of an Indian umpire by two arbitrators, of whom each side would nominate one, or requests to the United States, Canada, Australia, Eire, Sweden, China, the Soviet Union, the South American states, the Hague Court or the United Nations. But Jinnah soon denied that he had ever agreed to the principle of arbitration.[3]

After this, the two sides again reverted to rigid positions. Jinnah declared that the question of partition had been settled by the Muslim vote at the elections, but he was willing to agree to the sovereignty of Pakistan being 'delegated' to a Union for three subjects provided that sovereignty was recognized in the form of a group. Even communications were now limited to those necessary for defence. To this Jawaharlal retorted that the Congress and the League were completely opposed to each other on the question of partition, and it was essential to have a strong centre with control of many more subjects than the three basic ones. Alexander and Wavell were in sympathy with Jinnah, but to prevent public knowledge of the differences of opinion within the Mission, Pethick-Lawrence and Cripps vetoed Alexander's suggestion that he see Jawaharlal alone.[4] But even Alexander was compelled to recognize the next day, when the Congress formulated its position in writing, that it was nearer to a settlement than might have been imagined. While favouring a Centre with wide powers, the Congress accepted without qualification the Mission's suggestion that 'groups of provinces may be formed and such groups may determine the provincial subjects which they desire to take in common.'[5]

[1] Azad to Pethick-Lawrence, 8 May 1946, ibid., pp. 17-19.

[2] Cripps to Jawaharlal, 10 May 1946, with the enclosed note.

[3] Jawaharlal-Jinnah correspondence, 10 and 11 May 1946, *Papers relating to Cabinet Mission*, pp. 19-20.

[4] Alexander diary, 11 May 1946.

[5] Congress proposals 12 May 1946, *Papers relating to Cabinet Mission*, pp. 21-2; Alexander diary, 12 May 1946.

The conference, however, could make no further progress, and the Mission decided to issue its own plan. After obtaining the Cabinet's approval, delay in securing which had even led Pethick-Lawrence to consider resignation,[1] the Mission published its plan on 16 May. Partition, on the basis of either a large or a small Pakistan, was rejected. The Indian Union would deal with foreign affairs, defence and communications and have the powers necessary to raise the finances for these subjects. The idea of parity at the centre was dropped, but any major communal issue in the central legislature would require a majority of each community as well as an over-all majority. All other subjects and powers would vest in the provinces, which would be free to form groups, and each group could determine the provincial subjects to be taken in common. Any province could by a majority vote of its assembly call for a reconsideration of the Union and group constitutions periodically after ten years. The Constituent Assembly would be elected by the provincial assemblies, with each province being allotted a number of seats proportional to its population and this number divided between the communities on the basis of their population. The members so elected 'will divide up into three sections' — Section A comprising Madras, Bombay, U.P., Bihar, C.P. and Orissa; Section B Punjab, NWFP and Sind; and Section C Bengal and Assam. Each section would draw up provincial constitutions and, if desired, a group constitution. Any province could elect to come out of any group in which it had been placed after the first general elections under the new constitution. The framing of the constitution would obviously take time; but an interim government having the support of the major political parties and in which all the portfolios were held by Indians would be set up immediately.[2]

The Mission Plan was intended as a compromise, yielding some points to the Congress and some to the League in the hope that both would accept the whole even if not wholly satisfied. The idea of Pakistan as a sovereign state was rejected; and at the level of the Indian Union there was to be no weightage for the Muslims. Even in the elections to the Constituent Assembly the Muslims were not to have, as at the time, more seats than their numbers warranted. These were all concessions to the Congress. However, to make the Plan palatable to the League, Sections B and C, comprising the five Muslim-majority provinces, were created in the Constituent Assembly. But there was one major internal contradiction in the Mission Plan, which was to lead to disaster and which Cripps, at any rate, could not have failed to notice. Grouping of provinces was optional, but meeting of members of the Constituent Assembly by sections was compulsory. If a section met and decided on a group constitution, a province could opt out of the group only after the first general elections under the new constitution. In other words, grouping would in practice not be voluntary at all — unless the clause on optional grouping overrode that on compulsory

[1] Alexander diary, 15 May 1946.
[2] For full text of Cabinet Mission Plan, see M. Gwyer and A. Appadorai, *Speeches and Documents on the Indian Constitution, 1921-47* (London, 1957), vol. 2, pp. 577-84.

forming of sections. In fact, because of an assurance given by the Cabinet Mission to the League, of which the Congress was unaware,[1] that decisions in sections would be by a majority vote of the representatives of the provinces, it was the optional grouping clause which would be set aside; for the representatives of NWFP in Section B and of Assam in Section C would always be in a minority. The Congress was, at the time and later, criticized for being 'legalistic' and raising such issues as the binding nature of the document, the priority of clauses and the interpretation of the Plan. But it was to the Congress a matter of urgent practical importance: for the NWFP in Section B had no desire to find itself forced into a group with other provinces in that section even for ten years, nor did Assam wish to be coupled with Bengal.

Gandhi's interpretation was that the Plan was a recommendation to the Constituent Assembly which could vary, reject or improve upon it. No province could be forced to belong to a group.[2] Azad also wrote to the Mission on the same lines and said that the Congress would try to get the Constituent Assembly, which would be a sovereign body, to remove the defects in the Mission Plan. The only limitation which the Congress recognized was that decisions on certain major communal issues should be by a majority of each of the two communities.[3] Alexander and Wavell concluded that Gandhi was playing a deep game and that the real object of the Congress was to capture the interim government, eliminate British influence and then suppress the Muslims and displace the Princes before any constitution was drafted. The British, said Alexander in his most pompous manner, had not been stampeded at Dunkirk and should not be stampeded now.[4] He and the Viceroy prevailed on Pethick-Lawrence not to permit Cripps to see Gandhi alone and without notes being taken. But the Mission had to clarify its understanding of its Plan. So Pethick-Lawrence wrote to Azad that grouping was an essential feature of the scheme and it could only be modified by agreement between the two parties. As for the Constituent Assembly, there would be no interference with its discretion once it was formed and working on the basis of the various statements being made.[5] In other words, the sovereignty of the Constituent Assembly would be limited by the terms of reference under the Plan.

All this was dispiriting to Jawaharlal. Hopes of a settlement, on the basis of independence not in the future but at once, had been bogged down in a morass of interpretation. Despite everything, the old spirit and the old approach of the British did not appear to have greatly changed. Even while the Cabinet Mission was negotiating in India, the officials decided to institute fresh trials of INA officers.

[1] Menon, op. cit., p. 311.
[2] 19 May 1946, Tendulkar, *Mahatma*, vol. 7, p. 117.
[3] Azad to Pethick-Lawrence, 20 May 1946, *Papers relating to Cabinet Mission*, pp. 33-4.
[4] Alexander diary, 20 May 1946.
[5] Pethick-Lawrence to Azad, 22 May 1946, *Papers relating to Cabinet Mission*, p. 34.

The civil and military authorities of the Government of India function in a mysterious way. This, I suppose, is their method of preparing India for the freedom to come. Whatever they may have in their minds they succeed remarkably well in irritating public opinion and making a difficult situation even worse.[1]

In fact, the trials were soon abandoned, and Jawaharlal wrote a personal letter of thanks to the Commander-in-Chief.[2] But this was indicative of foresight in General Auchinleck rather than of a general change in the official outlook. In the formation of an interim government, the Viceroy laid emphasis on the British Parliament's ultimate responsibility and the Governor-General's prerogatives, and references to independence were linked with legal difficulties.[3] Wavell made no secret of his suspicion of the Congress, and thought that it intended to secure control of the centre and eliminate British influence in order to deal with the Muslims and the Princes with a high hand.[4] 'Don't lose heart', Pethick-Lawrence wrote to Jawaharlal,[5] 'in the independent India to come out of the Constituent Assembly. I feel so much depends on your courage in helping to bring it to birth and in guiding its destinies when it is born.' But whatever the long-term prospects, the attitudes of the Viceroy and the Government of India discouraged immediate confidence.

There was also the whole problem of the Indian States, of special interest to Jawaharlal in his capacity, at this time, as president of the All-India States People's Conference. It was difficult to believe that the widespread instances of repression in the States could occur without the support of the Political Department, for the maharajas and the nawabs were but shadows cast by the Paramount Power. Jawaharlal was for a friendly approach, urging the rulers to abandon autocracy and, where the lack of viability of their principalities was obvious, to merge them in the neighbouring province. There would then be left about twenty large States, autonomous units in the federation and with democratic governments under Princely figureheads.[6]

However, these sawdust autocrats, confident still of the support of the British, paid no heed. Reports continued to pour in from the various States of unwarranted firing, summary arrests, ill-treatment of prisoners and banning of popular organizations. These gave a touch of unreality to negotiations for British withdrawal from India. When Jawaharlal defied a ban on his entry into Faridkot State, the local authorities quickly reached a settlement. But soon after,

[1] Jawaharlal's statement to the press, 24 April, *National Herald*, 25 April 1946.
[2] 4 May 1946, Connell, op. cit., pp. 817-19.
[3] Jawaharlal to Wavell, 21 May, Wavell to Jawaharlal, 22 May, and Jawaharlal to Wavell, 25 May 1946.
[4] Viceroy's 'Note for talk with Pandit Nehru', 26 May 1946, Wavell, op. cit., pp. 278-9.
[5] Pethick-Lawrence's confidential and personal letter to Jawaharlal, 26 May 1946.
[6] Jawaharlal's presidential address to the All-India States People's Conference, 31 December 1945.

a crisis developed in Kashmir. There a strong, non-communal, political organization, the National Conference, had been built up by Sheikh Abdullah and
other leaders, who, though Muslim by faith, shunned the Muslim League and
were members of the Congress. Even the Political Department had to recognize
that during the years 1937 to 1943 Sheikh Abdullah had broadened out his
policy into one of sympathy with the Indian nationalist movement and gained
the support not only of a large number of the Muslim working-class element
but also of nationalist-minded Hindus and Sikhs in Kashmir.[1] That, in a state
with a Muslim majority and a Hindu ruler, popular feeling should lean towards
the Congress greatly irritated Jinnah, and he persistently urged the Viceroy to
appoint a 'strong Muslim' — i.e. a communally minded Muslim — and, failing
that, an Englishman, as prime minister of Kashmir.[2] The Political Department
had no liking for the National Conference, but was unwilling to upset the
Maharaja by insisting on a Muslim prime minister. They left it to him to deal
with the National Conference, which, though no revolutionary body, irked the
ruler by its very presence and made demands for responsible government and
civil liberties. After the failure of secret attempts in March 1946 to merge the
National Conference in the communal Muslim Conference and associate the
whole with the Muslim League, the Kashmir Government arrested Sheikh
Abdullah and the other leaders of the National Conference. This repressive
action was specially provocative to Jawaharlal, for at the time of his arrest
Sheikh Abdullah was on his way to Delhi to meet Jawaharlal at the latter's request. The Kashmir Government, complained Jawaharlal, seemed to be 'bent
on breaking and crushing the spirit of the people and are using their army as if
they were occupying recently conquered enemy territory'.[3] His first impulse
was to leave Simla for Kashmir to support his friends, but he curbed himself
so as to give the Viceroy a chance to intervene and not to worsen the situation
by disobeying any restraining order which might be served on him. But he made
it clear that if there were no improvement in the situation, he would not, whatever his other engagements, be able to keep away from Kashmir.

By the middle of June, Jawaharlal felt he had waited long enough and
decided to enter the State, along with some lawyers, to assist in Sheikh Abdullah's
defence. 'For my part I am not in the habit of giving up a cause I have espoused
or a comrade when he is in trouble.'[4] On 15 June he informed the Maharaja
that he would be arriving in the State four days later. Wavell asked Azad to
dissuade Jawaharlal and himself urged him to desist — but in vain. The Viceroy
then informed the Kashmir Government that any untoward incident involving

[1] A record of recent political events and tendencies in Kashmir prepared by the Political Department, 17 June 1947, Gov.-Gen. Sectt. File 295(4) — G/ 43.
[2] See Jinnah to Linlithgow, 23 August and 20 September 1943, and to Wavell, 27 September
1943, Gov.-Gen. Sectt. File 295(2) — G/ 43.
[3] Jawaharlal to Wavell, 25 May 1946.
[4] Statement to the press, 12 June 1946.

Jawaharlal during the next ten days would be highly embarrassing for all-India reasons, and suggested that the trial of Sheikh Abdullah be postponed, in which case Jawaharlal too might postpone his visit. But the Kashmir authorities refused and prepared to arrest Jawaharlal on the border. The Maharaja offered to abdicate and his prime minister to resign if the Government of India compelled them to take no action against Jawaharlal, and Wavell and the Political Department hastened to reply that no such pressure was being applied.[1] On the other hand, they informed the Cabinet Mission that in this very awkward and embarrassing situation there was nothing to be done but let events take their course. There could be no more striking testimony to the fact that misrule in the Indian States was made possible only by the permissive attitude of the Government of India and that the latter were willing to sacrifice all Indian interests to this.

Jawaharlal abided by his programme, and, on 19 June, was stopped by the Kashmir authorities at the State border. They served an externment order and organized black flag demonstrations. Jawaharlal was in a high rage. He condemned the extreme discourtesy shown him and the Congress organization and expressed scorn for the Maharaja's official and military minions. He waited for five hours to give the State government time to reverse their orders and then informed the magistrate that he was crossing into Kashmir.

> During the past twenty-five years I have never obeyed a single order of the British Government in India or any Maharaja which came in my way . . . When once a course of action is taken Jawaharlal never goes back, he goes forward; if you think otherwise then you don't know Jawaharlal. No power on earth can prevent me from going anywhere in India unless I am arrested or forcibly removed.[2]

On stepping across the border, Jawaharlal was arrested. The offer of the Kashmir Government to hand him over to the British Indian authorities was rejected by the Viceroy and the Political Department, who had no wish to be openly involved. The Government of India did nothing to prevent this episode jeopardizing the Cabinet Mission's negotiations, nor did the Secretary of State and his colleagues exercise their authority to reprimand the Kashmir Government. In the event, it was the adjournment of the trial of Sheikh Abdullah and the insistence of the Working Committee which led Jawaharlal to return to Delhi on the clear understanding that he would be back in Kashmir.

Meanwhile, the discussions on the Mission Plan had continued. The question of the formation of an interim government mainly concerned the Viceroy, who by now had irritated not merely Cripps but even Pethick-Lawrence by his

[1] Pol. Dept's telegram to Resident Kashmir, 18 June, Resident's telegram to Pol. Dept., 19 June and Pol. Dept's telegram, 19 June 1946. Gov.-Gen. Sectt. File 295(4) — G/43.
[2] Note on Jawaharlal's visit to Kashmir, 1946, prepared by his assistant.

attempts to control the latter's interviews.[1] Azad had the impression that the Viceroy had promised to function as a constitutional head of state. Wavell denied this but appealed to the Congress to place its trust in him rather than worry about assurances. In fact, he made it clear to the Mission that he would rather resign than function as a figurehead. He told Alexander that 'with all the private interviews which had been going on, Sir Stafford Cripps in particular might have committed himself more specifically than the Viceroy would desire, and that of course if he was to be expected to carry on he must have some powers and that in certain circumstances he would of course have to ask them to get somebody else.'[2]

As for the composition of the interim government, in his talks with Jinnah, Wavell committed himself to Congress-League parity and also not just to 'Caste-Hindu'-Muslim parity as in 1945 but to Hindu-Muslim parity. Nor was the Viceroy now thinking of including Muslims other than the nominees of the League. Both at Simla in May, and again in Delhi on 3 June, he informed Jinnah that the interim government would consist of 12 members — 5 Congress, 5 League, one Sikh and one Indian Christian or Anglo-Indian.[3] The Congress rejected this and insisted on 8 Hindus, including a non-Congressman, and 5 Muslims, including a non-member of the League. Despite the protests of Alexander, who even threatened to leave for London the next day if any member of the Mission saw Gandhi alone,[4] Pethick-Lawrence met Gandhi, who gave the friendly advice that each side be asked to submit a list and the Mission select one of the lists.

The Viceroy now suggested a formula of 6 Congress (including a Scheduled Caste representative), 5 League and 2 minority representatives. Rajagopalachari told the Mission on 15 June that the limit of Congress concession would be 7 Congress Hindus (including a Scheduled Caste representative), 5 Muslims and 2 minorities. Cripps was for accepting this but Wavell and Alexander insisted that the 'Caste-Hindu'-Muslim parity should be maintained. So on 16 June the Mission announced a list of 14 names — 6 Congress Hindus (including a Scheduled Caste representative), 5 Muslim Leaguers and 3 minority representatives. In case either party or both refused, the Viceroy would form an interim government representative of those who had accepted the Mission Plan.

On 6 June the Muslim League had announced its acceptance of the Plan 'inasmuch as the basis and the foundation of Pakistan are inherent in the Mission's plan by virtue of the compulsory grouping'. Now it was for the Mission to win over the Congress. Wavell informed Azad that grouping was

---

[1] Alexander diary, 3 June 1946.

[2] Ibid.

[3] Jinnah to Wavell, 8 June 1946, *Papers relating to Cabinet Mission*, pp. 37-8. Wavell later realized that he might have erred in beginning with this formula, and also in not pressing Jinnah to agree to the appointment of a Congress Muslim. See his retrospect of the Cabinet Mission's work, written on 1 July 1946, Wavell, op. cit., p. 313.

[4] Alexander diary, 11 June 1946.

not compulsory, and it was for the representatives of provinces meeting in sections to decide whether or not they wished to form groups.[1] Some days later, Gandhi was given a more specific assurance, when he raised the question of Assam, that grouping was not an essential part of the scheme.[2] The Congress was, therefore, justified in adhering to its own interpretation of the Plan, and was now more concerned with the inclusion of a Congress Muslim in the interim government. The Mission, misled by Azad and Rajagopalachari into believing that the Congress would not insist on this, blamed Gandhi for this development and rejected the demand. Jinnah now expected to be invited to join the interim government. Indeed, he had told Cripps of his specific desire to hold the defence portfolio.[3] Any hope that Jinnah's acceptance of a portfolio without securing a full commitment to Pakistan might prove a turning-point was diverted by the reluctance of Cripps to allow the League alone to enter the government; Cripps had seen the danger of the latter policy, and he wanted the Mission, in these circumstances, to ask Jinnah on what conditions he would join. Wavell and Alexander objected, for — knowing Jinnah — they knew that this would be tantamount to inviting him to put forward unacceptable conditions. Cripps replied that if that happened a fresh approach should be made to the Congress, and he was prepared to resign if his suggestion were rejected without consulting the Cabinet. Cripps prevailed to the extent that the League was not invited to join the government: but on the other hand Alexander and Wavell vetoed Pethick-Lawrence's willingness to accommodate the Congress on the question of including a non-League Muslim. Wavell also, in a letter to Jinnah, tacitly conceded the latter's request that the Scheduled Castes be treated as one of the minorities in the selection of whose representatives the League should be consulted. This seems to have been done by the Viceroy on his own initiative, but it served to alter his earlier formula of 6 Congress (including a Scheduled Caste representative) and 5 League into 'Caste-Hindu'-Muslim parity of 5-5. Even more important to Gandhi, it gave recognition to the claim that the Scheduled Castes formed a minority and were not Hindus. The substance of this letter to Jinnah leaked to the press, and had to be released.[4] When read along with Wavell's letter to Azad that the Congress would not be allowed to nominate a Muslim, it is not surprising that the Congress replied by refusing to join the interim government, while continuing to accept the long-term proposals as the Congress understood them.[5]

[1]Wavell to Azad, 15 June, *Papers relating to Cabinet Mission*, p. 42.
[2]See Wavell's diary entry for 24 June, and his note of 25 June 1946, Wavell, op. cit., p. 303 and appendix VII, respectively.
[3] Alexander diary, 12 June 1946.
[4]Wavell to Jinnah, 20 June 1946, *Papers relating to Cabinet Mission*, pp. 46-7.
[5]Wavell to Azad, 22 June, and Azad to Wavell, 25 June, and Congress resolution, 25 June 1946, ibid., pp. 48-52.

21

The Interim Government

Seemingly satisfied with the response of the Congress, the Cabinet Mission left on 29 June, leaving it to the Viceroy to negotiate the formation of an interim government on the basis of the acceptance of the Mission Plan by both the major parties. Soon after, Jawaharlal was elected in succession to Azad as president of the Congress. Azad's handling of the Congress case in the discussions with the Cabinet Mission had merited no confidence, and there was general agreement that Jawaharlal should take over. Hindsight has led to much significance being read into his election, it being seen as part of the Gandhian technique to ease Jawaharlal into the prime ministership which was looming ahead and deprive Patel of what was his by virtue of his control of the party machine. But at that time no one saw it in that light. In the summer of 1946 the presidency of the Congress seemed to bestow immediate responsibility rather than imminent office.

The new president summoned a meeting of the AICC in Bombay and secured its approval of the conduct by its leaders of the negotiations with the British Government. Both there and at a press conference a few days later, Jawaharlal reiterated, in sharp and emphatic terms, the Working Committee's interpretation of the Cabinet Mission Plan. 'We are not bound by a single thing except that we have decided to go into the Constituent Assembly.'[1] What he meant was that the Constituent Assembly would be a sovereign body with whose procedures and decisions, once the Assembly had been elected, the British Government could not interfere. The Assembly would meet in sections but it did not follow that there would be grouping.

> Obviously, Section A will decide against grouping. Speaking in betting language, there was a 4 to 1 chance of the NWFP deciding against grouping. Then Group B collapses. It is highly likely that Assam will decide against grouping with Bengal, although I would not like to say what the initial decision may be, since it is evenly balanced. But I can say

[1] Speech at the AICC, 7 July, *The Bombay Chronicle*, 8 July 1946.

with every assurance and conviction that there is going to be finally no grouping there, because Assam will not tolerate it under any circumstances whatever. Thus you see this grouping business approached from any point of view does not get on at all.[1]

These statements were seized upon by Jinnah to withdraw the League's acceptance of the Cabinet Mission Plan. He had never been happy about this commitment[2] from which he had failed to draw all the advantage he had expected; and he now charged the Congress with having circumscribed its own acceptance with so many conditions that it released him from his own pledge. The fact that, for once in its negative history, the League had bound itself to co-operate had roused such astonishment and expectation that Jawaharlal has been roundly castigated for helping Jinnah back to his normal, obstructive road. 'Now happened', wrote Azad in his memoirs,[3] 'one of those unfortunate events which changed the course of history . . . he [Jawaharlal] is at times apt to be carried away by his feelings. Not only so, but sometimes he is so impressed by theoretical considerations that he is apt to underestimate the realities of a situation.' More telling are Patel's views, expressed even at the time. Writing on the day Jinnah announced his withdrawal, Patel criticized Jawaharlal for often acting

with childlike innocence, which puts us all in great difficulties quite unexpectedly . . . acts of emotional insanity and it puts tremendous strain on us to set matters right. His mind has been exhausted by overwork and strain. He feels lonely and he acts emotionally and we have to bear with him in the circumstances. Opposition sometimes drives him mad, as he is impatient. [4]

However, it is unfair to blame Jawaharlal merely because Jinnah used this as the chance to break out of the cage of acceptance. Jawaharlal was not acting in a mood of pique. To make clear that these were not casual statements, he reiterated his views in the following weeks.[5] His utterances were deliberate and in line with Congress policy. Jawaharlal and the Congress believed that the League derived its main sustenance from the support of the British and without this, whatever its successes in the elections, its tissue would weaken. That support had been withdrawn by the Cabinet Mission and Jinnah was

[1] Interview to the press, 10 July, *National Herald*, 11 July 1946.
[2] It is said that Jinnah began to fret within hours of giving his acceptance. M.A.H. Ispahani, *Qaid-e-Azam Jinnah as I knew him* (Karachi, 1967), p. 209.
[3] Azad, op. cit., pp. 138 and 143.
[4] To D. P. Mishra, 29 July 1946, *Sardar Patel's Correspondence*, 1945-50 vol. 3 (Ahmadabad, 1972), pp. 153-4.
[5] Speech at Delhi, 21 July, interview at Lahore, 30 July, and speech at Allahabad, 1 August, *The Hindustan Times*, 22 July, 31 July and 3 August 1946, respectively.

aware of it. The important thing now was to make it clear to the British that the Congress intended India to conduct herself as a fully independent sovereign state. Fair treatment to the minorities was the obligation of a free India and not enforceable by the British. Jawaharlal's speech at the AICC and his statement at the press conference conveyed this message. When, after the press conference, one of those present said to him, 'You have changed the entire basis of the agreement with England', he smiled and replied, 'I am fully aware of that.'[1] His reference to groupings and sections contained nothing new. The Congress, said Jawaharlal, would go into sections but groupings were optional; and this was in accordance with the Plan. The difficulty was created by the Mission's unwarranted and clandestine assurance to Jinnah that a majority vote in a section would ensure compulsory groupings, and Jawaharlal's assertion that a sovereign Constituent Assembly would settle its own procedures dealt with this commitment effectively even if unknowingly. That the Congress accepted the Cabinet Mission Plan in accordance with its own interpretation had been repeatedly asserted by the Working Committee both before and after Jawaharlal's statements in Bombay in July. The Muslim League too had done the same and proclaimed that it accepted the Plan so as to be in a better position to work for a full Pakistan. It can, of course, be argued that, once the League was committed to the Plan, it would have been wise tactics for the Congress to adopt a low posture and give Jinnah no opportunity to withdraw from the Constituent Assembly. But it is difficult to see the Plan as a conversion of Jinnah which had been set at naught by Jawaharlal. As Jawaharlal said later while commenting on Azad's book, this was to think too much in individual terms and not in terms of the historical forces at work.[2] Pakistan was not made inevitable by two statements of Jawaharlal. They, at the most, provided Jinnah with an opening.

From Bombay Jawaharlal set off again for Kashmir. This visit, unlike the previous one, passed off quietly. Patel and Azad persuaded the Viceroy to secure the lifting of the ban on the entry of Jawaharlal, who promised not to raise any major issues or address any public meetings.[3] He attended Abdullah's trial and had four long private interviews with him, but was unable to meet the Maharaja who pleaded illness.[4] Jawaharlal's honour was now satisfied, and Kashmir faded, for the time at any rate, into the background. As president of the Congress, all-India issues demanded his prime attention. On his way to Srinagar he had met Wavell in Delhi, and this seems to have been one of the rare occasions when the Viceroy and Jawaharlal attained a measure of *rapport*. Jawaharlal said he did not wish to insist on any general inquiry into the conduct of

[1] Louis Fischer's introduction to the American edition of Azad's book (1960), p. xvii.

[2] Statement at press conference, 7 February 1959, *The Hindu*, 8 February 1959.

[3] Patel to Wavell, 8 July, and Azad to Wavell, 9 July 1946. Gov. Gen. Sectt. File 295(4)-G/43; Wavell to Jawaharlal, 17 July and Jawaharlal to Patel, 20 July 1946.

[4] Jawaharlal's note on Kashmir, 12 August 1946.

officials in 1942 and after, and would be satisfied with the retirement of some individuals. Wavell responded by offering, if the demand for a general inquiry were dropped, to direct Governors to discuss individual cases where there was well-substantiated evidence. Jawaharlal wrote on these lines to the premiers of Congress provinces, and the Government, which read these letters in the mail, was satisfied.[1]

Jawaharlal raised various other matters — the Governor's partisanship in Sind, the participation of Europeans in elections to the Constituent Assembly, judicial appointments in the U.P., the future of the Sikhs — and found the Viceroy willing to listen, discuss and explain.[2] Wavell, on his part, secured from Jawaharlal a public appeal to the employees of the postal department to call off their strike.[3] On the major constitutional issues also they seem to have reached some understanding; for the same day Jawaharlal wrote to the Premier of Assam not to confuse sections with groups and boycott the former, and the Viceroy wrote to Jawaharlal and Jinnah offering to form an interim government consisting of six Congress (including one Scheduled Caste representative), five League and three minority representatives.

Jinnah replied on 31 July, two days after the League had revoked its acceptance of the Mission Plan, rejecting the offer of five seats in the interim government. The Congress too had been unwilling to join until the status and powers of the interim government had been clarified and 'independence in action' assured.[4] Wavell had regarded this as practically amounting to an ultimatum, almost a declaration of war, and prepared for a show-down with the Congress; but he was curbed by the Cabinet.[5] Now the vehemence of Jinnah's attitude and the League's threat of direct action made both the British and the Congress more anxious to push ahead. The Viceroy invited Jawaharlal as president of the Congress to submit proposals for the formation of an interim government, repeated his assurance that he would act constitutionally and asked Jawaharlal to consider an approach to Jinnah before submitting his proposals to the Viceroy.[6] The Congress accepted this offer but insisted on a public announcement of the Viceroy's invitation before they sought Jinnah's co-operation. 'We shall welcome that co-operation but, if this is denied us, we shall be prepared to go ahead without it.'[7]

Such an announcement was made, and thereafter, armed with a resolution of the Working Committee that it accepted the Mission Plan in its entirety but

---

[1] Wavell's note of interview with Jawaharlal, 22 July 1946, Viceroy's Sectt. File 1252(2) GG/1943; Jawaharlal to Congress premiers, 22 July 1946, AICC File 71/1946-47.
[2] See Jawaharlal's letters to Pant, Azad and Patel, 22 July 1946.
[3] Wavell to Jawaharlal, 22 July, and Jawaharlal's statement to the press, 23 July, *The Hindustan Times*, 24 July 1946.
[4] Jawaharlal to Wavell, 23 July 1946.
[5] Wavell, op. cit., p. 322.
[6] Wavell to Jawaharlal, 6 August 1946.
[7] Jawaharlal to Wavell, 10 August 1946.

with its own interpretations to resolve the internal inconsistencies and fill the omissions, Jawaharlal met Jinnah. The talks failed as expected, for Jinnah would obviously not accept from the Congress what he had refused from the British. But it really seemed as if the British would ignore the League and work with the Congress on the basis, as Attlee had once suggested, that they could not allow a minority to place a veto on the advance of a majority. 'I have just', wrote Cripps to Rajagopalachari, 'had the news of Jinnah's speech and action and I hope that his "bark will prove worse than his bite". Whether we shall now get the Constituent Assembly going or not I don't know, but I very much hope so and I trust his withdrawal, if it takes place, will not lead to any stopping of the work by others. I still hope of course that the Muslims may join in when it comes to the time.'[1]

The Government's alliance with the Congress, however, went against Wavell's grain, and the killings in Calcutta in mid-August saw him scurrying back to the policy of appeasement of the League. Jinnah had fixed 16 August as the day for direct action, and H. S. Suhrawardy, the chief minister at the head of a League ministry in Bengal, declared it a public holiday in the province. Armed Muslim communal groups in Calcutta looted and murdered while the administration watched and the Governor took no action to call in the army. It was only after three days, when the Hindus and Sikhs took the law into their own hands and indulged in savage reprisals, that the army took charge; and even then the Bengal Government remained inactive. As the British commander observed later, 'Neither then [in August 1946], nor afterwards, did one member of that Government give me any real assistance in bringing order out of disorder.'[2] The obvious answer was to dismiss the ministry, and indeed Cripps had promised the Congress that this would be done in any such contingency as this.[3] But Wavell's reaction was the opposite. He told Jawaharlal, who was for firm action against gangsterism, that he wished to send for Jinnah, and it was only the threat of the Congress to refuse to form an interim government if he did so that led him to desist.[4] Jawaharlal wanted a ministry of 15 — five 'Caste Hindus', five Muslims, one Scheduled Caste and four minority representatives — but as Wavell insisted on the number being 14, the Anglo-Indian representative was dropped.[5]

Jawaharlal insisted that this ministry should function as a strong and stable government and not merely as a stop-gap arrangement till the League was willing to join. The Congress was anxious to have a coalition but this could not mean a surrender to the League. Jinnah could nominate his five representatives

---

[1] Cripps to Rajagopalachari, quoted in the latter's letter to Patel, 14 August 1946, *Sadar Patel's Correspondence*, vol. 3, p. 38.

[2] Sir Roy Bucher to Jawaharlal, 13 November 1954, Nehru papers.

[3] See Patel to Cripps, 19 October 1946, *Sardar Patel's Correspondence*, vol. 3, pp. 131-2.

[4] Jawaharlal to Cripps, 18 August, and to Wavell, 19 August 1946; Wavell to Jawaharlal, 19 August 1946.

[5] Jawaharlal to Wavell, 20 August, and Wavell to Jawaharlal, 22 August 1946.

but not interfere with the nominations of the Congress, including a nationalist Muslim. Jawaharlal repeated that the only proper approach was to make clear that while the Congress would always welcome co-operation, they would govern on their own even if this co-operation were denied.

> Calcutta has been a horrible shock to you and to all of us. And yet may I say that it has a personal significance for us which it cannot have even for you. Our friends and relatives are involved in these bloody murders, and our children and dear ones may have to face the assassin's knife at any time. It is this grim reality that we face. We shall face it of course without shouting, but we are not going to shake hands with murder or allow it to determine the country's policy. We shall still continue to reason with Hindu and Muslim and Sikh and others and try to win them over to the path of friendly co-operation, for there is no other way for the advancement of India. But we do not believe that co-operation will come out of appeasement of wrongdoing.[1]

Such firmness cowed the Viceroy for the time being. He announced the list of ministers and, in a broadcast, associated himself with the offer of the Congress to refer to the Federal Court all questions of interpretation of the Cabinet Mission Plan. But a visit to Calcutta and talks with a representative of the League revived Wavell's persistent desire to do all he could to bring the League into the interim government. He sent for Gandhi and Jawaharlal, presented them with a draft committing the Congress to groups as well as sections, and said he would not convene the Constituent Assembly unless the Congress made this declaration. He now brushed aside the suggestion of reference to the Federal Court by asserting that the problem was not a legal but a practical one. But the Working Committee rejected what seemed to it a new effort at blackmail and Gandhi had the matter referred to London.[2]

Wavell had meantime to go ahead with the reconstitution of the Government, and on 2 September what the Congress liked to regard as the provisional national government was sworn in. Jawaharlal was vice-president of the executive council and held the portfolios of external affairs and Commonwealth relations. Now at last he seemed to have come to the end of a long and irregular road and to be able to move away from conflict and struggle to constructive effort. 'Too long have we been passive spectators of events, the playthings of others. The initiative comes to our people now and we shall make the history of our choice.'[3] Jawaharlal organized his team to work as a Cabinet representative of the people. Rajagopalachari was pulled up for informing not Jawahar-

---

[1] Jawaharlal's personal letter to Wavell, 22 August 1946.
[2] Letters of Jawaharlal and Gandhi to Wavell, 28 August 1946; Wavell to Jawaharlal, 29 August and Jawaharlal's reply, 29 August 1946.
[3] Jawaharlal's broadcast, 7 September, *National Herald,* 8 September 1946.

lal but the Viceroy of the date of his taking up his portfolio. [1] Wavell had to agree not to receive secretaries of departments, as was the custom till now, and to deal only with the members of his council. The Viceroy's efforts to administer those departments whose members could not join at once were firmly resisted; and so was the Political Department's attempt to supervise the visits of Jawaharlal and his colleagues to the Princely States. [2] The members met informally every evening without Wavell to take decisions on major issues and agreed on no account to refer any matter to the Viceroy. When the British Government, in consultation with the Viceroy before Baldev Singh had taken over as defence minister, took steps to retain British troops in India while Indian troops were being demobilized, Jawaharlal, who came to know of it by seeing a chance telegram, sharply objected. This might have blown up into a crisis, for Wavell held that the question of stationing British troops affected vitally his responsibility to the British Parliament; but a way out was found by asking Baldev Singh to look into the matter with the help of the Commander-in-Chief. [3]

More serious points of friction between the Viceroy and the interim government were the conduct of the Governors and the League ministries in Sind and Bengal. In the former province the Governor used every method to thwart the Congress and keep the League in office, while in Bengal the Suhrawardy Government, with the passive acquiescence of the Governor, behaved 'essentially like the Hitler government in Germany during its early years . . . People who come from Bengal remind me forcibly of the refugees from the Hitler terror. I have never seen anything exactly like this in India before.'[4] The authorities of both provinces were supported by the Viceroy and the British Government, and Wavell prevented the intervention of the central government on the ground that it could not interfere with provincial autonomy which fell within the personal purview of the Governor-General. [5] Jawaharlal demanded that his government's views be forwarded to the Secretary of State and sharply rebutted Wavell's feeble efforts at defending the action of the Governor of Sind. 'If what I consider a racket and a public scandal has your approval, then it is obvious that our standards and sense of values differ considerably. It would also appear that our objectives are different.'[6] As for Bengal, violence was spreading in the districts with the government unable or unwilling to control it.

Indeed I have come seriously to think whether it serves any useful purpose for me to be in the Interim Government if an important part of

[1] Jawaharlal to Rajagopalachari, 30 August, and Rajagopalachari's reply, 3 September 1946.

[2] Wavell to Jawaharlal, 3 September, Jawaharlal's two letters to Wavell, 4 September and Wavell to Jawaharlal, 5 September 1946.

[3] Jawaharlal to Wavell, 18 September, and Wavell's reply, 19 September 1946.

[4] Jawaharlal to Krishna Menon, 6 October 1946.

[5] Wavell to Jawaharlal 8 September 1946

[6] Jawaharlal to Wavell, 23 September 1946.

India sinks to barbarism or something much worse . . . What is the good of our forming the Interim Government of India if all that we can do is to watch helplessly and do nothing else when thousands of people are being butchered and subjected to infinitely worse treatment? [1]

The case of the NWFP was entirely different. Here the Congress Party had a clear majority; and of the total Muslim votes cast in the elections, the Congress and Nationalist Muslim candidates had secured 208,896 and the League candidates 147,880. But so long as the Frontier Province, of which only about 3 per cent of the population was non-Muslim, was outside the League's control, Jinnah could not claim to be the unqualified representative of Muslim India, and Pakistan could be no more than a dream. So British officials set themselves to destroy the popularity of the Congress and rectify 'the bastard situation'. [2] Their first opportunity came when Jawaharlal decided to visit the NWFP. Tribal relations formed a part of his portfolio and he was anxious to make a first-hand appraisal. It was also obviously important for the leading figure of the Congress to undertake a flag march, as it were, and across terrain which had cast its spell over Jawaharlal. He was, as he told the Governor, Sir Olaf Caroe, himself regarded by many of his friends as being more than half a Pathan by nature. Caroe came to Delhi to dissuade Jawaharlal from visiting the province till after the League had joined the interim government, but Jawaharlal refused to postpone his visit, and toured the province and the tribal areas in the middle of October. The League organized demonstrations against him and sent the Mulla of Manki for this purpose into tribal territory. Such activities directed against the Vice-President of the Viceroy's Council should obviously have been taken serious note of; but Caroe was unwilling to restrain the Mulla and his men. His justification makes curious reading. 'I think that in the circumstances, and given the fact that Nehru's tour was obviously intended to push the Congress cause, it would have been wrong to put active restraint against the League's propagandists going into tribal territory, and an attempt to do so would certainly have led to disturbances.' [3] The result was that throughout his tour Jawaharlal faced hostile receptions and stone-throwing, which Caroe had no doubt had been organized by the League. Bruised, but fortunate not to have been killed, Jawaharlal completed his programme with courage. But the officials had succeeded in exploiting this visit to begin the weakening of Congress authority in the NWFP. As Caroe reported later, tongue in cheek,

Most of our troubles were started when Nehru took tribal affairs under his wing and followed this up with his ill-starred visit. Before that time

[1] Jawaharlal to Wavell, 15 October 1946.
[2] The phrase is Lord Ismay's. A. Campbell Johnson, *Mission with Mountbatten* (London, 1951), p. 54.
[3] Caroe to Wavell, 23 October 1946, Caroe papers.

the Province was going along very nicely all things considered, but it was an impossible thing to do to bring these tribals under a Pandit. Practically all our frictions and tensions date from that time. [1]

There was no cause for surprise in this curbing by Wavell and his governors of the functioning of what was virtually a Congress government at the centre. 'Almost everywhere in India it has been obvious that governors and others favour the Muslim League as against the Congress. Some of them do it inadvertently and almost unconsciously; others do it deliberately and obviously and sometimes even twist the law to this end.' [2] Alongside this hampering of the Congress, frantic efforts continued to bring the League into the interim government. In this the Viceroy now had the full support of the Cabinet in London. Cripps urged the Congress to go as far as it could in conciliating the League.

You know how earnestly — even if mistakenly sometimes — I have worked for Indian independence which I now see on the eve of accomplishment if only Congress can have the statesmanship and magnanimity to act the part of the strong man and give way to the weak. The possibility is in your hands and unborn generations will hail the act of Congress now as the great decisive gesture for Indian freedom and self-government.
It is not I am sure a question of hard bargaining now — that will get us nowhere, it is a question of supreme statesmanship and only you can solve the problem at this stage.
Jawaharlal — with all my heart and mind I beg and pray that you may be guided to right action in this difficult moment. [3]

Wavell, working on the premiss that the convening of the Constituent Assembly was the prerogative of the Viceroy and not of the Government of India, was unwilling to take action until agreement had been reached with Jinnah on both the long-term plan and a coalition government.[4] Now, once again, was revealed the pertinence of Jawaharlal's statements at Bombay in July on the sovereign nature of the Constituent Assembly and therefore the minimum amount of extraneous action in its procedures. The Viceroy started discussions with Jinnah who, having no wish to be left out of office, was willing to respond. The only point on which he now insisted was that the Congress should not nominate a Muslim in the government, and Wavell appealed to Gandhi and Jawaharlal to waive its right to do so for the sake of a settlement.

[1] Caroe to Mountbatten, 23 June 1947, Caroe papers.
[2] Jawaharlal to Caroe, 16 November 1946.
[3] Cripps to Jawaharlal, 16 September 1946.
  Wavell to Jawaharlal, 13 September 1946.

To this appeal was added a threat that if the Congress declined, the Viceroy doubted if he could allow the interim government to continue as it was.[1] Pethick-Lawrence backed up Wavell and added that the League would have to be brought into the Constituent Assembly if that body was to be of any use.[2]

Resentful though they were of these pressure tactics, the leaders of the Congress realized that there would be some advantages in bringing in the League. If this were effected in such a way as to bind the League to a proper working of both a coalition government and the Constituent Assembly, it might lighten the tension in the country and put events back on an even keel. So Jawaharlal called on Jinnah on 5 October, and found him considerably toned down. Though Jawaharlal repudiated a formula unthinkingly accepted by Gandhi that the League had an unquestionable right to represent all the Muslims, Jinnah did not break off the discussions. Rather, he assured Jawaharlal that he would never side with the British and would in no event permit the Viceroy to function as an umpire in any coalition government. In return Jawaharlal offered to have any fresh appointments of minority representatives considered by the whole Cabinet, to refer major communal issues, if necessary, to arbitration and, instead of rotating the Vice-Presidentship, to create an additional vice-chairmanship of the Cabinet co-ordination committee.[3] These concessions seemed to satisfy Jinnah; but within hours he reverted to his usual attitude of refusing to reach any agreement with the Congress and relying on the British. He insisted on Gandhi's formula and the exclusion of any Nationalist Muslim from the Government. The Congress replied that it could go no further than what had been offered by Jawaharlal, who added that he could never be a party to disowning the Muslims in the Congress. This was to him a personal as well as a national question of honour.[4] But discussions with Jinnah were resumed by Wavell. He accepted Jinnah's nomination of five members including one person belonging to the Scheduled Castes, but without securing a precise commitment on the part of the League to the Cabinet Mission Plan, a renunciation of the League's policy of direct action and a pledge to co-operate in the Government. Indeed the deliberate choice (apart from Liaqat Ali Khan) of second-rate diehard members of his party, and of a Harijan who represented nobody, established beyond any doubt that Jinnah's sole aim was to share power and disrupt the interim government. But so eager was Wavell to destroy the control by the Congress of immediate authority that he brought the League in, despite Jawaharlal's repeated protests,[5] unconditionally. It was among the most serious of Wavell's many disservices to India.

[1]Gandhi to Wavell, 27 September 1946.
[2]Krishna Menon to Jawaharlal, 26 September 1946.
[3]Jawaharlal's notes of conversations with Jinnah, 5 October, and letter to Jinnah, 6 October 1946.
[4]Jawaharlal to the Nawab of Bhopal, 10 October 1946.
[5]See Jawaharlal's letters to Wavell, 13, 14, 15 and 23 October 1946.

Once the League had agreed to join the Government, Wavell asked the Congress to hand over either external affairs or home or defence. When the Congress refused to transfer any of these portfolios and offered only finance and commerce, the Viceroy decided that the home portfolio should be taken away from Patel and given to the League. At this all the members of the interim government decided to resign,[1] and the crisis was only solved by the League agreeing to take finance. On this basis the five nominees of the League were sworn in on 26 October.

The working of the Congress-League government must be unique in the annals of modern administration. Each group met separately before a Cabinet meeting and there functioned in opposition to the other. This suited Wavell. He forgot the specific assurance he had given to the Congress that he would prevent any attempt to make the interim government a battleground of communal politics instead of an instrument for administering India.[2] He encouraged the League in its obstructive attitude by referring every major issue to the two sides for opinion rather than insisting on the government functioning as a team, and himself acted as umpire.

Jawaharlal's handling of external relations became one of the chief targets of the League's attack. As the first step in building up an independent foreign policy unaligned to any Power, Jawaharlal had preferred to develop informal contacts rather than utilize British diplomatic representation. Acting as Jawaharlal's personal envoy, Krishna Menon met Molotov, conveyed the new government's earnest desire for friendly relations with the Soviet Union and sought assistance in foodgrains.[3] He also, stepping beyond his brief, spoke to Molotov about the possibility of Soviet military experts visiting India. This upset not only the Foreign Office and the Indian external affairs department but also some of Jawaharlal's colleagues in the Congress; and Krishna Menon received the first of, over the years, very many mildly worded cautions from his chief.

I want to make it clear that I have complete faith in you and I am quite sure that whatever step you will take will be taken after full consideration and with a view not to create any difficulties. So far as I am concerned, that is all right. But other people, who do not know you well, have also to be taken into consideration and hence I have suggested to you that you might bear these people also in mind.[4]

When the League came into the government, Jawaharlal had to abandon his ideas of sending Menon to Moscow or appointing him as high commissioner

[1] Jawaharlal to Wavell, 24 October 1946.
[2] See his own report of his interview with Patel, 12 June 1946, Wavell, op. cit., p. 291.
[3] Jawaharlal's letters to Molotov, 21 September and to Krishna Menon, 25 September; note to the Viceroy, 24 September 1946.
[4] To Krishna Menon, 13 October 1946.

in London, for that post was technically attached to the commerce department, administered by one of the representatives of the League. Menon was asked to work with the Indian delegation to the United Nations. When the League sought representation on that delegation, Jawaharlal replied that it was too late to alter the composition. However, the League, with facilities provided by the Viceroy and the India Office, sent two representatives to the United States where they denounced the Congress, the Indian delegation to the United Nations and the working of the interim government. In the Cabinet and outside, the League expressed no views on foreign policy but merely repudiated Jawaharlal's efforts and appointments and demanded the creation of Pakistan; and Wavell repeatedly called upon Jawaharlal to discuss even matters pertaining to his own department with Liaqat Ali Khan.

More vital, of course, were developments in the various parts of India which were aptly described as being in a state of spontaneous combustion. 'Murder stalks the streets and the most amazing cruelties are indulged in by both the individual and the mob. It is extraordinary how our peaceful population has become militant and bloodthirsty. Riot is not the word for it — it is just a sadistic desire to kill.'[1] News of the slaughter of Hindus in Bengal percolated to Bihar and roused the local peasants to attack the Muslims. Gandhi and Jawaharlal urged the Congress ministry to deal sternly with the guilty, and in this received the firm support of the Viceroy and the League, whose concern for the sanctity of provincial autonomy was presumably reserved only for Bengal and Sind. Jawaharlal and one of the League ministers in the central government toured Bihar and helped to bring the province under control. The army was called in, and rioting crowds dispersed by fire and, on a few occasions, by aerial bombing. Such firm and decisive action was possible only because of Jawaharlal's initiative.

His intervention, however, was in his personal capacity. The interim government itself could do, and did, little. It was riven by dispute and powerless in action. Matters came to a head on the question of convening the Constituent Assembly. It was scheduled to meet in December but the Viceroy and his advisers, 'functioning more and more openly as if they were allied with the Muslim League,'[2] wished to postpone it on the ground that the League had not yet accepted the long-term plan rather than to press Jinnah to reach an early decision.[3] Jawaharlal insisted that as the League was making clear that it would not accept the Plan it should not continue in the interim government.[4] Attlee now decided to intervene and wanted the Congress, the League and the Sikhs to depute their representatives to London. The Congress declined to go as this was tantamount to reopening the whole question; nor did Jawaharlal have much confidence in Attlee, who, as reported by Krishna Menon, not

[1] Jawaharlal to Krishna Menon, 11 November 1946.
[2] Idem, 17 November 1946.
[3] Jawaharlal to P.S.V., 15 and 16 November and P.S.V.'s reply, 16 November 1946.
[4] Jawaharlal to Wavell, 21 November 1946.

only had shown 'no warmth at all for the new government or for you personally' but had made 'no response to the message of goodwill' and evinced 'certainly no anxiety or desire to be fraternal!'[1] But Attlee now sent a personal message urging Jawaharlal to come and assuring him that there was no intention to abandon the Plan or the Constituent Assembly, and the Congress authorized Jawaharlal to go, if only because persistence in refusal would have been discourteous.

The talks in London in December confirmed the misgivings of the Congress and served to strengthen Jinnah's position. The British Government declared that, according to the Cabinet Plan, decisions in the sections would be by a simple majority vote. They urged the Congress to accept this view and suggested, as a sop, that it could be referred, along with other questions of interpretation, to the Federal Court by the Constituent Assembly. Jinnah was delighted. He had, with the help of the British, recovered much ground. The League had, after an initial setback, moved into the government and brought administration to a standstill without any commitment on the Mission Plan; and now the Congress was being pressed to abandon its position and accept an unfavourable interpretation of the Plan so that the League could be cajoled into attending the Constituent Assembly. Pakistan seemed to be in sight, and to make it a large and powerful state he sought the collaboration of the Sikhs. At a private session with Baldev Singh, the Sikh representative at the talks in London, he offered the Sikhs any guarantees they might require. 'Baldev Singh, you see this match-box. Even if Pakistan of this size is offered to me I will gladly accept it, but it is here that I need your collaboration. If you persuade the Sikhs to join hands with the Muslim League we will have a glorious Pakistan, the gates of which will be near about Delhi if not in Delhi itself.'[2]

The Constituent Assembly met as scheduled, on 9 December, but adjourned repeatedly without taking any controversial decisions or breaking up into sections so as to enable the League to make up its mind. To provide Jinnah with no substantial argument for declining to join, the Congress, while voicing its disapproval of the manner in which the British Cabinet had elaborated its Plan to suit the League, accepted this interpretation and gave up its proposal of a reference to the Federal Court. All that it now stipulated was that there should be no compulsion of a province and the rights of the Sikhs should not be jeopardized. If such compulsion were attempted, a province or a part of a province should have the right to take whatever action was required to give effect to the wishes of the people concerned.[3] But Jinnah was still in a grandiose mood. The Working Committee of the League declined to reconsider its decision, and asked the British Government to declare that the Cabinet Mission Plan had failed and to dissolve the Constituent Assembly.[4]

[1] Krishna Menon to Jawaharlal, 18 October 1946.
[2] Baldev Singh to Jawaharlal, 19 September 1955, Nehru papers.
[3] Resolution of the AICC, 6 January 1947.
[4] Resolution of the Muslim League, 29 January 1947.

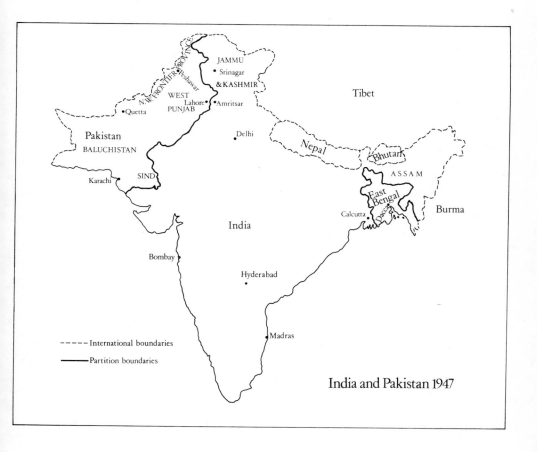

N.W. FRONTIER PROVINCE

JAMMU
• Srinagar
&KASHMIR

• Peshawar

WEST
Lahore•
PUNJAB   •Amritsar

•Quetta

Tibet

Pakistan

BALUCHISTAN

• Delhi

Nepal

Bhutan

ASSAM

Karachi   SIND

East
Bengal

Calcutta •   Dacca

Burma

India

Bombay •

Hyderabad
•

- - - - International boundaries

Madras •

Partition boundaries

India and Pakistan 1947

So, by the end of January 1947, it became clear that no further negotiations and compromises were possible, and the efforts of the Congress in this direction had only resulted in confusing its followers and dividing its leadership. With the League adamant and the Princes taking their cue from it and avoiding a decision on joining the Constituent Assembly, with the virus of communal rioting spreading across the face of northern India and the interim government resolution was about as bad as it could be. Perhaps there was a virtue in it for it makes the position quite clear.'[1] The Congress took the stand that the League, having rejected the Plan, should be told to leave the interim government. They had merely used it as a forum to harass the Congress and, with the Viceroy's assistance, raised the communal issue at every step. Even the appointments of ambassadors had been held up because they had wanted every second post to go to nominees of the League irrespective of merit, and Wavell had supported them by suggesting that all appointments in India and abroad should be considered by Cabinet committees.[2] This was hardly the atmosphere for the furtherance of Jawaharlal's many ideas, such as the development of a foreign policy which would show the world that the new India had iron in it and was not to be patronized or trifled with, the building up of the defence forces without any foreign element, the promotion of scientific research, the renewal of planning and the rapid industrialization of the country.

On 5 February, nine members of the interim government — all except the five nominees of the League — wrote a joint letter to the Viceroy that in their opinion the League could not continue in the government. Jawaharlal followed this up eight days later by stating that if a quick decision were not given he and his colleagues would leave the government. The League, of course, had no intention of resigning and Wavell, instead of pointing out to Jinnah that he was having the best of both worlds, still wished to press the Congress for further — and futile — concessions. But the British Government's decision was different. Attlee announced that the British would withdraw from India not later than June 1948, handing over, if there were no government established by a fully representative assembly, to the central government or in some areas to existing provincial governments. He added that Wavell would be replaced by Mountbatten.

Jawaharlal and the Congress welcomed this statement because, despite the clear hint that a Constituent Assembly without the representatives of the League would not be recognized, it seemed to show a way out of the deadlock so created. That Assembly could continue to function for the areas represented in it and without the limitations imposed by the Mission Plan. The statement also implied a partition of the Punjab and Bengal, because eastern Punjab and

[1] Jawaharlal to Gandhi, 9 February 1947.
[2] Jawaharlal to Wavell, 23 and 31 January 1947.

western Bengal were represented in the Assembly and had no intention of being cut off from the Indian Union. 'The truncated Pakistan that remains will hardly be a gift worth having.'[1] Economically and for defence it seemed impracticable and Jinnah might well prefer joining the Indian Union on special terms. So the Working Committee passed resolutions along these lines and invited the League to a joint consideration of these issues. The Congress also decided not to press for the resignation of the League's nominees in the central government till the general situation had been clarified; and Jawaharlal made a personal approach to Liaqat Ali Khan. 'The British are fading out of the picture and the burden of this decision must rest on all of us here. It seems desirable that we should face this situation squarely and not speak to each other from a distance.'[2] But the League did not respond to these gestures. Liaqat Ali Khan made no response to Jawaharlal's informal approach but introduced a wide-ranging budget without full discussions with his colleagues or even Jawaharlal on at least the general nature of his proposals.

The League was also not prepared to discuss constitutional developments with the Congress even on the basis of partition. Jinnah embarked on a cruise in the Arabian Sea, while his henchmen continued to clamour for direct action, brought down the ministry in the Punjab and fomented an agitation in the Frontier Province. Jawaharlal decided to visit these provinces, but while at Lahore received a message from Wavell requesting him to proceed no further. This injunction he attributed to Sir Olaf Caroe and demanded his removal. 'Am I to be prevented from performing my duty and shouldering the responsibility which has been cast upon me, because someone does not like me or does not approve of my going to the Frontier? . . . It is an extraordinary position. Almost anyone can go to Peshawar but I must not do so, even for a brief and informal visit.'[3] But no action was taken on his demand for Caroe's dismissal before Wavell's departure a few days later.

---

[1] Jawaharlal to Krishna Menon, 23 February 1947.
[2] Jawaharlal to Liaqat Ali Khan, 9 March 1947.
[3] Jawaharlal to Wavell, 19 March 1947.

22

The Transfer of Power

On 24 March 1947, Mountbatten was sworn in as Viceroy. Romantic myth has been built, not without encouragem-nt, round his short term of office. Books have been written depicting the I rince Charming who appeared in the last scene of the Indian drama, dominated the British Cabinet and imposed his will on Indian politicians. 'I was governing by personality.'[1] Taking, we are told, firm hold of a crumbling situation, he decided to partition the country and effected it in just over four and a half months, thus solving a problem which had baffled statesmen in Britain and India for years.

Mountbatten had, of course, great personal assets: good looks, links with royalty, a dazzling war reputation, a wife of charm and intelligence. But it is childish to suggest that these even helped to solve the Indian question by bemusing those concerned into accepting his solution. In fact, even before Mountbatten came to India, both the British Government and the Congress Party had come round to the view that there was no alternative to accepting Jinnah's demand in some form or another. It was now an axiom of official British thinking not only in Delhi but in London as well that the Congress represented the Hindus and the League the Muslims. Cripps, for example, said of the 1946 elections: 'For the first time since the beginning of the war the full strength of the rival *communities* was made clear and it became apparent that Indians had ranged themselves substantially upon a communal basis behind the Congress and the Muslim League.'[2] Attlee's statement of 20 February clearly recognized that the Mission Plan was dead and the British would transfer authority, if need be, to governments other than that at the centre. Even the fixing of the date by which the British would leave would seem to have been Attlee's idea, and therefore one for which Mountbatten cannot take the main credit. It has been ingeniously suggested that it was Mountbatten who was most insistent on a firm date and decided that the best way to secure

[1] Mountbatten's interview with the author, 28 May 1970.
[2] 3 March 1947. Italics mine. In the original draft the word had been 'parties' but it was altered to 'communities' to leave no doubt about what was meant. Cripps papers, File 13.

it was to impute it to the Prime Minister. [1] But perhaps it is best to rely in this matter on the testimony of Lord Ismay, who served on Mountbatten's staff in India and, besides being well-informed, was if anything prejudiced in Mountbatten's favour. Congratulating Attlee on the outcome of the Commonwealth Prime Ministers' Conference when India, though a republic, was enabled to remain in the Commonwealth, Ismay wrote:

> It was a wonderful personal triumph for you — as was the original decision to appoint a definite date for the handing over of power in India and to send Dickie [Mountbatten] as Viceroy. You have, if I may be so bold as to say so, ridden an absolutely consistent and far seeing line on India from the very outset . . . Anyway you have brought off a wonderful right and left, which history will certainly acclaim. [2]

The Congress Working Committee too had, early in March, reconciled itself to the partition of the Punjab and recognized that the same principle would also be applicable to Bengal. To Gandhi the unity of India was still important, but he had by now departed into the shadows. His role in the Congress was similar to that of a head of an Oxbridge college who is greatly revered but has little influence on the governing body. Jawaharlal and Patel had come to the conclusion that there was no alternative to at least temporary secession. Various psychological tensions seemed to them to have developed among the Indian people, and especially among the Muslims, and these could not be resolved by reason or dealt with by force. To insist on the maintenance of the Indian Union could only mean continuing trouble. Even a very loose union seemed out of the question and efforts to sustain it could only result in weakening the country and halting all social and economic progress. The total inability of the interim government to reach a decision on any major issue was powerful testimony in favour of division. So Jawaharlal and the Congress, while rejecting the two-nation theory, agreed to the separation of those parts of the country which wished to break away. Indeed, that might make it easier for reason and the compulsion of logic ultimately to prevail. There were some subjects like defence which, even after partition, would not of choice but of necessity have to be looked after in common, and this might lead gradually back to a reintegration of India. 'I have no doubt whatever that sooner or later India will have to function as a unified country. Perhaps the best way to reach that stage is to go through some kind of a partition now.' [3] It was wise to let events have their course for a while so that they might return on their own to the normal equilibrium. 'But of one thing I am convinced that ultimately there will be a united

---

[1] Hodson, op. cit., p. 194.
[2] Ismay to Attlee, 6 March 1949, Attlee papers, Box 6.
[3] To K. P. S. Menon, 29 April 1947.

and strong India. We have often to go through the valley of the shadow before we reach the sun-lit mountain tops.'[1]

Mountbatten's task, therefore, was merely to work out the details and effect the partition demanded by the League and accepted by both the British Government and the Congress; and this the new Viceroy moved commandingly to perform. Before Mountbatten's arrival, Jawaharlal had been concerned by the inclusion in his staff of Ismay and Sir Eric Miéville, who had last been in India with Willingdon, but he was soon impressed by Mountbatten's goodwill, commonsensical directness and sense of urgency — all in such sharp contrast to Wavell's dithering and prejudice. In the first few weeks of the viceroyalty, while Mountbatten went through the motions of consultations and seeking to breathe life into the Cabinet Mission Plan, Jawaharlal was content to be a mere spectator.

He first gave all his attention to the Asian Relations Conference. The idea of such a conference had been in Jawaharlal's mind from December 1945, and, after preliminary arrangements had been made, invitations were sent out in September 1946. It was to be a non-official conference representative of all shades of opinion in the countries of Asia (plus Egypt). So each country was requested to send a delegation of sixteen chosen by established institutions (where they existed) which were interested in world affairs; and these delegations were to be supplemented by four observers nominated by the government of the country and by distinguished scholars invited in their individual capacity. Convened in the uninhibited times before India was free and Jawaharlal was restricted by the requirements of official policy, the conference could hear the views of both the Kuomintang and the Communists, of the Arab League as well as the Hebrew University. The Soviet Central Asian republics were represented; and in addition the Soviet Union, along with Australia, New Zealand, Britain and the United States, sent observers.

There was, in fact, an euphoric atmosphere about the Conference. Its main purpose was to enable the leaders of Asia, on the threshold of a new world, to meet. Not only controversial issues involving these countries, but even matters like defence and security which concerned powers outside Asia were excluded from the agenda, which listed only such innocuous subjects as national freedom movements, migration and racial problems, economic development and the status of women. But the agenda was the least important part of the conference. For ten days, from 23 March to 2 April, Delhi saw itself as the natural centre of a resurgent continent, conscious of its glorious past and forging links for the future.

Standing on this watershed which divides two epochs of human history and endeavour, we can look back on our long past and look forward to

[1] To Brigadier (later General) Cariappa, 29 April 1947.

the future that is taking shape before our eyes . . . An Indian, wherever he may go in Asia, feels a sense of kinship with the land he visits and the people he meets . . . For too long we of Asia have been petitioners in Western courts and chancelleries. That story must now belong to the past. We propose to stand on our own feet and to cooperate with all others who are prepared to cooperate with us. We do not intend to be the playthings of others.[1]

Nothing came of the Asian Relations Organization set up by the Conference, and no participant country acted on the resolution to set up national units of this Organization or academies of Asian studies. There was not even a second session of the Asian Relations Conference, though one may trace its influence in the origins of the Asian-African Conference held at Bandung in 1955. Yet Jawaharlal was satisfied with the Conference as the expression of an emotion which he personally felt deeply. So to him the Conference was

an amazing success from every point of view. I think we can definitely call it the beginnings of a new era in Asian history. All those who came from the four corners of Asia felt the importance and significance of the occasion and went away duly impressed. Delhi did them well. India as a whole suddenly became conscious not only of all our neighbours but of Asia. We are all Asia-conscious at present.[2]

Even after the Conference, Jawaharlal took no active part in the constitutional discussions. 'He is very tired mentally and physically', commented Ismay after an interview with him,[3] 'and he's subject to emotion to an alarming degree. But he has courage and statesmanship of a sort.' Convinced of Mountbatten's *bona fides,* his main objective at this time was merely to clear the way for the Viceroy to concentrate on the major problems by shelving or disposing of the minor ones. He did not press for Caroe's removal. He resolved the minor crisis which had developed on the eve of Wavell's departure over the release of the members of the Indian National Army still in prison. This was the only issue on which the members of the interim government were united, and they were supported by the Legislative Assembly. Wavell, however, with the approval of the British Government exercised his veto. Normally any government could have been expected to resign, but the interim government was not a normal government. It is extremely doubtful if the representatives of the League, despite the common viewpoint, would have joined the Congress in such a step. This probably also influenced Jawaharlal in yielding to Mountbatten's pressure

[1] Jawaharlal's inaugural address to the conference, 23 March 1947, reprinted in *Asian Relations* (report of the proceedings), New Delhi, 1948, pp. 20-27.
[2] To Asaf Ali, 7 April 1947.
[3] 6 April 1947, R. Wingate, *Lord Ismay* (London, 1970), p. 153.

and suggesting reference of all these cases to the Federal Court for advice. He was resentful of Jinnah's insistence that he would sign an appeal for communal peace only with Gandhi and not also with J. B. Kripalani, who had taken over the Congress presidency from Jawaharlal. Jinnah's intent was clearly to imply that Gandhi represented Hindu India, and he, Muslim India — an approach unfair to Gandhi and contrary to the policy of the Congress. Yet Jawaharlal agreed to abide by Mountbatten's decision and the appeal was issued by Gandhi and Jinnah alone.[1]

Jawaharlal, therefore, even to the detriment of his own party, gave the Viceroy full scope to work out the best way in which the country could be partitioned. Mountbatten and his advisers drew up a 'Plan Balkan', whereby power would be demitted to the provinces and they would be left to decide whether they would form any groups.[2] The plan was not shown in detail to the Congress leaders, and Jawaharlal knew only the general outlines. He certainly does not seem to have known that power was being transferred to the provinces, and was assuming that partition would involve no more than a division of the Punjab and Bengal. It has been stated that Miéville showed the draft proposals to Jawaharlal and had a satisfactory interview with him.[3] But the evidence is all the other way. 'Neither I nor my colleagues of the Interim Government who were present at our meeting', wrote Jawaharlal to Mountbatten on 1 May, 'know the full extent of the proposals that Lord Ismay is taking with him to London. But you have been good enough to keep me informed of the broad outlines of these proposals and I placed these before the [Working] Committee . . . I have not entered in this letter into any detailed consideration of all your proposals as we have not got them before us in their final form.' So, apart from reiterating that the Congress would accept the principle of partition based on self-determination as applied to definitely ascertained areas, Jawaharlal stressed only the unfairness of attempts to dislodge the Congress ministry in the Frontier province in order to make Pakistan a practical proposition. To yield to the demands of the League, backed up by terrorism and rioting, for fresh elections would be a surrender which would have far-reaching repercussions not only in the Frontier province but in the rest of India.[4] But far from putting down this violence and the policy underlying it, the Governor and some of his advisers were encouraging the League; and Jawaharlal now hinted at resignation if Caroe were not removed. 'I find it increasingly difficult to continue to be in charge of a Department which is responsible in some way for the activities of officials who function wrongly and are completely beyond my control.'[5] Mountbatten could have had no doubts about Caroe's abuse of his position.

[1] Jawaharlal to Mountbatten, 14 April, and Mountbatten's reply, 15 April 1947.
[2] Hodson, op. cit., pp. 229-30.
[3] Ibid., p. 293.
[4] Jawaharlal to Mountbatten, 17 and 26 April 1947.
[5] Idem, 1 May 1947.

The New Cabinet

The New Cabinet, which will function from
August 15th 1947, will consist of the following members.
Their portfolios are indicated opposite their names:

Jawaharlal Nehru - Prime Minister; External Affairs
                and Commonwealth Relations; Scientific Research.
Sardar Vallabhbhai Patel - Home; Information and
                Broadcasting; States.
Dr Rajendra Prasad : Food and Agriculture.
Maulana Abul Kalam Azad : Education.
Dr John Matthai : Railways and Transport
Sardar Baldev Singh : Defence
Shri Jagjivan Ram : Labour
Mr C. H. Bhabha : Commerce
Mr Rafi Ahmad Kidwai : Communications
Rajkumari Amrit Kaur : Health
Dr B. R. Ambedkar : Law
Shri R. K. Shanmukham Chetty : Finance
Dr Shyama Prasad Mukherji : Industries and Supplies.
Shri N. V. Gadgil : Works, Mines and Power

                                Jawaharlal Nehru
                                August 14. 1947

Jawaharlal's first Cabinet List

The Governor openly acted on the premiss that 'the Congress is not natural here' and it was but proper that the province, sandwiched between the Punjab and the tribes, should have a League ministry. As the League lacked leaders in the province of the calibre of Abdul Gaffar Khan and his brother Dr Khan Sahib, the Congress premier, Caroe repeatedly urged the latter to oust the Hindus in his ministry and sever his connection with the Congress[1] — advice which was hardly in keeping with the Governor's constitutional position. But Mountbatten was not prepared, at this stage at any rate, to remove Caroe. Wavell had advised strongly against it and the dismissal of a senior I.C.S. governor at the request of half his government was not a step to be taken lightly. Moreover, on a visit to the Frontier province, Mountbatten seems to have been impressed by the mass demonstrations organized to establish the growing strength of the League. On the other hand, he protested against the agitation promoted by the Congress in various cities for the removal of Caroe, and Gaffar Khan's public criticism of the Governor, as attempts to make him act under duress.[2] In fact, Mountbatten decided to adopt Caroe's policy and make it acceptable to the Congress, when the time came, by getting rid of Caroe. He told Khan Sahib that he could only remove Caroe if the Congress agreed to a referendum; they could work out which they preferred.[3]

Even after Ismay had secured the Cabinet's approval, with minor amendments, to Mountbatten's Plan Balkan, Jawaharlal and Mountbatten continued primarily to discuss its application to the Frontier province. Jawaharlal was, on 10 May, Mountbatten's guest at Simla. There the Viceroy wrote to him that instead of Governor's rule or fresh elections in the NWFP, a referendum should be held on the issue of partition by an organization under the control not of the Governor but of the Viceroy. 'I will tell Caroe to tell Dr Khan Sahib that you are in general agreement with the procedure.' Jawaharlal promptly denied this and refused to be hustled. This was a matter on which the Working Committee felt very strongly and had specifically directed Jawaharlal to convey its feeling to the Viceroy. All that Jawaharlal had agreed to was that the people of the Frontier province should be consulted before final decisions were taken, but it was very important when this was done and in what context, and any referendum would require the full concurrence of the provincial government.[4]

On the night of 10 May Mountbatten, acting on 'an absolute hunch', gave Jawaharlal the complete text of the Plan Balkan as revised by the Cabinet. 'The moment', writes the chronicler of the Mountbatten phase in India, 'was a watershed in the history of three nations.'[5] This is to overrate the importance

[1] Caroe to Mountbatten, 22 March and 7 April 1947, Caroe papers.
[2] Mountbatten to Jawaharlal, 6 May 1947.
[3] Interview with the author, 28 May 1970.
[4] Mountbatten to Jawaharlal, 10 May, and Jawaharlal's reply of the same date.
[5] Hodson, op. cit., pp. 295-6.

of the event if Jawaharlal was merely being shown again a text which he had already seen, but with some minor alterations. In fact, he was seeing the full text for the first time, and was so upset that he burst into Krishna Menon's room at 2 a.m., speechless with indignation.[1] That certain features of the Plan came as a complete surprise to him demands emphasis, for an understanding of Jawaharlal's reaction hinges on this. Jawaharlal places this beyond doubt in a note recorded by him at the time:

> *At Simla*
> On the 10th May night I was given some idea of the draft proposals as they had been sent to London. I considered them that night and early next morning I dictated a long note. As there was delay in typing this note and events were marching fast, I sent a brief hand-written letter to Lord Mountbatten. I kept no copy of this. This letter produced an immediate impression and led to a talk. Later I handed over to Mountbatten the typewritten note of 11/5.
>
> On the 11th afternoon it was decided to postpone the Conference called for May 17th to June 2nd.
>
> J.N.

The hastily written note which he sent to Mountbatten shows signs of excitement and is in places incoherent. But it made clear that the Congress would not accept the break-up of the Indian Union and the transfer of sovereignty to the provinces. Any plan should start with the Union and the opting out of certain areas rather than a number of sovereign units coming together if they so desired. To jettison the basic conception of India and denude the Constituent Assembly of its significance was to yield to the League and ignore the views of all other sections of opinion in India. The 'preposterous' suggestion to settle the future of Baluchistan in accordance with the wishes of a few nominated Sirdars, the insistence that the NWFP be given a fresh opportunity to reverse its decision to form a part of India and the refusal to apply to Sind the formula enforced on Assam that a Muslim-majority part of it should be attached to the contiguous seceding area were all intended as special favours to the League. The inevitable consequences would be to invite the Balkanization of India, provoke civil conflict and add to violence and disorder, ensure a further breakdown of the central authority and demoralize the army, the police and the civil service. The States would also declare themselves independent kingdoms, probably in subordinate alliance with Britain, and this would create an almost

---

[1]Mountbatten's speech on the occasion of the third Jawaharlal Nehru Memorial Lecture, London, 12 November 1970.

unbridgeable gulf between the peoples of India and Britain. The public assurance to the tribes on the frontier that they could have treaties with whomsoever they liked was to invite them to profit by internal difficulties in India.

Jawaharlal's reaction surprised Mountbatten. He attributed it, as did Ismay later, to old suspicions of the British Government, and he believed that Jawaharlal resented the mere fact that the Plan had been revised in London.[1] A later interpretation draws on psychology. Jawaharlal, it is said, was prone to amnesia; even while discussing partition he had been entranced by the vision of a united India, and at the moment of truth reacted violently. The development at Simla is seen as essentially an internal crisis in the mind of an emotional dreamer; Jawaharlal was unconsciously balancing two sets of attitudes, experiencing one of his unpredictable, moody interludes, at odds with himself and with others, rebelling against the fact that he, the revolutionary, was putting himself into the hands of the Viceroy and the British Government.[2] But this interpretation assumes that Jawaharlal had seen the full text of the proposals which Ismay took to London; and he clearly had not. In his eagerness to get things done, Mountbatten was inclined to wishful believing. 'He's a grand chap in a thousand ways but clarity of thought and writing is not his strong suit.'[3] He had convinced himself that he had secured Jawaharlal's approval of the Plan Balkan and interpreted Jawaharlal's personal cordiality for whole-hearted acceptance of his scheme. But no doubt there was a gnawing sense of reality at the back of his mind and it was this which inspired his 'hunch'. Jawaharlal, taken aback by the concept of fragmentation, had too much faith in Mountbatten's integrity to believe either that he had introduced this feature into the Plan or that he had failed to inform Jawaharlal of it. He assumed, therefore, that it had been introduced by the British Cabinet and blamed them severely for it. This, and not the suggestion that he was so petty as to resent even minor alterations made in London, explains the language of his letter to the Viceroy. 'The relatively simple proposals that we had previously discussed now appeared in garb that HMG had provided for them in an entirely new context which gave them an ominous meaning . . . The picture of India that emerged frightened me . . . HMG seem to function in an ivory tower of their own isolated from realities in India . . .'[4]

Nor were Jawaharlal's fears wholly unreal and theoretical. There were powerful forces at work seeking to break up India into a number of units. Suhrawardy put himself at the head of a movement to create an independent Bengal and gained the support of some influential Congressmen. In the NWFP

---

[1]Campbell Johnson, op. cit., p. 90; Hodson, op. cit., p. 297; Ismay, *Memoirs* (London, 1960), p. 421.

[2]H. Tinker, *Experiment with Freedom* (Oxford, 1967), p. 112; and 'Jawaharlal Nehru at Simla May 1947', *Modern Asian Studies*, October 1970, pp. 349-58.

[3]Ismay on 23 April 1947, Wingate, op. cit., p. 153.

[4]This extract from Jawaharlal's handwritten letter (of which he kept no copy) of 11 May, is taken from Tinker's article, op. cit., p. 354.

also, many Congressmen talked loosely of independence as being preferable to being coerced into joining Pakistan. With the coming lapse of paramountcy the Political Department, over which the interim government had no control, was suspected by the Congress of encouraging the leading Princes to set themselves up as independent rulers.[1] The Nawab of Bhopal and the Nizam of Hyderabad were known to be toying with the idea of independence, and the Dewan of Travancore announced that this State would assume sovereign power. If the British Government had declared the Plan Balkan to be their policy, partition might well have expanded into fragmentation, and India as such ceased to exist.

After Jawaharlal's rejection of the Plan, Mountbatten, hurriedly plastering over his cracked confidence, postponed his meeting with the Indian leaders scheduled for 17 May, and directed his advisers to recast the Plan to meet Jawaharlal's main objection. The Constituent Assembly would continue to meet; and there would be a second Constituent Assembly for those areas which decided not to participate in the existing Assembly. The Punjab and Bengal would be partitioned if the representatives of either the Muslim-majority districts or the rest of the province desired it, and boundary commissions would be set up later to demarcate the boundaries on the basis of contiguous majority areas and other factors. It would not, however, be possible to provide a separate state for the Sikhs. Though Sylhet district was a part of Assam, as it was predominantly Muslim and contiguous to Bengal, a referendum should be held there to determine whether it should also be divided. Sind would decide through its assembly which state to join, and an appropriate mechanism would be devised to enable British Baluchistan also to choose. The real problem was with the NWFP, the majority of whose representatives were already participating in the Constituent Assembly. Here democratic principles were frankly set aside to enable Pakistan to become a reality. 'But it is clear, in view of its geographical situation, and other considerations, that if the whole or any part of the Punjab decides not to join the existing Constituent Assembly, it will be necessary to give the NWFP an opportunity to reconsider its position.' So if the Punjab decided on partition, a referendum would be held in the NWFP under the aegis of the Governor-General and in consultation with the Provincial Government. Agreements with the frontier tribes would be negotiated by the appropriate successor authorities. As for the Indian States, British policy would continue as before and the Plan would not apply to them.

This Plan was broadly acceptable to the Congress because it accepted the premiss that India was a continuing entity, with the separation of those areas the majority of whose inhabitants desired it. Jawaharlal and his colleagues were anxious too for quick and final decisions. Lahore was being gradually reduced to ashes while Calcutta prepared for another round of killings; but the admini-

[1] Jawaharlal to Krishna Menon, 27 February 1947.

stration was doing little to stem the spread and intensification of communal fury. 'We are at present living in the midst of crises and the situation is volcanic. The only comfort one can derive from it is that some solution must come soon. We have to face very hard realities now and the time for vague resolutions is passed. Definite choices have to be made and the choice is often a very difficult one.'[1] The first thing to be done was to effect an immediate transfer of power out of British hands, for British officials seemed neither willing nor competent to deal with the situation. Knowing that they would soon depart, many of them often showed little interest, while some appeared to derive satisfaction at the thought that India was going to pieces. 'The situation has become intolerable and all the evident goodwill of Mountbatten does not make it more bearable.'[2] With no one assuming responsibility, there was mere drift from bad to worse. As Patel told the Viceroy, 'You won't govern yourself, and you won't let us govern.'[3]

Catching Jawaharlal in this mood, Mountbatten induced him not only, despite all his earlier reservations, to agree to a referendum in the NWFP, but also to accept Dominion Status. From the start the Viceroy's objective had been to achieve a solution which would retain the Indian parties within the Commonwealth, and Jinnah, at one stage of the negotiations, sought to promote the chances of Pakistan by offering to accept Dominion Status. But obviously the prime importance was attached to the attitude of the Congress. Patel, with his conservative tendencies, and Krishna Menon, with his Anglophile attitudes, saw eye to eye on this. But Jawaharlal, occupying a central position, was adamant in opposition. His position had not changed since the days when he had moved the independence resolution at Madras in 1927 and presided over the Congress at Lahore in 1929 which had resolved on civil disobedience if independence was not granted. Thereafter every year Independence Day had been celebrated; and in December 1946 Jawaharlal had moved in the Constituent Assembly the resolution that India should be an independent sovereign republic. His speech on that occasion reflected his bitterness with the British authorities for their rejection of the interpretation of the Mission Plan put forward by the Congress. In the following months Mountbatten's personal friendship had made Jawaharlal less edgy but he had not altered his views on this subject.

> Under no conceivable circumstances is India going to remain in the British Commonwealth whatever the consequences. This is not a question for me to decide or for any few of us to decide. Any attempt to remain in the Commonwealth will sweep away those who propose it and might bring about major trouble in India. We must, therefore,

[1] Jawaharlal to S. Radhakrishnan, 14 May 1947.
[2] Jawaharlal to Vijayalakshmi Pandit, 22 May 1947.
[3] Campbell Johnson, op. cit., p. 72.

proceed on the assumption which is a practical certainty that India will
go out of the British Commonwealth by the middle of next year.

Friendly arrangements could be made with Britain on many matters, including
defence, but only on the basis of independence. If British army officers threatened to leave, 'I shall accept that without losing a night's sleep.'[1] It might
immediately mean some weakness in the higher ranks, but in the long run
it would build up India's self-reliance as well as give reality to India's independence. Severance from the Commonwealth would also in a sense strengthen
India's security, for Britain was incapable of defending India and the main
result of being in the Commonwealth would be to drag India into Britain's
foreign commitments and animosities, while India herself was threatened by
no major power.[2]

In May, however, Jawaharlal's keenness for an early *de facto* transfer of
power was exploited in favour of Dominion Status. In his note of 11 May he
had suggested that even before the British withdrew, the interim government
should be treated as a Cabinet with joint responsibility based 'upon full Dominion autonomy'; and if the League refused to accept this, its representatives
should be told to resign. Mountbatten at first agreed to this, subject to the
Viceroy retaining his overriding power to safeguard the interests of minorities; but then, presumably because of Jinnah's objection, he withdrew his
consent. The Congress strongly objected and there was a fairly heated argument. 'Mountbatten, almost for the first time, took up an entirely contrary
view and said that he thought we were unreasonable in insisting on this even
to the point of breaking when it was only a question of two or three months.'
Jawaharlal and Patel replied that this was a vital matter and if they were asked
once again to give in to Jinnah they would prefer to resign. But Mountbatten
refused to yield and accused the Congress of wanting to crush the League
during the coming months, and possibly to interfere with the Muslim-majority
areas to the League's disadvantage. In the end the Congress had to give way.[3]
It was finally decided that, to enable a speedy transfer of power once partition
was decided upon, there should be two Dominion Governments with a common
Governor-General or two separate Governors-General; and the armed forces
would also be divided in accordance with the territorial basis of their recruitment.

On the main clauses of the May Plan the Congress had little objection at
this stage, except that they wished certain Hindu-majority areas in Sind to be
given the right to secede from the province, and proposed the deletion of all
reference to the Sikhs unless it could be said that the boundary commission
would bear in mind their desire that as far as possible the majority of their

[1]To Baldev Singh, 14 April 1947.
[2]Idem, 8 April 1947.
[3]To Krishna Menon, 17 May 1947.

community should be included in eastern Punjab. Mountbatten rejected the first suggestion on the ground that it would open the way for the League to lay claim to little pockets elsewhere[1] — an argument which would have applied to Sylhet as well; but here again the Congress, now almost desperate for finality, did not pursue its case. On the question of the Sikhs, it was decided to make no reference to them at all.

Seeing that the Congress was continually yielding and that Mountbatten, for all his personal liking for Jawaharlal, was not favouring the Congress, Jinnah continued to pitch his claim high. Despite his verbal message to Mountbatten that the Plan as it stood was acceptable to the League, he continued — for the record, at any rate — to ask for more. The Constituent Assembly should be dissolved and two new Assemblies, for India and for Pakistan, should be convened; the Punjab and Bengal should not be partitioned; Calcutta should not be given to India, and, at the worst, should be made a free port; and the Congress ministry should not be consulted on a referendum in the NWFP. Then, when Mountbatten was in London for consultations with the Cabinet, he publicly formulated a demand for a corridor between western and eastern Pakistan. It is unlikely that Jinnah expected anything more at this stage than what had been conceded in Mountbatten's plan; but nothing was lost by playing this game of nerves. As Miéville commented, 'it was all so disappointing to me and yet at the same time not wholly unexpected.'[2] Jawaharlal's reply to this claim was that Jinnah obviously wanted no settlement and Mountbatten's plan should therefore be abandoned, the Cabinet Mission Plan imposed and the interim government treated as a Dominion government.[3]

Ignoring these demands of both sides, the Cabinet approved the plan as it stood, with only one major addition: that the date for the transfer of power could be brought forward from June 1948 by conferring Dominion Status on one or two successor authorities even in 1947. Mountbatten presented this plan to the Congress and the League, secured their agreement to work it, and asked Jawaharlal, Jinnah and Baldev Singh to follow him and broadcast to the nation on the evening of 3 June. Jawaharlal's effort was one of his outstanding performances. He was normally no orator but could, with genuineness and spontaneity, rise to the occasion. He stumbled along on the plains but was at home in the heights. His rhetoric was never over-blown, his prose never over-excited. He now spoke of the past nine months when the Congress had been in office at the centre, months of sore trial and difficulty, of anxiety and sometimes even of heartbreak. There was much on the credit side, for India had advanced nationally and internationally; but his mind was heavy with the thought of the tragedy and suffering which the Indian people had

[1] Jawaharlal to Mountbatten, 16 May, and Mountbatten's reply of the same date.
[2] To Jawaharlal, 22 May 1947.
[3] Jawaharlal's press statement, 23 May, and letter to Miéville, 25 May 1947.

undergone. It was with no joy that he now commended the proposals for secession, though he had no doubt that this was the right course. It was an India united not by compulsion but by the free and willing association of a free people that they laboured for, and it might be that these proposals would enable them to reach such an united India sooner than otherwise and with a stronger foundation.

> We are little men serving a great cause, but because the cause is great something of that greatness falls upon us also. Mighty forces are at work in the world today and in India, and I have no doubt that we are ushering in a period of greatness for India. The India of geography, of history and tradition, the India of our minds and hearts, cannot change.

It was with that faith that they should bury the bad past and make a fresh start.
   This was the appropriate blend of sadness and commitment, courage and magnanimity; and even a tough soldier like Ismay was moved.

> I hesitate to add to the number of papers that you have to read, but I must beg leave to send you my warmest congratulations on your splendid broadcast last night. It was, if I may say so, brave, generous and deeply moving; and I cannot imagine any words that are more likely to inspire us all to do our utmost in the days that lie ahead. I particularly liked your reference to 'small men' and 'big causes'. It so exactly describes the feeling that I have entertained about my own unworthy self ever since I undertook my task.
>
> Believe me in gratitude,
Yours very sincerely
Ismay.[1]

It now remained only to implement the plan, to ascertain the wishes of the people in the areas concerned and to arrange for separation if it were desired by the majority. Curiously, Jawaharlal expected little trouble. He regarded the communal frenzy as a fever which would pass once the decision about Pakistan had been taken. He had too noble an idea of his countrymen to believe that the desire to kill and torture, born of religious zeal, had any deep root in their nature. He was wrong, but so was everyone else in a position of responsibility at this time; and all were surprised and caught unprepared by the widespread and savage killings that disfigured India before and after partition. After 2 June, Jawaharlal, in the belief that the present had been settled, thought mainly of the future. It was a difficult time but India would muddle her way through, and once they had settled down to the new order they should move fast. In these summer months Jawaharlal, for the first time since his

[1] Ismay to Jawaharlal, 4 June 1947.

release in 1945, was not caught up in the rush of events. The loss of certain parts of India seemed to him a temporary phenomenon which would soon right itself. This was a view shared even by Cripps. He also did not see the June Plan as a complete severance of the seceding areas, and advised Professor Morris-Jones, who was going out to India at the end of May as constitutional adviser to Mountbatten, to make a study of such joint organizations as the Austro-Hungarian Empire and the International Postal Union.[1]

Nor did Jawaharlal see partition coming soon. Once partition had been decided on, Mountbatten believed that if it were not done rapidly 'the thing would have blown up under my hands'.[2] He had therefore announced, without any consultation with the Congress or the League, that the division would be effected and the two Dominion Governments come into existence by 15 August. But Jawaharlal does not seem to have taken this in. He was still thinking in terms of the British leaving in June 1948, when alone India would attain full independence. Dominion Status was nothing more than an interim arrangement. 'an ex gratia gift' from the British, advantageous to them in the long run because it increased their prestige and helped to produce good-will.[3] Mountbatten tried to clear this confusion,[4] but obviously in vain; for even later Jawaharlal was writing 'that from the 15th August onwards our Government will be a substantially free Government.' A measure of British control over the Indian army would still continue, and even by 1 April 1948 the Indian Government hoped to have 'substantial' — but presumably not full — control.[5] To Jawaharlal Dominion Status had never meant full independence, and he had not now changed his views. So long as India was a Dominion, the interim phase was not for him over. It was only when India had become a republic that she could be considered as fully free.

In acting on the clauses of the plan creating Pakistan, the Congress was chiefly concerned about its betrayal of the NWFP. At the meeting of the Working Committee which accepted the plan, Gandhi and Abdul Gaffar Khan were the only regular members who spoke against partition, and Gaffar Khan asked his colleagues to find out, as a small mercy, if the plebiscite in the NWFP could include the third alternative of independence as well.[6] The president of the party wrote accordingly to the Viceroy, and Gandhi took Gaffar Khan to meet Mountbatten. But Mountbatten refused to consider the suggestion and silenced the Congress by pointing out that it was Jawaharlal himself who had strongly objected to the grant of independence to any province. Jawaharlal had agreed to a referendum in the NWFP, as in Sylhet, as part of a larger pattern of consulting the people of the areas concerned; and the Congress could not retract.

[1] Professor W. H. Morris-Jones to the author, 11 March 1970.
[2] Interview with the author, 28 May 1970.
[3] To M. Chalapathi Rao, 6 June 1947.
[4] Campbell Johnson, op. cit., pp. 116-17.
[5] To Amir Sjarifoeddin, Prime Minister of Indonesia, 6 July 1947.
[6] Proceedings of the Wkg. Ctee., 2 June 1947, AICC File G 43(Part I)/1947; R. M. Lohia, *Guilty Men of India's Partition* (Hyderabad, 1970), p. 21.

If they had, as the Viceroy pointed out to Jawaharlal, both their positions would become untenable.[1] A further complication was the lack of clarity about the concept of independence. What the Congress leaders of the NWFP had in mind was apparently only a Pathan state enjoying full provincial autonomy within India,[2] but this was merely a confused way of demanding accession to India; and the confusion served to drag in issues of foreign policy and encourage Afghan irredentist ambition. The most striking feature of the negotiations for partition and the transfer of power in the summer of 1947 was the ambiguity on most of the vital issues. Was secession to be total or partial, would power be handed over by the British wholly or only in a measure, and what were the implications of a referendum in the Frontier province? — on none of these matters was there any clear understanding. The Congress, in its eagerness for finality, lost hold of certainty; and for this it could, to a large extent, blame Mountbatten's tactics of stampede. Only two men were clear-sighted. Gandhi had an overwhelming sense of disaster, and Jinnah knew precisely what he wanted and where he was going.

Jawaharlal urged the Khan brothers to abandon ideas of independence and to rally their forces to secure a majority vote on the straight issue of accession to India or to Pakistan. A number of officials from the Governor downwards, who were antagonists of the Congress, had expressed their opinion that its chances were still fifty-fifty; and the party should be prepared to put it to the test. Even if the Congress lost by a small margin, it could renew the struggle later.

Another factor to be borne in mind is the personality of the present Viceroy, Lord Mountbatten. He is obviously playing and going to play an important part in various developments. I have no doubt about his sincerity and bona fides and his desire to do the right thing. To some extent he is naturally bound by the past and the present set-up; but he is trying his best to go ahead in the right direction. He realizes the difficulties of the Frontier problem and wants to do everything in his power to solve them. I think he will prove helpful. He is convinced, however, that in the peculiar conditions that are arising in India now owing to possible secession of some parts, a chance must be given to the Frontier people to decide themselves by means of a referendum. He has definitely committed himself to this and he cannot get out of it without grave injury to his own prestige and impartiality. He would probably prefer to resign than to face such a situation.[3]

The only concession Mountbatten made to the Congress was to replace Caroe by General Lockhart. This ensured a fair election, and it is probable that if the

[1] Mountbatten to Jawaharlal, 17 June 1947.
[2] Khan Sahib to Jawaharlal, 2 July 1947.
[3] Jawaharlal's note on the position in the NWFP, 8 June 1947.

Congress had accepted battle it would have polled a large vote. As it was, the provincial party decided to abstain, suggesting timidity and even a certain lack of integrity. Despite this, out of an electorate of 572, 798, only 289,244 (50·49 per cent) were in favour of Pakistan, with 2,874 against. This hairline majority in favour of Pakistan justifies Jawaharlal's acceptance of a referendum, for the Congress might have won it or at worst lost very narrowly; and this would have exploded the case for Pakistan. In fact, the League was given a walk-over.

The other problems created by the transfer of power and the process of partition were sorted out, though not without acute bickerings. A partition committee representative of the two parties and boundary commissions with Sir Cyril Radcliffe as the chairman with the decisive voice were set up. But the relationship of the partition committee with the interim government, and the role of the interim government after the decision to divide had been taken, caused controversy. Jawaharlal proposed that the government work as two committees, each dealing with all subjects, one for India and the other for the future Pakistan. Mountbatten was willing to act on this sensible suggestion but Jinnah objected, and as the letter of the law was on his side nothing could be done and the administration continued to be ineffective. Jawaharlal was driven to offer his resignation, and this crisis was only averted by Mountbatten dividing the Cabinet as soon as the Indian Independence Act had been passed. The wording of this statute also caused concern, especially to Gandhi, who feared that it would grant recognition to the two-nation theory; and arrangements were made for its scrutiny before passage by the Indian leaders.

The aspect of the future that was of chief interest to Mountbatten at this time was the possibility of his continuance as the governor-general of both the new Dominions. As early as 17 May, Jawaharlal had agreed to this. Apart from his desire to oblige Mountbatten, he saw in this a means, however tenuous, of holding the old India together and enabling other ties to develop. Indeed, it is possible that Mountbatten did not provide in his plan for common councils or agencies, to which Jinnah might well have agreed, because he saw himself as the common link. But now, after the plan had been accepted, Jinnah refused to commit himself to a common governor-general and then put himself forward as governor-general of Pakistan, inviting Mountbatten to remain as an arbitrator between the two countries. Mountbatten fumed and blustered but to no avail.[1] He had to content himself with the governor-generalship of India and chairmanship of the joint defence council. Even to the latter Jinnah gave his assent in terms characteristic of his method of functioning. 'I have considered your suggestion and wish to state that if you decide to accept the Governor-Generalship of the "Dominion of India" and if your future Government will permit you to act as an independent and impartial chairman of the joint defence

[1] C. Muhammed Ali, *The Emergence of Pakistan* (New York, 1967), p. 177; Hodson, op. cit., pp. 330-31.

council, I would be glad to agree on behalf of the Dominion of Pakistan to your acting in this capacity.' This could hardly be called an invitation to serve as chairman. 'You will note', reported Mountbatten to the Secretary of State, 'that Jinnah consistently refrains from committing himself in writing to asking me to do anything. He merely agrees in a form that implies that I asked for his agreement.'[1]

India's decision to retain Mountbatten as governor-general did not, therefore, help in the way Jawaharlal had expected; but in another respect it paid prompt dividends. Lahore continued to smoulder and there were rumours that Calcutta would be set on fire once it was announced that it had been awarded to India. Some precautions were taken both in the Punjab and Bengal, though in no way adequate to the horrors that finally engulfed these provinces. But the full intensity of this savagery and large-scale migration still lay unexpected in the future. What worried the Congress at this time was the conduct of the Indian States. The Political Department had always, but with added emphasis since the formation of the interim government, been shoring up the Princes in their autocratic pretensions and aspirations of sovereignty; and Jawaharlal had repeatedly to complain to Wavell and Mountbatten about this. But Wavell had refused to interfere; and the Political Department began to burn records, wind up the Residencies and Political Agencies and transfer railways, cantonments and other government property. Hyderabad, a large state in the core of India, which since the'thirties had been seeking to increase its viability by securing access to the sea,[2] was now invited to acquire financial and industrial concessions in neighbouring principalities such as Bastar. Encouraged by all this, many of the Princes openly prepared for independence, the expansion of their armies and the acquisition of modern arms. One of them, Travancore, guided by a dewan of unbalanced ambition and vanity, declared that it would assume sovereignty on15 August, nominated a representative at Delhi and appointed an agent to Pakistan.

Jawaharlal held strong views on this subject of the States. He detested the feudal autocracy and total suppression of popular feeling, and the prospect of these puppet princes, with the encouragement of the Political Department, setting themselves up as independent monarchs drove him into intense exasperation. The whole policy of the Political Department was one of 'operation scuttle', with the deliberate intent of breaking up the unity of India and introducing anarchy by the back door; and Jawaharlal was prepared to thwart this even, as he hinted to Mountbatten, by using force if necessary. 'It must be remembered also that the right of protection which the States possess will also go with paramountcy.'[3] In this matter even Mountbatten had little influence over him. On one occasion, arguing that paramountcy did not lapse but was inherited by

---

[1] Both Jinnah's letter and Mountbatten's telegram are in Gov. Gen. Sectt. File 38/19/GG 43.
[2] See Lord Birkenhead, *Walter Monckton* (London, 1969), pp. 116 and 221.
[3] To Mountbatten, 4 June 1947.

the successor Government, he demanded that the Political Adviser to the Viceroy be tried for unlawful exercise of his authority. 'In fact', wrote Mountbatten,[1] 'as usual he completely lost control of himself.'

To Jawaharlal the test case was Kashmir. Not only had he close personal links with this State and the National Conference under Abdullah; it irked him that, despite his two visits in 1946, Abdullah and many of his colleagues remained in prison. So he planned to go there again, and Mountbatten's effort to dissuade him made him only the more determined. 'For many months — ever since Mountbatten came —' he wrote to Gandhi,[2] 'this question of your going or mine has been discussed and postponed. I have had enough of this business. This is not my way of doing anything. I hardly remember anything that has exasperated me quite so much as this affair . . . I shall go ahead with my plans. As between visiting Kashmir when my people need me there and being Prime Minister, I prefer the former.' In fact, he did not go, Gandhi and Mountbatten going instead; but the Maharaja succeeded in evading a decision on accession to either India or Pakistan.

However, apart from Kashmir, Hyderabad and Junagadh, all other States acceded to one or other of the two new Dominions before 15 August; and Mountbatten served India well in laying the bogy of independence. In view of the coming constitutional changes, he decreed that the Political Department should die a natural death and be replaced by direct relations between the States and the new Dominion governments. Patel took charge of the new States portfolio. He was essentially a man of government, unhampered by theoretical considerations. Though Mountbatten had a greater personal liking for Jawaharlal, it is clear that he found it easier to work with Patel. From the start they understood each other. At first, according to Mountbatten, Patel tried to bully him and demanded that he dismiss the chief commissioner of Delhi. The Viceroy replied that he would instead telegraph home his resignation and leave the next morning after publicly disclosing the cause of his departure.[3] Patel did not press the issue and thereafter the two worked well together.

Patel's willingness to reach agreements with the rulers and to give lower priority to popular representation facilitated Mountbatten's task in securing the accession of the States on the three subjects of defence, external affairs and communications. It was Jawaharlal and his way of thinking which the Princes and their advisers resented, and by setting him aside Mountbatten made it easier for the Princes to accede. He even got Travancore to retrace its steps by sternly telling the dewan to 'be your age'[4] and keep in line with all-India trends and the unanimous feeling of the people of Travancore. Working against the text

[1] 27 June 1947, quoted in Hodson, op. cit., p. 363.
[2] 28 July 1947, quoted in Pyarelal, *Mahatma Gandhi The Last Phase* (Ahmedabad, 1958), vol. 2, p. 354.
[3] Mountbatten's interview with the author, 28 May 1970.
[4] Idem.

of the British Government's statement and disregarding their directive not to apply pressure on the States,[1] brushing aside the advice of the Political Department, countering the wishes of the Princes for, if not sovereignty, at least higher privileges, and ignoring Jawaharlal's desire to involve the people of the States, Mountbatten ensured the continuance of an integrated India but, in doing so, strengthened right-wing elements in Indian politics.

It seemed that all was over now bar the shouting and the ceremonial. To the latter Mountbatten devoted considerable attention, and in his preoccupation with such detail was a true successor of Curzon. He invited Jawaharlal and Patel to drive on the great occasion either with him and his wife in the State carriage or in a semi-State carriage on their own; but he added to this invitation private advice that acceptance might weaken their political position. Jawaharlal's reply was characteristic. He said that 'he would have hated not to have been asked, but would equally have hated to have had to accept.'[2]

On 4 August Jawaharlal sent Mountbatten the names of the members of what would be the first Cabinet of free India. Though formed by the Congress, it was given the image of an all-party coalition by the inclusion of a loyalist, a leader of the Hindu Mahasabha, and Ambedkar, the extremist leader of the Scheduled Castes. It also, from the start, included Patel — a fact which would not require mentioning but for the story that Jawaharlal had decided to omit him but was persuaded by Mountbatten not to do so.[3] Were this so, Jawaharlal would have been lacking in not only integrity and loyalty but common sense; but the truth is very different. On 1 August Jawaharlal wrote to Patel formally inviting him to join. 'This writing is somewhat superfluous because you are the strongest pillar of the Cabinet.' Patel replied in the warmest terms. 'My services will be at your disposal, I hope, for the rest of my life and you will have unquestioned loyalty and devotion from me in the cause for which no man in India has sacrificed as much as you have done. Our combination is unbreakable and therein lies our strength.'[4] Jawaharlal also utilized Patel's services in recruiting other members of the Cabinet.[5] What lies behind the absurd story was that an unconfirmed rumour to this effect was carried to Mountbatten, but was not even mentioned by him to Jawaharlal when he saw that Jawaharlal was not only including Patel in the Cabinet but making him Deputy Prime Minister.[6]

At midnight on 14 August the Constituent Assembly met to usher in the

[1] See Secretary of State's telegram, 1 August, and Viceroy's reply, 4 August 1947, Attlee papers, Box 7.

[2] Mountbatten's report at his staff meeting, 28 July 1947, Gov. Gen. Sectt. File 1446/33/ GG 43.

[3] Hodson, op. cit., p. 389.

[4] Jawaharlal to Patel, 1 August, and Patel's reply, 3 August 1947. *Sardar Patel's Correspondence*, vol. 4, (Ahmadabad, 1972), p. 537.

[5] Jawaharlal to Patel, 30 July 1947, ibid., p. 536.

[6] Mountbatten to the author, 28 May 1970, and Mr H. V. Hodson's letter to author, 5 June 1970.

dawn of freedom. Jawaharlal once again made one of his most movingly appropriate speeches and, in the process, coined an undying phrase.

> Long years ago we made a tryst with destiny, and now the time comes
> when we shall redeem our pledge, not wholly or in full measure, but very
> substantially. At the stroke of the midnight hour, when the world sleeps,
> India will awake to life and freedom. A moment comes, which comes but
> rarely in history, when we step out from the old to the new, when an age
> ends, and when the soul of a nation long suppressed finds utterance. It
> is fitting that at this solemn moment we take the pledge of dedication to
> the service of India and her people and to the still larger cause of humanity.

The next morning — 'The Appointed Day!' as Jawaharlal had noted in his
pocket diary — Mountbatten was invited to continue as Governor-General and
he in turn swore in Jawaharlal as the first Prime Minister of a free India. For
the next few days Delhi and India seethed with joyous excitement. Only Gandhi
celebrated independence in Calcutta by fasting, and was not surprised when
the country was overtaken by the disillusion which was round the corner.

Biographical Notes

Abdullah, Sheikh Mohammed (b.1905). Organized the National Conference in Kashmir State in 1938; president of the All-India States Peoples Conference 1946; Prime Minister of Kashmir from 1948 to 1953, when he was dismissed and arrested; thereafter served long terms in prison assumed office again as Chief Minister of Kashmir in 1975.

Aga Khan (1875-1957). Spiritual head of the Ismaili Muslims; was active in Indian politics till 1947, and a loyal supporter of British rule.

Alexander, A. V., first earl Alexander of Hillsborough (1885-1965). Labour M.P. 1922-31 and 1935-50; First Lord of the Admiralty 1929-31, 1940-45 and 1945-6; member of Cabinet Mission to India 1946; Minister of Defence 1947-50; Chancellor of the Duchy of Lancaster 1950-51.

Ali, Asaf (1888-1953). Barrister of Delhi and Congress Member of Central Assembly 1934-46; member of Interim Government 1946; Indian ambassador in Washington 1947-8; Governor of Orissa 1948-52; Indian ambassador in Switzerland, 1952-3.

Ali, Maulana Mohamed (1878-1931). Interned 1915-19; a leader of the Khilafat agitation; in jail for sedition 1921-3; President of the Congress 1923, but thereafter gradually moved away from the Congress.

Ali, Maulana Shaukat (1873-1938). Elder brother of Maulana Mohamed Ali; and like him served long terms in prison; helped to organize the Khilafat campaign and then drifted away from the Congress.

Ambedkar, B.R. (1891-1956). Harijan leader and a signatory of the agreement of 1932 which rejected separate electorates for the Harijans and enabled Mahatma Gandhi to end his fast; member of the Viceroy's council 1942-6; Law Minister in Nehru's cabinet 1947-51 and one of the principal draftsmen of the Indian constitution.

Amery, L. C. M. S. (1873-1955). Conservative M.P. 1911-45; First Lord of the Admiralty 1922-3; Colonial Secretary 1924-9; Secretary of State for India 1940-45.

Andrews, C. F. (1871-1940). Came to India in 1904 as a member of the Cambridge brotherhood but left the mission nine years later; a friend of Gandhi and Tagore and closely identified with the nationalist movement.

Ansari, M. A. (1880-1936). Leading doctor of Delhi; participated in the home rule and Khilafat campaigns and organized a medical mission to-Turkey; president of the Madras session of the Congress in December 1927.

Attlee, C. R., first earl (1883-1967). Labour M.P. 1922-55; Under-Secretary for War 1924; member of the Indian Statutory (Simon) Commission 1927-30; Chancellor of the Duchy of Lancaster 1930-31; deputy leader of the Opposition 1931-5 and leader 1935-40; Lord Privy Seal 1940-42; Deputy Prime Minister 1942-5; Prime Minister 1945-51.

Azad, Maulana A. K. (1888-1958). Scholar and nationalist who served long terms in prison; President of the Congress 1923 and 1940-46; Minister for Education from 1947 to 1958.

Baldev Singh (1902-61). Sikh leader; Minister in the Punjab 1942-6; member of the Interim Government 1946-7; Minister for Defence 1947-52.

Banerji, S. N. (1848-1925). Entered Indian Civil Service 1871; dismissed 1874; President of the Congress 1895 and 1902; left the Congress in 1918; Minister in Bengal 1921-3.

Besant, Annie (1847-1933). Came to India in 1893 after a varied record of activity in Britain to serve the Theosophical Society of which she later became the president; started the Home Rule League during the First World War and was interned by the government; President of the Congress in 1917.

Bhave, Vinoba (b. 1895). Disciple of Mahatma Gandhi, who chose him to inaugurate civil disobedience in 1940; after 1947 started the movement to donate land to the poor.

Bhopal, Nawab of (1894-1960). Succeeded his mother 1926; Chancellor of the Chamber of Princes 1931-2 and 1944-7; transferred the administration of his state to the government of India in 1949.

Birkenhead, first earl (F. E. Smith) (1872-1930). Conservative M.P. 1906-19; Attorney-General 1915-19; Lord Chancellor 1919-22; Secretary of State for India 1924-8.

Birla, G. D. (b.1894). Leading industrialist who was on friendly terms with Mahatma Gandhi and many Congress leaders.

Bose, Subhas Chandra (1897-1945). Educated in Cuttack, Calcutta and Cambridge; qualified for the I.C.S. but resigned in 1921; detained or exiled for long terms; President of the Congress 1938 and 1939; resigned in 1939; escaped to Germany 1941; organized the Indian National Army in South-East Asia; died in an aircraft accident August 1945.

Brabourne, fifth baron (1895-1939). Conservative M.P. 1931-3; Governor of Bombay 1933-7; Governor of Bengal 1937-9; acting Viceroy 1938.

Brockway, Fenner, (baron) (b.1888). For many years Secretary of the Independent Labour Party; attended the Congress session at Madras in 1927; rejoined the Labour Party in 1946.

Butler, Sir Harcourt (1869-1938). Entered I.C.S. 1890; Foreign Secretary 1908-10; member of Viceroy's council 1910-15; Lieutenant-Governor of the U.P. 1921-3; Lieutenant-Governor of Burma 1923-7; Chairman of the Indian States Committee 1928.

Caroe, Sir Olaf. Entered I.C.S. 1919 and served in NWFP; Foreign Secretary to Government of India 1939-45; Governor of NWFP 1946-7.

Chhatari, Nawab of (b.1888). Minister of Industries, U.P., 1923-25; Home Member U.P. 1926-33; Prime Minister of Hyderabad 1947.

Crerar, Sir James (1877-1960). Entered I.C.S. 1900; Home Secretary, 1922-7; Home Member 1927-32.

Cripps, Sir Stafford (1889-1952). Solicitor-General in the Labour Government 1930-31; expelled from the Labour Party for advocating a united front 1939; visited India after the outbreak of war 1939; British ambassador in Moscow 1940-42; member of War Cabinet and deputed by it to India 1942; Minister of Aircraft Production 1942-5; President of the Board of Trade 1945-7; member of Cabinet mission to India 1946; Chancellor of the Exchequer 1947-50.

Dalton, Hugh (1887-1962). Labour M.P. 1924-31 and 1935-59; Minister of Economic Warfare 1940-42; President of the Board of Trade 1942-5; Chancellor of the Exchequer 1945-7.

Das, Chitta Ranjan (1870-1925). Leading barrister of Calcutta; joined the Congress in 1906; formed with Motilal Nehru the Swaraj Party within the Congress in 1922 to contest the elections; President of the Congress in 1922.

Emerson, Sir Herbert (1881-1962). Entered I.C.S. 1905; Home Secretary 1930-33; Governor of the Punjab 1933-8.

Erskine, Lord (1895-1953). Assistant Government Whip in House of Commons 1932; Governor of Madras 1934-40.

Gandhi, Mahatma (M. K.) (1869-1948). A barrister of Gujarat who trained Indians in South Africa to resist injustice by non-violent passive resistance; on return to India in 1915 adopted same methods to resist British rule; assassinated by a Hindu fanatic.

Ghose, Rash Behari (1845-1921). Lawyer of Calcutta and a leader of the moderates in the Congress; President of the Congress at Surat 1907, when the organization split, and again at Madras in 1908.

Gidwani, A. T. (1891-1935). An educationist from Gujarat; was arrested along with Jawaharlal Nehru at Nabha in 1923.

Gokhale, Gopal Krishna (1866-1915). The most outstanding of the moderate leaders in the Congress; a teacher in Poona who soon became known for his well-documented and analytical speeches in the Bombay and Central Assemblies; President of the Congress in 1905; founded the Servants of India Society in 1905.

Haig, Sir Harry (1881-1956). Entered I.C.S. 1905; Private Secretary to Viceroy 1925; Home Secretary 1926-30; Home Member 1932-4; Governor of U.P. 1934-9.

Hailey, Sir Malcolm, later first baron (1872-1969). Entered I.C.S. 1895; member of Viceroy's council, 1919-24; Governor of the Punjab 1924-8; Governor of U.P. 1928-30 and 1931-4.

Hallett, Sir Maurice (1883-1969). Entered I.C.S. 1907; Chief Secretary, Bihar and Orissa 1930-32; Home Secretary 1932-6; Governor of Bihar 1937-9; Governor of U.P. 1939-45.

Haq, Fazlul (1873-1962). Lawyer of Calcutta and member of Bengal Legislative Council 1913-20; President of the Muslim League 1916-21; Chief Minister of Bengal 1937-43.

Hoare, Sir Samuel, later Viscount Templewood (1880-1959). Conservative M.P. 1910-44; Secretary of State for Air 1922-3 and 1924-9; Secretary of State for India 1931-5; Foreign Secretary 1935; Home Secretary 1937-9; Lord Privy Seal 1939-40; British ambassador in Spain 1940-44.

Husain, Sir Fazl-i (1877-1936). A lawyer of the Punjab and chief organizer of the Unionist Party; member of Viceroy's council, 1930-35.

Iqbal, Sir Mohamed (1876-1938). An influential Islamic philosopher and poet in Persian and Urdu.

Irwin, baron, later Earl Halifax (1881-1959). Under-Secretary for Colonies 1921-2; President of the Board of Education 1922-4, 1932-5; Minister for Agriculture 1924-5; Viceroy of India 1926-31; Foreign Secretary 1938-40; British ambassador in Washington 1941-6.

Ismay, first baron (1887-1965). Commissioned in British Army 1905; Military Secretary to Viceroy 1931-3; Chief of Staff to Winston Churchill 1940-45; Chief of Staff to Lord Mountbatten in India March-November 1947; Secretary of State for Commonwealth Relations 1951-2; Secretary-General of NATO 1952-7.

Ispahani, M. A. H. (b.1902). Businessman of Calcutta and member of Working Committee of Muslim League; Pakistan's ambassador in the United States 1947-52.

Jayakar, M. R. (1873-1959). Barrister and judge; leader of the Liberal Party who worked closely with Sapru.

Jayaprakash Narayan (b.1902). One of the founders of the Congress Socialist Party 1934; member of Working Committee of Congress 1936; after 1947 was for some time a leading member of the Socialist Party.

Jinnah, M.A. (1876-1948). A barrister of Bombay and President of the Muslim League 1916, 1920 and from 1934 till his death; a nationalist who later campaigned for the creation of Pakistan, of which he was Governor-General 1947-8.

Jones, Thomas (1870-1955). Assistant and then Deputy Secretary of the British Cabinet, 1916-30; trusted friend of Lloyd George, Bonar Law and Baldwin.

Khaliquzzaman, Chaudhuri (1889-1973). A friend of Jawaharlal Nehru and a prominent member of the Congress in the U.P. till 1937, when he joined the Muslim League.

Khan, Abdul Gaffar (b. 1891). Congress leader of the NWFP; founded the 'Red Shirt' volunteer organization in 1929; detained by the Pakistan Government from 1947 to 1955.

Khan, Hakim Ajmal (1865-1927). Well-known physician of Delhi and President of the Congress in 1921.

Khan, Liaqat Ali (1895-1951). General Secretary of the Muslim League from 1936; member of Interim Government 1946-7; Prime Minister of Pakistan from 1947 till his assassination in 1951.

Khan, Sahib (1882-1958). Brother of Gaffar Khan and personal friend of

Jawaharlal Nehru; Cheif Minister of Congress ministries in NWFP 1937-9 and 1945-7; Chief Minister of West Pakistan 1955-7; assassinated in 1958.

Khan, Sir Sikandar Hyat (1892-1942). Served in the First World War; revenue member of Punjab Government 1930-35; Deputy Governor of Reserve Bank of India 1935-7; Chief Minister and leader of Unionist Party in Punjab 1937-42.

Kher, B. G. (1888-1957). Solicitor and Congressman of Bombay; Chief Minister of Bombay 1937-9 and 1946-52; Indian High Commissioner in London 1952-4; Chairman, Official Language Commission 1955-6.

Khwaja, A. M. (1885-1962). A lawyer of Aligarh and a friend of Jawaharlal Nehru; joined the Congress in 1915 but retired from politics in 1926.

Kidwai, R. A. (1894-1954). A Congressman of the U.P. and a close associate of Jawaharlal Nehru; Minister in the U.P. 1937-9 and 1946-7; Minister in the central government (with short intervals) from 1947 till his death.

Kripalani, J. B. (b.1888). General Secretary of the Congress 1934-46 and president in 1946; later resigned from the Congress.

Linlithgow, second marquis (1887-1952). Chairman of Royal Commission on Indian Agriculture 1926-8; chairman of Joint Select Committee on Indian Constitutional Reform 1933; Viceroy of India 1936-43.

Lothian, eleventh marquis (1882-1940). Editor *The Round Table,* 1910-16; Secretary to Lloyd George 1916-21; Parliamentary Under-Secretary for India 1931-2; Chairman of Indian Franchise Committee 1932; British ambassador in Washington 1939-40.

Lumley, Sir Roger, later Earl Scarbrough (1896-1969). Conservative M.P. 1922-9 and 1931-7; Governor of Bombay 1937-43; Lord Chamberlain 1952-63.

Mahmud, Syed (1889-1971). Lawyer of Patna and personal friend of Jawaharlal Nehru and his wife; Minister in Bihar 1937-9 and 1946-52.

Mahmudabad, Raja of (1914-73). A landholder of the U.P. and member of the Working Committee of the Muslim League.

Malaviya, K. D. A lawyer of Allahabad who worked for some time with Motilal Nehru.

Malaviya, M. M. (1861-1946). President of the Congress 1909 and 1918; later developed a Hindu outlook in politics; founder of the Banaras Hindu University.

Menon, V. K. Krishna (1896-1974). Secretary, India League in London

1929-47; borough councillor St Pancras 1934-47; Indian High Commissioner in London, 1947-52; Minister without Portfolio 1956-7; Minister for Defence 1957-62.

Miéville, Sir Eric (1896-1971). Private Secretary to Viceroy 1931-6; Assistant Private Secretary to King George VI 1937-45; member of Lord Mountbatten's staff in India 1947.

Montagu, E. S. (1879-1924). Secretary of State for India 1917-22; visited India in 1918 and, with the Viceroy, Lord Chelmsford, made proposals which formed the basis of the reforms of 1919.

Mountbatten of Burma, first earl (b. 1900). Chief of Combined Operations 1942-3; Supreme Allied Commander South-East Asia 1943-6; Viceroy of India March-August 1947; Governor-General of India August 1947-June 1948.

Munshi, K. M. (1891-1971). Home Minister of Bombay 1937-9; Union Minister of Food and Agriculture 1950-52; Governor of Uttar Pradesh 1952-7; later joined the conservative Swatantra Party.

Naidu, Sarojini (1879-1949). Poet and politician; President of the Congress in 1925; Governor of Uttar Pradesh 1947-9.

Narendra Deva (1889-1956). First President of the Congress Socialist Party 1934; member of Working Committee of Congress 1936; resigned from the Congress in 1948.

Nehru, Motilal (1861-1931). Lawyer of Allahabad and President of the Congress in 1919 and 1928; founder with Das of the Swaraj Party within the Congress and leader of that Party in the Central Assembly 1924-6.

O'Dwyer, Sir Michael (1864-1940). Lieutenant-Governor of the Punjab 1913-19; authorized in 1919 the imposition of martial law, which made possible the massacre at Amritsar.

Olivier, first baron (1859-1943). Civil servant in Colonial Office 1882-1920; Secretary, Fabian Society 1886-90; Secretary of State for India 1924.

Pal, B. C. (1858-1932). One of the extremist leaders in the agitation against partition of Bengal 1905; editor in 1920 of Motilal Nehru's newspaper *The Independent;* disagreed with Gandhi's programme and left the Congress.

Palme Dutt, R. (1896-1974). Member of executive committee of British Communist Party 1922-65; editor of *Labour Monthly* from 1921till his death.

Pandit, R. S. (1893-1944). A barrister of Rajkot who married Jawaharlal

Nehru's sister, Vijayalakshmi, in 1921; a scholar who translated Sanskrit works into English while in prison during the non-co-operation campaigns.

Panikkar, K. M. (1895-1963). Historian; for a short while a Member of the Congress; thereafter served in the Princely States; after 1947 served as ambassador.

Pant, G. B. (1887-1961). Advocate of Allahabad; leader of Swaraj Party in U.P. Council 1923-30; severely beaten along with Jawaharlal Nehru at Lucknow in the demonstration against the Simon Commission, 1928; Chief Minister of U.P. 1937-9 and 1946-55; Union Home Minister 1955-61.

Patel, Sardar Vallabhbhai (1875-1950). Congressman of Ahmadabad who organized the no-rent campaign in Bardoli 1928; President of the Congress in 1931; member of the Interim Government 1946-7; Deputy Prime Minister and Minister for Home, States, Information and Broadcasting 1947-50.

Patwardhan, Achyut (b.1905). Member of the Congress Socialist Party, 1934; member of Working Committee of Congress 1936.

Pethick-Lawrence, first baron (1871-1961). Labour M.P. 1923-31 and 1935-45; Secretary of State for India 1945-7; member of Cabinet Mission to India 1946.

Prasad, Rajendra (1884-1963). Lawyer of Patna who joined Mahatma Gandhi in 1917; President of the Congress 1934, 1939 and 1947-8; President of the Constituent Assembly 1946-50; President of India 1950-62.

Rai, Lala Lajpat (1865-1928). A Congressman of the Punjab who sided with the extremists in 1907 and was imprisoned in Mandalay for six months; President of the Congress 1920; member of the Swaraj Party but later broke away to found the Nationalist Party; was beaten by the police in the demonstration in Lahore against the Simon Commission and died a few days later.

Rajagopalachari, C. (1878-1972). A lawyer from Salem in Madras who joined the non-co-operation movement in 1919; member of Working Committee of Congress 1922-42, 1946-7 and 1951-4; Chief Minister of Madras 1937-9 and 1952-4; left the Congress in 1942 but rejoined in 1946; Governor of West Bengal 1947-8; Governor-General of India 1948-50; Union Minister without Portfolio and then for Home Affairs 1950-51; founder of the conservative Swatantra Party.

Ram Chandra, Baba (1875-1950). A settler in Fiji who returned to the U.P. after 1918 and organized the peasant movement in several districts.

Reading, first marquis (Rufus Isaacs) (1860-1935). Solicitor-General 1910; Attorney-General 1910-13; Lord Chief Justice 1913-21; ambassador in Washington 1918; Viceroy of India 1921-6; Foreign Secretary 1931.

Roy, B. C. (1882-1962). Physician and Congressman of Calcutta; Chief Minister of West Bengal from 1948 till his death.

Roy, M. N. (1893-1954). Left India in 1915 and participated in revolutionary movements in Mexico and Europe; attended Second World Congress of the Comintern in 1920; representative of the Comintern in China 1927; differed from the Comintern 1928; arrested on return to India in 1930 and sentenced to six years imprisonment; supported the British Government during the Second World War.

Sampurnanand (1891-1969). A Congressman of the U.P.; Chief Minister of Uttar Pradesh 1955-60; Governor of Rajasthan 1962-7.

Santanam, K. (b.1895). Lawyer of Madras who joined the non-co-operation movement in 1920; arrested with Jawaharlal Nehru at Nabha in 1923; joint editor of *Hindustan Times* 1943-8; Union Minister of State 1948-52.

Sapru, Sir T. B. (1875-1949). Advocate of Allahabad; law member of Viceroy's council, 1920-23; the most eminent of the Liberal leaders.

Satyamurti, S. (1889-1943). Advocate and Congressman of Madras; member of Madras council 1923-30 and of Central Assembly 1935-43; served several terms of imprisonment in the non-co-operation campaigns.

Saxena, M. (1896-1965). Chief whip of Swaraj Party in U.P. council 1924-6; helped to organize boycott of Simon Commission in Lucknow 1928; Secretary, U.P. Provincial Congress Committee 1928-35; Union Minister for Rehabilitation 1948-50.

Sherwani, T. A. K. (d.1935). Landlord and barrister of Aligarh; President, U.P. Provincial Congress Committee 1931.

Siddiqi, A. R. A prominent member of the Muslim League in Bengal.

Sitaramayya, B. Pattabhi (1880-1959). A leader of the Congress in Andhra who took interest in the states peoples movement; President of the Congress 1948; Governor of Madhya Pradesh 1952-7.

Sri Prakasa (1890-1971). Contemporary of Jawaharlal Nehru at Cambridge; secretary, U.P. Provincial Congress Committee 1928-34; Secretary of the Congress 1927 and 1931; after 1947 served as Indian High Commissioner in Pakistan, Union Minister and Governor of Assam, of Madras and of Maharashtra.

Suhrawardy, H. S. (1893-1963). Leader of Muslim League in Bengal; Minister 1943-5 and Chief Minister 1946-7; Prime Minister of Pakistan 1956-7.

Tagore, Rabindranath (1861-1941). Poet, novelist, essayist and dramatist primarily in Bengali but also in English; recipient of the Nobel Prize for

Literature 1913; was involved in India's political and social problems and renounced his knighthood as a protest against the massacre at Amritsar.

Tandon, Purushottam Das (1882-1962). A Congressman of Allahabad; Speaker, U.P. Assembly 1937-9 and 1946-50; President of the Congress 1950 but resigned because of differences with Jawaharlal Nehru.

Tilak, Bal Gangadhar (1856-1920). Teacher in a college at Poona and editor of journals in English and Marathi; regarded as the leader of the extremists and sentenced to long terms of imprisonment; also wrote scholarly works in Indian history and philosophy.

Vansittart, Sir Robert (1881-1957). Permanent Under-Secretary at the Foreign Office 1930-38; Chief Diplomatic Adviser 1938-41; determined opponent of Nazi Germany.

Wavell, Sir Archibald, later first earl (1883-1950). Commander-in-Chief, Middle East 1939-41; Commander-in-Chief, India 1941-3; Viceroy of India 1943-7.

Webb, Beatrice (1858-1943). With her husband, Sidney Webb, a pioneer of research in social and industrial conditions; a leading figure in the Fabian Society and the British Labour Party.

Wedgwood Benn, William, first viscount Stansgate (1877-1960). Joined Labour Party in 1927; Secretary of State for India 1929-31; Secretary of State for Air 1945-6.

Willingdon, first marquis (1866-1941). Governor of Bombay 1913-19; Governor of Madras 1919-24; Governor-General of Canada 1926-31; Viceroy of India 1931-6.

Zafrulla Khan, Sir Mahomed (b. 1893). Barrister at Lahore 1916-35; member of Viceroy's council, 1935-41; Judge of the Federal Court 1941-7; Foreign Minister of Pakistan 1947-54; Judge of the Hague Court 1954-61.

Zetland, second marquis (1876-1961). Governor of Bengal 1917-22; Secretary of State for India 1935-40; biographer of Curzon and Cromer.

Glossary

Ahimsa : non-violence
Anna : one-sixteenth of a rupee

Baba : religious leader
Bapu : father
Begari : forced labour
Brahmin : the highest, priestly, caste among the Hindus

Chapati : flat unleavened bread
Charka : spinning-wheel
Crore : ten millions or one hundred lakhs

Dāl : lentils
Darshan : sight of a person which is believed to be auspicious

Ekka : horse-carriage
Ekkawala : driver of a horse-carriage

Gurdwara : Sikh temple

Hartal : strike
Hindustani Seva Dal : Indian volunteer corps

Id : a Muslim festival

Jatha : squad
-Ji : a suffix added to a person's name to denote respect

Karma : fate

Khadi, Khaddar : cloth woven of handspun yarn
Kharif : autumn harvest
Khilafat : the agitation after the First World War to protest against the dismemberment of the Turkish empire. It lasted from 1919 to 1921.
Kisan : peasant
Kisan sabha : peasant association
Kshatriya : the second, warrior, caste among the Hindus
Kumbh Mela : a festival held once in twelve years on the banks of the Ganga in Allahabad

Lakh : one hundred thousand
Lathi : baton

Madrasa : Islamic school
Majlis : society (of Indian undergraduates at Cambridge)
Maulana : a learned Muslim

Nazarana : illegal cesses
Newar : broad cotton tape used in making a bed

Panchayat : village council
Panchayat raj : regime of village councils
Pandal : tent
Pandit : a learned Brahmin
Pie : one-twelfth of an anna
Punkha : ceiling fan worked by a pulley

Rabi : spring harvest
Rai Bahadur : a title given by the British Government to Indians
Rishi : saint

Sadhu : ascetic
Sahayak : assistance
Sanyasini : woman who has renounced the world
Satyagraha : literally 'truth force'; Gandhi's technique of passive resistance
Seva Samiti : social welfare association
Sharad purnima : the night of the full moon in October
Shikar : hunting
Sir : lands held for personal cultivation
Swadeshi : produced in one's own country
Swaraj : freedom

Takli : a hand spindle

Talukdar : a landowner, particularly in Avadh

Talukdari : the rights of a talukdar

Tehsil : a revenue sub-division of a district

Tehsildar : official in charge of a tehsil

Thana : police station

Tilak Swaraj Fund : a fund started by the Congress in memory of Tilak in 1920 for financing national service and the non-co-operation movements.

Vakil : lawyer

Zamindar : a landowner, particularly in Bengal

Bibliography

Manuscript Sources

Jawaharlal Nehru Papers

This book has been built round the letters, diaries and notebooks of Jawaharlal Nehru. These, from the start up to September 1946, are in the Nehru Memorial Museum and Library at Delhi. The letters have been arranged according to the correspondents, except (at the time of writing) for some letters and papers which have been recently transferred from Anand Bhawan, Nehru's home at Allahabad. The letters and papers of the period after September 1946 are in the custody of Shrimati Indira Gandhi. These are in chronological order, except for correspondence with some leading personalities, which have been kept in separate files.

Nehru Memorial Museum and Library

Motilal Nehru papers
A. M. Khwaja papers
Sri Prakasa papers
Purushottamdas Thakurdas papers

The files of the All-India Congress Committee

These include the correspondence of the presidents and secretaries of the Indian National Congress, the minutes of the Working Committee and papers relating to organizational matters. The record is, however, incomplete, as, apart from other hazards, the party was frequently, during this period, declared unlawful and its files seized by the police. Some files and proceedings of Allahabad municipality for the years 1923-5, when Nehru was chairman, have now been transferred to the N.M.M.L.

National Archives of India

Sampurnanand papers
Rajendra Prasad papers

Gandhi Smarak Sangrahalaya

The papers of Mahatma Gandhi

Jamia Millia, Delhi

M. A. Ansari papers

National Library, Calcutta

Sapru papers

The papers of Sachidananda Sinha at Patna have also been consulted.

Office of Uttar Pradesh Provincial Congress Committee, Lucknow

The papers of the United Provinces Provincial Congress Committee for the years 1921-47. But most of the files of this committee have been lost.

India Office Library, London

Sir Harcourt Butler papers	Mss. Eur. F. 116
Reading papers	Mss. Eur. E. 238
Sir Malcolm Hailey papers	Mss. Eur. E. 220
Halifax (Irwin) papers	Mss. Eur. C. 152
Templewood (Hoare) papers	Mss. Eur. E. 240
Zetland papers	Mss. Eur. D. 609
Erskine papers	Mss. Eur. D. 596
Brabourne papers	Mss. Eur. F. 97
Sir Harry Haig papers	Mss. Eur. F. 115
Linlithgow papers	Mss. Eur. F. 125
Sir Maurice Hallett collection	Mss. Eur. E. 251

Trinity College Library, Cambridge

Minutes of the Magpie and Stump Debating Society
Minutes of the Boat Club

Churchill College Library, Cambridge

A. V. Alexander papers

Nuffield College Library, Oxford

  Cripps papers (some only have been transferred)

University College Library, Oxford

  Attlee papers (some only have been transferred)

British Library of Political and Economic Science, London

  The diaries of Beatrice Webb in the Passfield papers

Caroe papers, in the possession of Sir Olaf Caroe.

R. Palme Dutt's correspondence with Nehru, in the possession of Palme Dutt at the time of writing.

Kingsley Martin papers and Harold Laski papers, at the time of writing in the possession of Miss Dorothy Woodman.

Official records

The records (mostly of the Home Dept. Political Series) of the Government of India in the National Archives of India.

The files of the Governor-General's Secretariat in Rashtrapati Bhavan (formerly the Viceroy's House) in New Delhi; but these files are not many, most of them presumably having been either removed by the Viceroys on their departure or destroyed.

The file of intercepted letters of the years 1921-47 in the possession of the Maharashtra Government.

The records of the United Provinces Government (home and revenue departments) in the U.P. Government archives at Lucknow.

The intelligence reports of the U.P. police which are in the custody of the U.P. government.

Confidential Government of India publications:

  C. Kaye, *Communism in India* (1926)
  India and Communism (1933)
  The Civil Disobedience Movement 1930-34 (1936)
  History of the Civil Disobedience Movement 1940-41 (1942)

Published Sources

Asian Relations: report of the proceedings of the Asian Relations Conference 1947 (New Delhi, 1948).

Bose S. C., *Correspondence 1924-32* (Calcutta, 1967).

Collected Works of Mahatma Gandhi (Delhi, 1958-   ). 56 volumes have been published so far.

Foreign Relations of the United States, 1942, vol. 1 (published by the State Department, Washington).

Nehru, J., *A Bunch of Old Letters* (Delhi, 1958).

——*Letters to his Sister*, ed. K.N. Hutheesing (London, 1963).

Papers relating to the Cabinet Mission to India (New Delhi, 1946).

Patel, Sardar, *Correspondence 1945-50* (10 vols., Ahmadabad, 1971-4).

Selected Works of Jawaharlal Nehru (Delhi, 1972-   ). 6 vols., have been published so far.

Speeches and Documents on the Indian Constitution 1921-47 ed. M. Gwyer and A. Appadorai (2 vols., London, 1957).

The Transfer of Power, ed. P.N.S. Mansergh (H.M.S.O., 1970-   ). 4 vols., have been published so far.

Wavell: The Viceroy's Journal, ed. P. Moon (Oxford, 1973).

Newspapers and Journals

Aaj (a Hindi newspaper of Delhi).

The Bombay Chronicle (Bombay).

The Hindu (Madras).

The Hindustan Times (Delhi).

The Independent (Allahabad, 1919-21). This newspaper, started by Motilal Nehru, contains articles and dispatches, signed and unsigned, by Jawaharlal Nehru.

The Leader (Allahabad).

National Herald (Lucknow). Jawaharlal Nehru started this newspaper in the summer of 1938. It carried his articles; he also wrote many of its editorials.

Pioneer (Lucknow).

The Tribune (Lahore).

Young India and *Harijan,* weeklies edited by Mahatma Gandhi.

Oral testimony

Names of those who have granted interviews to the author have been mentioned in the footnotes. The records of oral testimony in the Nehru Memorial Library of the following have also been found useful:

Roger Baldwin
Lord Brockway
Kailas Kaul
Sri Prakasa
Woodrow Wyatt

Secondary Works

Many books and articles have been cited in the footnotes; only those that require more than a passing reference are listed here.

Agrarian Distress in the United Provinces, report of the U.P. Congress Sub-Committee (Lucknow, 1931).
Ali, C. Muhammed, *The Emergence of Pakistan* (New York, 1967).
Azad, A. K., *India Wins Freedom* (Indian edition, 1959, repr. Calcutta, 1967; American edition with introduction by Louis Fischer, 1960).
Bayly, C. A., 'The Development of Political Organization in the Allahabad Locality 1880-1925' (Oxford D. Phil. thesis, 1970).
Bipan Chandra, *Elements of Continuity and Change in Early Nationalist Activity,* Indian History Congress proceedings, 1972.
────── *The Indian Capitalist Class and Imperialism before 1947* (Delhi, 1972).
Lord Birkenhead, *Walter Monckton* (London, 1969).
Bose, S. C., *The Indian Struggle* (London, 1935; Calcutta edition, 1964).
Campbell Johnson, A., *Mission with Mountbatten* (London, 1951).
Chablani, S. P., and Chablani, P. (ed.), *Motilal Nehru* (Delhi, 1961).
Chattopadhyay, G., *Communism and Bengal's Freedom Movement,* vol. 1, (Delhi, 1970).
Connell, J., *Auchinleck* (London, 1959).
Coupland, R., *The Cripps Mission* (Oxford, 1942).
Curie, E., *Journey among Warriors* (London, 1943).
Desai, M., *Maulana Abul Kalam Azad* (Indian edition, 1945).
────── *Day to Day with Gandhi* (5 volumes, Banaras, 1970).
Druhe, D. N., *Soviet Russia and Indian Communism* (New York, 1959).
Fischer, L., *Men and Politics* (London, 1941).
────── *A Week with Gandhi* (London, 1943).
Lord Glendevon, *The Viceroy at Bay* (London, 1971).

Gopal, S., *The Viceroyalty of Lord Irwin* (Oxford, 1957).

Haksar, U., *The Future That Was* (Delhi, 1972).

Hodson, H. V., *The Great Divide* (London, 1969).

Hutchins, F. G., *Spontaneous Revolution* (Delhi, 1971).

Lord Ismay, *Memoirs* (London, 1960).

Jayakar, M. R., *The Story of My Life* (2 vols., Bombay, 1959).

Jog, N. G., *In Freedom's Quest* (Delhi, 1969).

Kalhan, P., *Kamala Nehru* (Delhi, 1973).

Khaliquzzaman, C., *Pathway to Pakistan* (Lahore, 1961).

Low. D. A., *Lion Rampant* (London, 1973).

—— (ed.), *Soundings in Modern South Asian History* (London. 1968).

Mathur, R. D., *British Policy towards the Volunteer Movement in India during the Non-Cooperation Campaign,* Indian History Congress proceedings, 1970.

Menon, V. P., *The Transfer of Power in India* (paperback, Madras, 1968).

Molesworth, G. N., *Curfew on Olympus* (London, 1965).

Lord Mountbatten, *Reflections on the Transfer of Power and Jawaharlal Nehru* (Cambridge, 1968).

Munshi, K. M., *Pilgrimage to Freedom* (2 vols., Bombay, 1967).

Musgrave, P. J., *Landlords and Lords of the Land,* Modern Asian Studies, July 1972.

Nanda, B. R., *The Nehrus* (London, 1962).

Narendra Deva, *Socialism and the National Revolution* (Bombay, 1946)

Nehru, J., *Soviet Russia* (Allahabad, 1928).

—— *Letters from a Father to His Daughter* (Allahabad, 1929).

—— *Whither India?* (Allahabad, 1933).

—— *Glimpses of World History* (2-vol. edition, Allahabad, 1934).

—— *An Autobiography* (London, 1936; Indian edition, 1962).

—— *India and the World* (London, 1936).

—— *The Question of Language* (Allahabad, 1937).

—— *Eighteen Months in India* (Allahabad, 1938).

—— *Where Are We?* (Allahabad, 1939).

—— *China, Spain and the War* (Allahabad, 1940).

—— *The Unity of India* (London, 1941).

—— *The Discovery of India* (Calcutta, 1946).

Nehru Abhinandan Granth, presented to Nehru on his sixtieth birthday (New Delhi, 1949).

Norman, D., *Nehru: The First Sixty Years* (2 vols., London, 1965).

Personality and Power (B.B.C. publication, 1971).

Philips, C. H., and Wainwright, M.D. (ed.), *The Partition of India* (London. 1970).

Pyarelal, *Mahatma Gandhi: The Last Phase* (2 vols., Ahmadabad, 1958).

Reeves, P. D., 'The Politics of Order', *Journal of Asian Studies* (Feb. 1966).

Sayeed, K. B., *Pakistan, the Formative Phase* (London, 1968).

Siddiqi, M. H., 'The Peasant Movement in Pratapgarh, 1920', *Indian Economic and Social History Review* (Sept. 1972).

Sitaramayya, B. P., *Feathers and Stones* (Bombay, 1946).

Snow, E., *Journey to the Beginning* (London, 1959).

Stark, F., *Dust in the Lion's Paw* (London, 1961).

Tendulkar, D. G., *Mahatma* (8 vols., Bombay. 1951; repr. 1961).

Thompson, E., *Enlist India for Freedom!* (London, 1940).

Tinker, H., *Experiment with Freedom* (Oxford, 1967).

'Jawaharlal Nehru at Simla, May 1947', *Modern Asian Studies* (Oct. 1970).

Tuker, F., *While Memory Serves* (London, 1950).

Venkataramani, M. S., and Shrivastava, B. K., 'The United States and the Cripps Mission', *India Quarterly* (July-Sept. 1963).

Whitcombe, E., *Agrarian Conditions in Northern India*, vol. 1 (Los Angeles, 1972).

Wingate, R., *Lord Ismay* (London, 1970).

Woolf, L., *Downhill All the Way* (London, 1967).

Zakaria, R. (ed.), *A Study of Nehru* (Bombay, 1959).

Lord Zetland, *Essayez* (London, 1957).

Index